Lecture Notes in Computer Science 13522

Vincent G. Duffy · Pei-Luen Patrick Rau (Eds.)

HCI International 2022 – Late Breaking Papers

Ergonomics and Product Design

24th International Conference on Human-Computer Interaction
HCII 2022, Virtual Event, June 26 – July 1, 2022
Proceedings

 Springer

Editors
Vincent G. Duffy
School of Industrial Engineering
Purdue University
West Lafayette, IN, USA

Pei-Luen Patrick Rau
Department of Industrial Engineering
Tsinghua University
Beijing, China

ISSN 0302-9743   ISSN 1611-3349 (electronic)
Lecture Notes in Computer Science
ISBN 978-3-031-21703-6   ISBN 978-3-031-21704-3 (eBook)
https://doi.org/10.1007/978-3-031-21704-3

This Springer imprint is published by the registered company Springer Nature Switzerland AG
The registered company address is: Gewerbestrasse 11, 6330 Cham, Switzerland

Foreword

Human-computer interaction (HCI) is acquiring an ever-increasing scientific and industrial importance, as well as having more impact on people's everyday life, as an ever-growing number of human activities are progressively moving from the physical to the digital world. This process, which has been ongoing for some time now, has been dramatically accelerated by the COVID-19 pandemic. The HCI International (HCII) conference series, held yearly, aims to respond to the compelling need to advance the exchange of knowledge and research and development efforts on the human aspects of design and use of computing systems.

The 24th International Conference on Human-Computer Interaction, HCI International 2022 (HCII 2022), was planned to be held at the Gothia Towers Hotel and Swedish Exhibition & Congress Centre, Göteborg, Sweden, during June 26 to July 1, 2022. Due to the COVID-19 pandemic and with everyone's health and safety in mind, HCII 2022 was organized and run as a virtual conference. It incorporated the 21 thematic areas and affiliated conferences listed on the following page.

A total of 5583 individuals from academia, research institutes, industry, and governmental agencies from 88 countries submitted contributions, and 1276 papers and 275 posters were included in the proceedings that were published just before the start of the conference. Additionally, 296 papers and 181 posters are included in the volumes of the proceedings published after the conference, as "Late Breaking Work". The contributions thoroughly cover the entire field of human-computer interaction, addressing major advances in knowledge and effective use of computers in a variety of application areas. These papers provide academics, researchers, engineers, scientists, practitioners, and students with state-of-the-art information on the most recent advances in HCI. The volumes constituting the full set of the HCII 2022 conference proceedings are listed in the following pages.

I would like to thank the Program Board Chairs and the members of the Program Boards of all thematic areas and affiliated conferences for their contribution and support towards the highest scientific quality and overall success of the HCI International 2022 conference; they have helped in so many ways, including session organization, paper reviewing (single-blind review process, with a minimum of two reviews per submission) and, more generally, acting as good-will ambassadors for the HCII conference.

This conference would not have been possible without the continuous and unwavering support and advice of Gavriel Salvendy, Founder, General Chair Emeritus, and Scientific Advisor. For his outstanding efforts, I would like to express my appreciation to Abbas Moallem, Communications Chair and Editor of HCI International News.

July 2022   Constantine Stephanidis

Foreword

HCI International 2022 Thematic Areas and Affiliated Conferences

Thematic Areas

- HCI: Human-Computer Interaction
- HIMI: Human Interface and the Management of Information

Affiliated Conferences

- EPCE: 19th International Conference on Engineering Psychology and Cognitive Ergonomics
- AC: 16th International Conference on Augmented Cognition
- UAHCI: 16th International Conference on Universal Access in Human-Computer Interaction
- CCD: 14th International Conference on Cross-Cultural Design
- SCSM: 14th International Conference on Social Computing and Social Media
- VAMR: 14th International Conference on Virtual, Augmented and Mixed Reality
- DHM: 13th International Conference on Digital Human Modeling and Applications in Health, Safety, Ergonomics and Risk Management
- DUXU: 11th International Conference on Design, User Experience and Usability
- C&C: 10th International Conference on Culture and Computing
- DAPI: 10th International Conference on Distributed, Ambient and Pervasive Interactions
- HCIBGO: 9th International Conference on HCI in Business, Government and Organizations
- LCT: 9th International Conference on Learning and Collaboration Technologies
- ITAP: 8th International Conference on Human Aspects of IT for the Aged Population
- AIS: 4th International Conference on Adaptive Instructional Systems
- HCI-CPT: 4th International Conference on HCI for Cybersecurity, Privacy and Trust
- HCI-Games: 4th International Conference on HCI in Games
- MobiTAS: 4th International Conference on HCI in Mobility, Transport and Automotive Systems
- AI-HCI: 3rd International Conference on Artificial Intelligence in HCI
- MOBILE: 3rd International Conference on Design, Operation and Evaluation of Mobile Communications

Conference Proceedings – Full List of Volumes

http://2022.hci.international/proceedings

24th International Conference on Human-Computer Interaction (HCII 2022)

The full list with the Program Board Chairs and the members of the Program Boards of all thematic areas and affiliated conferences is available online at:

http://www.hci.international/board-members-2022.php

HCI International 2023

The 25th International Conference on Human-Computer Interaction, HCI International 2023, will be held jointly with the affiliated conferences at the AC Bella Sky Hotel and Bella Center, Copenhagen, Denmark, 23–28 July 2023. It will cover a broad spectrum of themes related to human-computer interaction, including theoretical issues, methods, tools, processes, and case studies in HCI design, as well as novel interaction techniques, interfaces, and applications. The proceedings will be published by Springer. More information will be available on the conference website: http://2023.hci.international/.

General Chair
Constantine Stephanidis
University of Crete and ICS-FORTH
Heraklion, Crete, Greece
Email: general_chair@hcii2023.org

http://2023.hci.international/

Contents

Product Design

Human Motion and Ergonomics

Computer-Aided Ergonomic Analysis for Excavator Using RAMSIS Software

Utkarsh Arora[1], Andre Luebke[2], and Vincent G. Duffy[1]([⊠])

[1] School of Industrial Engineering, Purdue University, West Lafayette, IN 47906, USA
{arorau,duffy}@purdue.edu
[2] Human Solutions, Morrisville, USA

Abstract. In this ergonomic analysis, an excavator cabin environment is optimized according to the manikins modeled in the 3D analysis software RAMSIS (developed by Human Solutions). This is a preliminary analysis, and based on this report, further changes and optimizations in the environment are possible depending upon the skill level of the user. In this analysis, the focus is primarily on two key roles, which will be performed by the operator in the excavator, driving and digging. This analysis will give an insight into the discomfort and obstruction in vision which will be experienced by the operator while performing different tasks. The cabin environment is modified to provide a decent level of comfort to the operator in both roles. Adjustments are made to the position of the touch panel, armrest, and steering wheel. Vision analysis is done to determine any obstruction in the visual field while working inside the cabin. The steering position is brought closer to the manikin, the touch panel is repositioned for comfortable access and the armrests are also adjusted for improved comfort of the manikins. A literature review is also done for the topic "digital human modeling". The results are analyzed using software such as VOSviewer, Web of Science, Scopus and MAXQDA.

Keywords: Excavator · RAMSIS · Ergonomics · Digital human modeling · Literature review

1 Introduction and Background

Excavators are heavy construction equipment that is used for removing a vast amount of soil from a place. It is mostly used in construction activities. An excavator consists of a long boom, cabin, and wheels/track. At the end of the boom, there is a shovel, which is used for digging the surface. This analysis aims to model the environment of the excavator cabin best suitable for the manikin. For this analysis, the manikins are modeled after two data sets to include a wide range of individuals. A 40-year-old male is modeled as per the anthropometric data published by NASA for the year 2000 [1] and a short male is selected from the RAMSIS software database. All the analysis of the cabin environment and manikin modeling is done using RAMSIS software. The 3D CAD model of the excavator is introduced in the software and then manikins are created

© Springer Nature Switzerland AG 2022
V. G. Duffy and P.-L. P. Rau (Eds.): HCII 2022, LNCS 13522, pp. 3–22, 2022.
https://doi.org/10.1007/978-3-031-21704-3_1

as per the anthropometric data. A role is defined to each one of them once they are created, to simulate the different roles of the operator. In this analysis only driving and digging role analysis is performed as these are the 2 main activities performed by the operator. The comfort level of different body parts is analyzed using the software along with visibility from inside the cabin. Multiple iterations are done in the environment to improve the comfort level of the operator and vision limitations while engaged in the activity.

1.1 Problem Statement

When all the manikins are placed in the cabin environment, their reachability to the steering wheel, joystick, and control panel is not suitable. This results in discomfort of the operator, which can be linked to the low height of the steering wheel, incorrect positioning of the panels, and poor location of the armrest. Due to the poor design of the cabin, the operator is prone to health issues such as fatigue, joint pain, and back pain. The vision of the operator is also affected while working inside the excavator cabin.

All these factors can add up and cause a serious accident while working in heavy machinery. Therefore, the use of simulation is necessary to address all such situations and improve operator safety. Nearly 1 out of every 5 fatally injured workers was employed as a driver/sales worker or truck driver [2]. The analysis done previously [5] did not consider the placement of the touch panel, access to controls, and the reachability of the manikin. The joint capacity of the manikin will also be analyzed, to determine if any joint is experiencing discomfort.

2 Literature Review

2.1 Trend Analysis

The trend analysis is based on the results of Web of Science and Scopus data. Analysis tools available in Web of Science and Scopus are utilized for analyzing the trend. The first paper related to "digital human modeling" in Web of Science was published in the year 2002, and maximum research on the topic was published in the year 2007. Figure 1A shows the trend for papers published in the field over the years. The research in digital human modeling dipped after the year 2007, and this dip continued till 2019, but it improved in the year 2020. A similar trend can be seen in the data collected from Scopus. The number of articles published in 2020 improved greatly from the previous years. This indicates that in the year 2020, a lot of new research was done in the field of digital human modeling (See Fig. 1A and B).

Figure 2C and D show the analysis done in Web of Science and Scopus based on Authors, which published the greatest number of articles related to digital human modeling. Duffy published the most articles with 21 entries in Web of Science, while the average number of articles per author was 10. Whereas, in the case of Scopus Duffy published 17 articles and the maximum number of articles (28) was published by Hogberg.

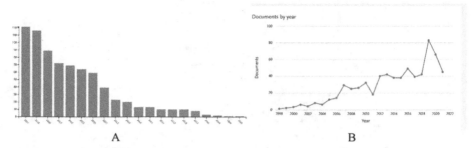

Fig. 1. A and B: Trend analysis for articles published in Web of Science and Scopus database related to "digital human modeling" till November 2021 respectively.

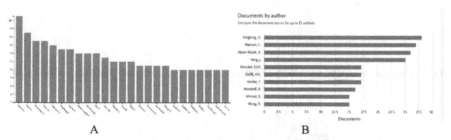

Fig. 2. C and D: Trend analysis by author for articles published in Web of Science and Scopus database related to "digital human modeling" till November 2021.

2.2 Co-citation Analysis

Co-citation is defined as the frequency with which two documents are cited together by other documents [6]. The articles in the co-citation analysis were taken from the Web of Science database. The parameters were set to only acknowledge articles with three or more co-cited references. 22 articles matched the search. See Fig. 3

2.3 Word Cloud

Two data set were collected from Web of Science and Scopus, which was used for bibliometric analysis. Articles were imported into MAXQDA to generate a word cloud. The top terms were "human" and "digital" with more than 500 search results each. The top authors with the most numbers of publications who appeared in the word cloud are Duffy (136), Skövde (102), and Zhang (76). Country-wise frequency of appearance in the word cloud is shown in Fig. 4.

3 RAMSIS Software Procedure

Multiple steps are performed to carry out the ergonomic analysis for the excavator. The details of each step, along with images, are mentioned in this section. The first step in the procedure is to launch the RAMSIS software by clicking on the

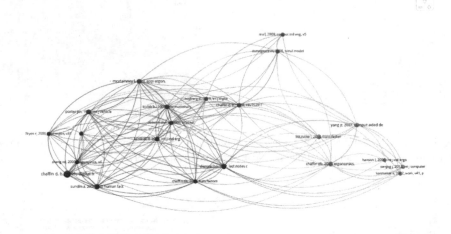

Fig. 3. Co-citation analysis for Web of Science database related to digital human modeling.

S.No.	Country	Frequency
1	USA	495
2	Sweden	240
3	Germany	129
4	Japan	81

Fig. 4. Word cloud generated using MAXQDA and country-wise appearance in the word cloud.

"*launchNextGenAutomotive*" file and to load the excavator geometry file into the software environment, click on *File-open*-select *geometry.sat-open*.

Step 2 is to create the manikins using the *NextGen body builder* plug-in from the start menu. Select the anthropometric database from the drop-down list, then add the control measurements (body height, waist circumference, sitting height) into the window (See Fig. 5). Add the Body Measure list to the structure tree. Exit the *NextGen body builder* plug-in.

Step 3 will create two manikins by clicking on the test sample icon and selecting the body measure list which was created in the previous step. Next, the role will also be assigned to the manikin using the role icon. 2 roles are assigned, driving, and digging. Click Create and both the manikins will appear on the screen (See Fig. 6).

Step 4 is to hide all the objects except the cabin environment, where the manikin will be placed, and operate the excavator. Select the geometry to hide with the left mouse button-right click on the mouse-from the list select hide/show.

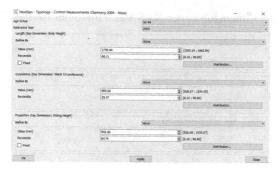

Fig. 5. Control measurements to create manikins.

Fig. 6. Manikins were created from the dimensions listed above (50th percentile male, 2000).

Before Step 5, the manikins that were created do not have shoes. To add shoes to their feet double click on the created manikin, an editor window will pop up, select the *additional options* tab, then click on the *shoe model* dropdown list and select *workshoe* and click *apply* (See Fig. 7).

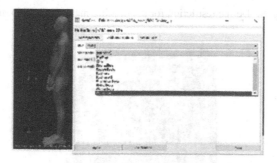

Fig. 7. Add shoes to the manikin.

A set of short manikins are created in the next step with body dimensions selected as per Fig. 8. So, now we have 2 sets of manikins for the cabin environment. One set with the average body dimension as per NASA and the other for the shorter individuals (test manikin).

Fig. 8. Control measurements to create test manikins.

Step 6 place the NASA manikin into the seat of the excavator by following the steps, clicking on the *define constraints* icon-in *manikin comp.*-type "PHPT"- in *Env. Obj.*-select seat surface (See Fig. 9)-*create-posture calculation*. Then the manikin will be placed in the seat (See Fig. 10).

Fig. 9. Define restriction for positioning manikin in the seat.

Fig. 10. Manikin in the seat.

Step 7, the seating position of the manikin is checked to determine if any adjustment in seat position is required. Change the display of manikin from texture to wireframe by clicking on the icon shown in Fig.

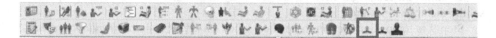

Now, calculate the distance between the manikin hip position and the seat. Click on *Analysis-Distance*-new window will appear. In the *From geometry*-select *PHPT*-To *geometry*-select middle point of hip position-*calculate*. Selection and distance calculated is shown in Fig. 11.

Fig. 11. 50th percentile male (NASA) hip position distance from the seat surface.

Since the larger manikin sits approximately 16 mm higher from the seat. The seat position must be adjusted for it. To adjust the seat position, create a new group of the seat and the surface selection. Figure 12.

Fig. 12. Surface selection for creating a new group.

Step 8 is for creating kinematics of the seat. *Geometry-Define Kinematics-origin-* select a point on seat surface-*Add DOF-direction*-right click select *z-axis-maximum limit*-50 mm-*close. Add Objects*-click on the seat-select group created in the previous step-*create-close.*

To adjust the seat, right-click on the geometry kinematics created-object properties-set the distance to 16 mm.

Step 9 is to position feet on the pedals. Click on *define constraint-manikin comp.-* select a point on the left heel of the manikin *(LeftOuterHeel)-Env. Obj.*-select floor surface-*create-posture analysis.* Repeat the same for the right leg. The heel of the manikin is placed on the floor (Fig. 13).

Fig. 13. Manikin heels constrained.

The foot of the manikin is placed on the floor and not aligned with the pedals. Step 10, place the feet on the pedal, follow the same steps as above. Replace the point on the heel with *LeftBallOffse*t point and surface with the centerline of the pedal. Repeat the same for the right leg. The foot of the manikin is now aligned with the pedal (See Fig. 14).

Fig. 14. Manikin feet on the pedal.

The steering position is made more comfortable and accessible for the manikin in the next step and made to adjust in 2 directions.

Step 11, hide steering geometry with the name TRIM 14 and TRIM 15. Only TRIM 13 steering geometry should be visible (See Fig. 15).

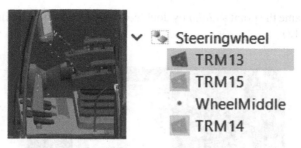

Fig. 15. Steering geometry visible (TRIM 13).

Step 12, To adjust the steering wheel in angular and translational direction, we will define new points on geometry to control this movement. Click on *Geometry* menu at the top of the window select *Point* -window will appear. In *Point type* select *Point on Object*. For *Object* select TRIM 13 and create 2 diagonally opposite points (See Fig. 16).

Fig. 16. New point creation for steering adjustment.

Step 13, a point is required at the center of this geometry in line with the steering wheel center. To create a point at the center, follow the same steps as above. In *Point type* select *create between points*. For the *First* and *Second point* select the points created in the previous step. After the selection is complete click on *Create*. The point created will be like the one in Fig. 17.

Fig. 17. Center point creation for steering adjustment.

Step 14, Rename the point as *Joint* by double-clicking on it and deleting the diagonal points (See Fig. 18).

Fig. 18. Renaming the center point

Step 15, Unhide TRIM 14 and create a new point in the middle of the steering wheel geometry (See Fig. 19). Rename the new point as *wheelcenter*.

Fig. 19. Creating new point at steering wheel center

Step16, Click on *Geometry* menu at the top of the window-*Define kinematics*-window will appear. *Origin*-select any point in the environment-click on *Add degree of freedom*-a new window will appear- select *Rotational* in *Type of DOF*-*starting point*-select *Joint*-*direction*- right-click in the dialogue box- select *y axis-minimum limit-negative 30°*-*maximum limit-positive* 30°-*create*. This will adjust the steering in an angular direction (See Fig. 20).

For translational motion, in the same kinematic window *Add degree of freedom*-a new window will appear- select *Translation* in *Type of DOF – direction*- right-click in the dialogue box- select points *Joint* and *wheelcenter-maximum limit-positive* 300 mm-*create*. *Add object*-select TRIM 14-*close*. Again, *Add object*-select TRIM 15-*close* (See Fig. 20). Under geometry kinematics-right click-*object properties-set value* = *10°* for rotational motion-*close*. For translational motion set value = 60 mm-*close-posture calculation*. See Fig. 21.

Fig. 20. Rotational and translational kinematics of steering

Fig. 21. Steering adjustment.

Step 17, for placing hands on the steering wheel. Define new skin points on the hand of the manikin. Click on *Ergonomics-manikin-skin points,* a new window will open select a point on the right-hand *MG1R_0_8-change activity-close*. Similarly, select a point on the left-hand *MG1L_0_8* (See Fig. 22).

Fig. 22. New skin point creation

To position right hand, *Define restriction-manikin comp.- MG1R_0_8-Env. Obj-Point_17-Apply-Posture calculation*. For left-hand *manikin comp.- MG1L_0_8-Env. Obj*-Point_9-*Apply-Posture calculation* (See Fig. 23).

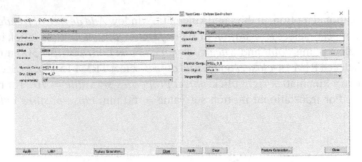

Fig. 23. Positioning hand on the steering wheel.

Fig. 24. Discomfort analysis of driving position.

Step 18, discomfort analysis is done on the driving position manikin and compared with the neutral position manikin. See Fig. 24.

NASA_male_50% Driving manikin analysis is complete. The driving position of the manikin inside the cabin can be seen in Fig. 25.

After this analysis, the NASA manikin restrictions are copied and pasted onto the shorter manikin (test manikin). Select the NASA manikin-*Edit-Special Copy*-Select the test manikin-*special paste*-select all restrictions, positions, and points. Now, the test manikin is also positioned inside the cabin in a driving position see Fig. 26.

Fig. 25. 50th percentile male driving position.

Fig. 26. 50th percentile male and test manikin driving position.

Step 19, To place the digging role manikin in the seat, deactivate the tasks for placing the hands on the steering wheel. Double click on the task and then click on posture calculation. See Fig. 27.

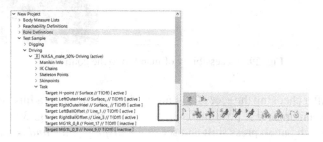

Fig. 27. Removing hands from the steering wheel.

Seat and steering wheel position analysis is also done for the test manikin. It was found that the original seat position was suitable for the manikin as there was only a difference of 3 mm from the position.

The position of the steering wheel for the test manikin was the same for the NASA manikin. The steering was within reach of the test manikin.

Test_Driving manikin analysis is complete. The driving position of the manikin inside the cabin can be seen in Fig. 28.

Fig. 28. Test_driving manikin position inside the cabin

Step 20, select the NASA manikin placed in the seat, then click on *Edit-special copy*, select the NASA-digging-manikin- *Edit-special paste*. Now, both the manikins are placed in the seat with the same pedal position and hip position. Hide both the driving role manikin. Now, the adjustment will be done for the digging role of the manikin.

Step 21, Check if the manikin can access the controls on the right side. Create a new point on the controls. The manikin also needs to see the controls while accessing them, so the line of vision must be checked. *Define restriction-manikin comp.-indexfinger3-sf-r-Obj- Point_14-Apply-Posture calculation.*

For adjusting the line of vision *Define restriction-manikin comp.- line of vision-Obj-Point_14 -Apply-Posture calculation.* See Fig. 29.

Fig. 29. Accessibility of manikin to the controls.

Step 22, After checking the access to controls, the touch panel is adjusted and brought closer to the manikin access position using the *move* icon (See Fig. 30) in the toolbar. To move the touch panel, press shift and select the *display_ face and display_frame.* A crosshair will appear in the middle of the geometry, reposition the touch panel using it inside the cabin environment.

Fig. 30. Move icon.

Step 23, To develop an envelope for the comfortable access of the right arm of the manikin. Click on *Analysis-Reach definition-*a new window will appear, enter the name as *comfortable-start joint*-select *shoulder-joint-r-body point-indexfingerjoint2-r-create-close*. While selecting these points, the manikin must be in wireframe mode. See Fig. 31.

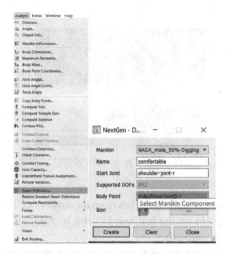

Fig. 31. Setting reach definition of the manikin

Step 24, Click on *Analysis-compute reachability-comfortable*. To find out the maximum reachability of the manikin arm click *Analysis-compute reachability-right arm*. Now, 2 envelopes are visible for the manikin, the one closer to the manikin is of comfortable reach and the outer one is of maximum reach of the manikin. To change the color of the envelope, double click on it and select the desired color and click on *apply*. See Fig. 32.

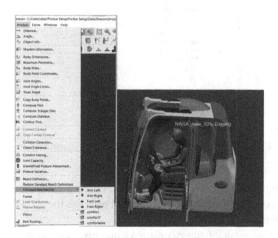

Fig. 32. Reachability analysis of manikin.

Kinematics is defined for the left and right armrests in 2 directions, to adjust them horizontally and vertically. Refer to document [5] for detailed steps.

Step 25 create skin points on the hand and elbow of the manikin (on both sides). *Ergonomics-manikin-skin points-select the point-change activity-close* (See Fig. 33).

Fig. 33. Create skin point.

Step 26 place hands-on joystick and elbows on the armrest. Click on *define constraint-manikin comp.*, select a point on the left hand of the manikin-*Env. The obj.*-select point on joystick-*create-posture analysis.*

Click on *define constraint-manikin comp.*-select a point on the left elbow of the manikin-*Env. Obj.*-select armrest top surface-*create-posture analysis.* Do the same for the right side.

Step 27, calculate the comfort feeling of the manikin in the digging position and compare it with the neutral position (See Fig. 34).

Fig. 34. Comfort feeling of NASA digging manikin.

The digging position of the manikin inside the cabin can be seen in Fig. 35.

To visualize the operator's eye perspective and analyze the view. Select the Analysis tab – Vision – Internal.

From Fig. 36. The view of the operator is not obstruction-free. The boom of the excavator and touch panel is in his field of view. This is not a bad condition since

Fig. 35. 50th percentile male digging position.

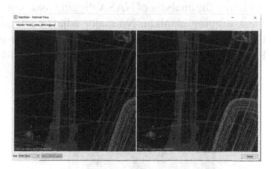

Fig. 36. Operator's view from the cabin.

the operator will be required to access the panel and needs to know the direction and movement of the boom being executed.

Step 23, analysis is carried out to determine the joint capacity of the operator. Select the *Analysis* tab – *Joint Capacity*. A new window will open, select the *whole body* under the *body region* selection, and for analysis select NASA. The joint capacity for the whole body will be visible. Figure 37.

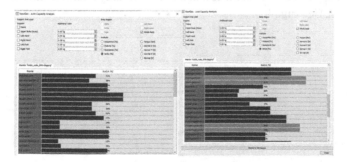

Fig. 37. Joint capacity analysis for digging manikin.

Joint capacity for the neutral position is shown in Fig. 38.

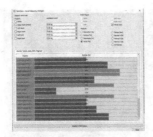

Fig. 38. Joint capacity analysis for manikin in a neutral position.

Step 23, After completing the analysis of NASA digging manikin, a similar analysis is carried out on the test_digging manikin. No major adjustments are required in the cabin environment. The joystick, armrest, control panel are all within comfortable reach of the manikin. See Fig. 39.

Fig. 39. Comfort and extended reach of arms for the test_digging manikin.

Some parts of the touch panel will have to be accessed by stretching out the arm completely, but it is not considered a big problem since it is not required to be accessed all the time.

Comfort analysis is done on the test manikin in digging position and compared with neutral position. See Fig. 40.

NextGen - Discomfort Assessment		
Manikin "Test-Digging"	Maximum	
Name	Value	Reference
Neck	2.59	1.64
Shoulders	2.33	1.44
Back	2.31	1.19
Buttocks	1.43	0.87
Left Leg	1.96	1.39
Right Leg	1.90	1.39
Left Arm	2.56	1.60
Right Arm	2.13	1.60
Discomfort Feeling	3.82	2.53
Fatigue	2.93	1.99
Health	4.89	4.92

Fig. 40. Comfort feeling of test_digging manikin

3.1 Analyses

Manikins are in a neutral position when they are positioned in the seat without any other restriction in place. The neutral position is considered the best comfort feeling for the operator. The comfort analysis is done on the manikin in this position and the value is set as reference data. The digging and driving positions are compared to the neutral position and iterations are done to bring down the level of discomfort to resemble the neutral position more closely.

In the case of driving position, the manikin is most affected when his hands are placed on the steering wheel. The manikin leans forward to meet this condition, and as a result, the discomfort feeling increases significantly. To improve the condition of the manikin, the steering is tilted by 10°, and it is also brought closer to the operator by 60 mm. This adjustment of the steering wheel resulted in it being inside the reach envelope of the manikin, hence manikin can access comfortably to some extent. The steering wheel may not need to be in the comfort zone of the operator because they will not be engaged in driving it around for a long time, the main activity will be digging [7]. In the case of digging position, the hands of the manikin are placed on the joystick and arms placed on the armrest. Upon analysis of this position, severe discomfort is observed. To ease the manikin discomfort, armrests are moved in the z-direction by 50 mm and x-direction (towards the manikin) by 25 mm. The joysticks are not needed to be adjusted separately, as we have already improved the armrest position. The touch panel inside the cabin is also brought within the comfort reach envelope of the operator. A comfort analysis for the right arm is performed to check if the controls on the right side are accessible to the operator, and they were found to be within the comfort envelope). The pedals are not adjusted for the manikin, instead, they are taken as a reference and everything else is adjusted around it.

The joint capacity analysis is done for the manikin in the digging position and compared with the manikin in the neutral position. Any value of joint outside the green zone is a potential area for improvement. The red zone is not preferred. A yellow zone is observed for shoulder joints in the neutral position and the digging position. The difference in value is small and can be ignored for now. After all the adjustments in the cabin environment for the different roles of the operator, the discomfort feeling for the digging role is 3.83 and for the driving role is 4.38, whereas, in the neutral position, the comfort feeling is 2.53. This is an improvement over the previous analysis done by Utkarsh [5].

During the vision analysis, it is seen that the boom is in the field of vision of the operator and might be considered as an obstruction. But it is not, as the operator will need to look where and how the boom is moving. So, having it in the field of view is considered good.

4 Discussion

During this analysis of the excavator operator, limitations in reachability were identified, comfort level for different positions was calculated, and the cabin environment was ergonomically improved. It was concluded that if the operator worked in that environment for a long duration time, then the most affected area will be his neck and shoulders.

One of the best features of RAMSIS is the comfort level calculator, based on my prior experience in the automotive industry, where we were designing jigs and fixtures for operators. This tool would have given us critical data and saved up a lot of time during the prototyping and approval process. Currently, the manufacturer develops a standard manikin and places it in the 3D CAD model environment, and measurements are taken to calculate the reach and height. There is no provision to find out how and where the operator will experience discomfort while operating. Currently, all the designing and tooling is done based on experience and standard data no simulation or analysis is done for it.

The training sessions provided by Andre Luebke have been instrumental in learning the software. The training manual is a very useful resource in getting familiar with the software environment and basic functions. Initial troubleshooting of any problem can be done by referring to the training videos or the manual [3]. One challenge which I faced while using the software was adjusting the steering wheel. I was able to overcome this challenge by referring to the training sessions given by Andre, and now I can adjust it according to any manikin in 2 directions. This helped me with the analysis in this project, where I positioned the steering wheel hands of the manikin to minimize the discomfort.

4.1 Future Work

Even though RAMSIS is a powerful tool in the ergonomic analysis of digital human models, certain limitations can be addressed to further strengthen it. As pointed out by Dr. Duffy, the software cannot model the behavior of humans in different conditions and environments [4]. It cannot model someone talking on the phone or running away. These simulations will give out essential data for improving the safety of the people in and around the environment. Similarly, introducing a feature in the software that can compare how well a task can be performed with bare hands and with gloves will give crucial insight into what can be the downside of both the conditions, for example, if gloves are used, they may reduce the operator's grip on a part, but they are essential for their safety. Information such as how much force will be needed for using a tool and how the performance of the operator will be impacted when wearing PPE. These are some of the features which will provide the organizations with more accurate data and enable them to build an optimized workspace.

References

1. National Aeronautics and Space Administration. Anthropometry and Biomechanics. https://msis.jsc.nasa.gov/sections/section03.htm. Accessed 25 Oct 2021
2. United States Bureau of Labor Statistics: National Census of Fatal Occupational Injuries in 2019. https://www.bls.gov/news.release/pdf/cfoi.pdf. Accessed 25 Oct 2021
3. Human Solutions. RAMSIS NextGen 1.8 Framework User Guide. Accessed 25 Oct 2021
4. Duffy, V.G.: Digital human modelling. In: Handbook of Human Factors and Ergonomics, pp. 773–774
5. Arora, U.: Computer-Aided Ergonomic Analysis for Excavator. Accessed 25 Nov 2021
6. Small, H.: Co-citation in the scientific literature: a new measure of the relationship between two documents. J. Am. Soc. Inf. Sci. **24**(4), 265–269 (1973)
7. Lubeke, A.: IE578 Applied Ergonomics (Project 2 Meeting). Posted 16 Nov 2021

Using Bibliometric Analysis, Ergonomic Principles and a Perching Stool to Prevent Injuries in the Workplace

Sachin Asokan and Vincent G. Duffy^(✉)

Purdue University, West Lafayette, IN 47906, USA
{asokans,duffy}@purdue.edu

Abstract. This paper outlines the importance of Musculoskeletal Disorders (MSDs) in the workspace and addresses the issue in the Industrial case where the operator has suffered a shoulder injury. There are two operations involved: 1. Cutting and 2. Assembly of die-cuts. Also, the workers are subjected to repetitive tasks which enable the participants to be injury-prone. The literature review has been done to find articles related to the problem area to provide solutions. Several design recommendations are provided with the help of ergonomic principles to address issues in the workstation which allows injuries to occur. Based on research and multiple factors it was found that a perching stool to be a viable option to address this issue. The stool acts as an amalgamation of sitting and standing postures and provides a balance between those two. It also provides better maneuverability and comfort to the operator performing the assembly and cutting operation.

Keywords: Musculoskeletal disorders · Workstation ergonomics · Workplace injuries

1 Introduction

The biomechanics of humans and other sociological and psychological factors need to be realized to prevent MSDs (Musculoskeletal Disorders) in the workplace [1]. Since our problem statement involves Lever-system (refers to Lever system in Mechanics) in the Human body, it is vital that they need to be studied to provide a viable solution. Lever systems are used to denote tissue loads in MSDs in Biomechanics [1]. Two loads act on the tissue namely: 1. External and 2. Internal Loads [1]. To design an established ergonomic workstation internal load must be minimized [1]. MSDs are more widespread and costly to deal with. They are comprised of about 15% of all injuries and accounts for 48% of the money paid to resolve them [2]. In 2011, MSDs comprised about 33% of injuries [2]. According to ErgoPlus the total costs to treat MSDs are to be 20 billion dollars every year [11]. Hence MSDs are of importance and must be prevented by designing an ergonomic-based workstation. Ergonomics Analysis should be done to locate the source of injuries and hazards in the workspace and rectify them [3].

© Springer Nature Switzerland AG 2022
V. G. Duffy and P.-L. P. Rau (Eds.): HCII 2022, LNCS 13522, pp. 23–33, 2022.
https://doi.org/10.1007/978-3-031-21704-3_2

Several studies have been accumulated and a meta-analysis has been done by Susan R Stock. It was found that there is a relationship between repetitive tasks, forceful work, and the occurrence of MSDs [5]. Anthropometric data of the workers in the industry is essential to design a workspace of optimum comfortability for all the participants. Colim et al. redesigned a workstation using Anthropometric data and RULA assessment in the furniture manufacturing industry [6]. The activities done by the workers in this research study were like those done in the industrial case presented here and are thus of prime importance. Mital et al. provide approaches to prevent injuries by applying ergonomic and design engineering principles [7]. Also, Mital et al. provide the means of identifying and quantifying risk factors related to MSDs [7].

The Hayman perching stool is of importance related to this topic since it accommodates better mobility and comfort of the user [8, 9]. Dickerson et al. provide guidance to design workstations to avoid shoulder injuries by realizing the mechanics of the shoulder [10]. In this paper, there are several recommendations and possible solutions provided to the industrial case at hand. Modifications to the workspace will be provided to improve the ergonomic aspect and to prevent MSDs in the workspace.

2 Problem Statement

A woman suffered a shoulder injury while performing an assembly operation to grab the filters and die cuts locks the frame in place and sends it to the glue machine. From the data provided it could be seen that the operator was in an inconvenient position and had to turn around to pick up the die cuts with a hip flexion of 90° from the stack and place them on the table to carry out the assembly operation. The operator was a short woman and the tables used in the plant necessitated her arm to be in awkward posture while operating.

There is also a cutting operation where the operator performs at least 10,000 cuts per day. The issue associated with this is the sharpness of the blade. This could of a problem in the future for the operator since they would have to impart more force to accomplish the task, which in turn would put a strain on his shoulder and arms. Repetitive motion is also involved in a hip twist to pick up die-cuts which could cause injuries. Another factor that needs to be considered is the anthropometric data of the workers. Redesigning the workspace should suit all the participants. Therefore, this paper aims to make design recommendations for the workspace based on ergonomic principles to ultimately prevent injuries and provide comfort for all the operators present.

3 Literature Review

3.1 Google Ngram

Google Ngram was used to check the frequency of terms in the literature. The search terms were Workstation Ergonomics, Workplace Injuries, Manufacturing Ergonomics, Musculoskeletal Disorders. It was found from the graph the frequency of the terms Musculoskeletal Disorders and Workplace injuries are higher compared to the ergonomics search terms. However, the frequency trend is increasing for an ergonomic search term which implies a lot of research has been conducted in the recent past and more information and data can be extracted through a literature survey for the problem at hand. Ngram call attention to the importance of MSDs in preventing injuries in the workplace (Fig. 1).

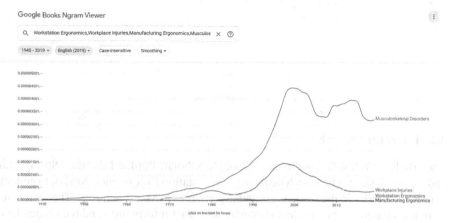

Fig. 1. Ngram viewer for the search terms: Workstation Ergonomics, Workplace Injuries, Manufacturing Ergonomics, Musculoskeletal Disorders between the year 1940–2019.

3.2 Vicinitas

The hashtag "Workstation Ergonomics" was searched in Twitter vicinitas to check the recent trends in the twitter-verse. The word cloud generated by Twitter has some interesting insights. It contained terms like MSDs, Workload, environment, and stress which are of importance to the problem at hand. Also, the tag had an influence of 18.6k which is not a small number. Moreover, there has been an increase in engagement in the past ten days. This implies that people are now more interested in workstation ergonomics and the importance of the topic is being shown (Fig. 2 and Fig. 3).

Fig. 2. Word cloud generated using vicinitas

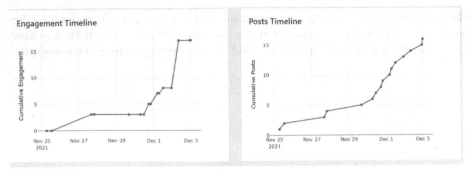

Fig. 3. Engagement and post timeline

3.3 Literature Search

The article search was done by using Google Scholar, Purdue Libraries, SpringerLink, and Research Gate. The search items were Workstation Ergonomics, MSDs, Ergonomics to prevent injuries in the workspace, and Ergonomics in Manufacturing. The search items were used based on the problem statement to extract information and recommendations to provide design suggestions for the problem. Appropriate articles related to the problem statement were selected. The criteria for the selection of articles were based on MSDs in the workspace. Articles that addressed the issue and provided ergonomic suggestions were selected. From that, information on the perching stool was discovered, which would be discussed later in the report and is of importance.

3.4 MAXQDA

All ten articles were uploaded to MAXQDA to perform content analysis. Irrelevant words have been added to the stop list to make the word cloud more relevant to the topic. From the word cloud, it is apparent that words like Equipment, disorder, Occupational, Workstation, and Ergonomics have been given more emphasis and are related to the problem of interest (Fig. 4).

Fig. 4. Word cloud generated by the list of reference articles.

4 Procedure and Results

Initially, the problem statement and the data provided by the Plant manager are studied. Based on the data provided, it was found that the operator had suffered a shoulder injury that comes under MSDs in the workplace. Furthermore, the employee had to perform repetitive tasks with a hip twist of more than 90°. The keywords MSDs, repetitive tasks, and workstation ergonomics can be used to best describe the issue at hand. With these keywords, a literature survey is done using search engines like Google Scholar, SpringerLink, and ResearchGate. The articles which discuss workplace injuries and MSDs were selected and studied. The recommendations and suggestions provided by the articles were reviewed and the best method to solve the problem has been identified and provided in this paper.

Because of the biomechanical complexity, shoulder injuries are crucial and surgical repair may be bothersome [1]. A shoulder can produce a good amount of force between the angles of 30° and 90°; however, fatigue becomes an issue when the shoulder is abducted over 30° [1]. Therefore, shoulder abduction should be kept below or at a maximum abduction angle of 30° for a proper ergonomic posture [1]. Neck fatigue can be mitigated by tilting the head forward at an angle of 30° from the vertical position as shown in Fig. 5 [1, 14].

Fig. 5. Denotes the head tilt angle for Neck fatigue and muscle strength (Adapted from [14])

Tradeoffs must be done between workspaces accommodating shoulder and neck [1]. The trade-off did usually depend upon the type of work implemented by the operator in the workspace [1]. Work that requires more precision warrants a level of visual prowess and hence the station must be designed accordingly [1].

Modern workstations have seated workspace as the popular form and the load acting on the lumbar spine is lesser when the operator is in the seating position [1]. Although seating does provide comfort, standing offers greater maneuverability over tasks that cannot be overlooked [2]. A tradeoff between standing and sitting needs to be achieved and perching stool does provide the balance between the two [1]. Perching stools will be discussed in the next section exclusively as an optimal solution for the industrial case. If standing stations are preferred for operations that require greater mobility, then the following factors must be kept in mind. Firstly, the optimum table height for the operator needs to be selected. This can be done by adopting Fig. 6. Also, some form of footrest needs to be provided for the feet to prevent fatigue. Recommendations provided in [2] are depicted in Fig. 7.

Prolonged tasks without any breaks can lead to injuries. Hence it is advised that there should be timely breaks between each task to prevent injuries [3]. Anthropometric data is required to better design the workspace. The anthropometric data of the participants in the plant should be acquired to make inferences and design suggestions. RULA (Rapid

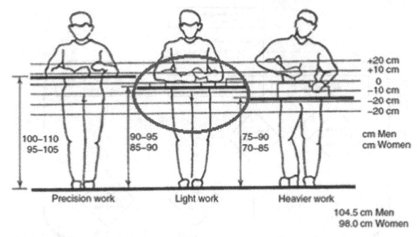

Fig. 6. Recommended heights of a bench for standing work (Adapted from [15])

Fig. 7. Footrest to prevent backache (Adapted from [16, 17]).

upper limb assessment) and REBA (Rapid entire body assessment) survey methods can be used to analyze upper limb disorders and posture analysis of the entire body [1]. Colim et al. through RULA analysis and anthropometric data of the workers have redesigned the workspace. Repetitive motion can be predicted using a motion analysis camera and a procedure for screening and analysis is provided by Gilad where the iterations for step by step procedure is highlighted [6]. The procedure for the analysis is depicted in Fig. 8.

5 Discussion

A systematic literature review shows HCI-related methods to identify key elements of ergonomic design for solving an industrial case. Detail related to the development of these methodologies was shared in prior articles [12, 13]. A perching stool is proposed

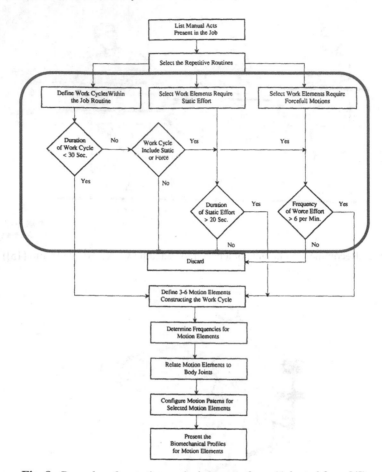

Fig. 8. Procedure for motion analysis camera from (Adapted from [4]).

as a possible solution for the industrial case at hand. The stool is an amalgamation of standing and sitting features that provides comfort for the operator. The blade sharpness of the cutting tool is a problem. The operator utilizing the cutting tool is more prone to MSDs since more force needs to be applied to perform the task when the blade is dull. For this, I would recommend self-sharpening, high-quality blades and timely change of the new ones depending upon the time and wear of the blade. These self-sharpening blades are found in agricultural applications where they are in contact with lawn clippings and their wear resistance needs to be high since resharpening maintenance is expensive [14]. From the last section, a shoulder abduction of more than 30° is undesirable. Thus, by following the table height level provided in Fig. 7 and by making the cutting blade to be at the level where shoulder abduction is 30°, we could prevent injuries from happening.

From Fig. 9 it could be seen that the operator has a hip twist of more than 90° while taking the die-cut for the assembly operation. This is undesirable and since the task is repetitive it could lead to injuries. Hence, the recommendation is that the die cuts be placed right next to her so that there is no hip flexion.

Fig. 9. Depicts the operator twisting to pick up die-cuts.

Fig. 10. Depicts the person using the perching stool from (Adapted from [9]).

The perching stool shown in Fig. 10 could be placed on the shop floor. It also has a feature to provide a cushioning effect for the feet to prevent fatigue. A chair could be placed in the workspace. Although sitting lowers physiological load considerably it does not offer better reachability for tasks [2]. Since the operators are required to perform tasks that require maneuverability, a chair is not an ideal choice. Therefore, a mixed posture of sitting and standing which offers comfortability and maneuverability needs to be realized and Perching stool provides the best trade-off.

6 Conclusion

Perching stool as an option to improve comfort, mobility and prevent injuries in the workstation. Accessibility of the operator has been improved by placing the die cuts next to her, thereby preventing a hip flexion of 90° which could be dangerous since the task is repetitive. The bench of the operator is lowered as per Fig. 6, consequently improving the shoulder dynamics by restricting the abduction at an optimum level of 30°. High-quality self-sharpening blades are used to rectify the sharpness situation of the cutting operation. Because of this, the operator will be imparting less force which improves the ergonomic aspect.

7 Future Work

Automating the process is a good idea, but there are hidden issues associated with it. For instance, the initial setup cost of the system is high. Also, after setting up such a system, it must be sustained by employing automation engineers in the plant which adds cost. We need to consider the application of the product being manufactured at the plant. From the looks of it, it is not a product that requires the help of autonomous agents to manufacture to perfection. I would recommend doing a cost-benefit analysis considering a variety of factors such as demand. A higher level of demand automating the process is an excellent idea.

References

1. WS Marras W Karwowski 2021 Basic biomechanics and workplace design Handbook of Human Factors and Ergonomics Wiley 303 357
2. S Konz S Johnson 2018 Work Design: Occupational Ergonomics CRC Press
3. CD Reese 2018 Occupational Health, and Safety Management: A Practical Approach CRC Press
4. I Gilad 1995 A methodology for functional ergonomics in repetitive work Int. J. Ind. Ergon. 15 2 91 101
5. SR Stock 1991 Workplace ergonomic factors and the development of musculoskeletal disorders of the neck and upper limbs: a meta-analysis Am. J. Ind. Med. 19 1 87 107
6. A Colim P Carneiro N Costa PM Arezes N Sousa 2019 Ergonomic assessment and workstation design in a furniture manufacturing industry – a case study Occupational and Environmental Safety and Health Springer Cham 409 417

7. A Mital A Pennathur 1999 Musculoskeletal overexertion injuries in the United States: mitigating the problem through ergonomics and engineering interventions J. Occup. Rehabil. 9 2 115 149
8. AS Dixon 1974 Hayman perching stool BMJ 2 5918 546
9. https://ergoimpact.com/blogs/news/is-perching-the-new-sitting-research-suggests-yes
10. CR Dickerson AC McDonald JN Chopp-Hurley 2020 Between two rocks and in a hard place: reflecting on the biomechanical basis of shoulder occupational musculoskeletal disorders Hum. Factors https://doi.org/10.1177/0018720819896191
11. https://ergo-plus.com/cost-of-musculoskeletal-disorders-infographic/
12. T Rostek W Homberg 2017 Locally graded steel materials for self-sharpening cutting blades Procedia Eng. 207 2185 2190
13. Z Zhang VG Duffy 2021 A systematic literature review of wireless sensor in safety application C Stephanidis Eds HCI International 2021 – Late Breaking Papers: HCI Applications in Health, Transport, and Industry 23rd HCI International Conference, HCII 2021, Virtual Event, July 24–29, 2021 Proceedings 2021 07 24 2021 07 29 Lecture Notes in Computer Science LNCS 13097 Springer Cham 653 667 https://doi.org/10.1007/978-3-030-90966-6_44
14. J Jiang VG Duffy 2021 Modern workplace ergonomics and productivity – a systematic literature review C Stephanidis Eds HCI International 2021 – Late Breaking Papers: HCI Applications in Health, Transport, and Industry 23rd HCI International Conference, HCII 2021, Virtual Event, July 24–29, 2021 Proceedings 2021 07 24 2021 07 29 Lecture Notes in Computer Science LNCS 13097 Springer Cham 509 524 https://doi.org/10.1007/978-3-030-90966-6_35
15. E Grandjean KHE Kroemer 1997 Fitting the Task to the Human: A Textbook of Occupational Ergonomics CRC Press
16. Chaffin, D.B., Andersson, G.B.: Occupational biomechanics (1991)
17. S Rodgers 1984 Working with Backache Perinton Press Fairport, NY

An Investigation of Ergonomic Injuries to Prevent Musculoskeletal Disorders and Control Risks in a Manufacturing Unit—An Industrial Case

Gnanaprakash Athmanathan and Vincent G. Duffy[✉]

Purdue University, West Lafayette, IN 47906, USA
{gathmana,duffy}@purdue.edu

Abstract. Ergonomic injuries also known as musculoskeletal disorders occur due to repetitive action for a long period. The National Centre for Health Statistics department states that more than 50% of Americans are facing musculoskeletal disorders. When physical and psychological demands are too strong, it leads to discomfort, pain, and functional impairment. In an air purifier manufacturing unit, the workers are facing ergonomic and soft tissue injuries while carrying out manual assembly operations. While looking at the microscopic level the operators across the assembly line with shorter height are facing discomfort in carrying out the process. Our study is focused on analyzing these ergonomic injuries using the ergonomic assessment report and operational video recordings. It is found that apart from the worker's anthropometry, the work layout, process sequence, and work allocations are some other factors that are responsible for these ergonomic injuries. We have analyzed those factors and provided viable solutions to resolve the ergonomic issues and enhance the wellbeing of the operators.

Keywords: Musculoskeletal disorder · Ergonomics · Assembly operations

1 Introduction and Background

Human factors, also known as human factors ergonomics (HFE), have evolved as a distinct and independent study focused on the nature of human–artifact interactions over the previous 70 years. Human factors experts help to design and evaluate tasks, jobs, goods, environments, and systems so that they are compatible with people's needs, skills, and limits. Much research has been carried out to address various HFE issues using various tools and methodologies. HFE has been classified as physical, cognitive, social, and organizational ergonomics. Physical ergonomics mainly focuses on human anatomical, anthropometric, physiological, and biomechanical traits as they relate to physical activity. Cognitive ergonomics is concerned with how mental processes such as perception, memory, and motor response affect human-machine interactions. The optimization of sociotechnical systems, including their organizational structures, policies, and processes, is the focus of organizational ergonomics (also known as macro ergonomics). Human

© Springer Nature Switzerland AG 2022
V. G. Duffy and P.-L. P. Rau (Eds.): HCII 2022, LNCS 13522, pp. 34–48, 2022.
https://doi.org/10.1007/978-3-031-21704-3_3

factor ergonomics deals with a wide spectrum of problems, in this context, it deals with human– machine-organization-environment interactions affecting human performance, well-being, and safety.

1.1 Musculoskeletal Disorder

Musculoskeletal disorders are ailments that affect the body's nerves, tendons, muscles, and supporting components. They are also referred to as Ergonomic injuries and diseases. These disorders are caused by regular and repetitive occupational activities, as well as activities that require abnormal postures. MSDs account for 40% of compensated injuries in the United States, costing between $45 to 54 billion a year [1]. In the year 2000, the province of Quebec spent $500 million on them, accounting for more than 40% of the money set aside for compensation for workplace injuries. MSD prevention is thus a critical topic, with ergonomic measures being one of the most well-known avenues of prevention. National center for health statistics (NCHS) [2] survey concludes that more than 50% of Americans suffer from musculoskeletal disorders, Fig. 1 represents the data survey by NCHS.

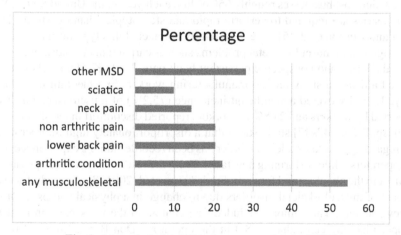

Fig. 1. Musculoskeletal disorders-survey data by NCHS

2 Aim

The overall objective of this project is to obtain a better understanding of the ergonomic injuries in the manufacturing industries to filter out the possible predictors of job induced strain and prevent them. The specific objective of this work is to analyze the factors affecting the operators and formulate viable solutions to establish a standard and safe working environment for the operators with a case study example.

2.1 Background of the Problem-Industrial Case

In the assembly line of a filter manufacturing unit in Indiana, the workers are facing ergonomic and soft tissue injuries due to certain processes. When the ergonomics team investigated the issue one of the reasons for injuries is the shorter operators are having discomfort in performing certain processes as the worktable is designed for average human heights. As a temporary solution, they have given platforms for shorter operators to adjust the height between the floor and worktable. However, this implementation might solve this specific problem and the organization is facing similar kinds of issues across the assembly, presumably involving ergonomic and soft injuries.

3 Literature Review

Workers in industries such as manufacturing, construction, retail, health care, and logistics engage in physically demanding activities, resulting in ergonomic injuries due to uncomfortable body postures and repetitive manual handling tasks (e.g., musculoskeletal disorders). SangHyun Lee [3] stated that absenteeism, lost productivity, and increased health care, disability, and workers' compensation expenditures are all linked to these injuries, which cost businesses roughly $50 billion each year in the United States. Workers in industries are required to perform rapid and stereotypical hand gestures. Hadler et al. [4] and Kurppa et al. [5] have anecdotally connected this type of manual activity to neurological and musculoskeletal problems such as carpal tunnel syndrome, tenosynovitis of the wrist, and nonspecific persistent hand pain. Paula K. Hembecker et al. [6] performed a detailed study on 226 manufacturing workers in a medium metallurgical industry. They discovered a significant incidence (75.2%) of musculoskeletal discomfort reported by workers and 24.8% of workers reported discomfort in the shoulder area. Michael Spallek et al.'s [7] study states that a disproportionately high number of complaints regarding musculoskeletal disorder has been recorded among experienced as well as new operators while performing new tasks. From the results, most of the operators had discomfort in the shoulder and forearm. Fredriksson et al. 2001 [8], the study focuses on the impact of musculoskeletal disorders due to change in a physical and psychological work environment. The author concluded that change in the work environment without proper planning can induce MSD in the operators. Don B. Chaffin's [9] research focused on how to design productive workspaces using digital human modeling tools. The author suggested that some basic advances in human modeling would be required to provide impactful ergonomics assistance in the design of various workspaces. Human reach analyses, sight-line determinations, and human fit and clearance simulations can all benefit from anthropometric data from a wide variety of sources, which can be easily accessed and combined with sophisticated statistical methods to ensure that a specific percentile of the population is accommodated. Sean Gallagher and John R. Heberger [10], had done an extensive study on the interaction between force and repetition on the musculoskeletal disorder. The result shows that out of the 12 epidemiological studies carried out between Force and Repetition interaction, 10 reported evidences of an interaction. Conducting developmental programs, ergonomic training, regular health checkup resulted in a decrease in musculoskeletal disorders. S.A. Pascual and S. Naqvi [11], focused relation between ergonomic analysis tools used for risk assessment in industries and musculoskeletal disorder. It is found that 78% of certified ergonomists use a check-list to assess the risk. It is also clear that there is a gap between what is recommended and what is taught in training by the Joint Health and Safety Committee of Canada. Therefore, a modification of the training curriculum might help ergonomists to assess the risk more accurately and this can help us to reduce the MSD's.

4 Research Methodology

Table 1. Research methodology description

Demo	Name of analysis	Description
1	BibExcel Website	BibExcel is designed to assist in analysis of bibliographic data and importing the data further to Excel [21]
2	VOS Viewer Website	VOS Viewer is used to construct and visually represent the bibliographic networks
3	Word Cloud	A word cloud is a graphic representation of text data that is frequently used on websites to display keyword metadata
4	Harzing Website	This site contains information, online papers, which includes software for citation analysis, as well as resources to help with academic publishing and research and journal quality assessment
5	Web of Science	Researchers can use web of science to collect comprehensive citation data for different academic disciplines
6	Google nGram	The Google ngram Viewer, is an online search engine that uses an annual count of n-grams found in printed sources to chart the frequency of any combination of search phrases [24]
7	NSF Website	The National science foundation award website is used to find the current and past grant projects related to the keyword entered
8	Cluster with Citespace	CiteSpace is used for visualizing and analyzing trends and patterns in scientific literature

These are the eight methodologies proposed to conduct this research and we used 4 demo to perform our study. These methodologies are widely used in various literatures to perform analysis [25, 26] (Table 1).

4.1 Demo 3: Word Cloud

A word cloud is a grouping of words that are displayed in various sizes. The more a specific term appears in a source of textual data (such as a database), the bigger and bolder it appears, and the more important it is. As our research is based on articles related to ergonomics and human factors, for demo 3 we have extracted top 10 articles from the web of science related to these keywords [19]. Using maxQDA we have created a word cloud as shown in this Fig. 2.

Fig. 2. Word cloud

4.2 Demo 4: Harzing and VOSviewer

From demo 4 harzing is performed in Publish or Perish software. In the harzing software, the keyword is searched in google scholar search tab. As our project is related to ergonomics and job design, we used those keywords for harzing [18]. From the Fig. 3 we can see the articles with author name, title, year related to those keywords.

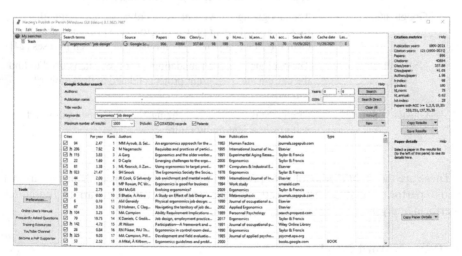

Fig. 3. Harzing

In the VOSviewer we used the dataset from the web of science to create cluster analysis [22]. In this we used musculoskeletal disorder as a keyword, exported data from the web of science and created a new map in VOSviewer. Figure 4 shows the cluster analysis of articles exported from the web of science.

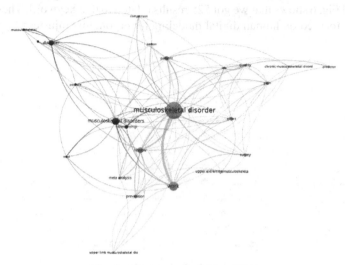

Fig. 4. Cluster analysis from WoS

Demo 8: Cluster with Citespace

The cluster analysis is carried out in citespace software [20]. The dataset from the web of science is downloaded in required format and we use citespace software to create the cluster with respect to the keyword. Figure 5 shows the cluster analysis for the keyword musculoskeletal disorder.

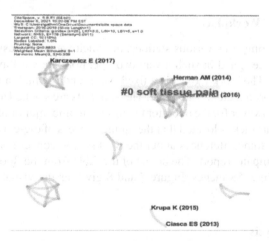

Fig. 5. Cluster analysis using citespace

Demo 7: NSF

The National science foundation award website is used to find the current and past grant projects related to the keyword entered [23]. In our case we used ergonomic injuries as a keyword and Fig. 6 shows that we got 525 results related to that keyword. These projects were mainly focused on human digital modeling for ergonomic injuries.

Fig. 6. NSF awards

5   Procedure

In our project we are focusing on an air filter manufacturing unit where in the assembly line the operators are facing ergonomic injuries. We have an industrial case to analyze the process and identify the root cause for these ergonomic injuries.

5.1   Description of Workplace

The assembly line comprises various stations, in which we are focusing on the die-cut zone. The layout is designed in such a way two operators are working simultaneously in the work fixture. The work fixture is a fixed pallet under which a moving conveyor carries the finished product to the next line. The materials are stacked aside the operators for ease of access, however for the operator facing ergonomic injury must grab them with discomfort as the part rack is located that the gluing process of die-cut can be performed easily. I have listed some inferences about the workstation concerning video recording of operation and company report. The height of the table from the floor is 36 inches and the operator 1 height is 58 inches. Figure 7 and 8 gives us the visual representation of the workstation.

5.2   Process Analysis

The process sequence of that specific station is described in the following Tables 2 and 3 from the reference of lecture videos and report from the manufacturing unit.

Fig. 7. Workstation

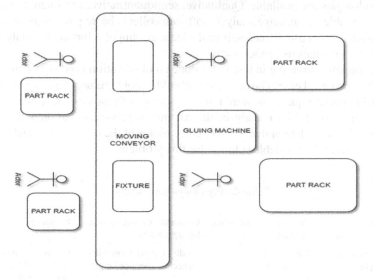

Fig. 8. Workspace layout

Table 2. Process description for operator 1

Operation No	Process description
P1	The operator 1 must turn back to grab the die cut from the part rack
P2	The op1 turns to the gluing machine, extends her arm, places the die cut and grabs the die cut after the gluing process
P3	The op1 places the die cut in the fixture and starts binding the RH side of part1 with part 2 which is placed by op2

Table 3. Process description for operator 2

Operation No	Process description
P1	The operator 2 turns to the part rack, grabs the part 2 of the filter and places part 2 over glued part1
P2	The operators bind the LH side of part 2 with part 1
P3	Once the binding process is over, then op2 places the finished product in the moving conveyor below the fixture

6 Ergonomic Assessment Report

Ergonomic assessment tool is used for the identification of risk in the process. For analyzing exposure to the risks associated with WMSDs, a variety of ergonomics analysis methodologies are available. Qualitative, semiquantitative, and quantitative analyses are all possible. Qualitative analysis software collects basic job observational data. These analytical tools usually necessitate the least amount of effort on the analyst's part. Checklists for job analysis is one example.

The ergonomist from the industry has done an observation type ergonomic assessment for this industrial case. The ergonomic checklist contains around 21 questions. Out of those 10 important questions were retrieved along with the comment/ recommendation of the ergonomist. I have analyzed the comments/ recommendation with reference to process video recording and inferred detailed issues of the operations which is shown in Table 4, to formulate a viable solution for this problem.

Table 4. Ergonomic assessment

S.no	Body part/attribute	Checklist question	Response	Comment/recommendation by ergonomist	Inferences
1.a	Workstation Heights	Is the work performed at an appropriate height?	No	Modify the platform with respect to operator height	In this case the operator is short, adding a platform will help, but for tall person, this solution won't be applicable
1.b		Is operator performing long reach?	Yes	Table width is too wide	The part rack (table) is too wide which makes the operator extend further to pick the part
2	Standing/sitting	Is the operator standing for long hours?	Yes	Provide an anti-fatigue mat	The operator in assembly line works 10 h long daily and 40 h weekly

(continued)

Table 4. (*continued*)

S.no	Body part/attribute	Checklist question	Response	Comment/recommendation by ergonomist	Inferences
3	Hand and wrist	Neutral wrist position?	Yes	Improve layout to minimize wrist bending	The gluing operation takes lots of wrist bending
4.a	Arm	Elbow forced away from body?	Yes	Change work height	The excessive arm movement is because of picking and gluing of die cuts operation
4.b		Excessive arm repetitions?	Yes	Automation required	
4.c		Excessive static load on arm?	No	Change work height	
4.d		Excessive push or pull?	Yes	Place the die cut instead of throwing	
5.a	Back	Excessive repetition of back movement?	Yes	Change work height	The part rack is located behind the operator, forcing her to twist her body to grab the part
5.b		Excessive twist?	Yes	Minimize twist by using feet to turn	

6.1 Inferences

1. From the ergonomic assessment report, the height of the operator is one of the factors of soft tissue injuries, the "Work Design" [12] book states that the work height should be 50 mm below elbow and table height should be 100 mm below elbow. In our case the height of the operator is 58 inches (1473 mm), and table height is 38 inches (915 mm). Figure 9 indicates that the elbow and worktable are the same height and the distance between elbow and table is less than 100 mm (presumably).

Fig. 9. Showing elbow and worktable are on same height

2. In chapter 11 from the "Occupational health and safety management" [13] book, it states that when an operator's motion frequency repetition of shoulder is more than 2.5 per minute, there is a high risk of injury. In our case the operator motion is more than 5 per minute. Therefore, the process sequence also accounts for these injuries
3. In our case, the operator is performing the same task for 10 h in a day and weekly 40 h. As per "Work design" book, any highly repetitive tasks should not be performed more than 6 h in a day. This can be another factor that induces soft tissue injuries.
4. The operator must extend her arms to reach the die cuts and gluing machine. The arm extension causes her discomfort in her arms and shoulder area. "Design for tall, Fit the short", as per this ergonomic phrase we must design the workspace for a more common population. This helps the manufacturing unit when they go 3 shifts a day where different set populations will come into consideration.
5. Adapt automation when we face one of the 4D- "Dangerous, Dirty, Difficult, Disappointing" in our process. Rather than automating the whole process which involves extensive capital, automating the risk involved process can reduce these soft tissue injuries. In our case picking the die cut and placing it in a gluing machine has a high risk involved process.

Therefore, we must consider all these factors and formulate a viable and generic solution which can address the soft tissue injuries in the assembly line of the manufacturing unit.

7 Results and Discussion

7.1 Platform Modification

In the first inference, as the table height is inappropriate for the operator, she was facing discomfort. From the "Work design" book, one of the guidelines for designing a workstation is accommodating a larger population. Designing the worktable with respect to a taller population and using adjustable height platforms as shown in Fig. 10 [17] while accommodating shorter operators are one of the sensible ideas to prevent discomfort in performing the operations.

Fig. 10. Height adjustable platform

7.2 Work Layout Modification

Extended arm action is another factor which is causing soft tissue injuries in operators. From the works of Wick and DeWeese (1993) [14], altering a packing workstation by adjusting the height, tilting the workstation table, and rearranging the supplies can help to prevent musculoskeletal diseases. Redesigning the layout in such a way that both tall as well as shorter operators can access the part rack and gluing machine is the ideal way to eliminate soft tissue injuries in operators. Reducing the reaching distance to the part rack and glue machine will eliminate the extended arm actions.

Process Sequence Modification

The repetitive actions of operation can be avoided by process sequence modification. Adapt automation when we face one of the 4D- "Dangerous, Dirty, Difficult, Disappointing" in our process. Rather than automating the whole process which involves extensive capital, automating the risk involved process can reduce these soft tissue injuries. In our case picking the die cut and placing it in a gluing machine has a high risk involved process. The new process sequence would be,

Process 1: The glue machine automatically grabs the die cut from the part rack.
Process 2: The operator 1 will grab the glued die cut and place it on the worktable.
Process 3: The operator 1 and 2 will bind the glued and counterpart

From this new process sequence, the repetitive arm movements, twisting back to grab die cuts which are the most risk included process, can be automated thereby reducing the risk in the operation.

Job Rotation.

Job rotation is defined as a strategy for alternating workers between jobs with varied exposure levels and occupational demands with the goal of avoiding overloading certain body parts. From the works of Guimarães et al. (2012) [15] when the operators are under job rotation it reduces fatigue, Musculoskeletal disorders, Absenteeism, Rework, Spoilage and increases the production rate. In our case we can relocate the operators after every break, which can reduce these soft tissue injuries.

Various study and research had been conducted to evaluate the importance of safe working conditions of the operators. The safe working conditions not only ensure the safety of the worker but also ensure an effective working environment. This effective environment not only reduces the ergonomic injuries, but indirectly helps in increasing the production rate as well as profit of the organization.

8 Conclusion

The workplace, process sequence, resources, work planning and operator's anthropometry are some of the factors that cause musculoskeletal disorders in a manufacturing unit. Using ergonomic tools to identify the risk and eliminate them is important. However, rather than controlling these issues, eliminating the soft tissue injuries in the initial design phase should be our goal. There is enough data to support the fact that an enormous amount of money is spent on performing reactive actions such as medical treatment to injured operators, disability pensions, etc. Proactive measures such as ergonomic training, workshops, automatic risk assessment tools should be enforced in the system to ensure the safety and wellbeing of the workers.

9 Future Scope

Manual observation-based ergonomic assessments (e.g., checklists) have been widely utilized to identify uncomfortable or repetitive working postures in order to treat musculoskeletal disease injuries. Manual observation methods, on the other hand, are time-consuming, costly, and prone to errors, making them difficult to implement in many organizations. The lack of qualified analysts is another roadblock to promoting ergonomic examinations in the workplace. As a result, to diagnose and minimize the risks of ergonomic injuries in a timely way, an effective and simply accessible tool for ergonomic examinations is required. The suggested computer vision-based automatic posture analysis approach uses motion capturing devices and automatic risk assessment tools such as REBA (Rapid Entire Body Assessment). In our proposal, the virtual machine with a learning pattern will assess the risk of the process and give the user a detailed report on risk factors in the existing process. This input can be used to redefine the process and eliminate the risk in the system. Eric H. Grosse [16] proposes a conceptual framework for integrating risk assessment into planning models of assembly activities that improve the performance of a system. Integrating the design of the production system with process risk assessment will provide us valuable insights into ergonomic hindrances in each process which can be resolved in the initial stage of allocations.

References

1. National Research Council: Musculoskeletal disorders and the workplace: low back and upper extremities (2001)
2. Clarke, T.C., Nahin, R.L., Barnes, P.M., Stussman, B.J.: Use of complementary health approaches for musculoskeletal pain disorders among adults: United States, 2012. National Health Statistics Reports 2016 (98). National Center for Health Statistics (2016)

3. Lee, S.H.: I-Corps: Automated Postures Analysis for Ergonomic Risk, Regents of the University of Michigan, National Science Foundation (2016)
4. Hadler, N.M.: Industrial rheumatology. Arthritis Rheumatol. **20**(4), 1019–1025 (1977)
5. Kurppa, K., Waris, P., Rokkanen, P.: Peritendinitis and tenosynovitis. A Review. Scand. J. Work Environ. Health. https://doi.org/10.5271/sjweh.2690
6. Hembecker, P.K., Reis, D.C., Konrath, A.C., Gontijo, L.A., Eugenio, E.A.: Investigation of musculoskeletal symptoms in a manufacturing company in Brazil: a cross-sectional study. Brazilian J. Phys. Ther. **21**(3), 175–183 (2017). Revista Brasileira de Fisioterapia. https://doi.org/10.1016/j.bjpt.2017.03.014
7. Spallek, M., Kuhn, W., Uibel, S., Mark, A.V., Quarcoo, D.: Work-related musculoskeletal disorders in the automotive industry due to repetitive work - implications for rehabilitation. J. Occup. Med. Toxicol. **5**(1) (2010). https://doi.org/10.1186/1745-6673-5-6
8. Fredriksson, K., Bildt, C., Hägg, G., Kilbom, Å.: The impact on musculoskeletal disorders of changing physical and psychosocial work environment conditions in the automobile industry. Int. J. Ind. Ergon. **28**(1), 31–45 (2001)
9. Chaffin, D.B.: Digital human modeling for workspace design. Rev. Human Factors Ergon. **4**(1), 41–74 (2008). https://doi.org/10.1518/155723408x342844
10. Gallagher, S., Heberger, J.R.: Examining the interaction of force and repetition on musculoskeletal disorder risk: a systematic literature review. Hum. Factors (2013). https://doi.org/10.1177/0018720812449648
11. Pascual, S.A., Naqvi, S.: An investigation of ergonomics analysis tools used in industry in the identification of work-related musculoskeletal disorders. Int. J. Occup. Saf. Ergon. **14**(2), 237–245 (2008). https://doi.org/10.1080/10803548.2008.11076755
12. Konz, S., Johnson, S.: Work Design: Occupational Ergonomics, 1st edn. CRC Press (2008). https://doi.org/10.1201/9780203733714
13. Reese, C.D.: Occupational Health and Safety Management: A Practical Approach, 2nd edn. CRC Press (2008)
14. Wick, J.L., Deweese, R.: Validation of ergonomic improvements to a shipping workstation. In: Proceedings of the Human Factors and Ergonomics Society, vol. 2, p. 808. Human Factors and Ergonomics Society, Inc. (1993). https://doi.org/10.1177/154193129303701034
15. Guimarães, L.B.M., Anzanello, M.J., Renner, J.S.: A learning curve-based method to implement multifunctional work teams in the Brazilian footwear sector. Appl. Ergon. **43**(3), 41–47 (2012). https://doi.org/10.1016/j.apergo.2011.08.008
16. Grosse, E.H., Glock, C.H., Jaber, M.Y., Neumann, W.P.: Incorporating human factors in order picking planning models: framework and research opportunities. Int. J. Prod. Res. **53**(3), 695–717 (2014)
17. LTW Ergonomic Solutions, Adjustable Steps Platform (Gen II). https://ltw1.com/adjustable-height-steps-operator-platform-gen-2/ (2021)
18. "Harzing's Publish or Perish: https://harzing.com/resources/publish-or-perish
19. MAXQDA: https://www.maxqda.com/
20. CiteSpace: https://citespace.podia.com/ (n.d.)
21. BibExcel: https://homepage.univie.ac.at/juan.gorraiz/bibexcel/
22. VOS Viewer: https://www.vosviewer.com/
23. NSF: https://www.nsf.gov/
24. Google ngram viewer: https://books.google.com/ngrams

25. Sheikh, A., Duffy, V.G.: Ergonomics training and evaluations in a digital world using collaborative technologies: a bibliometric analysis. In: Stephanidis, C., et al. (eds.) HCII 2021. LNCS, vol. 13097, pp. 639–652. Springer, Cham (2021). https://doi.org/10.1007/978-3-030-90966-6_43
26. Cistola, J.T., Duffy, V.G.: Systematic review on how the internet of things will impact management in the manufacturing industry. In: Stephanidis, C., et al. (eds.) HCII 2021. LNCS, vol. 13097, pp. 427–443. Springer, Cham (2021). https://doi.org/10.1007/978-3-030-90966-6_30

Preparation of a Selection System for Ergonomic Risk Assessment Methods

Mária Babicsné-Horváth[1]([✉]), Dorina Bór[2], Bianka Balla[1], and Károly Hercegfi[1]

[1] Budapest University of Technology and Economics, Műegyetem rkp. 3, Budapest 1111,
Hungary
babicsne.horvath.maria@gtk.bme.hu
[2] Eindhoven University of Technology, 5612 AZ Eindhoven, The Netherlands

Abstract. Ergonomic risk assessment and worker protection are more important today than ever before. Several summaries and evaluation articles on ergonomic risk assessment methods can be found in the literature. Still, most of these are field- or evaluation approach-specific and thus not well generalisable. We have conducted a comprehensive search in the present work and focused on creating a comprehensive and extensive collection of ergonomic risk assessment methods. The study aimed to prepare a selection system for ergonomic risk assessment methods by organising these methods using a systematisation framework applicable for industry work. The new categorisation could help industry professionals select the best-fitting ergonomic risk assessment method for their field. It could be helpful for academic teachers and DHM developers as well. We categorised the methods into three categories, namely General Risk Assessment Methods, Manual Material Handling Risk Assessment Methods and Specific methods. The techniques were analysed based on aspects that help highlight their strengths, weaknesses, and potential fit for assessing defined industry workplaces. The analysis approaches we used were body part-based analysis, field-specificity analysis, output-analysis and specific aspects for pushing and pulling and lifting in the case of Manual Material Handling methods.

Keywords: Ergonomic risk assessment · Industry · Industrial ergonomics · Ergonomics

1 Introduction

Nowadays, ergonomic risks are more and more common due to the different types of industrial workplaces and sitting work. Companies are focusing more on the employees' health as the regulations and standards are getting stricter. There are many ergonomic risk assessment methods in the literature, and it is hard to keep track of them all. Several articles can be found to compare ergonomic risk assessment methods. Most of them focus on examples of particular industrial fields and workflow (e.g. forest nursery [1, 2] furniture manufacturing [3], warehousing [4], pharmaceutical [5], construction [6]). In addition to area-specific papers, there are some more general methods introduced, which

© Springer Nature Switzerland AG 2022
V. G. Duffy and P.-L. P. Rau (Eds.): HCII 2022, LNCS 13522, pp. 49–58, 2022.
https://doi.org/10.1007/978-3-031-21704-3_4

can be categorised pen and paper methods [7], or, more broadly, a general overview and description of self-report, observation-based, and direct-measurement-based methods [8].

In our review, we would like to give a bigger picture of 40 observation-based ergonomic risk analysis methods. We do this in an area-specific way and not only for specific work processes, but we also classify which method considers what body part, what kind of loads, effort, lifting into account. That way, we can choose the evaluation method that best suits a given movement, workload, or even for several different work processes within a company.

The rise in the development of ergonomic risk assessment methods starting from the 1990s entailed a line of comparative and review articles to classify, analyse, and sort these methods. Our research supports this claim since the publishing year of the earliest review article [8] studied by us follows the first wave of the larger-scale appearance of ergonomic articles by approximately ten years. These articles either focus on a specific field of application [9, 10] or specific assessment aspects such as posture and body parts [11]. David took an approach to classify ergonomic risk assessment methods into three categories: self-reports, observational methods, and direct measurements using monitoring instruments [12]. The author recognises the problem of choosing the most appropriate risk assessment method in industry settings considering available resources. The study gives a qualitative rationale and concludes that observation-based methods are the most appropriate for industrial use. The limitation of the study is that focusing on the method-categories examined overshadows the assessment of specific methods, which entails that more elaborate, specifically method-focused research is needed as a continuation of David's work. It is one of the reasons why we choose observation-based methods as the focus of our work.

We could conclude the following remarks about the field or ergonomic risk assessment research. Meta-analyses compare only a few ergonomic risk assessment methods, with 19 being the most [13]. Some methods occur more frequently in comparisons, probably due to their wide recognition and use. However, some papers fail to explain why the given methods were chosen for comparison precisely. Additionally, in some articles, the field of application of some methods is unclear, which might confuse in cases of method selection in industrial settings. Moreover, even though certain articles draw up frameworks for comparing and analysing ergonomic risk assessment methods, the approaches of these frameworks differ significantly, complicating the comparison and evaluation of these frameworks. Consequently, we designed a larger scale study that considers a larger pool of ergonomic risk assessment methods and analyses the same methods from multiple aspects, such as definite field of application and body part-based assessment. Such a study adds to the literature of the field of ergonomic risk assessment research by providing a unified framework and thus common vocabulary to talk about the methods and has practical relevance for industry professionals struggling with choosing the appropriate method for ergonomic risk assessment.

2   Methods and Data Collection

It is important to note, that the aim of our research is to find ergonomic risk assessment methods, not exact experiments where they were used. Therefore, this is not a systematic review, although the beginning of our work is similar. With the help of the collection and categorization, eventually, our goal is to create a practical selection system.

The search was done on the main databases: Web of Science, Scopus, Google Scholar, Research Gate, PubMed, Taylor & Francis Online and SpringerLink. Various keywords were applied, like ergonomic risk analysis, ergonomic risk assessment, ergonomic assessment, ergonomic evaluation methods. The keywords which we used gave us too many scientific papers, so we have decided to look at the first 20. We have filtered out the irrelevant ones based on the title and continued with the abstract. In cases a specific method was mentioned, we looked to see if there was enough material to fully understand the method.

We also looked into different books in the field of ergonomics. The inclusion criteria were papers had to be in the English language; interpretable, feasible method based on existing freely accessible data; and must have presented ergonomic risk assessment methods based on observation.

After the searching phase, we compared the methods found, excluded the duplicates, and categorised the 59 different methods found. In the next few months, we gathered information about these methods. We were focusing on the following aspects: Abbreviation meaning; Place and time of development; Place of application; Field of application; Conditions of use; Main characteristics; Inputs; Outputs; Steps of use; Postures/body parts considered; Limitations of the method; Uses a standard or other method. Finally, based on the data collected, it is possible to categorise the methods according to different aspects.

3 Results

As a result of our study, we sorted the examined observation-based risk assessment methods into four main categories: General Methods, Lifting Methods, Push-Pull Methods, and Specific Methods.

The broadest category is General Methods, with 27 methods belonging here. These methods usually give an overview about several types of ergonomic risks present in the observed tasks and workflows, which are described in detail later. The methods in the category General Methods are the Washington State Caution and Hazard Checklist [14, 15], REBA [16], RULA [17], JSI [17], OWAS [18, 19], CERA [19], ART, PLIBEL, QEC [20], NERPA [21], RSI, the ACGIH TLV/HAL [22, 23], OCRA [23], the Utah Shoulder Movement Estimation [24, 25], the RMFA [25], ULA-UC and LBA-UC [26], HARM [22], the Keyserlings Cumulative Trauma Checklist [27, 28], KIM-MHO [29], LUBA [30], PATH [31], TDA [31], BRIEF, PRASAD [32], the Cube Model and the Automotive Industry Postural Assessment.

The following categories contain more specified methods than the general methods focus on one specific aspect of ergonomic risk assessment. The second and third categories, namely Lifting Methods and Push-Pull Methods, include methods that focus on manual material handling (MMH) tasks. Several methods focus on Lifting Methods counts eight methods, namely MAC [33], NIOSH RLE [18], the OHIO BWC Lifting Guidelines [34], the corresponding subset of questions from RAMP [35], the WISHA

Lifting Calculator [36], the corresponding sections of the Liberty MMMH (mutual manual material handling) Tables, the Low Back Compressive Force Model [37] and KIM-LHC. Each method takes a different approach to assessing lifting workflows, which is described in more detail in Table n. Push-Pull Methods includes six methods, namely the corresponding subset of questions from RAMP, the push-pull tables of the Liberty MMMH Tables, RAPP, the OHIO BWC Push-Pull Guidelines, the Utah Shoulder Movement Estimation and KIM-PP. Details about the methods are discussed in the section, specifically about our findings regarding Push-Pull Methods.

The last main category we identified is Specific Methods counting three methods, AWBA [38, 39], ROSA [40], MAPO [40] and Hand-Arm Vibration Calculator. We assigned methods to this category which either assess workflows in a specific domain, such as agriculture in case of AWBA, or take into account environmental factors that are related to ergonomic risks, as in computer workplaces for ROSA, hospital work for MAPO or examine a specific type of ergonomic risk, such as risks of exposure to vibration in Hand-Arm Vibration Calculator [41].

3.1 General Risk Assessment Methods – Based on Body Parts

The General Methods category is the largest and most diverse of all. Additionally, the methods in the category aim for an overall, general assessment of ergonomic risk in various contexts. This initial screening assessment of workplaces and processes can be interpreted from ergonomic risk related to the movement and exertion of particular body parts. In the following table, we introduce a framework based on earlier work and analyse our selection of General Methods based on that. The structure of the framework consists of a distinction between upper and lower body parts. These subcategories are further detailed based on the moving body parts divided by joints, such as upper arms and lower arms (divided by elbows) or trunk and legs (divided by hips). Joints are considered if their movement (such as shoulder shrugging) is significant from ergonomic risk but not included if they only actuate the movement of a body part (e.g. in case of the elbow moving the forearm).

Table 1. Analysis of general risk assessment methods based on body parts

Method	Upper body							Lower body		
	Neck/head	Shoulders	Upper arm	Forearm	Hands/wrists	Fingers	Trunk/back	Hips	Legs	Feet/toes
REBA	×	×	×	×	×		×		×	
RULA	×	×	×	×	×		×		×	
JSI				×	×					
OWAS			×				×		×	
CERA	×		×	×			×		×	

(continued)

Table 1 shows the classification of the examined methods according to the framework. Most of the General Methods assessed are comprehensive and consider the whole body (REBA, RULA, CERA, NERPA, RSI, RMFA, PATH, BRIEF and Automotive

Table 1. (*continued*)

Method	Upper body							Lower body		
	Neck/head	Shoulders	Upper arm	Forearm	Hands/wrists	Fingers	Trunk/back	Hips	Legs	Feet/toes
ART	×		×		×	×	×			
Washington State Caution & Hazard	×	×	×	×	×					
QEC (Quick Exposure Check)	×		×	×	×		×			
NERPA	×	×	×	×	×		×		×	
OCRA			×	×	×					
ACGIH TLV/HAL					×					
Utah Shoulder Movement Estimation			×	×						
RSI	×	×	×		×	×	×		×	
RMFA	×	×	×	×	×	×	×		×	×
ULA-UC & LBA-UC	×	×	×	×	×		×		×	
HARM			×	×	×					
KC				×	×	×				
LUBA	×		×	×	×		×			
PATH	×		×	×			×		×	
BRIEF	×	×	×	×	×	×	×		×	
Automotive Industry Postural Assessment	×		×	×	×		×	×	×	

Industry Postural Assessment). Additionally, the distinction of upper and lower body assessment appears in the structure of some of the General Methods (ULA-UC & LBA-UC). Interestingly, assessing solely the upper body was present in the selected methods (ART, QEC, LUBA), but none assessed the lower body exclusively. General Methods in our selection focused explicitly on one body area, such as JSI, OCRA, the ACGIH TLV/HAL, HARM, Utah shoulder movement estimation, and the Keyserlings Cumulative Trauma Checklist, which concentrate on the assessment of upper extremities. It is important to note that not all methods fit the categories mentioned above. Some general methods include body parts only tangentially, making them difficult to classify (OWAS, Washington State Caution & Hazard Checklist, KIM III.) Another notation of ours is that joints and body parts are used interchangeably in the description of methods, which makes them difficult to compare. Overall, the more body parts are considered in a given method, the more general the picture of the risk of the work process. Methods that focus on only a few body parts give a more detailed risk result for that body part.

3.2 Manual Material Handling Risk Assessment Methods

The different types of lifting, lowering, carrying, and push-pull ergonomic risk assessment can be grouped by different ways. One of the most significant differences between the general risk assessments and the manual handling risk assessments is the focus: the second one does not conclude the detailed body part movement and posture assessment. Therefore, two additional tables were needed for comparison. One for the lifting, lowering and carrying type risk assessment methods (Table 2) and one for the push-pull type methods (Table 1). Noticeable duplication between methods is possible due to the separate part of the method; for example, the Ohio BWC or Snook tables methods have separate modules for load lifting and push-pull.

As can be seen in Table 2, all of the listed assessments include criteria for the mass of the load to be lifted and the vertical lifting zones. These two aspects are essential for the risk assessment, but several methods also consider the horizontal lifting zones and the frequency of load lifting. A smaller number of additional aspects are indicated. The methods that take most aspects into account are RAMP and KIM I, followed by NIOSH, WISHA, Snook tables and MAC.

Table 3 shows that several load-lifting methods have a push-pull component, but the number of these is small In contrast to the previous table, there is no criterion other than the mass of the load that is taken into account by a significant number of methods. It may be explained by the fact that the methods operate according to different principles. Some methods, such as the OHIO BWC push-pull guidelines or the Snook tables, take into account the worker's height or determine for a given height what percentage of the population it corresponds to. In addition to these, there are more straightforward methods, such as RAPP, where height is not included, but environmental factors and distance travelled are. The methods that take most aspects into account are RAMP and the OHIO BWC push-pull guidelines.

Table 2. Analysis of risk assessment methods for lifting loads

Method	Weight/Load	Hand grip	Horizontal lifting zone	Vertical lifting zones	Environmental factors	Frequency of elevation	Duration of elevation	Several people lifting	One-handed lifting	Two-handed lifting	Trunk twisting	Gender of lifter
MAC	×	×	×	×	×							
NIOSH = RLE	×	×	×	×		×	×					
Washington State Caution & Hazard	×			×		×						
OHIO BWC lifting guidelines	×		×	×		×			×	×		
QEC	×			×		×						
RAMP	×	×	×	×	×	×		×	×	×		
WISHA Lifting Calculator	×		×	×		×	×				×	
Snook tables	×		×	×		×						×
Low Back Compressive force model	×		×	×						×		
KIM I. (KIM-LHC)	×		×	×	×	×	×				×	×

Overall, unlike the general methods, where we have found that the more body parts considered, the more general the picture, the more detailed the methods that focus on push-pull and load lifting are in the more aspects considered.

3.3 Specific Methods

We classified four methods as Specific in our framework. AWBA, ROSA and MAPO belong here due to their specificity in the field of application. AWBA was developed

Table 3. Analysis of push-pull risk assessment methods

Method	Initial force (N)	Continuous force (N)	Grip quality	Load weight	Environmental factors
RAMP	×	×	×	×	×
Snook tables	×	×		×	
RAPP	×		×	×	×
OHIO BWC push-pull guidelines		×	×	×	
KIM II. (KIM-PP)				×	×

for agricultural posture assessment, and ROSA assesses office workplaces. MAPO is a method specifically developed for risk assessment in hospitals and thus includes situations characteristic for health care explicitly taking place in hospitals. The Hand-Arm Vibration Calculator was classified as unique for another reason. It assesses tasks in which vibrations specifically may have adverse health-related effects on workers. However, it is worth noting that vibrations mainly occur in industrial and agricultural workplaces, which again narrows down the Hand-Arm Vibration Calculator application domain.

3.4 Insights and Limitation

A limitation of the research is that although we have searched for methods for an extended amount of time, using several keyword variations, it cannot be said that we have found all methods, and thus their classification cannot be complete. As experts, we see that there are many possible ways of defining categories. The categorisation we presented earlier is just one which we have chosen and considered the best. In several methods, it appears that repetitive work is recommended, but we could not place this information in the categories because, in other methods, the nature of the work process is not highlighted. From the keywords, methods applicable to more screen-based workplaces were not highlighted, probably because environmental factors are the main focus there. A limitation is that, in addition to categorising and analysing methods, it is important to be detailed, which we have only partially highlighted. For example, the strain load can be determined on both a two- and four-point scale for the methods analysed by body strain.

4 Conclusion

Overall, the research was successful because many methods were collected and systematised. However, the field is fragmented in many areas, and a great deal of professional collaboration would be needed to provide a comprehensive guide. The methods have different structures in that they are observation-based. In addition to the frequently occurring action analysis, questionnaire elements can be observed in the methods (e.g. Washington State Caution & Hazard Checklist, QEC). The differences also make them difficult to compare. Thus, further research is worthwhile. We strongly believe that the creation of a taxonomy of ergonomic risk assessment methods would be of valuable help to the industry.

Acknowledgments. This research was supported by the Ministry of Human Capacities of the Hungarian Government.

References

1. Unver-Okan, S., Acar, H.H., Kaya, A.: Determination of work postures with different ergonomic risk assessment methods in forest nurseries. Fresenius Environ. Bull. **26**(12), 7362–7371 (2017)
2. Chiasson, M.É., Imbeau, D., Aubry, K., Delisle, A.: Comparing the results of eight methods used to evaluate risk factors associated with musculoskeletal disorders. Int. J. Ind. Ergon. **42**(5), 478–488 (2012). https://doi.org/10.1016/j.ergon.2012.07.003
3. Amjad, H., Keith, C., Russell, M., Steve, S.: Using ergonomic risk assessment methods for designing inclusive work practices: a case study. Hum. Factors Ergon. Manuf. **16**(1), 337–355 (2006). https://doi.org/10.1002/hfm
4. Waters, T.R., Putz-Anderson, V., Baron, S.: Methods for assessing the physical demands of manual lifting: a review and case study from warehousing. Am. Ind. Hyg. Assoc. J. **59**(12), 871–881 (1998). https://doi.org/10.1080/15428119891011045
5. Yazdanirad, S., Khoshakhlagh, A.H., Habibi, E., Zare, A., Zeinodini, M., Dehghani, F.: Comparing the effectiveness of three ergonomic risk assessment methods—RULA, LUBA, and NERPA—to predict the upper extremity musculoskeletal disorders. Ind. J. Occup. Int. Med.**23**(1), 8–13 (2018). https://doi.org/10.4103/ijoem.IJOEM
6. Inyang, N., Al-Hussein, M., El-Rich, M., Al-Jibouri, S.: Ergonomic analysis and the need for its integration for planning and assessing construction tasks. J. Constr. Eng. Manag. **138**(12), 1370–1376 (2012). https://doi.org/10.1061/(asce)co.1943-7862.0000556
7. Rahman, M.N.A., Razak, N.S.A.: Review on pen and paper based observational methods for assessing work-related upper limb disorders. Ind. J. Sci. Technol. **9**(S1), 1–11 (2016). https://doi.org/10.17485/ijst/2016/v9is1/106822
8. Li, G., Buckle, P.: Current techniques for assessing physical exposure to work-related musculoskeletal risks, with emphasis on posture-based methods. Ergonomics **42**(5), 674–695 (1999). https://doi.org/10.1080/001401399185388
9. Jones, T., Kumar, S.: Comparison of ergonomic risk assessments in a repetitive high-risk sawmill occupation: saw-filer. Int. J. Ind. Ergon. **37**(9–10), 744–753 (2007). https://doi.org/10.1016/j.ergon.2007.05.005
10. Enim, N., Voluptatem, I., Voluptas, Q.: Ergonomic assessment methods for the evaluation of hand held industrial products: a review 2016-05-16-2, vol. I, pp. 1–22 (2016)
11. David, G., Woods, V., Buckle, P.: Further development of the usability and validity of the Quick Exposure Check (QEC). Ergon. Res. Rep. **211**, 1–68 (2005)
12. David, G.C.: Ergonomic methods for assessing exposure to risk factors for work-related musculoskeletal disorders. Occup. Med. **55**(3), 190–199 (2005). https://doi.org/10.1093/occmed/kqi082
13. Grooten, W.J.A., Johanssons, E.: Observational methods for assessing ergonomic risks for work-related musculoskeletal disorders. A scoping review. Revista Ciencias de la Salud **16**(PE), 8 (2018)

14. McGaha, J., et al.: Exploring physical exposures and identifying high-risk work tasks within the floor layer trade. Appl. Ergon. **45**(4), 857–864 (2014). https://doi.org/10.1016/j.apergo. 2013.11.002
15. Hignett, S., McAtamney, L.: Rapid entire body assessment (REBA). Appl. Ergon. (2000). https://doi.org/10.1016/S0003-6870(99)00039-3
16. McAtamney, L., Corlett, E.N.: RULA: a survey method for the investigation of work-related upper limb disorders. Appl. Ergon. https://doi.org/10.1016/0003-6870(93)90080-S(1993)
17. Moore, J.S., Garg, A.: The Strain Index: a proposed method to analyze jobs for risk of distal upper extremity disorders. Am Ind Hyg Assoc J (1995). https://doi.org/10.1080/154281195 91016863
18. Karhu, O., Kansi, P., Kuorinka, I.: Correcting working postures in industry: a practical method for analysis. Appl. Ergon. **8**(4), 199–201 (1977). https://doi.org/10.1016/0003-6870(77)901 64-8
19. Szabó, G., Mischinger, G.: Just an other ergonomic tool: the 'Composite Ergonomic Risk Assessment'. In: Ergonomics 2013 : 5th International Ergonomics Conference, pp. 169–174 (2013)
20. Li, G., Buckle, P.: Practical method for the assessment of work-related musculoskeletal risks – Quick Exposure Check (QEC). Proc. Hum. Factors Ergon. Soc. **2**, 1351–1355 (1998). https:// doi.org/10.1177/154193129804201905
21. Sanchez-Lite, A., Garcia, M., Domingo, R., Sebastian, M.A.: Novel ergonomic postural assessment method (NERPA) using product-process computer aided engineering for ergonomic workplace design. PLoS ONE **8**(8) (2013). https://doi.org/10.1371/journal.pone. 0072703
22. Garg, A., et al.: The Strain Index (SI) and Threshold Limit Value (TLV) for Hand Activity Level (HAL): risk of carpal tunnel syndrome (CTS) in a prospective cohort. Ergonomics **55**(4), 396–414 (2012). https://doi.org/10.1080/00140139.2011.644328
23. Savino, M., Mazza, A., Battini, D.: New easy to use postural assessment method through visual management. Int. J. Ind. Ergon. **53**, 48–58 (2016). https://doi.org/10.1016/j.ergon. 2015.09.014
24. Steele, T., Merryweather, A., Dickerson, C.R., Bloswick, D.: A computational study of shoulder muscle forces during pushing tasks. Int. J. Hum. Factors Model. Simul. **4**(1), 1 (2013). https://doi.org/10.1504/ijhfms.2013.055781
25. Rodgers, S.H.: Rodgers muscle fatigue analysis. Consultant **7**(1992), 5–7 (2006)
26. Janowitz, I.L., et al.: Measuring the physical demands of work in hospital settings: design and implementation of an ergonomics assessment. Appl. Ergon. **37**(5), 641–658 (2006). https:// doi.org/10.1016/j.apergo.2005.08.004
27. Keyserling, W.M., Stetson, D.S., Silverstein, B.A., Brouwer, M.L.: A checklist for evaluating ergonomic risk factors associated with upper extremity cumulative trauma disorders. Ergonomics **36**(7), 807–831 (1993). https://doi.org/10.1080/00140139308967945
28. Klußmann, A., Gebhardt, H., Rieger, M., Liebers, F., Steinberg, U.: Evaluation of objectivity, reliability and criterion validity of the Key Indicator Method for Manual Handling Operations (KIM-MHO), draft 2007. Work **41**(Suppl. 1), 3997–4003 (2012). https://doi.org/10.3233/ WOR-2012-0699-3997
29. Kee, D., Karwowski, W.: LUBA: an assessment technique for postural loading on the upper body based on joint motion discomfort and maximum holding time. Appl. Ergon. **32**(4), 357–366 (2001). https://doi.org/10.1016/S0003-6870(01)00006-0
30. Buchholz, B., Paquet, V., Punnett, L., Lee, D., Moir, S.: PATH: a work sampling-based approach to ergonomic job analysis for construction and other non-repetitive work. Appl. Ergon. **27**(3), 177–187 (1996). https://doi.org/10.1016/0003-6870(95)00078-X
31. Mitropoulos, P., Namboodiri, M.: The task demands assessment methodology. Proc. Inst. Civ. Eng. Manag. Procur. Law **164**(1), 9–17 (2011). https://doi.org/10.1680/mpal900087

32. Micheli, G.J.L., Marzorati, L.M.: Beyond OCRA: predictive UL-WMSD risk assessment for safe assembly design. Int. J. Ind. Ergon. **65**, 74–83 (2018). https://doi.org/10.1016/j.ergon.2017.07.005
33. McCabe, P.T.: Development of manual handling assessment charts (MAC) for health and safety inspectors. In: Contemporary Ergonomics 2003, 2020. https://doi.org/10.1201/b12800-2
34. Wireman, I.: The process of identifying and implementing ergonomic controls in the packaging of motors. In: Advances in Human Factors, Ergonomics, and Safety in Manufacturing and Service Industries (2010). https://doi.org/10.1201/EBK1439834992
35. Lind, C.M.: Pushing and pulling: an assessment tool for occupational health and safety practitioners, vol. 24, no. 1. Taylor & Francis (2018). https://doi.org/10.1080/10803548.2016.1258811
36. Paulus, P., Langenhorst, R.: WISHA lifting analysis. Quantum **24**(8), 1519–1523 (1988). (WISHA Lifting Analysis, Authors: Peter PaulusRalf Langenhorst, Quantum (1988))
37. Merryweather, A.S., Loertscher, M.C., Bloswick, D.S.: A revised back compressive force estimation model for ergonomic evaluation of lifting tasks. Work **34**(3), 263–272 (2009). https://doi.org/10.3233/WOR-2009-0924
38. Kong, Y.K., Lee, S.J., Lee, K.S., Kim, G.R., Kim, D.M.: Development of an ergonomics checklist for investigation of work-related whole-body disorders in farming – AWBA: agricultural whole-body assessment. J. Agric. Saf. Health **21**(4), 207–215 (2015). https://doi.org/10.13031/jash.21.10647
39. Sonne, M., Villalta, D.L., Andrews, D.M.: Development and evaluation of an office ergonomic risk checklist: ROSA — rapid office strain assessment. Appl. Ergon. **43**(1), 98–108 (2012). https://doi.org/10.1016/j.apergo.2011.03.008
40. Battevi, N., Menoni, O., Ricci, M.G., Cairoli, S.: MAPO index for risk assessment of patient manual handling in hospital wards: a validation study. Ergonomics **49**(7), 671–687 (2006). https://doi.org/10.1080/00140130600581041
41. Douwes, M., de Kraker, H.: Development of a non-expert risk assessment method for hand-arm related tasks (HARM). Int. J. Ind. Ergon. **44**(2), 316–327 (2014). https://doi.org/10.1016/j.ergon.2013.09.002

Analysis and Recommendations for an Automotive Manufacturing Assembly Station Ergonomic Risk

Jessica Backstrom(✉) and Vincent G. Duffy

Purdue University, West Lafayette, IN 47907, USA
jbackst@purdue.edu

Abstract. Warn Automotive is a medium manufacturing company that supplies Tier 1 automotive parts to OEMs. Their newly implemented lines contain automation and opportunities for improvement. Detailed analysis and risk assessment were completed for a station on one of the assembly lines that has had many complaints from operators. After risk tasks were identified, potential solutions are generated by attempting to eliminate, prevent or protect from the risk. The final solution includes Warn approval to begin to validate and test a robotic arm that eliminates an operator lifting task, a tool that takes the required force away from the operator's fingers, and other smaller improvements to the layout or fixture design.

Keywords: Manufacturing ergonomics · Automation · Solution

1 Executive Summary

Warn Automotive has recently implemented a new assembly line over 2019 and starting production in 2020. The last operator assembly station on this line has caused an issue as many operators complain of it being too difficult and painful – causing refusal to work at the station and need for engineering intervention. The cell was analyzed to have four main assembly tasks: (1) installing a vent gore, (2) screwing on bolts, (3) adding a sleeve and cap to the product, and then (4) putting the FAD into the dunnage. Tasks 1, 2, and 4 have ergonomic issues with the thumb, shoulder, and back respectively through poor posture, required installation force, and pinch risk. RULA and NIOSH analysis confirm that the positions are over the safety threshold.

The team then generated solution options that could eliminate, prevent, or protect from the safety risk. All solutions were presented to Warn management where desired solutions were selected for further validation and testing with the operators. The chosen solutions included (1) a hand tool to assist the operator in installing a component with a power grip instead of their thumb alone, (2) adding a lever on the part fixture to hold the bracket component while torquing the bolts, (3) providing an adjustable handle for the operators to find the most comfortable wrist position and (4) utilizing a robot arm to fully eliminate the operators from having to lift the 13 lb. Part.

© Springer Nature Switzerland AG 2022
V. G. Duffy and P.-L. P. Rau (Eds.): HCII 2022, LNCS 13522, pp. 59–79, 2022.
https://doi.org/10.1007/978-3-031-21704-3_5

2 Introduction and Background

2.1 Background

Warn Automotive is a tier 1 automotive supplier. The company was split from Warn Industries in 2017 to separate the OEM (original equipment manufacturer) and the aftermarket business. Warn Automotive makes the OEM drive train components that function for fuel efficiency: (1) front axle disconnects (FAD), (2) integrated wheel ends (IWE), and (3) hub locks. In the past 3 years, Warn has acquired new business programs and implemented new assembly and manufacturing lines consisting of more automation than their previous contracts, making assembly more efficient and less labor-intensive. Warn is classified as a low mix, high volume assembly plant with dedicated assembly and manufacturing cells at demand volumes up to 1 million annually for some products. Takt times on high volume cells reach as low as 9 s, providing an opportunity for injury from frequent ergonomically unsafe movements or positions.

The implementation of the Rogue assembly line – an electromagnetic FAD – was in September of 2020 after years of designing, planning, manufacturing, and debugging the entirety of the system. The Rogue assembly line has one main process flow consisting of 12 manned and unmanned stations and 5 different sub-assembly stations. Processes range from operators loading a FAD pallet with components to a fully automated function tester loaded by a robotic arm. The desired takt time of the cell is 45 s to meet their 450,000-component annual demand from the customer. Overall, through automation and engineering advances, the Warn engineering team has created a safer assembly line that eliminates the timeliest and ergonomically dangerous process steps. However, there are a few stations that remain an issue for the operators and have the potential to cause long-term musculoskeletal injury.

2.2 Problem Statement

The focus of this paper will be on the last assembly station in the Rogue assembly line named Bracket Install Station. This station has not only been a bottleneck efficiency-wise, but half of the operators refuse to work at the station at all because of the physical effort it takes. The goal is to analyze the station for its highest-risk tasks and positions to then create a solution to eliminate the risk and allow operators to feel more comfortable and safer at the station. A secondary goal is to improve the cycle time of the station.

3 Literature Review

The Warn bracket install issue relates to general manufacturing solution-based research as well as the potential for automation. Those two topics were what I chose to approach my bibliometric analysis on. This section will look at overarching themes in the research papers relating to both as well as some insight into specific, noteworthy papers and articles.

Books Ngram viewer shows manufacturing automation hitting its peak in the mid-1990s while manufacturing ergonomics seems to be more stable and truncated by the automation results (shown in Fig. 1). Manufacturing ergonomics alone peaks in 1998 itself at a similar time to automation, but at a much lower level. There is also a rise in authorship towards the end of the graph as well – indicating increasing interest in the topic. I suspect that is due to the increased well-being culture of the past 10 years as well as increasing regulation due to entities like OSHA.

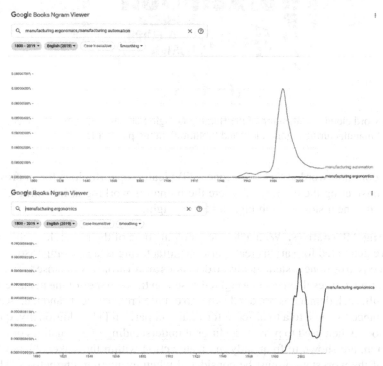

Fig. 1. Shown at the top of this Figure is the Ngram book search for both "manufacturing ergonomics" and "manufacturing automation". The picture on the bottom is the isolated search for "manufacturing ergonomics" alone.

3.1 Manufacturing Solution-Based Research

To get to this information, a Harzing Google Scholar search was utilized with the title keyword of "solution", keywords "manufacturing ergonomics" and a date range from 2010 to 2021. 315 papers and articles were found and analyzed.

Shown in Fig. 2 is a word cloud of the Harzing search results detailed. This gives a representation of the common words and themes in all of this research. Data visualization-style methods are introduced and utilized to highlight important aspects in the ergonomic field, represented by this Harzing search [7]. Intervention is an interesting insight, as it correlates to the need for engineering or safety support in a workstation from what was initially designed. Words such as task, tool, assessment, and time refer to the most common methods of analysis to understand task design and measure risk. "Workstation" was

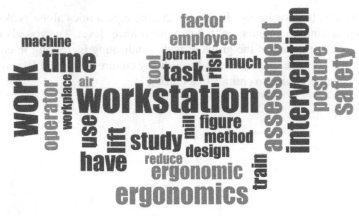

Fig. 2. A word cloud visualization of the Harzing Google Scholar search of 315 papers with the keywords "manufacturing ergonomics" and "solution" in the paper title.

the most common word at 241 occurrences. Typically, opportunities for improvement happen considering the entirety of where the human is working at including elements such as component storage, lighting, and table height.

Comparing Alternatives. With a detailed look at some of the research, multiple solutions were generated for various real-world manufacturing issues. Comparison of alternatives needs to be done systematically so decisions aren't arbitrary or biased. The "Voice of the Customer" is evaluated and weighted based on the demands of the management in a paper mill, each demand is broken down into detailed requirements and then weighted by importance to come to a total score for final comparison [1]. Additionally, quantitative methods, when used to provide additional understanding of alternatives or need for intervention, are shown to frequently motivate action within the stakeholders [8]. The entirety of the workstation must be considered when evaluating alternatives. Through an operator questionnaire and observation, engineers at a milling machine shop were able to identify poor posture partially due to insufficient lighting and faded markings [5]. Findings such as these are important to solution generation especially when they are the true cause of the issue and other options are unavailable (ex. Raise table height).

3.2 Manufacturing Automation Research

Automation research within the manufacturing field was found through a similar Harzing Google Scholar search containing keywords "manufacturing automation" with a limit of 500 papers. The title and abstracts were extracted from Harzing and imported into VOS Viewer to create a word map shown in Fig. 3. Words are enlarged by frequency of occurrence and connected and sorted through relevance to each other. The green section to the right seems to be correlated to utilizing manufacturing automation to improve safety, efficiency, and productivity. The red side on the left, equally dense in content, focusing on the implementation, specific technology, and integration of these automated solutions and products.

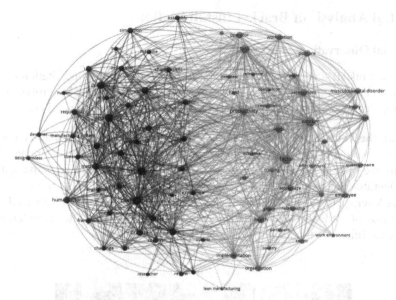

Fig. 3. A VOS Viewer common word analysis with relevance connections in references to 500 papers with "manufacturing automation" as a keyword from 2010 to 2021.

Justification for Automation. Automation has a wide range of benefits in a manufacturing setting, producing efficiencies in cycle time, safety, and consistency. Manual tasks, while having an increased ability to be flexible, lack overall productivity, the accuracy of tasks, and usually ergonomic working conditions [2]. A specific 2021 study of automation implementation was shown to reduce cycle time by 35%, improve ergonomic postures by 15% and increase the overall productivity of the system by 15%. Through all these improvements, however, current automation lacks effective collaboration and cannot be utilized in areas with irreplaceable human activities [2].

Automation is generally best utilized in a manufacturing setting for simple tasks. Generic solutions that automation can solve are component "feeding" or presentation and pick and place tasks [4]. However, automation can be costly to implement and not get enough return for investment if not utilized correctly. A Sweden study shows that the three most important parameters for a successful implementation of an automated solution are (1) safety aspects, (2) lack of technology and knowledge of interaction design, and (3) having a product not designed for automation [3].

3.3 Conclusion

Three of the Eight methods shown in the lecture were utilized to review the research data in Sect. 3: Ngram Viewer, VOS Viewer word analysis, and a word cloud.

4   Initial Analysis of Bracket Install Station

4.1   Initial Observations

The Bracket Install station is the final assembly step to the Rogue line. Station height is at 36″ and is part of a round, rotating fixture that is initially loaded by a robot arm out of the function tester. The station consists of four general steps outlined here:

Installing the Vent Gore. The vent gore is a small plastic seal 2 cm that the operator must press into the FAD using their hand, usually their thumb. The hole on the FAD is a tight fit and operators must use a considerable amount of force to press the vent into place. Operator stance is shown in Fig. 4. I observed several operators use their whole bodies as leverage to get enough force to install it. The installation spot is located on the operator side of the FADs towards the underside shown in Fig. 5. After completing this step several times, my thumb was sore and I had to switch hands.

Fig. 4. Operator installing the vent gore at the bracket install station. Notice the poor posture as they lean oversee the correct location of installation.

Fig. 5. Shows the location of the vent gore on the FAD.

Installing the Bracket. The operators pick up one of the aluminum brackets from the pallet sitting next to the station and put it in place on the underside of the FAD. Then they will pick up two screws from the bucket next to the cell and place them in the magnetized ends of the torques wrench shown in Fig. 6. Next, the operator will hold the bracket in place on the FAD and bring the torque wrench towards the part, activating the wrench when screws are in place. The operator needs to hold the bracket in place and provide resistance to start the screw threads – without it, the wrench would just push the bracket out of position (shown in Fig. 7). Operators must hold the wrench button until the automatic process is finished, where the light on the handle will turn green. The fixture then releases the part from its grips. I observed many operators bent over to what I assumed to be the height and the force needed to pull the screws into place. Management has also expressed concern about this station due to the fact the operators are holding the bracket and potentially causing a pinch risk.

Fig. 6. The operator is shown placing screws into the torque wrench on the left. Notice the operator lean over the FAD to reach each side of the wrench.

Fig. 7. The operator uses the torque wrench by pulling it to the FAD and activating it by pressing the button on the handle. The operator also holds the bracket in place with their left hand.

Installing the Cap and Spline Cover. This step is relatively simple as operators need to pick up the red cap and press it into the right end of the FAD with minimal force. The installed cap and sleeve are shown in Fig. 8. Next, they will grab a mesh cover and stretch it around the spline end of the shaft. This component also takes minimal force or effort to stretch or install. I see little risk in this part of the process.

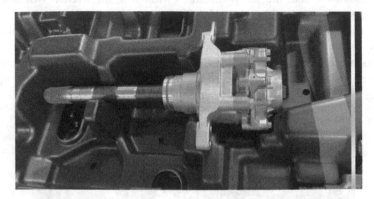

Fig. 8. Shows the red sleeve and red cap on either end of the FAD while sitting in the dunnage.

Moving FAD into Dunnage. When all components are installed onto the exterior of the FAD through the previous steps, the operator then lifts the finished good out of the fixture, turns and walks to the dunnage container, and places it in its spot. The dunnage container is on a pallet rotate and lift station so that operators can use a foot pedal to adjust the height of the dunnage. The FAD fully complete is 13 lbs. Which makes this task high risk for shoulder injuries when completed so frequently throughout the day. The dunnage requires a specific orientation, so I observed operators rotating the part and flipping it over to set it in the dunnage. An operator is shown placing the unit into dunnage on Fig. 9.

Fig. 9. The operator places the finished FAD into the dunnage. This image shows them reaching to place the 13 lb. Unit on the other side of the dunnage.

Overall, there were multiple elements of each task that were observed as being at risk of injury. Table 1 shows the observed risky task elements we will focus on and attempt to improve or eliminate.

Table 1. A summary of the high-risk tasks of the bracket install station and how they will be analyzed.

Task	Short name	Element of risk	Related musculoskeletal injury	Analysis method
Vent Gore Install	A	Pressing vent into the hole	Finger / Wrist	RULA
Bracket Install	B1	Holding bracket in place while torquing screws	Pinch Risk	RULA
	B2	Pulling torque wrench into place to install screws	Shoulder	RULA
FAD into Dunnage	D1	Taking FAD out of fixture	Low Back	NIOSH
	D2	Placing FAD into dunnage	Shoulder	NIOSH

4.2 Cycle Time

A video was recorded for 45 min over 2 different operators and cycle time was taken for each step and the whole-cell shown in Table 2. Overall, the station took an average of 45.51 s to complete all the tasks, which is above the 35 s desired takt time. Secondary to decreasing the ergonomic risk of the station, management would also like to see a reduction in time to help make more products in time.

Table 2. The breakdown of each task component by time to equal to a total cycle time of 45.51 s, 10 s over the desired takt time for the assembly line.

Process step	Cycle time
Install Vent Gore	9.14
Install Bracket	19.26
Install Cap and Sleeve	5.42
Place FAD into dunnage	5.71
Operator Dunnage Tasks	6.59
Total Cycle Time	*45.51*

4.3 Risk Assessment

RULA. The RULA (Rapid Upper Limb Assessment) was chosen for tasks A, B1, and B2 since they are all in similar upper-body positions [6]. The operators range in heights but overall, all have to tilt their head down at more than a 20-degree angle as well as hold their arms away from their body 20 to 30 degrees. The main difference between the 3 different task positions is in the wrist – where scores differed. However, the outcome, was the same for all three with a score of 7 – indicating "investigate and implement change" (Fig. 10 and Appendix A).

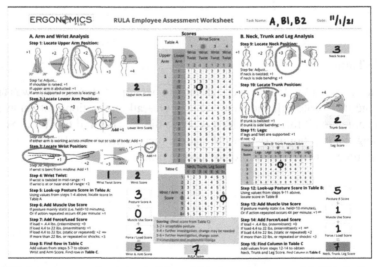

Fig. 10. RULA assessment for tasks A, B1, and B2 showed a score of 7. This indicates a need for intervention in the given position.

NIOSH. The NIOSH lifting assessment was chosen for lifts D1 and D2 where the operator lifts the FAD out of the fixture and into the dunnage. The vertical distance of the FAD will be different for each operator as it is dependent on their height and comfortable holding position. For NIOSH calculations, a taller operator was used to represent the worst-case scenario. Results using the NLE App show a lifting index of 0.7 for D1 and 0.9 for D2 shown in Fig. 11. These are both within the threshold of 1.0 for risk.

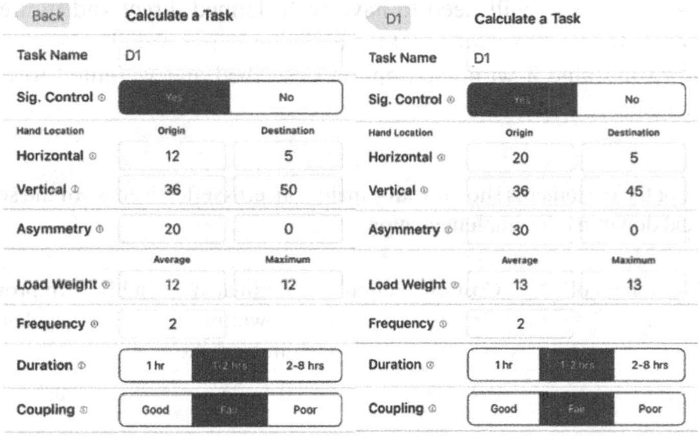

Back	Calculate a Task			D1	Calculate a Task		
Task Name	D1			Task Name	D1		
Sig. Control ⊙	Yes	No		Sig. Control ⊙	Yes	No	
Hand Location	Origin	Destination		Hand Location	Origin	Destination	
Horizontal ⊙	12	5		Horizontal ⊙	20	5	
Vertical ⊙	36	50		Vertical ⊙	36	45	
Asymmetry ⊙	20	0		Asymmetry ⊙	30	0	
	Average	Maximum			Average	Maximum	
Load Weight ⊙	12	12		Load Weight ⊙	13	13	
Frequency ⊙	2			Frequency ⊙	2		
Duration ⊙	1 hr	1-2 hrs	2-8 hrs	Duration ⊙	1 hr	1-2 hrs	2-8 hrs
Coupling ⊙	Good	Fair	Poor	Coupling ⊙	Good	Fair	Poor

Fig. 11. The requirements are used to evaluate the movement of tasks D1 and D2 respectively. Calculations are 0.7 and 0.9, under the 1.0 threshold.

However, the NIOSH equation does not consider the poor shoulder motion that operators need to flip the part to the correct orientation to match the dunnage. To provide additional information, RULA analysis was completed for the peak to the motion shown in Fig. 12. The RULA analysis shows that the position shown is also rated at a 7, which indicates implementation of change is needed (Appendix B).

Fig. 12. The operator is shown at a peak position of D1 – taking the FAD out of the assembly fixture.

4.4   Voice of the Customer

Warn management was initially the one to point out the station as one that needed change – more than the operators. The VP of Operations had expressed concerns specifically with the B1 task but also with the overall cycle time. Most management and engineers have at some point run the station in efforts to increase production rates on off-hours or fill in – creating good firsthand accounts from all parties. Warn is open to spending money to find a solution especially if it will increase output or reduce labor costs. Solution alternatives will need to have well-defined direct and indirect savings outlined as well as the cost to implement for budgetary approval. The needs of the customer are shown in Table 3 with each option described and weighted to be used for alternative analysis.

Table 3. Voice of the customer is shown with 4 main concerns: effectiveness of the solution, cost of a solution, and downtime for implementation.

	Effectiveness of solution	Cost of solution	Estimated assembly downtime to limplement	Improvement to cycle time
Weight	0.6	0.2	0.1	0.2
Score				
1	Issue is not fixed	> $50,000	2 + days of downtime	No Improvement
2	Issue is PROTECTED from operator	$25,000 - $50,000	1–2 days of downtime	Save up to 3 s
3	Issue is PREVENTED from exposure	$5,000 - $25,000	< 6 h of downtime	Save up to 7 s
4	Issue is completely ELIMINATED	< $5,000	No Downtime	Save 10 or more seconds

5   Results

Solutions for the bracket install station ergonomic issues were discussed with priority to (1) eliminate the risk, then (2) prevent the risk, and finally (3) protect from the risk – the last form of protection.

5.1   Task A – Vent Gore Installation

Eliminate. To eliminate the risk – we would need to automate the process. To automate would require a precision robotic arm, vacuum, or suction head to pick up the vent gores, and consistent vent gore presentation. This would be a very expensive solution as all three components would require engineering design and expert programming. Warn management has expressed concern with a solution like this as it would take a considerable amount of time and more effort than they are looking to accomplish.

Prevent. If automation is in-feasible, the next step is to prevent injury and reduce risk. One option to accomplish this is a hand tool that can grab the vent gores using suction and press the component into place using a power grip instead of their thumb – which is a more effective and safe way to apply pressure with our hands.

While this solution would greatly reduce the risk to the thumb – the position of the installation location is still inconvenient. Another option presented is to offload this installation, with the added power grip tool, to a different time in the assembly process where access to the location is in a better position. Another assembly station was identified as having additional time (within takt) and access. This would require Warn to do further investigation on their end about the feasibility of testing the product with the vent installed - since it is currently tested without the component installed and may cause other quality issues. It is not necessary but a further addition to a solution that may help.

Another prevention option is to change the design of the part to reduce the force needed to press the vent gore into the FAD. Engineers were questioned about the feasibility of this option and it was denied because the unit needs to be vacuum sealed – any looser and parts would fail a leak test and be unusable.

Protect. Lastly, the final option is to protect and a few potential options are available. Thick gloves can be provided to help hold some of the force needed to press the vent in. However, gloves like these would make other station tasks more difficult because they would restrict their hand movements.

5.2 B1 – Holding the Bracket in Place

Eliminate. Elimination of this task would simply be to have another force serve as resistance for starting the threads. Multiple options were brainstormed including a manual option like a gate-latch hook or spring-operated lever, or an automated holding lever on the part holding fixture. Implementation of either of these types of solutions would require a hand "tie-down". This refers to an opti-button or something similar that the operator has to be touching for the machine to operate. This is to avoid the operator, now with a free hand, from placing it somewhere that could get pinched or hurt in the torquing process.

A manual solution would be a simple and cheap solution as Warn would only need to buy enough for each fixture (about 16) and install them once. However, figuring out a convenient place to install this hold may be difficult because of the space needed to place the bracket in the correct spot and then eventually remove the whole FAD from the fixture. Another factor to consider is the rigidity of the solution needs to be just enough to start the threads (a small amount of force usually) and doesn't cause any other issues.

An automated hold is also a possibility as an elimination solution. This would look like a spring-loaded lever that when activated, would hold the bracket in place and then retract when the torquing operation is complete. This solution would have significantly more investment for the same outcome as the manual solution – it would require reprogramming the entire cell and making mechanical modifications to the assembly table and every fixture. However, the pallet does contain similar switches on the outside to hold the pallet – so Warn already understands that process.

Protect. Like other solutions, last resort options would include providing thicker gloves to protect from a pinching risk. As mentioned before, the operators would not prefer to wear gloves like this because it limits their hand motions and makes other tasks difficult.

5.3   B2 – Pulling Torque Wrench into Place

Eliminate. This is a great example of an opportunity for automation as elimination of risk. The FAD position is consistent, and the operator would only have to insert the screws into the gun. This could consist of the same torque wrench put placed on a track that when activated, will advance and tighten the screws. This automation would be costly and take programming and engineering time and would need to be paired with one of the elimination solutions for task B1. Together, the operator would be able to place the bracket and screws, step back from the area or press a button to activate, and the machine will run on its own.

While this eliminates ergonomic risk, that process step may take more time and become another point of failure and needed maintenance. The safety of the employees comes first, but it is a consideration when choosing alternatives.

Prevent. The current layout of the cell includes a caged area so to prevent risk when the assembly table rotates. Currently, operators need to step into the assembly area, and some reach to the left to grab the handle of the torque wrench. However, this can be avoided if we simply widen the opening to the assembly area. This would be a simple increase in comfort and allow the operator to have a little more room regardless.

Secondly, there is an opportunity to change the orientation of the torque wrench's handle or make it customizable. It currently sticks out perpendicular to the torque wrench. If we were to trade out the handle for one that could be bent 90 degrees down or up it would allow for a better wrist angle. This would also be a relatively cheap solution as Warn would need to buy only one handle and keep the old one as a spare with minimal installation time.

5.4   D1 and D2 – Moving the FAD

Elimination. Warn has a similar product to the rogue line – a heavy FAD that similarly engineers wanted to reduce the number of times the operator needed to pick up the part. The final solution that Warn came to was a robotic arm that would lift units out of the assembly line and into the dunnage. The same solution is being proposed for a solution for the Rogue line. The operator would finish their last operations and instead of picking up the FAD, it would advance to the next area where it would then be picked up by the robot and placed into dunnage. Warn already has similar robot programming code that would make the process easier as well as familiarity with these robots that are used in other locations in the assembly line and the plant. To accomplish this solution, a new robot would need to be purchased and the layout of the assembly and cell layout would need to be redone.

Prevent. Warn currently has precautions that are like a prevention solution. The dunnage is on a rotating pallet lift so operators don't have to reach as far to place a FAD in the dunnage. Additionally, the assembly table height was designed to be lower to accommodate for the lift of the FAD, even though other issues are the result of that issue as well.

If an elimination solution is not an option, then the current precautions help reduce the risk of the lift.

6   Discussion

6.1   Comparison of Alternatives

Table 4 shows each alternative presented in Sect. 5 against the voice of the customer. All current situations were rated at a score of 2 while proposed solutions showed improvements up to 3.7. Highlighted solutions are the highest scoring alternative in each task category and were presented as a recommended solution for each task shown in Table 4.

6.2   Final Recommendations and Warn Decisions

Options and analysis were presented to senior leadership at Warn and the following were designated as the solutions that were to be further investigated and implemented that met their preferences and made sense to the business direction.

A1 Vent Gore Installation. The hand tool was chosen as the desired option. The hand tool will spread the force needed to install the vent over the surface area of the power grip instead of being forced to use one's thumb. The cost of this solution was identified as being less than $5,000 – which is a good threshold for Warn improvements like this. Automation was discouraged for this task due to the amount of change and downtime the assembly cell would need to occur.

B1 Holding the Bracket. The desired option for this was a manual hold. Similarly, to A1, it would be a very simple solution that costs even less than $500 and utilize minimum downtime to implement. An automated solution is closer in possibility only if a manual improvement proves to not be effective (doesn't hold threads or breaks easily).

B2 Pulling Torque Wrench. An automated elimination solution was also discouraged due to similar reasons. A prevention solution to have an adjustable handle and opening the assembly area was chosen. I agree this is the best solution so that Warn will not need to compromise assembly takt time or additional downtime.

Table 4. Presented alternatives compared to the voice of the customer demands. The highest-rated scores for each task are highlighted in yellow.

SOLUTION	Effectiveness of Solution	Cost of Solution	Assembly Downtime	Improvement to Cycle Time	TOTAL
	0.6	0.2	0.1	0.2	
Task A - Vent Gore Installation					
Automate vent gore installation	4	1	1	1	2.9
Hand tool	3	4	2	1	3
Thick Gloves	2	4	4	1	2.6
CURRENT	1	4	4	1	2
Task B1 - Holding Bracket in Place					
Automated fixture hold	4	1	2	1	3
Manual latch or lever	3	4	2	1	3
Thick Gloves	2	4	4	1	2.6
CURRENT	1	4	4	1	2
Task B2 - Pulling torque wrench into place					
Automation of screw installation	4	1	1	1	2.9
Open up the layout of the area	3	4	3	1	3.1
Adjustable Handle	3	4	3	1	3.1
CURRENT	1	4	4	1	2
Task D1 & D2					
Robotic Arm	4	2	1	4	3.7
CURRENT	1	4	4	1	2

D1 and D2 Moving FAD. Lastly, it was decided that an automation solution was best to improve this operation. This was justified because (1) current preventative solutions are not as effective as desired, (2) Warn has some discount opportunity with the company supplying the robotic arms, and (3) it would incur a significant reduction in cycle time (about 9.5 s) as it eliminates the whole step to load the dunnage. This solution would incur the most cost at $50,000 and additional downtime to re-organize the cell.

6.3 Analysis Limitations

All of the potential and chosen solutions to the bracket install ergonomic risks have not been proven out yet. Warn has agreed to the implementation of these solutions with the contingency that they are trialed and tested beforehand. This will require a trial part fixture so that operators can try out as well as timely programming of a new robot in a different location.

Assemblers in the Rogue assembly area are mostly female and shorter than average American height. Due to this, we didn't want to make table height suggestions based on the current ten assemblers that are in the area. Warn utilizes temporary labor and assemblers are frequently helping in other areas, meaning the designing for the current population could result in a similar ergonomic risk for others. Optimal solutions may have been avoided because of this reason.

7 Conclusion

7.1 Important Insights

Overall, the team was able to provide meaningful insight into potential improvements to the bracket install station. By elimination of the lifting risk and providing tools to support more ergonomic hand and shoulder positions, we can reasonably reduce the musculoskeletal risk of the tasks. After working at Warn for over 3 years, this is one of the more complex ergonomic problems I have faced and will require significant timing and effort to plan a successful implementation.

Automation vs Manual Solutions. The range of solutions to the bracket install station could have ranged from almost full automation to little improvement. As shown in the literature, there are quantitative ways to address the need for automation but in the end, it comes down to the cost and perceived need for it. In the case of Warn, only one automated solution was of interest to management while simultaneously being the task with the least amount of risk according to the NIOSH lifting equation. From my experience working in a manufacturing environment, it is hard to get buy unless it has actualized savings (direct line to profit, not indirect like cost avoidance). I think this ideal has good and bad consequences. It functions well because it holds engineers accountable when coming up with solutions. It's hard to find a place with deep pockets and by forcing these profitable solutions, businesses can remain sustainable through improvement and innovation. However, it can also function as a safety limitation. There are situations where intervention is desperately needed, and management can be too eagerly focused on money to give it the financial support it needs. In these scenarios, you hear of companies who cut corners on cost, and it resulted in injury or long-term harm. Finding that balance is crucial to finding the best solution and unfortunately, there is not a formula that will work for all.

Company Culture. The initial course of operators when the line had started at the beginning of this year would heavily complain about the cell more than they do now. I assume this is due to a couple of things:

1. *Station Skills* Increased – As operators began to run the station more often, these actions would become more comfortable and "learned".
2. *Giving Up* – With incorrect management or lack of resources, ideas can be talked about but never acted upon. As time goes on, it seems fruitless to continue to complain than to come up with your own ways to make things better.
3. General Safety Culture – If the culture discourages speaking up for even the smallest discomfort, it can be difficult to feel like you can speak your mind.

For example, some operators claimed that their fingers were unphased by the vent installation or liked the height of the assembly table. This is a difficult situation as both are obvious ergonomic issues – but as an engineer, you don't want to "impose" your ideas on them without their buy-in.

7.2   Opportunities for Further Improvement

The biggest opportunity for improvement is the table height. Assembler postures were poor and even a small increase in table height (1.5 inches) could make a considerable difference. To do this effectively, we will need to better educate the operators about the risk of their postures with better visibility of their risks as well as proving to them it will result in a safer solution. While not all decisions need to be made with the operator's 100% approval, especially in safety scenarios, I think this is an important moment that we can educate and have them feel involved in their well-being at Warn.

Additionally, the use of human digital modeling would be useful within Warn's assembly creation to avoid situations like these in the future. Engineers create detailed 3D models of the assembled cells before creation – and the addition of human manikins and comfort analysis would be extremely beneficial.

Appendix A

See Fig. 13.

Appendix B

See Fig. 14.

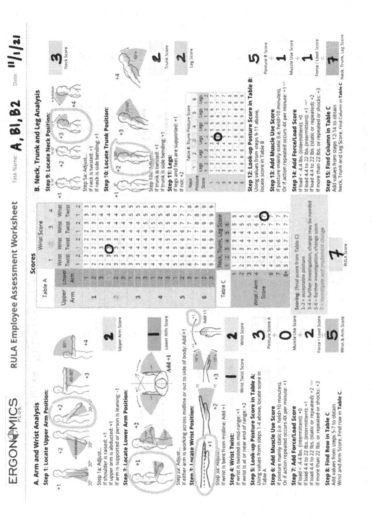

Fig. 13. RULA assessment completed for tasks A, B1 and B2.

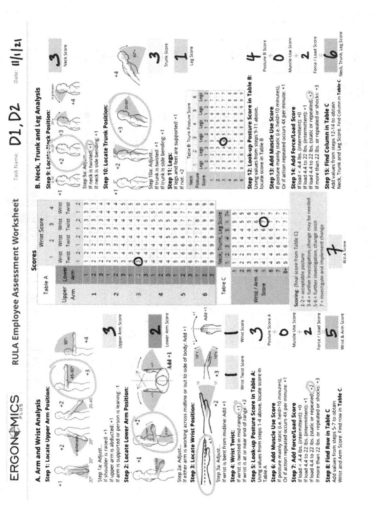

Fig. 14. RULA assessment completed for tasks D1 and D2.

References

1. Borg, H., Bergstrom, K.: Review of Ergonomic Concept Solution - for Cartoning Machine. Linnaeus University (2014)
2. Bortolini, M., Faccio, M., Balizia, F.G., Gamberi, M., Pilati, F.: Review of Adaptive Automation Assembly Systems in the Industry 4.0 Era: A Reference Framework and Full–Scale Prototype. In: Antonella, P. (ed.) Applied Sciences **11**(1256) (2021). https://www.mdpi.com/2076-3417/11/3/1256
3. Fast-Berglund, A., Salunkhe, O., Akerman, M.: Review of Low-Cost Automation – Changing the Traditional View on Automation Strategies Using Collaborative Applications. In: Vol. SE-412 96. Chalmers University of Technology (2020)
4. Hansen, G., David, A.A.M., Bilberg, A.: Review of Generic Challenges and Automation Solutions in Manufacturing SMEs. In: 28TH Daaam International Symposium on Intelligent Manufacturing And Automation (2017)
5. Halim, I., Radin Umar, R.Z., Syed Mohamed, M.S., Jamli, M.R., Ahmad, N., Pieter, H.H.I.: Low cost ergonomics solution for safe work posture at conventional milling machine: A case study. Journal of Advanced Manufacturing Technology **12**, 327-340 (2018)
6. Middlesworth, M.: A Step-by-Step Guide to the Rula Assessment Tool. ErgoPlus, January 30 (2020). https://ergo-plus.com/rula-assessment-tool-guide/
7. Pattanaik, S.N., Wiegand, R.P.: Data Visualization, In: Salvendy, G., Karwowski, W. (Eds.) Handbook of Human Factors and Ergonomics, 5th Ed., pp. 1209-1236. Wiley, New Jersey (2021)
8. Wells, R.P., Patrick Neumann, W., Nagdee, T., Theberge, N.: Review of solution building versus problem convincing: ergonomists report on conducting workplace assessments. IIE Transactions on Occupational Ergonomics and Human Factors **1**(1), 50–65 (2012)

Excavator Comfort-Height Dependence for 2010 German-Modeled Manikins

Garrett Behrje[✉] and Vincent G. Duffy

Purdue University, West Lafayette, IN 47906, USA
gbehrje@purdue.edu

Abstract. Comfort and posture analysis was conducted on 10 modeled individuals in a pre-designed excavator using the CAD-based software, RAMSIS. Individuals' anthropometry was based on the distribution of 2010 German Males and Females, and they were seated and replicated into the pre-determined position before posture and comfort calculations were performed. All individuals in the analyzed sample were given medium torsos and waists, predetermined by the software, and the heights of the individuals were varied based on a statistically normal (Z) distribution. Analysis was also performed to see if there was any functional dependence between the heights of the operators and the level of discomfort calculated by the software. Based on the analysis we found a weak positive association between operators' heights and the discomfort value. Additionally, optimization calculations were performed to determine the ideal male and female operator height to operate a statically designed (no adjustable features to increase comfortability) excavator seat. These heights were found to be 1.77 m and 1.66 m and correspond to the 39th and 52nd percentiles of 2010 German males and females respectively.

Keywords: Optimal operator height · Comfort · Excavator

1 Introduction and Background

Supply chains across the world have been disrupted from COVID-19 resulting in economic and labor inadequacies. Labor shortages in many industries have led to impacted production and have put an overall strain on the production facilities and industries responsible for essential products and resources. This also includes the workers apart of said production and manufacturing industries. With fewer workers present in these areas, burnout, fatigue, and injuries have been on the rise. Employee shortages have led to the inability in alleviating physical, mental, and societal pressures of increased demand with the limited resources. The increased demand and pressure on workers still on-site attempting to repair the supply chains to pre-pandemic levels is boiling over. To assist in this endeavor, analysis and modeling of safe and productive workplaces is imperative to recovering and meeting the necessary societal demand. Designing machinery and tasks to fit certain workers' skills and abilities is one of the many areas being explored. Work in this area has prompted the question of how an equally comfortable and productive work environment can be constructed for workers of drastically different heights,

© Springer Nature Switzerland AG 2022
V. G. Duffy and P.-L. P. Rau (Eds.): HCII 2022, LNCS 13522, pp. 80–95, 2022.
https://doi.org/10.1007/978-3-031-21704-3_6

weights, and torso sizes. Optimizing this design before implementation is necessary and beneficial for both parties, allowing for better comfort and productivity in workers, and indirectly improving profits for said industries. Modeling and analysis on various specimens in an excavator seat were recreated with RAMSIS software and the corresponding analysis and recommendations are provided below. In a complicated problem consisting of many inter-connected and conflicting variables and objectives, tradeoffs for various musculoskeletal systems were necessary to consider [1]. Figure 1 shows common strains encountered in muscles modeled with our manikins in the excavator seat [1].

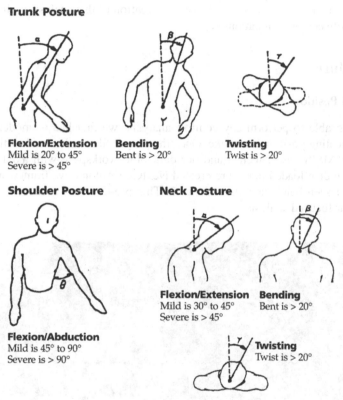

Fig. 1. Motions and posture that create stress buildup in various musculoskeletal systems as observed by the CDC [1].

Workers in manufacturing and other fields requiring the use of heavy machinery sometimes sit their full 8-to-10-h shift in an excavator or seat of other heavy machinery [2]. As such, this analysis was centered around determining the optimal size for a trained operator under those static conditions. Applying dynamic workplace design principles would allow abnormally tall or short or operators to experience a similar level of comfort in comparison to their "average" counterparts [2]. However, with the confined workspace of the excavator pulpit, it would be challenging to adapt and build-in adjustable features for increased ergonomics if not built into place when first assembling the excavator. As such this study will assume none of these features are built-in and that all work is conducted in a static workplace environment. Working with the excavator as designed and determining which features are most desirable to increase operator comfort are discussed in Sect. 5 and may be covered in future work.

RAMSIS was chosen as the CAD (Computer-Aided Design) software of choice due to its ability to handle complex workspaces consisting of several manikins and geometry groups going into the excavator design. Additionally, RAMSIS provides a quick and easily replicable way to run simulations through the use of skin points. By assigning actions to pre-set skin points when creating geometry on manikins in the workspace, one is easily able to carbon copy the procedure outlined in this study, allowing individuals of all technical backgrounds to experience a re-creation of this analysis with little to no variability between other iterations.

2 Procedure

2.1 Seated Position

Before being able to perform any comfort analysis, we first had to model what our designated seating position looks like. Once the proper files had been downloaded and installed, RAMSIS was launched and our dark blue workspace with axial directions appeared. We then loaded in the pre-created NextGen Automotive framework to show the excavator seen below as a part of Fig. 2. This pre-designed excavator will be the setting of our focused analysis.

Fig. 2. RAMSIS software with the loaded in automotive file, showing the pre-designed excavator in the workspace with the pink ground layer selected.

Since we are only concerned with the operators' position in the excavator seat, we have a lot of components that are in excess and not relevant for this analysis. By selecting a group of geometry on the excavator, we see the objects turn pink as shown in Figs. 2 and 3. Right-clicking this group of geometry and navigating the resulting dialog allows us to hide unnecessary geometry for this analysis and makes the design more streamlined and focused for both the designers and viewers of this analysis. Geometry that is hidden can reappear by switching to the hidden negative workspace, shown as the grey background in Fig. 3, and completing the tasks described above again.

Fig. 3. Negative (Hidden) workspace used to hide any unnecessary excavator geometric components for the ergonomic seat position analysis.

Upon removing a large portion of the excavator, we have just the seat and other features needed to operate the excavator including the steering wheel + column, pedals, and joysticks for digging. Now that we have our desired portion of the excavator, we can instruct our manikin to sit inside the excavator seat (more details on creating the manikin in Sect. 2.2). After creating a manikin of desired gender and size, we now can assign tasks for our manikin to perform.

Assigning tasks is completed by defining restrictions to the selected manikin, where it prompts the designer to select a series of functional skin or object points to model a scenario as shown above in Fig. 4. By creating new points or using points pre-created from our manikin we can build a series of restrictions that will sit the manikin into the excavator seat to progress with the analysis (Fig. 5). The resulting tasks assigned to each manikin appear in the project workflow shown in the left sidebar of the workspace as seen in Fig. 6.

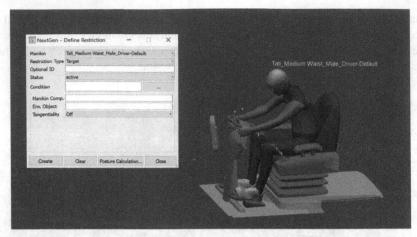

Fig. 4. Define Restrictions dialog box along a seated manikin in the excavator seat. This dialog adds tasks to a selected manikin to help position the necessary limbs into the desired position.

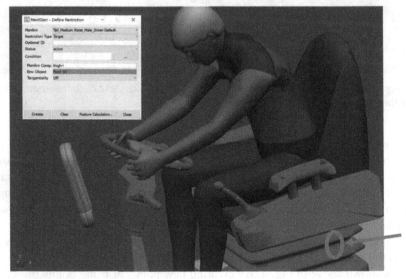

Fig. 5. Performing a target restriction on the manikin positioned in the seat to bring their left thigh to contact the point on the left joystick highlighted in purple (Point_61). The active point is also emphasized with the orange arrow to further distinguish it from inactive points. This restriction was not used in the comfort analysis and is purely a visual example for viewers.

After a series of restrictions has been applied to the manikin, we get the driving posture shown below in Fig. 7. This is the posture we will apply to all the manikins in the study and analyze how their comfort changes as a result of their height according to a normal distribution. It is important to note that multiple manikins can be present in a single workspace and can even be overlapped. We see this below in Fig. 8 where

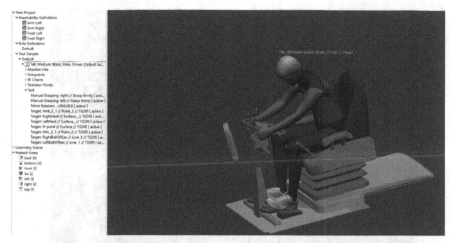

Fig. 6. Seated manikin with the list of tasks (shown in the left sidebar) applied to achieve said orientation. Tasks can be double-clicked in the sidebar to deactivate.

the first two manikins used in this study, the 50th height percentile male and female are shown in the same driving posture. In theory, all 10 manikins used in the study could be overlapped in the seat, but as manikins are added, it becomes increasingly difficult to differentiate which body parts belong to which manikin.

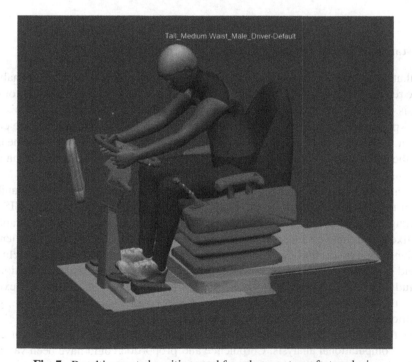

Fig. 7. Resulting seated position used for subsequent comfort analysis.

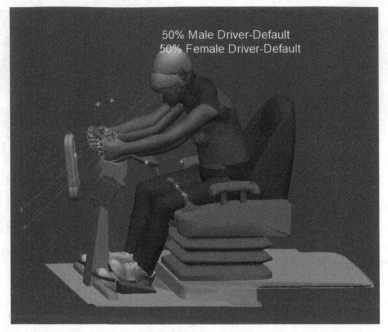

Fig. 8. 50th percentile 2010 German Male (outer) and Female (inner) by height overlapped in the resulting seated position.

2.2 Statistical Anthropometric Building of Manikins

Now that we can position our manikins into the necessary position for comfort analysis, we are ready to begin purposefully designing our manikins to various sizes for comfort analysis. We begin by specifying a database from which we want the manikin's data to be exported from through RAMSIS's test sample option. For this analysis, we chose German individuals from the year 2010. However, without providing a body measure list to the dialog shown below in Fig. 9, there is no way to quantitatively build a manikin as we are only given relative measures for length, corpulence, and proportion.

To create a body measures list and specify quantitative measures for the manikins used in the study we had to use the body-builder plug-in as a part of RAMSIS. By switching to the plug-in and opening the typology dialog window we are now able to enter fixed quantitative values or a specific percentile of the collected data for length, corpulence, and proportion. Additional options can also be added to manikins including hair and other cosmetic features, however, the only feature added from these options in this study was the inclusion of work shoes. Restrictions of certain values only exist if outside the data range of individuals apart of the database characterized by age, year, and nationality.

For this analysis, length or body height was the only variable modified for comparative computational analysis. Corpulence and proportion could have been varied as well, but to understand the related effects of height and comfortability, it is easier if the

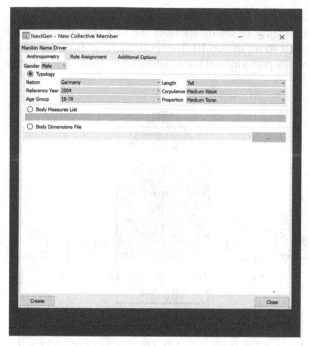

Fig. 9. Dialog window for the creation of a new manikin in RAMSIS

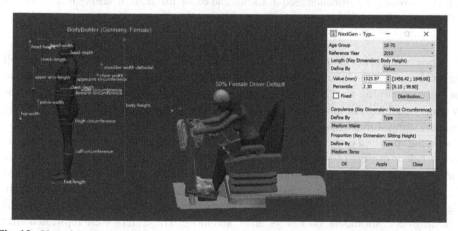

Fig. 10. Use of the Body-builder plug-in to quantitatively build body measure lists for use in our excavator seat comfort analysis.

other two variables are kept static. The value for the body height dimension in each of the 10 manikins was chosen in accordance to a normal (Z) distribution shown below in Fig. 11. Mu, μ represents the population mean or in context the average height of the selected database in RAMSIS and sigma, σ represents the standard deviation or squared variance of the population. To capture a majority of operators, five manikins of each gender were created, each one with the percentile value associated with −2 σ up to + 2 σ. The resulting heights of the manikins created for this analysis were specified and subsequently created above in Fig. 10. The resulting heights of our manikins along with their comfort analysis performance are summed up in Table 1 as a part of the following section.

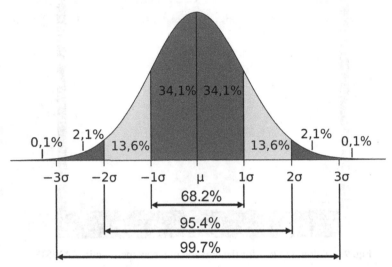

Fig. 11. Normal (Z) distribution used to assume and create manikins of various heights for this performed comfort analysis.

Upon configuring all the body measure lists planned for this analysis, we now had all the tools necessary to build our manikins and perform our comfort analysis. Returning to the ergonomics plug-in of RAMSIS, we can apply our body measures for the 10 manikins by simply clicking our manikin in the seated position and then double-clicking the body measure string stored in the project workflow along the left sidebar. RAMSIS would then load in the specified dimensions of our manikin to the seated driver. A posture analysis shown below in Fig. 12 was run to ensure all tasks assigned to the manikin were run under the new manikin dimensions. After the iteration had been completed, we opened the analysis window and ran a comfort analysis using the comfort analysis tool, shown in Fig. 13. This displayed the level of discomfort in a multitude of musculoskeletal systems including neck, shoulders, back, legs, arms, and more. These steps were replicated after applying all 10 body measures lists onto the manikins and subsequent data analysis was performed to see if there is a functional dependence between operator height and comfort in the static excavator position. Our findings are shown and summarizing in the following sections.

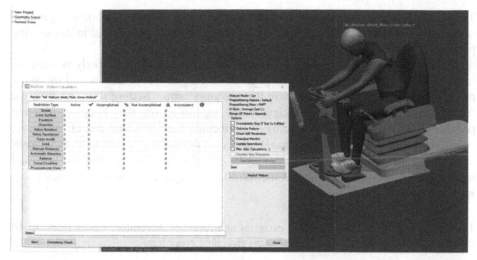

Fig. 12. Posture analysis iteration to ensure the target, grasping and rotation tasks assigned from prior work outlined in Sect. 2.1 are completed successfully under the new manikin dimensions.

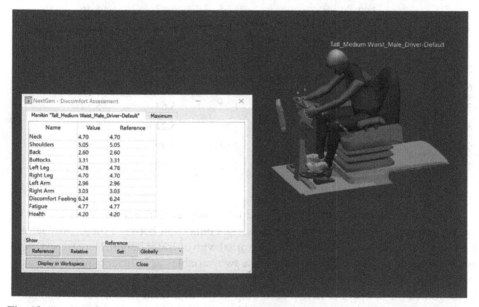

Fig. 13. Resulting posture analysis table for a test manikin not used in this study. This tool allows for quantification of posture and can help designers gauge if their design will yield bad posture in certain musculoskeletal systems amongst a majority of operators.

3   Results

After performing the 10 iterations of the above procedure on the manikins of various sizes based on the normal (Z) distribution, we see the resulting discomfort values outlined in

Table 1 below. Anything above 3.5 is indicative of noticeable discomfort, so regardless of the operators' dimensions, they all were uncomfortable when placed in this driving position.

This study focused on a static driving position, but stress could likely be relieved in the neck and shoulders with an adjustable seat height, which also would move the armrests up in the event pain arises in the operators' arms. Setting the correct height for the driver would also lower fatigue in the legs to ensure they could operate the pedals correctly without overextending or scrunching their legs into a confined space. Additionally, an adjustable and rotatable feature on the steering wheel to bring it closer or further from the operator in the seat may be effective in relieving shoulder, arm, and back pain. These modifications and the resulting changes in discomfort values likely will be studied in future work.

Table 1. Summary table of the body measures and resulting discomfort values from the 10 manikins chosen for this study according to the preceding procedure.

Manikin identifier	Gender	Height percentile	Height (m)	Height (Feet)	Discomfort value
1	Male	50	1.78	5.87	5.82
2	Female	50	1.65	5.42	5.46
3	Male	84.1	1.86	6.10	6.38
4	Female	84.1	1.72	5.63	5.72
5	Male	97.7	1.93	6.34	6.36
6	Female	97.7	1.78	5.84	5.92
7	Male	15.9	1.72	5.63	5.52
8	Female	15.9	1.59	5.21	5.77
9	Male	2.3	1.64	5.39	5.94
10	Female	2.3	1.53	5.00	5.62

While both pictorially and through the table, we see that our manikins are not in an ergonomically fit position, we can see some connection between these two factors. Figure 14 shows how the Discomfort value varied with operator height. Here we see there is a weak positive association between these two variables as indicated by the R^2 value of 0.5542, indicative that approximately 55% of the variability in the Discomfort value is accounted for in operator height according to the best linear fit for our 10 manikins tested. Additional analysis was done to see if operator gender (male or female) changed the level of strength in the functional analysis. This is shown below in Fig. 15 where relative height percentiles by gender are plotted against the resulting discomfort values. Here we see a parabolic fit where individuals closer to the population mean experienced less discomfort, despite still be above the 3.5 threshold value. We can estimate the operator height resulting in the minimum discomfort value by finding the vertex of both polynomials for each gender below in Fig. 15 by using Eq. 1.

For the parabola, $F(x) = ax^2 + bx + c$ with vertex (h, k)

$$h = -\frac{b}{2a}k = F(h) \qquad (1)$$

Equation 1: Vertex of Parabola formula to find size resulting in minimum discomfort when placed into the static excavator driving position.

Upon applying Eq. 1 to both of our polynomial fits, we see that the male manikins yield a minimum discomfort value is 5.66 and is achieved with a male at the 39th percentile in height for our seated position. Meanwhile for the female manikins tested, the minimum discomfort value predicted by the polynomial fit is 5.48 for a manikin at approximately the 52nd percentile in height. These correspond to heights of 1.77 m and 1.66 m respectively. Both the males and females have results near the population mean which makes sense as the design is often done based on average or typical human measurements, as opposed to someone abnormally tall or abnormally short as seen by testing the values at ± 2 σ. Individuals differing significantly from the mean are more likely to encounter increased discomfort if the design is not adaptable to their proportions.

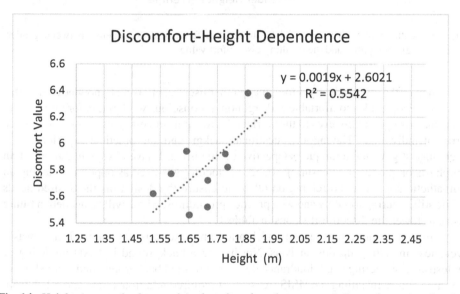

Fig. 14. Height (on an absolute scale) plotted against the outputted discomfort value for the analysis, there is a slight positive linear association between operator height and discomfort in the driving position.

4 Discussion

Prior experience in a manufacturing setting working with heavy machinery motivated me to pursue this work and remediating potential problems I've observed from operators of cranes, trains, and pulpits monitoring steel production at a distance. While I did not have a chance to operate this equipment during my time this summer observing the inner

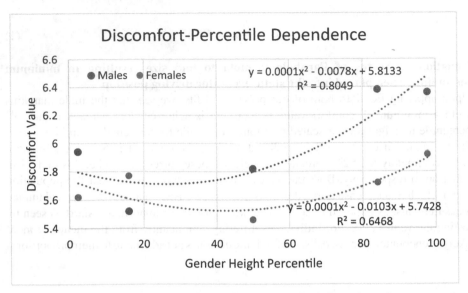

Fig. 15. Scatter plot with polynomial fits to analyze functional dependence between gender-specific height percentile and the resulting discomfort value.

workings of the steel industry, I took many other user accounts and knowledge into this analysis. People take comfortable and ergonomic-conscious workplaces for granted and this analysis opened my eyes to the work and effort put into efficient designs for a wide array of individuals. Having an educational background and practical experience as a metallurgist gave me a unique perspective of this issue. I have always had more of an emphasis on process and ensuring sound methodology is used as opposed to taking an empathetic approach and relying on others to ensure the design fits the desired needs while still adhering to safety and well practice procedures, which will be needed in future work to lower the discomfort values in Table 1.

While my unique perspective and limited knowledge is a strength, it also was a weakness in setting up this analysis. Not having a background in CAD modeling or Industrial engineering was a hindrance due to my limited background and prior skills in this area before installing RAMSIS. As such, it required additional time and effort from me to navigate the RAMSIS functionality and learn principles of modeling Industrial Engineering students have had years of practice with. Despite this original hindrance, I was able to prepare this report summarizing the analysis performed pursuing additional help from individuals at Human Solutions who helped provide the instructions in installing the software. Additionally, conversations with those of different educational backgrounds in engineering, including aerospace, industrial, and engineering management helped opened my eyes to the many angles that could be taken in this analysis. This analysis has formally introduced me to CAD and modeling principles not emphasized in my educational background as a materials engineer and I am grateful to add to my toolkit and subsequentially apply it to the metallurgy industry. For those motivated to replicate the analysis in RAMSIS and are intimidated that you do not have the educational background or skills, I ask you to try. Trying and failing with an open mindset is the only way you can learn. Even if you have a background in CAD, ergonomics, and industrial engineering, try and approach the problem from a perspective you are unfamiliar with. In any work setting, you will be faced with problems you do not know have to solve immediately or will be tasked with reframing a problem in a way that you are not as adept at solving. As such, use this exercise as a way to practice reframing a problem or taking a leap of faith to learn new practical skills.

Modeling provides many benefits when designing, including the opportunity to attempt many workarounds of potential issues before spending and fully implementing a given design. However, it is important not to lose sight of modeling never fully encompassing the reality of the application. Modeling approximations have an intrinsic amount of error as they usually are based on a database of old records and past experiences. This is described in Chapter 35 of the Handbook of Human Factors and Ergonomics by Vincent Duffy. He outlines the types of modeling and the information that can be obtained from corresponding analyses. Generally, a spectrum can be made to describe the types of modeling used to make meaningful designs in industry, based on the impact of interaction within the model [3]. The spectrum is pictorially depicted below in Fig. 16. Modeling that requires little to no interaction has often been termed a simulation. It is effective in automated systems for maintenance and routine applications where a lot of trials are performed giving the model a chance to learn potential errors and how to filter them correctly, ensuring a high efficacy rate [3]. Meanwhile, the other end of the spectrum entails a prototype where interactivity is necessary to obtain data and make necessary improvements before the final design is implemented.

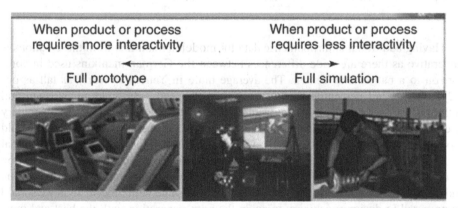

Fig. 16. Spectrum describing key differences in what is defined as a prototype and a simulation. It also provides a sense of what can be determined from the modeled results in RAMSIS [3].

5 Future Work and Conclusions

While this analysis has defined the optimal proportions and highlighted a possible dependence in operator size (specifically body height) and comfortability or lack thereof, much is still to be done. Analyzing other dimensions like corpulence and proportion in either isolated studies or alongside this analysis may help further understand how these factors affect worker fatigue and the connection to days missed. Another area that could be explored is replicating this analysis on a wider manikin base. Only German-based manikins were used in this analysis as they were the only nationality of manikins available in the version of RAMSIS installed. It is important to note that different nations have varying height distributions, so the optimal operator measurements could likely be improved over a test sample encapsulating a larger and more global perspective of excavator operators. Average heights of males and females from select nations are shown below in Table 2 [4].

Table 2. Average height of males and females across the world in both metric and US Customary units [4].

Nation	Average male height (m)	Average male height (Feet)	Average female height (m)	Average female height (Feet)
Germany	1.80	5.91	1.66	5.45
Netherlands	1.84	6.04	1.70	5.58
United States	1.77	5.81	1.63	5.35
Chile	1.73	5.68	1.59	5.21
Yemen	1.63	5.35	1.54	5.05
New Zealand	1.78	5.84	1.65	5.41
Philippines	1.65	5.41	1.54	5.05

Having additional anthropometric data for modeled manikins from these nations is imperative as there are wide differences between the German manikins used in comparison to a nation like Yemen. The average male in Yemen is nearly as tall as our -2σ male (~2nd percentile by height) used in the study. By building cross-cultural anthropometric comparisons, manufactures would be able to design heavy machinery like excavators more accommodating to a wider range of customers. This in turn would project an increased supply base and revenues as a result. This also provides additional motivation to study the extremes of the distribution not accounted for in the selection of our 10 manikins. Additionally, it is important to note that individuals are dynamic and height distributions amongst these nations will change with time, as such we should be prepared to design machinery to equip the next generation with the best and most ergonomically sound gear possible. While dynamic workplace design was not used in this study, it can be used to mediate issues in this space, despite it not being full proof. As such, thoughtful ergonomic design based on global anthropometry results is essential for all fields of work going forward.

Acknowledgments. This analysis was only made possible thanks to Purdue University and the school of Industrial Engineering for providing the resources to allow for the completion of this analysis. A special shoutout goes out to Andre Luebke from Human Solutions for assisting both virtually and in person to instruct the full functionality of the RAMSIS software and troubleshoot any errors found in the installation of the software and during preliminary stages of using the software.

References

1. Kittusamy, N.K.: Ergonomic Risk Factors: A Study of Heavy Earthmoving ... CDC Archives (2002). https://www.cdc.gov/niosh/mining/Userfiles/works/pdfs/erfas.pdf
2. Kittusamy, N.K., Buchholz, B.: An Ergonomic Evaluation of Excavating Operations: A Pilot ... CDC (2011). https://www.cdc.gov/niosh/mining/UserFiles/works/pdfs/aeeoe.pdf
3. Duffy, V.G.: Human digital modeling in design. Essay. In: Salvendy, G. (ed.). Handbook of Human Factors and Ergonomics, pp. 1016–30. Wiley, Hoboken, NJ (2012)
4. Average Height of Men and Women Worldwide: Worlddata.info (2019). https://www.worlddata.info/average-bodyheight.php

Developing Ergonomic Design Recommendations Using Human-Centric RAMSIS Analysis

Jonathan T. Breese, Adam M. Fuhrmann$^{(\boxtimes)}$, Vincent G. Duffy, and Andre Luebke

Purdue University, West Lafayette, IN 47907, USA
fuhrmann.adam@gmail.com

Abstract. This analysis was conducted to determine the utility of the advanced ergonomic analysis tools in the RAMSIS software. Specifically, this report demonstrates how RAMSIS can be effectively used to provide detailed design recommendations which improve operator comfort in an excavator control cabin. A literature review of similar ergonomic investigations in heavy machinery and construction was conducted to provide background information to guide the analysis and context for future work. The ergonomic issues in the cabin design which were analyzed were the steering wheel positioning, armrests, wrist pads, joysticks, seat, floor pedals, touchscreen, and field of view. The step-by-step approach to this analysis was documented to provide a guide for readers to conduct a similar analysis in other applications. Steps for the analysis include creating manikins to represent edge percentiles of operator population, evaluating the comfort ratings of the default control and seating positions, adjusting cabin components translation and rotation to improve comfort, improving touch screen reach and interaction, and evaluating visibility and comfort during control actuation. A table of cabin components, translation, rotation, and nominal position summarizes the key relevant findings. These data provide useful bounds for excavator designers to make more ergonomically beneficial design decisions earlier in the product's development. With little cost, relative to trial-and-error prototyping, RAMSIS can provide useful insights for a human-centric design.

Keywords: Ergonomics · Comfort · Human performance · RAMSIS · Computer-aided design

1 Introduction and Background

1.1 Introduction of RAMSIS

When designing heavy machinery controls, human comfort is often a lesser priority but is a critical consideration when trying to maximize the performance of a human-machine system. Additionally, when these ergonomic factors are addressed, there is often an insufficient range of human body dimensions considered to effectively conform the work environment to each operator [1]. Traditionally, these ergonomic analyses

© Springer Nature Switzerland AG 2022
V. G. Duffy and P.-L. P. Rau (Eds.): HCII 2022, LNCS 13522, pp. 96–112, 2022.
https://doi.org/10.1007/978-3-031-21704-3_7

are made via inspection of a physical prototype which is costly and prevents rapid design adjustments to arrive at the best solution. This report investigates a method of using computer-aided design of the environment along with ergonomic analysis software (RAMSIS) to generate detailed and actionable design recommendations. The focus is to alleviate awkward joint angles, enhance the field of view, improve the reach of controls, prevent repetitive stress injuries, and create adjustability to fit the operator's dimensions.

RAMSIS is an ergonomic analysis software with embedded tools to create human representative manikins and place them into the human-machine CAD model to quantitatively assess comfort and other ergonomic interactions. The software is an applied example of the concept of digital human modeling (DHM), more commonly referred to as human digital modeling in human factors contexts. The basic premise of DHM is creating a digital representation of a human being and evaluating it in a simulated environment to facilitate the ergonomic assessment of that interaction [2]. In an excerpt from the *Handbook of Human Factors and Ergonomics: Chapter 35*, "For the practicing engineer, human digital modeling represents the opportunity to reduce the need for physical prototyping as it typically makes the analyses available through commercial computer-aided engineering CAE)" [3].

1.2 Background and Literature Review

To provide some guiding background information for this analysis, the initial steps of a systematic literature review were conducted. The purpose of this effort was to reveal current research trends relative to this RAMSIS ergonomic analysis and establish context for future work. The protocol for this search was to begin with keyword searches of "heavy machinery ergonomics" and "construction machinery ergonomics" on multiple research databases (Google Scholar via Harzing's Publish or Perish, SpringerLink, Scopus, and Web of Science). The search date ranges were from 1990 to 2021 and no other filters were applied. The number of relevant articles yielded for each database is summarized in Table 1 below.

Table 1. Search results per database

Keywords searched	Heavy machinery ergonomics	Construction machinery ergonomics
Database	**# of Results**	**# of Results**
Google Scholar (Harzing)	1,000	1,000
SpringerLink	1,399	1,794
Scopus	57	271
Web of Science	31	41

The abstract, author, citation, and reference data were then exported from the databases which support this functionality for further bibliometric analysis and visualization. A word cloud using *maxQDA* software was created using the plain text keywords from each search. This cloud, shown in Fig. 1 emphasizes the most common keywords within the articles from the initial database search. This image provides an initial practical screening tool and helps to highlight more relevant search terms for iterating database searches for more targeted and refined results. The keywords: safety, design, construction, engineering, machinery, and ergonomics are the most common, so those articles which focus on those terms were sorted as most relevant.

Fig. 1. Word cloud from database search results

The export files of the abstract, author, and citation information were also used to generate a co-citation visualization web through *VOSviewer* software. Co-citation analysis displays instances of articles being cited together in another publication which reveals clusters of related research. The co-citation visualization in Fig. 2 shows a clear cluster of co-citation in the red area. Further inspection of these sources reveals a cluster of similar topics relating to ergonomic improvement in construction equipment via operator body sensors detecting vibration and shock as well as deep learning predicting sources of operator injury. The general trend of these articles is a retroactive analysis of existing equipment to determine potential ergonomic pitfalls. This points to a potential area of future work, where pairing the results of studies like these with focused analysis in RAMSIS could eliminate the discovered sources of operator discomfort.

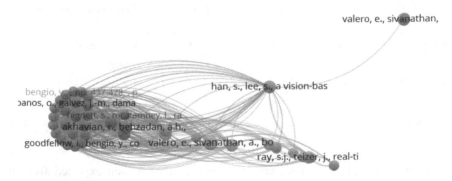

Fig. 2. Co-citation web of search results in scopus

Another method of filtering out relevant research from a large set of database results is to create a pivot chart. This can display top authors, institutions, countries, etcetera which contribute the most to the field of study. Figure 3 shows the most productive authors within the database search for "machinery ergonomics". This table displays only those authors who produced four or more relevant articles to the keyword search. This provides a useful list to focus the literature review investigation on since the number of publications of an author may indicate their depth of research into that subject.

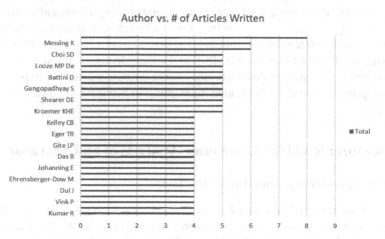

Fig. 3. Most productive authors within search result field

The trends in existing research show a clear need for improved ergonomic design considerations in heavy machinery over a wide array of industries. For example, operators of pit mining vehicles in the artic are at a high risk of discomfort, musculoskeletal disorders, and occupational accidents due to ergonomic failings in the design of their equipment [4]. Additionally, a study of heavy earthmoving machinery operators which characterized the level of increased exposure to ergonomic hazards such as vibration and poor postural requirements, recommended engineering improved ergonomic controls in the industry [5]. These concerns extend not only to the operation but to the maintenance of these machines, which the operators often need to do themselves in the case of forestry machinery [6]. In all these examples, there is a clear need for improving the ergonomic design considerations in the development of heavy machinery operator environments. The analysis in this report will demonstrate how DHM and the use of RAMSIS and CAD can fulfill this need.

2 Problem Statement

The problem statement leading to this analysis is: can the use of RAMSIS DHM software yield detailed design change recommendations for articulating seating and operator control components in the design of an excavator cabin. Initial work on this topic was documented in *Human-Centric Product Development: Using RAMSIS Ergonomic Analysis to Incorporate Operator Comfort into Excavator Design* [9]. This initial report demonstrated the viability of using RAMSIS to incorporate ergonomic design consid-erations early on in system development. The following report expands on that analysis in a few areas. It covers a wider percentile of operator body types, and more targeted body positions required for driving, excavator joystick manipulation, and touchscreen interface reach. It also introduces more advanced analysis techniques such as assessing the operator's visual field of view during the various task posture positions.

Similar to the initial analysis, this more in-depth problem is of interest to many indus-tries since this methodology can be applied to any product which encounters ergonomic challenges during its lifecycle due to the human operator being a design afterthought [7]. The methodology for this analysis was based on in-class demonstrations of the software in IE 578 as well as referenced techniques and procedures in the RAMSIS help menu documentation [8]. The following RAMSIS procedures document the steps the authors took to complete this analysis demonstration but are written in a manner to be a helpful, step-by-step instruction flow for readers attempting to replicate the analysis for their learning.

3   Procedure: RAMSIS Ergonomic Analysis of an Excavator

3.1   Creating Boundary Manikins for the Tasks

Reference *Human-Centric Product Development: Using RAMSIS Ergonomic Analysis to Incorporate Operator Comfort into Excavator Design* [9], under the *Procedure* section to set up the RAMSIS software. Multiple manikins are required to assess the ergonomic requirements of a multitude of body shapes and sizes.

The creation of manikins begins with selecting the *Next-Gen Body Builder* tab under the *Start* menu. Select *Anthropometry - > Germany 2004* then *Apply*. Once selected, a manikin will appear with the adjustment settings shown in Fig. 4. Control measurements of *Body Height, Waist Circumference, and Sitting Height* can be adjusted by selecting *Anthropometry - > Typology - > Control Measurements* then selecting *Value,* as seen in Fig. 4 To adjust Dependent Measurements, select *Anthropometry- > Typology - > Dependent Measurements.* Adjust Dependent Measurements by dragging the slider on the left or bottom of the window, while being careful to maintain within the boundary of the blue lines.

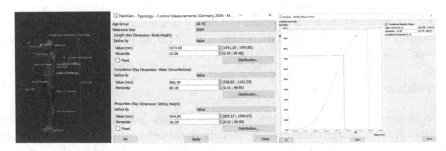

Fig. 4. Manikin control and dependent measurement tabs

Once the values are adjusted, select *Anthropometry - > Add Body Measure List to Structure Tree* to have it selectable for a manikin. Repeat the steps by changing gender and body size to have a wide array of manikins to choose from for ergonomic analysis.

Create a Role for the manikins by selecting the *Role Definition* icon ✦, and creating a Role of *Operator*. Select *PHPT* for the prepositioning point and *Heavy Truck* for the Posture Model as seen in Fig. 5.

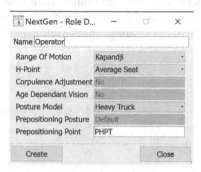

Fig. 5. Operator role defined

Now select the *Test Sample* button ⚕, to create multiple manikins with the *Operator Role*. Select *Male/Female* in the *Gender Category* and select the *Body Measure List* radial to select the manikin body measure generated from the previous steps, as seen in Fig. 6. Under the *Role Assignment* tab, select *Operator* and ensure that no shoes are selected under the *Additional Options* tab. Repeat the process to create multiple manikins, ensuring to name them in the Manikin Name section. Reference Fig. 6 to see the variety of manikins included in this analysis. Attach body points by loading the file via *File- > Open* and merging the .*bpt* files included in the RAMSIS setup file. Add work shoes by right-clicking on a manikin, select *Object Properties - > Additional Options,* and select *Work Shoe*.

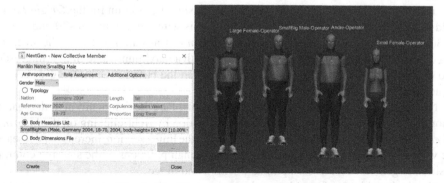

Fig. 6. Manikins of varying sizes and shapes

3.2 Evaluate the Location, Adjustment Range, and Comfort for the Overall Driving Posture

To manipulate the steering wheel components, a *Joint* and *Wheel Point* must be created for rotation and translation of the steering column. First, hide the top components of the steering column to view the base of the steering components. Select *Geometry - > Point - > Create on Object* to create a point on the object in the top right and bottom left as seen in Fig. 7 and Select *Create* for both points. Then change Point Type to *Create Between Points* and select the points for First and Second Points Respectively. Next, create a point on the middle of the steering wheel itself using the same instructions.

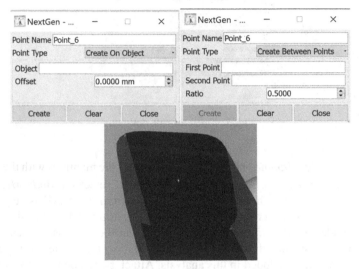

Fig. 7. Creating rotation and translation points

To move the steering group to a nominal ergonomic position, select *Geometry - > Define Kinematics*. When the *Object Kinematics* screen displays, change the name to Steering Wheel. Select the point at the base of the steering column for the *Origin Point*. Add a *Degree of Freedom* of *Rotation* in the Y-axis with a minimum of -30 and a max of 30 degrees. Add the second *Degree of Freedom* of translation between the steering wheel point and steering column points created with a maximum value of 200 mm. Add two objects, first the Steering Wheel itself and then the base of the steering wheel, as depicted in Fig. 8. Click *Create*.

Now that the steering wheel can be manipulated, place the first manikin in the seat to a nominal position. Adjust the steering wheel position by right-clicking on the *Steering Wheel Kinematic,* then select *Object Properties*. In the limits section, increase or decrease the values for rotation and translation. Repeat the manipulations to the steering column position to generate results for nominal position and range.

Nominal positioning for each manikin is determined by iterating adjustment of cabin components and seeing how those changes affect overall manikin comfort. The *Comfort Feeling* and *Joint Capacity* tools are useful ways to quantify the comfort levels of various

Fig. 8. Define geometry object kinematic input screen

body areas and joints when the manikins are positioned. When using the *Comfort Feeling* Analysis tool as depicted in Fig. 9 set the reference values with no manipulation done to the steering column. Once manipulation is made, select *Posture Calculation* to assess the result of the manipulation to the manikins overall *Comfort.* Continue to manipulate the steering column position until the lowest possible values are achieved and repeat the process for the other manikins. A similar process is done with the *Joint Capacity* tool depicted in Fig. 10, although with this analysis, specific joint discomfort capacity can be used to guide more targeted adjustments. For the steering column and all the following excavator cabin components in this report, these tools were used to derive the nominal position and ranges provided in each section table.

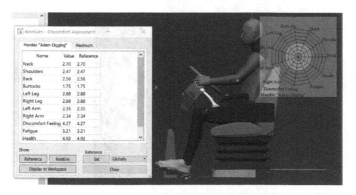

Fig. 9. Using comfort feeling to guide adjustment

After determining nominal steering column positioning using the four manikins, create a rotation of 20 degrees about the Y-axis and a translation of 150mm axially along the steering column. The nominal position of the steering column is depicted in Fig. 11. The range of adjustment to account for the comfort of all the manikins is the adjustability of 5 degrees in rotation and 20mm in translation as seen in Table 2 which displays the optimal position for the individual manikins as well as the range.

3.3 Evaluate the Location, Adjustment Range, and Comfort for Joysticks

To evaluate a range for the joysticks, *Group* the armrests and label them *Armrests.* The joysticks require a translation along the X and Z axes as well as a rotation about the

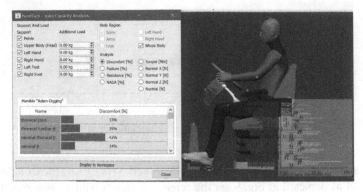

Fig. 10. Using joint capacity to guide analysis

Table 2. Steering column nominal position and range

Steering column	Tall big male	Small big-male	Small female	Large female	Range
Rotation (degrees)	15	20	25	15	20 ± 5
Translation (mm)	150	165	190	170	170 ± 20

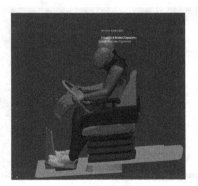

Fig. 11. Nominal position of the steering column

Y-Axis to increase the *Comfort Level.* To do so, follow the directions above for *Object Kinematics* and create all three axes for *Degree of Freedom* of *Translational* or *Rotational* respectively with the *Object* as the *Armrest* group created. Ensure the manikin is grasping the joysticks on the left and right. Adjust the armrests for each manakin to decrease the *Discomfort Feeling.* As a technique adjust the manikin to aneutral posture to assess the most relaxed position to attempt to achieve.

The differences between the manikins were more pronounced with the joysticks due to the massive differential in size between the manikins. Table 3 shows the delta between four and shows the range for Rotation (Y-Axis), Translation (X-Axis), and Translation

Z-Axis. Reference Fig. 12 to visualize the results of the range described in Table 3 and the different body positions required without the ability to adjust the armrests.

Table 3. Joystick nominal position and range

Joystick armrests	Tall big male	Small big-male	Small female	Large female	Range
Rotation Y-Axis (degrees)	15	10	5	12	10 ± 5
Translation X-Axis (mm)	0	10	50	20	20 ± 30
Translation Z-Axis (mm)	−40	−50	−60	−50	-50 ± 10

Fig. 12. Nominal position of the joysticks

3.4 Evaluate the Location, Adjustment Range, and Comfort of Wrist Pads

To evaluate a range for the wrist pads, start by performing similar grouping steps and degree of freedom generation as described in Sect. 3.3 but only select the wrist pads and wrist pad supports for grouping. Only a single axis of movement needs to be generated which is parallel with the top of the armrest. This axis will allow the wrist pads to slide forward and aft along the armrest while maintaining their connection regardless of armrest Y-axis rotation. Adjust the wrist pad fore-aft position along the armrests for each manakin to decrease the *Discomfort Feeling* following the same steps as outlined for the armrests.

In the case of the different manikins, the nominal wrist pad range was limited in variability. This is expected because when different body types are gripping the joysticks, their wrists naturally rest in a smaller area towards the front of the armrests. Table 4 shows the delta between the four body types and shows the range for translation along the armrest parallel axis (with negative values being closer to the joystick). Reference Fig. 13 to visualize the results of the range described in Table 4 and the different body positions required to rest the manikin forearm on the wrist pads.

Table 4. Wrist pad nominal fore-aft position and range

Wrist pad position	Tall big male	Small big-male	Small female	Large female	Range
Translation Armrest-Axis (mm)	−15	−20	−25	−15	−25 ± 15

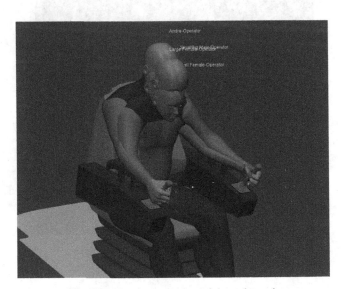

Fig. 13. Nominal position of the wrist pads

3.5 Evaluate the Location, Reach, and Comfort to Touch Screen

To assess the original location of the touchscreen, *Hide/Show* components to have the Touchscreen in view. Define a restriction to reach out and touch the touchscreen via the *Define Restriction* button . Choose the *indexfingertip-r* for the manikin component

NextGen - Define Restriction   —   □   ×

Manikin	Andre-Operator
Restriction Type	Target
Optional ID	
Status	active
Condition	
Manikin Comp.	indexfingertip-r
Env. Object	Display_Face
Tangentiality	Off

Apply   Clear   Posture Calculation...   Close

Fig. 14. Defined restriction for touchscreen

and choose the *Display Face* for the environment object as seen in Fig. 14. Ensure to change the line of vision to be looking at the Touchscreen.

Select *Analysis - > Compute Reachability - > Arm right.* Notice in Fig. 15 that all the manikins can reach the top of the touchscreen but are unable to reach the bottom. It is also apparent that the posture required to simultaneously operate the left control and touch the touchscreen is uncomfortable.

Fig. 15. Manikins unable to reach the bottom of touchscreen.

The touchscreen needs to be moved along the X-axis and the Z-axis to be in reach for the manikins. Define a kinematic with the touchscreen as the object and the degree of freedom as translational in both the X and Z axes. Reference Table 5 to see the ranges of movement required for each manikin to maximize *Comfort Feeling.* The ideal location for the touchscreen is a movement of 120mm and 190mm in the X and Z axes respectively.

Reference Fig. 16 to visualize the final touchscreen location with reachability range included.

Table 5. Touchscreen nominal position and range

Touch screen	Tall big male	Small big-male	Small female	Large female	Range
Translation X-Axis (mm)	100	120	140	120	120 ± 20
Translation Z-Axis (mm)	200	190	180	190	190 ± 10

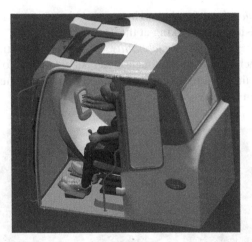

Fig. 16. Final touchscreen location inside reachability range

3.6 Evaluate Visibility and Comfort While Actuating Controls

To assess whether the changes made to the locations of components of the excavator affect the visibility while actuating the controls, first create a point on the display screen using the *Geometry - > Point* tool. Select *Operations - > Move Eye* to adjust the settings of where the manikin is looking. Select the *Viewing Task* to *Lok at Object*, the *Geometry Point* to the point created on the touch screen, and *Move Starting with* to *Neck*. Checkmark *Consider Posture Model* as seen in Fig. 17 and select *Apply*.

Now that the manikin is looking at the touchscreen, bring back the steering wheel components via *Hide/Show*. Select *Analysis - > Vision - > Internal View* to view the visibility from the manikin's perspective. Repeat the process with the manakin operating both controls and reaching to manipulate the touch screen while operating the left control. Finally, repeat the process with the varying-sized manikins to assess their sightlines. Figure 18 shows that in both positions, the changes made to the locations of the controls and touch screen give the manikins a clear sightline to the touch screen itself.

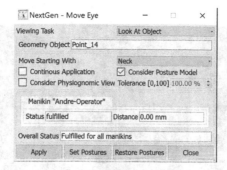

Fig. 17. Move eye input parameters

3.7 Recommended Design Changes

The recommended range of adjustments for each component of the cabin that interfaces with the operator are summarized in Table 6. These adjustment ranges support the ergonomic development of the excavator which will be adaptable to manikin ranges from the 5th-95th percentile of human body type based on the RAMSIS demographic records used. This approach of using RAMSIS to incorporate DHM, allows engineers to start from confidently derived nominal ergonomic design ranges to develop the adjustment mechanisms which conform to operator comfort instead of forcing operators to fit into uncomfortable environments. This is not to imply that design tradeoffs and limitations of cost, materials, schedule, etc. won't still exist, but the process can now fully incorporate ergonomic variables into those decisions.

In addition to supporting better human-centric design, RAMSIS analysis has the added benefit of generating these design parameters without requiring the time and cost-intensive construction of a full-scale prototype. While a prototype may still be prudent to test operator interaction, rapid iterations in the design to improve ergonomics can be done with RAMSIS comfort analysis tools before any physical prototype is built. In the case of this analysis, there are clear changes that need to be made in the steering column, joystick/wrist pad orientation, and position of the touch screen to support operator comfort and visibility to prevent unnecessary fatigue and repetitive stress injuries.

4 Discussion

Both authors have experience as Air Force pilots being in the operator role of a human-machine system and having to compensate because of poor ergonomic decisions in cockpit design. In many cases, these drawbacks in ergonomics are not just an impediment to comfort and a source of repetitive stress injury, but significantly impact the maximum capable human performance that can be expected of the operator. Even though humans are excellent at adapting to challenging situations, any level of pilot compensation required due to poor ergonomics still taxes the finite resources of human processing power and can therefore hinder tactical execution. Often, these poor ergonomic decisions are not a necessary tradeoff for the priority of aircraft performance but simply an oversight or lack of considering operator comfort during early design and prototyping.

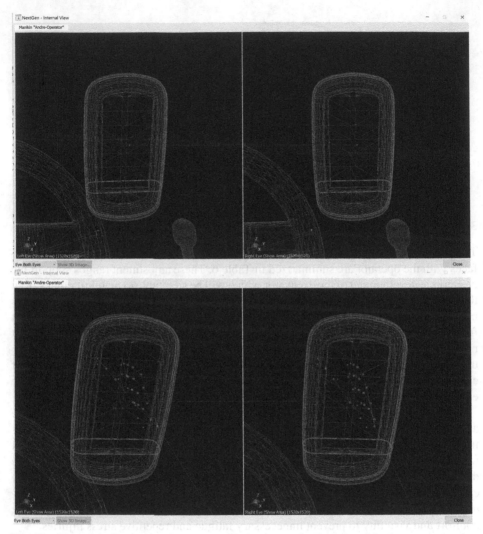

Fig. 18. Clear sight lines to touch screen panel (Top: operating both joysticks, bottom: operating left joystick and reaching for touch screen)

When contractors bring in pilots to assess ergonomics it is often well into the prototype stage where major cockpit configuration changes can be schedule and cost-prohibitive. An alternative approach could be to introduce DHM tools during very early cockpit design mockups in CAD to make those changes while the design is still fluid.

A challenge we faced during this analysis was encountering posture calculations which resulted in the manikin "clipping" with components of the seat. Specifically, armrest adjustments were forcing the manikin to lean back through the physical structure of the seatback. This can be prevented by creating a restriction from the skin point on the manikin's back to a geometry point on the chair, effectively pinning the manikin to

Table 6. Summary of comfort adjustment ranges

Steering column	Tall big male	Small big-male	Small female	Large female	Range
Rotation (degrees)	15	20	25	15	20 ± 5
Translation (mm)	150	165	190	170	170 ± 20
Joystick Armrests					
Rotation Y-Axis (degrees)	15	10	5	12	10 ± 5
Translation X-Axis (mm)	0	10	50	20	20 ± 30
Translation Z-Axis (mm)	−40	−50	−60	−50	-50 ± 10
Touch Screen					
Translation X-Axis (mm)	100	120	140	120	120 ± 20
Translation Z-Axis (mm)	200	190	180	190	190 ± 10
Wrist Pad Position					
Translation Armrest-Axis (mm)	−15	−20	−25	−15	-25 ± 15

the chair back. If there is an easier way to address this such as a setting that prohibits manikin clipping, that would be useful information to present future students.

5 Future Work

The capability of RAMSIS to aid designers in evaluating many details of operator comfort has been demonstrated. Specific translation and rotation ranges of cabin components provide a clear operating envelope for engineers to design adjustment mechanisms to suit operators of different sizes. However, these investigations were all conducted in a static environment within the RAMSIS software. Heavy machinery like an excavator will introduce abrupt movements and steady vibrations to the operator regardless of the positioning of their joints and reach. Future investigation into the excavator should address dynamic ergonomic considerations such as vibration, shear load, impact, sound, etcetera, and how those could negatively affect operator performance and health. Ways to address these dynamic issues could include seat bolstering, seatbelts or straps, and pliable seat material like foam or large spring dampers. The adjustments determined in RAMSIS to support nominal posture are a solid foundation but are just the starting point to develop an operator environment that will promote maximum human performance and support long-term health.

References

1. Rajhans, N.: (PDF) Study of Human factors in designing (2010). [online] ResearchGate. Available at: <https://www.researchgate.net/publication/326369408_Study_of_Human_fac tors_in_designing> Accessed 10 October 2021
2. Sinchuk, K., Hancock, A.L., Hayford, A., Kuebler, T., Duffy, V.G.: Rep. A 3-Step Approach for Introducing Computer-Aided Ergonomics Analysis Methodologies, n.d
3. Salvendy, G., Duffy, V.G.: Chapter 35: Human Digital Modeling in Design. Essay. In: Handbook of Human Factors and Ergonomics. S.l.: John Wiley & Sons (2021)

4. Reiman, D., Sormunen, A., Morris, E.: Ergonomics in the Arctic - A Study and Checklist for Heavy Machinery in Open Pit Mining. Work (Reading, Mass.). U.S. National Library of Medicine (October 2016). https://pubmed.ncbi.nlm.nih.gov/27792027/
5. Kittusamy, N.K.: Ergonomic Risk Factors: A Study of Heavy Earthmoving Machinery Operators. CDC.gov (2002). https://www.cdc.gov/niosh/mining/Userfiles/works/pdfs/erfas.pdf
6. Väyrynen, S.: Safety and ergonomics in the maintenance of heavy forest machinery. Accident Analysis & Prevention. Pergamon (16 July 2002). https://www.sciencedirect.com/science/article/pii/0001457584900368
7. Xue, H., Yuan, Y., Chen, J.: A Software Approach of Human–Machine Interface Ergonomics Evaluation. Essay. In: Man-Machine-Environment System Engineering. Springer Singapore (2020)
8. RAMSIS NextGen 1.8 User Guide: Kaiserslautern, Germany: Human Solutions GmbH (6 April 2021)
9. Fuhrmann, A.M.: Rep. Human-Centric Product Development: Using RAMSIS Ergonomic Analysis to Incorporate Operator Comfort into Excavator Design. West Lafayette, IN (2021)

Simulation and Ergonomic Analysis of a Very Tall Male Driving an Excavator in RAMSIS

Philippine Buisson and Vincent G. Duffy[✉]

Purdue University, West Lafayette, IN 06883, USA
{pbuisson,duffy}@purdue.edu

Abstract. This paper aims to analyze the comfort level of a very tall mall driving an excavator. An ergonomic analysis is then performed on the manikin to examine areas of discomfort while in the driving position. This analysis is particularly interesting to people in industries where excavators are used, but it can also be applied to the general population as cars have a similar interior setup consisting of a steering wheel, seat, and the floor between. Therefore, the conclusions drawn and recommendations made at the end of this paper could be made applicable to standard driving scenarios. This model was made in Human Solution's RAMSIS and the analysis was performed using the same software. It was found through the "Comfort Feeling" analysis that discomfort occurred mostly in the shoulders and neck as well as in the left and right legs. The only areas that did not experience as much discomfort were the right and left arms, back, and buttocks. It is worth noting however that this could be due to most of the strain being put on the previously mentioned areas that experience the highest discomfort. There was an overall very high discomfort feeling of 6.46 (compared to a discomfort threshold of 3.5), with uncomfortable fatigue and health values. Recommendations to reduce these include seat adjustment and steering wheel adjustment.

Keywords: Ergonomic design & neuroscience cooperation · Job design and changing nature of work · Occupational health & operations management · Task analysis · Quality & safety in healthcare · Driving · Excavator · Comfort · RAMSIS · Anthropometry · Ergonomic analysis · 3D-CAD-ergonomics simulation

1 Introduction and Background

The purpose of this ergonomic analysis is to understand how larger typologies can be better accommodated in excavators and how to use the RAMSIS "Comfort Feeling" analysis tool to determine what these accommodations should be. The goal of ergonomics is to achieve an optimized fit of the job and work environment to the worker [1]. More precisely, chapter 35 of the Handbook of Human Factors and Ergonomics states that "efforts to measure male and female hand, arm, and leg lengths are intended to better design products and workstations with a focus on minimizing the number of people excluded" [2]. Thus, Ergonomic analysis can be used to understand how anthropometric measures affect comfort levels.

© Springer Nature Switzerland AG 2022
V. G. Duffy and P.-L. P. Rau (Eds.): HCII 2022, LNCS 13522, pp. 113–126, 2022.
https://doi.org/10.1007/978-3-031-21704-3_8

On a personal note, the first author had an internship in a manufacturing plant where she noticed that a lot of workers were not properly informed on how to adjust their desks, chairs, and monitor heights to be accommodating to them. Many were also unaware of how beneficial these seemingly small adjustments could be. Ergonomic analysis can show which of these adjustments need to be made to reduce the risk of musculoskeletal disorders, improve productivity, and boost job satisfaction [3]. This analysis aims to show how much accommodations can impact a worker's comfort level.

2 Problem Statement and Project Scope

As previously stated, this paper analyzes the comfort level of a very tall mall driving an excavator. A driving task means that the manikin has both hands on the steering wheel. It should be noted that other postures relevant to the work system exist, such as having both hands on the joysticks to dig but are considered outside the "driving" scope of this paper. The analysis and subsequent recommendations covered in this paper are specific to the driving posture.

This design was chosen because it is particularly applicable. Although excavator seats, pedals, and steering wheels differ from those found in cars, the conclusions drawn from the excavator design could be similar to those drawn from ergonomic analysis of a car. It would be interesting to perform the analysis in this report on an "average" car and compare the results to those mentioned in this paper. A downside to performing ergonomic analyses is that creating and correctly positioning the model in the computer-aided design (CAD) environment can be a time-consuming process [2]. However, the RAMSIS software designed by Human Solutions offers particular advantages over other modeling software, including automatic posture prediction for digital human models [4].

The only manikin used was a "very tall male" to represent how a male in the ~ 95th percentile would be accommodated in this excavator seat. However, RAMSIS is capable of modeling any type of manikin. It is possible to specify different typology characteristics including population percentile, nationality, reference year, age group, length, corpulence, and proportion [4]. Thus, it would be interesting to perform the simulation and redo the analysis in this paper for a ~5% female, who would be "very short," and compare with the analysis performed in this paper. By calculating comfort levels for these two populations with drastically differing anthropometric measures, it can be determined which percentiles are most comfortable in the simulation setting and how to better accommodate all of the different typologies.

3 Procedure

3.1 Step-by-Step Explanation of In-Class Demonstration

Using RAMSIS to complete the demonstration shown by Andre Luebke in class, it was possible to create a model of a "very tall male" manikin in an excavator seat and then perform an ergonomic analysis on the manikin. The steps for this procedure are outlined below with a corresponding image for each step shown to its right (Fig. 1):

Fig. 1. Procedure step 1.

1. First, one should load the excavator by opening Automotive RAMSIS and going to File - > Load Session - > Data - > Session - > Training Day 1 (Fig. 2).

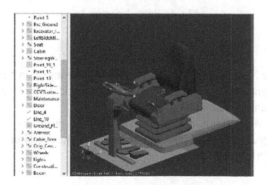

Fig. 2. Procedure step 2.

2. Next, "Hide/Show Spaces" can be used to hide all parts of the excavator except for the steering wheel, seat, and the floor directly surrounding them. An item's hidden status can be confirmed by seeing a greyed-out icon next to the item's name in the structure tree (Fig. 3).

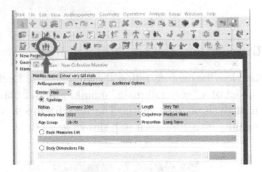

Fig. 3. Procedure step 3.

3. Then, one should create a very tall manikin with a long torso using the "Test Sample" option in the toolbar (circled in the image on the right) (Fig. 4).

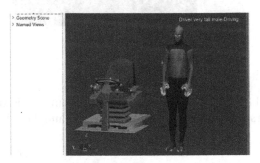

Fig. 4. Procedure step 4.

4. Under the "Role Assignment" tab, a role called "Driving" can be created where the manikin is assigned the role of driving a heavy truck. Hitting the "Create" button results in the manikin shown on the right.
5. After loading "Male Manikin Skin Points" into the program, "Object Properties" should be changed. In the "Additional Options" tab, the manikin is now assigned the shoe model "Workshoe (Fig. 5)."

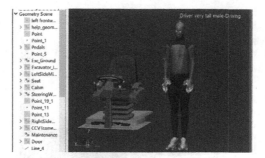

Fig. 5. Procedure step 5.

6. The next step is to position the manikin in the seat. Using the "Define Restriction" icon, one can connect the manikin's H-point (between his hips) to the surface of the chair (purple square defining the chair's range of movement). A connecting red line should appear (Fig. 6).

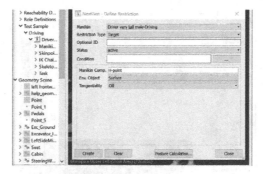

Fig. 6. Procedure step 6.

7. Next, one can put the mannikin's feet on the floor using the "define restriction" icon, filling them out as shown for both heels (Fig. 7).

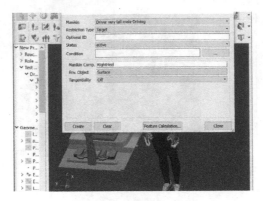

Fig. 7. Procedure step 7.

8. To put the balls of the manikin's feet on the two larger pedals, defined restrictions can connect "LeftBallOffset" to "Line_1" and "RightBallOffset" to "Line_3" (Fig. 8).

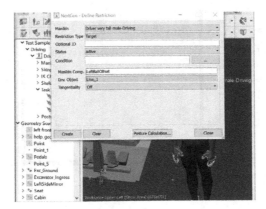

Fig. 8. Procedure step 8.

9. Next, to keep the manikin from tilting or rotating in the seat (while still allowing him to lean), another restriction can be created for pelvis rotation, as shown (Fig. 9).

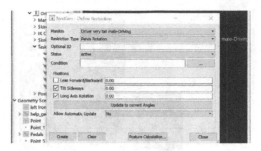

Fig. 9. Procedure step 9.

10. To insert the manikin in his seat, one can press "Posture Calculation." Any visual overlap between the manikin and the seat is of no concern as the seat can move up and down, forward and backward which will accommodate for this (Fig. 10).

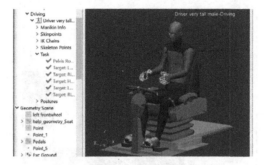

Fig. 10. Procedure step 10.

11. The next phase is to put the manikin's hand on the steering wheel. To do this, created points on the steering wheel should be placed at "10 and 2 o'clock." An example of this process for "10 o'clock" is shown (Fig. 11).

Fig. 11. Procedure step 11.

12. Then, a restriction can be defined with these new points so that the manikin's hands are connected to them. This is done by connecting HAR_2_1 to the newly created 2 o'clock point and HAL_2_1 to the 10 o'clock point (Fig. 12).

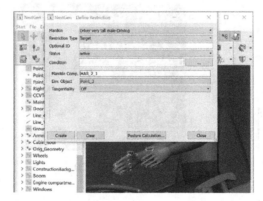

Fig. 12. Procedure step 12.

13. Pressing "Posture Calculation" once more yields (Fig. 13):

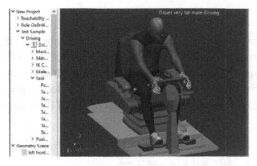

Fig. 13. Procedure step 13.

14. To make the manikin's hands grasp the steering wheel instead of touching it, one can include the NextGen Ergonomics module by clicking Start - > NextGen Ergonomics followed by Operations - > Hand Posture - > "Grasp Firmly" for both hands, as shown. Clicking "Apply" finalizes the manikin (Fig. 14),

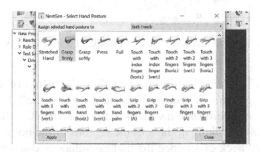

Fig. 14. Procedure step 14.

This is the final very tall male manikin in the driving position. It is now possible to perform an ergonomic analysis on this model (Fig. 15).

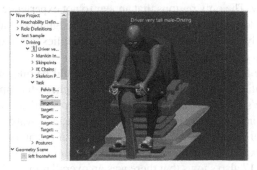

Fig. 15. Very tall male driver manikin.

3.2 Analysis

Now that the manikin is complete with all the necessary attributes and posture definitions, it is possible to perform the Comfort Feeling ergonomic analysis. This particular analysis was chosen as the authors felt that was the most applicable to examine the Manikin's level of discomfort. Specifically, the analysis was performed by going to the "Analysis" toolbar and selecting "Comfort Feeling." the first result of this analysis is shown below.

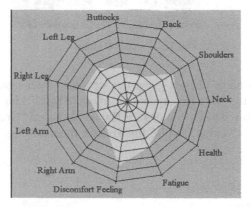

Fig. 16. The first result of the "Comfort Feeling" analysis.

The diagram in Fig. 16 can aid in understanding the values of discomfort relative to each other. Looking at this, it becomes evident that the overall discomfort feeling is exceedingly high, even in comparison with the fatigue and health values, which pass the "discomfort" threshold. Looking at the specific regions of the body, it is also apparent that the shoulders and neck experience the highest values of discomfort as well as the right and left legs. For a more quantitative interpretation, one can look at the second result of the analysis. This result is shown in Fig. 17 below.

To interpret Fig. 17, it is important to remember that 3.5 is the threshold where the manikin begins to experience discomfort. Any value above this represents increasing discomfort. So, the manikin is least comfortable in his shoulders, followed by his neck and legs, respectively. The only regions that appear to not experience a sense of discomfort are the right and left arms, back, and buttocks. Although these values are below 3.5, they are still relatively close to this threshold, which implies that these regions are still not in ideal positions and there is room for improvement.

Additionally, the lower values shown in Fig. 17 could be due to most strain being put on the aforementioned areas that experience the highest discomfort. For example, because the manikin's shoulders and neck are leaning forward so much, this alleviates pressure on the arms and back, since they do not have to lean forward as much. Therefore, it would be beneficial to improve comfort in all regions of the manikin's body to ensure that no regions are experiencing significantly higher strain than others.

The table in Fig. 17 also shows that there was an overall remarkably high discomfort feeling of 6.46, with uncomfortable fatigue and health values of 4.94 and 3.97, respectively. These are all high values and can certainly be cause for injury in the worker,

Manikin "Driver very tall male-Driving"

Name	Value	Reference
Neck	4.89	4.89
Shoulders	5.27	5.27
Back	2.71	2.71
Buttocks	3.43	3.43
Left Leg	4.44	4.44
Right Leg	4.37	4.37
Left Arm	3.20	3.20
Right Arm	3.16	3.16
Discomfort Feeling	6.46	6.46
Fatigue	4.94	4.94
Health	3.97	3.97

Fig. 17. The second result of the "Comfort Feeling" analysis.

especially over a prolonged period. Thus, it is necessary to implement changes that would decrease all of the aforementioned discomfort values.

3.3 Recommendations

Certain adjustments could be made to reduce the simulated worker's postural discomfort. These include adjustments made to the steering wheel and seat position.

It would be most beneficial to move the seat further back. It is worth noting that, as briefly mentioned in step 6 of the step-by-step procedure (Sect. 3.1), RAMSIS accounts for the excavator seat's adjustability by having a rectangular surface on the top of the seat that the manikin is targeted to touch with "H-point" (between the hips). Since this surface is a rectangle, the manikin's H-point can make contact with any point on that rectangle. This accounts for the seat's ability to move forward, backward, up, and down. Even though RAMSIS automatically connects the H-point to the optimal point on the rectangle, we see in the analysis that this is still making the worker uncomfortable. Thus, one recommendation is that the size of this rectangle be increased so that the chair can move even further back than it currently does. This would cause the legs to be in a more natural position, increasing comfort for both legs.

The second modification would raising the steering wheel and bringing it closer to the manikin. The steering wheel would be closer to the worker by going between his legs or switching to a more curved model where the base does not change position, but the steering wheel is closer to the manikin. This would allow his arms to not need to be as stretched out, thus decreasing discomfort in the neck, back, and shoulders. These changes would also reduce the amount of discomfort experienced in the worker's arms as the new position would be significantly more relaxed and natural.

An added benefit of raising the height of the steering wheel would be lifting the worker's natural gaze (or line of sight) to a more optimal position. If the worker were digging, it might be beneficial for him to be glancing down at what is being dug. However, because the assigned task was driving, the natural gaze should be directed slightly more upwards than shown in Fig. 18.

Fig. 18. The final model of the very tall manikin in the excavator seat (side view).

4 Discussion

As previously mentioned, the lower values output in the "Comfort Feeling" analysis (arms, back, and buttocks) could result from most of the strain being put on the areas that experience the highest discomfort (shoulders, neck, and legs). In reality, a very tall male driving the excavator might react to the discomfort in the shoulders by arching his back to distribute the discomfort, which would make the shoulder strain more tolerable. The person might prefer to have more even discomfort values around four for both back and shoulders rather than having the values for back and shoulder discomfort shown in the table.

Personally, when the first author of this paper injured her left shoulder earlier this year, she noticed that she performed more tasks with her right shoulder. For example, she found herself carrying her backpack only on the right shoulder because although this caused strain and discomfort in the right shoulder, it eased the pain in her left one and balanced the discomfort rather than having most of it in her left shoulder. A comparable situation could be present with this model in actual industry scenarios. However, RAMSIS, like many other modeling software [2], unfortunately fails to account for these reactions or adaptations which could also vary between individuals.

The biggest challenge for both authors was finding the balance between benefits and drawbacks of moving the seat and moving the steering wheel. At first, they thought that an obvious solution would be to move the seat so that the worker would be more comfortable. However, by revisiting the screenshot of the final manikin (Fig. 18), it can be deduced that if the seat were to be moved backward or upward, this would increase strain on the shoulders and neck, although the legs would be in a more natural position, thereby increasing comfort. On the other hand, if the seat were to be adjusted by moving forward or downward, this could provide relief by reducing strain in the arms, neck, and shoulders while the legs would be in a more unnatural and uncomfortable position. Since adjusting the seat would not provide more comfort to a body region without reducing the comfort in another, they had to look at other aspects of the problem to solve it. They ended up finding that moving the steering wheel would solve the problems that moving the seat would cause. Examining these solutions as a duo rather than looking at their impacts individually enabled them to overcome this challenge and eventually find recommendations that would be feasible and beneficial.

Professional experiences helped overcome this challenge and find a solution. Specifically, the first author was inspired by a certain moment in her internship where her workstation was not set up correctly and the table was very low, resulting in having to hunch over to perform work. So she examined the desk and saw that it had an adjustable height feature. This solved her problem, and she was able to complete her work more comfortably and efficiently. This is similar to the problem encountered during this project where the excavator cabin setup is causing the manikin postural discomfort. The desk in the aforementioned author's situation is comparable to the steering wheel in the excavator example.

The authors deem it would be beneficial for future students and researchers to bear in mind that although individual items can be changed to accommodate the worker, it could also be beneficial to look at how the combinations of changed items would help. For example, just moving the seat would not have improved the manikin's posture, but rather caused more discomfort. However, combining seat placement change with steering wheel change would prove beneficial to the worker. So they would recommend that future students consider the impact of individual changes as well as multiple changes at the same time that could interact to better the manikin's postural comfort.

5   Future Work

As mentioned and shown in this paper, ergonomic analysis is crucial to ensuring workers' comfort as well as boosting efficiency and task performance [3]. Thus, it might be beneficial to companies to gather anthropometric data on employees (anonymously for ethical reasons) and run simulations to determine what percentile is accommodated in the excavator. Using the NextGen Body Builder, it is possible to create a manikin that precisely reflects certain measurements [4]. This is especially useful as it can model the "average" employee as well as the 5th percentile and 95th percentile ones. It would be beneficial in this case to be able to upload a data set where RAMSIS automatically calculates the 5th, 50th, and 95th percentiles and corresponding manikins for each.

In the first author's senior design class as an undergraduate at Purdue University, she got to collaborate with a local pipe manufacturing company on a scrap-reduction project. When her and her team visited the plant, the director showed us a set of vehicles that were used in the manufacturing process to transport processed goods or raw materials. He said that the employees who worked for him tended to be larger (height and weight) than the average American and thus some of them would complain about discomfort in the vehicles. If RAMSIS had the data capability mentioned above, then maybe the company could have used RAMSIS to determine ways to accommodate for the typology of their employees.

An additional limitation of RAMSIS, and human modeling designs in general, relate to sensing and reacting [2]. The modeling does not account for human emotions or reactions to certain stimuli, discomfort, or pain. This would be particularly interesting to track over time as there might be a point where a period of adjustment to discomfort would interact with restlessness or fatigue from performing the task.

It would also be interesting for RAMSIS to include data regarding hearing or lighting. For example, the data for hearing could be relevant to calculating or comparing discomfort levels related to occasional alarms versus consistent noises in the environment. Similarly, the data for vision could examine the discomfort regarding a bright and/or flashing light, or how a dimly lit workspace creates headaches. Although there are guidelines and calculations for these, RAMSIS would be able to customize these guidelines and cater them to the thresholds of the particular worker. In other words, the calculations only account for the characteristics of the environment whereas RAMSIS would be able to account for the interaction between those characteristics and the worker. Again, it would be very interesting in this case to be able to track the discomfort level over a period of time. This would make it possible to notice trends and even help determine at what time the user should stop performing the task.

References

1. Sánchez, A.: The Importance of Ergonomics in Industrial Engineering. Industrial Engineering & Management **03**(01), OMICS (2014)
2. Duffy, V.G.: Human digital modeling for design. In: Salvendy, G. (ed.) Handbook of Human Factors and Ergonomics, 4th Ed., 1016–1030. John Wiley & Sons, Inc., Hoboken (2012)
3. Coelho, C., Oliveira, P., Maia, E., Rangel, R., Dias-Teixeira, M.: The importance of ergonomics analysis in prevention of MSDs. Occupational Safety and Hygiene II. 1st edn. CRC Press (2014)
4. Human Solutions: RAMSIS NextGen 1.8 Ergonomics User Guide. HUMAN SOLUTIONS GmbH. Kaiserslautern, Germany (2011)

Understanding Musculoskeletal Injuries, Their Causes, Potential Mitigation Solutions, and Recommendations for Future Prevention Within the Manufacturing Industry

Philippine Buisson, Matthew Chang, and Vincent G. Duffy[✉]

Purdue University, West Lafayette, IN 47907, USA
{pbuisson,chang841,duffy}@purdue.edu

Abstract. This paper was written to explore solutions to the following problem: an employee at a die-cutting station in a manufacturing plant is experiencing pain in her right shoulder. It is deduced that this pain results from improper posture due to a disproportionate height difference between the employee and the workstation, which is consequently too tall for her. Using different types of literature review, we first examined the topics of workplace injury and ergonomics, workstation design, and height, to gain a better understanding of the issue itself before focusing on its solutions. Next, we compared five potential solutions: (1) implementing an adjustable chair that the user can sit on while performing the task, (2) placing the die-cutting station on a height-adjustable table, (3) alternating between sitting and standing with an adjustable chair and adjustable workstation, (4) having the user stand on an aerobic platform, and lastly, (5) increasing job variety. Following a comparison of these five options, recommendations were made to justify the implementation of any or all of these five solutions.

Keywords: Workstation design · Height · Ergonomics · Musculoskeletal injury

1 Introduction and Problem Statement

1.1 Problem Statement and Purpose of Analysis

In this project, an industrial case study was presented where an employee reported pain in her right shoulder following completing a certain task within a manufacturing environment. Known as a musculoskeletal disorder, these injuries are defined as consequences of a bodily reaction, for example, excessive bending, climbing, crawling, reaching, twisting, overexerting, or repetitive motions (Centers for Disease Control and Prevention 2012). As stated in the case, this employee works as an assembler at a manufacturing facility where her primary responsibilities are to throw die cuts through a glue machine to pass further down the assembly line. Upon further investigation of the work environment, contributing factors, and a recommendation from the worker's doctor, it was determined that there may be two leading variables that caused this injury, these being constant

© Springer Nature Switzerland AG 2022
V. G. Duffy and P.-L. P. Rau (Eds.): HCII 2022, LNCS 13522, pp. 127–145, 2022.
https://doi.org/10.1007/978-3-031-21704-3_9

repetitive motion and height of employee relative to the workstation. A representation of the tasks this worker was responsible for as well as the height difference between table and employee can be seen in Fig. 1 below. In this project report, potential solutions to mitigating this injury hazard will be provided as will recommendations to prevent similar and related musculoskeletal disorders from occurring in the future, regardless of environment or influencing factors.

Step 1 Reach back and twist Pick up Die Cut. Step 2 Deliver to glue machine. Step 3 Place in Glue machine.

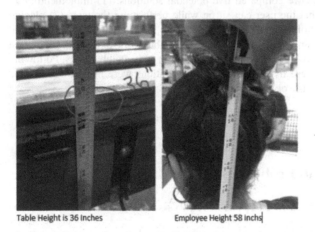

Table Height is 36 Inches   Employee Height 58 inchs

Fig. 1. Photos of worker's primary responsibility and height vs. workstation

In evaluating this case, the purpose of this analysis is to determine why such an injury occurred, understand what factors influenced this event to happen, and offer solutions to mitigate the same or similar issues from occurring in the future. While the solutions offered in this report will be specific to this example, the general recommendations that will be provided can be applicable and adopted in any working environment.

1.2   Statement of Relevance

According to the World Health Organization, over 1.71 billion people suffer from musculoskeletal disorders worldwide. Among all injuries, these conditions are the leading contributor to disability worldwide, causing individuals to retire early and suffer from lower levels of well-being due to limitations in mobility and dexterity. (World Health Organization 2021) From these statistics, it is evident that musculoskeletal disorders are serious, and measures should be taken to mitigate risks that can cause such injuries. This design problem is of interest and relevance to this project as it can affect all lines of work and business; while certain industrial environments may have higher associated risks, no single employee or position is exempt from these risks. In response to this, the World Health Organization has created the Rehabilitation 2030 initiative to bring attention to the need for rehabilitation services globally and spotlight the importance of developing strong healthcare systems to heal related injuries (World Health Organization 2021).

2   Literature Review

Fig. 2. Vicinitas analytics search of 'Workplace Injury'

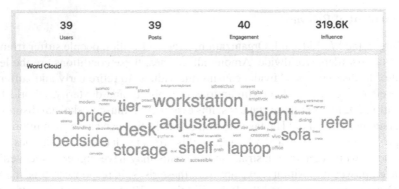

Fig. 3. Vicinitas analytics search of 'Workstation and Height'

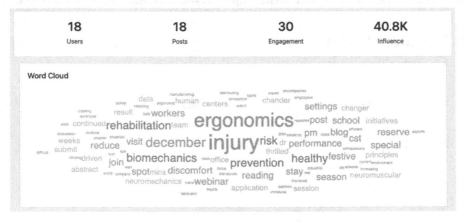

Fig. 4. Vicinitas analytics search of 'Ergonomics' and 'Injury'

As shown in Figs. 2, 3, and 4, various Vicinitas Analytics searches were run, each with different key terms that are important to this overall case study. Beginning with 'Workplace Injury', individuals are more engaged as compared to 'Ergonomics and Injury', which while enclosed within the workplace setting, is a more specific subset. Similarly, looking at the figures, we can deduce that less emphasis is placed on ergonomics within the workplace as is height and workstations. This is important to note as this case study investigates varying worker heights within a manufacturing environment and how ergonomically friendly designs can mitigate these risks and prevent musculoskeletal injuries.

Fig. 5. MAXQDA word cloud and lexical search

In Fig. 5 above, a lexical search and word cloud was created using MAXQDA and several scholarly articles related to this case study. The articles used in this literature review were obtained through Google Scholar using the following keywords: height, workstation design, ergonomics, and injury. The articles used are cited and can be found in Sect. 9 of this report. The word cloud above represents a correlation of these terms within the articles used in this analysis and throughout this project report.

Looking at the word cloud, it becomes apparent that the most frequently used terms that were not selected as keywords are: work, manufacturing, posture, musculoskeletal, simulation, workers, and technology. From these words, we can gather that these are the topics most related to the keywords input into MAXQDA. It is interesting to note that the word "simulation" is one that appeared often in this word cloud. This is perhaps due to the fact that many simulation softwares, such as Human Solutions' RAMSIS, can be used to analyze posture models based on anthropometric measures. However, because RAMSIS specifically models vehicle occupants, it is not particularly applicable in this case study. Nevertheless, other similar human modeling softwares could be used to investigate ergonomic hazards in the plant. Comparing and contrasting the impact of each proposed solution in this report through simulations could save time, money, and potentially convince other manufacturing plants to implement ergonomic safety measures as well.

Figures 6 and 7 represent co-citation analysis completed in VOSViewer using data gathered from Scopus. To find this bibliometric information, the following search terms were used: workstation, ergonomics, and injury. This resulted in 276 unique documents. In generating the VOSViewer map, binary counting was used, the minimum number of occurrences of a term was set to two, and the number of terms to be selected was 100. As seen in the above images, the primary terms highlighted in the articles were analysis, task, ergonomic assessment, musculoskeletal injury, method, discomfort, among others.

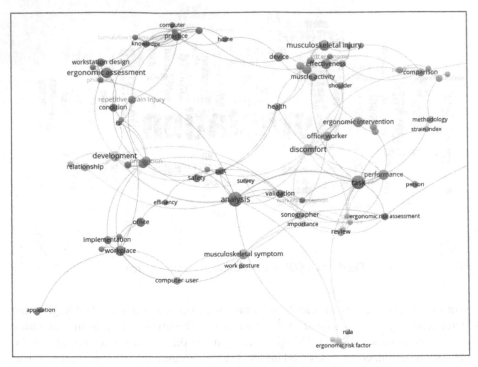

Fig. 6. Enlarged photo of co-citation analysis to aid readability

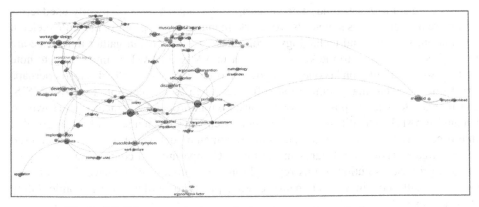

Fig. 7. VOSViewer co-citation analysis using search results from scopus

In Figs. 8 and 9, an analysis was performed in BibExcel to generate lists of publications and their authors using bibliometric data gathered from the Web of Science database. In this search, the keywords used were workstation, ergonomics, and injury, which yielded a total of 146 unique documents. As seen in the above photo, while there are numerous documents with these key terms, the maximum publications a singular author contributed to were two. From these results, it can be inferred that while scholarly

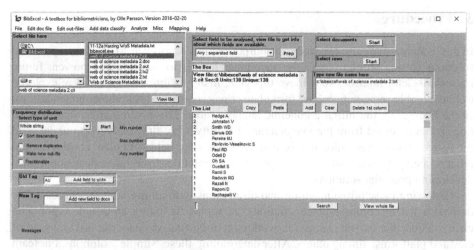

Fig. 8. BibExcel leading table analysis

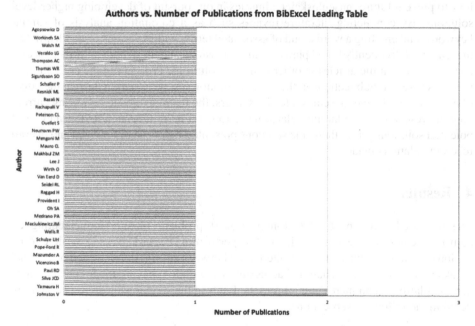

Fig. 9. PivotChart using BibExcel leading table

work is being done in these fields, there is not enough publishable material specifically highlighting the effects of an environment's workstation, its specific ergonomics, and their overall influences on hazards or potential injuries.

3 Procedure

In this evaluation of this case study, the purpose of this report was to determine potential solutions to this problem and offer recommendations to mitigate and prevent future musculoskeletal injuries. To achieve this goal, many different avenues were explored to find suitable remediations and formulate strong, research-backed recommendations. In the beginning, the initial ergonomic analysis, observation summaries, and medical documents received from the manufacturing facility were first analyzed to understand the issue at hand. In addition to this, conversations were held with plant employees and other related parties to widen our perspective and point our team into a direction to start developing potential solutions.

Following these initial meetings and discussions with all individuals, our team first derived a list of common-place solutions, examples including adjustable ergonomic chairs, adjustable tables, changes in work pattern (sitting vs. standing tasks), usage of elevated platforms, among others. After determining these 'simple' solutions, our team sought to use the literature analysis methods taught in class to gain a scholarly and research-based understanding of why these hazards occur, how to mitigate them, and how to prevent future musculoskeletal injuries in our pursuit of developing higher-level solutions. By conducting literature reviews such as a co-citation analysis of similar keywords and creating a word cloud of associated terms within various research articles, the team took frequently found phrases and expressions and used them to further specify and narrow down the articles in order to derive solutions. Proceeding the evaluation of previous research publications in the field of ergonomics, workstation design, the effect of height on work, and musculoskeletal disorders, the team pivoted to reviewing current ongoing research in similar and related fields to get a more thorough understanding of potential solutions. From there, the solutions presented below were finalized and overall recommendations made.

4 Results

The proposed solutions to the aforementioned problem include implementing an adjustable chair that the user can sit on while performing the task, placing the de-cutting station on a height-adjustable table, alternating between sitting, standing, and occasional breaks with an adjustable chair and adjustable workstation, having the user stand on an aerobic platform, and increasing job variety. Each of these options is discussed in more detail in the following subsections.

4.1 Adjustable Chair with a Footrest and Armrests

Fig. 10. Ergonomic chair with a footrest and two armrests. (NOUHAUS 2019)

The first option that we thought would be interesting to analyze is an adjustable chair, an example of which is shown in Fig. 10 above. There are several benefits to implementing this chair, including the fact that the chair is adjustable and customizable to accommodate each user. Therefore, this chair can be modified to accommodate short and tall users alike. Implementing this solution would "reduce tension in the shoulder-neck area and the foot support will improve body balance and minimize the static load on the worker's back." (Bejide 2014) In addition, further research suggests that "prolonged standing at work has been shown to be associated with several potentially serious health outcomes, such as lower back and leg pain, cardiovascular problems, fatigue, discomfort, and pregnancy-related health outcomes." (Waters and Dick 2014) Sitting also uses less energy than standing and thus can help stabilize the body. This can especially be beneficial if the worker is performing fine motor tasks. (UCLA Health n.d.) So, having this ergonomic chair could alleviate the risks of these injuries in addition to those caused by lack of footrests, bad posture, improper lumbar support, or a combination of these.

As previously mentioned, the plant manager was in contact regarding specific requirements and reservations the plant has for viable solutions. When the case manager brought up the potential implementation of stools or chairs, the plant manager stated that standing was more productive, and they were not willing to consider that as a feasible option. However, we would urge the plant manager to reconsider.

Research has previously stated that standing is preferred and more productive when the user must move to different workstations frequently, the work task lasts less than 5 min, or the workstation is too large to be comfortable reached when seated. (WFU Environmental Health & Safety n.d.) On the other hand, sitting is preferred when "visually intensive or precise work is required, the activity is repetitive; longer tasks are completed (greater than 5 min), and when everything can be placed within easy reach." (WFU Environmental Health & Safety n.d.) This second description better matches the tasks performed by the user, as outlined by the plant manager. Thus, we would highly recommend looking into adjustable and ergonomic seating.

This chair also boasts more ergonomic features than many of its competitors, with height-variable arms, a high back design providing total thoracic support, an adjustable headrest for ideal neck placement, a recline lock, solid footrest, anti-roll wheel lock, and a heavy-duty hydraulic gas lift. (NOUHAUS 2019) All of the features of this tall office chair ensure that no matter the ergonomic measures of the user, they are safe, healthy, and comfortable.

A few disadvantages to this proposed solution exist. The main one is that when an employee sits, there is decreased muscle activity compared to standing and the lack of movement can result in things like the employee's legs fall asleep, or soreness from remaining relatively static. (UCLA Health n.d.) Prolonged sitting could also cause strain on the employee's back, especially if the employee has poor posture or has a more physically demanding task.

4.2   Adjustable Table Height

Fig. 11.   Adjustable height desk. (Uline n.d.)

The next option we investigated was an adjustable height table, such as the one shown above in Fig. 11. This table's useful and most impressive features include "simple-to-use push-button control with four programmable heights, durable, 1″ thick laminated tops, 2 cable grommets, and telescoping legs." (Uline n.d.) With a varying height of 23 ½″ to 48," this desk could be used for taller and shorter people, sitting and standing alike, especially with the addition of adjustable seats for those who sit. This is further explored in the next section. Weighing 115 lbs., this table also has a weight capacity of 275 lbs. And can therefore be used for a variety of workstations, including those where heavier jobs and tasks are being carried out.

It is very common for workstations, such as the ones in this plant, to lack opportunities for individualization and personalization. Not permitting precise "adjustment to the ergonomic needs and personal preference of the particular user [can lead employees to] complain about the challenging environment, physical strain and health problems leading to absenteeism and a high turnover of personnel." (Mayrhofer et al. 2019).

Options for adjustments	Utilization for individualization	Expected benefits
1) Dimension: working height		
• Height of work surface • Utilization of work surface for seated and standing work positions	• Adjustment of optimal work height according to body height • Adjustment of optimal work height according to specific task • Change of work surface height according to defined use-time to foster switching from seated to standing work positions	• reduction of musculoskeletal strain due to avoidance of ergonomically unfavorable body positions • Efficiency improvements due to suitable working height (better gripping area, lower fatigue levels, fewer mistakes)

Fig. 12. Working height for individualized workstations. (Ware et al. 2005)

As shown in the table that constitutes Fig. 12 above, having height-adjustable workstations can be used to accommodate the user's body height as well as the work height needed for a specific task. Individually or as a combination, these can result in a reduction of musculoskeletal strain as "ergonomically unfavorable body positions" (Mayrhofer et al. 2019) have been avoided. In addition, a suitable working height can provide benefits like "better gripping area, lower fatigue levels, and fewer mistakes" (Mayrhofer et al. 2019) which will all improve efficiency and greatly benefit the plant's production numbers.

In summary, height-adjustable workstations can be very useful as they can be accommodating to each individual user. An article written by Dr. Olugbenga Bejide, a health physician and current Chief Consultant, states that "engineering control measures should be addressed as the first line of defense to eliminate or reduce ergonomic hazards that employees are exposed to." (Bejide 2014) These controls include the implementation of height-adjustable workstations.

However, disadvantages to this proposed model exist. These include the fact that many adjustable tables, such as the one shown in Fig. 12 above, are powered by electricity to ensure that that adjusting the table is as easy and efficient as possible and does not put any strain on the employee. Therefore, there are power cords attached to each table that need to be less than 10 ft away from an outlet. In a manufacturing plant, this could be difficult or unrealistic to achieve and the floors can sometimes be very large and thus the workstations will rarely be within 10 ft of an outlet. A potential solution to this could be looking into other non-electric, purely mechanically-adjustable tables that could use a crank to be modified, at the price of perhaps having employees experience strain from the cranking.

Another disadvantage is that if the plant has consecutive, touching workstations where the product flows from one workstation to another, utilizing tables of different heights could cause flow problems. More precisely, rather than sliding the finished product onto the next workstation, employees will have to lift the product and carry it to the next station so as not to damage it. This lifting could cause musculoskeletal problems for the employees.

The last disadvantage we found was that "the use of sit-stand stations rapidly declines so that after 1 month, a majority of people are sitting all the time." (UCLA Health n.d.)

Compliance could be problematic thus reducing the use of these desks. But the fact remains that whether the employee is sitting or standing at the height-adjustable desk, they can be accommodated, which as previously mentioned, can cause great benefits on its own.

4.3 Alternating Between Sitting and Standing with an Adjustable Chair and Adjustable Workstation

There is also the possibility of creating a workstation where the user can alternate between sitting in an ergonomic chair and standing with an adjustable workstation position. A graphic demonstrating the ideal work pattern resulting from research is shown in Fig. 13 below.

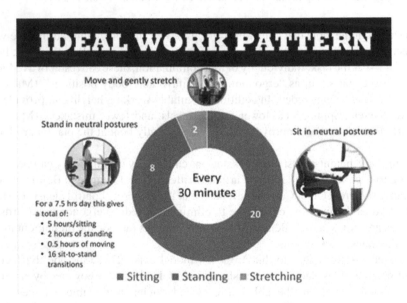

Fig. 13. Proposed ideal work pattern (Adapted from Waters and Dick 2014)

The figure above shows that for every 30-min block of work, 20 of those minutes should be spent sitting, 8 should be spent standing, and 2 should be spent stretching (or even walking as any non-static activity could be beneficial here). The figure also shows that when in the standing and sitting portions of the task execution, the user should try to stand and sit in neutral positions. For the stretching portion of the 30-min block, the user should very gently stretch and move, to increase blood supply to the muscles (Waters and Dick 2014).

Having such a workstation would reduce the discomfort and increased pressure on the neck and shoulders that are caused by prolonged sitting and the discomfort and pressure exerted on lower extremities from prolonged standing. The workers in the plant are almost certainly experiencing these effects, whether mild or severe. Alternating between these two work postures could "allow for increased rest intervals of specific body parts and reduce the potential for risk factors commonly associated with MSD [musculoskeletal disorders] development." (WFU Environmental Health & Safety n.d.).

In an ideal work situation, workers would have a workstation and job tasks that allow for "frequent changes of working posture... If either sitting or standing is feasible but only one possible, sitting in a properly designed chair is preferable." (WFU Environmental Health & Safety n.d.) This is because, as much research has shown, the human body best responds to "a balance between static and dynamic activity, between activity and recovery," (UCLA Health n.d.) or in other words, between sitting and standing.

4.4 Aerobic Platform

Fig. 14. Aerobic exercise platform with non-slip surface. (Amazon n.d.)

This image in Fig. 14 above shows a stackable, non-slip exercise platform that the plant manager had proposed to the case manager as a solution to this problem that the plant was looking into. The company stated that they investigated platforms to reduce soft tissue injuries for short employees when working on assembly lines. The platform shown above is made from "durable, recyclable high-density polyethylene [that] features a nonslip, textured surface for added safety [and] eight nonskid feet to prevent the platform from sliding or scratching floors" (Amazon n.d.) and hold the platform in place.

Another advantage of these 6″ tall steps is that, as stated by the plant manager, they are stackable. This means that employees who are too short to be comfortable performing their tasks without the platform could use more than one platform to be accommodated if one is not enough. This also means that the platforms can be stacked when not in use so that they can easily move between work cells. Utilizing these platforms can provide the user with the aforementioned benefits of standing while their cushioning can mitigate some of the risks that standing with no platform could create. Platforms could especially be useful in workstations that don't have adjustable heights.

Research has shown that platforms are optimal when they are light, sturdy, and have anti-fatigue matting. (Ware et al. 2005) The size recommendation is at least 24 inches deep and 32 inches wide so that the worker can comfortably change foot positions, turn around, and stand. Having stackable platforms (with each being approximately 2 inches tall) is especially beneficial so that "workers can select a platform that will put them within one inch of the proper working height allowing them to work in neutral wrist postures and maximize the forces generated." (Ware et al. 2005).

A few disadvantages of this model exist. Although this platform would elevate the shorter employees to a more suitable level for their workstation and task, this proposed solution would not help people who are too tall. To help solve this problem, the tables could be set to accommodate the large individual at the plant, therefore leaving the other smaller employees with the platforms to increase their height. (Ware et al. 2005) Though this could be somewhat impractical, it might be the only way to ensure all employees are accommodated if the fixed-height workstations remain.

In addition, platforms such as the one in Fig. 14 could pose danger to plant employees as people can forget that they are on it. If they want to reach for something slightly out of reach, they would have to get off the platform and could potentially forget that they are elevated, especially if in a rush or under stress. The platform is also small and could pose a risk to the user if they accidentally step off. The inability of the user to move could also cause the employee to experience stiffness in the legs from standing immobile for so long.

There is also a possible trip hazard while the platforms are in use. To mitigate this, "the edges of all platforms should have yellow and black tape to provide an additional visual indication of the platform" (Ware et al. 2005) and they should be placed in areas where they are not blocking aisles and would not obstruct people or moving machinery from moving past them.

The last disadvantage to implementing this model is related to the "Cost of Compliance." Practically, this means that workers may not be willing to spend the time needed to get the platform and bring it back to the workstation before beginning the work. This could be due to them feeling that the "time spent setting up the workstation prior to work decreases their output or is taking away from their productivity." (Ware et al. 2005) To counter this issue, the platforms should be as light as possible and stored as close to the workstation as possible or practical. It is even suggested that "workstations be set up such that the platform can be fixed so near the workstation that it can be flipped down for use and then flipped back up when the worker is not standing on it." (Ware et al. 2005) This could effectively solve the potential problems arising from the use of platforms in the plant.

4.5 Increased Task Variety Through Job Enlargement

The three steps that brought on the initial complaint by the short female employee are shown in Fig. 1 above. The employee must first face the production table and reach up and behind to grab a "die cut." Then, she must lower her arm to pass the "die cut" through a glue machine. The plant manager mentioned that this repetitive motion of the process is what initially brought on the complaint about a soft tissue injury. However, this issue has arisen in other circumstances and other processes at the facility. Although the plant manager concluded that the pain the employee was feeling in her right shoulder was a result of being too short for the workstation, there is also the possibility that this could also be due simply to the nature of the repetitive behavior.

Repetitive tasks are considered to be psychosocial hazards, ergonomic stress factors, and overall industrial health hazards. (Ware et al. 2005) Similar to excessive force, awkward or static postures, vibration, contact stress, and environmental factors, repetition can lead to an increased risk of developing upper extremity MSDs and other physical repercussions. Research also states that repetitive movements are hazardous when they "involve the same joints and muscle groups over and over, especially when the same motion [is performed] too often, too quickly and/or for too long." (CCOHS 2014) When work involves movements that are repeated, this can cause the worker to tire because they are unable to fully recover in the short periods of time between the repeated movements. Eventually, "it takes more effort to perform the same repetitive movements. When the work activity continues despite fatigue, injuries can occur." (CCOHS 2014) A study performed in 2016 analyzing the interaction between repetition and force on MSDs showed that out of 12 epidemiological studies testing this interaction, 10 reported evidence of this Force X Repetition interaction. (Gallagher and Heberger 2013) The researchers also noticed that "repetition seems to result in modest increases in risk for low − force tasks but rapid increases in risk for high − force tasks." (Gallagher et al. 2014) This makes sense since, as previously mentioned, there is not enough time for recovery when working on a repetitive job. Therefore, more forceful movements will cause the employee to develop fatigue at a higher rate.

This could potentially be remedied by taking breaks, but a more effective approach to solving this problem would be increasing task variety so that employees perform more than one part of a job during their shift as opposed to solely one specific task repeatedly. This would mitigate the risks of developing MSD as well as avoiding the aforementioned problems that arise from workers performing repetitive tasks.

5 Discussion

Considering the solutions proposed in the Results section above, it is clear that to decrease the risk of injury and avoid further musculoskeletal damages, engineering changes must be made to the workstation layout and the task should accommodate users through ergonomic and anthropometric considerations. The most common engineering changes made to workstations include workstation "height and layout, modifications to hand tools, selection of a chair that meets the task criteria, and the implementation of document holders and footrests." (Ware et al. 2005) Furthermore, although any of the five solutions discussed at length in the previous section could benefit the female employee who complained of shoulder pain, these changes could benefit all the employees at the plant. Although some may not have come forward to complain about pain, there is a chance that many employees in the plant have injuries that are too small to notice until they develop into an MSD (as they develop gradually over time) or the employees did not realize that the injury could be due to an unaccommodating workstation or task methodology. Regardless, it is widely understood that all of the proposed changes would benefit the employees at the plant. Similarly, it might be interesting to consider the possibility of implementing more than one of these solutions, if not all.

Figure 15 above shows a sample workstation that is similar to one where all five potential solutions are implemented. This workstation includes an adjustable chair that the user can sit on while performing the task, a height-adjustable table, thereby creating the possibility for the user to alternate between sitting and standing with occasional breaks, having the user stand on an aerobic platform (labeled "soft mat" in the picture above), and lastly, increasing job variety to minimize repetition.

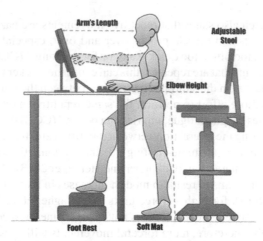

Fig. 15. A combination of the options discussed in "Results." (UCLA Health n.d.)

It is worth noting, however, that there exists a discrepancy between the pictured workstation and the one that would be implemented in the plant since the one in Fig. 15 shows a computer desk and the one in the plant would be a workstation where a task, like die-cutting for example, would be performed. Since the task performed in the plant requires more force exertion than is needed to type on a laptop, it is more likely that the exact dimensions and layout will slightly differ from that shown above. More precisely, the "elbow height" and "arm's length" measures in the figure may vary from the ones found in the plant and could even vary between workstations within the plant. Ideally, the essential part is to "provide workers with an accommodating workstation and job tasks that allow frequent changes of working posture, including sitting, standing, and walking." (WFU Environmental Health & Safety n.d.) The article also states that if it is unfeasible to implement sitting and standing, "sitting in a properly designed chair is preferable." (WFU Environmental Health & Safety n.d)

Nonetheless, implementing a workstation that includes all these accommodations and modifications will not only eliminate the pain that the female employee stated she was feeling in her right shoulder, but also reduce the strain, stress, and risk of developing a musculoskeletal disorder in all of the employees using these workstations.

6 Conclusion/Future Work

While improvements are being made in the designs and usability of workstations, there is still much work to be done in order to reduce the risks of musculoskeletal and related injuries. As highlighted in this report, there are several practical solutions that would immediately mitigate hazards for specific employees. These include adjustable chairs, new work schedules and patterns, a raised standing platform, an adjustable table, and more. While these are all valid recommendations, none of these are universal to employees of all shapes, sizes, and anthropometric measurements. Research should be continued in this field and case studies such as this that involve real-world individuals and first-hand experiences will continue to direct designers and researchers alike in developing innovative solutions that can be used by all individuals.

Looking to the future, the amount of work left in this field before eliminating all potential injury hazards is immeasurable. However, there are several significant options that can and should be evaluated going forward. These include the financial implications of injury, cognitive aspect of having to work physically and be prone to musculoskeletal conditions, options of remote work or hybrid (specifically in this COVID-19 era), difficulty of returning to work following an incident and missing time, organization within businesses and company structure, inclusivity of employees of all backgrounds and abilities, various human anthropometric measurements and their effects on completing a task/performance, the emotional response to injury, and the overall safety and health of employees within any working environment.

Currently, work is still being done in understanding how to reduce musculoskeletal disorders, specifically for individuals performing labor-intensive repetitive tasks. As seen in Fig. 16 below, a recent project beginning on December 1, 2021, was just funded by the National Science Foundation to develop technology that employs machine learning techniques to identify potentially hazardous situations and offer optimal ergonomic solutions.

While not all the aforementioned potential future research topics may contribute specifically to preventing and mitigating musculoskeletal injury risks in the workplace, all are equally important, not only for the employee, but also the employer. From reducing the loss of time missed due to injury to greater inclusivity and promotion within to higher levels of performance and efficiency, continued investigation in this field will impact working environments for generations to come.

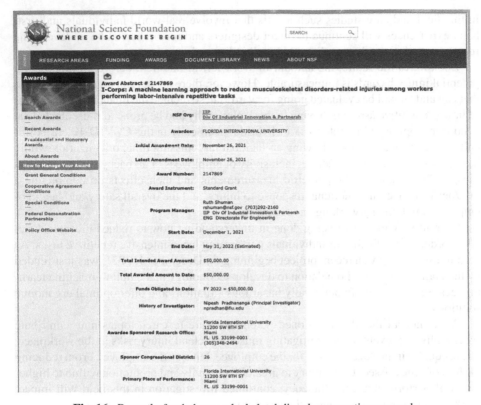

Fig. 16. Recently funded musculoskeletal disorder prevention research

References

"Ergonomics." Ergonomics – Overview | Occupational Safety and Health Administration. United States Department of Labor. Accessed 6 Dec 2021. https://www.osha.gov/ergonomics

Work-Related Musculoskeletal Disorders & Ergonomics: Centers for Disease Control and Prevention. Centers for Disease Control and Prevention. 12 Feb 2020 (2012). https://www.cdc.gov/workplacehealthpromotion/health-strategies/musculoskeletal-disorders/index.html

Musculoskeletal Conditions: World Health Organization. World Health Organization https://www.who.int/news-room/fact-sheets/detail/musculoskeletal-conditions. Accessed 3 Dec 2021

"NOUHAUS® ErgoDraft Drafting, Tall Office, Stool Chair or Standing Desk Chair." Nouhaus Inc. https://www.nouhaus.com/products/ergodraft?variant=31451688796194 (2019)

Bejide, O.: Managing ergonomic Challenges in the Manufacturing Industry. Prevention Ergonomics. Jabulani Consults Limited. http://www.prevention-ergonomics.com/ar/Managing%20Ergonomic%20Challenges%20in%20the%20Manufacturing%20Industry%206%20Dr%20%20Olugbenga%20%20O.%20%20Bejide.pdf (2014)

Waters, T., Dick, R.: Evidence of health risks associated with prolonged standing at work and intervention effectiveness. Rehabil. Nurs. **40**(3), 148–165 (2014). https://doi.org/10.1002/rnj.166

Sitting to Standing Workstations: UCLA Health. University of California: Los Angeles. https://www.uclahealth.org/safety/sitting-to-standing-workstations (n.d.)

Sitting versus Standing Work: Environmental Health & Safety. Wake Forest University. https://ehs.wfu.edu/health-safety/ergonomics/sitting-versus-standing-work/ (n.d.)

Adjustable Height Desk - 60 X 30, White. www.uline.com. https://www.uline.com/Product/Detail/H-7598W/Office-Desks/Adjustable-Height-Desk-60-x-30-White?pricode=WB6643&gadtype=pla&id=H-7598W&gclid=Cj0KCQiAtJeNBhCVARIsANJUJ2HQCf2fGrk-29mI7zc1-ifs98ID1Y8uZrU5QSOIAir7Ptf2SFTSJogaAvEbEALw_wcB&gclsrc=aw.d (n.d.)

Mayrhofer, W., Rupprecht, P., Schlund, S.: One-fits-all vs. tailor-made: user-centered workstations for field assembly with an application in aircraft parts manufacturing. Procedia Manufact. **39**, 149–157 (2019). https://doi.org/10.1016/j.promfg.2020.01.287

Ware, B., Supreeta, A., Jeffrey, F.: Multi-worker standing workstation accommodations: a practical guide." ResearchGate (2005). https://www.researchgate.net/profile/Jeffrey-Fernandez/publication/341050067_Multi-Worker_Standing_Workstation_Accommodations_A_Practical_Guide/links/5eaada1ea6fdcc70509c4a27/Multi-Worker-Standing-Workstation-Accommodations-A-Practical-Guide.pdf 29 Jun 2005

"The Step (Made in USA) 4 Stackable Aerobic Exercise Platform with Non-Slip Surface and Nonskid Feet." Amazon.com. https://www.amazon.com/Step-Stackable-Exercise-Non-Slip-Platform/dp/B000BO8AAM/ref=asc_df_B000BO8AAM/?tag=hyprod-20&linkCode=df0&hvadid=217041414866&hvpos=&hvnetw=g&hvrand=6573371704805552567&hvpone=&hvptwo=&hvqmt=&hvdev=c&hvdvcmdl=&hvlocint=&hvlocphy=9016200&hvtargid=pla-368267259973&th=1 (n.d.)

Government of Canada, Canadian Centre for Occupational Health and Safety: Work-Related Musculoskeletal Disorders (WMSDs) - Risk Factors. Ccohs.ca (2014). https://www.ccohs.ca/oshanswers/ergonomics/risk.html

Gallagher, S., Heberger, J.R.: Examining the interaction of force and repetition on musculoskeletal disorder risk: a systematic literature review. Human Factors: The J. Hum. Factors Ergon. Soc. **55**(1), 108–124 (2012). https://doi.org/10.1177/0018720812449648

MAXQDA Word Cloud Search Article Citations

Choobineh, A., Hosseini, M., Lahmi, M., Jazani, R.K., Shahnavaz, H.: Musculoskeletal problems in Iranian hand-woven carpet industry: guidelines for workstation design. Appl. Ergon. **38**(5), 617–624 (2007). https://doi.org/10.1016/j.apergo.2006.06.005

Colim, A., Carneiro, P., Costa, N., Arezes, P.M., Sousa, N.: Ergonomic assessment and workstation design in a furniture manufacturing industry—a case study. In: Arezes, P.M., et al. (eds.) Occupational and Environmental Safety and Health. SSDC, vol. 202, pp. 409–417. Springer, Cham (2019). https://doi.org/10.1007/978-3-030-14730-3_44

Das, B., Sengupta, A.K.: Industrial workstation design: a systematic ergonomics approach. Appl. Ergon. **27**(3), 157–163 (1996)

del Rio Vilas, D., Longo, F., Rego Monteil, N.: A general framework for the manufacturing workstation design optimization: a combined ergonomic and operational approach. Simulation **89**(3), 306–329 (2013). https://doi.org/10.1177/0037549712462862

Hernandez-Arellano, J.L., Nieves Serratos-Perez, J., de la Torre, A., Maldonado-Macias, A.A., Garcia-Alcaraz, J.L.: Design proposal of an adjustable workstation for very short and very tall people. Procedia Manuf. **3**, 5699–5706 (2015). https://doi.org/10.1016/j.promfg.2015.07.796

Khan, M.I., Khan, S., Haleem, A.: Modernizing ergonomics through additive manufacturing technology. In: Muzammil, M., Khan, A.A., Hasan, F. (eds.) Ergonomics for Improved Productivity. DSI, pp. 157–163. Springer, Singapore (2021). https://doi.org/10.1007/978-981-15-9054-2_17

Lin, R.-T., Chan, C.-C.: Effectiveness of workstation design on reducing musculoskeletal risk factors and symptoms among semiconductor fabrication room workers. Int. J. Ind. Ergon. **37**(1), 35–42 (2007)

Ergonomic Simulation and Analysis of Manikins Working in a Pre-designed Excavator

Mengzhou Chen[1]([✉]), Andre Luebke[2], and Vincent G. Duffy[1]

[1] Purdue University, West Lafayette, IN 47906, USA
{cloris,duffy}@purdue.edu
[2] Human Solutions of North America, Morrisville, NC 27560, USA
aluebke@human-solutions.com

Abstract. Digital human modeling has been one of the topics studied in the field of human factors and ergonomics. With a high amount of literature in the databases, researchers have conducted and analyzed many different applications in digital human modeling. In this paper, a brief bibliometric analysis of digital human modeling was conducted to provide some background on the topic based on the existing literature. Four sample manikins were created, and a pre-designed excavator was imported into the virtual environment in the 3D computer-aided design (CAD) software RAMSIS. The purpose of this study is to conduct ergonomic simulations and analyses of the manikins, to discover areas of improvement in the components of the excavator, and to determine the optimal adjustment ranges for the components. The positions of the manikins, the comfort of the manikins' positions, and a few adjustments were analyzed when the manikins performed specific tasks in the excavator. Eight components of the excavator were analyzed with the analysis functions in the RAMSIS software and adjustment ranges of the relevant components of the excavators were tested. As a result, the optimal possible adjustment ranges were determined so that the design of the excavator supports the decrease of discomfort feelings of the manikins.

Keywords: Manikin · Excavator · Discomfort Feeling · RAMSIS

1 Introduction

According to the Handbook of Human Factors and Ergonomics (Salvendy and Karwowski 2021), digital human modeling is a field that projects the safety and performance of the individuals in a variety of work environments, by modeling human models in simulated environments (Duffy 2009; Demirel and Duffy 2007). Using digital human models not only decreases the necessity of producing physical prototypes but also enhances efficiency and satisfaction in the workplace (Duffy 2010; Applied Human Factors and Ergonomics International 2012; Maurya et al. 2019).

Digital human modeling has been studied and applied to different fields and settings by many well-known authors over the years, including applications to human-machine systems, injury prevention, human-robot collaboration, and so on. In this paper, digital human modeling is being applied to a work environment with an excavator.

© Springer Nature Switzerland AG 2022
V. G. Duffy and P.-L. P. Rau (Eds.): HCII 2022, LNCS 13522, pp. 146–162, 2022.
https://doi.org/10.1007/978-3-031-21704-3_10

2   Bibliometric Analysis

To begin with the topic of digital human modeling, a brief bibliometric analysis was conducted to provide some foundation on the existing literature on this topic. Literature was gathered from Google Scholar, SpringerLink, Scopus, and Web of Science. MAXQDA and VOSViewer were used to analyze the literature (Sheikh et al. 2021). Top keywords in digital human modeling were extracted using the MAXQDA, a powerful tool for qualitative data analysis. Additionally, VOSViewer is a tool for creating maps based on network data and visualizing them by creating relationships between the data. It was used to generate a co-occurrence and a co-citation map to visualize the relationships between pieces of literature.

2.1   The Emergence of Digital Human Modeling in Corpus

As shown in Fig. 1, the Google Ngram Viewer displays the results of the appearance of keywords "Digital Human Modeling", "Office Ergonomics", "Human Supervisory Control", and "Automation Design" in the corpus from 2000 to 2019. "Digital Human Modeling" appears in corpus much more frequently than other topics in human factors and ergonomics.

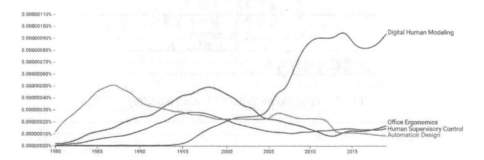

Fig. 1. Google Ngram viewer result (2000–2019)

2.2   Literature Search

Using the same term "Digital Human Modeling" in a few literature databases, many works of literature were found in Google Scholar, SpringerLink, Scopus, and Web of Science. The number of literature found in each database is shown in Table 1.

2.3   Top Keywords in the Word Cloud

MAXQDA was used to find the top keywords within the topic of digital human modeling. Among all the top keywords, a few ones with high frequencies were selected to be

Table 1. Results of literature search

Site	Term	Results
Google scholar	Digital human modeling	3,040,000
SpringerLink	Digital human modeling	363,831
Scopus	(Digital AND human AND modeling)	266,401
Web of science	Digital Human Modeling	23,381

included in Fig. 2. Other than "digital", "human", and "modeling", "design", "simulation", "analysis" and other keywords affirm the importance of computer software application in the topic of digital human modeling. This further validates why an ergonomic simulation software, such as RAMSIS, could be very beneficial in performing digital human modeling.

Fig. 2. Top keywords in digital human modeling

2.4   The Term Co-occurrence Map in VOSViewer

First, Google Scholar was used for literature search in Harzing's Publish or Perish software to extract literature with the keyword "digital human modeling" from 1990 to 2021. Due to the limited capacity to extract all relevant papers on this topic, only 250 papers were extracted.

A term co-occurrence map was generated based on text data from each literature to create a cluster of keywords. The map displays the keywords that share between each literature. With selections of binary counting, a minimum number of occurrences of a term of 5, the largest set of connected terms that include 47 terms were selected. A total of 250 papers were included in the co-occurrence map. From Fig. 3, it is not difficult to see that the term "ergonomic" is connected to "computer", "digital human model", "user", and more. A strong connection between "computer", "assessment", "research" and "digital human modeling" further validates the meaningfulness of conducting this study.

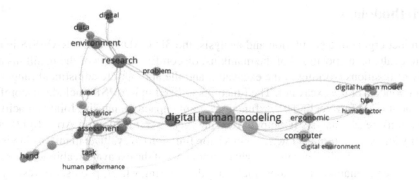

Fig. 3. The term co-occurrence map for digital human modeling

2.5 The Co-citation Map in VOSViewer

A co-citation analysis was conducted and A co-citation map was created to display the co-cited literature. Authors' work is being cited between literature. Based on the bibliographic data from 510 papers, only 95 authors have a minimum of two papers. The largest set of connected co-citation authors has 11 authors, and this is displayed in Fig. 4.

Fig. 4. The co-citation map of the largest set of connected co-citation authors

3 Purpose of Study

The purpose of this study is to determine the optimal adjustment ranges of the components of the excavator that would generally support the minimal discomfort feelings of the manikins. To do that, three specific goals are made to achieve the final purpose:

1. Conduct ergonomic simulations and analyses of the manikins
2. Discover areas of improvement in the components of the excavator
3. Determine the optimal adjustment ranges of the components

Because the design of the excavator is to fit a variety of manikins with different anthropometric measurements, the optimal possible adjustment ranges for positions of the manikins when performing different tasks or using specific components would vary from manikin to manikin and change from task to task.

4   Methodology

To conduct ergonomic simulation and analysis, the 3D CAD software RAMSIS is utilized to evaluate the positions of the manikins, discomfort feelings of the manikins at a variety of positions working in the excavator, and the appropriate adjustment ranges of the components of the excavator. The functions utilized in RAMSIS include discomfort assessment (Comfort Feeling... function), joint capacity analysis (Joint Capacity... function), reach analysis (Compute Reachability... function on Arm Right), and visibility analysis (Internal View... in Vision function) to evaluate manikins in visual or quantitative methods. Therefore, eight components of the excavator cabin were examined at different manikin positions, including the steering wheel, pedals, armrests, joysticks, wrist pads, touch screen display, and control panel. Four sample manikins (5% Annie-Operator, 5% Andy-Operator, 50% Annie-Operator, and 50% Andy-Operator) were created to determine the best adjustment ranges for the relevant components of the excavator. To decrease discomfort for the manikins, discomfort assessment was the main analysis function used to assess the adjustments of the components of the excavator.

5   Procedure

5.1   Designing Boundary Manikins and Defining Tasks

Start a new project file by going to *File > New... Go to Start > NextGen Body Builder* to switch to BodyBuilder mode in RAMSIS. To build a bodybuilder, go to *Anthropometry > Select Anthropometric Database...*. Select "Germany 2004" for *Nation* and "Male" for *Gender* and click *Apply*. The bodybuilder will appear and all the named labels around the manikins are the measurements on the human body that can be changed. The reason that we need to select the "Germany 2004" bodybuilder is that the bodybuilders from other nations, such as the "USA (Nhanes III)", have some measurements that are not adjustable. The "Germany 2004" bodybuilders provide more flexibility and adjustability on body measurements.

Then, go to *Anthropometry > Toggle Measuring Posture* to change the bodybuilder from a standing posture to a sitting posture. Then, go to *Anthropometry > Topology > Control Measurements...* and input values for each dimension at about 50% percentile. Note that we can only define three key dimensions, including body height, waist circumference, and sitting height because these are the three size-defining measurements. Any other body measurements are correlated with these three measurements. Click *Apply* to allow changes to be effective.

Next, go to *Anthropometry > Add Body Measure List To Structure Tree...* and name it "50% Andy". Now, this should appear on the left column under *New Project*. To create a female bodybuilder with the same *Nation*, go to *Anthropometry > Select Anthropometric Database...* again. Select "Female" as the *Gender* this time and click *Apply*. Go to *Anthropometry > Add Body Measure List To Structure Tree...* and name it as "50% Annie". The female bodybuilder should have the same body measurements as the male bodybuilder, as no measurements have been adjusted after the female bodybuilder was created. Use similar steps to create two more manikins, which are "5% Andy" and "5% Annie".

5.2   Creating Male and Female Manikins

Now, we switch to NextGen Ergonomics as all things are set in NextGen Body Builder. Go to *Start > NextGen Ergonomics*. Now the male and female bodybuilders need to be defined with roles. It is recommended to assign them one role, as they need to sit in the excavator. Click on *Role Definition...* , type "Operator" as the *Name*, and choose "Heavy Truck" as the *Posture Model*.

Click *Create*, then you create a manikin. Click on *Test Sample...* . Change the *Manikin Name* to be "Andy" then choose *Body Measure List*. Go to the next tab *Role Assignment*, choose "Operator" as a role, then click *Create* and *Close*. Click *Change* display of active manikins to be "textured", then the Andy-Operator should show up with body texture.

Next, to load skin points, we go to *File > Open...*, then find the "Manikin Body Points (Skin Points)" folder in the C:\Purdue Setup\Data. Change the Files of type to be "Manikin Body Points (*.bpt)", and then select "Male no Shoes.bpt". Then, on the manikin and right-click to select Object Properties.... In the Additional Options tab, select "Workshoe" as the Shoe Model, then click *Apply*.

Now, use the same steps to create a female manikin. Click on *Test Sample...* . Change the *Manikin Name* to be "Annie" then choose *Body Measure List*. Go to the next tab *Role Assignment*, choose "Operator" as a role, then click *Create* and *Close*. Change display of active manikins to be "textured" , then the "Annie-Operator" should show up with body texture rather than linked body points in. Next, to load skin points for the female manikin and not apply them to the male manikin simultaneously, first hide the "Andy-Operator" by double-clicking the manikin under the Test Sample on the left column. Then, select "Female no Shoes.bpt". Then, click on the manikin and right-click to select *Object Properties...*. In the Additional Options tab, select "Workshoe" as the *Shoe Model*, then click *Apply*. Double click on the "Andy-Operator" manikin again on the left column to unhide it. Use similar steps to create four manikins, "50% Andy", "5% Andy", "50% Annie", and "5% Annie", as shown in Fig. 5. To save manikin test samples, go to *File > Save As...*, then choose "Project File (*.prj) for *Files of type*. To open the project file, go to *File > Open...*, and then click on the project file you just created.

Fig. 5. "50% Andy", "5% Andy", "50% Annie", and "5% Annie" Manikins

5.3 Activating Additional Skin Points on Manikins

To activate skin points that are inactive on the manikins, go to *Ergonomics > Manikin > Skin Points….* First, for the male manikin "Andy-Operator", find the skin point named "UAL_1_9" and click *Change Activity* to activate it. The *Skin Points* window is shown in Fig. 6. To create a corresponding skin point on the right arm on the male manikin, simply change the "L" in the Name to "R". Use the same steps to activate this skin point set on the female manikin "Annie-Operator" as well. These skin points would help them to rest their arms on the armrests when they sit in the excavator. The result is shown in Fig. 7. The skin points were activated and are shown in yellow.

Fig. 6. The *Skin Points* Window to Activate "UAL_1_9" on the "Andy-Operator"

Fig. 7. The activated skin points "UAL_1_9" and "UAR_1_9" on the "Andy-Opera- tor" and "Annie-Operator" manikins

6 Evaluation of Overall Driving Position

6.1 Positioning Manikins onto the Excavator Seat

To position the manikins onto the excavator seat, we define restrictions. Go to *Define Restrictions…* , then enter "PHPT" for *Manikin Comp.* And click on the grey surface above the seat named "Surface" for *Env. Object.* Click *Create*, then the first restriction is created. Select "Pelvis Rotation" for *Restriction Type* and select "Tilt Sideways" and "Long Axis Rotation" under *Fixations*, then click *Create*. The third restriction is a target constraint, so select "Target" back for *Restriction Type*. And then select the point named "LeftHeel" on the backside of the manikin's left shoe for *Manikin Comp*. And the grey surface for the pedal named "Surface_" for *Env. Object*. To create the same constraint for the right shoe, simply change the name to "RightHeel" for the *Manikin Comp*. Next, click on the point on the bottom of the manikin's left shoe named "Left-BallOffset" for *Manikin Comp*. And click on the line in the middle of the left pedal named "Line_1" for Env. Object. Do the same to the right shoe. Change the name to "RightBallOffset" for *Manikin Comp*. And select "Line_3" for Env. Object. Now, go to Posture Calculation... > Start. The manikin should sit on the seat with both feet on the pedals shown in Fig. 8.

Fig. 8. The four seated manikins

6.2 Defining Steering Wheel Kinematics

To be able to rotate and extend the steering wheel further close to the manikin, kinematics needs to be defined. First, a point needs to be defined on the steering support as the joint. Starting with creating points on the surface, go to *Geometry > Points...*, and then define two points on a diagonal on the corners of the surface with "Create On Object" as the *Point Type*. Then, create a point in the middle of these two points. Select "Create Between Points" as the *Point Type*. Select one point as the *First Point* and the other point as the *Second Point*. Click *Create*. Then, delete the points other than the point in the middle. Name the point "Joint". Then, use the same steps to create a point in the middle of the steering wheel. To define degrees of freedom, go to Geometry > Define Kinematics..., and select "Add Degree Of Freedom...". Select "Rotation" for the *Type of DOF* with the "Joint" as the *Starting Point*. Select "Y-Axis" as the *Direction*, "−30" degrees for *Minimum* and "30" degrees for *Maximum*. Add another degree of freedom with "Translation" as the *Type of DOF*. Click the "Joint" and then the middle point on the steering wheel as the *Direction*. Enter "100" for *Maximum*. Then, select *Add Objects* and click on the steering wheel (TRM14) and the steering wheel support (TRM15). Now, when adjusting the values of the two degrees of freedom (DOF), the steering wheel may be adjusted in rotation and translation.

6.3 Discomfort Assessment and Comparisons

To assess the current positions of the manikins, we use *Analysis > Comfort Feeling...* to discover the current discomfort levels of the manikins at the seating positions. Before that, other restrictions were defined to make sure the manikins are looking at a certain point in the boom. The initial discomfort levels were set as a reference. Next, different adjustments were made to discover adjustments that would improve or worsen the discomfort of the manikins.

6.4 Determining Adjustment Range of Seat

First, it was noticed that the seat could be adjusted forward to make it more comfortable for both manikins. As a first trial, "−30 mm" was entered in x-direction so that the seat moved forward for 30 mm. The discomfort feeling of the male manikins (5% and 50% Andy-Operators) decreased by 0.15 and 0.12, respectively. The discomfort feeling of the female manikins (5% and 50% Annie-Operators) remained unchanged. This proved that moving the seat forward made a positive impact on male manikins' positions. When the seat was moved forward by 35 mm, the discomfort feeling of the male manikins remained the same as prior adjustment for the 5% Andy-Operator but increased by 0.02 for the 50% Andy-Operator. The female manikins remained the same as prior adjustment for the 5% Annie-Operator but decreased by 0.01 for the 50% Annie-Operator. When the seat was moved forward by 25 mm, the discomfort feeling of the male manikins (5% and 50% Andy-Operators) decreased by 0.15 and 0.03, respectively. The dis- comfort feeling of the female manikins (5% and 50% Annie-Operators) remained unchanged. Comparing the results of improving discomfort for the manikins with different seat adjustments, it can be concluded that the adjustment range for the seat would be between 25 mm to 35 mm.

6.5 Determining Adjustment Range of Steering Wheel Position

Second, it was observed that the steering wheel could be moved up more and tilted more towards the manikins to make it more comfortable to grab the steering wheel. As a result, the steering wheel was first moved up in an x-z direction by 70 mm. Note that our goal is to keep each value equal to or below 3.5, as it considers to be acceptable for a manikin. Because all values are above 3.5 when moved up by 70, adjustments need to be further made to allow four manikins to experience less discomfort. According to Table 2, the first row displays the adjustment made, and the red-shaded cells represent values equal to or above 3.5. It can be concluded that the steering wheel should allow being tilted from 10° to 30° and moved upward by 100 mm to 150 mm, or even higher.

Table 2. The discomfort feeling values of the steering wheel adjustments

	up by 70mm	up by 100mm	up by 100mm & tilted 5°	up by 100mm & tilted 10°	up by 100mm & tilted 15°	up by 100mm & tilted 20°	up by 150mm & tilted 20°	up by 150mm & tilted 30°
5% Andy	4.75	4.51	3.93	3.33	3.18	3.18	3.37	3.41
5% Annie	3.97	3.58	3	3.1	2.99	2.95	3.21	3.57
50% Andy	5.05	4.69	4.24	3.85	3.84	3.82	3.41	3.36
50% Annie	4.65	4.28	3.63	3.19	3.12	3.21	3.16	3.17

6.6 Determining Adjustment Range of Pedal Position

First, it is determined that the pedals could be moved in x and/or z directions. By trying different adjustments, the following Table 3 was made with the two best discomfort feeling values highlighted in yellow. It was found that the adjustment of "x = 10 mm and z = −10 mm" was the best adjustment among the six trials. Note that the discomfort feeling values for the 5% and 50% Annie increased after the best adjustment was applied, and no adjustment was found that allow all four manikins' discomfort feeling values to be below or equal to 3.5, even trials were beyond six times.

Table 3. The discomfort feeling values of the pedal adjustments

	Reference	x = 10mm	x = 10mm z = -10mm	x = 20mm	x = 20mm z = -10mm	x = 30mm	x = 30mm z = -10mm
5% Andy	5.33	4.77	4.83	4.83	4.87	5.16	4.93
5% Annie	3.57	5.02	4.73	4.97	4.77	5.01	4.81
50% Andy	5.79	5.42	5.16	5.58	5.23	5.75	5.6
50% Annie	3.16	5.09	4.86	4.87	4.92	5	4.73

7 Evaluation of the Joysticks

7.1 Grouping Components of the Right and Left Armrests

To adjust the height of the armrests along with the other components on them, such as joysticks and points on the joysticks, select all the corresponding objects and then they're shown in pink in Fig. 9. Then, right-click and choose "Group…". Name the group to be "Armrests" to create the group. To double-check if it's created successfully, find if it's included under the *Geometry Scene.*

7.2 Defining the Kinematics for the Armrests

To define a point on the "Armrests" that are grouped above, go to *Geometry > Define Kinematics…*, Change the *Name* to be "Armrests", and click a random point on the armrest to be the *Origin*. Then, click on *Add Degree of Freedom…*, right-click to select "Z-Axis" for *Direction* and enter "150 mm" for *Maximum*, then click *Create*. Then, click "Add Objects" and click on "Armrests", then click Create. Now, at the bottom of the structure tree, there's the "Geometry Kinematics". To increase the height of the armrests, right-click "Armrests (active)" after expanding the *Geometry Kinematics* from the left column, and then enter any value on the Value column of the first row.

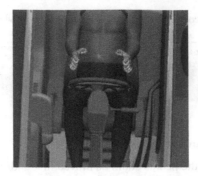

Fig. 9. Grouping components of the armrests (Color figure online)

7.3 Determining the Adjustment Range of Armrest Position

To find the best possible position for the four manikins, multiple trials were performed to find the lowest discomfort feeling values. First, manikins' positions were adjusted to allow the arms to be put on the armrests. This is shown in Fig. 10. Second, Table 4 was made to compare the discomfort feeling values between different adjustments. The armrests were lifted at different heights (z), and the maximum height adjustment is 150 mm. The table below suggests that the adjustment range would be 60 mm to 150 mm.

Fig. 10. The manikins' arms rested on the armrests

7.4 Putting the MANIKIN'S Hands on the Joysticks

To put the hands of the manikin on the joysticks, define restrictions to allow the manikin to grab the joysticks. Go to *Define Restrictions…* ✎ and select the point "HAR_2_1" from the manikin's right hand for *Manikin Comp.* And the point "Point_55" from the right joystick for *Env. Object.* Do the same for the left. Type "HAL_2_1" for *Manikin Comp.* And find "Point_60" from the left joystick. To allow the hands to grab the joysticks

Table 4. The discomfort feeling values of the armrest adjustments

	Reference	z = 40mm	z = 60mm	z = 80mm	z = 100mm	z = 150mm
5% Andy	5.32	4.66	4.52	4.57	4.58	4.64
5% Annie	5.89	5.32	5.07	4.78	5.05	5.74
50% Andy	5.22	4.84	4.29	4.27	4.3	4.15
50% Annie	5.36	5.12	4.7	4.48	4.49	4.57

firmly, select "Manual Grasping" for *Restriction Type*, and choose "Grasp firmly" for *Grasping Mode*, and do this step for both hands for all four manikins. Go to *Posture Calculation...* > *Start*, and the result manikin is shown in Fig. 11.

Fig. 11. The manikins grabbing the joysticks

7.5 Defining Geometry Object Kinematics for the Joysticks

To find a better position to grab the joysticks for both manikins, first group the components of the joysticks together. Then, go to *Geometry > Define Kinematics...* and select the grouped joysticks after clicking *Add Objects*. Then, choose *Add Degree Of Freedom...* and set limits to be [−150.00, 150.00] in the x-direction.

7.6 Determining the Adjustment Range for the Joysticks

By using multiple trials and starting with joysticks moving forward by 40 mm (x = − 40 mm), the best discomfort feeling values were found after the adjustments. Since the maximum they can be moved backward is 150 mm by Andre's demonstration, the best two sets of values out of all trials were when x = 140 mm and x = 150 mm. As shown in Table 5 below, the light-yellow cells indicate the better discomfort feeling values and the dark-yellow cells indicate the comparably worse discomfort feeling values. Except for the 50% Annie, all other manikins have better discomfort feeling values when the joysticks moved forward by 150 mm (x = 150 mm). It implies that the joysticks should be able to at least be moved backward 140 mm and maybe even further.

Table 5. The discomfort feeling values of the armrest adjustments

	Reference	x = -40mm	x = 40mm	x = 60mm	x = 80mm	x = 100mm	x = 120mm	x = 140mm	x = 150mm
5% Andy	4.5	4.94	4.35	4.29	4.09	4.01	3.96	3.91	3.88
5% Annie	4.42	4.72	4.15	4.15	3.89	3.75	3.67	3.59	3.57
50% Andy	5.44	5.56	5.29	5.31	4.86	4.9	4.81	4.32	3.93
50% Annie	4.38	4.42	4.87	4.07	3.82	4.01	4	3.65	3.75

8 Evaluation of the Wrist Pads

To create kinematics for the wrist pads, first group all the components of the wrist pads together. Then, go to *Geometry > Define Kinematics…* and then define a range of [−200, 200] for movement in the x-direction. Then, set up restrictions to allow the manikins to lie the arms on the wrist pads. The manikins' new positions are shown in Fig. 12.

Fig. 12. The manikins' arms resting on wrist pads

8.1 Determining the Adjustment Range for the Wrist Pads

With multiple trials performed in RAMSIS with a variety of adjustments, it was determined first that moving the wrist pads forward decrease the discomfort feeling across all manikins. Based on Table 6 below, moving the wrist pads forward by 180 mm (x = −180 mm) yielded the best discomfort feeling among all trials. It can also be concluded that an appropriate range for adjusting the wrist pads would be moving them forward by 160 mm to 200 mm.

Table 6. The discomfort feeling values of the wrist pad adjustments

	Reference	x = 20mm	x = -20mm	x = -120mm	x = -140mm	x = -160mm	x = -180mm	x = -200mm
5% Andy	6.05	6.48	5.98	5.88	5.65	5.56	5.41	5.28
5% Annie	6.96	7.26	7.02	6.18	6.09	5.89	5.9	5.93
50% Andy	5.81	6.32	5.67	5.31	5.36	5.23	5.09	4.9
50% Annie	6.59	6.72	6.48	6.12	6.14	6.09	5.91	5.99

9   Evaluation of the Touch Screen

9.1   Computing Reachability on the Right Arms

It is critical to conduct a reach analysis when considering designing an excavator. According to the RAMSIS Ergonomics User Guide (Human Solutions GmbH 2021), the function *Compute Reachability* in RAMSIS computes the farthest reachable space that manikins can reach in their current positions. Because the manikins are supposed to be able to reach the touch screen when they sit, a reach analysis was conducted to determine whether the manikins can reach the touch screen at seating positions. To discover if the manikins can reach the touch screen, go to *Analysis > Compute Reachability > Arm Right*. Figure 13 below shows that the manikins are not able to do so, as the reachable space for each manikin (red surface) does not include the touch screen inside the surface.

Fig. 13. The reachable spaces (in red) for the manikins' right arms (Color figure online)

9.2   Defining the Kinematics of the Touch Screen

First, group all components that belong to the touch screen together. Then, go to *Geometry > Define Kinematics....* First, go to *Analysis > Vision > Internal View...* to show what

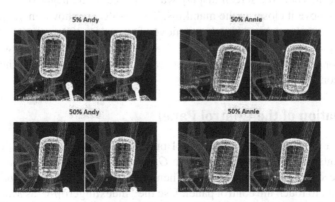

Fig. 14. The reachable spaces (in red) for the manikins' right arms (Color figure online)

manikins view from their eyes. From Fig. 14 below, the current position of the touch screen is in viewable position for all manikins, but the screen is not reachable for all manikins.

To allow the manikins' right arms to reach the touch screen at their current positions and make sure the touch screen is positioned in a better view for all four manikins, adjust using the reach spaces and discomfort feeling analysis. First, adjust the touch screen display so that it's inside all four surfaces of reachability. Then, move the touch screen so that all four manikins can see the entire screen. After fulfilling these prior two requirements, adjusting within the limits, and finding positions of the touch screen display would lower the discomfort feeling for all four manikins. Go to *Define Restriction...* and click on the point on the manikin's right index fingertip "indexfingertip-r" as *Manikin Comp.* And the "Point_13" on the touch screen as *Env. Object.* Right-click and select *Special Copy* and then *Special Paste...* to all other manikins to apply this same restriction to all other manikins. Go to *Posture Calculation...* and then all four manikins can touch the screen. This is shown in Fig. 15 below.

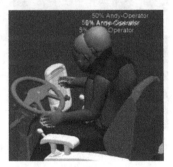

Fig. 15. The manikins touching the screen

Because lowering arms to touch the screen would be less tiring, the touch screen was first adjusted in the negative z-direction to lower the height of the touch screen so that the manikins may touch the screen with less effort on lifting their arms to reach and touch the screen. Then, the screen display was adjusted in the negative y-direction and x-direction to move it closer to the manikins. The results are shown in Table 7, and the most the screen could be moved is when it moved forward by 200 mm ($x = 200$ mm), left by 100 mm ($y = -100$ mm), and down by 10 mm ($z = -10$ mm). This also yielded the best values for discomfort feelings. Almost all four manikins are within the acceptable range of discomfort feeling of 3.5 or below.

10   Evaluation of the Control Panel

First, define a point on one of the control buttons. Group the point with the rest of the components of the control panel. Go to *Geometry > Define Kinematics...* and add degrees of freedom in x and z directions. Then, go to *Define Restriction* and set a target for the manikin to touch the control panel. Use the "indexfingertip-r" as *Manikin Comp.* And the "Point_8" on the control panel as the *Env. Object.*

Table 7. The discomfort feeling values of the touch screen adjustments

	x = 180mm y = -80mm z = -20mm	x = 180mm y = -80mm z = -10mm	x = 180mm y = -100mm z = -10mm	x = 200mm y = -100mm z = -10mm
5% Andy	3.94	3.89	3.72	3.54
5% Annie	3.97	3.92	3.79	3.61
50% Andy	4.3	4.26	4.19	3.91
50% Annie	3.94	3.89	3.79	3.5

Next, adjustments are made through the kinematics and multiple trials were performed. From Table 8 below, the cells for x = 10 mm and x = 30 mm adjustments were shaded with blue to indicate the better values in discomfort feeling. Light-blue cells represent the higher values whereas the dark-blue cells represent the lower values, meaning the discomfort feeling decreased for the manikin. Conflicting results were yielded in such two adjustments, so it implies that moving the control panel forward was not helpful for some manikins. The same idea applies to adjustment in the z-direction. Comparing the discomfort feeling between z = 10 mm and z = 30 mm, it can be concluded that moving the panel upward help most of the manikins in our samples (75%). Therefore, additional trials were performed by increasing z and decreasing x values. Comparing the discomfort feeling values between z = 60 mm and z = 70 mm, it can be concluded that it would be recommended not to exceed z over 60 mm. Based on such information, additional trials were performed to discover the best discomfort feeling values when decreasing x while maintaining a z value of 60 mm. Comparing the last two columns in the table, it can be seen that they have conflicting results on the better discomfort values. The minimum discomfort feeling value for each manikin was indicated in red font. It can be concluded that the best range for x is [−30, −80], among the trials that were performed. Because 5% Andy has the best discomfort feeling value when z = 10 mm, while all other manikins have the best when z = 60 mm, the best range for z is [10, 60], among the trials that were performed.

Table 8. The discomfort feeling values of the control panel adjustments

	Reference	x = 10mm	x = 30mm	z = 10mm	z = 30mm	z = 60mm	z = 70mm	x = -30mm z = 60mm	x = -60mm z = 60mm	x = -80mm z = 60mm
5% Andy	4.34	4.25	4.24	4.07	4.26	4.22	4.27	4.02	3.97	3.84
5% Annie	4.48	4.48	4.5	4.34	4.06	4.06	4.26	3.82	3.82	3.86
50% Andy	5.51	5.55	5.63	5.44	5.26	4.63	4.79	4.52	4.15	4.07
50% Annie	4.64	4.65	4.58	4.53	4.19	3.99	4.11	3.85	3.9	4

11 Discussion

Finding appropriate adjustment ranges was one of the challenges when completing the project. The specific key metrics to evaluate the adjustments were unclear at first. However, with technical consulting and assistance received at Purdue University, key metrics were identified and other analysis functions in RAMSIS were effectively utilized as well to determine the optimal adjustment ranges for manikins at different working positions.

There are a few limitations in the study, including limited manikin test samples, a limited number of trials performed, and a short project timeline before the deadline. Note that the tables shown in prior pages do not include all trials that were performed. Some were not included to reduce confusion for lay readers in understanding the progress of the project.

12 Future Work

Future studies should include more manikin test samples and perform more trials so that the optimal adjustment ranges would be more accurate. If the project is sufficiently funded with a longer timeline allowed, future studies should perform more analysis to examine other aspects of the simulation results. One type of data that RAMSIS does not include currently is data from specially abled and elderly. According to Maurya et al. (2019, 1), these two groups of people receive less consideration and limited applications in the digital human modeling field. However, they need to be considered as it will support these two vulnerable groups of people to work in the same workplaces other people work in. Incorporating their anthropometric data into RAMSIS would not only allow workplace design to be more inclusive but also would give them more independence and flexibility to be involved in work as others do (Maurya et al., 2019, 1).

References

Demirel, H.O., Duffy, V.G.: Applications of digital human modeling in industry. In: Duffy, V.G. (ed.) ICDHM 2007. LNCS, vol. 4561, pp. 824–832. Springer, Heidelberg (2007). https://doi.org/10.1007/978-3-540-73321-8_93

Duffy,V.G.: Introduction. In: Duffy, V.G. (ed.) Handbook of Digital Human Modeling, Chapter 1, pp. 1–5. CRC Press, Taylor & Francis Group, Boca Raton, FL (2009)

Duffy, V.G.: Advances in Applied Digital Human Modeling. CRC Press, Taylor & Francis Group, Boca Raton, FL (2010)

Human Solutions GmbH: RAMSIS NextGen 1.8 Ergonomics User Guide, pp. 3–7. Human Solutions GmbH, Kaiserslautern (2021)

Maurya, C.M., Karmakar, S., Das, A.K.: Digital human modeling (DHM) for improving work environment for specially-abled and elderly. SN Appl. Sci. 1(11), 1–9 (2019). https://doi.org/10.1007/s42452-019-1399-y

Salvendy, G., Karwowski, W.: Handbook of Human Factors and Ergonomics. John Wiley & Sons (2021)

Sheikh, A., Duffy, V.G.: Ergonomics training and evaluations in a digital world using collaborative technologies: a bibliometric analysis. In: Stephanidis, C., et al. (eds.) HCII 2021. LNCS, vol. 13097, pp. 639–652. Springer, Cham (2021). https://doi.org/10.1007/978-3-030-90966-6_43

Ergonomics and Musculoskeletal Injuries in a Manufacturing Setting

Sofia Katarina Chkautovich and Vincent G. Duffy(✉)

Purdue University, West Lafayette, IN 47907, USA
{schkauto,duffy}@purdue.edu

Abstract. An employee who works with die cuts complained about a soft tissue injury in her right shoulder. This injury was a result of repetitive motions occurring in a non-ergonomic fashion. Currently, the employee is required to reach up and around to retrieve the die cuts. This is an ergonomic analysis that studied the effects of a soft tissue injury in a manufacturing setting. The goal was to find a more ergonomic solution to lessen injury, or remove altogether, by analyzing the workspace, the worker's anthropometrics, and the tasks, repetitive or varying. The relevant findings of this study showed the task of throwing die cuts is repetitive, the employee in question faces another challenge of being shorter in height than her other coworkers, and injuries such as this are common and are occurring more often. An ergonomic plan showing recommendations and preventative methods is to be implemented and enforced by the employer and followed by the employees.

Keywords: Ergonomics · Musculoskeletal · Manufacturing

1 Introduction and Background

1.1 Ergonomics and Musculoskeletal Conditions

Human factors and ergonomics are sometimes used synonymously, resulting in the term "human factors ergonomics" (HFE). The International Ergonomics Association (IEA) defines ergonomics as "the scientific discipline concerned with the understanding of the interactions among humans and other elements of a system and the profession that applies theory, principles, data, and methods to design in order to optimize human well-being and overall system performance" (Spath et al. 2012).

Musculoskeletal refers to a person's muscles, bones, nerves, ligaments, and joints. Musculoskeletal injuries or disorders are typically caused by lifting, twisting, repetitive tasks, hyperextension, or foreign forces upon the body. The problem areas for these injuries are the back, neck, shoulders, and wrists.

This case study is an analysis of a musculoskeletal injury of an employee in an industrial, manufacturing setting. The employee in question sustained a soft tissue injury in the right shoulder. The notable features of the employee are she is a female of shorter stature and is right-hand dominant. Her task consists of constant repetitive motions of reaching up and behind to grab a die cut, then lowering her arm to "throw" the die cut through a glue machine. She works at a station without an adjustable platform or mechanism to aid in reaching or throwing.

© Springer Nature Switzerland AG 2022
V. G. Duffy and P.-L. P. Rau (Eds.): HCII 2022, LNCS 13522, pp. 163–180, 2022.
https://doi.org/10.1007/978-3-031-21704-3_11

Purpose of Analysis. There are multiple purposes of this study. The first is to provide the specific employee with a more ergonomic solution to complete her day-to-day tasks. The analysis also proposes potential changes for the company as a whole; catering to a variety of ergonomic concerns. All of these solutions should be considered permanent, with the intent of creating safer working environments and procedures. If a permanent solution is not feasible, temporary workarounds should be utilized until permanence is established. Preventing further injury is the ultimate goal for the analysis and the company.

Assumptions The author established six assumptions. First, the manager has looked into rectifying the problem. Included in this assumption is that upper management and the overall company are aware of the situation and its resolution status. Second, the employee is not continuing to perform the injury-inducing task. A doctor or physical therapist's note medically explaining the extent of the damage should be enough to halt the repetition until a solution has been established. Third, the manager and safety manager assessed other employees for similar or other ergonomic issues. Fourth, employees are wearing appropriate clothing, including personal protective equipment (PPE). Managers should conduct routine PPE inspections to ensure employees are compliant with safety standards. Fifth, the employee has thought of a better way to complete her task, with or without the help of her coworkers. Sometimes those who are deeply ingrained with the activity have greater insight as how to make it more conducive. Lastly, the employer has conducted employee safety surveys. This step can help the resolution and data analysis by eliminating options that are already implemented, do not work or are not feasible.

Relevance of the Problem. Ergonomics will never be obsolete. While completing this analysis, and simply being an observant individual, the author has found ergonomics and injury know no bounds. Age, gender, body type, work type, etc. are all affected differently. Creating and maintaining a safe work environment should be an employer's main goal. When an employee feels and is safe, they have the ability to put more focus on the tasks, rather than worrying about injuring themselves. Results of a safe environment are a reduction of injuries, improvement of production and quality, and employee satisfaction. Employers have the responsibility to provide employees with proper safety education, including, but not limited to ergonomics, well-being, first aid, fire, severe weather, etc.

2   Literature Review

2.1   Demos

The demos listed in Table 1 were conducted by the author to illustrate a systematic literature review. The method closely follows procedures outlined in Zimmerman and Duffy (2023). The table gives a brief overview of the methodologies used, the output for each demo, and which demos were included in this report. Beyond the table are individual descriptions of each demo, with accompanying figures. Additional figures for demos 2, 3, 4, and 5 can be found in the Appendix (Figs. 13, 14, 15, 16, 17, 18, 19 and 20).

Table 1. A visualization of a systematic literature review approach.

Demo	Software/methodology	Output	Used in report
1	Vicinitas, Google Ngram	Ngram graph	Y
2	'List of 10 ways'	List	Y
3	Harzing, maxQDA	Word cloud	Y
4	WoS, Vos Viewer	Network diagram	Y
5	BibExcel	Search results and pivot chart	Y
6	Scopus/Harzing	Network diagram	Y
7	nsf.gov	Search results for an award	Y
8	Citespace	N/A	N

Demo 1: Vicinitas, Google Ngram.
The first demo was conducted using Google Ngram instead of Vincinitas. By creating a set of search terms, narrowing the search by date range, and smoothing (a numerical scale used to determine raw data), a graph populates to show how the specific search terms appear in literature. The search terms used for this demo were "ergonomics, musculoskeletal, manufacturing safety" to stay within the topics of interest for this project. The date range was adjusted to try and create a better graph, but it did not change much. And the more search terms included in the viewer, the fewer generated results (Fig. 1).

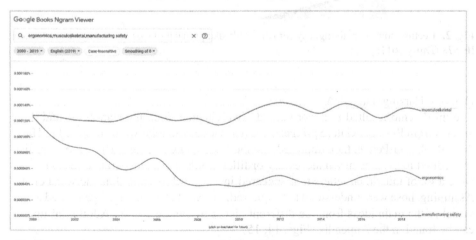

Fig. 1. Google Ngram plot of terms from 2000–2019, with a smoothing of 0 (Google 2022).

Demo 2: *List of 10 Ways*

To complete the second demo, the author searched Google Scholar, SpringerLink, and ResearchGate to find an article to analyze specifically using the *List of 10 Ways* (Fig. 2). The article chosen was "Ergonomic Design for Assembly Manufacturing Workstation Based on Universal Design Principles." This article because it specifically calls out ergonomic design for assembly manufacturing. It also has a similar endpoint of making sure the workstation fits the employee, in an attempt to be more ergonomic and productive. Additional figures can be found in the Appendix (Fig. 13).

Hambali, Ruzy Haryati, Effendi Mohamad, and Teruaki Ito. "Ergonomic Design for Assembly Manufacturing Workstation Based on Universal Design Principles." In Lecture Notes in Networks and Systems, 260:870–877, 2021.

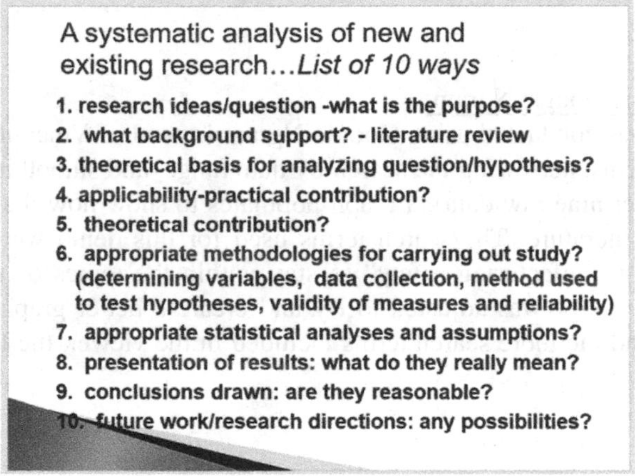

A systematic analysis of new and
existing research...*List of 10 ways*

1. research ideas/question -what is the purpose?
2. what background support? - literature review
3. theoretical basis for analyzing question/hypothesis?
4. applicability-practical contribution?
5. theoretical contribution?
6. appropriate methodologies for carrying out study? (determining variables, data collection, method used to test hypotheses, validity of measures and reliability)
7. appropriate statistical analyses and assumptions?
8. presentation of results: what do they really mean?
9. conclusions drawn: are they reasonable?
10. future work/research directions: any possibilities?

Fig. 2. Lecture notes explaining a systematic analysis approach of *List of 10* ways from Purdue IE 578 (Duffy 2011, p.58)

Demo 3: Harzing, maxQDA

The third demo resulted in a word cloud. Two chapters from the Handbook and three articles from ResearchGate, SpringerLink, and Google Scholar were compiled in Harzing's Publish or Perish, then imported into the MAXQDA software. The 'stop word list' was edited to exclude any unnecessary or filler words. For some strange reason, there were a lot of individual letters that appeared in the word list, and thus the word cloud. Assuming those were understood to be ignored, the word cloud in Fig. 3 generated a nice visual of the main ideas from the different pieces of literature used. Additional figures can be found in the Appendix (Figs. 14, 15).

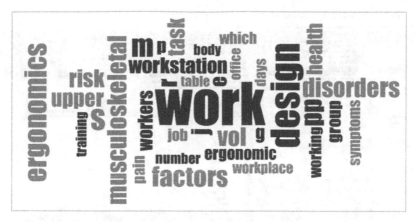

Fig. 3. A word cloud generated from MAXQDA (VERBI GmbH 2022)

Demo 4: Web of Science, VOS Viewer

After the word cloud, a density cluster was generated using VOS Viewer (Fig. 4). Articles were found using Web of Science and that data was imported to VOS. After a few iterations of filtering words and occurrence, the author was able to decrease the size of the clusters to then only show 70 items total. This allowed for a clearer visualization of the Harzing data. Additional figures can be found in the Appendix (Figs. 16, 17).

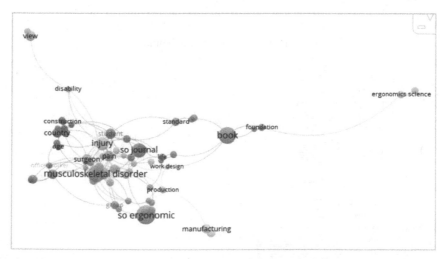

Fig. 4. VOS Viewer network diagram illustrating the density and connection of terms (Centre for Science and Technology Studies 2022)

Demo 5: BibExcel

BibExcel is a tool that utilizes the analytical portion of programs like Excel to process bibliometric data. The author searched Google Scholar via Harzing for the keywords "ergonomics in workplace" (Fig. 5).

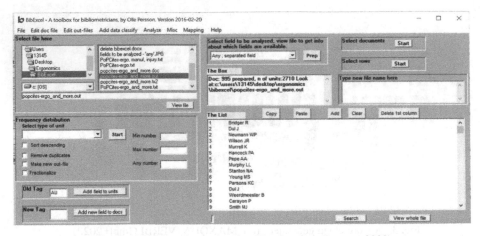

Fig. 5. A BibExcel search using Harzing data (Persson 2009)

A pivot chart of the leading authors in Google Scholar regarding 'ergonomics in workplace', with a detailed search on 'ergonomics and manufacturing and musculoskeletal injury' is seen in Fig. 6. For the purpose of brevity, a truncated chart was included in this report – the full chart contains 95 authors and it would not fit nicely to be able to clearly read the data. The steps to achieve these results can be seen in additional figures in the Appendix.

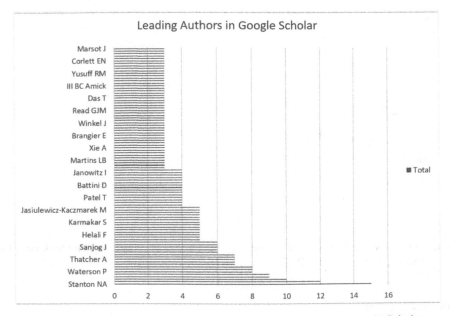

Fig. 6. A truncated pivot chart illustrating the leading authors in Google Scholar

Demo 6: Scopus

This next demo emphasized Scopus, but for this systematic review, VOS Viewer was used. This data came from Harzing and Google Scholar and the data text file from Demo 4 was repopulated. This time, the occurrences were increased to 25 and the number of terms to 30. This diagram also used full counting instead of binary counting (which Demo 4 used) (Fig. 7).

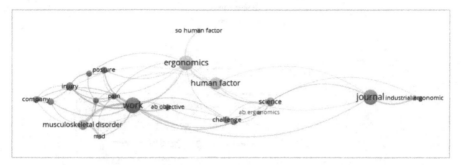

Fig. 7. A VOS Viewer network diagram (Centre for Science and Technology Studies 2022)

Demo 7: National Science Foundation (NSF)

To complete this demo, the author searched the awards section of the NSF website. Initially, 'workstation ergonomics' was searched, but it did not yield the results the author was hoping for. After a few iterations of the search terms, the author was able to find a decent award with the term 'anthropometry' which resulted in over 3,000 awards. Figure 8 is a screenshot of an award for "Designing for Human Variability: Allocation of Adjustability."

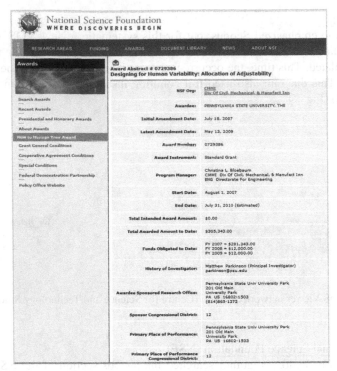

Fig. 8. A screen capture of an NSF award for an article about designing for human variability (National Science Foundation 2009).

3   Procedure and Results

3.1   Procedure

The procedure and analysis for this project were done at an academic level where every-thing was conceptualized and applied in a "what if" situation. The data and reports were presented to the author such that the majority of the situational data, directive from the manager, and die cut packaging information were given.

The first step was to learn about the presented problem; an employee sustained a soft tissue injury to her shoulder while on the job. After the problem was established, the safety reports were read. In this case, these reports came in the form of an "ergonomic analysis/observation summary" that was completed by the manager.

Once the reports were presented and inspected, data collection began. The biometrics of the employee in question were gathered, along with the components of her particular job. This employee is classified as short, measuring five feet in height, and right-hand dominant. There was no additional health data available that alluded to this muscu-loskeletal injury being caused by something else. When asked about her daily motions, she described the process of her task as the following: face the production table, reach up and behind to grab the die cut, lower her arm to pass the die cut through the glue machine, and repeat. This employee does this repetitive task for 10 h per day, 40 h per week.

Within the manager's letter stating that "other such cases" have occurred, additional data acquisition and research were needed.

Research. Soft tissue, more specifically musculoskeletal, injuries were researched. This author did not have a great deal of knowledge in this area, but in her search, she learned this type of injury is more common than realized. Shoulders and backs are the leading problem areas, but musculoskeletal injuries also affect joints (arthritis) and bones (osteoporosis) (World Health Organization 2021).

There are optimal movements and postures that experts have found for reducing injury and improving ergonomic work. Reach is one movement that is of utmost interest in ergonomics because it affects multiple body parts (shoulders, neck, wrists, elbows, etc.), sometimes simultaneously. This particular action tends to affect individuals of shorter stature. Bending is another movement that contributes to musculoskeletal injuries. Back and neck injuries are most common from this action, especially in taller individuals. And if someone picks up an object while bending, that increases the strain on the body. Figure 9 show the zones for each of these movements, reaching above shoulder height and bending below the waist.

Fig. 9. Illustrations of the danger and neutral zones for reach and bend (Adapted from Stone 2020).

Standing work is not thought of as hazardous work, but if not addressed properly, it can lead to neck, shoulder, back, or foot problems. The type of work will dictate the proper stance for an individual. Figure 10 shows Kroemer's diagram for standing work, ranging from precision to heavy work. While there are dimensions shown in the figure, it is to be assumed that the ratios change based on the worker's height.

Adjustable workbenches, moveable platforms, redesign of a work area, padded mats, and proper footwear can all be implemented to avoid injury or discomfort. Because all bodies are different and the goal is to have the job fit the worker, there are no standard motions or positions that all must follow.

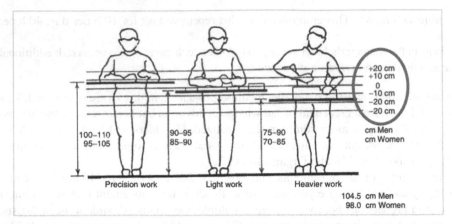

Fig. 10. Diagram illustrating standing work, with adjustable heights, based on the type of work ranging from precision to heavy work (Adapted from Kroemer and Grandjean 1997).

Analysis and Recommendations. As discussed, musculoskeletal injuries can affect the shoulders, joints, back, and neck. And in a manufacturing setting, workers become more susceptible to these injuries. Figure 11 illustrates the design of work tools, but the algorithm is a great model for how this industrial case can be corrected. Like most scenarios, there is a known problem and a (possibly) known solution, but the intermediate steps to achieve the solution are unknown. Trial and error or various assessments are done to eliminate unsuccessful efforts until the objective is within sight.

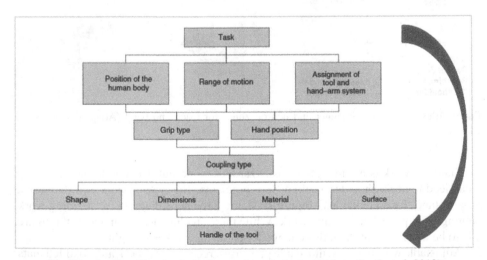

Fig. 11. An algorithm for designing work tools (Adapted from Spath et al. 2012)

Once an algorithm or process improvement chart is established, a model should be created. RAMSIS has shown to be a great modeling software that allows manikins to represent how the job should be fitted to the worker. Creating a model of this employee and her workstation allows for analysts to study her movements and identify problem areas. With specific issues brought to light, the process for engineering multiple recommendations becomes easier. Instead of using real resources to test the solutions, RAMSIS can be used to eliminate results that do not comply with ergonomic standards.

Establishing recommendations and possible solutions is the second to last step of the process. Once the company reviews recommendations, there should be a trial period to see how the ergonomics change for the better. If the problem is fixed, the process is complete. If the problem is still persistent, or worse, another issue arises, more specific recommendations should be provided.

4 Discussion

4.1 Recommendations

Prior to physical changes happening, a plan should be established so all are able to understand why changes are needed. The Centers for Disease Control and Prevention (CDC) recommends a three-tier hierarchy of controls. Tier one is for engineering controls, tier two is for administrative controls, and tier three is for the use of personal protective equipment (PPE) (Centers for Disease Control and Prevention 2020).

Some first step recommendations are adjustable platforms or workstations (tier one of the CDC plan), altering the way the die cuts are "thrown" (tier two of the CDC plan), reorganizing or redesigning the work area so the die cuts are not outside of normal reach, and if a reorder is not feasible, invest in a mechanical arm to retrieve the die cuts from a higher or awkwardly positioned location.

Another possible solution is for a fixed platform to be installed. This particular design has open sides so it could be butted against a table or piece of machinery without additional reach being imposed (see Fig. 12). It is understood that this type of platform cannot be easily folded, dismantled, or stacked when not in use, as stated by the plant manager, but it is an alternate option.

Fig. 12. A fixed-step platform to be placed against the work surface (LTW Ergonomic Solutions 2021).

In general, ergonomics should not need justification when implementing equipment or processes to increase safety in the workplace. Implementation of proper PPE is a solution that should be the cheapest since it is a standard across all industries. Once that has been established as mandatory, additional equipment is then considered. Standardized steps or platforms were a suggestion initiated by the plant manager, and as such, a form of this solution should be considered first. Anything adjustable is cost-beneficial because one item can be purchased to cater to multiple people instead of each employee ordering a personalized solution.

Potential Trade Offs. If a solution is not found or implemented, a series of issues can result. Simply, there could be an increase of new or recurring injuries, with potentially more severity.

While saving the shoulder, in this case, how is the neck affected? If a solution is designed for one body part, will that shift the stress to another area?

If companies do not respond to workplace injury, legal issues can also arise in the form of workman's compensation lawsuits.

Negligence on the company's part might also create issues for employee satisfaction and retention and quality of performance and production.

Like any project, budget and time are also essential for a successful study and implementation. Something for the company to consider is how much are they willing to invest in safety. Temporary fixes might be cheap at the moment, but will need to be replaced over time, and it may be costly. Another budgetary consideration is to implement a solution for one employee or task versus multiple areas and employees. With potential fixes available, it will take time to replace the old with the new, and train employees on proper usage. The adage is "time is money," but schedule should not take priority over safety. If multiple fixes are being worked on, it will take time and possible iterations to implement due to the difficulty of accommodating varying body types and needs, while keeping an ergonomic-centric design.

Ergonomic Fundamentals. Most objects, especially in manufacturing or industrial area, are designed with a male's anthropometrics in mind. These are typically referred to as the "5th to 95th percentile" measurements. According to the Handbook of Human Factors and Ergonomics, the 95th percentile weight has no relationship to the 95th percentile stature (Spath et al. 2012).

There are a variety of standards that govern ergonomics, specifically in the workplace. For example, the International Organization for Standardization (ISO) published standards, the United States government published MIL-STD-1472, Occupational Safety and Health Administration (OSHA) published *Ergonomic Program Rule*, and The American National Standards Institute (ANSI) published standards. These regulating standards are used to design everything from hand-held tools to aircraft to chairs.

If health and safety are not enough to convince employers to implement ergonomic changes, an incentive-type program may. Employer benefit programs include "reductions in numbers of lost workdays, workers' compensation costs, and MSD incidence rates" (Spath et al. 2012). Cost-benefit analyses are also used to demonstrate to companies the long-term savings that ergonomic solutions have, compared to their current methodologies.

Limitations. Due to this analysis being conducted at a brief academic level, there were some limitations. First, there was not enough time or data to complete an official study with full metrics and testing capabilities. The report from the plant manager stated there were "other such cases" similar to this, but that data (types of injuries, solutions, etc.) were not provided. Had the author been able to access the data, she could have used those metrics to enhance the analysis and potential solutions for this case. Modeling software could also have been used as well to test the practicality of the recommended solutions.

The analysis could have been improved with additional data, such as metrics from other employees who have experienced similar repetitive motion-induced injuries or other types of musculoskeletal discomfort.

5 Conclusion

5.1 Future Work

Most companies have the attitude of "this is how we've been doing it for years" and do not see an urgent need for change. If a study was done to show current processes versus new or modified processes, would the results be enough to evoke change within the company? Or would it take more, namely financial incentives?

There is also the notion of designing for not only the current issue but also the anticipation of side effects from the solution. Will the solution only fix the issue at hand or will it be adjustable for the future?

By completing an ergonomic study now, employers can get a head start on fixing any glaring ergonomic and safety issues. If these issues persist, there are possible solutions that exist or a strategy for assessing the problem and starting the pursuit for a new or better solution.

Future Ergonomic Questionnaire. As the situation was analyzed, the author asked the following questions to gain a better understanding of why ergonomic reports are not being conducted as frequently. Does the advent of bigger and better technology increase or decrease musculoskeletal conditions? If automation is taking over, will there be a need for ergonomics? Will the concepts of ergonomics stay relevant throughout time or will the "basics" become obsolete? Are there recovery plans established if the injuries become worse or more persistent? Do the employees have incentives or ramifications if the ergonomic plan is not followed?

Appendix

DEMO 2

1. Research ideas/questions – what is the purpose?
   a. Verify the ergonomic risk of workers and propose an ergonomic design for the manufacturing workstation.

2. Literature review – what background support?
   a. Nordic musculoskeletal questionnaire (NMQ)
   b. Interviews in the manufacturing department

3. Theoretical basis for analyzing question/hypothesis?
   a. Results obtained from the software can be used to validate any issues that involve the ergonomics problem occurrence
   b. An improvement can be made to achieve the best solution to eliminate the problem; thus, worker efficiencies and productivities could be enhanced.

4. Applicability – practical contribution?
   a. "Fatigue causes a slowing down of reaction times in which increases the time to complete a task. The longer time for a task to be done, the poorer the performance."

5. Theoretical contribution?
   a. Seven principles of the universal design: Unbiased, Flexibility, Simple and spontaneous, Noticeable information, Tolerance for mistake, Low physical struggle, Size and space for approach

6. Appropriate methodologies for carrying out study?
   a. Dimension of each station and jigs in the station for the layout of the selected department were measured using Stanley Metric Measuring Wheel; universal design was used in designing the existing workstation; CATIA V5 was used to model the design layout for the respective department; NMQ was used to compare body discomfort among the workers; DELMIA V5 was used to simulate the worker and working process involved

7. Appropriate statistical analyses and assumptions?
   a. Rapid Upper Limb Assessment (RULA) calculations were done to score workstation designs

8. Presentation of results – what do they really mean?
   a. NMQ: 96.77% experienced discomfort at spine and lower back after work. Meanwhile, only 3.23% experienced discomfort at thigh after work. However, more than 80.65% suffer discomforts at their arm, wrist, and lower back after work

9. Conclusions drawn – are they reasonable?
   a. Results showed that RULA and energy consumption of the proposed design were better than the existing design

10. Future work/research directions – any possibilities?
    a. "...this indicates software was powerful predictive tool to measure the ergonomic risk value and improve the workstation design of the industry"

Fig. 13. Screen capture of the author's 'list of 10 ways' article assessment.

DEMO 3

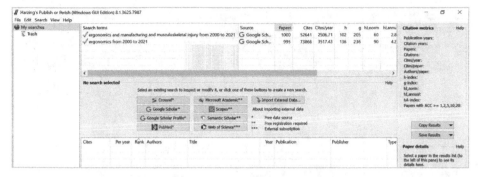

Fig. 14. Screen capture of a search done in Harzing (Harzing 2021).

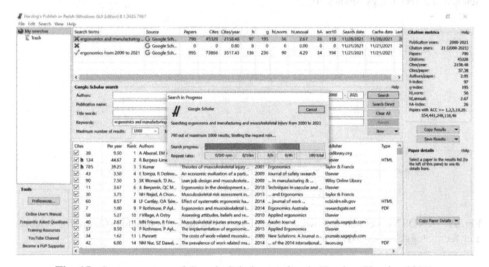

Fig. 15. Screen capture of Google Scholar results via Harzing (Harzing 2021).

DEMO 4

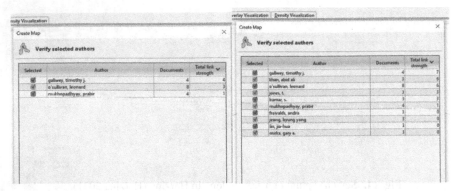

Fig. 16. A VOS Viewer 'selected authors' comparison of three results versus 10 (Centre for Science and Technology Studies 2022).

Fig. 17. A VOS Viewer notice showing three of the ten items are connected (Centre for Science and Technology Studies 2022).

DEMO 5

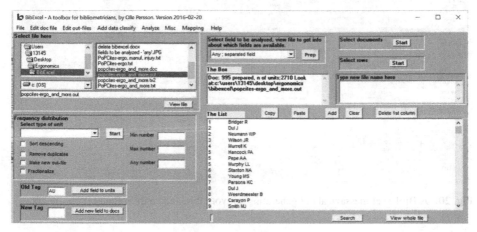

Fig. 18. A BibExcel screen capture showing the file locations and the list of authors (Persson 2009).

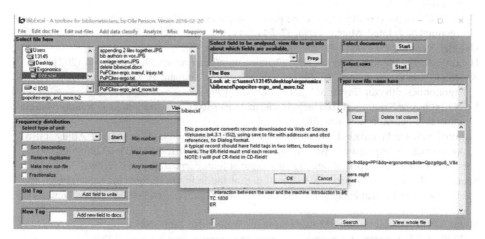

Fig. 19. An example of an error message from BibExcel (Persson 2009).

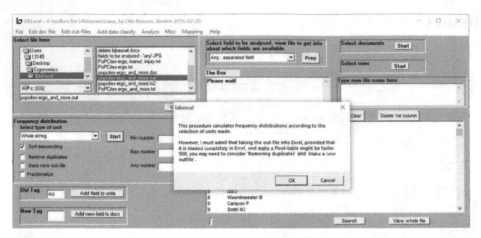

Fig. 20. A BibExcel message about generating a pivot table and chart in Excel (Persson 2009).

References

Centers for Disease Control and Prevention: Work-Related Musculoskeletal Disorders & Ergonomics. https://www.cdc.gov/workplacehealthpromotion/health-strategies/musculoskeletal-disorders/index.html (2020)

Centre for Science and Technology Studies: Leiden University. VOSviewer. https://www.vosviewer.com/ (2022)

Duffy, V.G.: Improving efficiencies and patient safety in healthcare through human factors and ergonomics. J. Intell. Manuf. **22**(1), 57–64 (2011)

Google: Ngram Viewer. http://books.google.com/ngrams (2022)

Harzing, A.-W.: Publish or Perish. https://harzing.com/resources/publish-or-perish (2021)

Kroemer, K.H.E., Grandjean, E.: Fitting the Task to the Human: A Textbook of Occupational Ergonomics, 5th edn. Taylor & Francis, London (1997)

LTW Ergonomic Solutions: Fixed Steps Platform. https://ltw1.com/fixed-steps-ergonomic-height-adjustable-operator-platform/ (2021)

National Science Foundation: "Designing for Human Variability: Allocation of Adjustability." Award Search. https://www.nsf.gov/awardsearch/showAward?AWD_ID=0729386 (2009)

Persson, O.: Bibexcel. https://homepage.univie.ac.at/juan.gorraiz/bibexcel/ (2009)

Spath, D., Braun, M., Meinkin, K.: Human digital modeling in design. In: Salvendy, G. (ed.) Handbook of Human Factors and Ergonomics, 4th edn., pp. 1643–1666. Wiley, New Jersey (2012)

Stone, S.: Eliminating Extreme Movements in the Warehouse. https://www.cisco-eagle.com/blog/2020/06/18/workstation-ergonomics-eliminating-extreme-movements/ (2020)

VERBI GmbH: *MAXQDA*. https://www.maxqda.com/ (2022)

World Health Organization: Musculoskeletal Conditions. https://www.who.int/news-room/fact-sheets/detail/musculoskeletal-conditions (2021)

Zimmerman, N., Duffy, V.G.: Systematic literature review of safety management in aviation maintenance operations. In: Duffy, V.G., Landry, S.J., Lee, J.D., Stanton, N. (eds.) Human-Automation Interaction: Transportation. Automation and Collaboration and e-Services, pp. 311–328. Springer Nature, Switzerland (2023)

Joint and Discomfort Analysis Using Ergonomic Software RAMSIS

Anthony DeInnocentes and Vincent G. Duffy[✉]

Purdue University, West Lafayette, IN 47906, USA
{adeinnoc,duffy}@purdue.edu

Abstract. Machine operators many times are involved in the constant precise movement with little room for error due to tight deadlines. With the use of the 3-D ergonomic software, RAMSIS, potential discomfort can be visualized and analyzed to provide insight into improvement in this industry for operators. The main impact of this software has the ability to provide biomechanical models (Duffy 2012) and ergonomic analysis including providing recognition for potential inside in joint and posture issues. More so combat joint and neck pain from lack of adjustable seating or out-of-reach equipment on an excavator. The evidence is shown for these needed changes by two analyses to provide specifics on what areas of the body and how simple changes of changing of hand grasps alone can affect an individual. Initial results showed 80–100% levels of discomfort in certain joints while operating the machinery. With multiple analyses, suggestions of adjustable seats and armrests provide the opportunity to reduce fatigue for workers in the process design phase. As well, the software provided insight into making analyses considering adjustments to parts of the seat, preventing potential overuse injuries in the shoulders and reducing potential for discomfort in lower back and potential chronic back pain. With modern information technologies coming into the industry as part an integration with heavy machinery, possible future solutions that could be considered by ergonomic analysis using digital human modeling tools. Others recently considered include adjustable joystick locations in the cabin itself and vibration reduction in the seats themselves to reduce fatigue for individuals (Du et al. 2018a, b).

Keywords: Joint pain · Discomfort · Manikin · Digital human modeling

1 Introduction and Background

The purpose of this study was to evaluate ergonomics risks for an excavator operator. The analyses helped to highlight potential joint problems and discomfort areas that are a common occurrence for excavator drivers. According to a prior Hazard Analysis, constant repetitive motion can lead to tendinitis in arm joints. After analyzing the operator-related manikins, solutions are proposed to reduce injury for operators and decrease overall fatigue.

© Springer Nature Switzerland AG 2022
V. G. Duffy and P.-L. P. Rau (Eds.): HCII 2022, LNCS 13522, pp. 181–189, 2022.
https://doi.org/10.1007/978-3-031-21704-3_12

2   Procedure

2.1   Opening up RAMSIS Software

The approach for introducing the ergonomic analysis modules follows similar a method to that which was introduced in "A 3-Step Approach for Introducing Computer-Aided Ergonomics Analysis Methodologies (Sinchuk et al. 2020). This study considers a different design application and ergonomic analyses than that shown in Sinchuk et al. (2020). The RAMSIS program used as part of ergonomics-related instruction in IE578 Applied Ergonomics in Fall 2021. The software was started by navigating to "Purdue Setup" folder and located in "RAMSIS–NextGen-stda_1-8-0203-64Bit" folder a windows batch file called "launchNextGenAutomotive." The analysis and re-design process began with the loading process for the program and creating a blank workspace for the user.

2.2   Loading the Machine

In order to initially display the excavator, the user needed to go to "File" in the taskbar and go to "Open…" where the user can locate "geometry.sat" in the session folder in the data folder in the program's files. Once loaded, the machine will be displayed, as shown in Fig. 1, and the user is able to move the viewpoint of the excavator by holding the scroll wheel on the mouse and moving around the machine or using defaulted views in Named Views on the left side of the main program window.

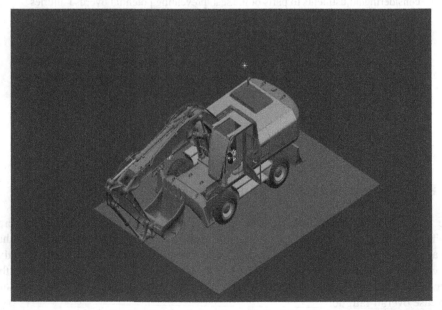

Fig. 1. The excavator is displayed using the iso viewpoint in the program once it is initially loaded into the software.

To focus on the seating arrangement of the excavator, the user must use the *show/hide* function in the program by highlighting any of the individual parts on the machine and then using the show/hide function. The user also can highlight parts of the machine by selecting body segments underneath the "Geometry Scene" folder on the left side of the main program window and using the function from there as well.

2.3 Loading the Manikin

In order to create a manikin in RAMSIS the user must initially create a role underneath the role definition tab located at the top of the main software/program window where the user will create a custom role based on different posture options that RAMSIS gives. For the excavator, the posture that is chosen is a heavy truck.

Users have option to create different sized manikins and customize different parts of the manikin, since some operators in the user profile may have, for example, longer arms and shorter legs, but may potentially not be uniformly proportional as 5%, 50% or 95%. The customizability of body part sizes for the manikins within RAMSIS allow a designer to match database information with potential users during design.

To load the manikin once a role is created, the user will select test sample and create a manikin based on different assumptions. For this analysis, each body segment was chosen to be medium for an overall average male height due to the lack of women operators. According to, U.S. Bureau of Labor Statistics, only 3.9% of total construction operators are female. The manikin will be displayed initially as just skin points seen in Fig. 2. In order to see lines that are used to retexture the manikin, the user needs to the select manikin display as textured and shown in Fig. 3.

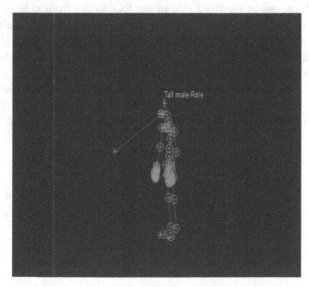

Fig. 2. This figure shows the manikin with just the skin point option chosen.

Fig. 3. This figure shows the manikin with the texture option chosen.

2.4   Position Manikin in Seat

To move the manikin to the seat of the machine, the user needs to select multiple skin points across the manikin and create target restrictions to the seat. For this analysis, 7 restrictions were made to adjust manikin to the seat, foot pedals, and joysticks on each side of the operator. A restriction was made from the H-point of the manikin to the surface plane of the seat. Four restrictions were made for the feet. Two restrictions were made for each foot, one at the front side of the foot to the front side of the pedal and one at the heel of the foot to the base of the pedal. For the hands, one restriction per each was made at the palm of the hand around the object points of the joysticks. Once all these restrictions were made, the user will select posture calculation for RAMSIS to adjust the manikin considering the created restrictions.

To fully replicate how one uses the joysticks, the manikin's hands are to be changed into the grasp position from the default open position. To change the handgrips, the user selects "Surround with hand" which is displayed in Fig. 4 and shown on the manikin in Fig. 5.

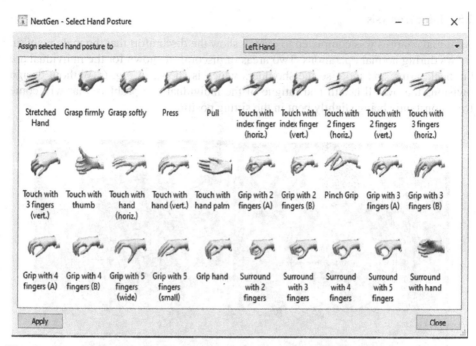

Fig. 4. This figure displays all the options that are available to change the position of the manikin's hands

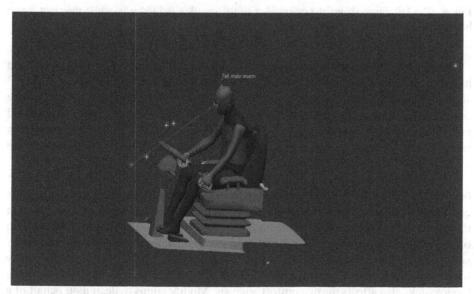

Fig. 5. This figure displays the manikin in the seat with all unnecessary objects of the excavator hidden and all restrictions applied.

2.5   Joint Analysis

An initial analysis was completed to overall show the discomfort that the male manikin shows during normal operations. Two areas of discomfort shown for the individual are the neck, arms, and more so the shoulders which is shown in Fig. 6. Without design revisions the overall health and fatigue of the individual is a problem that will come from constantly being slightly bent in the sitting position.

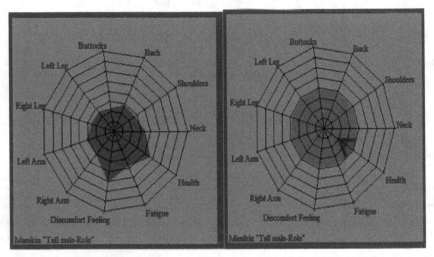

Fig. 6. The left figure shows the discomfort of the manikin individually while the right figure highlights the discomfort to global data.

Analysis of discomfort in each joint individually shows an expected high level and high percentage of discomfort in the shoulders, hips, and some in the spine. Figure 7 shows 100% discomfort in both hip joints while 84% in the cervical joint at the base of the skull. The sacrum joint in the spine shows 75% discomfort for the user. The red and yellow are used by the software to bring designer's attention to the need for design remediation. As shown in Fig. 8, both shoulder joints have a 92% discomfort level due to the position of grasping the joysticks.

The joint analysis selected with the posture percentage shows an overall discomfort between 80–89% for all finger joints in both hands. The hips joints in this analysis suggest caution and consideration for re-design as well with a 77% level. This corresponds with the previous analysis and provides reasoning to justify readjusting seating and/or position of joysticks for the operator. When the hand position is changing to pull from a position of surround with hand, the position percentage of thumb joint percentage goes from yellow to red with corresponding percentages of 89% to 90%. Validating that how the user holds the joysticks also affects the discomfort analysis. Modifications to design on behalf of a potential user and can either increase or decrease fatigue as well. So a task analysis and consideration for the anthropometry profiles of actual users is recommended.

To combat the overall discomfort of the manikin multiple solutions can be applied to create a more comfortable working environment. The most common and already applied

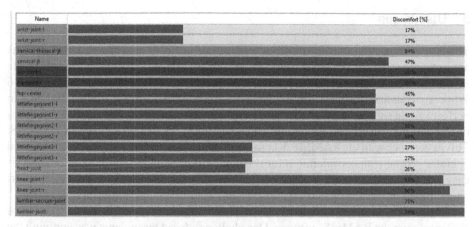

Fig. 7. This figure highlights the discomfort in the hip, cervical, and sacrum joints.

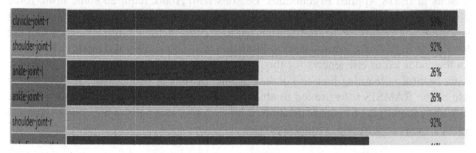

Fig. 8. This figure highlights the discomfort in both shoulder joints at 92% shown in red.

solution to many machines already is having adjustable armrests and seat heights. This was shown as useful in the study by Palega and Rydz, 2018. With adjustable armrests, the user reduces the amount of fatigue while operating the machine and less discomfort from less weight being applied on the finger joints. Having adjustable seat heights will allow the user to reduce the amount of pressure on their lumber joints and as well reduce the reach to the joysticks to decrease discomfort in shoulder joints. According to a 2018 study by Aparna Tripathy, in a study of 100 participants where 50 were male, there was a 2.6-inch variance in male overall height and 2.7 inches variance of length in the lower body alone. With even a relatively small sample of participants, the height difference shows justification for providing adjustable seats. A solution that could be applied in the future for these machines is the option to adjust how far or near the joystick is to the front side of the armrest. This will help individuals with shorter arms and reduce the amount of shoulder joint pain. As well, a study was done that showed reduction of vibration has the ability to reduce fatigue and joint pain for users (Du et al. 2018a, b). From individual use of heavy machinery, it was shown that a loss of feeling can come from constant vibration and forceful impact on joints.

3   Discussion

This study shows the overall the impact of sitting in heavy machinery when designs are not optimized for potential users. Project-related designs for the excavator made available to students in IE 578 Applied Ergonomics at Purdue. In prior course, IE486 Work Analysis and Design II, some students used a 3-D CAD software called 3D SSPP to perform some similar analyses for a different design application. The 3D SSPP focuses on general body segments versus more specific body segments analyzed in RAMSIS. This experience with the RAMSIS 3-D software with manikins inserted into the expected operator setting with consideration for task conditions made the application of analysis easy to interpret as evidence was gathered in visualization and tables for joint discomfort on the manikin.

The authors would like to thank Andre Luebke for his support in initial training of students to use the RAMSIS software. One challenge faced by students was applying the knowledge following a couple of fast-paced reviews and demonstrations during early lessons in IE578 Applied Ergonomics. Lessons with Andre required some brute force of some options in the software to figure what was needed for the analysis and exporting key elements for this report. Initial trials led to a lot of inefficient mistakes or using the long route from Andre's initial demos. Shortcuts based on images and icons in RAMSIS toolbar later led to efficiencies for this RAMSIS user. Initial demonstrations in lesson were helpful in learning how to conducting the movement of the manikin. Continued use of the RAMSIS software led to ability to meet analysis objectives for the project, including identifying a range of discomfort levels for various parts of the body on various subtasks expected for the (virtual) operator.

4   Future Work

RAMSIS has a vast amount of variability in the manikin placement but lacks the data of the specific machinery itself. One aspect of data that would be helpful for heavy machinery is the introduction of noise level data. More defined noise-related data in the area that is around the user during operation and as well vibrations felt by the individual would be helpful in further assessment. This kind of data related to vibrations could impact significantly on shoulder and hips joints as it supports the body and noise data could bring awareness about increases in potential hearing loss that is typically not currently available in commercially available digital human modeling tools.

References

"2020 Annual Averages – Employed Persons by Detailed Occupation, Sex, Race, and Hispanic or Latino Ethnicity." U.S. Bureau of Labor Statistics. U.S. Bureau of Labor Statistics, 22 Jan 2021. https://www.bls.gov/cps/cpsaat11.htm

"Hazard Analysis - Stressful Hand & Wrist Activity." Hazard Analysis | Heavy Equipment - Maintain heavy equipment - Stressful hand & wrist activity | Construction Solutions. https://www.cpwrconstructionsolutions.org/heavy_equipment/hazard/1084/maintain-heavy-equipment-stressful-hand-wrist-activity.html. Accessed 13 Oct 2021

Du, B.B., Bigelow, P.L., Wells, R.P., Davies, H., Johnson, P.W.: The impact of different seats and whole-body vibration exposures on truck driver vigilance and discomfort. Ergonomics **61**, 5258–5537 (2018)

Du, B.B., Bigelow, P.L., Wells, R.P., Davies, H.W., Hall, P., Johnson, P.W.: The impact of different seats and whole-body vibration exposures on truck driver vigilance and discomfort. Ergonomics **61**(4), 528–537 (2017). https://doi.org/10.1080/00140139.2017.1372638

Duffy, V.G.: Human digital modeling in design. In: Salvendy, G. (ed.) Handbook of Human Factors and Ergonomics, 4th edn., pp. 1016–1030. Wiley, New Jersey (2012)

Palega, M., Rydz, D.: Work safety and ergonomics at the workplace an excavator operator. Int. Sci. J. **3**(1), 25–29 (2018). https://stumejournals.com/journals/tm/2018/1/25.full.pdf

Sinchuk, K., Hancock, A.L., Hayford, A., Kuebler, T., Duffy, V.G.: A 3-step approach for introducing computer-aided ergonomics analysis methodologies. In: Duffy, V.G. (ed.) HCII 2020. LNCS, vol. 12198, pp. 243–263. Springer, Cham (2020). https://doi.org/10.1007/978-3-030-49904-4_18

Tripathy, A.: Contribution of upper and lower body lengths to the overall height of individuals: an anthropometric study among MMMC students (2018)

Ergonomic Analysis Through Targeted Industrial Case Review and Company Investment Benefit

Bethany Evans and Vincent G. Duffy[✉]

Purdue University, West Lafayette, IN 47907, USA
{evans349,duffy}@purdue.edu

Abstract. This report provides a brief analysis of a lab chair solution chosen for an industrial case study. It includes supporting documentation of company incentives to increase job satisfaction by means of ergonomic modification. The report provides a bibliometric review. Within this review demonstrations are utilized to highlight the research topic. This is accomplished through targeting source searches in google scholar, Scopus, and Web of Science (WoS). The collected data is then analyzed utilizing software such as VOS viewer, Max QDA, Harzing, and Bibexcel. Data synthesis and review are imperative to support the aforementioned claim. With limited exposure in this manufacturing environment, the credibility of the proposed solution comes from the experience and subsequent data of other researched cases. The literature review provides historical qualitative and quantitative data. Human factors methodologies have been historically utilized over the years and across organizations to resolve workstation inefficiencies. The targeted source search shows a strong pattern of profitability for companies that invests in employee ergonomics and increased job satisfaction. Data analysis concludes a universal solution is required to address height distributions to limit musculoskeletal injury. The ergonomic incorporation then leads to increased job satisfaction, and increased job satisfaction benefits business. Therefore, it is mutually beneficial for a company to invest in the well-being of its employees.

Keywords: Job satisfaction · Height · Task · Chair · Ergonomics · Operator

1 Introduction

The purpose of the following analysis is to provide the reader with a historically backed solution to an industrial case study. There is strong evidence that the physical work environment not only affects job satisfaction, but also employee performance, employee injury, behavior, communication patterns, fatigue, error rates, and physical and psychological stress. Lee et al. suggest that it is necessary to make improvements to the work environment and reduce work stress and strain to reduce employee turnover [8].

A literature review provides historical qualitative and quantitative data to support this claim. Historical human factors methodologies have been utilized over the years and across organizations to resolve workstation inefficiencies. With limited exposure in

© Springer Nature Switzerland AG 2022
V. G. Duffy and P.-L. P. Rau (Eds.): HCII 2022, LNCS 13522, pp. 190–206, 2022.
https://doi.org/10.1007/978-3-031-21704-3_13

this manufacturing environment, the credibility of the proposed solution comes from the historical data and experience of others. MaxQDA is utilized to compile the terms and Harzing will be operated to accumulate reference data that will be visually displayed in VosViewer. VosViewer will provide an analysis of many articles and emphasize the metadata from the bibliographic record. VosViewer is used to output a visualization of the similarities and co-citation analysis.

Ergonomics is the study of adapting the workplace environment to the worker's needs. Proper ergonomic design increases the efficiency and productivity of the worker and should be considered early in the development process for all workplace settings [5]. This is of interest since musculoskeletal disorders [MSD] are common workplace injuries. They are commonly found in industrial workers and contribute to not only a worker's absence but decreased job satisfaction [18]. "Light" assembly work contributes to MSD due to repetition. Even low-intensity work with repetition will elevate risks of neck and shoulder disorders [9].

1.1 Problem Statement and Assumptions

The problem statement for this case study is to reduce and ultimately eliminate soft tissue injuries for employees working on assembly lines. There is a specific emphasis on what is classified as "light" work when considering the demand of this industrial case study. An employee reported a soft tissue injury as a result of repetitive motion. The task requires employees to reach both up and behind to obtain a "die-cut". This leads to the assumption the assemblers are required to twist.

The operator/ assembler then lowers their arm to pass a "die-cut" through a glue machine. It is also assumed there is an additional downward force applied by the operator to press a filter piece into the "die-cut". A subsequent assumption is a solution should work in multiple axes. The z-axis for up downforce and x-y axes for the twist/ grasp behind motion and conveyor belt part placement. It is also assumed that the force required to push down is moderate effort, even for a short duration. This is an important assumption for assessment purposes in Sects. 3 and 4.

The stakeholder is the company that asked Purdue to assist in resolution. The stakeholder concludes it is likely the operator is too short for the task demands, repetitively applying a downward force to a "die-cut" on the conveyor belt. However, independent analysis is necessary as the chief complaining assembler may have sustained an injury at another task step/ motion. The assumption is the solution should not be task-specific or specific to the individual. It is also assumed that there is underreporting of MSD injuries amongst other members of the population. This assumption is supported in the article Trends in Work-Related Musculoskeletal Disorder Reports by Year, Type, and Industrial Sector: A Capture-Recapture Analysis, this article recollected data across 7 years. The data concluded upper-extremity MSD are significantly underreported when comparing physician reporting data and worker's compensation data [12]. If others are experiencing MSD the height distribution becomes a range.

Another important assumption is some operators are too tall for the demands of the task (require increased bending to apply force etc.). If there are operators that are too tall the repetitive motion (bending) will cause MSD that cannot be addressed with a step (stakeholder suggested solution). If the soft tissue injuries affect a wide height distribution of employees and the problem is not limited to a single target population, nor is it limited to a single task or motion. Then the solution needs to be equally universal. From a financial perspective, it is assumed the resolution must be a cost-effective solution. In other words, though automation may eliminate contact points and repetition by the assembler it is unviable as a solution since the implementation would cost time and money that is unreasonable.

The purpose of this analysis is to review historical decisions made by MSD resolution cases and create an ergonomically friendly solution for the assembler that will benefit the company. In short, the solution should cover a wide height population distribution. It should be cost-effective and storable. It will not limit employee work partnerships or require job task reassignment. It will address twisting motion (to obtain the cardboard) with the addition of a downward force (to place the filter into the cardboard product) and not be individual or task-specific.

2   Literature Review

2.1   Database Search

A database search is required to initialize analysis. The goal of database searches is to identify trends across numerous citations. Trend information allows the researcher to justify claims made across different papers and ultimately results in historically supported claims in this report.

The first step in a database search is finding the terms. Vicinitas, a data analytics tool, was used. Vicinitas tracks hashtags, and keywords associated with accounts to deliver in-depth engagement analytics from social media, in this case, Twitter. This tool measures user engagement and it is relevant to know what information the general population is aware of. Trends are used to find a potential relationship between terms. The terms, productivity, and safety were selected, since they're indirectly in the problem statement, and searched on the site. The output was an excel document and word cloud analytic. Figure 1 provides a view of the word cloud produced. There were 438 tweets on the topic from 370 users with engagement from 729 others and influence/ outreach of 1.8 million followers.

Fig. 1. Vicinitas word cloud

An intermediate step is used to compile data into a format that is compatible with analysis. Instead of using software such as Mendeley or in this case maxQDA. Terms found from the word cloud in Vicinitas were input into google scholar and web of science (WoS). Rather than an analysis based on tweets the terms were instead used to find articles related to job satisfaction, productivity, and ergonomic solutions. The next step was saving articles of interest from top relevance in the database. There were 6 sources utilized in the analytics tool maxQDA. As seen in Fig. 2 right, several articles in the green box, left of the image, were used to produce a content analysis. More specifically, 5 articles and 1 textbook chapter were used. The articles chosen for citation have a focus on job satisfaction and production. A textbook chapter related to the manufacturing side of ergonomics was selected for review.

The Word Cloud tool is visible while the 'Visual Tools' tab is activated and word cloud is selected as seen in the corresponding yellow boxes at the top right of Fig. 2 right. Non-substantial words were removed to produce the following word cloud Fig. 2 left. Common words such as Satisfaction, error, conditions, quality, health were highlighted in the maxQDA word cloud output. These terms all contribute to the idea of job satisfaction having an impact on production output in the company. The visualization of this effort is visible in the word cloud in Fig. 2 right.

Fig. 2. MaxQDA word cloud setup &word cloud [3, 7, 9, 10], adapted from [16]

An extended lexical search is created by selecting "Analysis" and "Lexical Search", shown in yellow boxes of Fig. 3 left. The lexical search is used to search within 6 documents the researcher chose. The search identification process is more efficient and meaningful when finding the key aspects of the topic that is selected. In maxQDA this report searched the term "ergonomics" and "Run search" executed the function shown in the red box in Fig. 3 left. In the 6 selected documents, there were 438 occurrences of the word, the right of Fig. 3 illustrates the output of "search and find" within the 6 documents. After execution of the "Run search", the results are displayed in the following manner, seen in Fig. 3 right.

Lexical data is pulled to narrow the search for more relevant data extraction from the databases. There were several databases utilized in this report: Scopus, Web of Science (WoS), Google Scholar, and Harzing. Table 1 shows a breakdown of the ultimate terms chosen and the results in each database. The output of each database search includes numerous results for each search return. Higher publication, documents, and citation

Fig. 3. Extended lexical search in maxQDA: ergonomic [3, 7, 9, 10, 16]

outputs are intentional. The documents are used to identify trending words as well as trends over time.

Citation data, for instance, is extracted from each of the resulting documents from the databases. The citations utilized are shown later in the analysis, but they can be used to find commonly cited works used across all documents. If a document has been cited several times over the years, the article is likely worth viewing as it may contain principles that are applied to a broad range of ergonomic solutions.

Table 1. Database search return

Database name	Search term	Results
Scopus	Ergonomics AND Productivity	2828 documents
Scopus	Anthropometry AND Productivity	260 documents
Web of Science	Ergonomics AND productivity	1662 publications
Web of Science	Under Reporting of Work Musculoskeletal Injury	190 publications
Web of Science	Workstation AND anthropometry	70 publications
Google Scholar	Ergonomics AND Productivity AND Job Satisfaction	56400 results
Google Scholar	Trends Workplace Musculoskeletal Injury Reporting	26100 results
Harzing's Publish or Perish	Job Satisfaction AND profit	710 publications
Harzing's Publish or Perish	Job Satisfaction AND Ergonomics	670 publications

The next step is to identify a reference management tool to keep track of relevant findings. Reference management tools locate existing strategic reviews that assist in giving structure or a path for research. There is strong evidence linking work environment to job satisfaction, there are also psychological performance factors that will affect company output. [4] Using the search databases articles of interest come up out of relevance. Within Lee's article [8] it is shown how necessary it is to improve the work environment. It increases productivity and safety which decreases work stress. These positive impacts are also expected to reduce employee turnover.

2.2 Term Analysis

Once database searches are compiled the next step is to run a citation analysis. A resource to assess journals quality called Harzing is a software that will assist to conduct citation/ text term analysis. Several searches are completed using Scopus/ Google Scholar. As seen in Fig. 4, several searches were completed using keywords from the database searches.

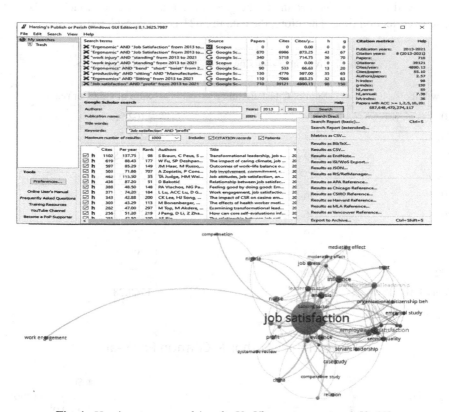

Fig. 4. Harzing- term search/results VosViewer: term network [3, 11]

Each search was truncated to only include 2013–2021 publications as seen in the search terms in Fig. 4 below. The data will be saved and can be concatenated using Bibexcel or individually saved as seen below as an "ISI/WOS Export". This will save the data for the searched terms selected as a text file to later be read in VosViewer. The terms "job satisfaction" and "profit" had 710 resulting papers, "ergonomics" and "job satisfaction" had 670 papers, and so on.

The search terms "job satisfaction" AND "profit" from Harzing were selected to form a text data network in VosViewer. The network with output terms that are shared across the 710 papers. A minimum term occurrence of 7 is selected for the network shown below in Fig. 4. The output for the network is 65 terms. The map provides a 10,000 ft visualization of the network before narrowing down the search. The map can be viewed below in Fig. 4. The largest term commonality exists for job satisfaction. Some terms of interest are systematic review, case/ comparative study, and job stress. Excel data was pulled from the Harzing search ergonomics and job satisfaction. From the data, the total cites per author and cites per year were analyzed from the year 2013–2021. The summation per year for each author and citations in each year is visible in Table 2.

Figure 5 below shows a pivot bar chart comparing author and citations in each year from 2013 to 2021. There was a spike in citations per author in 2014. Citations per year have stayed constant. The decline in the year 2021 may be due to a lack of data or a lapse in collection time. Therefore, the data in 2021 is not considered.

Table 2. Pivot table - harzing: job satisfaction and ergonomics

Row Labels	Sum of CitesPerAuthor	Sum of CitesPerYear
2013	287	102.95
2014	877	217.73
2015	249	107.18
2016	473	299.6
2017	396	264.5
2018	256	220.32
2019	180	220
2020	83	299
2021	10	37
Grand Total	**2811**	**1768.28**

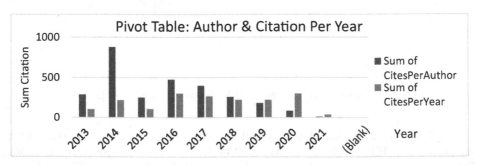

Fig. 5. Pivot Table Harzing (job satisfaction and ergonomics)- Sum cites per author per year

An additional analysis in VOS viewer is based first on occurrences of terms. In the following data map, text files that included "ergonomics" AND "job satisfaction". After extracting all terms, the output was 88 terms that met the threshold of a minimum of 8 common occurrences. From the 88 terms, the network was narrowed down further to 53 relevant terms selected. The network can be viewed in Fig. 6. The larger the ball behind the term the more frequently it is used. The color-coding denotes a cluster of like topics. The terms of interest from network Fig. 6 are safety, job stress (seen in job satisfaction and profit network), injury, workstation, and productivity.

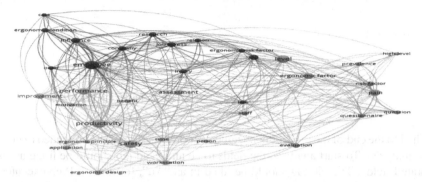

Fig. 6. VosViewer occurrence term network- job satisfaction and ergonomics

This research is to determine if stress affected job satisfaction if the environment influenced job satisfaction and if the work environment has a positive-negative or no effect on turnover intentions. The data analysis method used in this study is path analysis. This method of analysis is intended to test the linearity of the model and examine the relationship/ influence between the causal variables [11].

2.3 Co-citation/Co-occurrence Analysis

Co-citation analysis is completed by exporting metadata from Harzing. The search term outputs are then concatenated together. The results from BibExcel are used to generate an excel file of leading authors. Once the data is exported to excel a pivot chart and table are generated to illustrate the findings. VosViewer also provides useful visualization data links. The second analysis used bibliographic data and co-citation of the references in each document. First, the search terms were taken from Harzing, but the most valuable terms for this report came from export out of Scopus. More documents ensure meaningful connection across articles. The search terms workspace AND design AND ergonomics resulted in 383 documents, there were 8522 cited references, and 4 documents share at least 4 cited references shown below in Fig. 7. The effects of porter's research, (second most cited) aids in the development of new guidance for optimum posture for the comfort of drivers. Results from the study were measured instead of observation-based [14]. This is relevant when considering workers sitting in chairs to accomplish tasks.

Corlett's technique for assessing posture contains a technique for assessing postural discomfort (from 1976) [5]. Modern articles may still cite papers from several years back despite the truncated 2013–2021 criteria. The number of citations shared is especially relevant since the article remained applicable to numerous research topics.

Another example of co-citation used when BibExcel appended each search results for twist, work injury, standing, manufacturing, and productivity. One search term file is

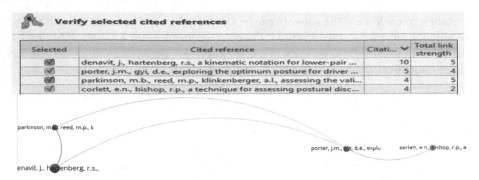

Fig. 7. VosViewer Co-Citation references and network [5, 14]

attached to the end of the preceding document. A.doc version of the appended document to be analyzed. To start analysis, the fields to be analyzed tab should be filled as "any; separated field". The old tag should be filled in as "Au", for author. Prep executes, in this case, a list of leading authors with their frequency across the appended documents. The list output (of BibExcel) can be seen at the top of Fig. 8.

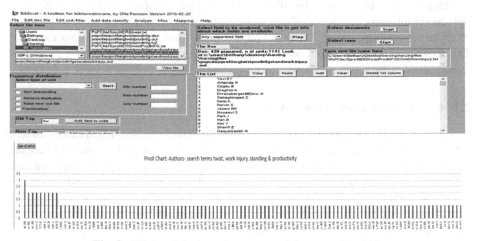

Fig. 8. BibExcel & pivot chart- sum articles vs authors [10]

The list is copied and pasted into an excel document to create a pivot chart. The pivot chart below in Fig. 8 illustrates the summation of articles vs leading authors for search terms twist, work injury, standing, manufacturing & productivity. Miguez's article on lean manufacturing and ergonomics [10] was found using this method. It reinforces the fundamentals of standing at work and efficiencies as a function of work injury. This also led to a Researchgate author lookup under Miguez. Miguez's article about reducing neck injuries for operators provides optimal work heights for assemblers referenced in Sect. 4 results.

3   Procedure

The first step is to evaluate the problem. There are a variety of potential issues that can be part of a problem conversely many things can contribute to the solution. It is imperative to understand the task requirements. Whenever there is a workplace injury data is collected about the site, injury, and those affected. It is up to the researcher to assess what may be contributing to the problem. In this section, the relevant data will be assessed, related to ergonomic fundamentals and recommendations will be made.

Task. From an interview with one of the company stakeholders, the task is described as follows. The operator reaches back to obtain the product. When the operator receives the product, it has been stacked and marked from a separate station. To receive the part though the operator reaches back to obtain the product and places it on the station's conveyor belt. The operators then add downward force to fit the filter in cardboard and pass the piece down the conveyor. Between the assemblers is a glue station with a large roller in a vat of glue. An operator twists and grabs the piece of cardboard to pile glue on the side. The assemblers grab the product and curl the cardboard ends to frame the edges on the side of the filter.

Data. The data measured at the time of injury is the table/ conveyor belt height is 36" and the height of the short individual is 58". Some workers are tall (74-75"). Workers are not standard height. Short operators work at chest height and tall operators must bend to apply downward force for 10 hours a day doing 3000 filters a shift.

Problem. Repetitive motion injuries are accumulating across operators. Shorter assemblers seek medical attention for shoulders, elbows, and upper back. Taller assemblers experience symptoms of lower back, knees, and ankles injury.

The repetition is a candidate for cumulative trauma disorder (CTD). As seen in Eq. 1 below, 3000 die-cuts/ shift, 1 shift is 10 h. 10 h equals 600 min which equals 1200 thirty-second intervals per shift.

$$3000 \frac{die\ cuts}{shift} * \frac{1\ shift}{1200\ thirty\ \sec interval} = 2.5 \frac{die\ cuts}{thirty\ second\ interval} \tag{1}$$

Solution. A solution must consider the best way to address individual variation. The business cannot avoid facing the issue since there all types of works big small young old etc. An optimum height cannot be obtained. The conveyor belt cannot be placed on individual varied heights for a task.

Operators should have an elbow height (height from floor to the elbow) around 7.5– 8″ above the conveyor belt/ station the task is completed on [16]. This is due to the force required to get the filter into the cardboard and to pass the weight of the product down the assembly line. This should also be paired with frequent (short breaks) to decrease the accumulated repetition.

An organization defines and influences ergonomic risk factors for musculoskeletal disorders (MSD). Policies and task definition can influence the extent of exposure to repetition, force, posture, and other ergonomic risk factors [15].

High turnover can cause or be caused by decreased job satisfaction. This impacts product quality and output speed with operators consistently coming in new and having lead times due to learning. This impacts quality and productivity. There are reductions in training costs, reduced time to complete tasks which increases the output of the product [11].

4   Results

The solution needs to be a holistic approach. It cannot compromise safety. The results from the above literature review contribute to the theory that a person's work environment is both a physical and nonphysical experience for the worker. When a company invests in the comfort and security for an employee job satisfaction occurs decreasing turnover [11] research supports investment in job satisfaction is mutually beneficial. The corporation has an incentive to invest in employee satisfaction as it leads to increased efficiency since operators are familiar with the parts they are working on [8]. There is a decrease in time per part which then increases output [4].

From a brief review of the data and onsite photos from the stakeholder, it is apparent the current process cannot remain. Duration and repetition are significant disadvantages for this case study. The output for a 10-h shift is 10,000 die cuts. The 10,000 cuts are split between 3 conveyor lines. Rounding down a single operator can be expected to make 3000 die cuts per shift. There is an increased risk factor for cumulative trauma disorder (CTD). Studies show if cycle time is less than thirty seconds between repeated motion the task becomes a candidate for CTD classification [16].

The task qualifies for CTD classification. This applies regardless of the downward force limit. The frequency of 2.5 die cuts per 30 s time interval is high for such a short duration. It is believed increased frequency increases the friction experienced in the tendons accelerating the progression of cumulative trauma (CTD) [16]. The concept behind CTD assumes that repetition of a task brings trauma to the tissue or joint that leads to trauma and in each repetition, the trauma (even minor) can build [16]. With increased task frequency/ repetition even minor injury will compound and become worse. Therefore even solutions that will decrease the impact of the trauma should be paired with sufficient rest time between the tasks.

The other objectionable aspect of the task is when operators are pressing the filter into the die-cut. The act of pressing down is impulse loading, which creates a problem for the lower back [16]. There is a height requirement above the conveyor belt needed to apply force with minimal operator strain. The average elbow-height for a person that is 58″ (4′10″) is 34.5–37″ [9]. With elbows at 90 degrees, the conveyor height falls within range (optimal arm positioning). However, the assumption that the operator should be working at 90 degrees does not apply in this task due to the impulse loading on the die-cut to press the filter and pass it through the glue station.

As highlighted in Fig. 9, in red, the operator should be 7.87 inches higher (20 cm)/ above the workstation to increase power to apply the downward force. Also shown in red is the selection of the operator performing "heavier work". When force is necessary the elbow angle should be more obtuse (over 90 degrees). Since the operator's task isn't precision or light work the shorter operator feels the impact of impulse loading after repetition which created the conditions for tissue damage. Figure 9 recommends a range of heights with the base elbow height at 20/ 7.87" [16]. This is regardless of sitting or standing conditions so long as elbow height displacement is approximately maintained.

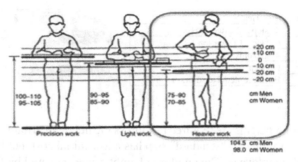

Fig. 9. Force required classification: Elbow positioning relative to height, adapted from [16]

Chair. The height of the conveyor belt is 36" to ensure elbow-height remains a minimum of 8" above Lab chairs are set on a continuous scale. The chair dimensions can be viewed in Fig. 10. It is not limited by conveyor height or tasks, there is flexibility in product tasks and processes in the future. As the comfort needs of the employees are addressed there is an increase in job satisfaction, this leads to increased output quality and lower turnover. With lower turnover, there is also increased productivity (since time to do a task decreases as task exposure increases) [4].

Fig. 10. Chair dimension to obtain proper elbow-height positioning [1]

For this task in particular each operator must set the chair height, so elbows rest a minimum of approximately 7.87" above the table height. This reduces shoulder discomfort [9]. The chair solution will take the load off of the operator's knees and lower back [16]. Frequently in industry static posture can be problematic. The nature of the work for the operator will require them to frequently stand from the chair solution to move the product down the conveyor belt and may become a non-issue. The twisting motion is also addressed with the chair on a pivot. It should not be overlooked that the chair can swivel therefore it can reduce the amount the individual twists. The foot positioning underneath the chair will reduce the risk to the spine. It addresses all height ranges.

Variable Step.

Table 3. Height limit variable step and dimension [2]

Operator Height	Step Height
4'10-5'0	8" step + 2 extensions
5'1"- 5'3"	6" step+ 1 extension
5'4"-5'6"	4"step only
5'7-5'10"	No step
Above 5'10"	Back Problem No solution

Steps of varying heights are required to address the height distribution across assemblers. The incorporation of a "standard" step has a low initial cost, but it does not solve health risks to all employees. The employee height ranges covered by this solution are 4'10–5'9" as seen in Table 3 above. It does not address twisting tasks or individuals "too tall" (above 5'10") for task demands. There are a variety of issues that can arise related to the duration of standing on a step. Twisting increases trouble with feet, knees, and lower back.

The business faces risk in both investment and storage demands (ensuring there is always an appropriate height step onsite). There are also safety implications with a step, as an individual may trip up/down, or block walkway hazard. It will need to be paired with frequent breaks. Those too tall for the task experienced will still experience back and knee pain from bending too far to apply force.

Tool. A tool to replace the frequent downward force applied to the filter will decrease injury across all height distributions. It has the potential to address tall or short individuals by limiting the stress and strain to the body. The downfall of this solution is it will not address twisting motion and will require time and skill to develop. Torso twisting is an objectionable action. Twisting leads to trouble with feet, knees, and lower back. The likelihood of employee injury increases. To develop the tool a mechanical designer with prior tooling knowledge and operator task familiarity are required. Tool development involves iterations including prototype costs, time delays, and eventually manufacturing costs for each workstation.

Though a viable solution it may be over-engineered for the problem statement. This alternative needs to be developed by an expert. It has been shown that workstation redesign with tooling can have positive effects on output quality [6]. Das' research highlights the use of tools and technologies for manufacturing work [6]. A process change or tool to reduce the downward force might make the necessity of workstation modification relatively unnecessary. Research by Nadadur details the limitations to overcome design that has been targeted to a narrow workforce population. It adapts anthropometric data to accommodate aging obesity and ethnicity distributions, models human variability, and develops virtual fits for large population groups with those considerations [13]. However, this is a heavy time and cost investment.

Job Rotation/Breaks. Other solutions were considered and ultimately eliminated such as job task rotation or "like-height" individual pairing. The application of either decreases job satisfaction (due to existing work relationships). Automation was also considered and quickly ruled out by stakeholder feedback (cost-benefit is not rational).

Breaks alone will not eliminate MSD issues, but they are necessary to incorporate into any solution selected to reduce the impact of the repetitions. This does not automatically equate to profit loss. Higher frequency over shorter duration bursts will reduce CTD impact. With infrequent breaks, there are few opportunities to take the load off the operators' knees and lower back. Job rotation is also not the overall solution. Occasionally rotation of tasks is enough however the stakeholder communicates this is not a potential solution as it would decrease job satisfaction since the assemblers have a preexisting relationship with their coworkers.

Assessment. The solutions will ultimately be assessed using a weighted decision table seen in Table 4 below. The weighted value is assessed by the researcher and multiplied by the rating (1–5) for the recommendation. The sum of the weight multiplied by recommendation divided by the total reveals the final score. The lab chair is the clear winner overall for the solution.

Table 4. Weighted solution alternatives [1, 2]

Objectives	Weight	Recommendation Alternatives		
		Lab Chair	Step	Tool
Initial Cost	0.2	($179) 4	($56 each) 5	(+$5k-$10k est.) 1
Ease Storage	0.05	3	5	2
Ease of Use	0.05	3	5	3
Safety/ Hazard Risk	0.15	5	3	4
Shop Floor Space	0.1	4	4	5
Variable Height Compatibility	0.2	5	2	5
Twist motion Compatibility	0.2	5	2	5
Productivity/Comfort	0.05	4	2	4
Total	1	33	28	29
Weighted Total		4.45	3.25	3.75

5 Discussion

Ultimately the lab chair is the optimal solution. The priority of solution alternatives is lab chair as a primary, development of a tool, then the varying height steps. When a company is experiencing challenges or vulnerabilities in its designs or processes it is important to draw reasonable conclusions. There are requirements the stakeholder (company) must stay within, and cooperation and communication are necessary to find the best fit. The solution must be inexpensive and the less invasive the better. The lab chair is adaptable for each operator to be comfortable at the conveyor. Though it isn't the least expensive solution it is the best overall solution that helps all individuals on multiple axes.

Static posture for the entirety of the shift cannot be the norm when using the chair as a solution otherwise new issues relating to bad posture may develop. A simple solution is frequent short breaks. Each time the operator gets up from the chair blood flows to the extremities. Neck, shoulders, back, and possibly wrist injuries may occur over time if nothing is done, and the operator remains static the entire shift.

Companies should invest in job satisfaction and safety. To increase both an ergonomic solution should be invested in. Even with an upfront cost, the money will come back to the company with an increased profit due to productivity and a decrease in new staff training. [8]. The findings of Beehr's research indicate that the work environment had a positive and significant effect on job satisfaction. Stress had a negative and significant effect on job satisfaction. [4] Work environment had a negative and significant effect on turnover intention. [8] Stress had a positive and significant effect on turnover intention. Job satisfaction had a negative and significant effect on turnover intention. [8] Based on these results, work environment, stress, and job satisfaction can be policy tools to reduce turnover intention, which can lead to a decrease in real turnover. These are reasonable and possible to apply to the workplace so long as management is willing to make an initial investment.

There are limitations to implementing a chair as the solution. People slouch in chairs as long the posture is varied big problems should not arise. However, if the same poor posture is repeated problems will come up and should be anticipated. Another limitation is when the feet do not touch the ground there is a lack of support. It is possible that the footrest on the chair will assist but it is not the same as the floor as support. [15] We need feet touching to get that support. The human body adapts so long as it is for short durations.

The trade-offs are resolved by considering the hierarchy of needs. There are tradeoffs for accommodating the back, shoulders, and neck. In Fig. 9 from Sect. 4 results above, shows the force requirement classification relative to height with elbow positioning. It illustrates the height of the task being performed as a function of the type of work/ effort to perform the task. [16] For example, heavier work requires higher strength, and visual accommodation does not have priority in the hierarchy. The shoulder position is ranked higher on the hierarchy of task needs. In this situation, ideal neck posture is sacrificed in favor of favorable shoulder/arm positioning and posture. [16] This is why heavy work is done with the table at a lower height, or in this instance, the operator must be raised to be above the set conveyor height. It makes sense to rank suboptimal neck positioning lower since the operator will not need to bend to focus on the part. At a height raised from the conveyor table, the position the elbow angles are between 90–135°, which maximizes strength, and the shoulders are close to 30° of abduction, which minimizes fatigue. The goal is to minimize negative posture impacts not to eliminate them.

6   Conclusion and Future Work

The research confirms the solution is to raise the operators on a chair to complete the task and reduce the occurrence of MSD in the workplace. There are drawbacks with static posture, feet not touching the ground, and neck discomfort. These drawbacks are mitigated by the benefit of this application. The need is based on reducing shoulder injuries, but also reaching an increased distribution of the employees. It is also important to solve for multiple axes. This solution resolves tall employees no longer needing to bend to apply force and it also resolves short employees no longer needed to reach and exert extra effort on part. A chair is used to pivot for twisting motion and can be used for a variety of tasks and part assembly. As highlighted in the literature review awareness and application of increased job satisfaction leads to employee retention (decreased turnover). There's increased profitability of the company with increased retention and a decrease in time/ training for employees learning the parts and tasks [11]. As it stands the processes in place are not adequate.

In future work, the company would benefit from further computer modeling of the task. If the task is broken down to the base movements a software can be used to evaluate and analyze the ergonomic of the task [17]. The movements and solutions can be applied to a variety of employee heights to see the effect. The software can be used to highlight the objectionable part of the task and takes into consideration what compensations are made given any solution. Future work could also compare businesses of the same field take job satisfaction categorization breakdowns to compare the profitability of the companies to associate real dollars with increased job satisfaction. Expansion on safety conditions is beneficial as well as time studies for the same company before and after implementation.

The company might also consider wellness incentives. Health incentives such as "step goals" or sports leagues after work promote comradery and increase movement to combat static lifestyles. There are productivity benefits for team building in the workplace that can be beneficial if explored. Grant money has been allocated to improving overall employee health/wellness with the design of products, tasks, and environments, to accommodate diverse populations.

References

1. Amazon: Giantex Mesh Drafting Chair, Standing Desk Chair. October (2021). https://www. amazon.com/dp/B09DYY7C88/ref=sspa_dk_detail_2?psc=1p13NParams&spLa=ZW5jcn lwdGVkUXVhbGlmaWVyPUFEV0pWS0pMTFNOTlMmZW5jcnlwdGVkSWQ9QTA 3MDczNjVWQVFaNkM0S1c1SkMmZW5jcnlwdGVkQWRJZD1BMDAxOTM2ODMy QUNXTzRFUFVFVFU0cmd2lkZ2V0TmFtZT1zcF9kZXRhaWwyJmFjdGlvbj1j
2. Amazon: Yes4All Aerobic Exercise Workout Step Platform. October (2021). https://www. amazon.com/Yes4All-KC6V-Adjustable-Aerobic-Platform/dp/B00WJK5SV0/ref=asc_df_ B00WJK5SV0?tag=bingshoppinga-20&linkCode=df0&hvadid=79989526348735&hvn etw=o&hvqmt=e&hvbmt=be&hvdev=c&hvlocint=&hvlocphy=&hvtargid=pla-458358910 2856358&psc=1
3. Butlewski, M., Misztal, A., Ciulu, R.: Non-financial factors of job satisfaction in the development of a safety culture based on examples from Poland and Romania. In: International Conference on Digital Human Modeling and Applications in Health, Safety, Ergonomics and Risk Management, pp. 577–587. Springer, Cham (2014)

4. Beehr, T.A., Newman, J.E.: Job stress, employee health, and organizational effectiveness: A facet analysis, model, and literature review 1. Personnel Psychology **31**(4), 665–699 (1978). Cox, S. J

5. Corlett, E.N., Bishop, R.P.: A technique for assessing postural discomfort. Ergonomics **19**(2), 175–182 (1976)

6. Das, B., Shikdar, A.A., Winters, T.: Workstation redesign for a repetitive drill press operation: a combined work design and ergonomics approach. Human Factors and Ergonomics in Manufacturing & Service Industries **17**(4), 395–410 (2007)

7. Falck, A.-C., Örtengren, R., Högberg, D.: The impact of poor assembly ergonomics on product quality: A cost–benefit analysis in car manufacturing. Human Factors and Ergonomics in Manufacturing & Service Industries **20**(1), 24–41 (2010)

8. Lee, B.-K., Seo, D.-K., Lee, J.-T., Lee, A.-R., Jeon, H.-N., Han, D.-U.: Impact of work environment and work-related stress on turnover intention in physical therapists. Journal of physical therapy science **28**(8), 2358–2361 (2016)

9. Miguez, S.A., Hallbeck, M.S., Vink, P.: Participatory ergonomics and new work: reducing neck complaints in assembling. Work **41**(Supplement 1), 5108–5113 (2012)

10. Miguez, S.A., Garcia Filho, J.F.A., Faustino, J.E., Gonçalves, A.A.: A successful ergonomic solution based on lean manufacturing and participatory ergonomics. In: International Conference on Applied Human Factors and Ergonomics, pp. 245–257. Springer, Cham (2017)

11. Mobley, W.H.: Intermediate linkages in the relationship between job satisfaction and employee turnover. J. Appl. Psychol. **62**(2), 237 (1977)

12. Morse, T., et al.: Trends in work-related musculoskeletal disorder reports by year, type, and industrial sector: A capture-recapture analysis. American journal of industrial medicine **48**(1), 40–49 (2005)

13. Nadadur, G., Parkinson, M.B.: The role of anthropometry in designing for sustainability. Ergonomics **56**(3), 422–439 (2013)

14. Porter, J.M., Gyi, D.E.: Exploring the optimum posture for driver comfort. International Journal of Vehicle Design **19**(3), 255–266 (1998)

15. Reese, C.D.: Occupational health and safety management: a practical approach. CRC press (2018)

16. Salvendy, G.: Handbook of Human Factors and Ergonomics, 4th edn. Wiley, Hoboken, NJ (2012)

17. van der Meulen, P., Seidl, A.: Ramsis – The Leading Cad Tool for Ergonomic Analysis of Vehicles. In: Duffy, V.G. (ed.) ICDHM 2007. LNCS, vol. 4561, pp. 1008–1017. Springer, Heidelberg (2007). https://doi.org/10.1007/978-3-540-73321-8_113

18. Walker-Bone, K., Cooper, C.: Hard work never hurt anyone: or did it? A review of occupational associations with soft tissue musculoskeletal disorders of the neck and upper limb. Annals of the rheumatic diseases **64**(10), 1391–1396 (2005)

Boundary Comfort: A RAMSIS Perspective

Aubrey Hocker[1(✉)] and Vincent G. Duffy[2]

[1] School of Mechanical Engineering, Purdue University, West Lafayette, IN 47906, USA
hockera@alumni.purdue.edu
[2] School of Industrial Engineering, Purdue University, West Lafayette, IN 47906, USA
duffy@purdue.edu

Abstract. The primary goal of this article is to review literature regarding ergonomics in relation to small/micro-businesses and the disconnect between knowledge and actualization. The secondary goal is to guide readers through an advanced process of ergonomic analysis through an example case study. Inspiration for the literature review stems from the commonly found tendency of small business to underestimate, or are not conscious of, the benefits of preventative care inherent to ergonomics. Those businesses that are knowledgeable but have not implemented any controls often cite the lack of capital required to effectively improve their operations. Using tools such as maxQDA, Vincinitas, Harzing's analysis, and CiteSpace to discover different sources of research helps establish a better understanding of the literature as a whole. The literature review conducted discovered many people, researchers, and organizations who are still trying to create innovations and that engagement in this area is rising. Using human digital modeling software such as RAMSIS can help alleviate this burden of capital restriction instead of costly trial and error. To help guide others through the process of adjusting rendered objects, the individual steps to accomplish this analysis and comparisons are discussed in detail. Through an example case study boundary manikins created for an excavator cabin needed significant adjustments to the steering column, seat, and touch screen for comfortable operation. Using a tool like RAMSIS allows designers/managers to save time and money by virtually interfacing with the design space to prototype different scenarios and configurations. Understanding the impact design decisions have on worker comfort and strain can help managers be more proactive with preventative care without expensive and time-consuming analyses.

Keywords: Discomfort · Ergonomics · RAMSIS · Small business · Reachability · Boundary anthropology

1 Introduction and Background

1.1 Problem Statement

For this paper, the emphasis of the case study will be on the analysis of a previously developed excavator. Hypothetical interested parties have decided to analyze the cabin design. Specifically, they wish to consider the potential need for improvements regarding

© Springer Nature Switzerland AG 2022
V. G. Duffy and P.-L. P. Rau (Eds.): HCII 2022, LNCS 13522, pp. 207–228, 2022.
https://doi.org/10.1007/978-3-031-21704-3_14

the necessary adjustment ranges required by the upper and lower population bounds. This allows for a complete view of the adjustable range required for the excavator cabins' instruments and tools. The literature review stems from a need to explore the challenges that small businesses face when considering ergonomics and preventative care who may be in similar circumstances.

Thus, a general review of literature is needed to show the kinds of solutions and questions raised when trying to bridge the gap between small businesses and ergonomic practices. This topic is not only an interest to companies or manufacturers that design excavators but also any industry that requires a human to be seated while operating a vehicle or other machinery [1]. An analysis of postures and their associated comfort levels is important not only for the initial acceptance but also for long-term health.

Effects of discomfort and pain that are caused by non-ergonomic work environments can affect not only physical well-being but also the psychological aspects of life. Some examples of problems caused by chronic pain include loss of sleep, cognitive processing, mood/mental health, and even cardiovascular health [2]. Noted in chapter 35 of the Handbook in Human Factors and Ergonomics, even well-known and established "industries ... need advanced methods and technology to measure safety" [3]. This text continues by saying how the "assessment capabilities, in the context of discomfort due ultimately to early design decisions, can provide insight into system incompatibilities" [3]. What the text emphasizes the most is that all areas of business can benefit from modeling human comfort in a variety of situations. With this in mind, one area that is in need of consideration are small business. The aim of this paper is thus to share the capabilities of the RAMSIS software and to show how adept it can be at analyzing the ergonomics comfort of a person.

1.2 Literature Review

Starting the review, by searched Google Scholar, Research Gate, and Springer Link using the terms "Ergonomics AND Small Business" as well as "small-business" and was able to find 3 relevant articles on small business [4–6]. Next, using chapter 21 from the Handbook of Human factors in ergonomics and the articles formed the following word cloud in Fig. 1. All of these articles relate to Chapters 21 and 56 from the Handbook because they relate how changes can be made within a workplace to improve the ergonomic benefits of the tools and products used by the employees. The articles go one step further and relate to how small businesses can benefit from the same concepts as the chapters describe but on a more manageable scale.

Trying to implement the kind of solutions that help lots of larger companies can be challenging due to a lack of ready capital and inherent need to rely on the equipment available/previously purchased. After importing the articles into the MaxQDA program the word cloud in Fig. 1 was produced with very detailed interpretations of the common terms found within the submitted material. This kind of word cloud teaches that among these articles the terms, "health, safety, small, business, [and] interventions" were all common enough to make the list. Knowing these terms can help drive search terms and lead to new articles that would not have been found through other means.

To further help the review we can also turn to the software known as Vicinitas. This program allows any user with a Twitter account to analyze recent activity to understand

Fig. 1. MaxQDA Wordcloud from 4 sources using search terms, "small business AND ergonomics".

how prevalent the subject is in multiple across the user base. The chosen search terms "ergonomics" and "small business" but didn't turn up too many results. In fact, only 5 tweets were able to be found that satisfied the combined search stretching back past November 5th as shown in Fig. 2.

Searching these terms separately showed that independently they have widely different trends. Firstly, "small business" has a user engagement profile that exceeded the 2K post maximum only going back a few hours. The term "ergonomics" on the other hand went back to November 5th. The quality of these word clouds are also nicer than wordcloud.com's since it seems they take out terms like "the, and, or" and so on by default. These terms were chosen because a small business may not have the kind of financial backing to do a complete overhaul of production to solve an ergonomic need.

Further, these businesses make up a vast percentage of business throughout both the United States and the World. This brought the idea forward that a review of smaller business literature could benefit countless people in the form of fiscally responsible ergonomic solutions. Creating a paper on this problem may help those who also haven't put thought into ergonomics because they assume they are too complicated or expensive.

Figure 2, above, resulting word clouds showed trends of "support, training, mentality, free, prevention, and options". What this can tell us is that when people talk about business, ergonomics, and/ or small business they think of support and the kinds of mentalities that ergonomics embodies. The context of many of the tweets is lost in these kinds of analyses which is a limiting factor. However, these visualizations help get a mind into the right space for context when thinking of search terms and reaching out for inspiration. The next phase of the literature review uses these terms in other search engines to find more relevant articles and ways to visualize their significance.

As seen above, by using the Web of Science (WOS) to search for the terms "Ergonomics AND Small Business" 126 articles were found. Of these, the program VOS Viewer, a reference analytical program, was able to show a connection between 3 major authors, one of which is Yazdani. The co-citation analysis within Fig. 3., right, was

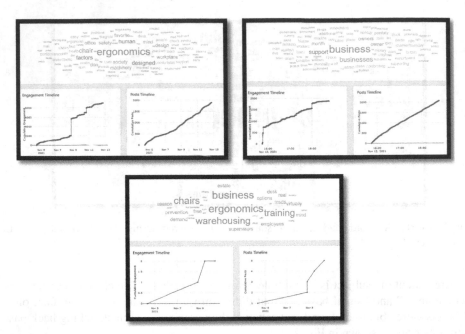

Fig. 2. Vicinitas analytics showing twitter trends and wordclouds generated from twitter user's tweets.

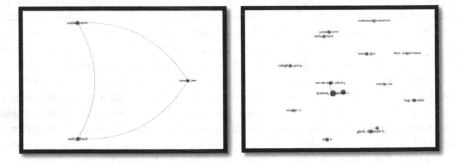

Fig. 3. VOS Viewer analytics (left) and Co-citation analysis (right).

done with the search engine known as HArzing's Publish or Perish software. This program searches Google Scholar for hundreds of articles related to the search terms provided. Once gathered, these were also fed into VOS Viewer for a comparison. This author also appeared in the co-citation analysis. Realizing this, after sorting through the WOS/Harzing results one article from Yazdani stuck out.

This article titled, "Awareness of Musculoskeletal disorders…in Micro and Small Businesses…" sheds light on how small and even micro-businesses are mostly unaware of the kinds of preventative controls and are often either overlooked or never considered [7]. Businesses need to take the time to learn about the proper controls, but also we need to take the time to make them more accessible. Next, we will see the results of a Citespace analysis of a new search done in Citespace with slightly different terms.

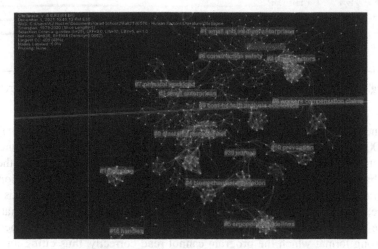

Fig. 4. CiteSpace Co-citation and word association analysis.

The node cluster, above, was formed after searching the WOS for articles using the terms "Ergonomics AND (small business OR low cost)" to expand the field to 1000 results. The reason for the adjustment in search terms was because the original terms that provided the word clouds and citation analysis did not produce enough articles to support a CiteSpace analysis. These new search terms were created from the wordclouds and consideration of the kinds of mentalities a small business would consider an ergonomic approach to a design problem. Mainly, the idea of "low cost" came to mind after seeing terms like "free" and "options" from the previous MaxQDA/Vicinitas assessment.

Clarivate, a company that manages the WOS search engine, has access to a wide array of articles accessible only through subscription. This allows a more thorough and reliable source of articles, assuming appropriate search terms. Access to Clarivate itself requires a subscription and or an affiliation with a contracted entity like Purdue University. This kind of privacy and contracts with large entities allow the service to have the capital necessary to access many restricted or pricey articles that would otherwise be lost to the average researcher.

After downloading the search data and importing it to the program known as CiteSpace, a Cluster analysis tool, Fig. 4. was made. The CiteSpace Cluster analysis shows how the different articles are connected through citation, authors, and similar terms like that of common word clouds. This cluster analysis showed that there were multiple terms commonly found, such as "small and medium enterprises, cost-benefit analysis, and prevention" which were among the top 10 terms for all clusters. Regarding the co-citation analysis, a visual representation of the most commonly cited authors is given by the citation burst comparison depicted in Fig. 5, below.

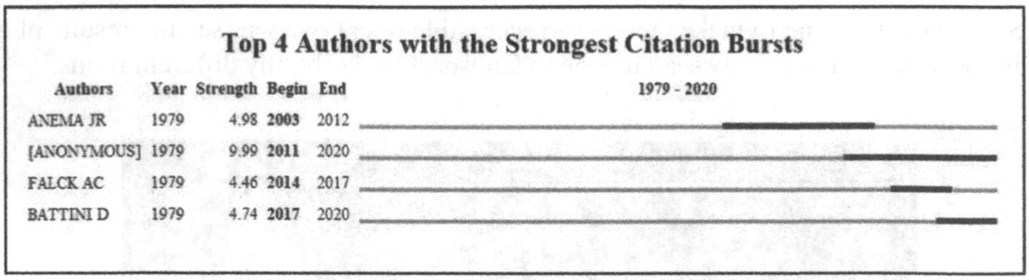

Top 4 Authors with the Strongest Citation Bursts

Authors	Year	Strength	Begin	End	1979 - 2020
ANEMA JR	1979	4.98	2003	2012	
[ANONYMOUS]	1979	9.99	2011	2020	
FALCK AC	1979	4.46	2014	2017	
BATTINI D	1979	4.74	2017	2020	

Fig. 5. CiteSpace citation burst analysis created from the optimized WOS search

Again, using the terms "Ergonomics AND (small bussiness OR low cost)" found nearly 1000 articles that created 4 authors with significant citation bursts. One author of interest was "ANONYMOUS", which is surprising. Digging deeper into the list of articles that referenced this anonymous author did not reveal a hidden citation. None of the articles that were searched through had any mention of an anonymous source. Therefore, it is conjectured that the result is most likely a computer error that cannot recognize a set of authors. It is also possible that there is a common reference that is in the wrong format which the program cannot read correctly, thus citing an error or "anonymous" value.

Once all of these analyses have been completed a review of individual papers that particularly influence the literature can be analyzed. One such method of analysis is referred to as the List of 10 Ways to analyze an article. In essence, the List asks questions about the research to guide the reader to create a well-rounded review. An example of this method has been provided below regarding one of the more influential articles cited by the previous CiteSpace method.

Dul et al's paper on Ergonomics Contributions to Company Strategies delves into multiple strategies and business goals to which ergonomics can contribute. This is in order to show more evidence and strengthen the argument that ergonomics isn't just about healthier people but also more productive people thereby incentivizing companies to take it more seriously. The authors use the standard definition of ergonomics but also that it optimizes the overall system. Their desire to investigate this topic comes from their research into articles that explored this space to find the underlying assumptions by such businesses. Many of the small and micro businesses showed reactive intervention instead of preventive and thus the need to explore multiple strategies. Their many examples on how to emphasize different aspects of ergonomics lend a practical perspective and create a useful reference for those struggling to communicate the benefits and necessity of ergonomic consideration. Future research can still be done regarding more specific guidelines and scenarios to help bridge the gap of understanding [8].

A critique of the references that fully captures all that is available to the reader is possible with the list of 10 Ways. It is important to consider why a research paper, or another article, is cited many times. Its popularity can be from sensational findings or its complete incompetence. Using this analysis tool helps create a more informed literature review that then has more impact on the readers' understanding of said literature.

In total, what was found through this literature review came down to two things. One is that, even though there has been significant progress in ergonomic solutions for businesses of all sizes, many companies and managers are reluctant to implement or simply unaware of them. The second concept is that there is not an accessible and economic solution for small and micro-businesses to implement all the recommendations by ergonomists. Innovations in communication, as well as innovations that reduce the reliance on management to fully protect individual employees, will create a better and efficient work environment for small businesses. Further, it is important to consider tools that can simulate an environment quickly to discover problematic setups without extensive and invasive methods of measurement that simply are not in the budget for small businesses. This is where RAMSIS comes in. In the following section, a detailed look at this modeling software will help the reader explore the many uses and kinds of results to expect.

2   Comfort Analysis Procedure

2.1   Anthropology Setup

To begin the comfort analysis the first step is to create the boundary manikins that will be analyzed by the software. This process has a detailed explanation created by Aubrey Hocker in the paper, "Discomfort To Comfort: The Excavator Story", that will not be reiterated in this paper [1]. What will be discussed is the individual characteristics of the manikins that were made. As mentioned in Sect. 1, the manikins are supposed to represent the boundary limits of the population. Thus, for this study 2 manikins will be created, one manikin will have a tall torso and short arms, and the other will have a short torso and long arms. Due to the time constraints of the case study, only male manikins will be considered. Their designations going further will be known as MTS and MSL, respectively.

The actual anthropology will be using lower minimum average percentiles and the upper maximum average percentiles for the forearm and upper arms of each manikin. Lower percentiles will be for the short arms and higher percentiles for the long arms. Torso height is simply a selected characteristic from the manikin builder. Figure 6, below, shows the process of selecting the individual percentiles for the specific characteristics.

Each manikin can be adjusted in a multitude of ways. After starting the NextGen Body Builder by selecting, 'Start > NextGen Body Builder' the anthropology of the manikins can be adjusted manually as needed. To do so, select 'Anthropology > Typology > Dependent Measurements' to open the Global Measurements window, see Fig. 6 (left). From there, any individual set of limbs can be selected for editing. Once a limb or segment of a limb has been chosen selecting the 'Modify Selected Measurement' button will open a new window to adjust the desired measurements, Fig. 6 (right).

There are many ways to make adjustments but the one implemented for this paper is to simply drag the 'Value' or 'Percentile' bars. By doing so their extremums are reached, symbolized by the corner boundaries of the population line (red). This is done to represent the most extreme case scenario for the excavator cabin while also being realistic to the

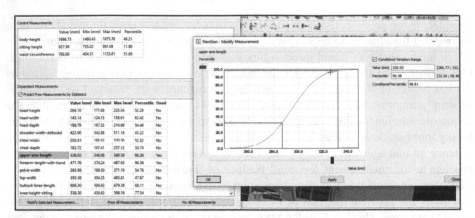

Fig. 6. Shown here is the process of adjusting the properties of individual limbs to meet boundary needs.

likely/expected boundaries that an employer might see. This is mostly calculated based on the minute the actual population boundaries seen in real life. Most of the distribution of males from the selected anthropology population never reaches beyond these corner plots. This process is repeated for both manikins and their respective roles as boundary representatives.

2.2 Kinematic Controls

Before the comfort analysis can truly begin, the tools needed to adjust the objects within RAMSIS need to be created. This allows the user to understand the kinds of relations objects and tools have with each other as well as the process of adjustments/ order of adjustments. This is where the Kinematic Controls can be implemented to aid in the study. To begin, it is common to consider which objects are of interest. In this case, the steering wheel, seat, joysticks, wrist pads, and the touch screen are focused on. From there the user needs to create reference points for the Kinematic Control(s) (KC) to use as a guide to moving the desired objects.

Steering Wheel Kinematics

For the steering wheel, the center of the steering column will be the main reference point. Figure 7, below, details the process of selecting the point creation tools. The reason for this reference point is so that the results from any movement of the object have a tangible and relevant relation to the rest of the cabin. This allows designers to easily identify where and how to adjust the design without having to make guesswork regarding what the numbers are really referring to. The process for reference point creation is fairly common for each of the interested areas and thus this subsection and series of figures will be cited frequently in later kinematic considerations. Finally, a reference point is created in the center of the steering wheel. Its purpose is to serve as a reference point for the KC to create a direction, this will be expanded upon later.

As seen in the figure above, the creation of anchor points follows that of the previous paper on RAMSIS by Aubrey Hocker [1]. Figure 8, below, depicts the process of creating

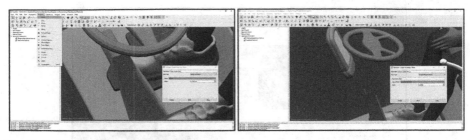

Fig. 7. In Fig. 7 (left) the process of creating an anchor point starts with selecting the point creation tool to create 2 points on opposite corners. This allows a third point to be created between them shown in Fig. 7 (right) after selecting the appropriate "Point Type" in the drop down menu.

a kinematic control. This is done by selecting, 'Geometry > Define Kinematics' and then selecting the origin point, which in this case is the point in the center of the column. Next, adding in the objects to be moved includes the neck and wheel of the steering column. This can be accomplished by left-clicking on the 'Add Objects' button to the right of the KC window.

Then, selecting 'Add Degree of Freedom' (DOF) opens the DOF window. For the first DOF, translation is to be selected from the 'Type' drop-down menu. Then, after selecting the 'Direction' box, the anchor point created needs to be chosen, and afterward the point created in the center of the steering wheel. This creates a direction for the control to move the selected objects through. Finally, add the amount of freedom to move that is expected, this can be adjusted later.

This particular direction is useful because it is an already established angle that the designers/engineers are aware of and it also allows for simultaneous x and z-axis movement which saves time. The next DOF is the rotational adjustment so that the steering wheel can be adjusted about the y-axis. This can be done by selecting 'Rotation' from the 'Type' drop-down menu and then selecting the typing '0 1 0' to signify the y-axis. Then, simply add the amount of rotational freedom needed. To end the list of DOF's a final x-axis translation needs to be added. Simply follow the same process as before but with a direction of '1 0 0' for the x-direction. An important note for future KC is that if there is a KC that moves an individual object, it cannot be a named object in another control. It can however be added to a group in another KC as long as the grouping itself is called into the KC.

Even though this process is fairly simple there are issues with having multiple DOF's. Specifically, when it comes to mixing translation with rotation. As noted in Fig. 9, below, once the rotation of the object is affected, the subsequent translation DOF no longer has a direction of '1 0 0'. This is only a minor inconvenience since the x-translation can be edited after creation. Simply select the DOF to be edited and then select 'Edit' on the side of the KC window. The difference is more tangible when comparing the left and right images of Fig. 9. And noticing the change in visual angle that the more horizontal line has after adjustment.

Something to note, in order to be efficient, it is important to add the intended point of contacts expected of the manikins to the KC window. This is because it allows the restrictions placed on the manikins to follow the intended objects to be interacted with.

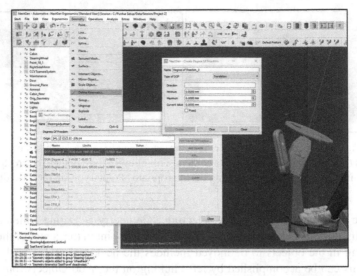

Fig. 8. This image shows that once the Geometry Object Kinematics toolbox is initiated it is possible to select the type of movement and the objects to move. Selecting the "Add Degree of Freedom" allows the creation of the kinematic control of the desired objects.

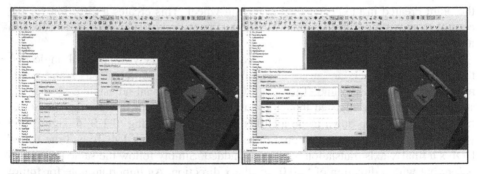

Fig. 9. The left figure shows how after adjusting both the diagonal translation and rotation the reference frame for the x-axis movement is now askew. This is something to consider and adjust for after each translation/rotation as well as the order of such movements. The right figure shows the adjusted line.

Without them, moving the objects is more or less an aesthetic action. Next, the Kinematic Controls will be discussed regarding the seat for the manikin.

Driver Seat Kinematics

Starting relatively the same way as the steering wheel kinematics, a point needs to be created in the center of the seat. In this case, the center of the plane at the top of the base of the chair will be the anchor point. Again, this is so that the numbers gathered by the different translations are relevant and easily identifiable to engineers and designers. One key difference between the KC's of the steering wheel and the seat is that only an x-axis and z-axis are needed. The objects to be added are the rest of the relevant objects for the task at hand. For efficiency, everything from the seat to the wrist pads is added so that the KC can be used for both driving simulation and the boom-arm operation (joysticks). As noted previously, for the later kinematic controls these objects should be added to a group and then called into the KC. This allows for later KC's to use individual controls for their adjustments (Fig. 10).

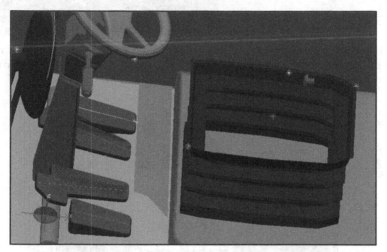

Fig. 10. The purple star is the origin point of seat translation. It was created from corner points and is the point centered but at the bottom of the seat.

Once again the necessary contact points either created or inherent to the object of interest need to be added to the KC list. The only other recourse is to add the points after the collection of objects have been moved to a position, but this is highly inefficient. A more detailed explanation of point creation can be found by reviewing Hocker's previous paper [1]. Next, the Kinematics for the wrist pads will be discussed.

Wrist Pad Kinematics
For the wrist pads, two KC's will be needed since the directions that are anticipated to be moved are in opposite vectors. The approximate center of the wrist pad at the top will suffice as an anchor point. Any point can be used but as previously stated, something that is recognizable and/or easily measurable is preferred. For the DOF's of each KC simply the translation in the x-axis and z-axis of each anchor point (Fig. 11).

Joystick Kinematics
The next KC is for the joysticks. Much like the wrist pads, there will need to be two kinematic controls because the expected translations are in opposite vectors. Instead of only the joystick objects, the entirety of the separate armrests will be added. Including their respective contact/anchor points. This inclusion of anchor points is to ensure the range of movements are relevant and understandable after analysis. The next figure shows the setup for the KC's (Fig. 12).

Fig. 11. Depicted here is the creation of an anchor point at the center and top of the wrist pad. This will act as a reference point for the KC. Keynote: ensure anchor points are added to the seat KC for efficient analysis.

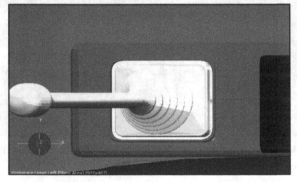

Fig. 12. The anchor point is placed at the center of the back portion of the joystick frame. The purpose is so that the location is recognizable to engineers in comparison to other features.

When it comes to anchor points it is hard to pick one that is both convenient for the analyst and engineers or designers. As mentioned previously, anchor points should be visible and their location should be easily measurable. This is so that they can be used in the design change process using the data collected from this study. For instance, a point that is randomly placed near the upper third of a panel is not as easily measured due to a lack of obvious features to relate to it. This anchor point is along the centerline of two different objects and is equidistant between the corners of the joystick base. Being in the center means that the measurement is the same from multiple directions allowing for individual engineers to have some freedom in their approach.

Touch Screen Kinematics
The final Kinematic Control necessary for a complete study of the cabin's interior is for the touch screen. This object will mostly be analyzed in terms of raw position and reachability. The reason for this restriction of DOF's is due mainly to a restriction of time for this study. For the translational directions, each of the axis' will be added so that any direction needed can be obtained. The figure below shows the anchor point and creation of touchpoints that will be studied in terms of comfort. Notice that there are

many potential touchpoints along the surface of the screen. This allows the different analyses a more complete view of comfort (Fig. 13).

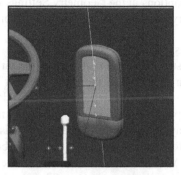

Fig. 13. Using the top and bottom center of the screen, an anchor point was created in the center.

2.3 Driving Posture

Reachability Analysis.
For the first portion of comfort analysis the driving position will be analyzed. Before any comfort analysis is done, a look at the reachability of the manikin is needed to see if there are any obvious seat adjustments to be done. After activating the manikin and performing the necessary H-point assignment [1] the following selection can be made: 'Start > NetxtGen Ergonomics > Analysis > Compute Reachability > [select limb]'. The figure below shows this process and the resulting scene in the Active Workspace (Fig. 14).

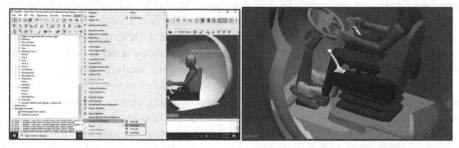

Fig. 14. An example of the reachability analysis for the left and right foot (Orange and Grey, Respectively)

From the reachability analysis, it was shown that the steering wheel, seat, and pedals are within initial reach of the manikins' legs. This does not mean that the current positions of the objects are comfortable. It does mean that the individual objects should not be adjusted to a new starting point. Going forward a reachability analysis will be beneficial to consider for different positions and roles. This bubble of reachability can be removed by deletion. It can also be recolored for comparison to other zones. To do so write-click on the bubble in question and select 'Object Properties' in the dropdown menu. Color selection is one of the first options in the Geometry Settings window that then pops up. Next, a look at the necessary seat adjustments for driving comfortability.

Seat Adjustment to Pedals

When it comes to the adjustments to the seat it is important to consider its relation to the pedals that are necessary for driving the excavator. For the interest of clarity and reference frame, the position of the feet regarding the pedals will be assumed correct. The main reason for this stipulation is because at some point moving the seat backwards will move the feet before any discomfort is displayed. This is not conducive to analysis because it would provide too wide a range of movement beyond the relevant scope. The hands of the manikin will not be restricted to the steering wheel yet because it would interfere with the seat adjustment ranges. The steering wheel will be adjusted later so that the suggested changes are separate from the pedals to protect from over or underestimation of the real adjustments needed.

Starting with the adjustment to the pedals, by using the kinematic control that was set up previously and confirming the results with a comfort analysis an easy way to quickly find the boundaries is possible. The figure below shows the general setup used after assigning the appropriate restrictions to the manikin. Further detail on setting up these restrictions to a manikin can be found in Hocker's paper on RAMSIS setup [1]. With the feet restricted to the middle two pedals and the manikin's H-point set to the seat, a comfort analysis needs to be done. To run a comfort analysis simply select 'Analysis > Comfort Feeling' and a new window will pop up and display the results. Pressing the "Set" button in the new window sets the current values as the reference for future analyses. Selecting the button "Display in Workspace" places the visualization of the comfort values separately. An efficient view of this setup can be seen in Fig. 15 below.

Now that the comfort analysis has been set up, adjusting the KC for the seat can be done by selecting the individual DOF and testing different X and Z direction locations. After an adjustment is made the next step is to rerun the posture calculation. This will adjust the manikin to the most comfortable position it can make with the new placement of the objects and their contact points. With the comfort analysis window already opened the new posture calculation will automatically update the analysis. By adjusting the seat in multiple directions any comfort attribute that reaches beyond 3 will be visible and indicate a boundary position. For optimal position, any directional movement that decreases overall values the most is considered to be the best for the manikins.

A significant improvement to the legs was noticed when the seat was moved along the x-axis 180 mm (in Fig. 5 to the right). Beyond −30 mm created discomfort more than 3 and beyond 220 mm the feet of the manikin needed to be moved when running the posture calculation. In this case, it was just below 3 (general limit). Height had additional requirements such as the legs should not make an angle beyond 105° by 5° while the thighs should be roughly parallel with the floor and the back should be angled 20–30° [9–11]. These requirements seemed to agree with the comfort feeling analysis with the lowest leg values, 1.40 each, while also matching the examples referenced. The figure above shows a small gap between the legs of the manikin and the seat when the seat has

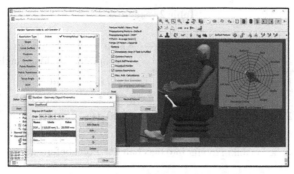

Fig. 15. Process of adjusting manikin/seat and running simultaneous comfort analysis(top right). Once the seat is adjusted via Kinematics window (bottom left) a posture calculation can start (top left/behind). This view also allows visual confirmation of the adjustments and fit.

not been adjusted in height that visually illustrates a lack of fit. The table below shows the results of seat adjustments. An asterisk indicates beyond this point moved the feet (Table 1).

Table 1. Seat Adjustment

	Optimal ΔX	Optimal ΔZ	Boundary X-axis	Boundary Z-axis
Optr 2 MSL	180.00 mm	0.0 0 mm	−40 mm: 220*mm	−10*mm: 10*mm
Optr 2 MTS	100.00 mm	−30.00 mm	−40 mm: 130*mm	−80*mm: 20*mm

* Boundary point pushed manikin too far into the chair.

Steering Adjustment
Now that the seat has been adjusted to the optimal position the steering wheel can be considered. This will primarily be done using the established kinematic control and two contact positions at the 8 and 4 o'clock positions for the left and right hand, respectively. The results of the analysis are listed below in the following table. Some general lessons learned were that finding the optimal position took a long time. This is because many positions that were as comfortable and no one single position was better. It was assumed that the position that was the lowest and most comfortable would be best so that visibility is greater (Table 2).

Visibility Analysis
Now that the manikins are in their most comfortable positions the visibility analysis can be done. There are a few ways to do a visibility assessment and the one used in this paper is the 'Move Eye' operation combined with the 'Internal View' assessment. Using these tools, the placement of different objects can be further assessed by the way they impact the line of sight. The Internal View window allows the user to see firsthand what the manikin sees. Something to note, highlighting an object of interest before entering

Table 2. Steering

	Optimal ΔAlongAngle	Optimal ΔX	Angle Appropriate	Boundary Along Angle	Boundary X-axis
Manikin MSL	115.00 mm	245 mm	25.00 deg	40**mm: 150*mm	110 mm: 270*mm
Manikin MTS	250.00 mm	170 mm	30.00 deg	130 mm: 320**mm	60 mm: 220*mm

* Boundary point pushed manikin too far into the chair; ** Point before steering wheel contacted legs

the view can amplify its appearance within the viewing window. This allows for a more comprehensive look at the potential obstruction. To use these functions some preparation is needed.

First, the point or object of interest must be established. In the example below the entirety of the touch screen was used as a focal point for the 'Move Eye' operation. By selecting 'Operations > Move Eye' a new window will appear. Within this click inside the 'Geometry Object' text bar and then select the object of interest. Next, click on the drop-down menu located to the right of the window and select 'Neck' to allow the whole head to move. Finally, click the 'Consider Posture Model' check box beneath the previous selection so that the work that has been done is considered when looking at the object. Once this is done select 'Apply at the bottom to run the operation'.

Now, the active workspace is ready for the 'Internal View' analysis. Simply select the object of interest so that it is highlighted and then select the following to start the analysis: 'Analysis > Vision > Internal View'. A new window should pop up and should show the view from the eyes of the manikin. Selecting the drop-down menu at the bottom of the window and then selecting 'Cyclopean Eye' will merge the left and right eye views. See Fig. 16. Below for an example of the process described.

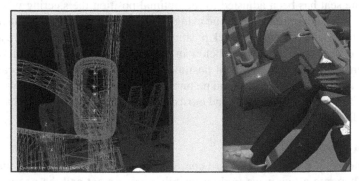

Fig. 16. Depicted here is the result of a visibility assessment using the Move Eye operation. By selecting an object of interest and aiming the sightline toward the desired object the interference of the object can be seen.

It is evident that in its current position the touch screen is almost half covered up by the steering wheel. If there were cameras displayed on this screen then the driver would need to move out of the proper driving position. Going forward this will be something to consider. For the rest of the driving assessment, this process was repeated for both manikins and the only view that was completely obstructed was the line of sight to the right mirror on the outside of the cabin. It was found that the boom arm was obstructing the view completely. An assessment of the TS manikin showed that the steering wheel covered nearly 85% of the touch screen. This means that the touch screen will likely need to be moved regardless of reachability.

2.4 Ripper Control Analysis

Reachability Analysis.

The reachability of the joysticks are well within the boundaries of the reach assessment and thus do not need to be moved to a new starting position for either manikin. It was noted that the reach of the SL manikin was considerably closer to the joysticks. This kind of realization is helpful for the next activity because it is clearer that the KC needs to be set higher when assessing the TS manikin. The legs of the manikin had roughly the same reachability as the SL manikin's which helps when considering lengths for the new pedal positions. Assessing the reach of the arms for the TS manikin showed that the joysticks were on the reachable edge.

Joystick and Wrist Pad Adjustment

For this analysis, the individual joysticks were treated as a pair because only the Y-direction needed to be adjusted with different signs to the movement. This means that the table below represents the values of both joysticks. Additionally, the Wrist Pads are done in this step since they are a part of the boom arm control system. In this case, they are the support to the arms to make sure the muscles and joints are not too strained from holding themselves aloft. An additional tool is used in this analysis. It is the joint capacity analysis tool because it helps to point out where discomfort is concerning the different components of the body.

This is different than the standard comfort analysis because it can assess the joints between the attributes listed in the comfort analysis. To access this tool simply select 'Analysis > Joint Capacity' and then select the options applicable to the support to different areas on the left of the pop-up window and then select 'Whole Body' under the body region section. Finally, select the 'NASA' radio button under the Analysis section. This tells RAMSIS to consider the comfort to that of a manikin in a neutral position as if it were floating in near zero-gravity. This analysis was particularly interesting because it was very hard to get the comfort values for the shoulders below 3 and without moving the wrist pad or the joysticks too far inward and thus hitting the body. It was impossible to get the shoulders to not be yellow in the Joint Capacity analysis. All other joints showed green. The theory with this problem was that the arms had to move outward too far and could not be adjusted back toward the center due to interference. Note that ' ± ' means positive for the left and negative for the right Joystick/ WP (Table 3).

Touch Screen Adjustment

The touch screen adjustments were not conducted for the driving position because it

Table 3. Joystick and Wrist pad

	Optimal Position (X,Y,Z)	Boundary X-axis	Boundary Y-axis	Boundary Z-axis	Joint Comfort
Optr 2 MSL JS	50, ± 50, 140 mm	−50 mm: 80 mm	± 50 mm*	100 mm: 180 mm	82% - Shoulders
Optr 2 MTS JS	160, ± 40, 240 mm	80: 200 mm	± 60 mm: 0 mm	200 mm: 250 mm	85% - Shoulders
Optr 2 MSL WP	0, ± 70, 80 mm	0**	± 70 mm: 0 mm	60 mm: 80 mm	79% Shoulders
Optr 2 MTS WP	100, ± 70, 160 mm	100 mm: 200 mm	± 70 mm: 0 mm	140 mm: 170 mm	80% Shoulders

* This means the value was at the threshold for the under 3 comfort value. ** Is for interference with objects

was assumed drivers would/should not have more distractions from driving than are necessary. As noted from the initial reachability analysis, the touch screen was just inside of the reachable zone. After adjusting the seat to the optimal position using the KC previously made, the reachability needs to be assessed again before considering optimal ranges. It was found that the starting point for the touch screen was now beyond the zone and need to be moved by the following amounts at least 300 – 400 mm in the X-direction and 200 mm in the Z-direction for each Manikin.

To get an optimal position the different touchpoints on the screen needed to be considered in the comfort analysis. After finding the position that resulted in the lowest average comfort values the following table was made. The NA results represent the efforts in trying to keep the comfort value below 3. The optimal positions, in this case, were also the boundary positions. It is definitely a possibility, however, that the angle/rotation of the touch screen could have really helped the analysis. Future studies should focus on this aspect of the assessment (Table 4).

Table 4. Touch Screen

	Optimal Position (X, Y, Z)	Boundary X-axis	Boundary Y-axis	Boundary Z-axis
Optr 2 MSL	200, 30, 0 mm*	NA	NA	NA
Optr 2 MTS	150, 30, 50 mm*	NA	NA	NA

* This is in reference to the adjusted starting position as a result of the reachability analysis.

3   Conclusions

3.1   Data Analysis

(Table 5)

Table 5. Adjustment Ranges.

	Seat Position (X, Z)	Steering Wheel Position (Path, X, Angle)	Joystick Position (X, Y, Z)	Wrist Pad Position (X, Y, Z)	Touch Screen Position (X, Y, Z)
Position Ranges	0:180 mm, −80: 20 mm	0:250 mm, 0:245 mm, 0:30 deg	0:160 mm, 0: ± 70 mm, 0:240 mm	0:100 mm, 0: ± 70 mm, 0:160 mm	0:600 mm, 0:40 mm, 0:50 mm

3.2   Design Recommendations

Steering Wheel: Because of the drastic changes in position required by the two manikins it is recommended that a new steering column design be created in order to accommodate this kind of telescoping. It was necessary to adjust the steering wheel in multiple dimensions and so it will be necessary to allow for such positioning. This would also allow for more visibility when readjusting the steering wheel back to the starting position when switching to boom arm operation.

Wrist Pads and Joysticks: Having a joystick and wrist pad that are adjustable is nice but having them rotatable would likely help reduce the interference with the seat that was seen during the comfort analysis. A configuration where the pad and sticks can swivel in front of the manikin would be ideal. This could be done with a rotating panel that swivels into place like a bar on a roller coaster for instance.

Touch Screen: Although numbers were found for the touch screen it would be more relevant to redo this analysis with the KC allowing for rotational adjustments. This would likely increase the range of comfortable DOF's and lead to better inspiration for design change. Ultimately, keeping the screen closer to the chair is preferable in any scenario.

Visibility: The recommendation for this would be to have the arm up and as far back as possible or to have the angle of the arm in such a position that the bucket(end of the arm) and the beginning of the arm are on either side of the mirror.

4 Process Discussion

One of the most influential aspects of prior experience that helped the most was understanding how CAD modeling and manufacturing process are done/ measured. This informed where to create the reference points for movement and kinematics so that the numbers were relevant and easily identifiable to designers/engineers. A challenge that proved difficult to overcome was determining where the reference frame should be for all the measurements. Trying to adjust all the objects in the cabin would be irrelevant and a waste of time without the constraint of a reference point. This is the same for the different kinematic controls.

Choosing the petals seemed to be the most appropriate choice for this matter since the feet could travel along a plane whereas the hands and H-point were stuck to one point of reference. What helped to make this idea come to like was when it was considered how other problems like in physics are solved. An assumption is made about temperature, time, material strength, and even the reference frame to consider the number for positive and negative values. The process of reflecting on similar situations and previous assignments from different classes has always helped put the current problem into perspective. It allows the user to think like they are a third party being asked to relate it to something they have more experience with.

For future practitioners, it is important to make assumptions about the work in order to make sure the numbers that are gathered are meaningful. There are going to be a lot of conditions that are not determined by the customer or by the managers in charge of supplying the objects to model against. It could be weather or boundary populations or even if all aspects of comfort are necessary. Making an educated guess about the safe and most encompassing assumptions will be a safe bet in this project. Just take care not to make too broad of assumptions or this kind of analysis can take forever to accomplish.

5 Future Work

Something that could help to improve the RAMSIS software would be to incorporate an analysis tool that could measure the blood flow restriction for a given posture. Deep vein thrombosis is a serious condition commonly found in industries whose worker's main tasks are to sit and do something for long periods of time [12]. This could be another factor in the overall health and could possibly be an optional attribute if the scenario is known to only have a sitting posture for small amounts of time. If this were combined with the interference measurements that RAMSIS is capable of then for different materials the analysis could have a more dramatic effect. For example, a metal chair can restrict blood flow more than a cushion.

Regarding the future of literature and research of small businesses, one can look to the National Science Foundation (NSF) and their recent awards. Depicted below is the result of searching the NSF'S database for awards related to the keywords, "Small business", "Ergonomics", and "Low Cost". Over 3,000 results were found and one, in particular, shows how relevant (within 6 years) small business ergonomic innovations are to the current day. Below is a literature review of the article in question using the List of 10 Ways.

This article describes how the Small Business Innovation Research (SBIR) Phase 1 project is attempting to, "study the feasibility of automatically evaluating the risk of musculoskeletal injury in the workplace using smart wearable devices". Musculoskeletal Disorders (MSD) caused by continuously poor ergonomic activities account for nearly $15.2 billion in direct costs per year which can often be prevented or mitigated with enough warning. Having a system to provide feedback to the workers at risk would both reduce the reliance on management and increase the health/longevity of the everyday worker. This would be invaluable to small businesses that do not have the background or resources to implement sweeping ergonomic changes to their facilities. Though still reactive, it is the next best way to progress toward the prevention of worse MSD [13].

What this review and database search show is that there are still many ways in which to improve the lives of workers in smaller businesses. There are still many people and organizations trying to create innovations for others to use which are economical as well as conducive to ergonomic health.

References

1. Hocker, A.: Discomfort To Comfort: The Excavator Story. West Lafayette: Purdue University (October 15 2021)
2. Fine, P.G.: Long-Term Consequences of Chronic Pain: Mounting Evidence for Pain as a Neurological Disease and Parallels with Other Chronic Disease States. American Academy of Pain Medicine. Oxford University Press (July 13 2011). https://academic.oup.com/pai nmedi-cine/article/12/7/996/1840819. https://doi.org/10.1111/j.1526-4637.2011.01187.x
3. Salvendy, G., Duffy, V.C.: CH 35 Human Digital Modeling in Design. Essay. In: Handbook of Human Factors and Ergonomics, 4th ed., p. 1025. John Wiley & Sons, Inc., Hoboken, NJ (2012)
4. Pakhomova, A., Salnikova, Y., Namestnikova, L.: Methods of Ergonomics and Social Technologies Application in Small Business. In: Kantola, J.I., Nazir, S., Barath, T. (eds.) AHFE 2018. AISC, vol. 783, pp. 46–54. Springer, Cham (2019). https://doi.org/10.1007/978-3-319-94709-9_5
5. Schwatka, N.V., et al.: Small business total worker health: a conceptual and methodological approach to facilitating organizational change. Occupational Health Science 2(1), 25–41 (2018). https://doi.org/10.1007/s41542-018-0013-9
6. Long, J., Burgess-Limerick, R., Stapleton, F.: Acceptance of participatory ergonomics in a healthcare setting. In: Proceedings of the 46th Annual Conference of the Human Factors and Ergonomics Society of Australia, pp. 46–52 (2010). https://www.ergonomics.org.au/docume nts/item/70#page=45
7. Yazdani, A., Sawicki, B., Schwenck, G., Wells, R.: Awareness of Musculoskeletal Disorders Hazards and Controls in Micro and Small Businesses in Ontario, Canada. IISE Transactions on Occupational Ergonomics and Human Factors 7(1), 12–21 (2019). https://doi.org/10.1080/24725838.2019.1565870
8. Dul, J., Patrick Neumann, W.: Ergonomics Contributions to Company Strategies. Applied Ergonomics 40(4), 745–52 (2009). https://doi.org/10.1016/j.apergo.2008.07.001
9. National Library of Medicine: Guide to good posture. Guide to Good Posture (25 October 2017). Retrieved 20 November 2021, from https://medlineplus.gov/guidetogoodposture.html

10. Cleveland Clinic: Is Your Driving Posture Causing You Pain? Cleveland Clinic. Cleveland Clinic (26 June 2019). https://health.clevelandclinic.org/is-your-driving-posture-causing-you-pain/
11. Yoo, K.-T., An, H.-J., Lee, S.-K., Choi, J.-H.: Maximal torque and muscle strength is affected by seat distance from the steering wheel when driving. J. Phys. Ther. Sci. **25**(9), 1163–1167 (2013). https://doi.org/10.1589/jpts.25.1163
12. MFMER: Deep Vein Thrombosis (DVT). Mayo Clinic. Mayo Foundation for Medical Education and Research (22 December 2020). https://www.mayoclinic.org/diseases-conditions/deep-vein-thrombosis/symptoms-causes/syc-20352557
13. Elhawary, H.: SBIR Phase I: Feasibility of Estimating Musculoskeletal Injury Risk of Material Handling Workers with Novel Wearable Devices. Award # 1548648 (2015). https://nsf.gov/awardsearch/showAward?AWD_ID=1548648&HistoricalAwards=false

Elimination of Shoulder Related Musculoskeletal Disorder's in Assembly Operations

Tanmay Kavathekar[1], Craig Zehrung[2], and Vincent G. Duffy[1(✉)]

[1] School of Industrial Engineering, Purdue University, West Lafayette, IN, USA
{tkavathe,duffy}@purdue.edu
[2] Purdue University, West Lafayette, IN, USA
czehrung@purdue.edu

Abstract. The project focuses on work-related musculoskeletal disorders of the shoulder muscle in assembly operations. The given shoulder injury problem is encountered by a short operator in a manufacturing assembly operation. The project aims to provide a solution to reduce shoulder injuries. The analysis starts with a bottom-up approach by conducting a task analysis of the operation followed by a Rapid Entire Body Assessment (REBA) to study the postures involved in performing the tasks. Based on this and available information on the process, a change in layout is suggested which can potentially reduce the stressful movements of the shoulder muscle. A cycle time study of the current process and the future process based on the proposed layout is conducted. Corresponding calculations for an estimated increase in productivity are also presented. Historical aspects underlying the importance of WMSD's are highlighted too. The project report concludes with a brief description of future work that can be done to further reduce work postures that lead to shoulder injuries.

Keywords: Work-related Musculoskeletal Disorders (WMSD's) · Task analysis · REBA · Cycle time

1 Introduction

Work-related Musculoskeletal Disorders (hereafter referred to as WMSD's) are the disorders that cause pain and discomfort in the body. They are mainly caused by stressful movements of the joints. WMSD's affect the muscles, tendons, ligaments etc. [1]. Some of the common work tasks that lead to WMSD's are twisting, bending, picking up a heavy object while bending, and reaching overhead objects [2]. Work tasks which are frequent and repetitive in nature are one of the major reasons for these injuries. Other reasons are constrained body motions in a limited space, significant speed of tasks, pressure on one or more body parts due to force exerted in completing the task etc. [2].

WMSD's pose a major threat to operators working in any industry. These injuries come with a cost.

The importance of WMSD's is discussed in this section. The graph below indicates the number of days missed or away from work (Fig. 1).

© Springer Nature Switzerland AG 2022
V. G. Duffy and P.-L. P. Rau (Eds.): HCII 2022, LNCS 13522, pp. 229–242, 2022.
https://doi.org/10.1007/978-3-031-21704-3_15

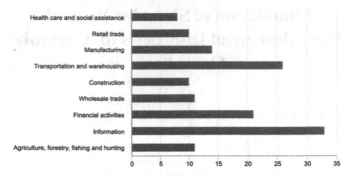

Fig. 1. Sector-wise days away from Work [1].

As is seen from the above graph, the number of days away from work is nearly equal to 15 days in a year for the manufacturing sector. Assuming minimum wage for a worker/operator as 10$/hour and hours worked per day as 10, the cost of missed day per operator for 15 days would be nearly 1500 dollars (values assumed for simplicity in calculations). Medication costs are added to this. These are direct costs. Other hidden costs include absenteeism, reduction in productivity, etc. (Fig. 2)

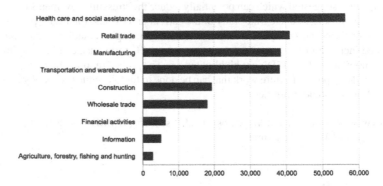

Fig. 2. Sector-wise injuries due to WMSD's [1].

The above figure shows the number of injuries due to WMSD's in the Manufacturing sector. Having an insight into the historical data gives us an idea of the prevalence of the problem. It also helps us to take steps in the right direction as an organization.

Shoulder injuries are one of the most common and major musculoskeletal disorders in the manufacturing or assembly industry. The shoulder muscle has a complex biological structure of various bones, tendons, and tissues. Even more complicated is the remedial surgery for a shoulder injury. Hence, it is preferred to avoid shoulder injuries altogether [3]. There are two major movements associated with the shoulder muscle, shoulder abduction and shoulder flexion. In the later sections, solutions are provided based on reduction of these two movements.

Shoulder abduction is defined as the posture of the shoulder in which the shoulder is raised or elevated sideways (lateral) [3]. Correspondingly fatigue increases as shoulder abduction level increases. Thus, it is imperative to relieve the shoulder of extensive abduction angles. It is recommended to have the shoulder abduction angle of a maximum of 30° [3].

Shoulder flexion is the movement of the shoulder in the front direction towards the head. Shoulder flexion is also related to fatigue and injury. More the flexion, more is the fatigue experienced.

2 Problem Statement

WMSD's are worth approximately $20 billion in the United States every year [4].

Out of the total WMSD's, injuries of the shoulder are approximately 15%. The following report is based on the problem of soft tissue injuries of the shoulder muscle for short operators in an assembly operation. In the manufacturing industry, operators are of various sizes and shapes. A 'one size fits all' approach in terms of workstation design is not always easy to implement. Moreover, the backend study and rationale for workstation design is also not robust in each industry. Work postures are essential to determine the right way of completing a task. If the work postures and movements are not established properly, they lead to incorrect postures which then lead to such injuries. The layout too plays an important role in deciding how tasks are performed. Designing a workstation with these things in mind, will help in reducing injuries, increasing operator comfort and in turn productivity. This will reduce the direct costs of injuries. Moreover, the hidden costs which arise due to injuries such as absenteeism, reduction in productivity, individual and team morale in doing that job and, job satisfaction can also be controlled. Lower the injuries, higher the productivity and in effect higher throughput. Throughput can be linked to a better dispatch rate and more sales opportunities. In this study, a solution is suggested to reduce shoulder-related WMSD's.

3 Literature Review

Work-related Musculoskeletal disorders exist in every industry. In some industries, the term Musculoskeletal disorders may not be used. But simpler terms like shoulder injuries, shoulder strain, muscle injuries, etc. may be prevalent. The importance of WMSD's is increasing day by day. The following literature review focuses on a few aspects which are later used in the analysis and subsequent conclusions. Multiple types of analysis tools are used with different search criteria to emphasize on different topics and terms which are used in the project report. The review starts with 'Musculoskeletal Disorders', to provide a background on the current prevalence of the problems. Vicinitas software was used to search for the term "Musculoskeletal Disorder" [5]. The results showed approximately 258 posts and an influence of 1.3 million (Fig. 3).

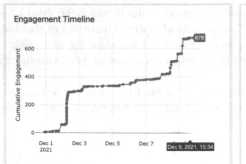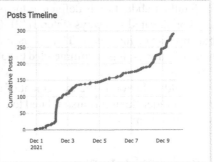

Fig. 3. Graphs indicating timeline for engagement and post using Vicinitas software [5].

The above graphs show the timeline of the use of the keyword. One graph is based on engagement, which can be seen to following an increasing trend in a period of 9–10 days. The second graph is based on the posts and its timeline. This follows a similar trend. As can be inferred, the posts are recent and can show the importance of musculoskeletal disorders. Social media is one of the most powerful tools of this century, hence it can be safe to say that many hidden costs or things (like WMSD's) can be highlighted using this medium [6].

The next analysis tool used was VOS viewer [7]. The data was extracted from Harzing software. (Publish or Perish) [8]. The keywords used were "Musculoskeletal Disorders, Workplace Ergonomics, Ergonomic Design, REBA, RULA, Anthropometry". Approximately 650 articles were found containing all the keywords from Google Scholar [9]. The exercise aimed to search for projects and articles that have focused on some or all these terms while determining a robust ergonomic solution (Fig. 4).

Fig. 4. Data extracted from Harzing's publish or perish software [8].

This data was then exported into VOSviewer software [7]. An analysis was done using keywords with a minimum occurrence of 10 (Fig. 5).

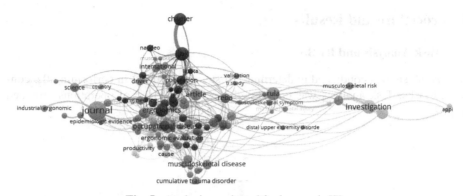

Fig. 5. Analysis conducted for keywords [7].

The above analysis shows clusters of words that occur the greatest number of times. As we can see, many these terms form the fundamentals of workplace ergonomics and are closely connected.

Additionally, an analysis was carried out for current research work. This was done by searching for awards funded by the National Science Foundation (NSF) [10]. The keyword used for the search was "Musculoskeletal Disorder's". The following image describes current work going on in the ergonomics domain related to Musculoskeletal Disorders. A search result of upward of 1000 awards is seen. From the results, the research work on 'Vision-based risk assessment of working postures' can be related to the study and analysis of postures presented in this report [11]. Using technologically driven software's, incorrect work postures could possibly be detected beforehand, thus reducing Work-related Musculoskeletal Disorders (WMSD's) [11] (Fig. 6).

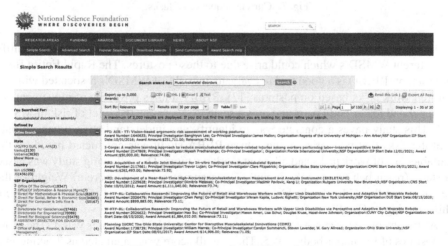

Fig. 6. Award search at NSF.gov [10].

4 Procedure and Results

4.1 Task Analysis and REBA

Task Analysis was conducted to determine all steps carried out in performing the concerned tasks. Task analysis was done by observing the video of operations provided (Fig. 7).

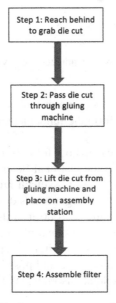

Fig. 7. Current sequence of tasks.

Identifying and studying the work tasks for stressful postures was essential to identify the different WMSD's which could arise due to these postures. The Rapid Entire Body Assessment (REBA) is a good tool to evaluate the risks of WMSD's associated with the required work tasks based on postures [12]. REBA studies positions of movements of the upper and lower body parts and uses a scale to determine the level of risk of MSD's [12]. This study paves a concrete way to identify and understand at an organizational level the risks that may arise in the future. REBA study was conducted based on the available data of work tasks and different work postures. The following study was based on step 1(reach behind to grab die-cut). The assumptions made were a) Weight of the die-cut is less than 11 pounds. b) Low to medium grip is required to grasp the die-cut while moving it (Fig. 8).

As per the operator's movement, the score for lower body postures was 4. The score for postures of the upper body was 5. The overall score was calculated as 7 taking into consideration the frequency and changes in posture while performing the tasks. Based on this score it was recommended that the risk of MSD's is medium to high, and changes should be made to prevent it from escalating [12].

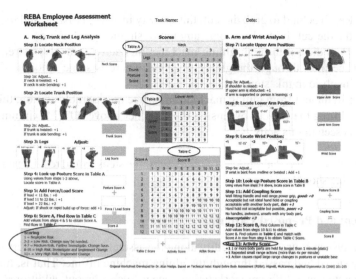

Fig. 8. Retrieved from www.ergoplus.com (Based on worksheet originally developed by Dr. Alan Hedge, adopted from Applied Ergonomics 31 (2000)) [12, 13] (Table 1).

Table 1. Adapted from www.ergoplus.com [12, 13]

Step No	Description	Score	Justification /Comments
Middle and Lower Body Postures			
1	Neck	2	0-20 degree inclination, twisted neck
2	Trunk	2	Twisted trunk
3	Legs	2	One Leg raised
4	Posture Score	4	Based on reference table
5	Force/Load	0	Assumption
6	Total Posture Score	4	
Upper Body Postures			
7	Upper Arm	3	Shoulder raised above 20 degrees and is in an abducted position.
8	Lower Arm	2	Motion between 0-60 degrees
9	Wrist	3	Wrist is bent greater than 15 degrees, slightly bent from midline.
10	Posture Score	5	Based on reference table
11	Grasping Force (to grasp object)	0	Assumption
12	Updated Posture Score	5	
13	Nature of Task	2	Frequency of task & changes in posture
14	Updated Posture score + Nature of task	7	

After conducting Task Analysis and subsequent REBA Study, the following motions were identified as the major cause of increased fatigue on the shoulder for the operator.

1. Step 1: Reach behind to grab die-cut, this activity involves twisting and reaching out to grab the die-cut. It involves some amount of shoulder abduction.
2. Step 2: Pass die-cut through gluing machine, this activity involves stretching and passing the filter through the gluing machine. There is some amount of shoulder flexion involved in this step.
3. Step 3: Lift die-cut from gluing machine and place on assembly station, this activity involves lifting the die-cut by raising the shoulder above 90°. Maximum shoulder flexion is seen in this activity.

The elimination and re-alignment of the above three steps would result in a significant reduction in the shoulder fatigue.

4.2 Current and Proposed Layout

A conveyor system is used in the facility along the assembly line. It is observed that the die-cuts are stored and passed through the gluing machine offline. That is, this activity is done separately at a different workstation. Due to such a layout, additional steps and movements are encountered by the operator. Some of these motions and movements are contributing to higher usage of the shoulder which leads to shoulder injuries. Thus, eliminating and re-aligning these steps will prove beneficial in limiting soft tissue shoulder injuries.

One method suggested here is to shift the gluing station onto the assembly line. That is, the gluing operation would take place on the assembly line itself. This would result in a few benefits. Firstly, the process would eliminate the task of twisting the body and extending the shoulder and arm to grasp the die-cut. (Step 1). Secondly, the action which contributes to maximum shoulder flexion and fatigue of lifting and carrying the die-cut to the assembly workstation can also get eliminated (Step 3). Elimination of these unnecessary motions would result in reducing the shoulder flexion and abduction, in turn reducing the shoulder fatigue. This is shown in the current and proposed layout diagrams, and in the proposed sequence of tasks, as follows (Fig. 9):

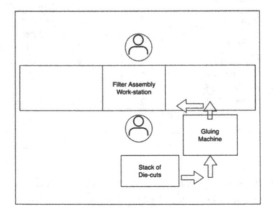

Fig. 9. Current layout.

The arrows indicate the movement of material (die-cut). As is explained above, the gluing station is not on the conveyor. Thus, there is an additional movement of the material and the operator. These directly contribute to the two types of waste of Lean Manufacturing principles, namely, Transportation and Motion. Transportation refers to the unnecessary movement of materials while Motion refers to the unnecessary movement of humans [14] (Fig. 11).

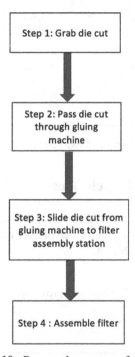

Fig. 10. Proposed sequence of tasks.

In the proposed layout, the gluing machine is shown to be shifted onto the existing conveyor system. This can be possible as the existing gluing machines have wheels for movement (as per given information). With certain modifications, this layout can be achieved. As compared with the existing layout diagram, there can be a significant reduction of material and operator movement, thus reducing the two wastes highlighted above (transportation & motion).

Additionally, it can bring the operations into an existing value stream, thus reducing the number of non-value-added activities. The discussed solution can also help to reduce cycle time as certain tasks in the operation would get eliminated /modified as is seen in the proposed sequence of tasks (Fig. 10).

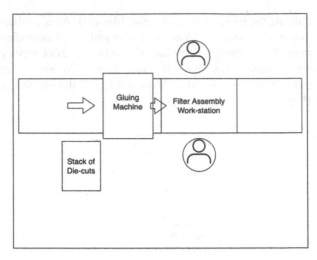

Fig. 11. Proposed layout.

5 Current and Projected Cycle Time

Cycle time for each activity was calculated using the Stop-watch Time Study method. This was achieved by observing the given video of operations. The following calculations are solely based on the video (Table 2).

Table 2. Current approx. Cycle time

Step No	Task	Approx. Cycle Time (secs)
1	Reach behind to grab die cut	1.5
2	Pass die cut through gluing machine	1.5
3	Lift die cut from gluing machine and place on assembly station	1.5
4	Assemble two parts of filter together	4.5
		9

Even though the above shoulder movements can be eliminated or re-aligned, it is important to note that some of these steps will still be required to perform the concerned operation. Thus, the steps (1&2) in effect can be modified, while step 3 can be eliminated.

After re-alignment and elimination of steps, estimated cycle times can be projected as follows (Table 3).

Table 3. Projected cycle time

Step No	Task	Approx. Cycle Time (secs)	Proposed % Reduction
1	Grab die cut	1	33% reduction
2	Pass die cut through gluing machine	1.5	-
3	Slide die cut from gluing machine to assembly station	1	33% reduction
4	Assemble two parts of filter together	4.5	-
		8	

The re-aligned step 1 of grabbing the die-cut will eliminate the motion of twisting and reaching behind. The proposed action will only lead to the operator extending the arm to the left to grab the die-cut. Due to this re-aligned movement, we can safely estimate a reduction of 0.5 s in performing the task. Similarly, due to the proposed location of the gluing machine, we can eliminate the lifting action (of the die-cut) and replace it with a 'sliding' action. Since this movement will require less force and motion of the shoulder, coupled with shortened distance between the gluing machine and filter assembly station, it can be a safe assumption to estimate a reduction of cycle time by 0.5 s for this task. The other two tasks (steps 2 and 4) shall on an average require the same time to perform and hence no reduction is projected for these steps. To manage the differences in height of the operator and the worktable, the operator can be provided a platform with small layer of foam. This layer of foam will help to counter any pressure on the knees or feet.

6   Discussion

After a thorough task analysis and REBA study, it was concluded that the nature of the tasks contribute more significantly to the shoulder injury than the height or reach of the operator. As explained above, moving the gluing station on the assembly line will help to tackle the problem of shoulder injuries at their root. The proposed layout can help to eliminate the twisting and reaching behind motion as well as the lifting motion. Re-aligning these steps as per the proposed layout will also help in reducing cycle time. Based on the available data, a current cycle time was calculated to be approximately 9 s. An estimated cycle time based on the proposed layout will be approximately 8 s. The layout above and the following cycle time calculations are representative but can provide a good direction in achieving the actual numbers. Thus, we can estimate a reduction of the cycle time by approximately 11%. As the cycle time is directly related to output and productivity, we can even project an increase in productivity as follows (Table 4):

Table 4. Estimated productivity increase calculations

Current Process			Projected Process			Approx. Productivity increase
Current Cycle Time (secs)	Production per hour (nos)	Production per shift (nos)	Projected Cycle Time (sec)	Production per hour (nos)	Production per shift (nos)	
9	400	4000	8	450	4500	13%

These calculations are based on assumptions such as a) Shift is of 10 h in duration. b) Production per hour and Production per day are calculated considering 100% efficiency. The overall increase in productivity can be approximately 13%. The changed layout can be coupled with providing a small platform to increase the reach of the short operators.

Summarizing the report, we can understand some key terms are connect in meaning and application and bring out an overall system improvement. As we have seen above, task analysis, ergonomics, layout, cycle time and productivity seem to be interlinked. They form the basis of industrial engineering. The following word cloud is created to summarize and lay emphasis on how they are interlinked (Fig. 12).

Fig. 12. Word cloud generated using MAXQDA software [15].

The above word cloud is generated in MAXQDA software [15]. It compares 4 articles related to 'cycle time', 'layout', 'ergonomics', 'productivity' [16–19]. These search terms were used in Google scholar [9]. Based on this, a word cloud was created, using 71 words, keeping a minimum frequency of 25 words [20]. An attempt was made to remove all uninfluential words, to make the word cloud more impactful. As can be inferred, terms like "ergonomics, work study, layout, system, production, assembly" are common terms and are closely tied as is the case in real-world situations.

7 Future Work

As explained in the above sections, shifting the gluing machine onto the conveyor will help to eliminate steps which cause a strain to the shoulder. These steps are, reaching behind to grab die-cut and lifting die-cut from gluing machine to filter assembly workstation. This proposed layout will also help to reduce the cycle time by approximately 11% and the productivity can possibly increase by 13%. A REBA study of the other operator movements such as step 3 (lifting die-cut from gluing machine) will help to strengthen the root cause analysis of the shoulder injury. Also, an actual time study at the shopfloor will help to determine the current state of the process. In addition to the proposed layout, a base plate can be fixed between the gluing machine and the filter assembly workstation. This will aid the operator in sliding the die cut from the gluing machine even more easily. A further modification could be done by keeping a certain height difference between the gluing machine and the filter assembly workstation. This height difference can be used to automatically feed the die-cuts from the gluing machine to assembly workstation by gravity (gravity feed). Considering the repetitive nature of the tasks and the proposed layout, the gluing operation can be explored for complete automation by providing an automatic feeder mechanism to continuously feed the die cuts. This can even lead to optimizing the number of operators required for the task.

References

1. U.S Bureau of Labor Statistics: Injuries, Illnesses, and Fatalities. (May 2020). https://www.bls.gov/iif/oshwc/case/msds.htm
2. Canadian Centre for Occupational Health & Safety: Diseases, Disorders and Injuries. Accessed 9 December 2021. https://www.ccohs.ca/oshanswers/diseases/rmirsi.html
3. Marras, W.S.: Basic Biomechanics and Workstation Design. In: Salvendy, G. (ed.) Handbook of Human Factors and Ergonomics, pp. 346–375. John Wiley & Sons
4. Middlesworth, M.: The Cost of Musculoskeletal Disorders (MSDs). Ergo Plus (July 2021). https://ergo-plus.com/cost-of-musculoskeletal-disorders-infographic/
5. Vicinitas: https://www.vicinitas.io/. Accessed 23 February 2022
6. Jiang, J., Duffy, V.G.: Modern Workplace Ergonomics and Productivity–A Systematic Literature Review. In: International Conference on Human-Computer Interaction, pp. 509–524. Springer, Cham (2021)
7. VOS viewer: https://www.vosviewer.com/. Accessed 23 February 2022
8. Harzing's Publish or Perish. https://harzing.com/resources/publish-or-perish. Accessed 23 February 2022
9. Google Scholar. https://scholar.google.com/. Accessed 23 February 2022
10. National Science Foundation. https://nsf.gov/. Accessed 23 February 2022
11. Lee, S., Mallon, J.: PFI: AIR - TT: Vision-Based Ergonomic Risk Assessment of Working Postures (2016). https://nsf.gov/awardsearch/showAward?AWD_ID=1640633&HistoricalAwards=false
12. Middlesworth, M.: A Step-by-Step Guide to REBA Assessment Tool. Ergo Plus. (October 2017). https://ergo-plus.com/reba-assessment-tool-guide/
13. McAtamney, L.Y.N.N., Hignett, S.: REBA: rapid entire body assessment. Appl. Ergon. **31**(2), 201–205 (2000)
14. Skhmot, N.: The 8 Wastes of Lean. The Lean Way (2017). https://theleanway.net/The-8-Wastes-of-Lean

15. MAXQDA: https://www.maxqda.com/trial. Accessed on 24 February 2022
16. Gnanavel, S.S., Balasubramanian, V., Narendran, T.T.: Suzhal–An alternative layout to improve productivity and worker well-being in labor demanded lean environment. Procedia Manufacturing **3**, 574–580 (2015)
17. Shinde, G.V., Jadhav, V.S.: Ergonomic analysis of an assembly workstation to identify time consuming and fatigue causing factors using application of motion study. International Journal of Engineering and Technology **4**(4), 220–227 (2012)
18. Neumann, W.P., Jörgen Winkel, L.M., Magneberg, R., Erik Mathiassen, S.: Production system design elements influencing productivity and ergonomics: A case study of parallel and serial flow strategies. International journal of operations & production management (2006)
19. Battini, D., Faccio, M., Persona, A., Sgarbossa, F.: New methodological framework to improve productivity and ergonomics in assembly system design. Int. J. Ind. Ergon. **41**(1), 30–42 (2011)
20. Alkhaleefah, A., Renardo, Q., Duffy, VG.: Injury Prevention for Transportation Safety: A Bibliometric Analysis.In: International Conference on Human-Computer Interaction, pp. 205–218. Springer, Cham (2021)

Ergonomics in an Industrial Setting – A Case Study

Michael Lambrosa[✉]

Purdue University, West Lafayette, IN 47906, USA
mlambrosa@purdue.edu

Executive Summary. An industrial manufacturing enterprise faces an ergonomic dilemma affecting operators stationed at their glue station work environment. Workers of shorter stature face a poor ergonomic scenario when moving pre-glued air filters to their glue station that is leading to strain on their shoulders and adverse working conditions. The goal of this project is to address the poor ergonomic working conditions specifically affecting shorter stature workers through several solutions options. Three solution options are proposed to address and the above problem statement: A process redesign through ergonomically advantageously placed conveyor systems, a work station redesign through the use of vacu-hoist lifting technology, and a work station remediation through the use of pneumatic lift tables. Consideration of solution details, the effects of KPIs of the enterprise and weighting affect on the overall process lead to the suggestion of the work station remediation through the incorporation of lift tables as the most optimal solution in addressing the ergonomic problem statement.

Abstract. The design of a workstation in an industrial setting must account for numerous factors; including production capacity, space limitations, cost, and human factors. Among the human factors that must be accounted for are human ergonomics and the effects that the work station has on a human's physical condition in the work station and their ability to complete their assigned tasks. Just as work station design must balance numerous factors in its construction, human ergonomics as a design factor in work station design must balance optimal ergonomic qualities with other variables such as cost, production capacity, and ease of use. The following proceeding outlines a case study in analyzing an ergonomic dilemma in work station design in an industrial setting and potential solutions to optimize ergonomic factors in the working environment. In order to accomplish the goals of this process a literature review supports gathering background information on three potential work station solutions; a work station process design, work station redesign, or work station mitigation.

Keywords: Industrial ergonomics · Work station

1 Introduction and Background

1.1 Background

Ergonomics can be defined as the "laws of work" when broken down from its Greek roots and focuses on designing work stations for human capabilities and work optimization

© Springer Nature Switzerland AG 2022
V. G. Duffy and P.-L. P. Rau (Eds.): HCII 2022, LNCS 13522, pp. 243–256, 2022.
https://doi.org/10.1007/978-3-031-21704-3_16

(I.A.H, 2). Ergonomics has been an informal factor in designing and analyzing human work stations and production systems for years but began gaining traction with and formalization in the 1940s in the military aircraft sector (Brauer, 594). It was during this time that the design of aircraft cockpits, functioning as the work station for the pilot, began to be analyzed quantitatively and scientifically to optimize the user's ability to accomplish their designated tasks in the environment. The environment of the pilot and the effects that prolonged exposure to a high altitude environment of an aircraft cockpit was also analyzed and factored into the overall work station design. The method and process of ergonomic design and evaluation soon branched out from aviation-specific focuses to more mainstream private sector environments; including white-collar office environments and industrial settings. A key piece of ergonomic analysis of a work station in weighing the variables that will affect the human in their work environment; psychological, physiological, and anthropomorphically among them. Each working environment poses unique ergonomic challenges to workers, including prolonged screen exposure in an office environment, increased decibel exposure in a construction environment, and repetitive twisting and lifting injuries in an industrial assembly line work process.

Twisting and lifting injuries often fall into the overexertion category of musculoskeletal disorders (MSDs) suffered by workers and affect nearly half a million workers each year, of which 60% fall involve lifting and back pain (Intro to Human Factors, 320). MSDs are often a result of improperly designed workstations (Introduction to Human Factors, 320). In the case of most workstation designs that play into MSDS, the workstation was not designed around the use but rather design for the user to conform to it. With the physical capabilities of the human body being limited in their abilities, it is of great importance to design a work station to fit a human, and not for a human to fit into a work station (Brauer, 584). When this factor is ignored, long-term MSDs may impact workers and lead to reduced production capacity due to reduced working capabilities, costly employer and employee medical expenditures, lost working days, and expensive work station remediation (Brauer, CH 31). The negative impacts of MSDs are more likely to impact work environments in which their employees rely on their physical capabilities to complete their work, such as those in industrial production line environments. The highly repetitive, physically demanding, and diverse employee base of assembly line-based production environments are critical candidates for ergonomic workstation design.

1.2   Introduction and Problem Statement

While the negative impacts of poorly designed workstations from an ergonomic perspective have been documented in workplace-related injuries and employer expenditures by organizations such as NIOSH, the work to incorporate optimal ergonomic design is far from a universally adopted practice in the industrial world (Introduction to Human Factors, 320). As is the case with most decisions faced by most privately held enterprises, factors such as cost, production, and ease of adoption must also be considered before implementing any changes to a working environment. Hesitancy to widespread adoption of ergonomic design can be seen in the case study of an air filter manufacturer and their production line system. In this production system, air filters are moved through an assembly line that encompasses multiple work stations designed to assist employees in completing tasks related to the synthesizing of the air filters. One of the multiple workstations included in the total production system involves moving the air filters through a glue machine before final packaging. This work station consists of an employee standing in front of two work platforms at different heights and transferring filters from a higher platform to a lower platform and glue station. This work station provides numerous ergonomic dilemmas to the employee; the repetitive motion of twisting and lifting the air filter from the higher table to the lower glue station among them. This workstation design poses an especially critical risk to shorter employees, as the need to lift to grab the air filters may strain their shoulders after repetitive moves. The scenario has played out in this industrial work setting and forms the basis of the case study in this work. The problem statement analyzed throughout this proceeding can be summarized as follows: Develop a solution to limit the shoulder strain faced by employees due to improperly heightened workstations while balancing the overall enterprise factors of cost, production, and ease of use.

2 Literature Review and Procedure

2.1 Data Collection

The ergonomic scenario introduced in the previous section poses multiple risks to an employee in the form of ergonomic hazards. To understand the best method for addressing the ergonomic inefficiencies of the current work station design, it is necessary to conduct a literature review to gain a better background of tools and methods to mitigate the problems in the statement. The literature review piece of the report was focused on scholarly and academic works as well as practical industrial case studies in trusted sources google scholar and web of science. Background and authoritative information were also collected from text sources like Roger Brauer's *Safety and Health for Engineers* and *An Introduction to Human Factors Engineering*. The searches conducted in these databases were centered around the key search term "Industrial Ergonomics" in the hopes of generating information that would be relevant to the air filter production system case study. Following searches in the three databases for "Industrial Ergonomics" the results of the searches were analyzed in metadata visualizing tools VosViwer and MaxQDA to better understand key terms and articles to focus research on in the solution development.

The first step in conducting the literary analysis was identifying the proper databases with which to pull articles from. Web of Science and Google Scholar databases were chosen as part of the literary analysis, as they have inclusion of cited references and size of search capabilities respectively. Web of Science and Google Scholar allow for the ability to conduct a co-citation and content analysis using other tools later in the study due to their inclusion of the above information. One keyword search was conducted in both of these databases to find relevant articles in the topic area. This search was done using the term "Industrial Ergonomics". The keyword was searched in Web of Science with search parameter years set at 2001–2021 and resulted in 7,739 article results. Keyword searches conducted in Google Scholar through Harzing were stopped at 400 results (*Harzing's Publish or Perish*, n.d.). Figure 2 shows the results from the

Web of Science search on the key term "industrial ergonomics" as it relates to various topic areas (Fig. 1).

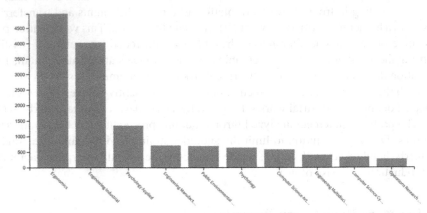

Fig. 1. Shows a bar chart grouping the 7,739 search results from the key term search "industrial ergonomics" in the date range of 2001–2021.

2.2 Co-citation Analysis

After data in the form of scholarly articles on the keyword search term "Industrial Ergonomics" was collected from Web of Science and Google Scholar through Harzing Publish or Perish, an analysis of the results for connections between the articles and

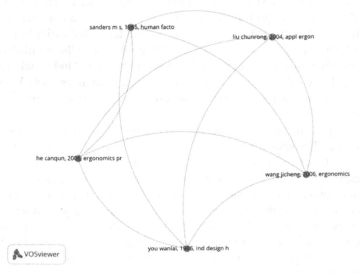

Fig. 2. Shows the results of the co-citation analysis performed using the keyword search industrial ergonomics in Web of Science as generated in VosViewer.

topic field was conducted. To complete this, a co-citation analysis, content analysis, and word cloud generation were undertaken. The co-citation analysis was undertaken first and was aimed at finding important articles in the keyword fields and give insights into articles to further dissect for reference in creating a solution recommendation for the industrial ergonomic scenario. VOSViewer was used for the co-citation analysis with results collected through Web of Science from the keyword search "Industrial Ergonomics". Articles from Web of Science were used for this task due to the resulting data including author citations. The results from the keyword search were limited to the latest 500 articles published as of 2020. The minimum number of citations of a cited reference was set a 3 of which 5 articles met the threshold.

2.3   Content Analysis

After the co-citation analysis was completed, a content analysis undertaken on the article results from the keyword search. The content analysis follows a systematic process of evaluating articles in the topic areas of industrial ergonomics for keywords and their occurrences within the title or abstracts of those articles. The data visualization was created using data from Google Scholar in the VOSviewer software. Google Scholar results were chosen due to their for the content analysis due to greater number of article results and inclusion of meta data in article extractions. The minimum number of occurrences for the terms within an article while conducting the content analysis was set at 15 occurrences. With the results from this analysis and data visualization, it was easier to identify an area with which to direct literature review (Fig. 3).

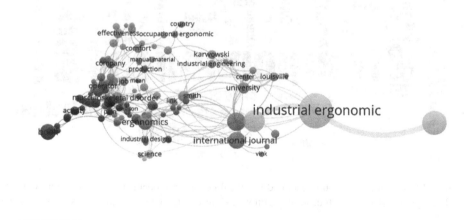

Fig. 3. Shows the results of content analysis using Google Scholar data drawn through Harzing.

Figure 5 shows the results of the content analysis conducted in Google Scholar using Harzing for the keyword search term "Industrial Ergonomics". The number of occurrences in the content analysis was limited to 15 occurrences with a relevance score of 60%. The content analysis generated in VosViewer shows over 50+ terms returned in which to direct further research in developing process improvements for the ergonomic situation. The terms shown in the image above are scaled based on occurrence. Connections between the term clusters are indicated with links, larger links correlating to stronger connections. Color coordination is also present in the content analysis image to separate clusters from one another. 10+ separate clusters of words exist from this content analysis. The results of this process indicate "Industrial Ergonomic" occurred the largest number of times for keywords.

2.4 World Cloud Analysis

The last data processing method undertaken was the creation of a Word Cloud from articles across both search databases searched in the literature review Generation of the word cloud was completed in the MAXQDA software using Google Scholar and Web of Science articles. Keywords and terms from this article field were extracted and displayed in a word cloud format. The data from the searches were refined to eliminate irrelevant words such as "the" and "is" with the top 50 words with a minimum of occurrences being present in the figure. In this data display, the larger the word in the figure, the greater the number of occurrences. Figure 6 below shows the figure of the MAXQDA generated word cloud (Fig. 4).

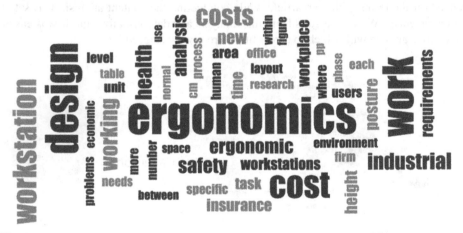

Fig. 4. Shows the word cloud generated to reveal commonly occurring and important content in the keyword search of "Industrial Ergonomics" across Google Scholar and Web of Science searches.

3   Results

3.1   Solution Options

Upon completion of the literature review and collection of critical background information that would guide the final solution options and recommendations, it was necessary to devise several solutions to the previously stated ergonomic scenario. To lessen the level of ergonomic distress incurred by the user in this scenario, the height varying heights of the workstation and the lack of height customization need to be addressed. It can be seen that designing the workstation with the principle of allowing for usage of the 5th percentile in height, or those that are shorter in stature than 95% of the population would be an appropriate design guider (Intro to Human Factors and Engineering, 316). It is important when designing the work station for the 5th percentile that the reach envelope of the user is quantitatively analyzed and considered for optimal placement of any work station remediations (Intro to Human Factors and Engineering, 316). To more effectively place the working environment into a 5th percentile worker's reach envelope, several improvement strategies can be undertaken to adjust the ergonomic quality of the work station: Process Redesign, Work Station Redesign, or Work Station Remediation.

3.2 Process Redesign

The first option for addressing the ergonomic gaps faced by shorter stature workers in this environment is through a work process redesign. Process redesigns are a common method in addressing ergonomic shortcomings in a workstation. As outlined in work done by Arijit Sengupta, poor process designs and layouts can often result in costly acute and chronic ergonomic stress and operators (Sengupta, 1). In the current process, air filters are moved through a multi-job station production line. While it can be assumed that prior to the glue station work station, the height of the work station is fairly consistent, the glue station involves work stations at various heights. When strategy to resolve this issue would be to redesign the entire work process to incorporate work stations at a height optimal for the 5th percentile reach envelope. This would presumably consist of lowering the conveyor system of the previous work station be lowered to the post glue station height, acceptable to the shorter user. This solution would offer a viable option to solve the height issue by allowing for all conveyor systems to be at an optimal and acceptable height to meet the 5th percentile rule of design. However, this would not eliminate the need for the worker to twist their entire body to reach behind them to grab the air filters and transfer them to the glue station. A design alternative to address this issue would be to create an extension of the conveyor system that can feed the unglued air filters to the employee at a level height and allow them to reach in front of them to feed the air filter into the glue machine. This design, while allowing for comprehensive elimination of the ergonomic issues in the form of lifting at different heights and twisting the body and the strain placed on the user, would prove to be quite expensive and time-consuming in completion. The above solution would necessitate the enterprise to layout their process and transportation of work, costing money and potential production during redesign completion and allow for retraining of employees and process changes.

3.3 Work Station Redesign

The second option that can work to reduce negative ergonomic stress on the employee would be through workstation redesign. Redesigning the glue station work environment would allow for the employee in that area to work in a more ergonomically friendly setting and reduce the negative enterprise impacts that come along with stress on the worker without redesigning the process flow. Work station redesigns often work to overhaul the principle layout of a singular work cell without interrupting the overall process or the work cell's purpose in the process. To effectively redesign a workplace for industrial ergonomics, it is first key to understand the population for which the work station will be redesigned (Baman, 1). Understanding the key population of interest, in this factor, shorter stature individuals, their applicable measurements, and applying them to the work station redesign is key to finding a solution to address the ergonomic inadequacy in question (Braman, 1). As is the case in the process redesign option, redesigning the work environment requires that the employee need not undergo the strain of twisting and lifting at different heights under weighted stress. To best accomplish this outcome while also limiting the redesign of the entire workplace, the usage of assistive technology in the workstation would be very beneficial. One such technology to consider would be a vacu-hoist assisted lift system. A vacu-hoist assisted lift system would allow an employee in the work environment to access an overhanging piece of equipment that can grab objects without the need for an employee to exert force in lifting. Figure 7. Shows an example of such a system. In the vacu-hoist work station redesign, the operator would only need to take the following steps to complete their tasks:

1. Gran vacu-hoist end effector arm handles
2. Guide end effector and suction head to pre glued air filters.
3. Engage end effector by pulling compressed air trigger to pick up pre-glued air filters.
4. Move pre-glued air filters to the glue station and disengage compressed air.

These tasks would largely mirror the current glue station operator's duties in moving air filters into the glue station but would reduce the strain placed on the worker by removing the force needed for the operator to grab the air filters. While this workstation redesign would require the installation of a vacu-hoist system and training on its use, it would not require any large-scale process redesign or multi work station changes. This issue would still require the operator to twist and interact with higher work stations, but would not require the strain to be placed on the operator of lifting while also completing these tasks.

3.4 Work Station Remediation

The third option proposed to address the ergonomic situation of the air filter case study involves mitigating the current work environment with minimally invasive adjustments. Work station remediation offers the least intrusive method of solving an ergonomic shortcoming and can easily be inserted into a workstation with minimal effort or change in environment function. The goal of the work station, similar to the process and work station redesigns is again to limit the negative impacts of twisting and lifting strain on the work station operator. Information from Ch 21. Of *Handbook for Human Factors and Ergonomics* on workplace design proves especially useful in understanding methods for addressing the ergonomic dilemma in the problem statement (Salvendy, 606). Potentially areas to consider in finding a solution in this workstation redesign are the worker's posture, stature, and task requirements (Salvendy, 606). The most logical area to introduce minimal change is in the height of the pre-glued air filter collection area.

Fig. 5. Shows an example of a vacu-hoist system that can be incorporated in the work station redesign solution.

Adjusting the height of this area to an optimal worker reach envelope would allow for the work to limit their shoulder strain while moving the relatively light air filters. A potential method to address this height differential would be with the incorporation of an adjustable pneumatic lift table with which to accumulate the pre-glued air filters. Pneumatic lift tables consist of a flat surface of equal size to the process conveyor flow that can, with power from a pneumatic airline, be adjusted in height to fit a user's preferences. Pneumatic lift tables air portable and easily set up to allow for easy changes in operator usage between multiple shifts and can allow for various heights that can optimally suit any anthropomorphic data set in the operation's resource pool. The operator would only need to move stacks of pre-glued air filters onto the lift table or place the lift table at a position in which air filters can simply flow onto it. Lowering the workstation to an optimal height for the operator will allow for the principle of designing the job to the human and not forcing a human to fit into a poorly agronomical workplace fit (Introduction to Human Factors Engineering, 309). While this process does require some setup time for the operator at the beginning of each shift, its relatively cheap expensive, adjustability, and ease of implementation make this option an enticing choice for addressing the industrial ergonomic dilemma faced by the air filter manufacturer.

Fig. 6. Shows an example of a pneumatic lift table that can be incorporated into the work station redesign solution.

4 Discussion

4.1 Decision Evaluation Criteria Matrix

After compiling three reasonable and practical solutions to addressing the ergonomic shortcomings in the current work station design, it was pertinent to begin weighing the solution options. To take a quantitative approach to select a solution, a decision evaluation criteria matrix (DEMC) was created to place quantitative values on each key factor within the solutions. The first step in constructing the DEMC was creating choosing the key process evaluation pieces (KPIs) to evaluate each scenario from. These KPIs are also assigned a weighting in the form of a percentage of their importance in the overall decision of the process change. With the industrial nature of this process the KPIs of cost, productivity, ease of use/implementation, quality, and safety were chosen for this purpose. In a private enterprise, the cost of any potential process change must be weighed and factored in as well as the effect the change will have on the productivity of the process. With this in the mind, the weighting of these two KPIs was chosen to be 40% of the final decision for each of the two. Ease of use and implementation of any solution must also be factored into a process change decision and is chosen at 15% of the final implementation decisions. Finally safety, and quality was chosen to be 5% of the total decision evaluation. Both of these factors are incredibly important in the overall process environment, but are also continuously incorporated in the other three decision levels and are thus independently only rated at 5%. Figure 7 shows a blank template of the decision evaluation criteria matrix used for this process change.

4.2 Recommendations

Once the KPIs and weighting of the importance of each KPI were compiled, each project alternative was evaluated to create a quantitative "score" with which to compare each solution with. Each solution was given a score of 1–5, 5 being the most optimal solution in the criteria field and 1 being the least optimal, to grade out each criteria area. The first criteria evaluated, cost/ROI, was analyzed based on the pure cost to implement each

			Recommended Change		
		Wt.	Process Redesign	Work Station Redesign	Work Station Remediation
Criteria	Cost / ROI	0.400	4	5	3
	Productivity	0.400	5	5	3
	Ease of Use	0.100	4	3	5
	Quality	0.050	5	5	5
	Safety	0.050	5	5	5
	Total	1.00	23	23	21
	Weighted Total		#REF!	#REF!	#REF!

Fig. 7. Shows the process evaluation criteria matrix, with the Wt. Column corresponding to the approximate weighting of each factor level and the criteria rows corresponding to each evaluated criteria factor.

one of the solutions. Using previous industrial experience as background and reference, a conveyor system redesign and rebuild as would be necessary to accomplish the gains of the process would be a costly endeavor, incurring costs well over $150,000 for a conveyor system of the process length in the air filter production environment. The Work Station Redesign option that would incorporate a new vacu-hoist system would incur significantly fewer costs than the process change but would still come in at a relatively high price tag of roughly $40,000 with installation and pneumatic airlines needing to be run to the area. Option 3, work station remediation, would net the least costs of the three options. The cost of purchasing a pneumatic lift table and running an airline costs the enterprise only around $7000 in total capital. This would net the scores of 1, 3, and 5 for project solutions 1,2, and 3 respectively.

Following the evaluation of the cost criteria, it is next relevant to move to the effect each solution will have on the productivity of the air filter manufacturing process. In the case of this productivity impact, we will look only at the short-term relationship between implementing each solution on the immediate impact on production. Solution 1 will most likely have a large impact on productivity due to the large scale necessitated by the change. While the productivity changes that follow a redesign of the production system may be equal to the current production system in the long run, short-term production will ultimately be affected negatively due to the large loss in the production time needed to implement such a large-scale change. Solution 2 will have a minimal impact on productivity overall. The implementation of a vacu-hoist system will slow the overall movement of air filters from one side of the glue work station to another (vacu-hoist overall work slower than human body movements through historical time studies) but would allow the operator to move more air filters at a time and work longer hours at a lower fatigue rate. In this rate, it can be seen that productivity will be minimally impacted, perhaps slightly positively affected. The lift table work station remediation shown in solution 3 will lead to nearly no production impacts, as the work station will remain nearly the same with only small adjustments made to the setup. As is the case with solution 2, introducing a pneumatic lift table may slightly positively affect production in reduced worker fatigue throughout a shift with minimal negative impacts. The reasonings mentioned form the basis for ranking solutions, 1,2, and 3 with a 3,4, and 4 respectively.

Ease of use and implementation is the next criteria evaluated for each solution method. This criteria field most closely captures the end-users adaptation and continued use of the process environment selected and its ease of introduction into the overall air filter manufacturing process. When analyzing the ease of use for the process redesign option, the ease of use will be very simple as the overall tasks and method of completion for the operator will go unchanged. While the layout and structural changes that accompany the process redesign option allow for high ease of use for the operator, the ease of implementation will be quite high and require a great deal of time and effort to implement. These factors combine to yield a score of 3 for option 1 of the proposed solution. The work station redesign would yield a different set of technology, in the form of a vacu-hoist system, that the operator would need to learn to use and become comfortable with using. While the incorporation and implementation of a vacu-hoist system is less cumbersome than an entire process redesign, the added difficulty of learning to use and incorporate new technology into the overall process would yield a score of 3 as well for option 2. Solution option 3, the work station remediation, would result in a low level of difficulty of ease of use and implementation, as introducing a pneumatic lift table would largely leave the tasks of the operation unchanged and introduce no new technology to become comfortable with. This would yield a score of 4 for ease of use and implementation for solution option 3.

The final criteria to evaluate, safety and quality, can largely be viewed together for each solution. Quality concerns would be minimal for each technology, with few new variables introduced to either hurt or benefit the quality of the produced air filters throughout this process. When considering safety as a criterion, we will isolate the ergonomic safety factors of any of the solution suggestions and focus only on safety concerns outside of these areas. Safety, as is the case with quality, is also largely unaltered by any of the solution recommendations. Introducing new technologies or power sources as is the case in the work station redesign and remediation solutions may pose new opportunities for safety risks, but they are fairly minimal when balanced with the existing process layout. With this in mind, all solutions will be scored with a 5 for quality and 5 for safety.

After evaluating each solution based on the criteria established in the decision matrix, the overall score of each solution is established using the previously quantified weighting for each criteria area. The values explained and justified above were imported into the decision matrix and yield the following weighted scoring results in Fig. 8.

As is demonstrated in the above figure, workstation remediation is the most optimal solution. This case can be clearly explained in the large balance this solution has between cost and easy understanding of the current process structure while also allowing for reduced strain on the glue station operator.

| | | | Recommended Change | | |
		Wt.	Process Redesign	Work Station Redesign	Work Station Remediation
Criteria	Cost / ROI	0.400	1	3	5
	Productivity	0.400	3	4	4
	Ease of Use	0.100	3	3	4
	Quality	0.050	5	5	5
	Safety	0.050	5	5	5
Total		1.00	17	20	23
Weighted Total			2.4	3.6	4.5

Fig. 8. Shows the scoring for each project solution based on the scoring results and criteria weighting.

5 Conclusion and Future Work

5.1 Conclusion

After analyzing the stance of each KPI on the selected solutions and options weighing them based on criticality to the overall enterprise operation, we can create quantitative values with which to compare the success each solution will have to solve the stated ergonomic problem As captured in the decision evaluation matrix in the previous section, the overall scores for each solution stack out to a score of 2.4 for the process redesign, 3.6 for the workstation redesign and 4.5 for the work station remediation. Scores from the matrix can be interpreted with a higher score correlating to a more optimal solution to the problem. Thus with the above values, we can conclude that the work station remediation is the best option to solve the ergonomic issue above and continue to assist in meeting the enterprise's operational goals. Analyzing the decision evaluation matrix further leads us to believe this conclusion is fairly intuitive. Solution 3 allows the enterprise to sacrifice the least in implementation costs and productivity while adequately addressing the issue introduced in the problem statement. In this way, the workstation remediation can be justified as the best selection for the problem statement.

5.2 Future Work

While the use of lift tables in support of a workstation remediation serves to address the ergonomic issue introduced in the problem statement, it is by no means the end of the work that can be done to optimize the ergonomic scenario of this glue station working environment. One potentially enhancement to this solution proposal process would be through the use of 3D CAD technology such as RAMSIS design software. RAMSIS and similar 3D CAD design software provide a realistic, simulative method for testing the ergonomic effects on human users in a proposed environment without the need to create design prototypes or sacrifice high viability data (Human Solutions, et al.). The use of such technology would allow a designer to propose multiple workstation/process redesigns with multiple operator placements and understand the scenario's ergonomic effects on the operator. 3D CAD would add another quantitative decision point and would greatly assist in the creation of future redesigns of future processes and workstation layouts.

Another area for opportunity in the future state of the current air filter manufacturing environment would be through the use of automation and robotics. Further use of autonomous robotics would serve to assist human operators in their tasks as part of the holistic operation. Robotics can likely serve to benefit both the ergonomic scenario of the glue station operator by reducing the manual tasks of the induvial while also potentially assisting in productivity with faster processing time and reduced fatigue and delay impacts (Sauppe,1). Research promoted at the University of Wisconsin studies the process of incorporating robotics into human-driven manufacturing systems and seeks to find best practices in carrying out this task. As outlined in the article, it is not sufficient to simply insert robotics and automation into a human-driven manufacturing system is not sufficient without understanding the tasks, goals, and constraints of the human and robotic elements of the process (Sauppe,1). Before beginning to incorporate the benefits of automation and robotics into this industrial process, the enterprise must first understand and quantitively measure the collaborative factors in the new human-robot interaction such as tasks assignment, tool allocation, and skills sets (Sauppe,1). While requiring further research and effort to understand a future state situation, the incorporation of robotics into the current manufacturing process will serve as a worthy endeavor and supplement to their industrial environment.

References

1. Brauer, R.L.: Safety and Health for Engineers. Wiley (2016)
2. Das, B., Sengupta, A.K.: Industrial workstation design: a systematic ergonomics approach. Appl. Ergon. **27**(3), 157–163 (1996). https://doi.org/10.1016/0003-6870(96)00008-7
3. "Industrial Ergonomics Backgrounder - Mhi." Accessed 3 December 2021. https://www.mhi.org/downloads/industrygroups/ease/technicalpapers/ERGOBACKGROUNDDOC.pdf
4. Salvendy, G.: Handbook of Human Factors and Ergonomics. Wiley (2012)
5. Sauppé, A., Mutlu, B.: Effective task training strategies for human and robot instructors. Autonomous Robots **39** (2015). https://doi.org/10.1007/s10514-015-9461-0 Citation Details
6. Sengupta, A.K., Sengupta, A.: (PDF) Industrial Ergonomics and Workstation Design. ResearchGate. unknown, (1 January 2004). https://www.researchgate.net/publication/228501116_Industrial_Ergonomics_and_Workstation_Design?enrichId=rgreq-d37b33c127ea3caf0da2d7cb3246f020-
7. Systemadministrator: RAMSIS 3D CAD Modeling. Human Solutions - Products - RAMSIS General. Accessed 9 October 2021. https://www.human-solutions.com/en/products/ramsis-general/index.html
8. Wickens, C.D., Lee, J., Liu, Y., Gordon-Becker, S.: An Introduction to Human Factors Engineering. W. Ross MacDonald School Resource Services Library, Brantford, Ontario (2015)

Improving the Ergonomics and Preventing Soft Tissue Injuries at an Air Filter Assembly Work Cell

Seanan C. Lee[1](✉) and Vincent G. Duffy[2]

[1] College of Engineering, Purdue University, West Lafayette, IN 47906, USA
seananlee@purdue.edu
[2] School of Industrial Engineering, Purdue University, West Lafayette, IN 47906, USA
duffy@purdue.edu

Abstract. Industrial ergonomics in manufacturing settings is often neglected during the design phase of work cells. An employee at an air filter manufacturer suffered soft tissue injuries to their shoulder due to the incompatibility between her stature and the production table's height. The improved ergonomics will increase the enterprises' competitiveness and employees' satisfaction index in the production department. Through a systematic literature review conducted with tools such as VOSviewer and CiteSpace, the authors identified high-impact research studies and incorporate their findings into the proposed solution. The recommendations from employees and the safety evaluator are also compared against other commercially available solutions and they are compared based on effectiveness, cost, and viability. It is recommended that height-adjustable swivel shop stools with backrests be made available to the employee to eliminate height incompatibility, the need to twist their body to retrieve die cuts air filter frames, and the need to stand for extended periods. Adjusting the shop floor layout such that all materials required at this work cell are all within easy reach of the assembler eliminates the potential for cumulative trauma disorder caused by throwing die cuts toward the downstream process. Following initial adoption, the safety evaluator should investigate further to validate the changes made before widespread adoption in the production department.

Keywords: Industrial ergonomics · Manufacturing · Cumulative trauma disorder · Soft tissue injuries · VOSviewer · CiteSpace

1 Introduction and Problem Statement

Industrial ergonomics encompasses the human factors concerns during the manufacturing phase of a product's lifecycle. The major manufacturing tasks include production, assembly, logistics, planning, control, maintenance, and quality management. Industrial ergonomics is a growing concern in today's workplace as manufacturing operations transition away from force-focused physical activities towards cognitive control activities [1]. Physically demanding work – i.e., not automated – can be improved via work structuring and ergonomic design to maximize productivity and minimize the potential for injuries [1].

© Springer Nature Switzerland AG 2022
V. G. Duffy and P.-L. P. Rau (Eds.): HCII 2022, LNCS 13522, pp. 257–274, 2022.
https://doi.org/10.1007/978-3-031-21704-3_17

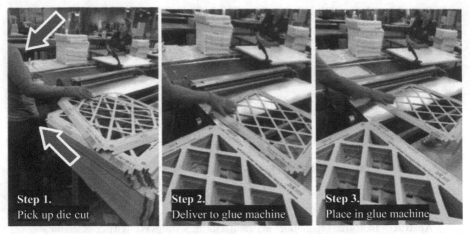

Fig. 1. Current glue station workflow at the work cell. Step 1 poses major ergonomic risks to the shoulders and waist as the employee must reach back and twist to retrieve die cuts.

The authors were tasked with improving the ergonomic design of an air filter assembly station. The current assembly station's workflow is shown in Fig. 1. Employees at the station reach up and behind to retrieve die-cut air filter frames, then pass the frames through a glue machine before sending them to the next station. A female assembler with a stature of 58″ reported pain in her right shoulder, and the post-incident ergonomics assessment – as seen in Appendix A – revealed that she was overextending her arm as the production table, which is 36″ tall, was too tall and too wide for her stature. There are several limiting factors for the redesign owing to the existing layout of the facility and the client's wishes. Limitations include requiring all non-permanent additions – steps, stools, etc. – to be easily stored when not in use, the table on which the glue machine sits cannot be adjusted, and the process will not be automated despite its repetitiveness.

Improving the ergonomics of this work cell is of interest to the authors as this is an avenue to apply state-of-the-art research in an industrial setting and the recommendations will help reduce injuries in the workplace. The technical assistance provided will culminate in the increased competitiveness of the manufacturing enterprise and a higher employee satisfaction index in the production department.

2   Literature Review

2.1   Trend and Source Analyses

The primary databases used during this study are Scopus and Web of Science. The two databases source their information from different journals and are complementary to one another. Using multiple databases allows us to gain a better understanding of the problem and offer viable and sensible solutions. The search terms used are "industrial ergonomics" and "manufacturing", which yielded 935 results in Scopus and 2,113 results in Web of Science.

Information from the two databases is used to study how often researchers studied industrial ergonomics in manufacturing environments throughout the years. The oldest entry found on Scopus is from 1958, and the oldest entry found on Web of Science is from 1989. Only sources published after 1990 are included in this analysis as material published before that may not reflect the current consensus within the scientific community on industrial ergonomics.

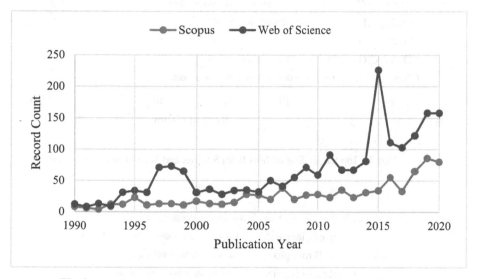

Fig. 2. Number of publications per year from Scopus and Web of Science

Figure 2 shows a general upward trend in the number of publications on the topic of industrial ergonomics in manufacturing within the last three decades. There are two notable increases in the number of publications found in the Web of Science data between 1997–99 and 2015. A similar, albeit less significant, year of growth in 2015 is also reflected in the data from Scopus. Industrial ergonomics is considered an emerging field as the number of articles published more than doubled – from 114 to 238 – between 2011 and 2020.

The data from Scopus and Web of Science is aggregated to identify the authors and institutions with the highest number of publications. Out of the 4,679 authors and 1,585 institutions, there are only a few that made significant contributions to the understanding of ergonomics in manufacturing. The top ten leading authors and institutions are shown in Fig. 3 and Fig. 4 respectively.

Of the top ten leading authors, six of them are based in the United States. Two of them – Peruzzini and Pellicciari – are based in Italy, and the remaining two – Neumann and Chan – are based in Canada and Hong Kong respectively. The United States has the most representation within the top ten leading institutions with four. The remaining institutions featured are from Taiwan, Sweden, China, the United Kingdom, Canada, and Hong Kong.

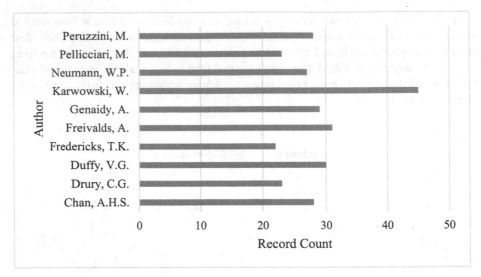

Fig. 3. Top ten leading authors from Scopus and Web of Science

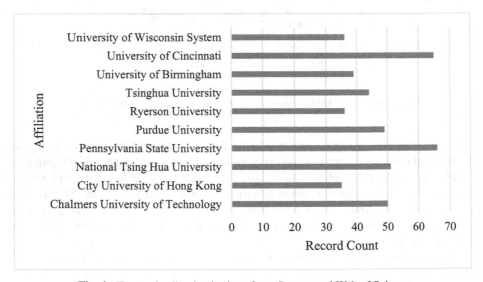

Fig. 4. Top ten leading institutions from Scopus and Web of Science

Source analysis is used to identify high-impact authors, and two publications – Genaidy et al. 1999 and Tuncel et al. 2008 via leading authors and leading institutions respectively – were identified using this approach. This process enables a more refined analysis beyond the capability of lexical search.

2.2   Co-citation and Co-authorship Analyses

Co-citation analysis was used to determine the relatedness of the documents from Web of Science based on the number of times they were cited together. Sources that were often cited together – connected with lines – suggest they are complimentary with one another. The 2,113 documents from Web of Science have a total of 45,842 cited references, and the 27 articles that have a minimum of 20 citations are visualized below in Fig. 5.

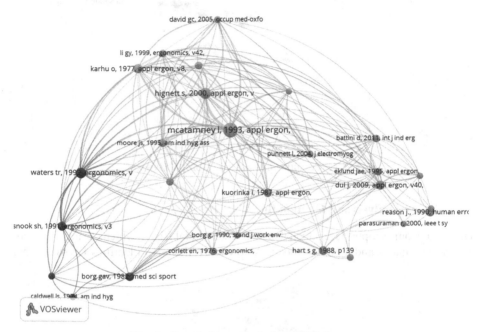

Fig. 5. Co-citation analysis from VOSviewer

Co-authorship analysis looks at the relatedness of documents through their authors based on the number of documents they have co-authored together. This information can be used to assess contribution trends within industrial ergonomics and supplement the source analysis in Sect. 2.1. Of the 4,921 authors whose work can be found on Web of Science, 379 of them have authored a minimum of three documents. The largest set of connected authors contains 60 names, and is shown in Fig. 6.

Co-citation and co-authorship analyses were used to identify seminal works that were often referenced by other authors and leading authors on industrial ergonomics. Two publications – Dul and Neumann 2009 from co-citation analysis and Kong et al. 2006 from co-authorship analysis – were identified as important texts due to their high impact and their high relevancy to the analysis detailed by this paper.

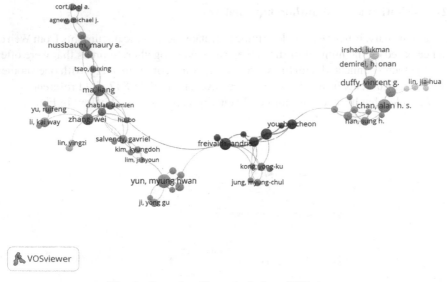

Fig. 6. Co-authorship analysis from VOSviewer

2.3   Cluster Analysis and Citation Burst

The data from Scopus is evaluated using cluster analysis – which results in a co-occurrence map – and a citation burst. A co-occurrence map identifies keywords that

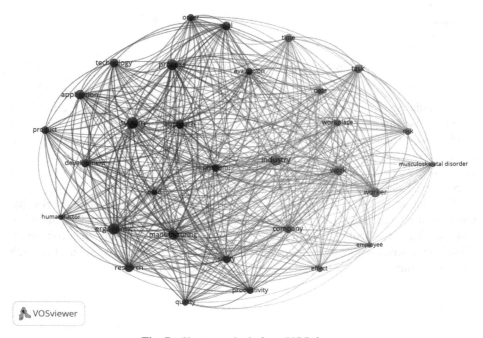

Fig. 7. Cluster analysis from VOSviewer

appear in articles' titles and abstracts, and how often they appear in conjunction. Of the 19,958 terms found, 36 of them appeared a minimum of 75 times. Eliminating words that do not add significant values – study, research, etc. – results in the slightly smaller cluster shown in Fig. 7.

Citation bursts detect whether a certain publication is associated with a surge of citations, which will suggest that the article has attracted significant interest from research communities. The top ten articles with the highest burst strength are all less than ten years old at the time of writing, and the longest bursts found lasted for four years. The citation burst is shown in Fig. 8, and the parameters used are listed in Table 1.

Table 1. Parameters for the Citation Burst

$f(x) = \alpha e^{-\alpha x}, \alpha_1/\alpha_0$	0.5
α_i/α_{i-1}	0.5
The number of states	2
$\gamma[0, 1]$	0.375
Minimum duration	2

References	Year	Strength	Begin	End	2016 - 2019
Caputo F, 2017, A preventive ergonomic approach based on virtual and immersive reality @ A preventive ergonomic approach based on virtual and immersive reality @ , V0, P0	2017	1.13	**2017**	2019	▬▬
Merletti R, 2016, Surface Electromyography, V0, P0	2016	0.75	**2016**	2019	▬▬▬
Arezes PM, 2015, Workplace ergonomics in lean production environments, V52, P57-70	2015	0.75	**2016**	2019	▬▬▬
Rashedi E, 2016, Cycle time influences the development of muscle fatigue at low to moderate levels of intermittent muscle contraction @ J Electromyogr Kinesiol, V28, P37-45	2016	0.75	**2016**	2019	▬▬▬
Battini D, 2015, Assembly line balancing with ergonomics paradigms, V48, P586-591	2015	0.75	**2016**	2019	▬▬▬
Wilson JR, 2014, Fundamentals of systems ergonomics/human factors @ Appl Ergon, V45, P5-13	2014	0.75	**2016**	2019	▬▬▬
Spada S, 2015, FCA ergonomics approach in developing new cars, V0, P0	2015	0.75	**2016**	2019	▬▬▬
Vignais N, 2017, Physical risk factors identification based on body sensor network combined to videotaping @ Appl Ergon, V65, P410-417	2017	0.75	**2017**	2019	▬▬
Grosse EH, 2015, Incorporating human factors in order picking planning models, V53, P695-717	2015	0.65	**2016**	2017	▬▬
Vignais N, 2013, Innovative system for real-time ergonomic feedback in industrial manufacturing @ Appl Ergon, V44, P566-574	2013	0.65	**2016**	2017	▬▬

Fig. 8. Top ten references with the strongest citation bursts from CiteSpace

Citation burst is used to identify high-impact publications, and one publication – Rashedi and Nussbaum 2016 – was identified during this analysis. The publications identified by the bibliometric analysis in this section are then supplemented with sources found using lexical search. The keywords found in the co-occurrence map are associated with two publications – Larson 2012 and Choobineh et al. 2021 – which were found through lexical searches on Web of Science.

2.4   Survey of Existing Literature

The sources identified in Sects. 2.1 through 2.3 suggest that industrial ergonomics in manufacturing is both a human factors problem and a business problem. Therefore, any proposed solutions must satisfy the needs of both parties and be determined after consulting all stakeholders. The cost associated with work-related musculoskeletal disorders – WMSDs – was estimated to be $13 billion to $54 billion annually, and more than 20% of those cases occur in manufacturing despite employing only 14% of the workforce. The two sources responsible for WMSDs are the elements of the work system – physical and nonphysical – and the capacity of the individual [2]. Both sources can be targeted by human factors practitioners to reduce the disparity between individual capacity and the work system.

Risk factors for WMSDs include repetitive wrist movements, awkward hand postures, and highly dynamic wrist motions. As arm and shoulder muscles are used to rotate the forearm and hand, the damages are often manifested in the form of soft tissue injuries in those areas [3]. For hand-intensive tasks, large and repeated tendon forces can be a contributing factor in tendon disorder even with relatively low applied force. The tendon forces were, on average, three times larger than the applied forces in pinches and power grips [3]. The larger forces experienced by the tendon may seem trivial at first, but repeated exposure can lead to pain in the arms and shoulders.

Reduction in localized muscle fatigue also helps minimize the risks of WMSDs. Improper working posture and sustained muscle contraction have been shown to cause soft tissue injuries if muscle fatigue is not properly alleviated. Higher exertion levels and duty cycles have been linked to higher rates of muscle fatigue and decreased endurance time [4]. The reduction in productivity can be minimized by providing tasks with shorter cycle times. The shortened cycle time is associated with lower rates of perceived discomfort and smaller force fluctuations due to the larger magnitude of task variation. Variations in biomechanical exposure are effective interventions for decreasing movement similarity in movements with high levels of repetition [4]. Work restructuring intended for lowering cycle time must take workplace-specific needs into account, and any intervention should be based on addressing those needs.

A successful ergonomics program should align with and supports a company's business strategy. While reducing musculoskeletal disorders can promote employee well-being as an application for ergonomics, it can also be used to increase operating efficiency and optimize human-system performance [5]. Training workshops, participatory ergonomics, and workstation redesign are often effective at facilitating long-term improvements to the workplace's ergonomics. For workers, ergonomics should be viewed not only as a science but also as a technological tool for solving workplace problems [6]. This view on ergonomics must be built upon a high level of awareness of its importance and an understanding that it should be applied to their subsystem.

A work system consists of a set of interlinked parts or processes that cannot be divided into independent processes. When optimizing a work system's performance, it must "simultaneously be optimized through its three components—the organization, the process, and the worker" [7]. If processes – die-cut retrieval, glue application, etc. – are evaluated and optimized individually rather than as a system, they tend to lose their ability to carry out their defining functions as their total identity is lost. As people commit more easily to changes that they help create, any proposed solutions should take the employees' recommendations and preferences into account [7]. Formalizing employee-initiated workplace improvement solutions can result in enhanced interpersonal relations, personal development, and a sense of contribution.

The limited integration of ergonomists into a company's structure results in ergonomics being considered too late in the design process. This timeline limits the potential for ergonomists' ability to make positive contributions to the design as any design changes will be a time-consuming and costly endeavor [8]. Ergonomists have a crucial role in developing possible links between ergonomics and the company's strategies, justifying those links, and communicating the links to business stakeholders [8]. When upgrading an existing design, the number of options available to ergonomists may be limited due to factors outside of their control. In this scenario, the company may wish to opt for incremental upgrades that are viable and sensible rather than major changes that come with significant time and financial commitment.

3 Procedure and Results

The air filter assembly work cell in this study is not optimized based on ergonomics principles. The post-injury investigation was performed by a safety evaluator, and they identified several serious shortcomings in the existing work cell design. An excerpt of that report is provided in Table 2.

Table 2. Problems identified during the ergonomic assessment

Category	Problem
Workstation heights	Work is not performed at appropriate heights
	Nearby work heights not in close relationship with one other
Posture	Standing in one position for long periods
Hand and wrist	Deviation from neutral wrist position
	Excessive wrist or hand repetitions
Arm	Elbows forced away from the body
	Excessive arm repetition
	Excessive pushing/pulling force on the arm
Back	Excessive repetitive back motions
	Excessive twisting

There are several proposed solutions to improve the existing work cell for shorter employees. As the table cannot be lowered, the improvement efforts will be focused on raising the employee's position. The evaluators' recommendations and comments – shown in Table 3 – will be used as a basis to identify potential solutions.

The recommendations and comments provide several potential solutions that require changing elements of the work system and the capacity of the individual through material

Table 3. Recommendations and comments from the evaluator

Recommendations	Comments
Provide an adjustable platform or stand	Modify a platform for the employee to stand on
Provide an anti-fatigue mat	
Add a footrest or stand	Some of the table widths are too wide and that creates [a need] for the employee to reach even farther
Improve layout to minimize bending wrists	
Change work heights	
Minimize twisting by moving feet to turn	Eliminate the need to throw die cuts

and nonmaterial means. Other solutions that were implemented by third parties were also identified through lexical search. All proposed solutions will utilize commercial off-the-shelf products that require little to no modification before being used by the production department. This allows for easy replacement if they are damaged in service or when they exceed their service life. Additionally, options that are lower cost and quicker to install are preferred over those that require significant modification to the existing production line structure.

Providing an adjustable platform or stand will reduce the height difference between the production table and the employee's natural arm positions. The introduction of anti-fatigue mats and footrest/stand can help reduce the stress experienced by joints during extended periods of standing. Additionally, a stool with back support can be placed in the work cell to reduce the amount of time the employee spends standing. Body measurement charts can be used to determine the optimal stool and footrest height for each employee, but they should still have the autonomy to determine what height suits them best [1]. The results of these efforts are a changed work height and improved ergonomics in the work cell.

The current work cell layout requires the employee to reach back and twist to pick up die cuts. This increases strain on the wrists, waist, and shoulder, and repeated exposure without adequate rest times in between increases the risks of cumulative trauma disorder significantly [9]. Changing the workflow to eliminate the need to throw die cuts after the glue is applied is recommended, as this process caused the pain experienced by the employee. The excessive forces experienced by the tendon when throwing die-cuts can cause a myriad of cumulative trauma, such as carpal tunnel syndrome and tendinitis [10]. The work cell can be reorganized such that the employee's twist angle between the die cuts and the glue machine is minimized. An alternative approach is to place the die cuts above or below the glue machine rather than behind it, which eliminates the need for the employee to twist their torso when retrieving die cuts.

If the employee is standing at a height suitable to their posture, they should not need to reach excessively to perform all their job functions. As the existing production table is unlikely to be replaced, reorganizing the table to ensure all functions – die cuts, the glue machine, and the downstream process – is easily reachable would be a viable approach. Another approach would be to use a conveyor belt to deliver the die cuts to the assembler rather than having them turn around to retrieve them. A conveyor belt could also be installed to eliminate the need to throw die cuts toward the downstream process. If conveyors are installed, they may create additional hazards such as falling material and elevate the risks for neck tension syndrome [9, 10]. The improved ergonomic design of the work cell will reduce the likelihood of soft tissue injuries caused by repeated motion and the costs of workplace injuries despite the implementation cost.

4   Discussion

There are three primary problems with the current layout of the work cell. The first problem is with the employee's standing height being too low in comparison with the production table. The second problem is related to the need for the employee to deviate from recommended postures and twist an excessive amount to retrieve die cuts. The third problem is that the employee is forced to throw die cuts towards the downstream process as they cannot comfortably reach other processes owing to the table's width. A secondary problem raised during the ergonomic evaluation pertains to the employee being required to stand in one position for long periods, which leads to fatigue. The assemblers' have ten-hour long shifts, and they are standing for most of those times. The four-day workweek provides some time for the assemblers to recover between days, but recovery times are often inadequate for front-line workers [6].

To reduce the height incompatibility between employees and the fixed production table and their need to stand for extended periods, it is recommended that height-adjustable swivel shop stools with backrests be made available to the employees. The price of a shop stool from online retailers range between $60 to $300 depending on quality and material, and they are also available at home improvement store at comparable prices. A work stool is selected over the other proposed solutions such as adjustable platforms and anti-fatigue mats as they only address one problem at a time, whereas the stool addresses the height, posture, and fatigue problems at once. An anti-fatigue mat can cost between $20 and $200 from online retailers, and an adjustable work platform from online retailers ranges between $100 and $300. The solution enables a more cost-effective and unified performance optimization that also limits the risk of work system incapacitation due to previously unrecognized interactions [7].

Poor workspace design can lead to the need for employees needing to twist excessively to reach parts or processes. The current work cell design requires the employee to reach up and behind to grab a die-cut, which places undue stress on their shoulder and back. To alleviate that, it is recommended that the die-cut be placed in a new location in which the employee can simply swivel the work stool to retrieve them without the need of reaching up. The angle between the two should be within 90 degrees, but within 180 degrees – i.e., not reaching behind – is also acceptable [11, 12]. The recommended distances and angles can be found in Fig. 9. This is preferred over placing the die-cut above or under the glue machine as this approach will create challenges associated with refilling the stock and the potential for soft tissue injuries caused by the need to reach inappropriate angles.

The need for the employee to throw die-cuts can be eliminated by changing the arrangement between the glue station and the downstream process. The elevated employee position provided by the stool will widen the reach of the employee, but the

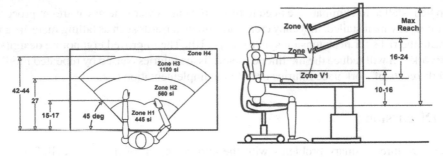

Fig. 9. Recommended reach zones and limits in inches (Harris 2018)

production table is still too wide for them to reach other processes comfortably, which creates additional ergonomic risk factors for the assemblers' forearms [10]. Moving the downstream process next to the gluing station rather than across the production table eliminates the need to throw die cuts, and this is preferred over installing a conveyor belt connecting the two processes. The conveyor belt can create additional risks for the assemblers, and their high cost – starting at $1,500 – makes this solution less desirable. The lower cost associated with process rearrangement means the capital can be used for other projects, such as studying the feasibility of using automation to replace the more monotonous tasks in the production department.

There are limitations to this analysis and the recommendation made, namely that the evaluations are primarily qualitative rather than quantitative due to the insufficient data available. Additionally, the study is limited in scope as only the stature of one employee was considered rather than all employees who may be utilizing the work cell. All benchmark products used to determine the cost and benefit associated with the options are listed in Appendix B. However, those products only represent a subset of all commercially available options available. Other vendors may offer more competitive prices when ordered in bulk which may sway the decision toward a solution not selected by the authors.

5   Conclusion and Future Work

The current work cell design at the gluing station did not consider the ergonomic impact it has on the employees during its design phase. There are several problems with the existing design. Shorter employees are standing too low for the production table as it is not adjustable, and they must twist their bodies and reach behind for a die-cut. Additionally, the assemblers are forced to throw die cuts toward the downstream process as they cannot reach it comfortably. This repetitive motion creates problems with soft tissue injuries, and it is exacerbated by the need for employees to stand for most of their ten-hour shifts.

The authors recommend providing height-adjustable swivel shop stools with backrests to the employees to eliminate height incompatibility, the need to twist their body to retrieve die cuts, and the need to stand for extended periods. Additionally, the authors recommend reorganizing the processes such that all materials required at the gluing station – die cuts, the glue machine, and the downstream process – are all within easy reach of the assembler. The reorganized process will eliminate the need for the assemblers to throw die cuts towards the downstream process and prevent cumulative trauma disorder caused by the forces exerted by the glued die cuts. These two recommendations are the most cost effective and viable solution based on the information available as it addresses all the identified problems without the need for significant capital investment. All the forgone solutions either failed to address the problem holistically or involve significant capital investment.

Industrial ergonomics in manufacturing settings is a topic that is still actively studied by researchers. As Industry 4.0 becomes more prevalent in manufacturing environments, researchers are focusing on designing tools and technologies that facilitate the transition without the need to halt operations. Offering tools to evaluate the ergonomic design of workstations and assembly lines will have tremendous impacts on employees' well-being and increase productivity [13]. Digital human modeling is also a viable approach as potential solutions can be modeled and tested before adoption. After the initial implementation of the proposed solutions, the safety evaluator should conduct further investigation to determine whether the implemented solutions have achieved their stated goals. If the solutions are performing as expected, it is recommended that they be adopted by other work cells as similar ergonomic shortcomings may also be present in other processes.

Appendix A: Ergonomics Report

Ergonomic Analysis / Observation Summary:
(Attach the completed analysis or observation form to this summary)

Employee Name: _____ Date: 6/15/2021

Plant/ Facility: L. _____ Department: Production

Job Title: Assembler _____ Machine: _____

Analysis Type: ☐ RULA   ☐ REBA   ☑ Observation   SAFETY TECH Signature:
SCORE: ____   ____   ____   _____

Define/List and provide details:
Explain all the Ergonomic Factors, Findings, of the Analysis or Observation:

Restrictions from Doctor: Employee is not to use Right Arm to twist or lift.

How has this injury possible:
She has been working here a few years and always an assembler. The repetitive motion may be one factor. She is a very short women, the tables we use cause her to lift her right arm up and then rotate her shoulder so as to move her arm up and back to grab die cuts.

On returning to work with restrictions:
Current assignment is making 2 piece filters and she only puts down the media and locks the frame in place and then reach's out to smooth the sides to help join the top of the frame to the bottom.

She is too short and is still extending her arm because the table is to tall and to wide for her. She reports moderate pain in her right arm and shoulder.

Recommendations: Changes to the JOB   Changes to the Employee
List all necessary changes and equipment to be added or modified:

She needs a platform. This will stop or reduce the reaching up motion if she is raised up. Additionally when stretching out, if she is raised up she will not need to stretch as far.

ERGONOMICS ASSESSMENT WORKSHEET

NAME: _C_   ATE: _6/15/2021_   EVALUATOR: _l_

DEPARTMENT: _Production_   LOCATION: _Manual 1_   SHIFT: _1st_

JOB / POSITION: _Assembler_   LENGTH OF TIME AT CURRENT POSITION: _10 hrs_

HOURS PERFORMING THIS JOB: DAILY: _10 hrs_   WEEKLY: _40 hours_

OTHER TASKS: _N/A_

HEIGHT: _5"0_   WEIGHT: _____   MALE / (FEMALE)   DOMINANT HAND: LEFT (RIGHT)

1. WORKSTATION HEIGHTS		RECOMMNDATIONS	COMMENTS
1a. Is work performed at appropriate heights?	Yes (No)	1aa. Adjust work height to _____ cm (1ab.) Provide an adjustable platform or stand 1ac. Provide an adjustable chair or stool	I recommend to modify a platform for the employee to stand on?
1b. Are nearby work heights in close relationship with each other?	Yes (No)	1ba. Align work heights to a most appropriate level of _____ cm 1bb. Align work heights to match a common work height of _____ cm	
1c. Are long or awkward reaches minimized?	(Yes) No	1ca. Move frequently used items within _____ cm 1cb. Remove less frequently used items 1cc. Eliminate obstacles 1cd. Tilt work surface 1ce. Use a Lazy Susan 1cf. Provide a cut-out	Some of the tables width are too wide and that creates for the employee to reach even farther
1d. Is the worker free from having to lean on edges?	(Yes) No	1da. Pad edges 1db. Adjust work height to _____ cm 1dc. Provide an adjustable platform or stand 1dd. Tilt work surface	

ERGONOMICS ASSESSMENT - PAGE 1 OF 4
ErgoEval_general

ERGONOMICS ASSESSMENT WORKSHEET

	(No)	3eb. Anti-vibration gloves 3ec. Different tool	
3f. Excessive static load on hand/wrist?	Yes (No)	3fa. Provide fixture for holding part / tool 3fb. Different tool (3fc) Eliminate or change task	Not throw the die cut.
4. ARM		**RECOMMNDATIONS**	**COMMENTS**
4a. Elbows forced away from body?	(Yes) No	4aa. Tilt work surface 4ab. Bend tool handle or pistol grip 4ac. Use fixture to hold part / tool (4ad) Change work heights	
4b. Excessive arm repetitions?	(Yes) No	4ba. Use machine or automation 4bb. Use fixture to hold part / tool 4bc. Eliminate task	
4c. Excessive static load on arm?	Yes (No)	4ca. Mechanical assist 4cb. Use fixture to hold part / tool (4cc) Change work heights	
4d. Excessive pushing / pulling force on arm?	(Yes) No	4da. Advise workers to push loads rather than pull 4db. Optimize work heights for muscle efficiency 4db. Provide wheeled cart 4dc. Mechanical assist	
5. BACK		**RECOMMNDATIONS**	**COMMENTS**
5a. Excessive repetitive back motions?	(Yes) No	5aa. Increase weight lifted (reduce repetitions) (5ab) Change work heights 5ac. Change workstation layout 5ad. Use scissors lift or mechanical aid	

ERGONOMICS ASSESSMENT - PAGE 3 OF 4
ErgoEval_general

2. SITTING/STANDING POSTURE		RECOMMNDATIONS	COMMENTS
2a. Sitting in one position for long periods?	Yes No	2aa. Add a dynamic (moving), adjustable footrest 2ab. Properly adjust lumbar support on chair to height of _____ cm 2ac. Adjust chair pan height to _____ cm 2ad. Tilt seat pan downward to _____ cm 2ae. Provide adjustable, ergonomic 5-wheel chair 2af. Provide a sit-stand workstation	
2b. Standing in one position for long periods?	Yes No	2ba. Provide an anti-fatigue mat 2bb. Add a foot rest or stand 2bc. Have workers use cushioned insoles 2bd. Provide a sit-lean stand 2be. Provide an adjustable stool with foot rest 2bf. Provide a sit-stand workstation	

3. HAND & WRIST		RECOMMNDATIONS	COMMENTS
3a. Neutral wrist position?	Yes No	3aa. Improve layout to minimize bending wrists 3ab. Angled tool grip 3ac. Different tool	
3b. Excessive wrist or hand repetitions?	Yes No	3ba. Utilize power tool 3bb. Different tool 3bc. Automate	
3c. Excessive grasping force?	Yes No	3ca. Improved tool grip 3cb. Grip wrap 3cc. Different tool 3cd. Gloves	
3d. Excessive pressure on palm?	Yes No	3da. Power tool 3db. Different tool 3dc. Angled tool grip	
3e. Excessive hand vibration?	Yes	3ea. Dampen vibration	

ERGONOMICS ASSESSMENT - PAGE 2 OF 4
ErgoEval_general

5b. Excessive lifting and / or carrying force required?	Yes No	5ba. Reduce weight lifted to _____ 5bb. Add another worker / lifter 5bc. Mechanical aid	
5c. Excessive pushing or pulling force required?	Yes No	5ca. Reduce weight to _____ 5cb. Advise to push loads rather than pull 5cc. Provide wheeled cart 5cd. Mechanical assist (jack or lift truck)	
5d. Excessive bending and awkward bending over postures?	Yes No	5da. Raise load off floor 5db. Place more often used items on middle shelves 5dc. Add handles to loads 5dd. Raise working heights to _____ 5de. Use mechanical aid (scissors or tilt load)	
5e. Excessive twisting?	Yes No	5ea. Minimize twisting by moving feet to turn 5eb. Change workstation layout 5ec. Reduce weight 5ed. Use mechanical aid	
OTHER		RECOMMNDATIONS	COMMENTS

Notes & Diagrams:

ERGONOMICS ASSESSMENT - PAGE 4 OF 4
ErgoEval_general

Appendix B: Selected Products From December 2021

Work Stool

Codnor Height Adjustable Lab stool, $63.99.

https://www.wayfair.com/furniture/pdp/orren-ellis-codnor-height-adjustable-lab-stool-
w003045331.html

Height Adjustable Industrial/Shop Stool, $299.99.

https://www.wayfair.com/furniture/pdp/interion-height-adjustable-industrialshop-
stool-w006720445.html

24 in. H x 16 in. W x 16 in. D Adjustable Shop Stool with Casters, $184.48.

https://www.homedepot.com/p/DEWALT-24-in-H-x-16-in-W-x-16-in-D-Adjustable-
Shop-Stool-with-Casters-DXSTAH025/304354683?

Masterforce Premium Shop Stool, $99.99.

https://www.menards.com/main/tools/automotive/automotive-tools-shop-equipment/
masterforce-reg-premium-shop-stool/85666/p-1558679410415-c-9113.htm?tid=768
1347647667512892&ipos=2

Anti-fatigue Mat

Office Fitness Ninjas' Best Standing Desk Mats for 2021, starting at $16.00.

https://www.workwhilewalking.com/best-standing-mat-reviews

New York Times' The Best Standing Desk Mats, starting at $28.00.

https://www.nytimes.com/wirecutter/reviews/best-standing-desk-mat/

Work Platform

Factory Supply Adjustable Work Platform, starting at $210.24.

https://www.factorysupply.com/product-category/rolling-ladders-platforms/industrial-
step-stools/adjustable-work-platform-industrial-step-stools/

Grainger Work Platforms, starting at $45.46.

https://www.grainger.com/category/material-handling/access-ladders-platforms-scaffo
lding/work-platforms

Conveyor

A-Lined Belt Conveyors, starting at $1,570.00.

https://a-lined.com/products/belt-incline-conveyors/

FloStor Hytrol Conveyor, starting at $1,980.00.

https://www.flostor.com/conveyor/FLOSTOR-hytrol-conveyor-price-estimates.pdf

References

1. Spath, D., Braun, M., Meinken, K.: Human factors in manufacturing. In: Salvendy, G. (ed.) Handbook of Human Factors and Ergonomics, pp. 1643–1666. John Wiley & Sons Inc, Hoboken, NJ (2012)
2. Tuncel, S., et al.: Research to practice: Effectiveness of controlled workplace interventions to reduce musculoskeletal disorders in the manufacturing environment—critical appraisal and meta-analysis. Hum. Factors Ergon. Manufact. **18**, 93–124 (2008)
3. Kong, Y., Jang, H., Freivalds, A.: Wrist and tendon dynamics as contributory risk factors in work-related musculoskeletal disorders. Hum. Factors Ergon, Manuf. **16**, 83–105 (2006)
4. Rashedi, E., Nussbaum, M.A.: Cycle time influences the development of muscle fatigue at low to moderate levels of intermittent muscle contraction. J. Electromyogr. Kinesiol. **28**, 37–45 (2016)
5. Larson, N.L.J.: Corporate ergonomics: it's musculoskeletal disorder management and system optimization. Ergon. Des.: The Quart. Hum. Factors Appl. **20**, 29–33 (2012)
6. Choobineh, A., et al.: A multilayered ergonomic intervention program on reducing musculoskeletal disorders in an industrial complex: a dynamic participatory approach. Int. J. Ind. Ergon. **86**, 103221 (2021)
7. Genaidy, A., Karwowski, W., Christensen, D.: Principles of work system performance optimization: a business ergonomics approach. Hum. Factors Ergon. Manuf. **9**, 105–128 (1999)
8. Dul, J., Neumann, W.P.: Ergonomics contributions to company strategies. Appl. Ergon. **40**, 745–752 (2009)
9. Rodrick, D., Karwowski, W., Marras, W.S.: Work-related upper extremity musculoskeletal disorders. In: Salvendy, G. (ed.) Handbook of Human Factors and Ergonomics, pp. 826–867. John Wiley & Sons Inc, Hoboken, NJ (2012)
10. Brauer, R.L.: Safety and Health for Engineers. John Wiley & Sons Inc., Hoboken, NJ (2016)
11. Harris, C.: 2-Minute Guide to Workplace Ergonomics (2018). https://www.treston.us/blog/2-minute-guide-workplace-ergonomics
12. Canadian Centre for Occupational Health and Safety: Working in a Sitting Position - Basic Requirements (2018). https://www.ccohs.ca/oshanswers/ergonomics/sitting/sitting_basic.html
13. Hsieh, S.-J.: NSF Award Abstract # 2026615 FW-HTF-P: Design of Tools and Technologies for Industry 4.0 Manufacturing Work (2020). https://www.nsf.gov/awardsearch/showAward?AWD_ID=2026615&HistoricalAwards=false

Review and Assessment of Excavator Operations Using RAMSIS Ergonomic Engineering Software

Andrea Mansfeld[1], Andre Luebke[2], and Vincent G. Duffy[1(✉)]

[1] Purdue University, West Lafayette, IN 47907, USA
{amansfel,duffy}@purdue.edu
[2] Human Solutions of North America, Morrisville, NC 27560, USA
aluebke@human-solutions.com

Abstract. Excavators are utilized for a wide variety of construction jobs and tasks that require moving large amounts of material. Excavator operation involves driving, manning controls, and ensuring the safety of the machine, the operator, and surrounding people and equipment. The cab of an excavator should be designed to facilitate comfort for a variety of operator body types for the tasks necessary for operation. The study brought forth in this paper uses RAMSIS ergonomic modeling software to assess various excavator operations concerning different body types. The operations assessed are driving, digging, touch screen operation, and use of controls. The differences in body type are modeled by creating a diverse sample of manikins that encompass differences along the spectrum of height and weight. Comfort, reachability, and visibility analysis were completed to optimize excavator cab design for each operator type. A literature review of research in autonomous vehicles was also conducted.

Keywords: Ergonomics · Excavator · Controls · Driving · Reachability · Visibility RAMSIS · Autonomous Vehicles

1 Introduction and Background to Excavator Operation

The following excerpt is from my Project 1 report:

"Excavators are utilized for a variety of projects that require digging into the earth and moving large quantities of matter. For example, construction projects need excavator machines to dig building foundations. Excavators are operated by a human that sits in the cab area and manually controls the movement of the vehicle and the machine arm via and steering wheel and controls. Figure 1 shows an excavator in action.

It is important to design the cab of an excavator to comfortably allow a wide variety of people to operate the machine safely and efficiently.

Statement of Project 1 Objectives. The RAMSIS software will allow the designer to model the placement of manikins for a variety of excavator tasks and assess the ergonomics of the design. RAMSIS will be used to identify the best conditions for excavator driving, digging, touchpad, and controls operation.

V. G. Duffy and P.-L. P. Rau (Eds.): HCII 2022, LNCS 13522, pp. 275–295, 2022.
https://doi.org/10.1007/978-3-031-21704-3_18

Fig. 1. A human being moving dirt with an excavator [1]."

2   Review in Literature Regarding the Ergonomics of Autonomous Vehicles

The rise of autonomous vehicles is becoming mainstream as they are being designed and manufactured with more sensors that can understand their surroundings. Furthermore, sophisticated algorithms have been developed to give vehicles full autonomy, allowing them to make decisions about how they should behave on the road and in dire situations.

This topic directly relates to the human-machine interaction and the ergonomics of the system. For example, the way truckers drive trucks across the United States is shifting as more functions become automatic. Some trucking cabs are designed to let the driver take a few hours of sleep while the vehicle still makes its way to the destination. In the consumer world, electric vehicles manufactured by Tesla have the option for the user to purchase a complete self-driving option. Although it is not advisable to fall asleep while driving one of these vehicles, the car can make driving decisions with minimal driver input and will even pull over if it senses that the driver has fallen asleep.

There have been many research studies into the area of vehicle autonomy, from technological advancements in artificial intelligence and automobile engineering to ethics and social impact. The following literary review consists of three different approaches to understanding the realm of works in the topic of autonomous vehicles and their impact on society.

2.1   Demo #3

A preliminary review of the literature was done using the Harzing software, VOS Viewer, and Word Cloud (Demo#3). Using the Google Scholar source option, I input keywords "ergonomics" and "automobiles" and a year range of 2017 to 2021. The maximum number of results was set to 50 to cut down processing time. The results are shown in Fig. 2.

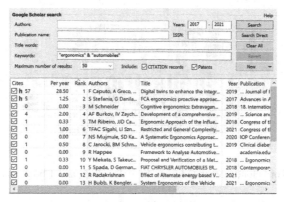

Fig. 2. Results for keywords "ergonomics" and "automobiles" on Google Scholar between the years 2017 and 2021.

Using this method, an article of interest was discovered that discusses the prominent collide between ethics and safety [2]. The analysis of the article is displayed in Fig. 3.

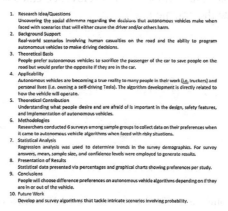

Fig. 3. 10 step analysis of "The social dilemma of autonomous vehicles" by Bonnefon, Jean-François, Azim Shariff, and Iyad Rahwan.

A word cloud generated from MAXQDA was created to understand the scope between 1 article from Google Scholar [2], 1 article from SpringerLink [3], one article from ResearchGate [4], Chapter 59 from the handbook [5], and a paper on bibliometric analysis [6]. Common words such as "the" and "a" were deleted from the word cloud. The words shown in Fig. 4 have at least 20 occurrences between the 5 sources.

Across all sources, consideration of the pedestrian is a common theme. This makes sense since in many cases with autonomous driving, many critical decisions involve the safety of the passengers inside and pedestrians around the vehicle exterior.

Fig. 4. Word clouds generated from 4 articles [2–5] and 1 book chapter [6].

2.2 Demo #4

Using the Web of Science, the keyword phrase "autonomous vehicles" was searched and 100 records containing the author, title, source, and abstract were exported into a.txt file. This file was uploaded to the VOS software. The settings were adjusted to encompass the title and abstract in the analysis and a threshold of at least 10 occurrences was chosen. 25 words met this threshold. Furthermore, with a relevance calculation of 60%, 15 words were chosen to generate the graphic in Fig. 5.

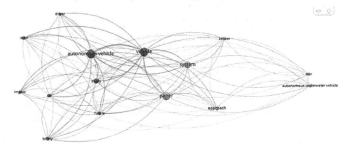

Fig. 5. VOS graphic of common word occurrences between 100 articles on autonomous vehicles.

This analysis shows that many articles address autonomous underwater vehicles, or AUVs, as well.

The methodologies for the literature review shown in this article are adapted from [7] and [8]. A co-citation analysis was performed using a similar method. In the Web of Science, "autonomous vehicles" was searched and 100 article Authors, Titles, and Abstracts were exported to a text file. This file was imported into VOS under the option "Read data from bibliographic database files". The type of analysis performed was co-authorship with authors as a unit, full counting, and a minimum number of documents set to 5. This yielded 11 results of 3,107 authors. When creating the graphic in Fig. 6, note that the largest cluster that could be generated was between 4 authors.

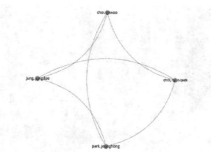

Fig. 6. VOS graphic of co-citation analysis between 100 articles on autonomous vehicles.

2.3 Demo #7

A search was performed on the National Science Foundation's (NSF) under the award tab for the keywords "ergonomics autonomous vehicles". The results of this search are shown in Fig. 7. Most awards fall into the $100k - $500k range, with some outliers.

Fig. 7. NSF awarded research under "ergonomics autonomous vehicles."

The first article on the list related to human digital modeling is titled: "Modeling Cyber Transportation and Human Interaction in Connected and Autonomous Vehicles." With the rising popularity and technical development surrounding artificial intelligence and machine learning/vision, modeling aspects of human and autonomous vehicle interaction will help design the cars and transportation vessels for the future.

3   RAMSIS Scene and Manikin Development

The following excerpt is from my Project 1 report:

"RAMSIS is equipped with a plugin that allows for the assessment of the manikin-excavator interaction. The software and plugins were downloaded and the session, shown in Fig. 8, started.

To focus on the cab of the excavator, the external excavator components were hidden from sight. Components of the excavator cab were grouped in preparation for kinematic

Fig. 8. The excavator session started in RAMSIS."

adjustment. Using the group function in RAMSIS, the seat, the steering wheel, the joysticks, the armrest, the touchscreen, and the control panel were identified as individual groups that will be assessed later in this report. Figure 9 shows the working space and the designated groups.

Fig. 9. Groups designated in the software. Top Row: Seat, Armrests, Controls. Bottom Row: Steering Wheel, Touchpad, Joysticks.

3.1 Object Kinematics

The groups designated in Fig. 9 can be translated in the X, Y, and Z directions as well as rotated around any of these axes. The object and degrees of freedom type and range are designated via the Geometry → Define Kinematic operation. Figure 10 shows the kinematics defined for the steering wheel.

The values can be adjusted within the defined range. The optimal values will vary with manikin type since taller manikins may require more space for the steering wheel whereas shorter manikins will need the position of the steering wheel to be closer. This process of defining kinematics was done across all operations groups.

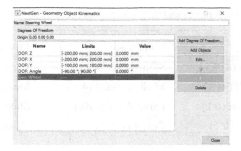

Fig. 10. Steering wheel geometry kinematics defined.

3.2 Boundary Manikins

Manikins were designed to optimize the ergonomics of the excavator cab for driving, digging, touchscreen, and controls tasks. The RAMSIS Body Builder plug-in provides software that allows the user to create manikins of unique dimensions. Utilizing this plug-in, 4 manikins were created. These manikins and their dimensions are shown in Fig. 11.

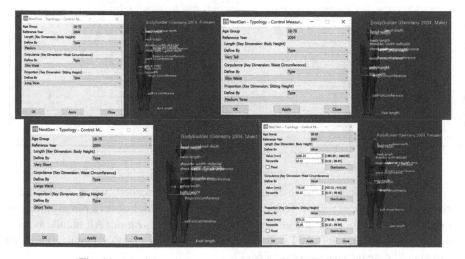

Fig. 11. Manikins were created using the Body Builder plug-in.

The manikins were personalized in height, waist size, and torso length. They have names, which will be used to denote them throughout this paper. Table 1 is a list of the manikins, body types, percentiles, and names. The body height, waist circumference, and sitting height were used as the percentile numbers for length, corpulence, and proportion, respectively.

Table 1. Manikin identities and their percentiles rounded to the nearest percent.

	Length	Corpulence	Proportion
Kyla	Medium (47%)	Slim Waist (14%)	Long Torso (74%)
Alex	Very Tall (94%)	Medium Waist (4%)	Medium Torso (88%)
Danny	Very Short (6%)	Large Waist (94%)	Short Torso (2%)
Andrea	Custom (10%)	Custom (70%)	Custom (29%)

Table 2 is a detailed list of their percentiles. These values can be identified by selecting "Body Dimensions" under the Analysis tab.

Table 2. Body dimensions (left number) and percentiles (right number) of created manikins.

Kyla Measurement	Value (mm)	%	Andrea Measurement	Value (mm)	%	Danny Measurement	Value (mm)	%	Alex Measurement	Value (mm)	%
body-height	1645.00	46.55	body-height	1600.20	10.41	body-height	1653.00	5.72	body-height	1885.00	94.09
sitting-height	893.00	74.21	sitting-height	870.00	29.08	sitting-height	843.00	1.72	sitting-height	970.00	87.66
head-height	201.00	40.60	head-height	201.07	38.29	head-height	212.00	21.88	head-height	227.00	72.96
head-width	143.00	33.94	head-width	144.67	60.20	head-width	154.00	56.42	head-width	150.00	32.27
head-depth	186.00	54.71	head-depth	182.70	27.03	head-depth	191.00	30.83	head-depth	200.00	76.54
neck-length	100.85	---	neck-length	95.66	---	neck-length	83.22	---	neck-length	104.85	---
shoulder-width-deltoidal	401.00	16.15	shoulder-width-deltoidal	419.97	55.17	shoulder-width-deltoidal	476.00	61.06	shoulder-width-deltoidal	433.00	7.67
upper-arm-length	289.00	30.56	upper-arm-length	286.33	20.23	upper-arm-length	318.00	32.66	upper-arm-length	344.00	83.06
forearm-length-with-hand	418.00	24.40	forearm-length-with-hand	411.58	13.75	forearm-length-with-hand	458.00	24.40	forearm-length-with-hand	490.00	79.63
forearm-circumference	226.00	19.02	forearm-circumference	238.12	60.91	forearm-circumference	283.00	62.34	forearm-circumference	255.00	11.90
chest-width	240.00	16.78	chest-width	254.07	53.83	chest-width	311.00	71.49	chest-width	263.00	6.48
chest-depth	166.00	20.82	chest-depth	180.59	66.21	chest-depth	256.00	92.53	chest-depth	180.00	9.92
waist-circumference	649.00	14.25	waist-circumference	736.60	69.60	waist-circumference	1073.00	94.54	waist-circumference	697.00	4.45
pelvis-width	267.00	21.55	pelvis-width	273.28	46.86	pelvis-width	306.00	71.92	pelvis-width	280.00	29.24
hip-width	350.00	20.02	hip-width	364.91	53.99	hip-width	376.00	72.72	hip-width	345.00	20.14
buttock-knee-length	560.00	15.25	buttock-knee-length	567.94	24.47	buttock-knee-length	605.00	35.19	buttock-knee-length	641.00	81.35
knee-height-sitting	496.00	27.50	knee-height-sitting	487.84	11.77	knee-height-sitting	537.00	18.66	knee-height-sitting	602.00	90.42
foot-height	71.00	50.54	foot-height	66.03	24.47	foot-height	72.00	30.32	foot-height	79.00	62.68
foot-length	237.00	25.23	foot-length	235.20	22.57	foot-length	259.00	26.41	foot-length	273.00	68.14
foot-width	90.00	32.05	foot-width	91.01	41.99	foot-width	100.00	41.36	foot-width	99.00	35.29
hand-length	173.00	33.23	hand-length	168.13	19.57	hand-length	185.00	24.73	hand-length	202.00	79.81
palm-length	100.00	35.60	palm-length	96.93	32.25	palm-length	109.00	30.94	palm-length	119.00	72.92
hand-breadth	74.98	34.34	hand-breadth	73.19	34.14	hand-breadth	85.97	36.29	hand-breadth	90.04	60.66
hand-depth	24.00	21.74	hand-depth	24.50	49.11	hand-depth	32.00	67.56	hand-depth	29.00	31.55
upperarm-circumference	266.00	19.69	upperarm-circumference	282.64	63.70	upperarm-circumference	336.00	62.34	upperarm-circumference	303.00	12.18
calf-circumference	346.00	27.00	calf-circumference	359.37	59.69	calf-circumference	395.00	76.85	calf-circumference	350.00	13.20
thigh-circumference	543.00	20.39	thigh-circumference	577.90	58.97	thigh-circumference	583.00	72.44	thigh-circumference	525.00	16.65

A diverse distribution of measurements is recommended when designing a workspace for a range of people. Kyla, Andrea, Danny, and Alex cover a range of heights and sizes and are a good sample group for ergonomic optimization. All manikins were created from the Germany 2004 option and designated as male or female. They are shown standing next to each other in Fig. 12.

The object properties of each manikin were toggled to include work shoes on their feet as well as to customize their hairstyles. It is important to note that the manikins were created without shoes to create skin contact points on their feet.

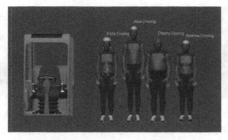

Fig. 12. Manikins Kyla, Alex, Danny, and Andrea lined up for comparison next to the excavator cab. They are identified as having the task of "Driving".

4 Tasks and Restrictions

Restrictions were applied on the manikins to get them into the correct posture for the following operations:

- Driving
- Digging
- Touchpad
- Controls

Target restrictions are created by selecting skin points on the manikin and skin points on the object that contact is desired with. Skin points are designated by little white stars. Figure 13 shows the restriction used to get the manikin "Kyla" to sit in the seat. Upon starting the posture calculation, Kyla was positioned in the seat.

Fig. 13. Positioning Kyla in the seat by creating a target restriction (left) and performing the posture calculation (right).

Another example in Fig. 14 is restricting Kyla's palm skin points to meet the contact points on the steering wheel, and implementing a manual grasping restriction to model holding the steering wheel.

This process of creating target restrictions, pelvis rotation, line-of-site direction, and manual grasping restrictions makes it possible to model the manikins' position for a variety of operations.

Table 3 shows the restrictions that were placed on the manikins to get them in place for each of the operations.

Fig. 14. Positioning Kyla's hands by creating target restrictions (left), completing the posture calculation (center), and implementing manual grasping restrictions (right).

Table 3. Restrictions for driving, digging, touchpad, and controls operations.

Driving Restrictions	Digging Restrictions
˅ Task	˅ Task
Direction: line-of-vision // T-C (-1.0 0.0 0.0) [active]	Direction: line-of-vision // T-C (-1.0 0.0 0.0) [active]
Manual Grasping: left // Grasp softly [active]	Manual Grasping: left // Grasp softly [active]
Manual Grasping: right // Grasp softly [active]	Manual Grasping: right // Grasp softly [active]
Pelvis Rotation: -//0.0//0.0 [active]	Pelvis Rotation: -//0.0//0.0 [inactive]
Target: H-Point // Surface // T(Off) [active]	Target: H-Point // Surface // T(Off) [active]
Target: hand5-sf-l // STW_L // T(Off) [active]	Target: hand5-sf-l-inwards // JSL // T(On) [active]
Target: hand5-sf-r // STW_R // T(Off) [active]	Target: hand5-sf-r-inwards // JSR // T(Off) [active]
Target: RightHeel // Surface_ // T(Off) [active]	Target: RightHeel // Surface_ // T(Off) [active]
Target: LeftHeel // Surface_ // T(Off) [active]	Target: LeftHeel // Surface_ // T(Off) [active]
Target: LeftBallOffset // Line_1 // T(Off) [active]	Target: LeftBallOffset // Line_1 // T(Off) [active]
Target: RightBallOffset // Line_3 // T(Off) [active]	Target: RightBallOffset // Line_3 // T(Off) [active]
Touchpad Restrictions	**Controls Restrictions**
˅ Task	˅ Task
Manual Grasping: right // Touch with index finger (horiz.)	Pelvis Rotation: -//0.0//0.0 [active]
Pelvis Rotation: -//0.0//0.0 [active]	Target: H-Point // Surface // T(Off) [active]
Target: H-Point // Surface // T(Off) [active]	Target: line-of-vision // Button // T(Off) [active]
Target: line-of-vision // Display_Face // T(Off) [active]	Target: indexfingertip-r // Button // T(Off) [active]
Target: indexfingertip-r // Touch // T(Off) [active]	Target: RightHeel // Surface_ // T(Off) [active]
Target: RightHeel // Surface_ // T(Off) [active]	Target: LeftHeel // Surface_ // T(Off) [active]
Target: LeftHeel // Surface_ // T(Off) [active]	Target: LeftBallOffset // Line_1 // T(Off) [active]
Target: LeftBallOffset // Line_1 // T(Off) [active]	Target: RightBallOffset // Line_3 // T(Off) [active]
Target: RightBallOffset // Line_3 // T(Off) [active]	

With the manikins in place, the cab can be optimized to provide maximum comfort, reachability, and visibility in the operation scenarios for each manikin.

4.1 Driving Operation

The driving restrictions were special copied from Kyla to the rest of the manikins, shown in Fig. 15.

Each manikin has its preference on cab design based on its body type. To accommodate this, the steering wheel group was shifted to provide optimized comfort for each manikin. For Danny and Alex, the shortest and tallest members of the group, the seat was also shifted to provide better comfort. The optimized driving positions are shown in Fig. 16.

The steering wheel assembly was adjusted to the values in Table 4 for each manikin accommodation.

Fig. 15. Comfort feeling analysis of unoptimized driving conditions for all manikins. These values are to be used as a reference.

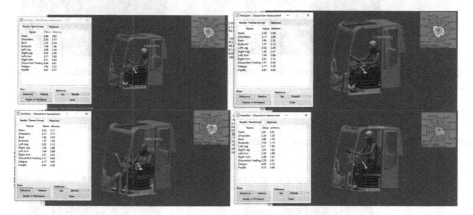

Fig. 16. Optimized driving positions via steering wheel adjustment.

Table 4. Optimal steering wheel adjustments in free space.

Manikin	X-Translation	Y-Translation	Z-Translation	Y-Rotation
Kyla	130 mm	0 mm	120 mm	20°
Danny*	140 mm	0 mm	150 mm	20°
Andrea	190 mm	0 mm	120 mm	20°
Alex**	0 mm	0 mm	250 mm	10°

* the seat was also lowered by 50 mm so that Danny's feet could comfortably touch and operate the pedals.

** the seat was also raised by 100 mm so that Alex's legs could comfortably fit inside of the cab.

4.2 Joystick Operation and Wrist Pad Usage

The restrictions for a digging operation were implemented and the comfort analysis was assessed for all the manikins to understand the current state of ergonomics in the cab for this operation. The manikins in the initial digging positions are shown in Fig. 17.

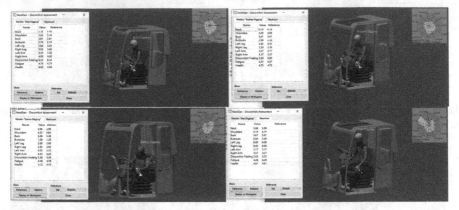

Fig. 17. Comfort feeling analysis of unoptimized digging conditions for all manikins. These values are to be used as a reference.

Optimizing the joystick position and the armrests, the manikins experienced greater comfort. The optimized positions are shown in Fig. 18.

Fig. 18. Optimized digging positions via joystick and armrest adjustments.

The joystick and armrest assembly were adjusted to the values in Table 5 for each manikin accommodation. The seat adjustments for Danny and Alex remain the same.

Table 5. Optimal joystick and armrest assembly adjustments in free space.

Joystick				
Manikin	X-Translation	Y-Translation	Z-Translation	Y-Rotation
Kyla	50 mm	40 mm	140 mm	0
Danny	0 mm	40 mm	120 mm	0
Andrea	50 mm	40 mm	100 mm	0
Alex	0 mm	0 mm	250 mm	0
Armrest				
Kyla	0 mm	120 mm	100 mm	0
Danny	0 mm	0 mm	0 mm	0
Andrea	0 mm	80 mm	120 mm	0
Alex	0 mm	-60 mm	300 mm	0

4.3   Touch Screen Operation

The restrictions for touch screen operation were implemented and the comfort analysis was assessed for all the manikins to understand the current state of ergonomics in the cab for this operation. To model touchscreen use, a skin point was created, circled in red, on the screen, shown in Fig. 19.

Fig. 19. Skin point created to model touch screen usage.

The manikins in the initial touchscreen-usage positions are shown in Fig. 20.

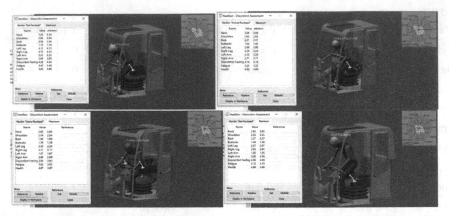

Fig. 20. Comfort feeling analysis of unoptimized touch screen conditions for all manikins. These values are to be used as a reference.

Most of the manikins need to stand up out of the seat to use the touch screen. The touchpad was adjusted to better suit the reachability of the manikins (Fig. 21). More information on the reachability analysis is discussed in a later section.

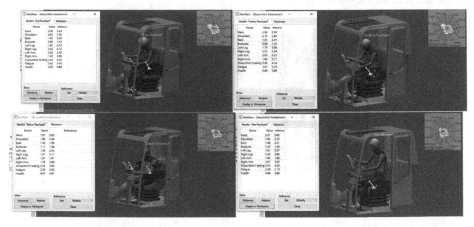

Fig. 21. Optimized touch screen positions via touchpad adjustment.

The touchpad was adjusted to the values in Table 6 for each manikin accommodation.

4.4 Controls Operation

The restrictions for controls operation were implemented and the comfort analysis was assessed for all the manikins to understand the current state of ergonomics in the cab for

Table 6. Optimal touchscreen assembly adjustments in free space.

Manikin	X-Translation	Y-Translation	Z-Translation	Y-Rotation
Kyla	300 mm	0 mm	300 mm	0°
Danny	300 mm	0 mm	300 mm	−15°
Andrea	300 mm	0 mm	300 mm	−15°
Alex	300 mm	0 mm	500 mm	−15°

Fig. 22. Skin point created on the control panel for usage modeling.

this operation. A skin point was created, circled in red, on one of the control buttons to model the usage of the panel (Fig. 22).

Manikin Kyla was restricted into the control-usage position, shown in Fig. 23.

Fig. 23. Comfort feeling analysis of unoptimized controls operations for Kyla.

The discomfort of this position is shockingly high; it was decided to optimize the position of the controls altogether before assessing the other manikins for this operation. After some toggling and more comfort assessments, the position of the controls was placed as such in Fig. 24.

If the steering wheel/controls assembly placed in the optimal steering wheel position allows the manikin to access the buttons with their thumbs, Fig. 25 is the optimal position for the steering wheel/controls assembly.

The steering wheel/controls assembly was adjusted to the values in Table 7 for each manikin accommodation. The seat height for Danny and Alex remains the same.

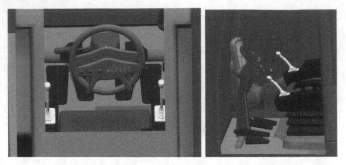

Fig. 24. New position for controls (left) and kinematic group was created to move the assembly as a whole (right).

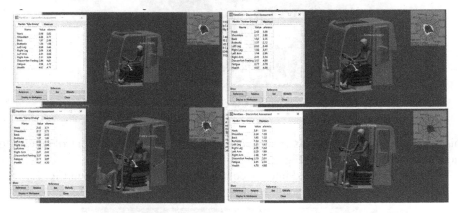

Fig. 25. Optimized driving positions applied to the controls usage.

Table 7. Optimal steering wheel/controls adjustments in free space.

Manikin	X-Translation	Y-Translation	Z-Translation	Y-Rotation
Kyla	130 mm	0 mm	120 mm	20°
Danny	0 mm	0 mm	150 mm	20°
Andrea	190 mm	0 mm	120 mm	20°
Alex	0 mm	0 mm	250 mm	10°

5   Reachability Analysis

The range of motion was assessed for each manikin in their optimal touchpad and controls operations to verify that their bodies can do these operations without overextension. Each manikin's reachability range from their shoulder joint to pointer finger is shown in Fig. 26.

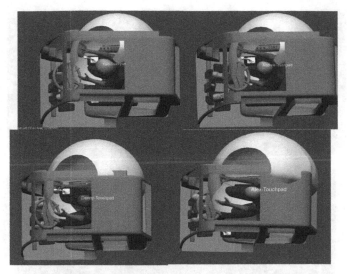

Fig. 26. Touchpad reachability for each manikin.

The touchpad falls into each manikin's range of motion with them still being able to bend their elbows comfortably. Furthermore, with the controls on the optimized steering wheel position, the buttons can be designed to be in reach of the manikins' thumbs, similar to the configuration in Fig. 27 for steering wheel buttons located in cars.

Fig. 27. Ergonomic button placement on a car steering wheel.

6 Visibility Analysis

Visibility analyses were conducted to understand what the manikins can see while performing certain operations. The range of vision for driving the excavator is shown in Fig. 28.

With the controls on the steering wheel and the touchpad off to the side, the manikins can see clearly out of the front window and to the sides.

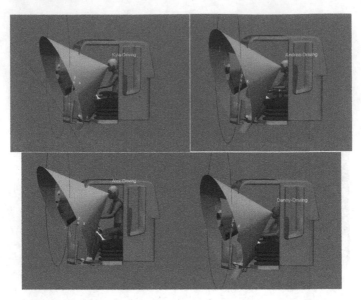

Fig. 28. Vision range for manikins while operating excavator.

When using the touchscreen, it is important to be able to see the screen with no obstructions. Using the RAMSIS Analysis tab, Vision was selected and the Internal View was displayed for each manikin. The results are in Fig. 29.

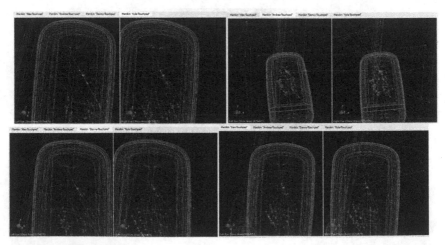

Fig. 29. Internal view analysis for touchscreen of each manikin: Kyla (upper left), Andrea (upper right), Danny (lower left), and Alex (lower right).

7 RAMSIS Study Conclusion

The cab was adjusted for all manikin types, ranging from the 6th percentile to the 94th percentile in body length, and the 4th percentile to the 94th percentile in waist thickness. This range accounts for most people that exist. This study was conducted to understand the adjustments to be made in an excavator cab to facilitate a variety of operations over a variety of people. The conclusive points are bulleted below:

- The seat of an excavator shall be able to be lowered to -50 mm and raised to 100 mm.
- The joystick and armrest assembly shall be able to be raised independently to 250 mm or be adjusted with the seat.
- The steering wheel of an excavator shall be able to be raised to 250 mm, brought forward to 190 mm, and have an option of rotation to 20° towards the driver.
- The touchpad of an excavator shall be brought closer to the operator by at least 300 mm and allow a tilt of 15 degrees up.
- The control buttons of an excavator shall be placed on the steering wheel for maximum ergonomic reach, comfortability, and ease of use.

The implementations described above allow for an ergonomic excavator cab for a variety of body types.

8 Discussion

RAMSIS allows one to virtually model a scenario in preparation for delivering it in real life. In the case of the excavator, it is important to analyze what changes could be made to the design before sending it for manufacture. Changes related to ergonomics are very important to consider when human-machine interaction is involved.

This work is an application of human digital modeling, a tool useful for predicting the safety and performance of work involving human interaction. It allows for virtual prototyping that helps designers understand the ergonomics of physical work aspects in an environment. Chapter 35: Human Digital Modeling in Design in Gavriel Salvendy's *Handbook of Human Factors and Ergonomics* covers applications of human digital modeling in the design of processes that are used by humans. A figure (Fig. 30) that caught my attention was the use of a motion capture suit to improve the prediction of performance and safety for an ATM.

The reflectors on this suit are reminiscent of the skin contact points on RAMSIS manikins and perform a similar function when modeling human positioning."

Fig. 30. A motion capture suit containing reflectors is used to assess the ergonomics of ATM design for wheelchair-bound people. (Adapted from [8]).

9 Future Work

Using this software to model components of one excavator was insightful. However, on a construction site, there are many large pieces of machinery and workers moving around. Human digital modeling in RAMSIS or another CAD software would benefit from being able to integrate many operations and machinery at a larger, more comprehensive scale. Understanding the ebb and flow of a worksite would be insightful to understanding where the high traffic areas, hazardous zones, and safe zones are in the area. This prediction would inform where machinery and tools should be placed as well as where safe rest areas for the workers.

Furthermore, modeling software at this level could be applied to operations that are not construction worksites. Understanding the movement of airports, hospitals, and schools would greatly facilitate improvement in resource distribution, safety, and security.

References

1. Admin: Use of excavator in construction. Basic Civil Engineering (23 April 2015). https://basiccivilengineering.com/2015/04/use-of-excavator-in-construction.html
2. Bonnefon, J.-F., Shariff, A., Rahwan, I.: The social dilemma of autonomous vehicles. Science **352**(6293), 1573–1576 (2016)
3. Rasouli, A., Tsotsos, J.K.: Autonomous vehicles that interact with pedestrians: a survey of theory and practice. IEEE **1524–9050**, 900–918 (2019)
4. Rosique, F., Navarro, P.J., Fernández, C., Padilla, A.: A systematic review of perception system and simulators for autonomous vehicles research. Sensors **19**(648), 1–29 (2019)
5. Maditatia, D.R., Munimb, Z.H., Schramma, H.-J., Kummera, S.: A review of green supply chain management: from bibliometric analysis to a conceptual framework and future research directions. Resources, Conservation & Recycling **139**, 150–162 (2018)
6. Salvendy, G.: Handbook of Human Factors and Ergonomics, 4th Edition. John Wiley & Sons, Inc., Hoboken, 1615–1638 (2012)
7. Cistola, J.T., Duffy, V.G.: Systematic Review on How the Internet of Things will Impact Management in the Manufacturing Industry. In: Stephanidis, C., et al. (eds.) HCII 2021. LNCS, vol. 13097, pp. 427–443. Springer, Cham (2021). https://doi.org/10.1007/978-3-030-90966-6_30

8. Duffy, B.M., Duffy, V.G.: Data Mining Methodology in Support of a Systematic Review of Human Aspects of Cybersecurity. In: Duffy, V.G. (ed.) HCII 2020. LNCS, vol. 12199, pp. 242–253. Springer, Cham (2020). https://doi.org/10.1007/978-3-030-49907-5_17
9. Duffy, V.G., Human Digital Modeling for Design. In: Salvendy, G. (ed.) Handbook of Human Factors and Ergonomics, 4th Ed. John Wiley & Sons, Inc., Hoboken, pp. 1016–1030 (2012)

Classification of Body Posture on TikTok Videos Using a Representation Based on Angles

Niels Martínez-Guevara[⊠], Hazan Orrico, and Jose-Rafael Rojano-Cáceres[⊠]

Facultad de Estadística e Informática, Universidad Veracruzana,
Xalapa, Veracruz, Mexico
{niemartinez,rrojano}@uv.mx, zs16013986@estudiantes.uv.mx

Abstract. Representing complex phenomena, such that coming from video sources, in order to build models for posture detection involves challenges such as: avoiding loss of relevant information, rely on that the representation fits the expectative, and avoid cost for specialized hardware [1,4,5,8].

According to Patel et al. [7] detecting corporal movement is gaining strength for tasks such as: personal health care, environmental awareness, human-computer-interaction and surveillance systems.

On the other hand, as we previously said, acquiring information based on corporal movement to feed the algorithms that build the models can be costly in time, computational resources, human participation, as well as the variety of representative movements to be studied. However, considering crowdsourcing coming from social networks which are focused in creating contents such as TikTok has facilitated collecting data from this nature. In particular, the contents in this social network are focused on corporal movements such as dancing, walking, speaking in sign language etc. which can be used to integrate large and diverse data sets.

The trending in the platform, which are mainly oriented to dancing, make it possible to collect postural data sets which are arranged into similar observations. Nevertheless, there exists a challenge to analyze these sources due to the diversity to record the videos, for example we can find different resolution, backgrounds, source light, clothes, spatial position from the individual, etc. In this sense, preprocessing video is one of the first tasks to tackle noisy or diverse information and provide reliable information in the subsequent stage of the analysis.

Therefore, in this article we propose a novel technique for extracting information that can be used to generalize postural information from the human body in TikTok videos without being affected by the differences in their capture methodology. To build a data set with the initial features from the videos we used the algorithm proposed by Cao et al. [2]. In our case, the novel technique is based on the representation of relationships between the corporal features which can form triangles in their significant positions within the posture. Due to such representation it is possible to search for equivalence in angles through different data sets. In that way, we reduce the number of variables used to find

V. G. Duffy and P.-L. P. Rau (Eds.): HCII 2022, LNCS 13522, pp. 296–307, 2022.
https://doi.org/10.1007/978-3-031-21704-3_19

similarities, enabling the possibility to create generalized models with lower costs. In this case we used a Naïve Bayes Network to verify the level of generalization and performance.

Keywords: Naive bayes · Body representation · Video analysis · Neural networks · Posture detection · Tiktok data · Data mining

1   Introduction

Nowadays, the big data which is generated through different platforms such as TikTok, dubsmash, byte, triller, funimate, chingari, between others, have served as a mechanism for getting significant information which can be used for the study of complex phenomena as the corporal movement. This phenomenon is represented by people exhibiting different memmetics characteristics (Dawkins & Suárez, 1979) which can be observed in the dancing through different trending within the platform. Such characteristics are present in the imitation or even replication with certain degree of precision a set of movements with a recreational purpose (for example replicating dancing steps). For the sake of the study of social phenomenon it is possible to collect data set which contain several observation for the same movement, in some cases it is possible to find out thousands of videos with the same movement.

Whereas generating postural corpus can be a costly task (in resource and time) because of it is necessary to coordinate participants to achieve the same movement or position arrange, besides to control the variability of the sampling suppressing the possible noise factors. Again, as it has been said, a platform as TikTok makes it possible not only to recover diverse sampling without taking care of noisy variables, but also providing an enriched sampling for the study only with using appropriately the hash tag to recover similar videos. However such richness has a downside, because it is necessary a procedure for the treatment of inconsistencies by adding a reliable pre-processing stage.

In this work we use a Bayesian classifier to recognize the postural position in 41 videos belonging to the treading "replay slow ver". We use the generated precision of the Bayesian model as a reliable factor of accomplishment for the task. And, as we said, the difference between the corpus elements makes it necessary to consider a way to minimize the impact of the variety. In our case we use the relationship between the limbs of the body for the representation of a posture as a invariant element.

1.1   Problem Statement

In spite of getting a big amount of data, the creation of a corpus from social networks entails the problem of gain a significant amount of noise caused from the capture process carried out in each video. For example, as a part of the computer vision process to obtain most relevant features from a trending set of videos in TikTok we would find so much diversity in the features selected which would directly affect the machine learning task. Some of the noisy sources can be:

- Position: the relative position between the subject respects to the camera is a problem considering the loss of referent points from the extremities; this happens when he/she is close to camera. On the other hand, if he/she is far it can be loss the visibility of the subject.
- Background: this variable is generally no controlled in social network videos, since each one select where to record the video. Therefore, the background affects the visibility of the subject as well as the points of interest, for example if there are other people behind or walking around.
- Lighting: the light as well as the background is very variable, each person chooses when to record the video along the day. So, it generates inconsistency from the source of illumination. Besides, if the source is artificial and inadequate avoids the tracking of body position and visibility of some parts of the body.
- Clothing: this variable when wrongly chosen can result in people is merged with the background, avoiding the subject identification.
- Occlusion: during the execution of dancing in videos is common that occlusion occurs. This happens when some object or human limb stands in front of another. As a consequence, it can't be identified correctly the posture or configuration in human body.
- Filters: TikTok offers as a part of their services the possibility to apply filters for sharing the video. Such filters can change aspects as brightness, lighting, tint, or even affect the human morphology. Besides, it's possible to add animations or labels which avoid the visibility of the subject.
- Camera: noticeably the camera aspects impacts in video results. Thus, in order to upload videos to the social network includes recording from professional cameras with postproduction stage to recording through the application in a mobile phone. This leads to videos with different quality, resolution, FPS, and formats, having as a result non-uniformity of recording sources.

Particularly, when it's analyzed the postural configuration in human body, the number of frames related with the FPS (frames per second), can complicate the analysis due to the considerable amount of data which entails a bigger of FPS sampling. For this particular case, our methodology proposes to analyze only the representative frames considering the fixed postures made at the beginning and the end of a movement.

Fig. 1. Sample of pictures conformed from one TikTok trending that shows the variability produced by noisy sources. In IV and VI it's exhibited lighting noise from different source of light. Clothes change in all the samples. Gesture occlusion can be seen in I, IV and V. Tags filter example can be seen in III. Finally, considering resolution it can be the difference in I, II and III with lower resolution in contrast with IV, V and VI.

Therefore, given such variability it is complex to achieve the postural analysis from corpus created from social networks in contrast with videos generated in a controlled environment. However, the advantages are also such representativeness and lower cost. Thus, in this paper we present a pre-processing stage to reduce the effect of such noisy source.

1.2   Contributions

In this work we propose a methodology of data pre-processing focused on the analysis of body posture in videos, through the use of several tools that allow improving the representation of the phenomenon for classification tasks. The pre-processing of data consists of two steps:

- The first step is focused on the automatic detection of fixed postures and has the objective of reducing the size of the data to be analyzed, going from a video to a selection of frames that represent body postures.
- The second step aims to eliminate possible noise variables that can be generated by capture methodologies, as mentioned in the problem section.

To get the representative movement frames we use the proposed algorithm of the work of Martinez et al. [6] where from a more complex phenomenon such as sign languages, it is proposed to detect the initial frame of a movement and the final frame of a body movement trajectory, which is of interest for this work.

Once with the collections of frames, it is necessary to eliminate as far as possible the noise variables present in the corpus, so the generalization of the identified positions becomes an essential task and for this, it is necessary to identify the parts of the body within the frame, for this the work of Cao et al. [2], is the implementation of a neural network, which identifies the extremities of the body and represents them in Cartesian values in pixel value in the frame. Once with the collections of frames, it is necessary to eliminate as far as possible the noise variables present in the corpus, so the generalization of the identified positions becomes an essential task and it is necessary to identify the parts of the body within the frame, for this the work of Cao, is the implementation of a neural network, which identifies the extremities of the body and represents them in Cartesian values in pixel value in the frame. However, the proposed representation in Cartesian values could cause noise if we analyze different videos with different capture methodologies. Now, starting from the points that the algorithm provides, we could establish relations of the parts of the body using a set of vectors that represent them. The problem of the vector representation it is becomes insufficient since it still has some drawbacks with the noise variables mentioned, which is why the proposal is to analyze the relationships that exist in the set of vectors that present in the posture, through a representation based on triangles. This is given the property of similarity of polygons, we can say that two triangles are similar regardless of the dimensions of their vertices, but they have the same internal angles on them, in Fig. 2 the similarity of polygons is exemplified [9].

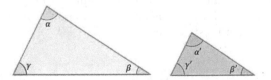

Fig. 2. Where if α and α', β and β', γ and γ' are equal we can say that the two polygons are similar.

Based on this premise, we proposed to define the following triangles from the points recovered by the algorithm, which can be seen in Fig. 3, a description of the set of internal angles.

Fig. 3. Description of the internal angles, blue triangles: the orientation of the head and torso, red triangles: the posture of the left and right arm, finally the yellow triangles position of the hands. (Color figure online)

Using the angles the relationship between the elements present in the posture in the creation of the database, we believe that it will have enough significant information to represent the phenomenon.

2 Related Work

In the literature it can be find related work with body postural analysis, for this purpose intrusive and non-intrusive methods has been used [7]. In the case of intrusive methods stand out the use of sensors such as gyroscopes and accelerometers. On the other hand, stand out the computer vision techniques for video analysis. In this work we mention some works which follows the last approach.

Thus, to detect fixed posture from an automatic way [6] perform an analysis through the arithmetic operation of frame subtraction to detect the movement presence. Such process is executed comparing a pair of adjacent frames and registering the changes between them by means of Otzu binarization. If the difference between frames becomes significant the Otzu function get a higher value, on the other hand if the difference is lower the function returns lower values. Therefore, considering this approach in this work we use such process to obtain automatically the representative frames in a TikTok video, assuming that if all the videos have the same movements the postural recovering should be the same for all the elements of the corpus.

In the work [2] the authors propose a mechanism to represent the body elements as set of 25 points. This is done by a trained neural network. The result is presented in Fig. 4, in one hand it can be visualized on the analyzed images. On the other hand, such set of points can be stored as a json file, which for each point it is represented as a Cartesian coordinates, with their respective reliability value that the neural network estimates for recognizing each human limb point.

Therefore, considering both works, it is possible to lead the analyze of postural positions from videos, regardless of the process performed to capture the video.

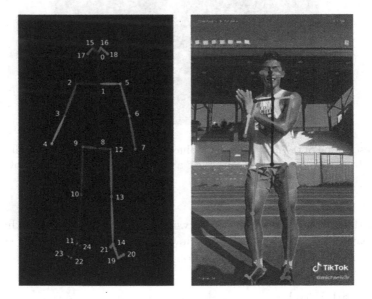

Fig. 4. Human body points detected by the OpenPose algorithm.

3   Methodology

In this work to verify that the proposed representation contained significant information, we define a methodology of experimentation collecting a corpus of TikTok videos, this social network was chosen because there are no watermarks, logos, video coding, or external elements on the videos, that could affect the experimentation. To obtain a number of significant observations in the corpus, it was decided to analyze a platform trend called: "REPLAY SLOW VER".

An important feature of selected trending is that, unlike others, it is done individually where a person is shown performing a set of well-defined movements without having the presence of displacements in the environment, this reflects the memetic phenomena shown in Fig. 5. For the experimentation, 42 videos were selected, which contain differences in the capture methodology, but the movements defined by the trending were clearly shown.

Fig. 5. Through words or emojis, the movements present in the trending are defined, this with the purpose of their instruction and propagation.

With the corpus complete, the set frames of occurrence of movement were detected, using the tool proposed by [6] et al. Where a set of frames is obtained, that represents the body posture before and after performing a movement. Something observable is that there is a relationship between the fps of the video and the frames recovered by the algorithm, where at a higher number of fps the frames recovered were higher, however, the fixed postures of the movements are recovered in all the videos, as shown in Fig. 6.

Fig. 6. Sample of frames on the identification of the fixed posture *arms up* in the TikTok corpus.

Analyzing the frames recovered by the algorithm, three postures are considered: *arms up, arms down and arms crossed* as shown in Fig. 7. From the selected postures, the Openpose [2] algorithm was used. This is to obtain the cloud of points that indicate the parts of the human body, using a set of coordinates based on the frame. Not all Openpose points were used because the movements present in the corpus involved only upper body movements. The result can be seen in Fig. 7.

Fig. 7. Sample of the point clouds obtained in the selected postures 7.1 Arms Up, 7.2 Arms Crossed, 7.3 Arms Down.

The point cloud of the human body is the first step to reach the proposed representation, which considers the angles that are formed between the different parts of the human body as they are: The wrists, the head, the torso, the elbows, and the shoulders. From the cloud of points obtained, triangles were generated as shown in Fig. 2. Once the polygons were defined, the angles of the vertices were calculated using the internal product between two vectors [9].

Once the angles were identified, the database was registered in a csv file, since the values obtained were in radians, a database of 18 variables with continuous values and a categorical variable as a class variable was obtained. Having variables with continuous values and using a probabilistic model such as a naive Bayesian network, it is necessary to carry out a discretization process. For this, a filtering algorithm was applied, included in the weka algorithm collection [3]. This discretization algorithm defines ranges in continuous variables making a fitting with the class variable, thus promoting the relationship between the data.

Once having the database with discrete values, a stratified segmentation of 10 fold cross-validation was applied to select the training and test sets for the learning process to the model. From the structure of the naive bayes network, see Fig. 8, the conditional probability tables were made to carry out the classification process using the weka tool [3].

Fig. 8. Naive Bayes model that represents the posture of the body using angles.

The results of the experimentation of the defined naive bayes network and the chosen data pre-processing are shown in Table 1.

Table 1. Results of the accuracy of the naive bayes model.

Naive Bayes Classifier	
Correctly Classified Instances	93.4959 %
Incorrectly Classified Instances	6.5041 %
Kappa statistic	0.9024
Mean absolute error	0.0378
Root mean squared error	0.1777
Relative absolute error	8.4946
Root relative squared error	37.679
Total Number of Instances	123

The naive Bayes model achieved an accuracy of 93.49% of correctly classified instances, in some cases, the model could not adequately identify the phenomenon, however, the statistics of error show a correct fit in the model.

4   Conclusions and Future Work

In this work, we found favorable results considering the model accuracy through the precise classification of the instances. On the other hand, with this process we achieve a significant reduction in the data processing.

As a conclusion, we can ascertain that the most representative to identify a postural position is the relationship between the human limbs elements, as well as, that the angles representation is proficient in such task.

We also achieved representativeness in pre-processing stage, obtaining as a result the elimination of noisy variables for each video, previously stated in the Sect. 1.1, as a consequence it is possible to analyze the posture avoiding such vices.

Finally, analyzing postural positions from TikTok videos allow us the possibility to understand complex phenomena such as corporal movements in videos.

Acknowledgements. We would like to thank CONACyT for the support for the preparation of this paper and the doctorate in Computer Science of the Veracruzana University for the support for the development of this project. Niels Martínez is supported by a CONACyT doctoral scholarship, No. 711994.

References

1. Alvarez-Alvarez, A., Trivino, G., Cordón, O.: Body posture recognition by means of a genetic fuzzy finite state machine. In: 2011 IEEE 5th International Workshop on Genetic and Evolutionary Fuzzy Systems (GEFS), pp. 60–65. IEEE (2011)
2. Cao, Z., Hidalgo, G., Simon, T., Wei, S.E., Sheikh, Y.: Openpose: realtime multiperson 2d pose estimation using part affinity fields. IEEE Trans. Pattern Analysis Mach. Intell. **43**(1), 172–186 (2019)
3. Frank, E., Hall, M., Holmes, G., Kirkby, R., Pfahringer, B., Witten, I.H., Trigg, L.: Weka-a machine learning workbench for data mining. In: Data mining and knowledge discovery handbook, pp. 1269–1277. Springer (2009). https://doi.org/10.1007/978-0-387-09823-4_66
4. Hu, F., Wang, L., Wang, S., Liu, X., He, G.: A human body posture recognition algorithm based on bp neural network for wireless body area networks. China Commun. **13**(8), 198–208 (2016)
5. Le, T.L., Nguyen, M.Q., et al.: Human posture recognition using human skeleton provided by kinect. In: 2013 international conference on computing, management and telecommunications (ComManTel), pp. 340–345. IEEE (2013)
6. Martínez-Guevara, N., Rojano-Cáceres, J.R., Curiel, A.: Detection of phonetic units of the mexican sign language. In: 2019 International Conference on Inclusive Technologies and Education (CONTIE), pp. 168–1685. IEEE (2019)

7. Patel, P., Bhatt, B., Patel, B.: Human body posture recognition-a survey. In: 2017 International Conference on Innovative Mechanisms for Industry Applications (ICIMIA), pp. 473–477. IEEE (2017)
8. Shirehjini, A.A.N., Yassine, A., Shirmohammadi, S.: Design and implementation of a system for body posture recognition. Multimedia Tools Appl. **70**(3), 1637–1650 (2014)
9. Shively, L.: Geometría moderna. Editorial Continental, México (1984)

Advanced RAMSIS. Analysis of Excavator Operator

William Raymer[✉] and Luisa Ciro[✉]

Purdue University, West Lafayette, IN 47906, USA
{wraymer,lciro}@purdue.edu

Abstract. This project consists of improving what was done in the previous project. The previous project was about using RAMSIS to run an ergonomic analysis of an excavator. This analysis allows the improvement of a workplace that matches the capabilities of the workers and operators. It also helps prevent injuries at a workplace by identifying tasks that are hazardous for work-related musculoskeletal disorders [1]. In the previous project, we concluded that the excavator needed improvement by adjusting the steering wheel, the display, the control panel, and the armrests of the seat. This project consists of making these adjustments and finding a range of adjustments that would be comfortable for 6 different manikins who cover a wide range of body types. The body types consist of both male and female operators, long and short torso, 95th, 5th, and 50th percentiles. We created points on the display, control panel, steering wheel, and created kinematics for these three objects which allowed us to create degrees of freedom so we can adjust by translating these objects along the x, y, and z axes and rotating them along the three axes. Once the adjustments have been made, we ran the ergonomic analysis by calculating the level of discomfort and the reachability of the manikins. The goal is to keep the level of discomfort below 3.5 and the manikin must touch the object without leaning forward.

Keywords: Ergonomic analysis · RAMSIS · Digital human modeling

1 Introduction, Background, and Problem Statement

When talking about the human factor and ergonomics, it is important to note that this discipline is capable to create the best solutions considering the design, well-being, and the systematical approach of the problem [2].

Karwowski introduced the term symvatology, which is defined as "the systematic study (which includes theory, analysis, design, implementation, and application) of interaction processes that define, transform and control compatibility relationships between artefacts (systems) and people" [3]. He also implies how important is to integrate this concept to build the fundamental of ergonomics science, considering that having this deep understanding of the interaction between people and artefacts, the designing of operations and products will be improved.

© Springer Nature Switzerland AG 2022
V. G. Duffy and P.-L. P. Rau (Eds.): HCII 2022, LNCS 13522, pp. 308–335, 2022.
https://doi.org/10.1007/978-3-031-21704-3_20

However, in recent times, there has been a recurrent necessity to explore and exploit its potential and make sure that the industry perceives the great value that an HFE can provide to any situation. Here is where Digital Human Modeling (DHM) starts playing a big role in providing further analysis to the solutions, especially its designs.

Digital Human Modeling complements the design and manufacturing process of any product, considering that the current market is highly competitive, they require a high-speed response to changes, without forgetting the safety of the users. There are multiple softwares for this modeling, as such Jack, SAFEWORK, RAMSIS, SAMMIE, and UM 3DSSP [4].

Considering the multiple usages of DHMs software to provide a deeper and proper understanding of the safety and well-being of a user interacting with a product, we used RAMSIS to simulate multiple tasks of manikins in an excavator.

RAMSIS provides a large number of analysis tools that complement ergonomic analysis, which is fundamental once a product is being designed. Taking as an example the model that is being used in this project, RAMSIS allows the designer to position the object inside the cabin, for example, going further than just the position of those as a matter of design but making sure that those are reachable and comfortable for most people. Then, changes can be made easily and at a low cost as the analysis and the decision are taken before manufacturing the product.

Moving to the relevance that this topic might have, the literature review was done using three bibliometric analysis tools, where the keywords were "Digital Human Modeling" and "Ergonomics".

The search was done using Harzing Publish or Perish for Digital Human Modeling, and Ergonomics through Web of Science. The metadata was subtracted from around 1100 papers found regarding these topics, including the author, title, keywords, and references.

Then the metadata was exported and appended in BibExcel. As shown in Fig. 1, there are a large number of authors writing about DHM (around 500). From this, it is possible to infer that this topic is currently relevant and there is a current interest for people in the Human Factors and Ergonomics file to research more about Digital Human Modeling.

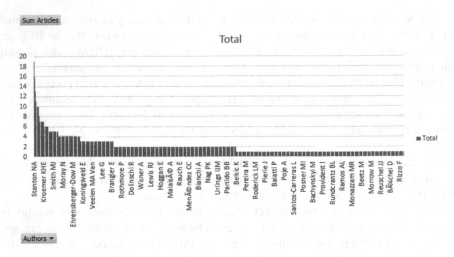

Fig. 1. Number of citations per author in BibExcel

Then, the appended metadata obtained in BibExcel was exported to VOSviewer, where the network regarding the co-citation of those papers was created. In Fig. 2 it is possible to see the connection between authors and, indirectly, their work. Authors such as Karwowski, Stanton, and Carayon have made a high contribution to the area, and they are connected in their research.

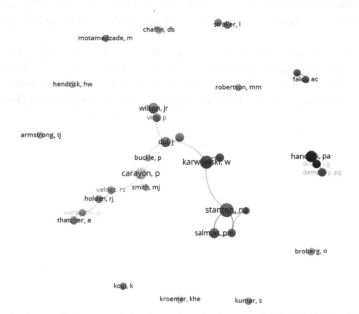

Fig. 2. Co-citation analysis network for the authors for key words Digital Human Modeling and Ergonomics

Finally, the data was exported to CiteSpace to get the top references in the citation burst analysis. On the first run, 14 references were found, most of them from the late '90s and early 2000. Then, it was run again, and 10 top references were found from 1999 to 2010. This shows how even Digital Human Modeling seems to be a new topic in ergonomics, research in this area has been performed for more than 20 years and considering that the industrial world is constantly changing, there is still room for improvement and contribution (Fig. 3 and Fig. 4).

Top 14 References with the Strongest Citation Bursts

References	Year	Strength	Begin	End	1996 - 2003
*AM PSYCH ASS, 1994, DIAGN STAT MAN MENT, V0, P0	1994	3.01	1996	1999	
ENDERS W, 1993, AM POLIT SCI REV, V87, P829	1993	2.46	1996	1997	
MALLONEE S, 1996, JAMA-J AM MED ASSOC, V276, P382	1996	4.69	1997	2000	
TUCKER JB, 1997, JAMA-J AM MED ASSOC, V278, P362	1997	3.49	1999	2001	
SIMON JD, 1997, JAMA-J AM MED ASSOC, V278, P428	1997	3.49	1999	2001	
FRANZ DR, 1997, JAMA-J AM MED ASSOC, V278, P399	1997	3.22	1999	2001	
CARTER A, 1998, FOREIGN AFF, V77, P80	1998	2.97	1999	2001	
OKUMURA T, 1996, ANN EMERG MED, V28, P129	1996	2.59	1999	2001	
ZILINSKAS RA, 1997, JAMA-J AM MED ASSOC, V278, P418	1997	2.36	1999	2001	
TOROK TJ, 1997, JAMA-J AM MED ASSOC, V278, P389	1997	3.62	2000	2001	
RICHARDS CF, 1999, ANN EMERG MED, V34, P183	1999	3.21	2000	2001	
HENDERSON DA, 1999, SCIENCE, V283, P1279	1999	2.66	2000	2001	
INGLESBY TV, 1999, JAMA-J AM MED ASSOC, V281, P1735	1999	2.65	2000	2001	
KEIM M, 1999, ANN EMERG MED, V34, P177	1999	2.26	2000	2001	

Fig. 3. Top references for Digital Human Modeling using Citation Burst analysis in CiteSpace from 1993 to 1999

Top 10 References with the Strongest Citation Bursts

References	Year	Strength	Begin	End	1996 - 2019
Yang JZ, 2006, J COMPUT SCI TECH-CH, V21, P189, DOI 10.1007/s11390-006-0189-3, DOI	2006	4.29	2007	2011	
Lamkull D, 2009, INT J IND ERGONOM, V39, P428, DOI 10.1016/j.ergon.2008.10.005, DOI	2009	4.28	2012	2014	
Cox IJ, 1997, IEEE T IMAGE PROCESS, V6, P1673, DOI 10.1109/83.650120, DOI	1997	4.19	1999	2001	
Lamkull D, 2007, APPL ERGON, V38, P713, DOI 10.1016/j.apergo.2006.12.007, DOI	2007	4.03	2009	2012	
Sechopoulos I, 2013, MED PHYS, V40, P0, DOI 10.1118/1.4770281, DOI	2013	4.01	2017	2019	
Chaffin DB, 2007, HUM FACTOR ERGON MAN, V17, P475, DOI 10.1002/hfm.20087, DOI	2007	3.68	2008	2011	
Barni M, 1998, SIGNAL PROCESS, V66, P357, DOI 10.1016/S0165-1684(98)00015-2, DOI	1998	3.59	1999	2001	
Xiang YJ, 2010, STRUCT MULTIDISCIP O, V41, P465, DOI 10.1007/s00158-009-0423-z, DOI	2010	3.48	2013	2014	

Fig. 4. Top references for Digital Human Modeling and Ergonomics using Citation Burst analysis in CiteSpace from 1999 to 2010.

2   Procedure

Before explaining the kinematics and adjustments created in this project for the armrests, steering wheel, display, and control panel, it is important to note how the manikins were created.

In this case, six different body measurements were created: 5th percentile Female, 5th percentile Female with a short torso, 5th percentile Female with a long torso, 50th percentile male, 95th percentile male with a long torso, and 95% percentile male with a big waist. Then, these were assigned to the manikins.

These body measurements enrich the modeling as we are considering a wide extension of measurements, then a wide extension of the population (Fig. 5).

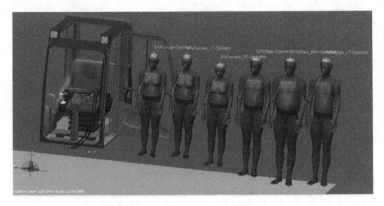

Fig. 5. The six manikins created in this project to simulate the tasks for an exactor operator

Once all manikins were created, we created the task required for them to sit on the seat in a neutral position. The discomfort feeling analysis (Table 1). Discomfort assessment values for the six manikins on sitting position (neutral) helped us to have a reference will we were adjusting the position of the objects (Fig. 6).

Table 1. Discomfort assessment values for the six manikins on sitting position (neutral)

Position	Manikin	Part name										
		Neck	Shoulders	Back	Buttocks	Left leg	Right leg	Left arm	Right arm	Discomfort feeling	Fatigue	Health
Neutral-Sitting	5% Female	1,64	1,50	1,24	0,88	1,53	1,51	1,57	1,58	2,57	2,02	4,72
	5% Female L-T*	1,64	1,46	1,12	0,83	1,50	1,50	1,59	1,60	2,53	2,00	4,72
	5% Female S-T**	1,64	1,56	1,28	0,92	1,62	1,60	1,64	1,64	2,61	2,04	4,72
	50% Male	1,64	1,79	1,45	1,30	2,08	2,04	1,40	1,40	2,89	2,17	4,72
	95% Male L-T*	1,64	1,88	1,52	1,66	2,57	2,51	1,26	1,26	3,13	2,27	4,72
	95% Male B-W***	1,64	1,86	1,50	1,54	2,17	2,13	1,34	1,34	3,04	2,23	4,72

* Long torso, ** Short torso, *** Big Waist.

Fig. 6. Manikins sitting in a neutral position inside the excavator cabin

For some of the tasks that will be described below, we also used the join capacity analysis. This report will show us the percentage of effort or discomfort that each part of the body is having regarding a specific task. In this case, as indicated in the demos, the analysis will be done with the NASA feature, this means that the percentages will be calculated in zero gravity. We will focus mainly on the parts in which the percentage is high, then the bar will be red, and for those with a percentage in the middle, then the bar will be yellow. However, we will discard from our analysis the fingers, as they usually will be in an uncomfortable position for any task (Fig. 7).

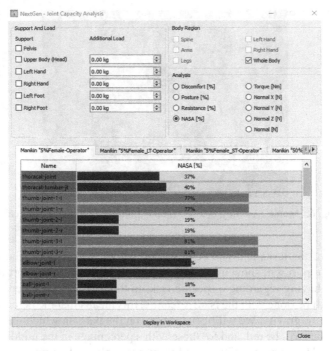

Fig. 7. Joint capacity analysis

2.1 Armrest

The first assessment for the manikins will be to grasp the joysticks that are located at the end of the armrests. For this object, André provides us with a new model for the seat. This one has the pad separate from the whole armrest in order to evaluate if there will be an improvement in the position if they move independently.

We created two kinematics, the first one for the group of bases, joysticks, and their points. This kinematics has a degree of freedom in the Z-axis, then this will move up and down.

The second one if for the pad (TRM 2 and TRM 9), and this has the degree of freedom on the X-axis (back and forth).

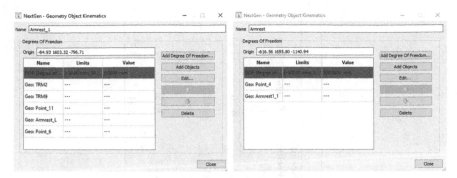

Fig. 8. Kinematics for armrest and pad

Once the kinematics were created, then we created the task required for the manikin to grasp the joystick firmly, by creating a restriction between the body point from the hand and the upper point on the joystick. As shown in Fig. 8 some of the manikins, especially the shortest ones, are leaning forward to complete this task and have an awkward position while doing so (Fig. 9).

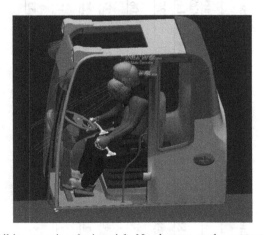

Fig. 9. Manikins grasping the joystick. No changes on the armrest position yet

We gather the data for the discomfort feeling analysis and the joint capacity report, in order to visualize the values for each one of the manikins. Looking at the information provided in Table 2 and Table 3, the values in both cases can be improved by reviewing the positioning of the armrest and the grasping, keeping in mind that we want to reach values in the discomfort feeling analysis below 3.5 and to keep to a minimum the percentage of discomfort in the joint capacity analysis.

Table 2. Discomfort feeling values for the armrest. No changes on the object

Position	Manikin	Neck	Shoulders	Back	Buttocks	Left Leg	Right Leg	Left Arm	Right Arm	Discomfort Feeling	Fatigue	Health
Joysticks-No Changes on Arm-rest	5% Female	4,63	3,88	3,37	2,46	3,31	3,27	3,53	3,53	5,97	4,58	4,70
	5% Female L-T *	3,99	3,74	3,03	2,45	3,11	3,06	3,21	3,23	5,52	4,20	4,33
	5% Female S-T**	4,49	4,08	2,94	2,61	3,32	3,27	3,34	3,36	5,81	4,46	4,31
	50% Male	2,97	2,38	2,28	1,83	2,26	2,25	2,51	2,58	4,28	3,26	4,71
	95% Male L-T*	2,83	2,27	2,19	1,75	2,18	2,17	2,45	2,52	4,13	3,15	4,72
	95% Male B-W***	3,07	2,41	2,45	1,98	2,34	2,33	2,70	2,78	4,51	3,41	4,72

Table 3. Joint capacity notes considering the parts with a high and medium percentage

Status	Manikin	Body parts high %	Body parts medium %		
Joysticks-No changes on armrest	5% Female	0	Fingers	Elbow-r 75%	Shoulders 81%
	5% Female Long Torso	0	Fingers	Shoulders 82%	
	5% Female Short torso	0	Fingers	Shoulders 81%	
	50% Male	0	Fingers	Shoulders 81%	
	95% Male Big waist	0	Fingers	Shoulders 80%	

With this information, we started changing the position of the armrest, by increasing the value of DOF (Degree of Freedom) in the Kinematic section for this object and testing it out with each manikin. The ideal position for each manikin was selected considering the results of the discomfort feeling analysis but also the percentages for the joint capacity. We found that the best value for the armrest, for all manikins, is +200 mm on Z-axis. The results are the following (Table 4 and Table 5):

Table 4. Discomfort feeling values when armrest changes in the Z-axis.

Position	Manikin	Part Name										
		Neck	Shoulders	Back	Buttocks	Left Leg	Right Leg	Left Arm	Right Arm	Discomfort Feeling	Fatigue	Health
Joysticks-Changing armrest	5% Female	3,12	2,97	1,93	1,57	2,66	2,60	2,36	2,40	4,05	3,21	4,60
	5% Female L–T *	2,97	2,83	1,85	1,47	2,44	2,38	2,26	2,31	3,86	3,06	4,60
	5% Female S–T**	3,64	3,35	1,97	1,70	2,87	2,82	2,57	2,60	4,40	3,56	4,60
	50% Male	2,51	2,11	1,66	1,19	1,80	1,78	2,04	2,14	3,37	2,66	4,63
	95% Male L–T*	2,43	2,04	1,65	1,21	1,79	1,77	2,03	2,12	3,34	2,63	4,63
	95% Male B–W***	2,71	2,21	1,94	1,49	2,00	1,98	2,29	2,37	3,95	3,04	4,64

Table 5. Joint capacity for the manikins when the armrest is +200 mm in the Z-axis

Status	Manikin	Body parts high %	Body parts medium %	
Joysticks-Changing armrest	5% Female	0	Fingers	Shoulders 82%
	5% Female Long Torso	0	Fingers	Shoulders 82%
	5% Female Short torso	0	Fingers	Shoulders 81%
	50% Male	0	Fingers	Shoulders 81%
	95% Male Big waist	0	Fingers	Shoulders 81%
	95% Male Long torso	0	Fingers	Shoulders 81%

In the data, we can see that for most manikins and body parts the discomfort feeling is below 3.5, as well as the percentages for the discomfort on the shoulders joint were reduced.

We also want to explore which will be the results of these two analyses if the way the joysticks are being grabbed changes. In this case, we moved the armrest to the original position and added a new point in the upper part of the joystick as shown in Fig. 10.

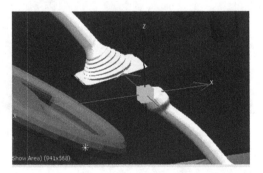

Fig. 10. New points in the joysticks to change the way the manikins grasp them

Then we added a new restriction again between the body points in the hand and these new points, and for making sure the manikin is grasping the joystick horizontally, we added a restriction of direction on each hand with a binormal axis (Fig. 11).

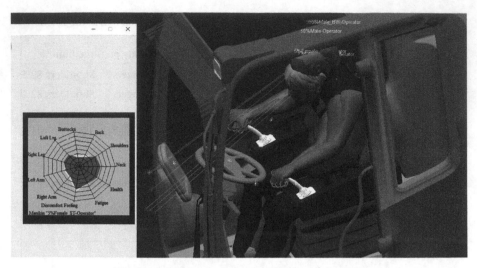

Fig. 11. Manikins grasping the joystick horizontally

With this change, we review again the results for discomfort feeling and joint capacity. As shown in Table 6 and Table 7, the manikins have good values in most parts, which leads us to infer that if the operator always grabs the manikin this way, then the armrest does not have to be adjusted, as the values are below or close to 3.5.

Table 6. Discomfort feeling values for the changes on the way to grab the joystick. No changes on the armrest

Position	Manikin	Neck	Shoulders	Back	Buttocks	Left Leg	Right Leg	Left Arm	Right Arm	Discomfort Feeling	Fatigue	Health
Joysticks- No Changes grasping joystick on top	5% Female	3,77	3,78	2,12	2,00	2,60	2,51	1,87	3,50	4,65	3,67	4,17
	5% Female L-T*	3,18	3,48	2,32	1,72	2,43	2,33	1,56	3,65	4,33	3,38	4,26
	5% Female S-T**	3,63	3,83	2,18	1,83	2,55	2,52	2,68	2,64	4,53	3,60	4,20
	50% Male	2,75	2,46	1,79	1,19	1,94	1,95	2,19	2,24	3,58	2,86	4,72
	95% Male L-T*	2,76	2,49	1,82	1,24	1,99	1,98	2,26	2,28	3,65	2,91	4,72
	95% Male B-W***	2,80	2,40	2,05	1,41	2,02	2,02	2,47	2,49	3,86	3,01	4,72

Table 7. Joint capacity results for changes on the way to grab the joystick. No changes on the arm-rest

Status	Manikin	Body parts high %	Body parts medium %	
Joysticks-No changes grasping joystick on top	5% Female	0	Fingers	
	5% Female Long Torso	0	Fingers	Shoulder 79%
	5% Female Short torso	0	Fingers	
	50% Male	0	Fingers	
	95% Male Big waist	0	Fingers	
	95% Male Long torso	0	Fingers	

2.2 Steering Wheel

Fig. 12. Steering wheel

From Fig. 12 Andre provided us with a steering wheel that was composed of a joint between the lower part and the top parts. This allows us to translate the steering wheel along the Y-axis and tilt it to find the best range that would keep the level of discomfort under 3.5 for all 6 manikins.

We first had to separate the bottom geometry piece and the top two geometry pieces to create kinematics that would allow us to tilt the steering wheel and adjust it up and down. To do this, we want to create a point in the middle of the surface of the bottom geometry piece. We first created to point diagonally opposite on the corners of the surface by cliquing on "Geometry" than "point" then selecting the "create on object" on the "point type". Now to create the point in the middle, we used the same steps as above but instead of selecting "create on object", we would select "between points" which would ask to select the two previous points where the new point would be created after which we can delete the previous two points and name this point "joint". We need another point on top of the steering wheel which was created the same way as above by using "created on object" for the point type which we named "wheelmiddlepoint".

We then created kinematics by cliquing on the geometry toolbar then "define kinematics". We then used the "joint" point as the origin and the starting point of the degrees of freedom where the type of DOF is "rotation". The direction of DOF is along the Y-axis where we set the minimum at -30 degrees and the maximum at 30 degrees. We also created a second degree of freedom where the origin is still the "joint" point and the type of DOF is translation. The direction now is defined by the "joint" point and the "wheelmiddlepoint" point. The minimum value is kept at zero mm and the maximum value is set at 200 mm. Then we added the objects TRM 14 and TRM15 which are the top two geometric pieces of the steering wheel (Fig. 13).

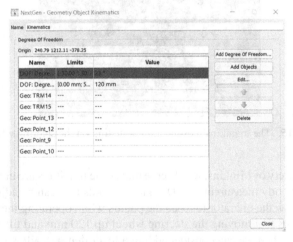

Fig. 13. Settings for steering wheel adjustments

After making several adjustments, trying to find the right adjustment that would meet the criteria for the comfort feeling analysis. After adjusting, we ran the posture calculation which is one of the icons on the toolbar. The posture calculation applies to all the adjustments made including tasks. We found that tilting the wheel by 23 degrees and moving the steering wheel 120 mm up is the right position for the steering wheel (Fig. 14).

1	Operator	Neck	Shoulders	Back	Buttocks	Left Leg	Right leg	Left Arm	Right Arm	Discomfort feeling	Fatigue	Health
2	0	4.44	3.22	2.92	2.78	2.96	2.93	3.94	3.97	5.94	4.5	4.62
3	1	4.71	3.39	2.9	2.82	3.01	2.95	4.45	4.4	6.1	4.67	4.64
4	2	4.75	3.78	2.86	3.67	2.95	3.08	3.82	4.27	6.45	4.77	4.63
5	3	4.94	3.82	2.78	3.55	3.05	3.01	3.91	4.25	6.47	4.85	4.62
6	4	5.63	4.55	2.91	3.52	3.32	3.27	4.86	5.1	7.1	5.51	4.64
7	5	4.79	3.56	3.03	2.89	3.11	3.1	4.53	4.58	6.3	4.82	4.64
8	Maximum	5.3	4.18	3.03	3.66	3.2	3.13	4.54	4.85	6.69	5.12	4.64

Fig. 14. Comfort feeling Analysis for the steering wheel

According to the comfort analysis, the goal is to keep the value below 3.5 and as we can observe, most values are below the threshold. The areas that need improvement are the neck, left and right arm, the discomfort feeling, fatigue, and health. These areas will improve as we adjust the seat and armrests (Fig. 15).

Fig. 15. The manikins' posture after adjusting on the steering wheel.

Due to the variety of Minkins, we observe that some manikins are unable to reach the floor due to their body measurements. Designing pedals that can be adjusted up, down, and tilted will allow the operator to reach the pedals while operating the machine. Since the analysis tells us that moving the steering wheel up 120 mm and tilting it 23 degrees is a good position, then we can consider adding a lever that will allow the operator who would struggle to get in and out of the seat to adjust the steering wheel preferably at the joint level.

2.3 Display

Fig. 16. Display

The operator uses the display of the excavator to monitor, and position select excavator attachments (Fig. 16). This means the display must be placed at a location that is easily accessible and at a direct line of sight of the operator. We first created a point on the display using the same method as the steering wheel. This point is used to calculate the reachability of the manikin which is done by cliquing the "Analysis" tab then "compute reachability". This allows you to see how far the manikin must learn to reach an object and does the manikin has to twist in uncomfortable positions to reach an object. This allows us to know in which direction we must move the object to improve the level of comfort of the manikin. We created a target between the point found on the right index finger of the manikin and the point found on the display. This is done under the "operations" tab then "define restriction" Then select which manikin then select "target" as a restriction type then select the point found on the right index finger as the manikin comp and the point on the display as the Env. Object. We then created kinematics for the display using a similar procedure as for the steering wheel. We then created the DOF consisting of 3 rotations and 3 translations. The translation DOFs were on the x, y, and z-axis. The x-axis had a minimum of −10 mm and a maximum of 500 mm, the y-axis had a minimum of −200 mm and a maximum of 500 mm, and the z-axis had a minimum of −200 mm and a maximum of 500 mm. The rotation DOFs were along the x, y, and z-axis. We created two sets of settings for the display by dividing the manikins into two different groups to give us a range of values.

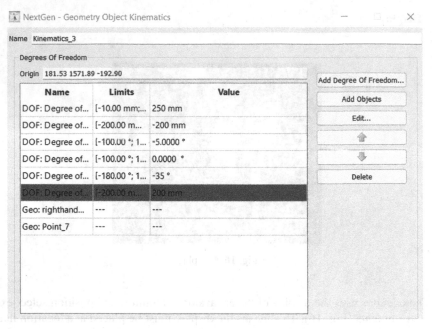

Fig. 17. The display kinematics for manikins' operators 1, 2, and 6

The first set of manikins were operators 1, 2, and 6 with the kinematics for these manikins are displayed in Fig. 17. The values obtained for their comfort analysis are displayed in Fig. 19. The values obtained were satisfactory.

The second set of manikins were operators 3,4, and 5. The kinematics for these manikins are displayed in Fig. 18. The values obtained for the calculation of the comfort analysis is shown are in Fig. 19. We are satisfied with the obtained values.

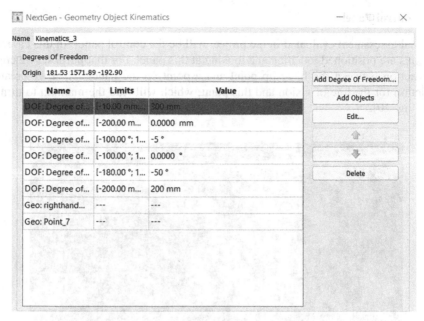

Fig. 18. The display kinematics for operators 3, 4, and 5

	Operator	Neck	Shoulders	Back	Buttocks	Left Leg	Right leg	Left Arm	Right Arm	Discomfor	Fatigue	Health
1												
2	0	2.3	1.75	1.49	1.06	1.81	1.81	1.72	2.25	3.15	2.51	4.66
3	1	2.29	1.82	1.44	1	1.77	1.78	1.7	2.11	3.08	2.47	4.65
4	2	2.17	1.91	1.25	0.77	1.56	1.62	1.6	1.67	2.75	2.25	4.65
5	3	2.14	1.88	1.42	0.87	1.62	1.72	1.72	1.75	2.9	2.33	4.64
6	4	2.63	2.24	1.62	1.32	1.9	1.9	1.57	2.44	3.47	2.74	4.65
7	5	2.22	1.72	1.51	0.98	1.73	1.78	1.94	1.96	3.07	2.44	4.65
8	Maximum	2.29	1.82	1.49	1	1.77	1.78	1.96	2.11	3.08	2.47	4.65

Fig. 19. Comfort Analysis for the display

Figure 19 shows the values obtained from the comfort analysis for all 6 manikins. As we can observe, all of the values are below the desired value of 3.5 except for "Health". This is because the calculation of the comfort analysis is taking other postures into account that we haven't considered. These postures may include the pedals, the back and the height of the seat, etc.

2.4   Control Panel

The final assessment evaluated in the project will be the control panel. In this case, the manikins are positioned touching and looking at this panel. For that purpose, we create a restriction between the fingertip point and a point on the panel. Then we create a restriction for the line of vision and this point, which will lead the manikin to turn its neck (Fig. 20).

Fig. 20. Manikins interact with the control panel. No changes on the object

We took the results of discomfort feeling and joint capacity for the manikins before doing any changes on the position of the control panel as a reference and to keep coming back to them while doing changes on the object (Table 8).

Table 8. Discomfort feeling values for the control panel task. No changes on the object

| Position | Manikin | Part Name | | | | | | | | | | | |
		Neck	Shoulders	Back	Buttocks	Left Leg	Right Leg	Left Arm	Right Arm	Discomfort Feeling	Fatigue	Health
Panel control- No changes	5% Female	3,78	1,59	3,49	1,93	3,40	3,16	2,80	3,09	5,22	3,89	4,94
	5% Female L–T *	3,90	1,62	3,54	1,99	3,48	3,22	2,77	3,25	5,36	4,00	4,96
	5% Female S–T**	3,73	1,78	3,43	1,74	3,23	3,19	2,87	2,68	4,98	3,76	4,93
	50% Male	4,42	2,05	3,70	2,16	3,53	3,37	2,88	3,75	5,57	4,20	5,01
	95% Male L–T*	4,49	2,17	3,68	2,16	3,54	3,50	2,86	3,82	5,63	4,27	5,03
	95% Male B–W***	4,47	1,92	3,67	2,32	3,70	3,43	2,85	4,13	5,88	4,42	5,04

Table 9. Joint capacity values for control panel without changes

Status	Manikin	Body parts high %	Body parts medium %			
Panel control-No changes	5% Female	0	Fingers	Head 79%	Shoulders 77–79%	
	5% Female Long Torso	0	Fingers	Head 79%	Shoulders 77–79%	
	5% Female Short torso	0	Fingers	Cervical joint 75%	Head 78%	Shoulder l 77%
	50% Male	0	Fingers	Cervical joint 79%	Head 78%	Shoulder l 77%
	95% Male Big waist	0	Fingers	Cervical joint 79%	Head 77%	Shoulder l 77%
	95% Male Long torso	0	Fingers	Elbow 77%	Head 79%	Shoulder l 77%

For the control panel, we created a kinematic for the object and the point created previously. The kinematic has DOF on X-axis, then it was adjusted moving it back and forth.

Similarly, as the way we did with the other three objects, we started changing the position of the control panel and reviewing the data for each one of the manikins. In this case, we also tried to reach the 3.5 value for the discomfort feeling. However, the priority was to improve the percentages in the joint capacity analysis, which as shown in Table 9, there is a high percentage of discomfort on the cervical joint, head, and shoulders.

We found that the best range for this control panel is between −90 mm and −70 mm on X-axis. The results for each manikin are shown below:

Table 10. Discomfort feeling for control panel considering the changes on the position in the X-axis

Position	Manikin	Neck	Shoulders	Back	Buttocks	Left Leg	Right Leg	Left Arm	Right Arm	Discomfort Feeling	Fatigue	Health	
										Part Name			
Panel control-Moving back and forth	5% Female	3,23	1,43	3,08	1,70	3,09	2,94	2,68	2,71	4,73	3,54	4,88	Change -90 mm
	5% Female L-T*	3,25	1,40	3,05	1,67	3,08	2,93	2,64	2,64	4,68	3,51	4,95	Change -90 mm
	5% Female S-T**	3,16	1,46	3,08	1,60	3,04	2,92	2,74	2,51	4,63	3,48	4,90	Change -70 mm x
	50% Male	3,72	1,62	3,19	1,92	3,29	3,09	2,68	3,41	5,08	3,83	5,03	Change -80 mm x
	95% Male L-T*	3,82	1,76	3,21	1,91	3,30	3,24	2,72	3,41	5,14	3,90	5,05	Change -80 mm x
	95% Male B-W***	3,81	1,68	3,38	1,96	3,53	3,27	2,45	3,57	5,32	4,00	5,00	Change -85 mm x

Table 11. Joint capacity percentage for the control panel considering the changes in the position in the X-axis

Status	Manikin	Body parts high %	Body parts medium %		
Panel control-Moving back and forth	5% Female	0	Fingers	Head 75%	Shoulders 77–80%
	5% Female Long Torso	0	Fingers	Head 76%	Shoulders 77–80%
	5% Female Short torso	0	Fingers	Shoulder 77%	
	50% Male	0	Fingers	Head 75%	Shoulders 77–79%
	95% Male Big waist	0	Fingers	Shoulder 77%	
	95% Male Long torso	0	Fingers	Head 77%	Shoulders 77–79%

As shown in Table 10 and Table 11 most values are below 3.5 and, the percentage and parts in the joint capacity analysis have improved. For the male manikins, we test multiple positions for the control panel in order to get values on the discomfort feeling for the neck, however, if we move it, for example, −90 mm on the X-axis we will reduce the discomfort feeling but the percentages in head and shoulders would increase. Therefore, we prioritize the joint capacity values over the discomfort feeling, keeping in mind that the latter is mainly used for driving positions.

We also make sure that the control panel was in the reachability definitions as shown in the following Figures (Fig. 21, Fig. 22, Fig. 23 and Fig. 24):

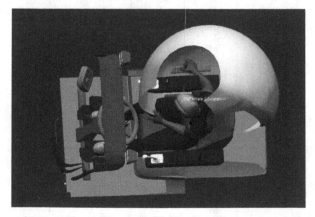

Fig. 21. 5th percentile Female and 5th percentile female Long torso interacting with the control panel.

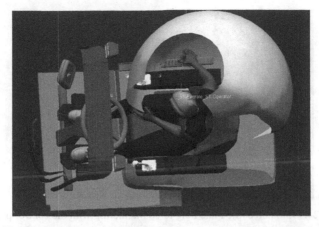

Fig. 22. 5th percentile female short torso interacting with the control panel.

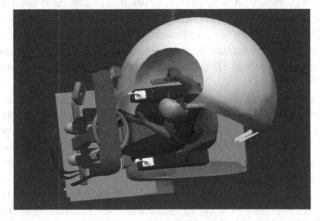

Fig. 23. th percentile Male and 95th percentile male big waist interacting with the control panel

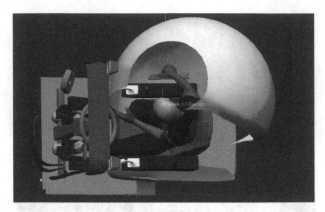

Fig. 24. 95th percentile male long torso interacting with the control panel

3 Discussion

From our prior experience, it was useful for us to already have used RAMSIS this semester in the first project of this course, as it was possible to go further in our modeling and analysis. The latter is complemented with the knowledge we acquire during this semester regarding human factors and ergonomics in different contexts. Also, knowing how to use additional 3D modeling software, help us to understand easier the functionalities of RAMSIS.

In this project, we think that the challenge was to find the proper range for each object and each manikin. The visualization of the analysis results for each manikin was not possible to have directly in RAMSIS as it was not possible to keep a value as a reference for all manikins. Therefore, we wrote down the results in tables, and in this way, it was easier for us to compare, prioritize certain values or analyses and, ensure the improvement of the results with every change.

We think that an important factor in this project, that will be useful for future students to have is the understanding of why we create the body measurements that we create. We think that, even if the explanation of how to build body measurements in our model was clear, the importance of the percentiles for each gender could be reviewed more in-depth, making sure that we are considering significant measurement if we intend to design an artefact that can be used by anybody, such as a car.

4 Future Work

In the Handbook of Human Factors and Ergonomics chapter 35, the author states: "Certainly health care is an application area that provides both opportunities and challenges concerning current and emerging human digital models" [5]. This is important for future work of the RAMSIS software because there are a lot of safety issues within the health care system that can be avoided if simulated beforehand. Some examples include the comfort of a patient before and after a medical procedure, the effect of the combination of administered medications, the duration, and rate of recovery of a patient after a medical procedure or sickness, etc. These are just a few examples of how the software can benefit the healthcare system and avoid mistakes in the process.

Another area that we think will be interesting would be to use RAMSIS to predict behavior. If RAMSIS could be used to predict and cognitive behavior, then we can look at the reaction time of when certain buttons or pedals are pressed which would benefit us by creating a forcing function of a specific movement of the body and different extremities [5]. We can use the ergonomic analysis to see what needs to be considered and get feedback on the discomfort and health of the operator.

References

1. Inyang, N., Al-Hussein, M., El-Rich, M., Al-Jibouri, S.: Ergonomic analysis and the need for its integration for planning and assessing construction tasks. J. Construct. Eng. Manage. **138**(12), 1370–1376 (2012). https://doi.org/10.1061/(ASCE)CO.1943-7862.0000556
2. Dul, J., et al.: A strategy for human factors/ergonomics: developing the discipline and profession. Ergonomics **55**(4), 377–395 (2012). https://doi.org/10.1080/00140139.2012.661087
3. Karwowski, W.: Ergonomics and human factors: the paradigms for science, engineering, design, technology, and management of human-compatible systems. Ergonomics **48**(5), 436–463 (2005). https://doi.org/10.1080/00140130400029167
4. Chaffin, D.B.: Human motion simulation for vehicle and workplace design. Hum. Fact. Ergon. Manuf. **17**(5), 475–484 (2007). https://doi.org/10.1002/hfm.20087
5. Duffy, V.G.: Human digital modeling in design. In: Handbook of Human Factors and Ergonomics. John Wiley & Sons, Inc. (2012). https://doi.org/10.1002/9781118131350.ch35

Effect Analysis of Each Reach Zone in Ergonomics During Putting and Pulling Movement of Shelf on VR Experiment

Satoki Tsuichihara$^{(\boxtimes)}$ ⓘ, Yuto Watanabe, Kaito Hara, and Yasutake Takahashi

University of Fukui, Fukui-shi, Bunkyo 3-9-1, Japan
satoki-t@u-fukui.ac.jp
http://ir.his.u-fukui.ac.jp

Abstract. In the imitation of human motion for humanoid robots, the variation of the motion should be satisfied, i.e., the efficiency of the paths and stability of the whole body. In ergonomics, reach zones have been defined to indicate safe and efficient positions of both hands for human movements. In a neutral zone of the reach zone, the humans can move using only their arms without other bodies. Outside of the neutral zone, humans need to use the torso and legs for the far target position of the hands, it is harmful to the chest and the legs. In this research, we believe that the robot can conduct the task outside the neutral zone instead of the human. In this paper, we measure the putting and pulling movement of shelf, which is necessary for a convenience store, to check the effect of each reach zone in a Virtual Reality environment. To verify the effect of each reach zone in the ergonomics, we change the distance between the shelf, which has a box to move, and the torso of the human as a percentage of the length of the human hand. In the evaluation of the posture of the torso and legs, it was found that the participants used their torso and knees more in the distance considered to be the maximum reach zone than in the distance considered to be the neutral zone.

Keywords: Reach zone in ergonomics · Posture evaluation · VR

1 Introduction

In recent years, due to the declining birthrate and aging population, the introduction of autonomous robots that can perform human tasks instead of humans has been active. In particular, humanoid robots, which have many joints, can perform motions by estimating human posture and design a variety of motions [1]. To satisfy the versatility of the measured human motions, it is necessary to measure the motions in the various configuration of the object's poses and prepare a large number of robot's movement data. As one of the motion measurement environments, there is the Virtual Reality (VR) environment. The VR environment

This work was supported by JSPS KAKENHI Grant Numbers JP21K13487.

V. G. Duffy and P.-L. P. Rau (Eds.): HCII 2022, LNCS 13522, pp. 336–347, 2022.
https://doi.org/10.1007/978-3-031-21704-3_21

is easy to change the configuration of the experimental environment flexibly and adjust the shape, size, and position of the objects and the workbench in the experiment, which are necessary to satisfy the versatility of human motion. The VR is also useful to require various scenarios of motion measurement.

The VR was used in a variety of research fields, for example, the implementation of an aircraft evacuation drill using VR [2]. Creating an environment similar to the actual environment to learn best close to actual experience was a study of how VR can provide knowledge and experience, the implementation of VR training which could not be tested in a real environment. There is a comparison between the results of training in a VR environment and a real environment [3]. The comparison was a study in which virtual training in a VR environment and physical training in a real environment are used to solve a puzzle, and the results of the puzzle and questionnaires were used to verify whether training in the VR environment is effective. In addition, online simultaneous learning and recognition of daily life activities were implemented in the VR [4]. This research used a VR training environment instead of a physical training environment, which is difficult to build in the cost issue, and used an inference system to classify known behaviors and learn new behaviors at the same time, extracting the task space used for the behavior and the available task space.

In the field of ergonomics, the reach areas are defined based on the damage of each human's body and joint part when a person works [5]. The work area is calculated by the length of a person's arm, and the work area in the horizontal plane can be further divided into a neutral reach zone and a maximum reach zone. The ratio of the neutral reach zone to the maximum reach zone is 15.5 inch to 20.0 inch, and in percentage terms, if the maximum range of the arm extension in the maximum reach zone is 100%, the neutral reach zone is 77.5%. Movements outside of the neutral reach zone are considered to reduce work efficiency and cause physical fatigue and are therefore tasks that we would like robots to perform on our behalf.

Related research on the relationship between VR and ergonomics was proposed, for example, the design of an ergonomically safe manufacturing site using VR technology by creating a virtual space that mimics a workplace and using VR to perform tasks in the same way as in the actual workplace [6]. Therefore, there was an effort to make a difference between the actual hand's movement and the modified movement in the VR, and to make the movement in the VR larger than the actual movement so that the body moves more in the VR even if it is moved a little [7]. There was also a study on a support system to design the reach zone using the VR [8]. In this research, a 3D magnetic sensor was used to perform movements in a VR environment, and the measured joint angles were used to determine the range of motion required for the subject to work in the VR environment. However, although several studies relate VR to ergonomics, there have been few studies that relate VR to the reach zone as the safety index.

In this study, we focus on the putting and pulling movement of the shelf (after this referred to as shelving motion), such as often conducted in a convenience store, to investigate whether the influence of the reach zone based on the motion data in the VR environment. During the shelving operation, the stability decrease because of both the weight of the object and the distance from the shelf. In the experiment, we implement a VR environment in which the distance between the subject and the shelf can be configured and configure the distance based on the subject's arm length. In this experiment, we measure the posture of the torso and legs and the ZMP (Zero Moment Point) [9] of the foot soles.

2   Evaluation of the Stability in Each Reach Zones

In the field of ergonomics, the reach zone is defined as the space used in planar or in three dimensions when a human moves [5]. The three-dimensional reach zone is composed of the horizontal and vertical reach zone of the two-dimensional reach zone. The reach zone is determined by the length of a person's arm, and the horizontal reach zone can be divided into the neutral reach zone and the maximum reach zone. Figure 2(a) shows the postures of the human body when

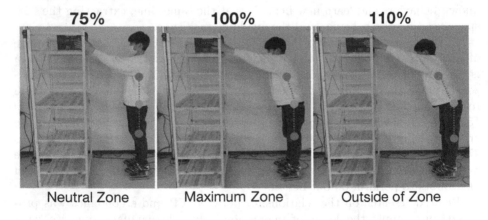

Fig. 1. The postures between inside and outside of neutral reach zone

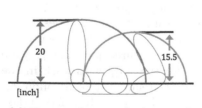

(a) Two reach zones (red: neutral, blue: maximum)

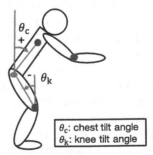

(b) The tilt angles of the chest and the knee

Fig. 2. The definition for calculating each evaluation score (Color figure online)

the person moves in the neutral reach zone (left) and maximum reach zone (middle) and outside of the zone (right). The neutral reach zone is the area that person can reach with the bending arm lightly, while the maximum reach zone is the area that person can reach without bending the arm. In the neutral reach zone, the hand can be reached without moving the torso, while outside the neutral reach zone, the body parts other than the arm, such as the torso and legs, must be used. The ratio of the radius of the neutral reach zone to that of the maximum reach zone is 15.5 inch to 20.0 inch, and in percentage terms, if the range of the maximum reach zone is 100%, the neutral reach zone is within 77.5% (Fig. 2(a)). The motion outside the neutral reach zone is an unreasonable motion for the worker, which may cause a decrease in work efficiency and physical fatigue, and is, therefore, a motion that we want the robot to perform for us.

The equations used in the evaluation are shown in Eq. (1), where E is the evaluation equation, E_c and E_k are the evaluation equations for the torso and knee, respectively. The weight of the chest and the knee are ω_c and ω_k. The tilt angles of the chest and the knee are $theta_c$ and θ_k. $theta_k$. Figure 2(b) shows the definition of the tilt angles of the chest θ_c and the knee θ_k. Using the tilt angles and the weight, the evaluation score E is calculated below.

$$E = E_c + E_k = \omega_c \Delta\theta_c + \omega_k \Delta\theta_k \tag{1}$$

The weights of the torso and knee were defined as in Eq. (2).

$$\omega_c = \frac{L_k^2}{\sqrt{L_c^2 + L_k^2}}, \omega_k = \frac{L_c^2}{\sqrt{L_c^2 + L_k^2}} \tag{2}$$

For the weights, we used the range from the minimum to the maximum values of the torso ($L_c = |\max(\boldsymbol{\theta}_c) - \min(\boldsymbol{\theta}_c)|$) and knee angles ($L_k = |\max(\boldsymbol{\theta}_k) - \min(\boldsymbol{\theta}_k)|$). For evaluation, the amount of change from the initial value at any given time i of the torso angle ($\Delta\theta_c = \theta_c(i) - \theta_c(0)$) and the knee angle ($\Delta\theta_k = \theta_k(i) - \theta_k(0)$).

3 Experiment

3.1 Outline

The experiment was conducted on four males who were 20 years old. As the examples of the posture, the feature during movements measured in the experiment is shown in Fig. 3. First, they put their hands out in front of them to grab a box on the top board of the shelf, pull the box to their bodies with their hands in their hands, and put the box on the middle-height board with their hands in front of them. This series of actions, called "shelving movement", was tested in a VR environment. The distance between the shelf and the person is changed using a percentage of the arm length, and the configured distance is changed every 5% from 65% to 110% for ten times to perform the shelving motion. The reason for starting the measurements at 65% is that 65% is the shortest distance

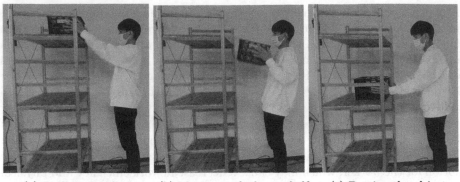

(a) Pulling the object   (b) Moving to the lower shelf   (c) Putting the object

Fig. 3. The postures during putting and pulling movement of shelf

at which the movement can be performed without straining, and the reason for measuring up to 110% is to check if the trend of the results is the same for distances after 100%. At each distance, we measured the posture of the torso and legs and the ZMP of the soles of the feet. In particular of Fig. 3 (a) and (c), the changes in posture were large to determine the degree of use of the torso and knees and the degree of ZMP use. To evaluate the reach zone in ergonomics for the VR environment, we evaluate the use of the torso and knees, as well as the ZMP.

3.2 Devices Used in the Experiment

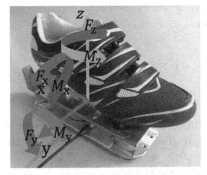

(a) VIVE Pro Eye

(b) Shoe which has 6-axes force and torque sensor

Fig. 4. Devices used in the experiment

VR HMD. To conduct the experiment in a VR environment, we use a VR device called VIVE Pro Eye from HTC (Fig. 4(a)). Figure 4(a) contains a Head-Mounted Display (HMD), a controller, and a base station. The HMD is used for viewing VR images, the controller is used for manipulating objects in the VR environment, the base station is used for calibrating the real space and the VR space, and the tracker is worn on a person's body to measure the poses of the body parts and joints.

Shoes-Type Foot Force Sensor. In the experiment, we measure the ZMP to investigate the stability of the whole body using a 6-axis force sensor. The 6-axis force sensor is Leptrino's FFS Series (FFS080YS102U6, sensor is located in the middle between the sole plate and the shoe as shown in Fig. 4(b)), which can measure the translational force (F_x, F_y, F_z in the x, y, and z directions) and the moment of force (M_x, M_y, M_z) around each axis.

In order to calculate the balance of the foot in the frontal direction of the human, it is necessary to measure the ZMP in the x-axis direction as shown in Fig. 4(b). Using translational forces (F_x and F_z) and moment (M_y) measured by the 6-axis force sensor, the ZMP can be calculated by Eq. (3).

$$p_{R_x} = \frac{-M_y - F_x d}{F_z} \tag{3}$$

3.3 Implementation of Putting and Pulling Movement in VR Environment

(a) Configuration with a real shelf

(b) Configuration in the VR environment

Fig. 5. Experimental environment

To implement the VR environment, we used Unity Technologies' game development platform. We add the floor and the player in the imported assets to the VR. The player contains a camera and a hand when the VR device is connected, and the camera is connected to the HMD, and the HMD shows the VR image from the camera. The hand is connected to the controller, and by moving the controller, the hand on the VR moves in the same way. Next, we created a shelf and a box with the same dimensions as the real shelf (860 mm wide, 500 mm depth, 1755 mm height) and the box (414 mm wide, 304 mm depth, 195 mm height).

The HMD is used to view the VR image, the controller is used to manipulate the objects in the VR, and the tracker is used to acquire the position and rotation angle of the body part by attaching it to the body. The controller and the hand on the VR move in the same way. In the experiment, we used the controller to move a box on a shelf board. When the controller is close enough to the box to grab it, the box is highlighted in yellow. In the VR environment, the box can be grasped by pulling the trigger of the controller, and while the trigger is pulled, the box follows the controller, and the hand is invisible. When the player releases the trigger of the controller, the player can put down the box. The box will not stay in the air because of gravity, and if the player releases the box in the air, it will fall to the ground. There is a collision detection function between the shelf and the box, and the controller will vibrate when they collide. We used three trackers (Fig. 5(a)), one for the right elbow, one for the chest, and one for the right knee. In the experiment, the distance between the shelf and the person was changed as a percentage of the arm length, so the distance could be adjusted by fixing the position of the shelf and changing the position of the player. In addition, to investigate the stability ZMP of the foot, we wore shoes with 6-axis force sensors.

3.4   Procedure of Experiment

The experimental procedure is shown below.

1. Measure the length of the subject's arm from the shoulder to the fingertip.
2. Enter the percentage of the measured arm length in the player coordinates in the VR to adjust the distance to the shelf.
3. Perform the shelving movement.
4. Measure the posture of the torso and legs and the ZMP of the feet at each distance.

Repeat the procedure of the measurement, changing the distance every 5% from 65% to 110% of the arm's length as a percentage.

Figure 6 shows the posture for one subject during the shelving movement. In each movement, Fig. 6(a) is the posture when grasping the box in the neutral reach zone, Fig. 6(b) is the posture when grasping the box in the maximum reach zone, Fig. 6(c) is the posture when placing the box in the neutral reach zone, and Fig. 6(d) is the posture when placing the box in the maximum reach zone.

3.5   Experimental Result

The angles of the torso and the knees during the shelving movement at each distance are shown in Fig. 7.

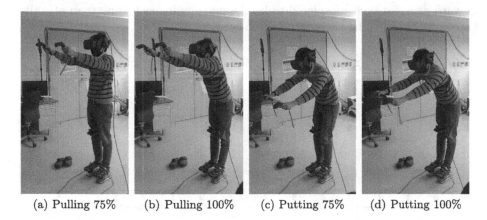

(a) Pulling 75%   (b) Pulling 100%   (c) Putting 75%   (d) Putting 100%

Fig. 6. Measured postures during the putting and pulling movement of the shelf in VR environment

The use ratio of the torso and knees (Eq. (1))during the shelving movement at each distance is shown in Fig. 8.

In the Fig. 9, the use of the torso and knees when putting the box does not show the same trend as when pulling, but appears to be decreasing. This shows that when grasping the box, the torso and knees move more at a distance around 100% of the arm length than at a distance around 75% of the arm length, but when placing the box, the torso and knees move less.

The right foot ZMPs in the forward and backward directions during the shelving movement at each distance are shown in Fig. 10.

3.6   Evaluation

In the evaluation of the posture of the torso and legs, subjects 1, 2, and 4 moved their torso and knees more at the distance of 100% than at the distance of 75% of the arm length through the shelving movement. So the safety index of ergonomic working range used in the real environment must be taken into account in the VR environment as well. However, the movements of subject 3 were generally the same, and except for when grabbing a box in the shelving movement, there was no particular reach zone to be considered. This may be due to their understanding of the shelving movement and their familiarity with the VR, and the fact that they were exposed to the VR several times in the process leading up to the experiment may have resulted in similar body movements at all distances.

ZMP evaluation did not show that the subjects moved with their body weight forward at a distance considered to be the maximum reach zone than at a distance considered to be the neutral reach zone.

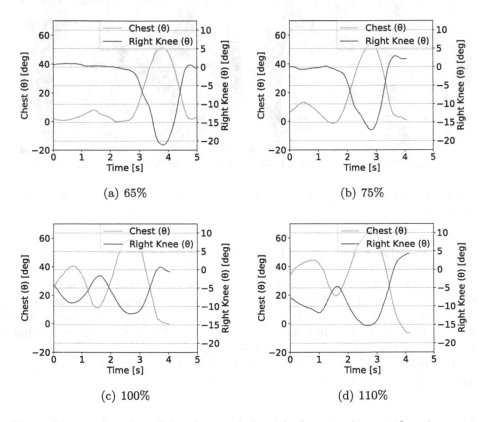

Fig. 7. Measured angles of the chest and the right knee in the actual environment during the putting and pulling movement of the shelf in VR environment

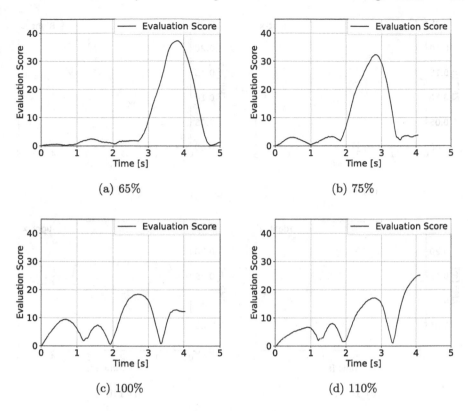

Fig. 8. Measured angles of the chest and the right knee in the actual environment during the putting and pulling movement of the shelf in VR environment

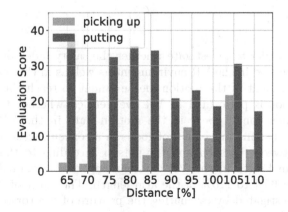

Fig. 9. The postures between inside and outside of neutral reach zone

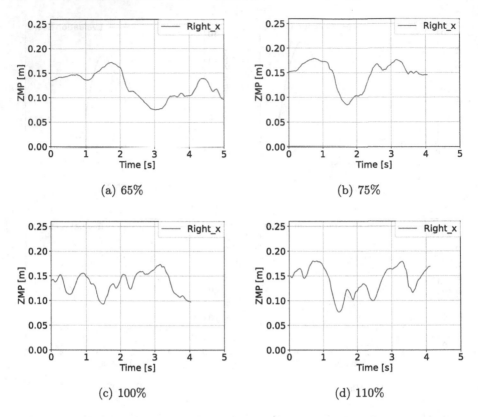

Fig. 10. Measured ZMP in the actual environment during the putting and pulling movement of the shelf in VR environment

4   Conclusion

In this study, in order to investigate whether the safety index of the ergonomic reach zone is required in the VR environment as well as in the real environment when the environment of the motion measurement to teach the motion to the autonomous robot is performed in VR, we verified whether the results that consider the reach zone appear in the motion data in the VR environment. Focusing on the shelving movement of goods in a convenience store, we changed the distance between the shelf and the person according to the percentage of the person's arm length in the VR environment, and measured a total of 10 movements from 65% to 110% of the arm length. The effect of distance on the posture was investigated by evaluating the posture of the torso and legs using three methods: the average torso angle, the average knee angle, and the degree of use of the torso and knees, and evaluating ZMP using two methods: the amount of change in ZMP and its average value.

The experimental results showed that three out of four subjects used their torso and knees more at the distance of 100% than at the distance of 75% of the arm length through the shelving movement in the evaluation of torso and leg posture, indicating that the working range of ergonomics must be considered in VR environments. However, the ZMP evaluation did not show that the four subjects put more weight forward at distances near 100% of the arm length than at distances near 75% of the arm length, and it was not clear whether the reach zone should be considered. This may be because we tried to match the start time of the ZMP measurement to the start time of the shelving movement, but in reality, the initial value of the ZMP was slightly off and different from the ZMP in the stable state of upright immobility. In the future, we would like to improve the method of the experiment a little, for example, to have the participants stand still in a cautionary posture when measuring the ZMP, and to have them perform the shelving movement after starting the ZMP measurement.

References

1. Yoshikawa, T., Losing, Viktor., Demircan, E.: Machine learning for human movement understanding. J. Robot. Mechatron. **34**(13) 828–844 (2020)
2. Sharma, S., Otunba, S.: Collaborative virtual environment to study aircraft evacuation for training and education. In: 2012 International Conference on Collaboration Technologies and Systems (CTS), pp. 569–574, (2012)
3. Murcia-Lopez, M., Steed, A.: Comparison of virtual and physical training transfer of bimanual assembly tasks. In: IEEE Transactions on Visualization and Computer Graphics, vol. 24, pp. 1574–1583 (2018)
4. Bates, T., Ramirez-Amaro, K., Inamura, T., Cheng, G.: On-line simultaneous learning and recognition of everyday activities from virtual reality performances. In: 2017 IEEE/RSJ International Conference on Intelligent Robots and Systems (IROS), pp. 3510-3515 (2017)
5. Ergonomics in daily life. Jikkyo Shuppan Co., pp. 90–95 (2011)
6. Grajewski, D., Gorski, F., Zawadzki, P., Hamrol, A.: Application of virtual reality techniques in design of ergonomic manufacturing workplaces. Procedia Comput. Sci. **25**, 289–301 (2013)
7. Montano Murillo, R.A., Subramanian, S., Martinez Plasencia, D.: Erg-o: Ergonomic optimization of immersive virtual environments. In: Proceedings of the 30th Annual ACM Symposium on User Interface Software and Technology, pp. 759–771 (2017)
8. Virtual reality system for designing working area. In: Proceedings of 6th Mechanical Engineering Congress (2017)
9. Kajita, S., Hirukawa, H., Harada, K., Yokoi, K.: Introduction to Humanoid Robotics. STAR, vol. 101. Springer, Heidelberg (2014). https://doi.org/10.1007/978-3-642-54536-8

Nagereru-Kun: Design and Implementation of a Bowling Form Reflection Support Application for Beginners

Shigetoshi Uraya, Yoshinari Takegawa[✉], and Keiji Hirata

Future University Hakodate, Hakodate, Japan
{g2120045,yoshi,hirata}@fun.ac.jp

Abstract. In this research, our goal is to design and implement an application to support reflection on bowling form, targeted at bowling beginners. Learning correct bowling form is a vital factor for steadily achieving high scores. The influence of physical ability, weight of the ball, fatigue, and so on can easily cause deterioration of form. By using a video camera to record form at the moment of bowling a ball, it is possible to confirm visually how one is bowling, yetit is difficult to notice deterioration of form, or errors. The proposed application uses a camera to record the conditions of a learner when bowling a ball. The application has a function that enables comparison of the recorded bowling images, example images, images of when the learner bowled correctly, and so on, in the form of frame-by-frame images. In addition, there is a function that cues several comparison images for each moment in bowling form, such as the moment the ball is released. An evaluative experiment was conducted to compare the proposed method, which is the application we developed that uses evaluation functions, and a comparative method consisting of watching video of bowling. As a result, in a quiz, the average correct answer rate of subjects who used the proposed method was 45% higher than that of those who used the comparative method and a significant difference was observed when a two-sided Student's t-test was applied at a significance level of 5%.

Keywords: Visualization · Learning support · Viewer

1 Introduction

The flow of a single turn in bowling comprises the decision of the bowling position to be assumed at the time of rolling the ball, the proceeding run-up, and the release of the ball. Learning correct bowling form is important for steadily achieving high scores. The influence of physical ability, weight of the ball, fatigue, and so on can easily cause deterioration of form. By using a video camera to record

This work was supported by JSPS KAKENHI Grant Number JP19H04157.

V. G. Duffy and P.-L. P. Rau (Eds.): HCII 2022, LNCS 13522, pp. 348–358, 2022.
https://doi.org/10.1007/978-3-031-21704-3_22

form when bowling a ball, it is possible to confirm visually how one is bowling, yet it is difficult to notice errors or deterioration of form, because this requires analysis of both brief motions lasting only tens of milliseconds and microscopic differences of motion.

In recent years, there has been a great deal of research involving introducing ICT into sports to support skill acquisition. Various systems have been proposed, such as a system that incorporates mixed reality into golf training and presents the user with an instructor's motion data [2] and a system that incorporates VR into skiing training and visualizes a coach's skiing, as well as visualizing differences between the movement of the learner and the coach, in the form of a graph [8]. There is also a skiing system that has a function to present example images of a coach's skiing form that are synchronized with images of the learner's form, to support repetitive practice [1]. It can be said that presenting example video, as in these systems, is effective for skill improvement, but when learners themselves are able to analyze disparity in their movements, we can expect not only promotion of learners' comprehension of their own mistakes, and creation of methods for improvement, but also metacognitive learning whereby learners comprehend the tendency of their mistakes.

Therefore, in this research, our goal is to design and implement a bowling form reflection support application - Nagereru-kun- to enable bowling beginners to notice disparity in their form.

2   Related Research

Currently, the application of IoT to sports equipment is progressing, beyond just the field of bowling. For example, in Technical Pitch, developed by Acrodea Inc., a 9-axis sensor is installed within a baseball and a specified application carries out analysis of data gathered when the ball is thrown [6]. Ogawa et al. [4], in their bowling-related research, propose software to record and feed back the appearance of a professional bowler when bowling. In our research, we refer to these previous works and propose visual support to enable users to reflect on their bowling form. While the aforementioned systems are video-based, our research differs in that it proposes reflection support by an image-based frame-by-frame playback format which has a function that can cue important events in bowling form.

There are many works of research that tackle the analysis or visualization of body motion, besides in bowling. For example, Urribarri et al. [7] apply time compensation by DTW (Dynamic Time Warping) to motion capture data obtained from karate moves, and propose a means capable of comparing multiple items of motion data. In addition, Liu [3] proposes a visualization method that expresses gestures as vectors and plots them on a sphere. Also, Sujino et al. [5] propose a visualization method that emphasizes focus points, such as where instruction is required. Yoshimura et al. [9] focused on head movement and rhythm to develop a dance mastery support system that enables easy comparison of the dancing of an instructor and that of a learner.

As we have shown, there is much existing research relating to visualization of motion. However, visualization in the form of frame-by-frame image playback, specified for bowling, has not yet been investigated.

3   Interview with Professional Bowler

To consider functions for reflection on bowling form, targeted at beginners, we conducted a depth interview with a professional bowler who teaches beginners at a bowling alley. The interview lasted approximately one hour and was carried out by one of the authors of this paper. Also, the interview was recorded with an IC recorder. Permission to record was obtained from the interviewee beforehand.

Two of the authors of this paper considered the interview method and question items based on the behavioral observation technique of observing the interviewee instructing beginners. As a result, to increase feasibility, it was decided to have the professional bowler watch video of three different beginners bowling and ask 'what aspects of bowling form would you focus on when giving instruction?'.

3.1   Interview Results

The content of the interview was written up and analyzed.

Focus Points of Bowling Form. We obtained the statement that there are certain points to focus on when providing instruction on bowling form, and these can be classified as the following five items:

- Standing position: Confirming whether the bowler is standing in an appropriate position in relation to the remaining pins on the lane, when beginning to bowl. Generally, it is desirable to bowl one's first ball down the center, then bowl the second ball at an angle so that it is more likely to touch the remaining pins.
- Backswing maximum: Confirming the height of the ball when it is lifted during backswing. Generally, the maximum height of the ball should be level with the bowler's hip.
- Moment of release: Confirming the state of the impact of the ball on the lane, after it is released from the bowler's hand. Generally, it is desirable for the ball to hit the lane with low impact.
- Directly after bowling: Confirming the bowler's pose after bowling, the angle of the feet in relation to the lane and the position of the bowling arm. Generally, the feet and arm should be horizontal to the lane.
- Four-step run-up: When bowling, after the ball is lifted level with the bowler's chest, in preparation, a four-step run-up is taken before releasing the ball. Generally, on the first step the bowler holds the ball at chest level. On the second step the bowler lowers the ball. On the third step the bowler raises the ball high behind himself and inclines his body forward, on the principle of a pendulum. On the fourth step the bowler releases the ball, assuming a posture that allows the ball to be thrust forward vigorously.

Past Bowling, and Instruction by Comparison to other Bowlers. The professional made the following comments: "Because most beginners can't correctly visualize what kind of form they have when throwing, it's important to get pupils to form a concrete image of how they themselves are bowling". "I explain to pupils, in words, about how they are bowling, and, when it's difficult to understand from words alone, I re-enact what they did. Also, because bowling form alters gradually due to exhaustion and so on, I give a tangible explanation of the deterioration or improvement of form by comparing it to the pupil's past form each time and showing how it differs from the directly preceding form." "For pupils learning in groups, it is easy for them to understand when I compare each person's bowling form to that of pupils of the same level or slightly higher, and explain how their form differs from the directly preceding turn". From these statements it is clear that the professional carried out bowling form reflection through comparison, to give his pupils a tangible understanding of their bowling form.

Difficulty of Confirming Focus Points from Video. The professional offered the following comments: "I think it is important for pupils to check their own bowling form from bowling footage like this, but I don't think they will improve simply by looking at video. It's important to enable them to check focus points properly and to check the difference between their form and that of an example. In particular, because each focus point of bowling form is only an instant within the video, I think focus points are difficult for beginner pupils to determine". From this it can be understood that simply showing learners video of their bowling is not sufficient. Furthermore, the professional remarked "I think it would be good if there was some means of presenting to what extent pupils' form is off".

3.2   Requirements

As a result of analyzing the interview with the professional bowler, the following functional requirements became evident.

(A) Effective presentation of focus points in bowling form
(B) Bowling form comparison focused on degree of incorrectness of focus points

4   Nagereru-kun

Based on the interview results, we propose a bowling form reflection support application, 'Nagereru-kun', targeted at beginners.

Figure 1 shows a screenshot from Nagereru-kun. The frame-by-frame playback image is presented in the center of the screen. The horizontal direction is the time axis, while the vertical direction represents each bowling turn. In Fig. 1, three turns of bowling are presented. One series of frame-by-frame playback images comprises the images from the start of bowling (the moment of holding the ball and standing on the lane) to the moment directly after bowling (the moment of assuming a pose after releasing the ball). Figure 1 shows three frames from one series of frame-by-frame playback images. Also, in frame-by-frame playback images corresponding to focus points, annotation on the relevant focus points has been added manually.

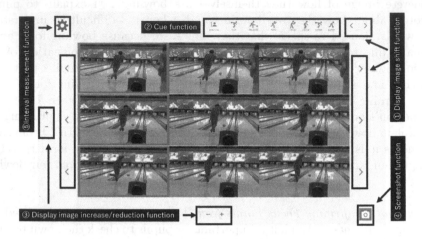

Fig. 1. Screenshot

(1) Display Image Shift Function

The display image shift function is a function that, taking the currently displayed frame-by-frame playback image as a basis, can shift to either the next frame or the preceding frame. This function has two types of buttons. The buttons to the right and left of the frame-by-frame playback image can progress or return the frames of each bowling turn one-by-one. This can be used to perform a detailed check, for example of a slight difference between the arm movement of the user and other bowlers. In contrast, the buttons at the top can be used to progress or return the entire set of frames for a turn.

(2) Cue Function

The cue function is used when comparing focus points. Clicking on each button causes the focus point frames corresponding to that button to be displayed. Based on the results of the interview with the pro bowler, we prepared focus point buttons corresponding to the timing of bowling position (POSITION), backswing maximum (MAX), the moment the ball is released from the hand (RELEASE) and the form after the ball has been bowled (POSE), as well as the timing of the four-step run-up (1st STEP - 4th STEP).

(3) Display Image Increase/Reduction Function

The display image increase/reduction function is a function that can alter the number of frame-by-frame playback images displayed on the screen. A maximum of 10 frames each for 6 people's worth of bowling images can be displayed.

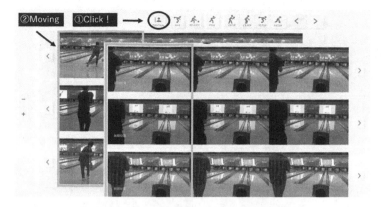

Fig. 2. Cue function

Fig. 3. Example of the number of displayed images

(4) Screenshot Function

The screenshot function is a function for saving the currently displayed image as a screenshot.

(5) Interval Measurement Function

Whereas the cue function concentrates on cueing up focus points in bowling, the interval measurement function visualizes the length of the intervals between focus points. The [START] and [STOP] icons at the bottom left express from what time to what time is being displayed. For example, in Fig. 4, the system displays all the bowling images from the interval between the third step of the four-step run-up to when the ball is raised highest. It is good if the timing from the third step to the maximum raise is mostly consistent. From the number of images being displayed, the user can see to what extent their timing is off. Incidentally,

Fig. 4. Zone function

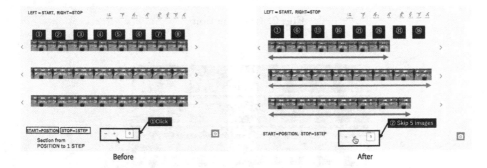

Fig. 5. Skip of zone function

when there are too many images to be contained within the frame, one to five display images can be skipped over by pressing the button at the bottom of the screen. Figure 5-After is the consecutive images displayed when five images have been skipped over from Fig. 5-Before and the next images displayed.

5   Evaluative Experiment

An evaluative experiment was conducted to investigate whether disparity in bowling form could be comprehended by using Nagereru-kun. A task was carried out in which, within a specified time, subjects answered a quiz about three rolls performed by the same person. Subjects were divided into two groups: a group who undertook the task using our system, Nagereru-kun, explained in Sect. 4, and a group who undertook the task using a pre-existing video playback application (Quick Time). It can be said that the higher the correct answer rate of the quiz, the more accurate the subject's judgement of disparity of form.

Table 1. Quiz

Question	Proposed method correct answer rate(%)	Comparative method Correct answer rate(%)
(1) On which turn was the ball raised highest?	90	100
(2) On which turn was the pose after bowling most correct?	81	36
(3) On which turn was the right shoulder lowered most in the zone between step 1 and step 2?	72	36
(4) On which turn was the ball raised highest from step 2 to step 3?	63	36
(5) On which turn was the body most inclined forward from step 3 to step 4?	54	36
(6) On which turn was the ball raised highest from step 4 to release?	100	81
(7) Which of the three turns exhibits the best form?	63	0
(8) Which turn took the longest time from starting position to step 1?	81	81
(9) Which turn took the longest time from step 1 to step 2?	100	36
(10) Which turn took the longest time from step 2 to step 3?	100	45
(11) Which turn took the longest time from step 3 to maximum lift?	100	9
(12) Which turn took the longest time from maximum lift to step 4?	100	36
(13) Which turn took the longest time from step 4 to the moment of release?	90	27
(14) Which turn took the longest time from the moment of release to the final pose?	100	18

Hereafter, Nagereru-kun is referred to as the proposed method and the pre-existing video playback application is referred to as the comparative method.

5.1 Subjects

The subjects who took part in the experiment were 16 males and females aged between 21 and 25 years old, all of whom were bowling beginners. 8 subjects each were assigned to the comparative method and proposed method respectively. Each subject completed the experiment using only one of the two methods. Also, how to operate the assigned methods was explained to the subjects.

5.2 Flow of the Experiment

The flow of the experiment was as follows.

(1) Subjects received instruction regarding how to operate the method they would use in the experiment, and actually practiced using the method to confirm that they understood.

(2) Within a 15 min time limit, subjects answered the quiz while using the application that had been assigned to them.

When the operation methods of the applications were explained, subjects were instructed "When you are answering the quiz, please tell us if there is any vocabulary you do not understand or any question you find difficult". In addition, subjects were told "Using your assigned method, please answer the quiz as quickly as possible, within the time limit". To check how the subjects used their assigned methods to answer the quiz, their screens were recorded during the experiment. Incidentally, in both methods, there were no subjects who found the task too difficult and gave up. Furthermore, there were no subjects who totally disregarded the functions of their assigned applications and used an individual method to practice.

5.3   Results

The results for the proposed method and comparative method are presented in Table 1. The higher the correct answer rate, the more accurately the subject was able to answer. The average correct answer rate of the proposed method was 85% (SD: 15%), while the average correct answer rate of the comparative method was 40% (SD:27%). When a two-sided Student's t-test was conducted at a significance level of 5%, a significant difference (t (14) $= 2.0$, $p = .05$) was observed. Accordingly, it can be said that the average correct answer rate of subjects who used the proposed method was significantly higher than that of subjects who used the comparative method.

5.4   Considerations

Average Correct Answer Rate. In comparison to the correct answer rate of the comparative method, the correct answer rate of the proposed method was high overall. As reasons for this, the proposed method's comparison of bowling in the form of frame-by-frame playback images, cue function and interval measurement function are considered to have contributed to the increased correct answer rate. The majority of the subjects who used the comparative method answered by repeatedly watching the video, concentrating on the places corresponding to the quiz questions. On the other hand, the subjects who used the proposed method answered by using the cue function and interval measurement function to quickly display the frame-by-frame playback images corresponding to the quiz questions, and comparing the frames from the three turns. From all the subjects who used the comparative method, we received the comment that it was difficult to judge a disparity of tens of milliseconds or a slight difference in movement from a video.

The one question in regard to which the correct answer rate of the proposed method was lower than that of the comparative method was 'on which turn was the ball raised highest?'. In this question, subjects click the MAX button of Nagereru-kun's cue function and determine on which turn the ball was raised highest. However, the only subject in the proposed method group who answered incorrectly said that the second highest ball was the highest. This is thought to be because the subject judged whether the ball was high or low by comparing the position of the raised ball with the position of the bowler's hip.

Points for Improvement of the Proposed Method. As a point for improvement of the proposed method, obtained through a questionnaire after the experiment was completed, it was pointed out that there was a time lag between pressing the cue function or interval measurement function button and the relevant results being displayed. This caused problems, such as subjects, before getting used to the time lag, repeatedly pressing the aforementioned buttons and no results being displayed. We intend to resolve this issue by means such as simplifying image display processing in the program, or having the buttons change color when pressed. Another issue raised was that the system included a lot of specialized terms that are difficult for beginners to understand. We plan to address this by providing a fully comprehensive user manual, for example.

6   Conclusion

In this research, we constructed a bowling form reflection support application, targeted at bowling beginners. We interviewed a professional bowler who instructs beginners, to formulate the necessary requirements for reflection on bowling form. The appearance of a learner when bowling is recorded and, based on the resulting camera images, the proposed application displays bowling footage as frame-by-frame playback images. The application has a function to display frame-by-frame playback images from multiple turns. There is also a function to cue frame-by-frame playback images corresponding to focus points in bowling form, such as the moment the ball is released. We conducted an evaluative experiment to investigate whether the proposed application contributes to determination of disparity in bowling form. As a result of conducting an experiment, with a proposed method using the application we developed and a comparative method of watching bowling video on a pre-existing video playback application, the average correct answer rate of the quiz for subjects who used the proposed method was 45% higher than that of the subjects who used the comparative method. Furthermore, when a two-sided Student's t-test was conducted at a significance level of 5%, a significant difference was observed between the correct answer rates of the proposed method and comparative method.

As future work, there is the implementation of a function to automatically extract each of the focus points. Also, in the evaluative experiment, we focused on whether disparity in bowling form could be correctly comprehended, but it is necessary to carry out evaluation concerning whether the application contributes to comprehension of errors in bowling form, improvement of form and increase of score.

References

1. Hamanishi, N., Rekimoto, J.: Poseasquery: Full-body interface for repeated observation of a person in a video with ambiguous pose indexes and performed poses. In: Proceedings of the Augmented Humans International Conference. AHs '20, Association for Computing Machinery, New York, NY, USA (2020). https://doi.org/10.1145/3384657.3384658
2. Ikeda, A., Hwang, D.H., Koike, H.: AR based Self-sports Learning System using Decayed Dynamic TimeWarping Algorithm. In: Bruder, G., Yoshimoto, S., Cobb, S. (eds.) ICAT-EGVE 2018 - International Conference on Artificial Reality and Telexistence and Eurographics Symposium on Virtual Environments. The Eurographics Association (2018). https://doi.org/10.2312/egve.20181330
3. Liu, L., Long, D., Magerko, B.: Moviz: A visualization tool for comparing motion capture data clustering algorithms. In: Proceedings of the 7th International Conference on Movement and Computing, pp. 1–8 (2020)
4. Ogawa, T., Kagawa, M.: Development and assessment of feedback software by image for bowling player. J. Inform. Educ. **7**, 1–7 (2010)
5. Sujino, S., Moriya, T., Takahashi, T.: Development of a hip-hop dance coaching system by using kinect. In: International Workshop on Advanced Image Technology (2013)
6. Technical Pitch: Technical Pitch. https://technicalpitch.net/ (9 2017) Accessed 27 Aug 2021
7. Urribarri, D.K., Larrea, M.L., Castro, S.M., Puppo, E.: Overview+Detail Visual Comparison of Karate Motion Captures. In: Pesado, P., Arroyo, M. (eds.) CACIC 2019. CCIS, vol. 1184, pp. 139–154. Springer, Cham (2020). https://doi.org/10.1007/978-3-030-48325-8_10
8. Wu, E., Nozawa, T., Perteneder, F., Koike, H.: VR alpine ski training augmentation using visual cues of leading skier. In: 2020 IEEE/CVF Conference on Computer Vision and Pattern Recognition Workshops (CVPRW), pp. 3836–3845 (2020). https://doi.org/10.1109/CVPRW50498.2020.00447
9. Yoshimura, M., Murasato, H., Kai, T., Kuromiya, A., Yokoyama, K., Hachimura, K.: Analysis of japanese dance movements using motion capture system. Syst. Comput. Japan **37**, 71–82 (2006). https://doi.org/10.1002/scj.20250

Development of a WBGT Index Meter Based on M5Stack Core2

José Varela-Aldás[1,2](✉) ⓘ, Jorge Buele[1,2] ⓘ, Hairo Mosquera[1] ⓘ,
and Guillermo Palacios-Navarro[2] ⓘ

[1] SISAu Research Group, Facultad de Ingeniería y Tecnologías de la Información y la
Comunicación, Universidad Tecnológica Indoamérica, Ambato 180103, Ecuador
{josevarela,jorgebuele}@uti.edu.ec, hmosquera@indoamerica.edu.ec
[2] Department of Electronic Engineering and Communications,
University of Zaragoza, 44003 Teruel, Spain
guillermo.palacios@unizar.es

Abstract. Environmental working conditions are of crucial importance for job
performance. Thus, thermal comfort helps the human body to withstand long
working hours without stress. There are several indicators of heat stress, but one
of the most complete is the WBGT (Wet Bulb Globe Temperature) index, which
considers 3 temperatures to determine the heat stress index, the dry bulb temperature, the wet-bulb temperature, and the temperature of radiation. For this reason,
this document describes the process of building a low-cost heat stress meter. Two
DHT22 sensors and M5Stack Core2 controller are used that includes a screen
for the presentation of the information. The user interface includes buttons for
changing the view type to show indoor or outdoor results, as well as the battery
level. In addition, all this information is sent to the IoT platform of ThingSpeak
through internet access using WiFi communication, this information can be displayed graphically from a web browser and from anywhere in the world. The data
are compared with a commercial meter to validate this prototype, obtaining an
error of less than 5% and no significant differences were found. In this way, it is
possible to offer equipment for industrial solutions, but at a fraction of its cost.

Keywords: Heat Stress Meter · IoT · WBGT Index · M5Stack Core2

1 Introduction

According to the International Labour Organization (ILO), despite advances in safety
and health at work, access rates remain high. It is estimated that 5,300 people die daily
from accidental causes and work-related illnesses [1, 2]. While, on an annual basis, there
are about 312 million accidents. In Nicaragua and El Salvador, temperatures reach 42 °C,
which harms young people and adults in their work activities. This classifies heat stress
as a "silent disease", with a high incidence in outdoor tasks [3]. Heat stress is a feeling
of discomfort that a person experiences as a result of being in an environment that has
not been suitable for them for a long time [4]. Given the low humidity of human skin,
overexposure to unfavorable thermal conditions leads to increased regulatory effort [5].

© Springer Nature Switzerland AG 2022
V. G. Duffy and P.-L. P. Rau (Eds.): HCII 2022, LNCS 13522, pp. 359–372, 2022.
https://doi.org/10.1007/978-3-031-21704-3_23

According to forecasts in the year 2045, at least 50% of the world population will live in high-risk areas [6].

In the floricultural sector, heat stress affects not only people but also the flora and fauna of every region. For this reason, recent studies describe the negative effects of high temperatures on crops in Costa Rica. This causes alterations in physiological processes such as accelerated development, stability of the membranes, and breathing. In Sonora, Mexico, wheat is impacted by the risk of climate change, damaging the region's ecosystems and industrial development [7]. The optimum environmental values for the development of greenhouse crops are greater than those which determine a comfortable working situation. Therefore, the work is specifically affected by conditions such as ventilation, radiant temperature, air humidity, and ambient temperature. Indicators of human heat stress refer to the function of physical activity and the temperature of the surrounding environment.

This risk is among the twenty-four main dangers of Non-Traumatic Forms of Work Accidents, mentioned by the National Institute of Safety and Hygiene at Work. Consistent measurements and analyses of radiation levels are the best way to address these concerns. In Iran, a comparison of different heat stress indices is made, where the validity of the WBGT (Wet Bulb Globe Temperature) index is evidenced, which is currently the most used [7]. In [8] several measurements of the heat stress index are made under different environmental conditions and clothing combinations in the USA. The results show that the work environment and clothing affect the comfort of the work done. While [9] describes the high values of the WBGT index that were measured at the 2014 Australian Open Tennis Championships and the precautions that workers and spectators should take. In [10] the changes in the WBGT index that currently exist as a result of climate change in China, Australia, Africa, and Central America are analyzed.

In Latin America, there are few studies on the work in which extreme temperatures are found [11]. For many businesses, there is a great lack of knowledge about its impact and the health issues that workers may present. In addition, the companies that perform this monitoring do so manually, which makes it a time-consuming and exhaustive process. A further disadvantage is a high cost that commercial meters can have and that low-income industries cannot afford. This demonstrates the need to make low-cost proposals that involve new technologies. The Internet of Things (IoT) and industry 4.0 systems are based on sharing information in real-time, which facilitates analysis and decision making. This is especially true in applications involving human well-being, such as ergonomics at work. Access to new, low-cost technologies offers the opportunity for more affordable and feature-rich solutions, including IoT [12, 13].

Good ergonomics maximize output and reduce medical costs due to occupational diseases and downtimes [14]. Exposure to these temperatures interferes with the accident rate and, in turn, with productivity rates, because of the low level of comfort. For this reason, in the present work, the development of a WBGT index meter using an M5Stack Core2 device is described. As a case study, there is a floricultural company and specifically the greenhouse area. The meter automatically acquires and processes data to send it to the cloud for remote viewing. Measurements are validated using a commercial device and performing statistical analysis.

This document has four sections, including the introduction in Sect. 1. The materials and methods used in the development of the prototype are described in Sect. 2. The results are presented in Sect. 3 and the conclusions in Sect. 4.

2   Methods and Materials

A hardware and software development methodology must be used to develop this system. The Top-Down methodology is used since a commercial device is taken as a reference and replicated with the greatest possible detail. This includes the phases of planning, design, development, and verification. Figure 1 shows the general scheme of the prototype to be made.

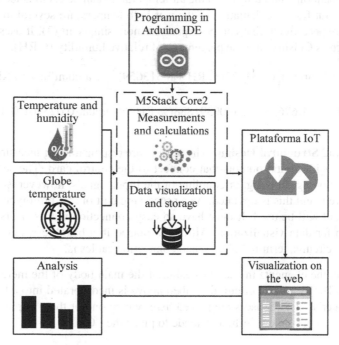

Fig. 1. WBGT index meter general diagram.

2.1   Planification

Staff meetings and on-site observation evidence the need to measure the thermal exposure of workers during their working day. Environmental conditions include relative humidity from 25 to 65%, temperature from 5 to 40 °C, and noise levels from 80 to 110 dB. Based on the bibliographic search and the local context, the SPER SCIENTIFIC 800036 commercial WGBT index meter was chosen as a reference. Its technical characteristics are presented later in Table 1 when compared with the developed prototype. Measurements are 248 x 51 x 32 mm, 4.6oz/130 g weight, and 38 mm globe diameter.

2.2 Design

Calculation of the WBGT Index. The WBGT index estimates the effects of humidity, temperature, wind speed, and visible and infrared radiation on the person. This indicator is based on the measurement of the wet bulb (Th) and globe (Tg) temperature. For the evaluation of interior environments, (1) is used, and for exterior environments, the ambient temperature (Ta) is added, as expressed in (2).

$$WBGT = 0.7 \, Th + 0.3 \, Tg \qquad (1)$$

$$WBGT = 0.7 \, Th + 0.2 \, Tg + 0.1 Ta \qquad (2)$$

Both the balloon temperature and the air temperature can be established by measuring a sensor. But for the calculation of the wet-bulb temperature several mathematical operations are performed, that can be expressed more simply in (3). It uses the values of Ta (in degrees Celsius) and the percentage of relative humidity (%RH).

$$Th = Ta \arctan\left[0.151977(\% \, RH + 8.313659)^2\right] + \arctan(Ta + \% \, RH)$$

$$-\arctan(\% \, RH - 1.676331) + 0.00391838(\% \, RH)^{3/2} \arctan(0.023101 \, \% \, RH) - 4.686035$$
$$(3)$$

Electronic and Structural Design. The sensors are responsible for measuring the TH, T, and %HR, with digital outputs that connect to the control card. The sensors could require conditioning, filtering, or coupling of the input signals, however, some models do not require it and this is obviated. As a processing unit of this prototype, a low-cost embedded card will be used. It must have an easy connection with sensors, actuators, and a screen for data visualization. All this is placed in a bakelite where the printed design of the circuits, terminal blocks, and connection cables is.

To protect the elements inside, the design of the main body of the meter is done in SolidWorks. The electronic circuit described above is incorporated into a box made of synthetic material. Two sensors are placed here, where one of them is placed inside a hollow black copper sphere. A hole is made to place the LCD.

2.3 Development

Hardware. - Some sensors measure temperature and humidity separately, but the DHT22 (AM2302) module/sensor for temperature and relative humidity with digital output does so in one. It has a resolution of 8 bits, with a calibrated digital signal output of a single bus (bidirectional), reduced size, and energy consumption. As the central processing unit of this system, we have the M5Stack Core2 m5 [15], which bases its operation on the ESP32 module. It has a 16 MB flash memory and a built-in LCD touch screen where the required information is displayed. This module has an internal 5 V battery with 390 mAh, which is charged through a USB type C connector. The charging time of it is between 2 and 3 h, while the discharge takes about 10 h on average. This is why the prototype cannot be turned on continuously and is limited to a staff working day (8 h). The general scheme of the electronic circuit is shown in Fig. 2.

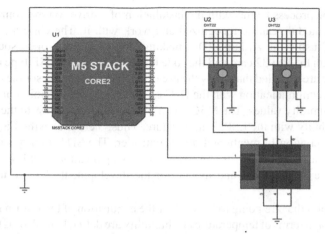

Fig. 2. Electronic circuit diagram

Structure. Based on the previous design, the structure of the device is built with a 3D printer. Using white PLA material, a light but the resistant case is built, with high protection against impacts and falls. The final product and its integration with the previous elements are in Fig. 3 (a). As indicated before, an opaque black balloon that completely covers it must be placed on one of the sensors. The globe made of copper (0.3 mm thick) has a thermal balance that isolates it from the effects of the exchange between ambient radiation and convection, which allows TR to be measured accurately. As shown in Fig. 3(b), it has a diameter of 60 mm.

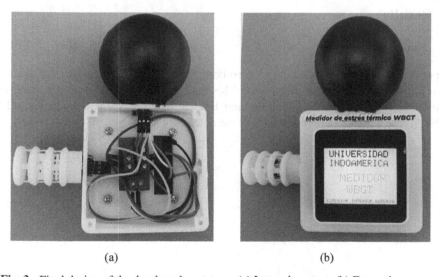

(a)   (b)

Fig. 3. Final design of the developed prototype: (a) Internal content. (b) External structure.

Software. The process begins with the installation of a driver on the computer so that the M5Core2 module can be recognized and work with it. The chosen programming language is C using the Arduino IDE, making it easy to write open source. This is compatible with the ESP32 card and the code is loaded through a USB type C connector. Some libraries are installed that allow the use of different external resources. The DHT.h library allows communication with the DHT22 sensor and the obtaining of temperature and relative humidity values. The M5Core2.h library supports access to the module due to its compatibility with the ESP32 architecture. Thus, there is also the FS.h library for managing the previously mentioned microcontroller. The SD.h library supports work with external SD cards which is important for this application. SPI.h is used for the handling of the SPI protocol and math.h for the development of basic mathematical operations.

The variables that are going to be used for the acquisition of the information coming from the sensor in terms of temperature and humidity are defined. So also, as the variables in which the result of the signal conditioning operations is saved. Using (3) the value of the wet-bulb temperature is obtained. Subsequently, the numerical value of the WBGT index is calculated using (1) and (2), depending on the location. The commands that allow messages to be displayed on the touch screen are added, as part of the information presented to the user. The three existing buttons and their respective events are also configured: measurement indoors, and outdoors, and checking the battery level. The values of the wet-bulb temperature (denoted Th), globe temperature (denoted Tr), dry-bulb temperature (denoted Ts), and the value of the WBGT index are displayed on the screen. At the same time, the script has been configured to record the data every 10 s. This information is saved in a file with a.txt extension and has been set to be stored on a microSD card.

3 Results

3.1 Experimental Tests

Experimental tests are carried out to corroborate the proper functioning of the device during a working day in a greenhouse. This data can be viewed remotely using the ThinkSpeak platform using the following link: https://thingspeak.com/channels/170 1479. Figure 4 shows the presentation of the data graphically.

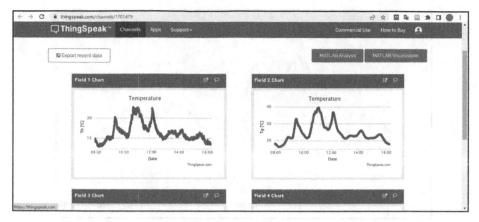

Fig. 4. Presentation of data on the web.

The data obtained in each of the variables that intervene in the calculation of the index (indoors) are presented below. Wet bulb and globe temperature graphs are provided in Fig. 5 and Fig. 6 respectively. Figure 7 shows the WBGT indices obtained.

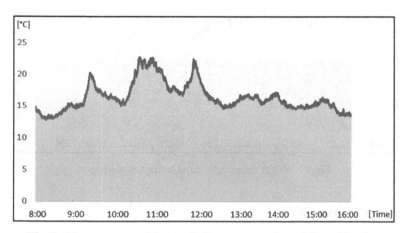

Fig. 5. Measurements of the wet bulb temperature in an 8-h working day.

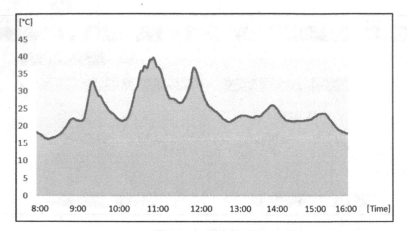

Fig. 6. Measurements of the globe temperature in an 8-h working day.

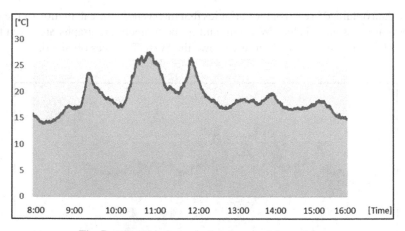

Fig. 7. WBGT index calculated on an 8-h workday.

3.2 Device Comparison

In the last stage of the methodology, the verification of the prototype is carried out and for this, it is analyzed if the technical characteristics of the prototype are similar to those of a commercial device that was previously presented. Their comparison is described in Table 1 and can be seen in Fig. 8.

Fig. 8. Comparison of the prototype device and a commercial

Table 1. Comparison of the technical characteristics of the devices.

	Device	Range	Resolution	Precision
WBGT	Commercial	0 to 50 °C. 32 to 122°F	0.1 °C/F	± 2 °C indoor and 3 °C outdoor
	Prototype	0 to 50 °C. 32 to 122°F	0.1 °C/F	± 1.5 °C indoor and ± 2 °C outdoor
Air temperature	Commercial	0 to 50 °C. 32 to 122°F	0.1 °C/F	± 0.6 °C
	Prototype	−40 to 80 °C. −40 to 176 °F	0.1 °C/F	± 0.5 °C
Globe temperature	Commercial	0 to 80 °C. 32 to 176°F	0.1 °C/F	± 2 °C (15 a 35 °C)
	Prototype	0 to 80 °C. 32 to 176°F	0.1 °C/F	± 2 °C
Relative humidity	Commercial	0 to 100%	0.1%HR	± 3% (10 a 90%) else ± 5%
	Prototype	0 to 100%	0.1%HR	± 1% increases ± 0.5% every year

3.3 Statistic Validation

Subsequently, a test has been carried out to validate this proposal, making measurements and obtaining the WGBT index that is compared with the commercial device. The tests took place on Saturday, February 19, 2022, from 1:25 p.m. to 2:25 p.m. In Table 2 it can be seen that the approximation error is less than 5%.

Table 2. Measurements with the commercial device and the prototype with its approximation error.

M	IC	IP	AE	M	IC	IP	AE	M	IC	IP	AE
1	17.2	17.88	3.94	21	20.3	20.69	1.90	41	19.1	19.60	2.61
2	17.2	17.83	3.65	22	21.1	21.41	1.47	42	18.3	18.87	3.14
3	17.4	18.06	3.78	23	21.2	21.50	1.42	43	18.4	18.96	3.07
4	17.6	18.24	3.63	24	21.5	21.77	1.27	44	17.8	18.42	3.49
5	17.3	17.97	3.86	25	21.4	21.68	1.32	45	17.7	18.33	3.56
6	17.3	17.92	3.57	26	21.3	21.59	1.37	46	17.1	17.69	3.43
7	17.2	17.88	3.94	27	21.2	21.50	1.42	47	17	17.60	3.51
8	17.4	18.06	3.78	28	21.2	21.43	1.09	48	16.9	17.51	3.58
9	16.8	17.51	4.25	29	21.1	21.41	1.47	49	16.6	17.23	3.82
10	16.8	17.47	4.02	30	21.1	21.35	1.19	50	16.4	17.05	3.98
11	16.7	17.42	4.34	31	21.4	21.68	1.32	51	16.5	17.14	3.90
12	16.9	17.61	4.17	32	21.1	21.41	1.47	52	16.3	16.91	3.75
13	17.3	17.97	3.86	33	20.5	20.87	1.79	53	16.2	16.82	3.83
14	17.8	18.42	3.49	34	20	20.41	2.07	54	16	16.64	4.00
15	17.9	18.51	3.42	35	19.3	19.78	2.49	55	15.7	16.37	4.26
16	18.5	19.06	3.00	36	19.2	19.69	2.55	56	15.6	16.28	4.34
17	19	19.51	2.67	37	19.2	19.70	2.60	57	16.1	16.73	3.92
18	19.4	19.87	2.42	38	19.2	19.66	2.39	58	15.9	16.55	4.08
19	19.7	20.14	2.24	39	18.8	19.33	2.80	59	15.6	16.28	4.34
20	19.9	20.32	2.13	40	18.9	19.42	2.74	60	15.5	16.19	4.43

M = Measurement; IC = WBGT Index - Commercial Device; IP = WBGT Index – Prototype; AE = Approximation error.

Using the SPSS version 26 software, the normality test (Kolmo-gorov-Smirnov) is executed, as shown in Table 3. Since the assumption of normality was met, the independent samples t-test was used. The value of the bilateral significance of the t-test is 0.102 and it is established that there is no difference between the means. This verifies that from the statistical point of view the measurements that both devices do not have a significant difference, validating the use of this proposal. As shown in Table 4.

Table 3. Data normality test.

Device	Range	Dof	Sig
Commercial	0.195	60	0.190
Prototype	0.141	60	0.200*

Table 4. Results of the t-test for independent samples

	Levene's test for equality of variances		t-test for equality of means				
	F	Sig	t	Dof	Sig	DM	SED
VI	0.586	0.445	−1.65	118	0.102	−0.53983	0.32792
VN			−1.65	117.32	0.102	−0.53983	0.32792

VI = Equal variances are assumed; VN = Equal variances are not assumed;
DM = Difference of means; SED = Standard error difference.

3.4 Costs Analysis

Based on what is established in Table 5, it can be seen that the element with the highest cost is the M5Stack Core2 module, after that the DHT22 sensor and the 3D printing of the cover. The remaining elements have very low values and with this, the total value that their manufacture represents can be obtained. This allows you to consider your commercial distribution at a higher value, obtaining a profit margin, while maintaining a lower value than the competition. As previously presented, commercial devices that identify the value of the WBGT index range from $500 to $2000. The investment made represents savings for the company in the future, since the presence of thermal risks can be evaluated periodically.

3.5 Discussion

The literature indicates that WBGT's measurement devices are varied, particularly when it comes to commercial equipment. Cooper et al. [16] make a comparison of the main commercial meters, where the variation between devices is very small. The results obtained in our research have been validated with a small variation, with which it can be inferred that it could be comparable to all other commercial equipment. There are innovative suggestions such as the use of sensors embedded in smartphones to measure heat stress [17]. However, the results show a lot of variabilities and are therefore unreliable, as opposed to our counter which keeps constant readings. Other devices are very similar to those presented by Vargas-Salgada et al. [18]. This prototype has an error of 9% versus a commercial device, whereas our device has an error of less than 5%. Finally, we compare our proposal with the device made by Varela-Aldás et al. [11] where an error of 3.26% is revealed. This ensures that the performance is up to expectations and

Table 5. Stress meter construction estimate.

Component	Amount	Value
DHT22 relative humidity and temperature sensor	2	$14.49
M5 Stack Core2	1	$63.99
Globe sphere	1	$0.50
3M x 2cm screws	8	$0.40
Male - female cables	9	$1.35
Male - male cable	2	$0.20
2-pin terminal block	1	$0.25
3-pin terminal block	2	$0.60
Bakelite 10x10	1	$0.80
3D printed box	1	$12.30
Total		$94.88

what has been reported in recent studies. A clear advantage of our proposal is the remote monitoring that can be done through the internet.

4   Conclusions

IoT applications make it easier to remotely collect and track physical variables, including heat indicators that affect human comfort. In this way, a direct application of technology in the workplace can be seen. These benefits are becoming more affordable and affordable, like the M5Stack Core2, which combines multiple IoT features and an OLED display. This work begins with a bibliographical review that allowed establishing the background, operation, and technical characteristics of the devices that measure the level of heat stress existing in the national and international market. Based on this, it was possible to determine the most appropriate model based on the specific requirements of this investigation.

Based on what was previously defined, the design of the prototype was carried out, for which the formulas for the calculation of the WBGT index were defined, as well as the electronic and structural designs, respectively. With this, the construction of the device started by selecting the materials which met the established technical requirements and their interconnection. The programming was developed in open source and considering the previously defined formulas. 3D printing is used to build the external structure where the PCB components are housed. Finally, the experimental tests and the statistical analysis carried out validate this low-cost prototype, whose operation resembles that of a commercial device. It can therefore be integrated as a valuable tool in the technical analysis of installations and their environmental conditions.

The authors of this study plan to continue researching this topic in the future and see the feasibility of developing a second version with more precise sensors. It is curious about the use of smartphones for measuring heat stress, for their daily use, and could be evaluated how to improve its accuracy in comparison to previous studies. Finally, its possible application in other workplaces considered dangerous because of the present environmental conditions is proposed.

Acknowledgments. Fraternal thanks are extended to the Universidad Tecnológica Indoamérica for providing the necessary resources for the development of this research and the dissemination of the results.

References

1. Lundgren-Kownacki, K., Kjellberg, S.M., Gooch, P., Dabaieh, M., Anandh, L., Venugopal, V.: Climate change-induced heat risks for migrant populations working at brick kilns in India: a transdisciplinary approach. Int. J. Biometeorol. **62**(3), 347–358 (2017). https://doi.org/10.1007/s00484-017-1476-0
2. Parsons, L.A., Masuda, Y.J., Kroeger, T., Shindell, D., Wolff, N.H., Spector, J.T.: Global labor loss due to humid heat exposure underestimated for outdoor workers. Environ. Res. Lett. **17**, 014050 (2022). https://doi.org/10.1088/1748-9326/ac3dae
3. Ordunez, P., et al.: Chronic kidney disease epidemic in central america: urgent public health action is needed amid causal uncertainty. PLoS Negl. Trop. Dis. **8**, e3019 (2014). https://doi.org/10.1371/journal.pntd.0003019
4. Sabrin, S., Zech, W.C., Nazari, R., Karimi, M.: Understanding occupational heat exposure in the United States and proposing a quantifying stress index. Int. Arch. Occup. Environ. Health **94**(8), 1983–2000 (2021). https://doi.org/10.1007/s00420-021-01711-0
5. Ramanathan, N.L.: Physiological evaluation of the WBGT index for occupational heat stress. Am. Ind. Hyg. Assoc. J. **34**, 375–383 (1973). https://doi.org/10.1080/0002889738506866
6. D'Ambrosio Alfano, F.R., Malchaire, J., Palella, B.I., Riccio, G.: WBGT index revisited after 60 years of use. Ann. Occup. Hyg. **58**, 955–970 (2014). https://doi.org/10.1093/annhyg/meu050
7. Zare, S., et al.: A comparison of the correlation between heat stress indices (UTCI, WBGT, WBDT, TSI) and physiological parameters of workers in Iran. Weather Clim. Extrem. **26**, 100213 (2019). https://doi.org/10.1016/j.wace.2019.100213
8. Seo, Y., Powell, J., Strauch, A., Roberge, R., Kenny, G.P., Kim, J.H.: Heat stress assessment during intermittent work under different environmental conditions and clothing combinations of effective wet bulb globe temperature (WBGT). J. Occup. Environ. Hyg. **16**, 467–476 (2019). https://doi.org/10.1080/15459624.2019.1612523
9. Brocherie, F., Millet, G.P.: Is the wet-bulb globe temperature (WBGT) index relevant for exercise in the heat? Sports Med. **45**(11), 1619–1621 (2015). https://doi.org/10.1007/s40279-015-0386-8
10. Newth, D., Gunasekera, D.: Projected changes in wet-bulb globe temperature under alternative climate scenarios. Atmosphere (Basel) **9**, 187 (2018). https://doi.org/10.3390/atmos9050187
11. Varela-Aldás, J., Fuentes, E.M., Ruales, B., Ichina, C.: Construction of a WBGT Index Meter Using Low Cost Devices. In: Rocha, Á., Ferrás, C., Montenegro Marin, C.E., Medina García, V.H. (eds.) ICITS 2020. AISC, vol. 1137, pp. 459–468. Springer, Cham (2020). https://doi.org/10.1007/978-3-030-40690-5_45
12. Matsui, K., Sakai, K.: A Proposal for a Dynamic Digital Map to Prevent Heatstroke Using IoT Data. In: Barolli, L., Takizawa, M., Xhafa, F., Enokido, T. (eds.) AINA 2019. AISC, vol. 926, pp. 1205–1216. Springer, Cham (2020). https://doi.org/10.1007/978-3-030-15032-7_101

13. Brik, B., Esseghir, M., Merghem-Boulahia, L., Snoussi, H.: An IoT-based deep learning approach to analyse indoor thermal comfort of disabled people. Build. Environ. **203**, 108056 (2021). https://doi.org/10.1016/j.buildenv.2021.108056
14. Varela-Aldás, J., Pilla, J., Andaluz, V.H., Palacios-Navarro, G.: Commercial Entry Control Using Robotic Mechanism and Mobile Application for COVID-19 Pandemic. In: Gervasi, O., et al. (eds.) ICCSA 2021. LNCS, vol. 12957, pp. 3–14. Springer, Cham (2021). https://doi.org/10.1007/978-3-030-87013-3_1
15. Miranda, M., Varela-Aldás, J., Palacios-Navarro, G.: Comparison of Blockly vs Arduino IDE for programming education using M5Stack Core2 ESP32 IoT Development Kit. In: 12th International Conference on Applied Human Factors and Ergonomics (AHFE 2021) and the Affiliated Conferences (2021). https://doi.org/10.54941/AHFE1001182
16. Cooper, E., Grundstein, A., Rosen, A., Miles, J., Ko, J., Curry, P.: An evaluation of portable wet bulb globe temperature monitor accuracy. J. Athl. Train. **52**, 1161–1167 (2017). https://doi.org/10.4085/1062-6050-52.12.18
17. Fujinami, K.: Smartphone-based environmental sensing using device location as metadata. Int. J. Smart Sens. Intell. Syst. **9**, 2257–2275 (2016). https://doi.org/10.21307/ijssis-2017-963
18. Vargas-Salgado, C., Chiñas-Palacios, C., Aguila-León, J., Alfonso-Solar, D.: Measurement of the black globe temperature to estimate the MRT and WBGT indices using a smaller diameter globe than a standardized one: Experimental analysis. In: 5TH CARPE CONFERENCE. pp. 201–207 (2019). https://doi.org/10.4995/carpe2019.2019.10203

An Industrial Ergonomic Analysis of Potential Techniques to Prevent Repetitive Stress Injuries in Employees Working on Production Assembly Lines

Olivia Villamagna and Vincent G. Duffy[✉]

Purdue University, West Lafayette, IN 47907, USA
{ovillama,duffy}@purdue.edu

Abstract. Many companies struggle with the balance of productivity and proper ergonomic work task design. However, it is extremely important to ensure the well-being of the employees. This is an ergonomic analysis of a plant that reported a repetitive stress injury in one of its employee's shoulders. A systematic literature review was completed, through co-authorship analysis, relevancy searches, and leading author analysis. The articles found through the literature review presented solutions to some of the identified issues with the workstation. These identified issues were determined through in-class lectures, Q&A sessions with one of the plant's stakeholders, and pictures from the plant. Many of the considerations were based of the ideals and quantitative values of the NIOSH lifting equation which puts emphasis on the angle of rotation and the overall reach movement of the operator [1]. Through ergonomic analysis, it was determined that the alternatives must limit twisting, reaching, and long, sedentary standing by the operators. These alternatives are intended to help prevent the introduction of more repetitive stress injuries in employees working on this production assembly line. Such alternatives include sit-stand stools, overhead storage, and other tools to help redesign the workstation to not only improve the health of the employees but does not disrupt production as well.

Keywords: Repetitive stress injuries · Work station · Ergonomics

1 Introduction

Assembly lines have been one of the most common layouts of manufacturing production since their invention by Henry Ford in 1913 [2]. Although efficient, assembly line workers find themselves doing the same task in the same position multiple times a day, multiple days a week. This can lead to repetitive stress injuries, which is "damage that occurs to musculoskeletal structures as the result of extended overuse" [3]. Repetitive stress injuries are also called repetitive motion injuries, repetitive strain injuries, cumulative trauma disorders, or musculoskeletal disorders. According to Otto and Scholl (2011), control of ergonomic risks at manual workplaces, such as the one referenced in this paper, is a necessity commanded by legislation, care for the health of workers, and economic

© Springer Nature Switzerland AG 2022
V. G. Duffy and P.-L. P. Rau (Eds.): HCII 2022, LNCS 13522, pp. 373–384, 2022.
https://doi.org/10.1007/978-3-031-21704-3_24

considerations [4]. Therefore, it is important for Human Factors and Ergonomic (HFE) professionals to be involved in task design to ensure companies are meeting ergonomic and employee health requirements. This paper will focus on the immerging importance of ergonomics in the manufacturing field, specifically assembly lines, and provide analysis and justification of solutions to the plant of focus described herein.

2 Problem Statement

A manufacturing plant, that uses the assembly line layout, recently had an employee report pain in her right shoulder while "throwing die cuts". Upon further investigation the plant manager reported:

- The woman who was too short in height but we could not lower the table. She faces the production table but reaches up and behind to grab a "die cut". See Fig. 1 for height measurements of table and employee.
- Then she lowers her arm to pass the "die cut" through a glue machine.
- This repetitive motion has brought on her complaint. See Fig. 2 for the repetitive motion sequence.

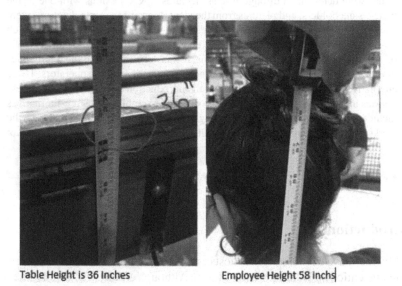

Table Height is 36 Inches   Employee Height 58 inchs

Fig. 1. This figure shows the height of the workstation table in review and the height of the worker that complained of right shoulder pain due to the repetitive and sustained motion of her job.

From these complaints, the plant manager reached out to Purdue for human factors and ergonomics professionals to analyze the workplace environment and suggest alterations to improve the employees' health. The analysis done in the paper can be applied across many industries that incorporate the same assembly line layout.

Step 1 Reach back and twist Pick up Die Cut. Step 2 Deliver to glue machine. Step 3 Place in Glue machine.

Fig. 2. This figure shows the steps that the employee that sustained the repetitive stress injury does daily.

3   Literature Review

Literature reviews are necessary to prove the relevance and value of the information presented to stakeholders; in this case the plant manager. The following section will describe how resources were found and their associated value-add to this analysis.

3.1   Data Collection

Data collection from reputable databases is the beginning of a valid literature review. Databases such as Harzing, Scopus, Google Scholar, SpringerLink, and Research Gate. Table 1 provides the search results per each database with the search terms "Assembly line" AND "Repetitive stress injury" OR "Assembly line" AND "Ergonomics" and the years 2010 and 2021 used as limiters.

Table 1. The number of article results for each search.

Database	Number of search results
Harzing	80*
Scopus	409
Google Scholar	118
SpringerLink	24
Research Gate	Unknown

* Limited by loading capability

3.2   Analysis and Results

The first analysis was completed using Vicinitas analytics, which takes data from the social media platform, Twitter, to analyze the trend of how often a term has been used and what related words were used in conjunction. This can current engagement with the term. This gives a broader idea of what the community is engaged in currently.

Figure 3 shows the word cloud of the related terms when I searched on "repetitive motion injuries". The engagement and posts timelines show the amount of traction these search terms got over about a week span, this could be related to events on that day that might have spiked engagement.

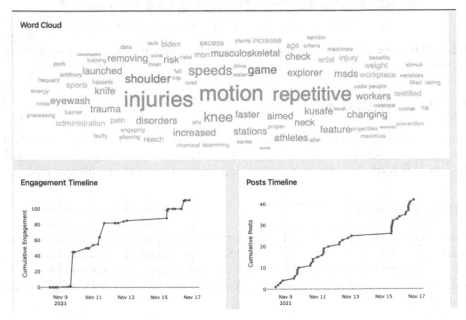

Fig. 3. This is a screen which shows trends in Twitter term use through Vicinitas analytics

Figure 4 shows another tool used for this literature review. I used the data from Harzing and imported it into another analytic tool, VOS Viewer. For this search, the terms "Human factors" AND "Assembly line" were used, with the limits that word should be used more than 7 times applied. It should be noted I did not delete any words before the map creation. Therefore, the 31 terms seen in the map are representative of the full search. This is a helpful tool during a literature analysis to show what other terms to search on to gather more data and resources. Some of the notable terms are "shoulder" and "stations" which relate very well to the case presented in this paper.

The same tool and terms/limitations were used for the next analysis in this literature review. Although the same tool was used, a different analytics method was applied to create a co-authorship map. This is one of the most important literature analysis methods because it shows which authors cite each other which can provide validity to the information presented since it has been cited in other similar works. Figure 5 shows this analysis with the settings to include authors that have 3 or more articles and only included authors that connected. This brought my count from 42 to 13, but I felt like this was more valuable data since they are more cited which, in our case, we are assuming correlated to the validity of the information.

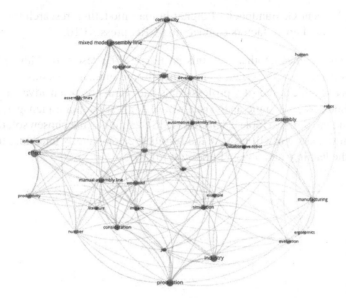

Fig. 4. This figure is the map that shows the relation of search terms. Color codes show different groups of word categories.

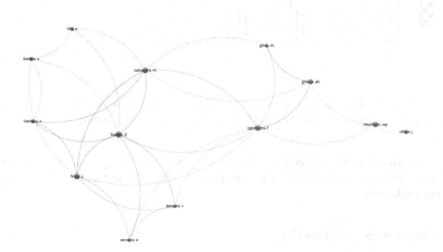

Fig. 5. This figure shows the co-author citation map.

I generated a table in BibExcel using data exported from the Google Scholar search within Harzing. The software generated a table in Excel and I created a pivot chart that shows the leading authors for the terms "Human factors" AND "Ergonomics" and "Ergonomics" AND "Repetitive stress injuries". Notably, professor Duffy is listed right in the middle at just over 20 articles found. An example of these articles includes:

1. Duffy, Vincent G. Handbook of digital human modeling: research for applied ergonomics and human factors engineering. CRC press, 2016.

This article outlines another way this issue could be resolved. Although, not the focus of this paper, it is important to note that digital human modeling tools, such as RAMSIS, as available to industry professionals and should be taken advantage of when doing sophisticated ergonomic analysis. I would suggest the plant manager, or a hired HFE professional, utilize a tool such as RAMSIS to simulate the chosen solution before purchasing it to ensure it will provide the results the company is intending to achieve. The rest of the leading authors can be seen in Fig. 6.

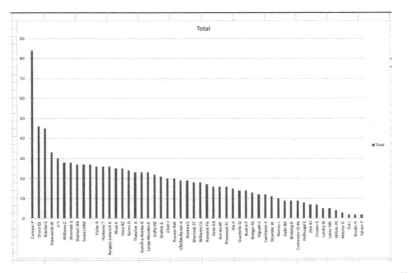

Fig. 6. This figure shows the leading authors, in descending order, for the search terms "Human factors" AND "Ergonomics" and "Ergonomics" AND "Repetitive stress injuries".

This final analysis concluded my literature and provides me with valid and useful articles to assess the workspace shown in the problem statement and make the following recommendations.

4   Procedures and Results

The first solution I analyzed was the alternative that the plant manager suggested as their preferred method to limit the repetitive stress injuries seen by the female employee and others. Figure 7 shows the stackable steps that the plant manager would like to use to limit the amount of time the shorter employees would be reaching while working at the workstation.

Fig. 7. This is an image of the step that the plant manager suggested to use to aid in the shorter employees' reach to the work station.

Figure 8 shows the effects of arm positions at a workstation for a prolonged period. According to the authors, "Fatigue occurs more rapidly as the worker's arm becomes more elevated" [5]. These deviations in shoulder/arm positions affect the length- strength relationship [5]. This concept would support the step alternative above, as it would put the workers at about 5cm over the workspace which would take about 10 min for the worker to feel significant fatigue holding a die cut (assuming a die cut is about 1 lb). Comparatively, the worker currently feels significant fatigue at 3 min since they are about 30–50 cm.

Although, this step solution fixes the reach problem there needs to be consideration for how the company will ensure employees do not fall or trip off the step and should consider how to continue to provide padded mats for knee and back support.

Another aspect of the workstation that should be evaluated is the duration the employees stand at work. "The prolonged standing posture during work affects the risk of developing musculoskeletal disorders of the lower limbs, especially in lack of alternative sitting" [6]. This could lead to other repetitive stress injury reports that are external to the shoulder issue already seen.

The last aspect I would like to address is the twisting motion done by the employees every time they have to reach for a new die cut behind them. According to Hamid, "awkward or static postures during treatment of patients result in stresses and strains which is another cause of such problems [musculoskeletal disorders]" [7]. The awkward postures noted in this article are consistent with the twisting motion the workers do to retrieve the die cuts. This has the potential to add to the repetitive stress injuries already reported in the plant.

The first alternative I have decided to present to the company is an overhead storage apparatus that would connect to the rafters of the manufacturing building. They would hold the die cuts on so that the employees do not have to reach behind themselves in

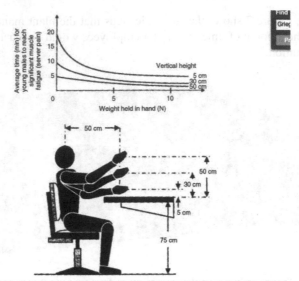

Figure 13 Expected time to reach significant shoulder muscle fatigue for varied arm flexion postures. [Adapted from Chaffin, D. B., and Andersson, G. B. (1991), *Occupational Biomechanics*, Wiley, New York.]

Fig. 8. This figure shows the expected time to reach muscle fatigue with varying postures with different weights.

a twisting motion. This would be a good combination with the steps to also ensure all employees could reach these with ease and not introduce other reach issues. This would reduce the chances of occupational lower back injuries which are usually associated with repetitive lifting tasks that involve twisting and bending [8]. Figure 9 shows an example of overhead storage that the company could buy from Amazon.com. The company could also use a less robust storage rack, as the die cuts are very light in weight.

Fig. 9. This is an overhead storage tool that could be used to store die cuts. Storing them above the employees instead of behind them could reduce twisting.

The next alternative I will present is a sit-stand stool. When deciding on the appropriate posture for a workplace it is important to consider the type of work being completed. William S. Marras states four types of tasks that would call for mostly standing-based workstations [5].

1. The task required a high degree of mobility (when reaching and monitoring in positions that exceed the employee's reach envelope or performing tasks at different heights or different locations)
2. Precise manual control actions are not required
3. Leg room is not available (when legroom is not available the moment arm distance between the external load and the back is increased and thus greater internal back muscle force and spinal load result)
4. Heavy weights are handled or large forces are applied.

Since none of these fully apply to the die cut station, I believe the sit-stand stool is a good option. I know the plant manager is concerned with employees consistently sitting because of the stigma around sitting in the manufacturing world. However, with an adjustable sit-stand stool the employees would be more leaning on the stools. This would take the stress off of the lower body, which is important because when employees are subjected to a full workday on their feet, joints, muscles, ligaments, and the vertebral column can be overstrained [9]. The stools would also provide height since the stools are adjustable and when not in use the stools reduce to a short enough height to store under the work station. Figure 10 is an example of one of these stools.

Fig. 10. This is an example of a sit-stand stool that could be used to reduce reaching, twisting, and prolonged standing by employees.

Another option to reduce the repetition of a task, without spending a significant amount of money, is described in the article "Incorporating ergonomic risks into assembly line balancing" by Alena Otto and Armin Scholl. This article talks about line balancing as an effective method to reduce the ergonomic risk [4]. Although this is not my main argument for my paper, this could be an alternative for the company, especially if the company would like to reduce costs. Figure 11 and Fig. 12 show how to balance a line to properly reduce the repetition of tasks that could induce injuries.

Line balancing helps diversify tasks for workers to allow for movement within the workday to reduce long periods of standing and moving in the same motions.

Table 1
Example of an assembly line. Task description for the right hand. Cycle time is 63 seconds.

TaskNo.	Task time (seconds)	Actions	Posture	Average force, % of max force capacity (MFC)
1	18	8	Hand grip (wide)	20%
2	6	2	Elbow flexion > 60°	5%
3	15	5	Elbow flexion > 60°	Insignificant
4	21	6	Elbow flexion > 60°	10%
5	3	5	Hand grip (wide)	33%
6	6	2	Neutral posture	1 lifting of 17 kg (avg. force of 70%)
7	9	2	Neutral posture	1 lifting of 15 kg (avg. force of 40%)
8	18	3	Dorsal flexion	20%
9	15	4	Neutral posture	33%
10	15	3	Dorsal flexion	25%
11	12	11	Dorsal flexion	10%

Fig. 11. This table shows an assembly line before balancing.

Table 5
Alternative balances of the assembly line described in Table 1 (OCRA index for the right hand).

Station load	Worst posture, duration in % of cycle time	Avg. force, %MFC	Actions per minute	PM	FoM	OCRA index	NIOSH index
First balance							
Station 1: 1, 2, 3, 4, 5	Elbow flexion, 67	11	25	0.7	0.83	2.4	0
Station 2: 6, 7	Neutral postures	12	4	1	0.80	0.3	1.1
Station 3: 8, 9, 10, 11	Dorsal flexion, 71	21	20	0.6	0.61	3.1	0
Second balance							
Station 1: 1, 2, 3, 6, 8	Dorsal flexion 29	19	19	0.7	0.68	2.2	0.98
Station 2: 4, 5, 7, 9, 10	Elbow flexion 33	24	19	1	0.52	2.0	0.86
Station 3: 11	Dorsal flexion 19	2	10	1	1	0.6	0

Fig. 12. This is a table of the same assembly line but balanced to reduce repetition to reduce injuries.

5 Discussion

As shown throughout this paper, the importance of ergonomics within manufacturing is very important for the overall health and wellness of employees. As an ergonomics professional, I would highly recommend using the overhead storage, the line balancing, and the steps in conjunction to get the best results. These would cover all aspects of the body to ensure the plant limits the exposure to all repetitive stress injuries. The overhead storage and the steps satisfy one of the human factors fundamentals of what is known as the "reach envelop". This refers to the "normal working area is described as a comfortable sweeping movement of the upper limb, about the shoulder, with the elbow flexed to 90 degrees or a little less" [10]. With the addition of line balancing, the workplace would also address an ergonomic concern of strain, which can be calculated through the Strain Index (SI). The SI takes into account the duration of the task per day and shows the benefits of task diversity such as job rotations, which is promoted in line balancing [11].

Although I do believe the sit-stand stool could also be a good addition to the overall solution, I understand the tradeoff the plant manager addressed and I think limiting the twisting motion and line balancing would also help relieve lower back joints. I do also realize I could have potentially come up with more plant-specific, appropriate alternatives if I had been able to physically visit the facility.

6 Conclusion

With all the considerations mentioned throughout this paper, including the literature review, it is evident there is much work to still be done to implement ergonomic practices into workplaces. The main suggestions should be taken seriously as they could prevent the plant from incurring more employee injury expenses.

I think the plant could implement many of these suggestions and would be happy with the results seen in the health of their workers. However, the most important implementations should be considered as determined in the Discussion section. It is always important to consider the other implications when implementing new tools or procedures. If the plant were to implement any or all of these suggestions, it is recommended to consider the trade-offs to their specific workplace, as I did not have access to tour the facility in person to get the feel of the environment.

In the future I think a digital human modeling tool would be a good next step to this analysis. Through utilizing the comfort analysis tools it would be a quantitative method of determining the preferred alternative for the plant. I also think a HFE professional should visit the plant again to assess the improvements after an alternative is chosen as sometimes solutions present other issues that were not foreseen.

References

1. National Institute of Occupational Safety and Health (NIOSH). Application Manual for the Revised NIOSH Lifting Equation. U.S. Department of Health and Human Services, NIOSH, Cincinnati, OH (1991)
2. History.com Editors. Ford's Assembly Line Starts Rolling. HISTORY. A&E Television Networks (2018). https://www.history.com/this-day-in-history/fords-assembly-line-starts-rolling. Accessed 13 Dec 2018
3. Rothfeld, G.S., Baker, D.: Repetitive stress injuries. In: Library of Health and Living: The Encyclopedia of Men's Health, 2nd edn. Facts On File (2017)
4. Otto, Scholl, A.: Incorporating ergonomic risks into assembly line balancing. Eur. J. Oper. Res. **212**(2), 277–286 (2011)
5. Marras, W.S.: Basic biomechanics and workstation design. In: Salvendy, G. (ed.) Handbook of Human Factors and Ergonomics, pp. 347–381 (2012)
6. Capodaglio, E.M.: Occupational risk and prolonged standing work in apparel sales assistants. Int. J. Ind. Ergon. **60**, 53–59 (2017)

7. Hamid, A., Ahmad, A.S., Dar, S., Sohail, S., Akram, F., Qureshi, M.I.: Ergonomics hazards and musculoskeletal disorders among workers of health care facilities. Curr. World Environ. **13**(2), 251–258 (2018)
8. Umar, R.Z.R., Lee, F.A.M.A., Khafiz, M.N., Ahmad, N., Abdullasim, N.: Space mapping of hip and wrists motions for different transfer distances in manual material handling task. IIUM Eng. J. **21**(2), 164–176 (2020)
9. Luczak, H., Kabel, T., Licht, T.: Task design and motivation. In: Salvendy, G. (ed.) Handbook of Human Factors and Ergonomics, pp. 397–440 (2012)
10. Plocher, T., Rau, P.L.P., Choong, Y.Y., Guo, Z.: Cross-cultural design. In: Salvendy, G. (ed.) Handbook of Human Factors and Ergonomics, pp. 252–279 (2012)
11. Rodrick, D., Karwowski, W., Marras, W.S.: Work-related upper extremity musculoskeletal disorders. In: Salvendy, G. (ed.) Handbook of Human Factors and Ergonomics, pp. 826–867 (2012)

Control Goals of Whole-Body Coordination During Quiet Upright Stance

Hongbo Zhang[✉]

Department of Engineering Technology, Middle Tennessee State University Murfreesboro,
Murfreesboro, TN 37132, USA
hbzhang@mtsu.edu

Abstract. Whole body coordination is essential for maintaining human posture stability. Yet the control goals and influences of individual differences and task-related effects have not been well investigated. Uncontrolled manifold method was used to assess whole-body coordination during upright stance with 16 young and 16 older individuals. These ratios were obtained for the head, shoulder, and whole-body center-of-mass, in both the mediolateral and anteroposterior directions. As evidenced by larger uncontrolled manifold ratios, the head and shoulder appeared to be more likely than whole-body center-of-mass as control goals for whole body coordination. The present results demonstrate that investigation of head and shoulder kinematics among upright stance posture could be likely yielding clinical meaningful results.

Keywords: Quiet upright stance · Whole body coordination · Uncontrolled manifold · Fall prevention

1 Introduction

Exploration of human postural control is quite crucial for human fall prevention. It is known that human falls are predominant leading to significant injuries and even death. On average, one in three elderly adults older than 65 years age fall annually. Falls lead to bone fracture, muscle injuries, and even death. Fall prevention is a tricky topic and hard to study. It is largely because of the intrinsic challenges of the research topic, research on fall prevention has been very slow. Especially, practical engineering intervention is either not quite useful or cumbersome to implement.

Previous research of falls have mostly focused on the study of human postural controller. Such controller can be PID controller, optimal controller, and intermittent controller [1, 7, 10, 14]. Such postural controllers are mostly inspired from the engineering design. It works well to model a biomechanical system but not necessarily is able to capture the neural muscular structure details. As such, it is desirable to view the postural control system with a new angle. Such new angle starts from the analysis of human postural control from a fundamental level.

Upright stance is inherently unstable due to gravitational torque and internal disturbances such as hemodynamic and neuromuscular noise [1–3]. Previous studies have

© Springer Nature Switzerland AG 2022
V. G. Duffy and P.-L. P. Rau (Eds.): HCII 2022, LNCS 13522, pp. 385–393, 2022.
https://doi.org/10.1007/978-3-031-21704-3_25

demonstrated that multiple joints contribute to balance control during quiet upright stance [4–14]. Several possible motor control goals have also been suggested, such as maintaining the projection of the center-of-mass (COM) [7, 15, 16] or the center-of-pressure [17] within the base of support and maintaining head and gaze stability [18–20]. Although this earlier work offers some clues as to how whole-body coordination is achieved, as yet there is no consensus. Such divergence provided one motivation for the current study, the aim of which was to explore the potential control goal used for whole-body coordination. Joint coordination is also known dependent on intrinsic aspects of the musculoskeletal system, which differ with age and gender [21–23]. As such, differences related to age and gender were also explored.

To explore potential control goals, kinematics of the head, shoulder, and whole-body COM were examined here. While the shoulder has not been explicitly regarded earlier as a control goal for whole body coordination, a strong biomechanical constraint exists between the head and trunk/shoulder, and these two segments have also been shown to move in a coordinated fashion [20, 24, 25]. Additionally, small relative movements between the shoulder and trunk imply that the shoulder could play an important role for ankle-trunk-shoulder coordination, which is essential for maintenance of quiet upright stance control [7, 26].

The uncontrolled manifold (UCM) ratio has been used for assessing whole-body coordination [27–30]. This approach assumes that control goals achieve minimum variation through coordination involving multiple limb segments [7, 9, 31, 32], and conceptually is similar to coherence analysis used to analyze signal similarities. Through comparison of UCM ratio magnitudes, it is possible to identify the most likely control goals [7, 29]. The UCM ratio method was thus used here for assessing control goals.

2   Methods

2.1   Experimental Data

A subset of data from an earlier experiment [33] were used herein. A total of 32 participants (gender balanced) were involved, half of whom were young adults (18–25 years) and half older adults (55–65) years. Repeated trials of quiet upright stance were measured involving participants standing without shoes, as still as possible, with their feet together, arms by their sides, head upright, and eyes closed. Each trial lasted 75 s, with at least one minute between two consecutive trials. Whole-body kinematics was estimated from surface markers that were tracked using a 6-camera system (Vicon 460, Lake Forest, CA, USA) at 20 Hz [5, 34]. Raw kinematics signals were low-pass filtered (Butterworth, 8 Hz cut-off frequency, 4th order, zero lag, bi-directional) and transformed to obtain body position time series; the first 10 s and the last 5 s of data in each trial were removed to eliminate any potential transition effects.

2.2   Kinematics and Uncontrolled Manifold

Following filtering and windowing of marker data, 3D marker locations were available. The 3D marker is used for calculation of the joint angle. In total, the following angles are calculated. It includes head angle, upper arm angle, lower arm angle, trunk angle, knee angle, ankle angle, and foot angle. For each joint, the distal d1(x, y, z) and proximal positions d2(x, y, z) of the respective body segment were used, along with the equations below, to estimate angles in both the sagittal and frontal planes.

$$\theta_{FPA} = \tan 2^{-1}\left(\frac{d1[z] - d2[z]}{d1[x] - d2[x]}\right) \tag{1}$$

$$\theta_{SPA} = \tan 2^{-1}\left(\frac{d1[z] - d2[z]}{d1[y] - d2[y]}\right) \tag{2}$$

All these angles are calculated in both ML and AP planes. The computed angles are shown in Fig. 1.

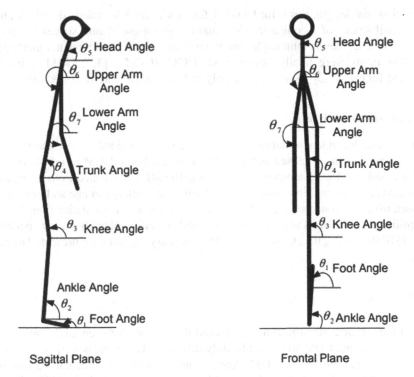

Sagittal Plane   Frontal Plane

Fig. 1. Kinematics system of the whole body joint angles during quite upright stance

From these, sagittal plane and frontal plane joint segment angles were derived, along with the whole-body center-of-mass (COM) locations, using approaches similar to earlier reports [5, 35]. Major joint angles including neck and trunk segmental joint angles and bilateral means of foot, ankle, knee, shoulder, and elbow segmental joint angles served as input for UCM analysis, along with the noted task variables (locations of the head, shoulder, and COM) [35]. For both the ML and AP directions, time series of these locations were computed using segmental models including the foot, lower leg, upper leg, trunk, head, upper arm, and lower arm, e.g., shoulder position is a summation of projected length of the foot, lower leg, upper leg, and trunk segments. Jacobian matrices were calculated using joint angle derivatives separately for each of these body location, and the null spaces of these were obtained [35].

Projections of variance on the UCM ($UCM_{\parallel}$) and orthogonal to the UCM ($UCM_{\perp}$) were determined as described by [35] with equations as Eq. (3) and Eq. (4),

$$
UCM_{\parallel} = \sqrt{[(n-d) \times N]^{-1} \sum_{i=1}^{N} \left(\sum_{j=1}^{n-d} e_j^T \theta e_j \right)^2 } \tag{3}
$$

$$
UCM_{\perp} = \sqrt{(d \times N)^{-1} \sum_{i=1}^{N} \left[(\theta - \overline{\theta}) - \left(\sum_{j=1}^{n-d} e_j^T \theta e_j \right) \right]^2 } \tag{4}
$$

where N is trial length, n is 6 for COM, 4 for head, and 3 for trunk, d = 1, e_j and e_j^T are the null spaces of Jacobian matrices and the transpose of null spaces of Jacobian matrices. θ is segmental joint angle, and the $\overline{\theta}$ is average of the segmental joint angle.

UCM ratios were finally obtained as: $UCM_{\parallel}/UCM_{\perp}$ [35]. UCM ratios were estimated for each body location, separately in both the AP and ML directions.

2.3 Statistical Analysis

Means of the dependent variable (UCM ratios) were obtained from three trials, and these means were used subsequently in statistical analyses. UCM ratios for the head, shoulder, and COM were compared separately in the ML and AP directions, using paired t tests corrected for multiple comparisons. Differences related to age and gender were assessed using separate two-way ANOVAs for each UCM ratio and direction. The level of significance for all tests was set at $p < 0.05$, and all statistical analyses were performed using JMP 9.02 (SAS Inc., Cary, NC, USA). Summary statistics are presented as means (SD).

3 Results

In both the AP and ML directions, all paired differences between UCM ratios of the head, shoulder, and COM were significantly different. These ratios were largest for the shoulder and smallest for the COM. Age x gender interaction effects were significant for several measures, and approached significance otherwise (Table 1 and Fig. 2). Older individuals had higher UCM ratios for Head$_{AP}$ and COM$_{AP}$, though this age-related difference was more substantial among females. For other measures, the interactive effects were more complex and less consistent.

Table 1. Summary of the effects of Age (A) and Gender (G) on UCM ratios in the antero-posterior (AP) and medio-lateral (ML) directions. Significant effects are bolded (i.e., p values < 0.05). The final column provides the mean (SD) of the UCM ratios across subjects.

		A	G	A x G	UCM ratio
AP	Head	**0.026**	0.44	**0.029**	0.82 (0.00078)
	Shoulder	0.39	0.35	**0.018**	1.34 (0.15)
	COM	**0.0175**	0.59	**0.021**	0.64 (0.0014)
ML	Head	0.60	0.17	0.083	0.84 (0.013)
	Shoulder	0.22	0.14	0.067	1.02 (0.0035)
	COM	0.57	0.95	**0.012**	0.048)

4 Discussion

We investigated whole-body coordination and moderating influences of age and gender during upright stance using the UCM ratio approach. Overall, the current results suggest the importance of the head and shoulder as control goals in quiet upright stance (i.e., larger UCM ratios than COM). The study results have profound applications for postural classification [42].

Regarding the control goal, UCM ratios for the shoulder were > 1 in the AP and ML directions. In contrast, UCM ratios for the COM and head were < 1 in both directions. If the UCM ratio is < 1 for a task variable, task variability is structured in such a way as to not minimize end-effector variability. Therefore, our results suggest that whole body COM is less likely to be a principal control variable during upright stance, supporting previous evidence of that alternative control goal (e.g. head or trunk) are used for whole body coordination [36, 37]. Instead, our results suggest that the shoulder may be more likely to be relevant control variables in both the sagittal and frontal planes. This result might stem from the arm and hand, which contribute to the center of mass position, having low coherence with trunk and leg motions in quiet upright stance (where the arm and hand remain relatively static), leading in turn to less coherent whole-body motion and thus a decreased COM UCM ratio. In contrast, the upper body and leg, which are involved in manipulating the shoulder and head positions, have more substantial coherent motions [6, 32, 38].

Older adults had larger initial UCM ratios in some cases. Though differences were of small magnitude, this may suggest a higher level of goal oriented postural coordination among older adults, perhaps as compensation of postural instability due to larger time delays in the control loop [39–41]. However, there were significant but inconsistent age x gender interaction effects (Fig. 1); further study is needed to better understand these.

The current study has practical research and clinical insights for human postural control and fall prevention. For a long time, it is highly suggested the control of human postural control is centered by the center of mass of human body. While center of mass might be important, according to our study, center of mass is unlikely the human coordination goal. In contrast, shoulder is more likely the whole body coordination goal.

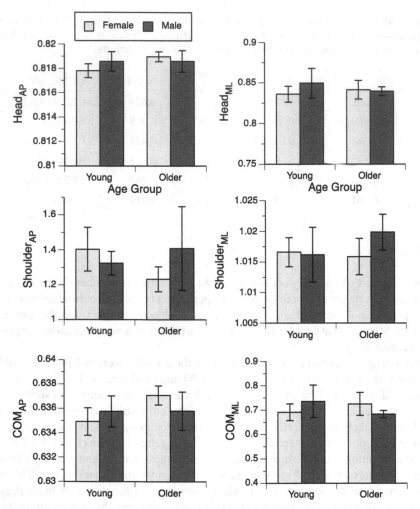

Fig. 2. Effects of age and gender on UCM ratios for the Head, Shoulder, and COM, in both the antero-posterior (AP) and medio-lateral (ML) directions.

As far as the rational behind of it, it is likely driven by the need of maintaining head stability which is a crucial task for human safety. Clinically, our study has important indications. It shows the importance of upper body coordination for fall prevention, which is largely ignored in the past. Hence, the lower and upper body coordination intervention such as Taichi could be likely useful for fall prevention.

The current study is potentially limited in that the UCM method was used in the time domain, though future analysis in the frequency domain may yield additional information. Further investigation of these limitations could help to improve our understanding of whole-body coordination.

Acknowledgments. The authors declare that there is not conflict of interest.

References

1. Peterka, R.J.: Sensorimotor integration in human postural control. J. Neurophysiol. **88**, 1097–1118 (2002)
2. Peterka, R.J.: Postural control model interpretation of stabilogram diffusion analysis. Biol. Cybern. **82**, 335–343 (2000)
3. Winter, D.A.: Biomechanics and Motor Control of Human Movement. Wiley, Hoboken (2009)
4. Pinter, I.J., Van Swigchem, R., van Soest, A.J.K., Rozendaal, L.A.: The dynamics of postural sway cannot be captured using a one-segment inverted pendulum model: a PCA on segment rotations during unperturbed stance. J. Neurophysiol. **100**, 3197–3208 (2008)
5. Zhang, H., Nussbaum, M.A., Agnew, M.J.: Use of wavelet coherence to assess two-joint coordination during quiet upright stance. J. Electromyogr. Kinesiol. **24**, 607–613 (2014)
6. Kiemel, T., Elahi, A.J., Jeka, J.J.: Identification of the plant for upright stance in humans: multiple movement patterns from a single neural strategy. J. Neurophysiol. **100**, 3394–3406 (2008)
7. Hsu, W.L., Scholz, J.P., Schöner, G., Jeka, J.J., Kiemel, T.: Control and estimation of posture during quiet stance depends on multijoint coordination. J. Neurophysiol. **97**, 3024 (2007)
8. Alexandrov, A., Frolov, A., Massion, J.: Axial synergies during human upper trunk bending. Exp. Brain Res. **118**, 210–220 (1998)
9. Krishnamoorthy, V., Yang, J.F., Scholz, J.P.: Joint coordination during quiet stance: effects of vision. Exp. Brain Res. **164**, 1–17 (2005)
10. Zhang, H., Nussbaum, M.A., Agnew, M.J.: Development of a sliding mode control model for quiet upright stance. Med. Eng. Phys. **38**, 204–208 (2016)
11. Zhang, H., Nussbaum, M.A., Agnew, M.J.: A new method to assess passive and active ankle stiffness during quiet upright stance. J. Electromyogr. Kinesiol. **25**, 937–943 (2015)
12. Gaffney, B.M., Harris, M.D., Davidson, B.S., Stevens-Lapsley, J.E., Christiansen, C.L., Shelburne, K.B.: Multi-joint compensatory effects of unilateral total knee arthroplasty during high-demand tasks. Ann. Biomed. Eng. **44**, 1–13 (2016)
13. Peng, Y., He, J., Khavari, R., Boone, T.B., Zhang, Y.: Functional mapping of the pelvic floor and sphincter muscles from high-density surface EMG recordings. Int. Urogynecol. J. **27**(11), 1689–1696 (2016). https://doi.org/10.1007/s00192-016-3026-4
14. Peng, Y., He, J., Yao, B., Li, S., Zhou, P., Zhang, Y.: Motor unit number estimation based on high-density surface electromyography decomposition. Clin. Neurophysiol. **127**, 3059–3065 (2016)
15. Reisman, D.S., Scholz, J.P., Schoner, G.: Coordination underlying the control of whole body momentum during sit-to-stand. Gait Posture **15**, 45–55 (2002)
16. Massion, J., Popov, K., Fabre, J.C., Rage, P., Gurfinkel, V.: Is the erect posture in microgravity based on the control of trunk orientation or center of mass position? Exp. Brain Res. **114**, 384–389 (1997)
17. Ferry, M., Martin, L., Termoz, N., Cote, J., Prince, F.: Balance control during an arm raising movement in bipedal stance: which biomechanical factor is controlled? Biol. Cybern. **91**, 104–114 (2004)
18. DiFabio, R.P., Emasithi, A.: Aging and the mechanisms underlying head and postural control during voluntary motion. Phys. Ther. **77**, 458–475 (1997)
19. Ledebt, A., WienerVacher, S.: Head coordination in the sagittal plane in toddlers during walking: Preliminary results. Brain Res. Bull. **40**, 371–373 (1996)
20. Mouchnino, L., Aurenty, R., Massion, J., Pedotti, A.: Coordination between equilibrium and head-trunk orientation during leg movement: a new strategy build up by training. J. Neurophysiol. **67**, 1587–1598 (1992)

21. Welch, T.D.J., Ting, L.H.: A feedback model reproduces muscle activity during human postural responses to support-surface translations. J. Neurophysiol. **99**, 1032 (2008)
22. Hsu, W.-L., Chou, L.-S., Woollacott, M.: Age-related changes in joint coordination during balance recovery. Age **35**, 1299–1309 (2013)
23. Kato, T., Yamamoto, S.-I., Miyoshi, T., Nakazawa, K., Masani, K., Nozaki, D.: Anti-phase action between the angular accelerations of trunk and leg is reduced in the elderly. Gait Posture **40**, 107–112 (2014)
24. Bloomberg, J.J., Peters, B.T., Smith, S.L., Huebner, W.P., Reschke, M.F.: Locomotor head-trunk coordination strategies following space flight. J. Vestibular Res.: Equilib. Orient. **7**, 161 (1997)
25. Keshner, E.A.: Head-trunk coordination during linear anterior-posterior translations. J. Neurophysiol. **89**, 1891–1901 (2003)
26. Zhang, Y., Kiemel, T., Jeka, J.: The influence of sensory information on two-component coordination during quiet stance. Gait Posture **26**, 263–271 (2007)
27. Hsu, W.-L., Lin, K.-H., Yang, R.-S., Cheng, C.-H.: Use of motor abundance in old adults in the regulation of a narrow-based stance. Eur. J. Appl. Physiol. **114**(2), 261–271 (2013). https://doi.org/10.1007/s00421-013-2768-7
28. Qu, X.: Uncontrolled manifold analysis of gait variability: effects of load carriage and fatigue. Gait Posture **36**, 325–329 (2012)
29. Wu, J., McKay, S., Angulo-Barroso, R.: Center of mass control and multi-segment coordination in children during quiet stance. Exp. Brain Res. **196**, 329–339 (2009)
30. Qu, X.: Uncontrolled manifold analysis of gait variability: effects of load carriage and fatigue. Gait Posture. **36**, 325–329 (2012)
31. Krishnamoorthy, V., Latash, M.L., Scholz, J.P., Zatsiorsky, V.M.: Muscle synergies during shifts of the center of pressure by standing persons. Exp. Brain Res. **152**, 281–292 (2003)
32. Creath, R., Kiemel, T., Horak, F., Peterka, R., Jeka, J.: A unified view of quiet and perturbed stance: simultaneous co-existing excitable modes. Neurosci. Lett. **377**, 75–80 (2005)
33. Lin, D., Nussbaum, M.A., Seol, H., Singh, N.B., Madigan, M.L., Wojcik, L.A.: Acute effects of localized muscle fatigue on postural control and patterns of recovery during upright stance: influence of fatigue location and age. Eur. J. Appl. Physiol. **106**, 425–434 (2009)
34. Zhang, H., Nussbaum, M.A., Agnew, M.J.: A time–frequency approach to estimate critical time intervals in postural control. Comput. Methods Biomech. Biomed. Engin. **18**, 1693–1703 (2015)
35. Black, D.P., Smith, B.A., Wu, J., Ulrich, B.D.: Uncontrolled manifold analysis of segmental angle variability during walking: preadolescents with and without down syndrome. Exp. Brain Res. **183**, 511–521 (2007)
36. Hollands, M.A., Ziavra, N.V., Bronstein, A.M.: A new paradigm to investigate the roles of head and eye movements in the coordination of whole-body movements. Exp. Brain Res. **154**, 261–266 (2004)
37. Kavanagh, J., Morrison, S., Barrett, R.: Coordination of head and trunk accelerations during walking. Eur. J. Appl. Physiol. **94**, 468–475 (2005)
38. Qu, X., Nussbaum, M.A.: Modelling 3D control of upright stance using an optimal control strategy. Comput. Methods Biomech. Biomed. Eng. **15**, 1053–1063 (2012)
39. Nishihori, T., Aoki, M., Jian, Y., Nagasaki, S., Furuta, Y., Ito, Y.: Effects of aging on lateral stability in quiet stance. Aging Clin. Exp. Res. **24**, 162–170 (2011)
40. Davidson, B.S., Madigan, M.L., Southward, S.C., Nussbaum, M.A.: Neural control of posture during small magnitude perturbations: effects of aging and localized muscle fatigue. IEEE Trans. Biomed. Eng. **58**, 1546–1554 (2011)

41. Qu, X., Nussbaum, M.A., Madigan, M.L.: Model-based assessments of the effects of age and ankle fatigue on the control of upright posture in humans. Gait Posture **30**, 518 (2009)
42. Zhang, H., Gračanin, D., Eltoweissy, M.: Classification of human posture with RGBD camera: is deep learning necessary? In: Stephanidis, C., Duffy, V.G., Streitz, N., Konomi, S., Krömker, H. (eds.) HCII 2020. LNCS, vol. 12429, pp. 595–607. Springer, Cham (2020). https://doi. org/10.1007/978-3-030-59987-4_42

Product Design

The Trend of Industrial Design from the Perspective of Metaverse

Yuehui Hu$^{(\boxtimes)}$ and Hong Chen

East China University of Science and Technology, Shanghai, China
engoy2008@163.com

Abstract. With the rapid development of the Internet, the concept of metaverse has been put forward, and the development of metaverse will affect all industries. At present, metaverse is still at the stage of infrastructure construction, but the development route is gradually clear. This paper summarizes the concept, formation factors and core of the metaverse, combs and analyzes the cutting-edge technologies and cases under the metaverse background, and comes to the conclusion that the core of the metaverse is the integration of virtual and reality, and "experience" is the core of the integration of virtual and reality. Under the metaverse background, there have been new changes in the field of industrial design, this paper analyzes the two realization paths and related technologies of metauniverse, as well as the development trend of industrial design in the direction of design tools, design performance and industrial chain. VR, AR, MR, game engine and digital Twin are important technologies affecting the field of industrial design. The value of "virtual" has been paid more and more attention. How to make good use of these technologies to combine virtual assets with reality is an important development trend in the field of industrial design.

Keywords: Metaverse · Industrial design · VR · AR · MR · Game engine · Digital twin

1 About the Metaverse

1.1 The Concept of the Metaverse

Metaverse is a highly integrated Internet application and social form of virtual world and real world. The metaverse provides immersive experience based on extended reality technology, generates the image of the real world based on digital twin technology, and builds an economic system based on blockchain technology. In the metaverse, the virtual world will be closely integrated with the economic system, social system and identity system of the real world, and each user is allowed to produce content and edit the world [1]. At present, due to the technical limitations of the equipment, metauniverse can only be displayed in a limited form through personal computers, mobile phones and VR glasses. In the future, the metaverse should be an all-truth form combining virtual and real, integrating social, economic, cultural and other real systems into it, and gradually realizing a new world that comprehensively simulates real perception.

© Springer Nature Switzerland AG 2022
V. G. Duffy and P.-L. P. Rau (Eds.): HCII 2022, LNCS 13522, pp. 397–406, 2022.
https://doi.org/10.1007/978-3-031-21704-3_26

In the concept of metaverse, the human sensory dimension will also be expanded into a comprehensive sensory integration of reality and virtual, including vision, hearing and touch. "You can think about the metaverse as an embodied internet, where instead of just viewing content—you are in it." said Zuckerberg, CEO of meta (formerly Facebook).

1.2   Formation Factors of the Metaverse

There are many factors for the formation of the concept of metaverse, but the most important factor is the inevitable result of mankind's unlimited pursuit of the authenticity of content carrier [1]. From the evolution of the Internet, we can see the evolution process of human content carrier from text to image, from static image to dynamic video, from text-based blog to image-based microblog to short video and video platform, The traditional transmission of text, pictures and video content is the "recording and transmission" of information. Under the concept of metaverse, it is to go further on the current basis to achieve the "experience" of information. The author summarizes the factors of the formation of the concept of metaverse from three aspects: Social factors, market factors and technical factors.

1) Social factors: The novel coronavirus (2019-nCoV) epidemic has prompted social virtualization, and online communication, work and study have become the new normal
2) Market factor: The market needs a more immersive and experiential interaction method, from 'seeing" to "experiencing". The combination of reality and virtual has broad commercial potential
3) Technical factors: The rapid development of AI, 5G, big data, cloud computing, digital twin, blockchain, VR, AR, MR and other technologies has laid a technical foundation for the Metaverse. At the same time, the recording and transmission capabilities of human media have greatly improved, making it possible to "record and transmit information" in the past to "record and transmit experience" today [2].

1.3   The Core of the Universe

The core of the metaverse is the integration of virtual and reality. The virtual world is more real and three-dimensional, and the real world surpasses reality by integrating with the virtual world. From the user level, it will change from "obtaining information" to "experiencing information" [1]. Therefore, the core of the integration of virtual and reality is "experience".

1.4   Influence of Yuancosmos on Various Industries

At present, the metaverse is still in the stage of infrastructure construction, but the development route has been relatively clear. The concept of metaverse will include social, economic, cultural, scientific and technological and other elements in reality, which is bound to affect various industries. This paper will focus on the impact of the concept of metaverse on the field of industrial design.

2 Industrial Design from the Perspective of Metaverse

Industrial design is committed to guiding innovation, promoting business success and providing a better quality of life. It is closely related to the development and changes of technology, culture and lifestyle. Metaverse brings broad development space for the future with diversified and integrated ideas and methods, which also creates more development opportunities for industrial design.

2.1 The Realization Path of Metaverse

The metaverse integrates virtual and reality to make the virtual world more real and three-dimensional, and the real world surpasses reality by integrating with the virtual world, which leads to two development paths: one is immersive path, that is, virtual reality (VR), the other is superimposed path, that is, augmented reality (AR) and hybrid reality (MR).

Virtual Reality. Virtual reality (VR) is a technology that uses computer simulation to generate a three-dimensional virtual world, provides users with visual and other sensory simulation, and makes users feel immersive [3]. 2016 is the first year of an era of VR. It has been six years since then, and VR has not been popularized on a large scale. However, with the continuous iteration of technology, today's VR equipment has become more and more mature [3, 4], and the ecology of software is gradually improving, playing an important role in the wave of metaverse.

The market demand brought by virtual reality technology is mainly divided into hardware and software. The hardware is mainly reflected in the design of VR helmet, VR experience cabin and other equipment. VR equipment needs to provide users with good "virtual experience", which puts forward requirements for industrial design. The release of oculus Quest 2 in 2020 has become a watershed in the industry, Oculus Quest 2 adopts wireless streaming technology, which makes the helmet get rid of the wired mode, makes the activity more convenient, and further improves the display and audio-visual effects. It is equipped with Snapdragon XR2 chip to provide performance guarantee. In 2021, the sales volume of oculus Quest 2 has reached 10 million units. From the development iteration of VR devices in the market, VR devices are moving towards lightweight, wireless, easy to operate and comfortable wearing experience High quality display effect.

In terms of software, the lack of high-quality and rich software content ecology has always been a major resistance for VR to enter the consumption field. With the gradual attention of software developers to the VR field and the expansion of VR market, more and more excellent software content landed on the VR platform. In 2020, the VR game "Half-Life:Alyx" developed by valve was sold and won wide praise from players, which is known as the "killer application" of VR, and won the annual VR game in 2020, and its user scale on steam has exceeded 2 million. The popularity of "Half-Life:Alyx" has also promoted the sales of valve index, valve's own VR device. Valve index has been sold out since the game was released.

Augmented Reality. Augmented reality (AR) refers to a technology that enriches people's interaction with the real world and digital world by superimposing computer-generated virtual information into the real environment, so as to achieve sensory experience beyond reality [5]. In 2017, apple and IKEA launched an interesting and useful AR application IKEA place, Through the mobile app, you can place the 3D model of IKEA furniture or home decoration into the real living environment, preview the placement effect of IKEA products at home in turn, support different styles and colors, and output the synthesized scenes and photos. However, the display effect of augmented reality is based on the screen of mobile phone and tablet computer, which is a flat display effect, and does not meet the requirements of "experience" from the perspective of metaverse. AR glasses and augmented reality head up display (AR-HUD) are the key development directions in the future AR field. Facebook, Google, apple, HTC, Lenovo and other technology giants have begun to layout AR glasses. Augmented reality head up display (AR-HUD) is another important application scenario of AR technology. The function of AR-HUD is to project important driving information such as speed and navigation on the windshield in front of the driver, so that the driver can see important driving information without looking down or turning around. AR-HUD is an important part of the future intelligent cockpit. FAW, GAC, Volkswagen, BMW and other manufacturers have begun to layout. The next two years will be the time of AR-HUD outbreak. The design of AR-HUD includes not only physical functions, but also interaction and guidance. How to display information safely, efficiently and reasonably and improve the driver's user experience and driving safety needs reasonable design.

Mixed Reality. Mixed reality (MR) is a new visual environment that combines the real and virtual worlds. In the new visual environment, physical and digital objects coexist and interact in real time. MR is a further expansion of AR technology. Both MR and AR emphasize the sense of scene and enhance the scene. Therefore, on the basis, MR and AR are consistent. Both MR and AR require to integrate the scene picture as much as possible, and both need to understand the scene in real time, and then integrate the computer-generated virtual image. Therefore, field enhancement is the same point of MR and AR.

The difference between MR and AR is that MR emphasizes the authenticity of the virtual image and needs pixel level intersection and occlusion with the real scene. It requires that the virtual scene has real lighting and is naturally mixed with the real scene. While AR emphasizes the information of the virtual image and needs to appear in the correct position to increase the amount of information for users, but it does not emphasize the occlusion and illumination of the real scene. AR superimposes virtual information in the real scene, MR is a virtual object that can interact with the real world.

The HoloLens2 released by Microsoft in November 2019 is an MR glasses priced at $3,500 and has been used in professional fields such as manufacturing, retail, and medical care. However, there are problems such as high price, small display viewing angle, and insufficient display quality. MR technology is still in the stage of exploration and development, and there is still a long way to go before large-scale use (Fig. 1).

VR, AR and MR represent the two major directions of the metaverse. VR is committed to building an immersive and realistic virtual world. AR and MR are both committed

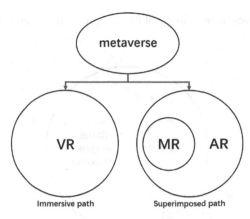

Fig. 1. Relationship among VR, AR and MR

to integrating virtual objects and information into real scenes, but MR goes further on the basis of AR, and virtual objects can interact with the real world.

2.2 The Influence of Metaverse Development on Industrial Design Tools and Design Performance

Modern Industrial Design Tools. The tool cornerstone of modern industrial design is undoubtedly CAD (Computer Aided Design). Since the 1970s, after Dr. Patrick Hanratt, a pioneer of CAD, designed the first computer-aided drawing system [6], the industrial design industry has undergone earth shaking changes. Industrial design moves from hand-painted drawings to digital design. The gap between design and production has been narrowed. Designers can easily make digital templates. Design does not always need to start from scratch. Subtle drawing errors no longer mean fatal defects. The commonly used software in the field of industrial product design are Rhino, Keyshot, Alias, CATIA, etc. the emergence of these CAD software has greatly improved the work efficiency of design, and designers can test their new ideas faster. So far, various CAD software is still a necessary tool in the field of industrial design.

Although the model data of the three-dimensional model made by CAD software can be directly used for production, the designer actually observes the model through a two-dimensional screen, and the model size displayed in the screen is not the actual size, so it is often necessary to make a 1:1 model for verification and review before actual production to test whether the design is reasonable and beautiful. Some designs are not feasible in actual production, and the design-test-redesign model undoubtedly needs to pay a lot of time and cost. This problem is caused by the inconsistency between virtual reality and reality.

Industrial Design Tools from a Metaverse Perspective. In the concept of metaverse, the integration of reality and virtual will bring a new revolution to the field of industrial design, and its impact is no less than the birth of CAD. In fact, many companies have been using the latest technology to gradually realize the integration of reality and virtual, which greatly improves the efficiency of design, production, sales and other links [3, 7] (Fig. 2).

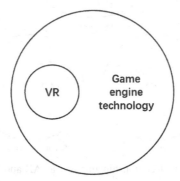

Fig. 2. Relationship between game engine technology and VR technology

Game engine technology and VR technology are the focus and trend in the field of industrial design. There is a strong correlation between game engine technology and VR technology. The realization of VR at the software level is based on the game engine. VR is one of the application directions of game engine.

Game Engine Technology. Game engine is an important content production tool and integration platform for content output in metauniverse. Game engine specifically refers to the core components of some compiled editable computer game systems or some interactive real-time image applications, which are widely used in game development. However, mainstream game engines such as Unreal and Unity have real-time visualization, real physical simulation, high picture quality More intuitive interactive performance and other advantages have been gradually used in the fields of architecture, film and television, simulation and design in recent years.

The advantages of game engine technology in the field of industrial design are as follows:

1. Real time visualization: a major advantage of game engine is "real-time visualization". Designers often need to render high-quality pictures through rendering software as the display effect of project review or product publicity. If it's just pictures, the current mainstream rendering software can quickly render high-quality renderings, but it still takes a long time for complex animation. However, the game engine can render in real time. In recent years, the addition of ray tracing and other functions can achieve photo level rendering quality, and the production efficiency of animation has been greatly improved. In 2017, the Volkswagen Group began to build an automotive visualization platform (AVP) based on the Unreal engine. AVP saves at least 30% of the cost, and the delivery time to the market has been shortened from weeks to hours [6].

2. Interactivity: more importantly, the interactivity of the game engine can jump out of the shackles of traditional plane renderings or plane videos, bringing a new possibility, that is, real-time display and interactivity, allowing designers or users to freely

rotate their perspective to observe the photo level product rendering model and interact, such as: check the effect of explosion diagram, different colors, materials and different functions and states of products, which improves the efficiency of design verification and inter department communication [8]. Designers and engineers of BMW Group are already using the powerful real-time workflow of unreal engine, so that the group can carefully evaluate the design of vehicles in a virtual environment. Now such cooperation can be carried out all over the world, and participants can interact and collaborate together, just like playing a multiplayer game [6].

3. Virtual assets: traditional industrial design models are generally used to produce and render renderings, but the virtual value of three-dimensional models can play a greater role through the game engine. At present, BMW, Toyota, Audi and other companies are using the point of sale (POS) and virtual exhibition hall technology supported by the virtual engine [6]. Connecting the configurator to your point-of-sale system means that the vehicle will be built and delivered exactly according to the consumer's configuration, thus improving consumer satisfaction. Users can also use the browser to view different accessories, stitches and decoration options from a 360-degree cabin perspective. Moreover, because these different experiences have equivalence and consistency, if consumers configure their favorite car at home, and then want to see the finished product with their own eyes in the dealer's video wall or VR. In the future, the metaverse will gradually become a reality, and the importance of virtual assets will be higher and higher.

VR Technology. The advantages of VR technology in the field of industrial design are as follows:

1. Experience: The first-person immersive visual experience brought by VR can simulate various perspectives of the real world and solve the visibility problem in design. For example, engineers at GM's Design Lab used VR to study the effects of shading from the dashboard to the driver's side window. Lighting algorithms have evolved to the point where light reflections can be accurately calculated and rendered. Using this technology, designers can better understand how the dashboard affects the driver's visibility when driving at night [3].

2. Ergonomics: VR can simulate the actual product size to solve ergonomic problems in design. At Ford Motor Company, ergonomic engineers are using VR to establish design standards related to the maximum allowable assembly force for installing various hoses [3]. Equipped with VR helmets, physical props and force sensors, ergonomic engineers estimate the force required to install the hose in a specific human posture. Using the results of VR experience, they set the design specifications for external suppliers with the maximum strength required for installation.

3. True perspective and size: At present, the mainstream design effect is observed through the 2D screen, which cannot show the real size of the design. Therefore, the design needs repeated proofing tests to confirm whether its appearance, size and structure meet the requirements. Through VR technology, designers can observe the real size of the design from a real perspective, so as to make more accurate judgments, so as to improve the design efficiency, save costs and shorten the development cycle. Engineers in Ford 5 laboratory use VR technology to understand the aesthetic

quality of 3D vehicle design [3]. Car models with different interior materials can be loaded into the virtual environment and compared in terms of appearance, feeling and personality. VR enables designers and engineers to present real postures and visual perspectives, and designs can be quickly changed and reassessed in a virtual environment.

Performance of Industrial Design from the Perspective of Metaverse. At present, the design expression is mainly based on renderings and videos, which belongs to a one-way and fixed expression form. Through the game engine technology, it can bring dynamic and interactive expression forms. Through VR, AR, MR and other technologies, it can get closer to the real experience, provide more possibilities for the expression of industrial design, and also provide a more intuitive and vivid expression for the marketing of products, From the perspective of metaverse, the marketing mode of products will not be limited to one-way output of product promotion content to users, but users can interact with product content interactively and actively according to their own preferences. In 2017, Epic Games, Chevrolet and visual effects production company TheMill jointly produced an interactive short film Users can make real-time choices of different models and colors, and they can see the high-quality details on the screen. Therefore, the expression of future design will be more interactive and experiential [6].

2.3 Industrial Chain from the Perspective of Metaverse

Industrial design is only one part of the whole product development process. In the traditional product development process, the communication cost between each link of the whole industrial chain is very high, because the knowledge fields and problems involved in each link are different. The lack of communication between links will directly affect the production time. If multiple processes are carried out continuously, the delay of one link may affect the whole downstream process. The emergence of game engine technology can get rid of the shackles of traditional linear process. It can realize parallel deployment of multiple tasks and share the created assets [6]. The concept, design, production and marketing of products can be unified and integrated through the game engine. The visual process also greatly reduces the communication cost between various processes. If it cannot be visualized, complex process communication will become extremely difficult. It is difficult for everyone to cooperate with each other and discuss solutions to challenges. Through the game engine, you can visualize the production process, show the operation mode of the facility to stakeholders and business partners, and even refine the work content of each employee.

Through the game engine, all processes can also be virtualized and simulated, which is the so-called digital twin. After the digital twin technology, the whole production system can provide efficient and low-cost solutions for the management, optimization and analysis of production processes, so as to make the operation of the whole industrial chain more efficient, so as to reduce production costs and improve the speed of R & D. For example, use game engine technology to create test scenes for autopilot AI, because they are customization tools that can provide unlimited possibilities, and can create photo images in real time. You can achieve a large number of test mileage required in the auto drive system through synthetic data. These simulations can be run on cloud-based hardware. In a few days, you can get a preliminary AI model. Within hours, you can get the perceptual training and testing effects that take years in the real world. Uber Technology Group (UTG) has been using game engine technology as a visualization and verification tool for its self-driving vehicle test scenarios [6]. Engineers will build a one-time scenario to further improve the capability of UTG autopilot suite and test its performance in a safe and interactive environment. In this way, the team can run thousands of tests in the simulation system every day and adjust various parameters, such as the speed, weather and traffic mode of oncoming vehicles, or the data of a car suddenly entering the lane of an autonomous vehicle. The new behavior will enter the test lane only after the actual test in the simulated environment, and then test on the real-world road.

3 Summary

This paper analyzes the basic concept, causes and core of metaverse, and analyzes the trend of industrial design in four directions: market demand, design tools, design performance and industrial chain from the perspective of metaverse.

Metaverse is a grand concept, which points to a highly integrated Internet application and social form of virtual world and real world, involving a wide range of fields and technologies. This paper only analyzes the parts related to the field of industrial design. Although the concept of metauniverse is complex, its core is the integration of virtual and reality. As long as we recognize this, the development trend of many fields will be very clear.

From the perspective of metaverse: VR, AR, MR, game engine, digital twin and other technologies are important technologies affecting the field of industrial design. The value of "virtual" has been paid more and more attention. Of course, "virtual" does not abandon reality, but combines "virtual" with "reality" to create a better "reality". How to make good use of these technologies to combine virtual assets with reality is an important development trend in the field of industrial design. Design tools will be more efficient, intuitive and close to reality, so as to improve the efficiency, accuracy and quality of industrial design, enrich the design forms, and greatly improve the communication and cooperation between design links and other links such as production, sales and publicity. Industrial design practitioners need to follow the trend and accumulate relevant knowledge and technology in order to make better design.

References

1. Wang, R., Xiang, A.: 2020–2021 research report on the development of metaverse (2021)
2. Jian, D.L.B.: 2021–2022 metaverse report (2021)
3. Berg, L.P., Vance, J.M.: Industry use of virtual reality in product design and manufacturing: a survey. Virtual Reality 21(1), 1–17 (2016). https://doi.org/10.1007/s10055-016-0293-9
4. Bastug, E., Bennis, M., Medard, M., et al.: Toward interconnected virtual reality: opportunities, challenges, and enablers. IEEE Commun. Mag. 55, 110–117 (2017)
5. Carmigniani, J., Furht, B., Anisetti, M., et al.: Augmented reality technologies, systems and applications. Multimed. Tools Appl. 51, 341–377 (2011)

6. Epicgames: automotive field guide (2020)
7. Berni, A., Borgianni, Y.: Applications of virtual reality in engineering and product design: why, what, how, when and where. Electronics **9**, 1064 (2020)
8. Tideman, M., Voort, M., Houten, F.: Using virtual reality for scenario based product design. In: Proceedings of Virtual Concept, Biarritz, France (2005)
9. Maples-Keller, J.L., Bunnell, B.E., Kim, S.J., et al.: The use of virtual reality technology in the treatment of anxiety and other psychiatric disorders. Harv. Rev. Psychiatry **25**, 103–113 (2017)
10. Mooradian, N.: Virtual reality, ontology and value. Metaphilosophy **37**, 673–690 (2010)
11. Nomura, J., Sawada, K.: Virtual reality technology and its industrial applications. Control. Eng. Pract. **7**, 1381–1394 (1999)
12. Ottosson, S.: Virtual reality in the product development process. J. Eng. Des. **13**, 159–172 (2002)
13. Parong, J., Mayer, R.E.: Learning Science in Immersive Virtual Reality. J. Educ. Psychol. **110**, 785–797 (2018)
14. Radianti, J., Majchrzak, T.A., Fromm, J., et al.: A systematic review of immersive virtual reality applications for higher education: design elements, lessons learned, and research agenda. Comput. Educ. **147**, 103778 (2020)
15. Regt, A.D., Barnes, S.J., Plangger, K.: The virtual reality value chain - ScienceDirect. Bus. Horiz. **63**, 737–748 (2020)
16. Shao, J., Zhang, Y., Yu, Z.: Research on development and application of virtual reality system for car styling review. In: China Society of Automotive Engineers (ed.) Proceedings of China SAE Congress 2019: Selected Papers. Lecture Notes in Electrical Engineering, vol. 646, pp. 903–912. Springer, Singapore (2021). https://doi.org/10.1007/978-981-15-7945-5_65
17. Shin, D.: Empathy and embodied experience in virtual environment: to what extent can virtual reality stimulate empathy and embodied experience? Comput. Hum. Behav. **78**, 64–73 (2018)
18. Thalen, J.P., Voort, M.: Facilitating user involvement in product design through virtual reality (2012)
19. Thomas, B.H.: Virtual reality for information visualization might just work this time. Appl. Sci. (2020)
20. Wang, L., Luo, J., Luo, G.L., et al.: Industrial product art design method based on internet of things technology and virtual VR. J. Ambient Intell. Human. Comput. (2021)
21. Balzerkiewitz, H.P., Stechert, C.: Use of virtual reality in product development by distributed teams. Proc. CIRP **91**, 577–582 (2020)
22. Cruz-Neira, C., Sandin, D.J., Defanti, T.A.: Surround-screen projection-based virtual reality: the design and implementation of the CAVE (1993)
23. Elbamby, M.S., Perfecto, C., Bennis, M., et al.: Towards low-latency and ultra-reliable virtual reality. IEEE Netw. **32**, 78–84 (2018)

Product Innovation Through A3 Problem-Solving: Improving the Design of a Commercial Beverage Dispenser

Yu-Hsiu Hung[✉] and Der-Wei Liao

Department of Industrial Design, National Cheng Kung University, Tainan, Taiwan
idhfhung@gmail.com, p36091113@gs.ncku.edu.tw

Abstract. The purpose of this study is to demonstrate that A3 problem-solving is able to enable design innovation in product development. A company that developed a commercial beverage dispenser participated in this study. The R&D manager of the company demonstrated to the research team three key problems that caused a long weekly cleaning cycle (complained by most customers): (1) complicated cleaning and sanitizing procedures; (2) inefficient water circulation; (3) poor fridge organization. Progressive A3s were then produced by our research team to solve each individual problem systematically. The iterative process allowed the team to actively collaborate with the R&D manager on the purpose, the goals, and the strategies of each problem. Results of this study revealed that the implementation of A3 not only generated innovative designs for reducing the weekly cleaning time by 38%, but also kept product development knowledge in one place. Outcomes of this study provide implications on team collaboration and knowledge-driven design in product development.

Keywords: A3 Problem-solving · Product development · PDCA · Knowledge management

1 Introduction

Due to the shortening of product innovation cycles and the changing needs of customers, product innovation is regarded as a key indicator of firm performance [1]. The term innovation can be interpreted as generation of new ideas and their implementation into profitable new products, processes or services [2], or as the improvement of existing products or services to meet customer needs or provide new value [3]. What these definitions of "innovation" have in common is that a new idea cannot be considered innovative unless it has been properly developed and transformed to create market value [4].

There are no shortcuts to successful innovation. Innovation occurs in the development process when members of an organization move back and forth from step to step and learning along the way [5]. For instance, Design Thinking, which focuses on customer requirements and generates innovative ideas through a series of problem frameworks for layer-by-layer thinking, it is applicable to a variety of industry sectors and is particularly

© Springer Nature Switzerland AG 2022
V. G. Duffy and P.-L. P. Rau (Eds.): HCII 2022, LNCS 13522, pp. 407–419, 2022.
https://doi.org/10.1007/978-3-031-21704-3_27

popular among designers [6]. TRIZ has a vast array of analytical tools that can be used to rapidly find effective and less risky solutions to customer problems and confirm the feasibility of solutions at an early stage of development process [7]. As a result, it often integrated with innovative development tools such as brainstorming and QFD to assist companies in developing innovative solutions to problems [8].

Nevertheless, when designers and engineers apply Design Thinking to the same product problem, the results may vary significantly depending on how well they comprehend the problem and how well they utilize their own expertise [9]. In addition, some academics have argued that design thinking lacks clear definitions and methods [10], which makes its application in industry challenging. TRIZ, on the other hand, is a "toolset" rather than a prefabricated framework [11], as it does not provide a strict sequence of tools or guidance for developers [12]. Although TRIZ is capable of intuitively resolving a single contradiction, there is no logical relationship between the TRIZ tools, which limits its application to complex problems [13]. Faced with ever-increasingly complex new product development [14], companies need a clear and structured approach to help them standardize their problem-solving process in all circumstances in order to maintain their innovative capacity.

A3 report is a tool for improvement in lean product development that assists companies in establishing a knowledge-driven product development environment and facilitating decision making through a standardized framework [15]. The A3 report has demonstrated its efficacy in problem solving and knowledge generation through its application in a variety of fields, continual implementation of problem solving will eventually lead to innovation by gradually altering the current situation. Sobek & Jimmerson's [16]implementation in hospital, for instance, demonstrates how A3 problem solving can be used to make significant improvements through multiple innovative problem-solving solutions, as well as the significance of objective data obtained from A3 reports in learning and continuous improvement. While Bassuk & Washington [17] utilized nine problem-solving A3 reports to improve animal health and care issues in a vivarium, they also improved the team's medical efficiency through ongoing implementation.

To the authors' best knowledge, the complete structured innovation process of product development is rarely disclosed, despite the increasing popularity of the term "innovation" in current times. In that case, the purpose of this study is to demonstrate how to gradually approach customer needs and achieve the goal of product innovation in the product development process by utilizing the repetitive operation of A3 report. A case study on improvement of a beverage dispenser's cleaning process was used as an illustration of the vital role A3 problem solving play in the innovation process. The research hypotheses are as follows:

H1: A3 report can accumulate changes to the status quo of the product and gradually approach the objective of achieving product innovation.

The case study reveals that product development innovation objectives can be met through the repetitive use of A3 problem solving. It is hoped that the results of this study will have significant impact on those companies expect to maintain innovation momentum in their product development departments.

2 Literature Review

2.1 Continuous Improving with PDCA Cycle

The ability to identify and solve problems can assist businesses in developing innovative products that solve customer problems [18]. Consequently, problem-solving skills in the product development process are viewed as a crucial competitive requirement for companies [19, 20]. In the past, continuous improvement was viewed as a never-ending process of performance improvement to maintain an efficient product development environment [21, 22], resulting in the widespread use of the PDCA (Plan - Do - Check - Act) cycle by many companies for problem solving and continuous improvement [23]. For instance, after implementing the PDCA cycle, a dairy laboratory was able to significantly reduce milk contamination, improve dairy yield and quality, and reduce production costs [24]. A PDCA cycle implemented in a teaching hospital in China decreased the inappropriate use of prescribed medications, which led to a decrease in adverse physiological effects on patients and a decrease in unneeded medication costs, resulting in improved cost-effectiveness for patients. The research also demonstrated the positive impact of PDCA cycles on the enhancement of healthcare quality [25].

A key principle of PDCA implementation is that it facilitates learning in the process through continuous iteration, with knowledge gradually expanding with each cycle [26]. Multiple cycles may be required to resolve complex problems encountered during product development [27]. Even after improvement objectives have been attained, the PDCA cycle should be repeated in an effort to improve product performance. However, despite the fact that an increasing number of businesses use the PDCA cycle as a tool for continuous problem improvement, it is simple for employees to grasp the PDCA process but the absence of guidelines to guide them through all the necessary analysis and evaluation results in deviation from the standard process and compromises the desired outcomes [28].

2.2 Accumulation of Knowledge and Product Design Through A3

Previous research has shown that mastering the processes by which knowledge is created, disseminated, and applied is a crucial prerequisite for the continuous improvement of product development and innovation [4, 29]. Yet the absence of standardized documentation and archiving makes it difficult for designers to locate the important information they have learned in the past, thereby impeding knowledge sharing [30].

The A3 report is a tool for establishing a knowledge environment that facilitates learning and knowledge accumulation [31, 32]. Comparing to traditional documents, A3 reports are more suitable as a standard communication tool because they are considered a concrete structure for implementing PDCA [33], information is presented in a simple and intuitive manner in A3 reports, and the problem solving process is clearly demonstrated, which not only helps the team to gain a deeper understanding of the problem in order to generate innovative solutions [22], but it is also easier to read and comprehend, enhancing communication among team members[34]. Moreover, it strengthens the PDCA cycle [26]. Long-term implementation of A3 thinking in a company can also foster a culture of learning among its employees, meanwhile, continuous improvement in every aspect of the company can bring a tremendous increase in revenue [35].

Several publications also indicate that the A3 report is an essential knowledge-building tool that contributes to innovative performance. For example, Alshahran et al. [36] applied A3 problem solving to improve a number of customer complaints an airline received. The study noted that the clear process of operating A3 problem solving assisted the airline in transforming these frustrating experiences into appropriate and useful knowledge that could be preserved and accumulated for reuse, thereby enhancing the service experience by preventing recurrences of problems and customer complaints. In the case of SKODA Automotive's green transport innovation, it was suggested that an A3 report would be an effective troubleshooting tool when addressing a broad issue by first breaking it down into smaller topics. The knowledge gained through careful examination of each topic would ultimately assist the organization in achieving its innovation objective [37]. A plastic injection molding company in Indonesia also implemented A3 to reduce defective labeling machines by making a series of improvements from the root cause of the problem, which led to an increase in the company's performance indicators, and emphasized the importance of avoiding hasty solutions from corporate employees before understanding the core of the problem [38].

3 Method

3.1 Objective

This study presents a commercial beverage dispenser cleaning process innovation as a case study to demonstrate how repetitive operation of A3 problem-solving can make improvements to get closer to customer needs and achieve the product innovation objective during the product development process.

3.2 Participants

Three product designers with backgrounds in industrial design and special training in A3 report operation participated in the study, while customer information was provided by the R&D manager of the beverage dispenser company. In order to complete the A3 report, the research participants disassemble and categorize the problems based on the provided customer needs and pain points and observation of the actual operation, and then delve into the problems using the product knowledge they possess.

3.3 Material

The Problem Solving A3 Report. A3 report is a knowledge visualization tool that improves organizations' problem-solving skills and facilitates communication [22]. As they are widely implemented across a variety of domains, the format and content are frequently slightly modified to accommodate various contexts. The following basic structure is commonly found in A3 reports [16, 21]: (1) Background (2) Current Condition (3) Future Goal (4) Root Cause Analysis (5) Countermeasures (6) Implementation and Follow-up Plan (7) Results.

3.4 Problem Description

On the current market, there are two primary methods for connecting the syrup tanks in commercial beverage dispensers. The first is to insert the syrup cartridges directly into the machine, and the second is to connect the syrup tanks stored in the lower portion of the machine via pipes. In the case of machines connected by pipes, the syrup tanks from the lower portion of the machine are connected to the nozzle on the upper portion of the machine for beverage output, and this type of machine includes a hot water tank for pumping and circulating clean water when cleaning the pipes. In the case of this study, the machine connects syrup tanks via pipelines, while the greatest issue with this type of product is its lengthy cleaning time. Take the Brand T product (the case in this study) for example, even though a portion of the cleaning process is automated, the entire cleaning process still takes nearly an hour.

3.5 Procedure

(1) Define development goals and improvement subjects

Significant problems with a product may be the result of a combination of multiple flaws, and past experience has shown that great problems are not easily resolved in one go [37]. This study decomposes the product problem into multiple improvement opportunities and forms multiple improvement subjects in order to delve deeper into the issue.

Through contextual inquiry, the researcher enumerated the cleaning steps (see Table 1), selected the time-consuming steps, categorized them by the components or location in the dispenser, and summarized several improvement subjects.

Table 1. Cleaning process of the beverage dispenser

Phase	Steps
Preparation	1. Fill the hot water tank 2. Remove the pipelines from the syrup containers 3. Put the pipelines into the hot water
Automated cleaning process	4. Discharge the syrup from the pipelines 5. Circulation cleaning 6. Circulation disinfection
Restoration	7. Plug the pipelines into the syrup containers 8. Organizing the pipelines and the syrup containers

(2) Outlining the PDCA Cycle in an A3 Report

The steps involved in creating an A3 report corresponded to the four phases of the Plan-Do-Check-Ack (PDCA) continuous improvement cycle [39]. Multiple improvement subjects posed in this study were resolved sequentially using the PDCA cycle to establish a culture of continuous improvement for product development. According to the standardized structure of A3 reports, which served as a communication tool for the development team, each issue's improvement process was documented in a concise and clear fashion. The stages of the PDCA cycle and the corresponding A3 reporting steps, as well as the actions taken in this study, are shown in Table 2.

Table 2. PDCA phases and corresponding 7 steps in A3 Report and actions in this research

Phase	Steps in A3 report	Actions
Plan	1. Background: 2. Current Condition 3. Future Goal 4. Root Cause Analysis 5. Countermeasures	1. Clarify the problem's context and significance, then measure the current state of the product by observing and operating the beverage dispenser in order to establish a specific improvement objective 2. Discuss the problem and the affected parameters with the R&D manager of the beverage dispenser company to determine the root cause of the issue and to propose solutions for resolving it
Do	6. Implementation	Experiments are designed and executed to evaluate the feasibility of the solution. During the experiment, any unusual occurrences should be recorded
Check	7. Results	Analyze the experimental results and evaluate the effectiveness of the improvement by comparing them to the original performance
Act	8. Follow-up Plan	Preserve the experimental outcomes as development knowledge that can be reused. Draw up the production plans, then return to the "Plan" stage for the next iteration of improvements

4   Results and Discussion

After conducting contextual inquiry and documenting the cleaning process, the research team and R&D manager of the company identified three major issues from the customer's pain point of "lengthy cleaning time", they are: (1) Complicated cleaning and sanitizing procedures (2) Inefficient water circulation, and (3) Poor fridge organization, as shown in Fig. 1. In this study, three PDCA cycles were conducted to address the three issues, and an A3 report was produced for each, as described below.

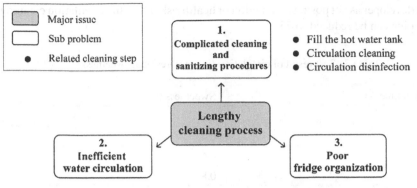

Fig. 1. Problem breakdown

4.1 The First A3 Report (from Step #1, #5 and #6 in Table 1): Complicated Cleaning and Sanitizing Procedures

Plan

Based on observations and customer feedback from the beverage dispenser developer, a significant portion of the cleaning time is spent on the machine's circulation cleaning by pumping hot water. It takes 360 s to cycle through twelve pipes. The 12 pipes were separated into four groups of three and cleaned for 90 s with 13 ml of water per second. We desired to clean using as little water as possible without sacrificing effectiveness. The investigation of the root cause revealed that in the past, it was believed that a cycle of longer seconds would have a better cleaning effect; however, the actual effect has not been verified, and people can only determine whether or not the pipes are clean by smelling them.

Do

In this study, an experiment was devised with the goal of minimizing the cleaning time for circulation. The research team filled a pipe from the beverage dispenser with syrup, connected it to a pump from the beverage dispenser, and placed the pipe in a tank containing water and detergent to demonstrate a cleaning cycle. The independent variable was the circulation time, which was set to 90 (original time), 75, 60 and 45 s respectively (because it takes at least 11 s for the water to flow through the entire pipe, so the experiment is performed in units of 15 s). Residual sweetness is the dependent variable, and residual sugar in the pipeline is measured by a digital saccharometer after the specified number of seconds of cleaning circulation.

Check

The test results are shown in Table 3. The difference in sugar residue between the 75-s and 90-s tubes was negligible (only 0.1% difference) and was evaluated by the beverage machine developer as not posing a sanitation or health risk. Thus, the circulation cleaning time per pipe can be reduced to 75 s.

Table 3. Test result of circulation time and residual sweetness

Circulation time (s)	Sweetness (%)
90	0.3
75	0.4
60	0.6
45	0.8

Act
Through an simple experiment to validate the cleaning effect, the company found that the cycle cleaning can be completed in less time. This experimental result can be applied to commercially available products, while the knowledge gained during this experiment can be saved as vital information for future product development.

4.2 The Second A3 Report (from Step #4, #5 and #6 in Table 1): Inefficient Water Circulation

Plan
The issue with the current product is that hot water is pumped from the lower half of the beverage dispenser to the nozzle on the upper half. Not only does it reduce pumping efficiency, but it also forces customers to spend considerable time cleaning in a squatting position. This study aims to reduce the circulation cleaning and disinfection time by 40% by rearranging the pipelines without compromising the cleaning effect, and to ensure that all pipes can absorb water efficiently. Through the discussion of the root causes, the developers found that the original design deliberately ask customers to add more water in the hot water tank than was necessary in order to let all the pipes extract hot water smoothly for the cleaning process, resulting in huge size of hot water tank, and led to the need for storage in the lower level of the machine.

Do
To improve the efficiency of pumping water, the designers rearranged the components of the beverage machine to reduce the distance between the hot water tank and the nozzle. The independent variables were the placement of the hot water tank on the lower and upper levels of the machine, while the dependent variable was failure to pump water from the tank. The cleaning efficiency of the hot water tank at various positions is determined by whether or not the hot water can be extracted smoothly with the same volume of water.

Check
The minimum amount of water required for circulation cleaning has decreased from 8

L to 6 L as the circulation cleaning time has been shortened to 75 s. Moreover, it has been discovered that if the hot water tank is placed on the work surface and hot water is pumped from the bottom of the water tank using pipes, the problem of being unable to pump water smoothly can be resolved and excess hot water can be reduced. The placement of the hot water tank on the work surface also allows the operator to reduce the amount of time spent in a squatting position during the cleaning process, thereby increasing their efficiency while operating the machine. Figure 2 depicts a comparison of the water flow path before and after the improvement.

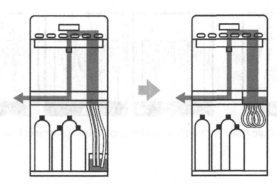

Fig. 2. Comparison of water flowing path in circulation cleaning process

Act

As a result of the relocation of the hot water tank, the ingredient area beneath the machine has more space for reorganization. This result demonstrates the knowledge reuse of the A3 report, which can also be regarded as an iterative PDCA cycle for knowledge expansion. Using the outcomes of previous experiments as the foundation for a new development plan can aid in the discussion of pertinent countermeasures and problem solving.

4.3 The Third A3 Report (from Step #2, #7 and #8 in Table 1): Poor Fridge Organization

Plan

The current beverage dispenser's fridge (ingredient area) lacks careful planning, requiring the user to spend additional time organizing the syrup tanks and pipes during cleaning or replacement of syrup tanks. The objective of this improvement is to reduce the time users spend searching for the syrup tank. The developers discovered that the current beverage dispenser makes inefficient use of space in the fridge, resulting in a significant amount of wasted space within.

Do

For each of the aforementioned issues, a solution was devised. By placing the syrup containers in a fixed location and size, reconfiguring the piping, and guiding the users with signs, the time spent organizing the fridge can be reduced dramatically. Meanwhile, to confirm that the operation of the beverage dispenser would not be affected by the new spatial planning, bending experiments on pipelines were conducted on a prototype. In this experiment, the independent variable was the pipeline connection method, and three options (A, B, and C) were presented in Fig. 3. The dependent variable is the smoothness of the pipeline, and the evaluation consists of determining whether the pipes are blocked when bending in order to determine the optimal configuration.

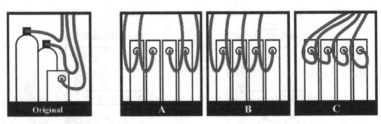

Fig. 3. Original storage room for Ingredients (left) and the improvement prototype A, B and C

Check
All of the different flavor syrups are now neatly arranged in uniform-sized boxes and labeled with the flavor name and pipe number, reducing the time required for users to sort syrup containers and pipes before and after cleaning by 5 min. The results of the bending test indicate that Solution A connects the pipelines from both sides without causing blockage due to excessive bending.

Act
The improved organization of fridge has successfully reduced user sorting time, and the new spatial layout has been tested to ensure that it does not cause pipeline blockage.

Using the three problem-solving A3s listed above, the total cleaning time was reduced by 38% by systematically addressing each issue. The results of the three A3 reports indicate that the structured framework of the A3 reports, which documented the process of product improvement, can contribute to the generation of development knowledge. Repeated PDCA cycles can aid in the development of new products, ultimately leading to product innovation by reducing cleaning times and user discomfort. At the same time, the results also confirm previous research showing that knowledge creation, dissemination, and application are essential foundations for continuous improvement in product development and innovation [4, 29], and as Fig. 4 shows, knowledge creation and accumulation in A3 can bring the organization closer to its development objectives.

In experiments on circulation cleaning time, A3 problem solving helped the company determine that similar cleaning results could be achieved in less time. The development knowledge was generated through experimental validation of A3 reports, which renders it reliable and usable in the future when confronting similar problems. The standardized process of the A3 report clearly documents the development process so that all company employees can comprehend the root cause of the problem and the context of the

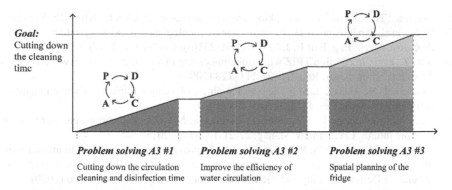

Fig. 4. Knowledge accumulation of implementing problem solving A3

improvement process. This will increase the company's overall knowledge and can be used as a reference to develop additional solutions to similar problems in the future. However, a limitation of this study is that it does not compare the A3 method to the traditional new product development process; we only examine how innovation is gradually realized through the A3 method. It is anticipated that future studies will include developer feedback and evaluation.

5   Conclusion

This study aims to demonstrate how to approach customer needs gradually and achieve the goal of product innovation in the product development process by utilizing A3 report repeatedly. To achieve cleaning process innovation, the primary customer pain point of lengthy cleaning time was broken down into three sub-problems, and these problems were progressively derived from the problem's root to the design solution using the standardized structure of A3 problem solving. The product's overall cleaning time was reduced by 38%, thereby not only achieving the team's development objective but also satisfying the customer's desire for a quicker, more intuitive, and simpler cleaning process. This also confirms the hypothesis of this study that A3 reports can accumulate changes to the status quo of a product and gradually approach the innovation objective.

References

1. Lee, H., Smith, K.G., Grimm, C.M.: The effect of new product radicality and scope on the extent and speed of innovation diffusion. J. Manag. **29**(5), 753–768 (2003)
2. Urabe, K.: Innovation and the Japanese management system. Innovation and management international comparisons. Walter de Gruyter, Berlin (1988)
3. Kanagal, N.B.: Innovation and product innovation in marketing strategy (2015)
4. Popadiuk, S., Choo, C.W.: Innovation and knowledge creation: how are these concepts related? Int. J. Inf. Manage. **26**(4), 302–312 (2006)
5. Manseau, A.: Redefining innovation, in Building Tomorrow: Innovation in Construction and Engineering, pp. 43–55. Routledge, Abingdon (2019)

6. Dorst, K.: The core of 'design thinking' and its application. Des. Stud. **32**(6), 521–532 (2011)
7. Li, M., et al.: An integrated TRIZ approach for technological process and product innovation. Proc. Inst. Mech. Eng. Part B: J. Eng. Manuf. **231**(6), 1062–1077 (2017)
8. Hua, Z., et al.: Integration TRIZ with problem-solving tools: a literature review from 1995 to 2006. Int. J. Bus. Innov. Res. **1**(1–2), 111–128 (2006)
9. Laursen, L.N., Haase, L.M.: The shortcomings of design thinking when compared to designerly thinking. Des. J. **22**(6), 813–832 (2019)
10. Johansson-Sköldberg, U., Woodilla, J., Çetinkaya, M.: Design thinking: past, present and possible futures. Creat. Innov. Manag. **22**(2), 121–146 (2013)
11. Da Silva, R.H., Kaminski, P.C., Armellini, F.: Improving new product development innovation effectiveness by using problem solving tools during the conceptual development phase: integrating Design Thinking and TRIZ. Creat. Innov. Manag. **29**(4), 685–700 (2020)
12. Thurnes, C.M., et al.: TRIZ events increase innovative strength of lean product development processes. In: Research and Practice on the Theory of Inventive Problem Solving (TRIZ), pp. 187–206. Springer (2016). https://doi.org/10.1007/978-3-319-31782-3_11
13. Mayda, M., Börklü, H.R.: An integration of TRIZ and the systematic approach of Pahl and Beitz for innovative conceptual design process. J. Braz. Soc. Mech. Sci. Eng. **36**(4), 859–870 (2013). https://doi.org/10.1007/s40430-013-0106-y
14. Kim, J., Wilemon, D.: An empirical investigation of complexity and its management in new product development. Technol. Anal. Strate. Manag. **21**(4), 547–564 (2009)
15. Saad, N.M., et al.: A3 thinking approach to support problem solving in lean product and process development. In: Concurrent Engineering Approaches for Sustainable Product Development in a Multi-Disciplinary Environment, pp. 871–882. Springer (2013). https://doi.org/10.1007/978-1-4471-4426-7_74
16. Sobek II, D.K., Jimmerson, C.: A3 reports: Tool for organizational transformation. In: IIE Annual Conference. Proceedings. Institute of Industrial and Systems Engineers (IISE) (2006)
17. Bassuk, J.A., Washington, I.M.: The A3 problem solving report: a 10-step scientific method to execute performance improvements in an academic research vivarium. PLoS ONE **8**(10), e76833 (2013)
18. Atuahene-Gima, K., Wei, Y.: The vital role of problem-solving competence in new product success. J. Prod. Innov. Manag. **28**(1), 81–98 (2011)
19. Barnett, B.D., Clark, K.B.: Problem solving in product development: a model for the advanced materials industries. Int. J. Technol. Manag. **15**(8), 805–820 (1998)
20. Sun, H., Zhao, Y.: The empirical relationship between quality management and the speed of new product development. Total Qual. Manag. **21**(4), 351–361 (2010)
21. Liker, J.K., Morgan, J.M.: The Toyota way in services: the case of lean product development. Acad. Manag. Perspect. **20**(2), 5–20 (2006)
22. Sobek II, D.K., Smalley, A.: Understanding A3 Thinking: a Critical Component of Toyota's PDCA Management System. Productivity Press (2008)
23. Gidey, E., et al.: The plan-do-check-act cycle of value addition. Ind. Eng. Manag. **3**(124), 2169–0316.1000124 (2014)
24. Kholif, A.M., et al.: Implementation of model for improvement (PDCA-cycle) in dairy laboratories. J. Food Saf. **38**(3), e12451 (2018)
25. Hong, Y., et al.: Continuous improvement on the rationality of prophylactic injectable PPIs usage by a clinical pharmacist-led guidance team at a Chinese tertiary teaching hospital. J. Int. Med. Res. **48**(10), 0300060520954729 (2020)
26. Loyd, N., Gholston, S.: Implementation of a plan-do-check-act pedagogy in industrial engineering education. Int. J. Eng. Educ. **32**(3), 1260–1267 (2016)
27. Nguyen, V., et al.: Practical application of plan–do–check–act cycle for quality improvement of sustainable packaging: a case study. Appl. Sci. **10**(18), 6332 (2020)

28. Lodgaard, E., Aasland, K.E.: An examination of the application of plan-do-check-act cycle in product development. In: DS 68–10: Proceedings of the 18th International Conference on Engineering Design (ICED 11), Impacting Society through Engineering Design, vol. 10: Design Methods and Tools pt. 2, Lyngby/Copenhagen, Denmark, 15–19 August 2011 (2011)
29. Bartezzaghi, E., Corso, M., Verganti, R.: Continuous improvement and inter-project learning in new product development. Int. J. Technol. Manag. **14**(1), 116–138 (1997)
30. Rasmussen, S., Fritsch, J., Hansen, N.B.: A design archival approach to knowledge production in design research and practice. In Proceedings of the 31st Australian Conference on Human-Computer-Interaction (2019)
31. Mohd Saad, N., et al.: A3 thinking approach to support knowledge-driven design. Int. J. Adv. Manuf. Technol. **68**(5–8), 1371–1386 (2013). https://doi.org/10.1007/s00170-013-4928-7
32. Tortorella, G.L., Fries, C.E.: Application of focus groups and learning cycles on the A3 thinking methodology: the case of increasing machinery capacity at a steel plant. In: Proceedings of the 2015 International Conference on Operations Excellence and Service Engineering (2015)
33. Shook, J.: Managing to learn: using the A3 management process to solve problems, gain agreement, mentor and lead. Lean Enterprise Institute (2008)
34. Anderson, J.S., Morgan, J.N., Williams, S.K.: Using Toyota's A3 thinking for analyzing MBA business cases. Decis. Sci. J. Innov. Educ. **9**(2), 275–285 (2011)
35. Flinchbaugh, J.: A3 problem solving: Applying lean thinking. Lean Learning Center, pp. 533–538 (2012)
36. Alshahran, B., Al-Ashaab, A., Mclaughlin, P.: The initial study of problem-solving in customer services in the airlines' sector. Int. J. Econ. Manag. Syst. **2** (2017)
37. Lenort, R., et al.: A3 method as a powerful tool for searching and implementing green innovations in an industrial company transport. Procedia Eng. **192**, 533–538 (2017)
38. Rini, S.: Implementation of lean thinking through A3 report in plastic injection company. Int. J. Ind. Optim. **2**(1), 63–68 (2021)
39. Parrish, K., Tommelein, I.D., Ballard, G.: Use of A3 reports to focus design and construction conversations. In: Construction Research Congress 2009: Building a Sustainable Future (2009)

Research on Generative Design of Car Side Colour Rendering Based on Generative Adversarial Networks

Yuanwei Ji and Yumiao Chen(✉)

School of Art Design and Media, East China University of Science and Technology, Xuhui District, No. 130, Meilong Road, Shanghai, People's Republic of China
jiyuanwei_iris@outlook.com, cym@ecust.edu.cn

Abstract. The traditional artificial color rendering process often relies on the limited personal design experience of the designer. Therefore, the design results are often uncertain. In order to help designers get inspiration for color rendering, a multimodal generation method for car side color rendering schemes was proposed through the multimodal unsupervised image translation framework MUNIT based on generative adversarial network. Firstly, based on the image crawling technology and image batch collection tools, the car colour rendering inspiration dataset consisting of hand-drawn colour pictures of the car side was constructed. After that, the car side hand-drawn images were processed through the image styling processing technology and deep learning pre-trained models to construct the car color rendering design object dataset. Next, the car color rendering generation experiment was conducted through MUNIT framework. Then, the generated images were evaluated in quantitative and qualitative methods to select the best iterative model. Finally, with the experimental data integrated, the intelligent generative design system Analogist for car color rendering was designed. The results of the research showed that the method we proposed can realize the multimodal generation of color rendering schemes of line drawings of car side through an image-to-image inspired approach. It can be concluded that Analogist can assist designers in stimulating design inspiration and improving design efficiency in colour rendering of car styling.

Keywords: Generative adversarial networks · Car colour rendering · MUNIT

1 Introduction

Image rendering can be divided into photorealistic rendering and non-photorealistic rendering. Photorealistic rendering is designed to simulate and reproduce real scenes. Non-photorealistic rendering aims to express the artistic style of the image, which is widely used in the field of art design. Non-photorealistic image rendering, also known as stylized rendering, was first proposed by David Salesin [1] in 1994. Car color rendering belongs to the category of non-photorealistic image rendering. In the field of automotive design, non-photorealistic rendering serves as a supplement and provides

© Springer Nature Switzerland AG 2022
V. G. Duffy and P.-L. P. Rau (Eds.): HCII 2022, LNCS 13522, pp. 420–434, 2022.
https://doi.org/10.1007/978-3-031-21704-3_28

designers with a lot of inspiration [2]. However, the traditional rendering process of 2D images of automobiles is time-consuming and labor-intensive. It poses a great challenge to the designers' creativity in terms of brush stroke style, light-shade contrast and color matching. It is difficult for designers to absorb a large amount of design work experience in a short period of time, and it is easy to fall into the dilemma of solidified color matching thinking and single style. The advance of artificial intelligence technology has given designers the ability to overturn old processes and standards, aiding designers in making more flexible and diverse design. Among them, machine learning provides new ideas and methods for car design.

Machine learning is the core research content in the field of artificial intelligence. It provides the system with the ability of learning automatically and improving from experience through the study of computer algorithms. As one of the latest trends in the field of machine learning, deep learning is widely used in speech recognition, object detection, image recognition and so on, bringing revolutionary progress to computer vision and machine learning. Among them, generative adversarial networks have received extensive attention since it was proposed by Ian Goodfellow et al. [3] in 2014. The variants are widely used in the fields of style transfer, semantic segmentation, natural language processing, super-resolution, 3D generation, image and video inpainting, etc.

In this context, this research proposes a generative design method for color rendering of the side view of the car based on the MUNIT framework [4] and conducts a prototype design to realize the multimodal output of the intelligent style rendering scheme of the car side line drawing.

2 Research Status of Generative Adversarial Networks

2.1 Principles of Generative Adversarial Networks

Generative Adversarial Networks is a leading generative model with the potential to learn high-dimensional and complex real-world data distributions [5]. GAN is mainly composed of generator G and discriminator D. G aims to learn the distribution of real data $Pdata(x)$ and deceive D by generating generated samples similar to the real sample x after receiving the random vector z. D aims to distinguish whether the received sample is a real sample or a generated sample. G and D continuously optimize in confrontation training, and finally achieve Nash equilibrium. The probability of judging real samples or generating samples is both 0.5. The objective function of Gan is expressed as follows:

$$\min_G \max_D V(D, G) = E_{x \sim p_{data}(x)}[\log D(x)] + E_{z \sim p_z(z)}[\log(1 - D(G(z)))] \quad (1)$$

E represents the expectation function; $Pdata(x)$ represents the probability distribution of real data; $Pz(z)$ represents the probability distribution of random vectors; $D(x)$ represents the discriminant probability after D receives the real sample; $D(G(z))$ represents the discriminant probability after D receives the generated sample. The goal of G is to generate realistic generative samples to deceive D with the discriminant probability as big as possible; In other words, G aims to minimize $\log(1 - D(G(z)))$. Since the objective function of G is independent, the objective function of G is:

$$\min_G V(D, G) = E_{z \sim p_z(z)}[\log(1 - D(G(z)))] \quad (2)$$

The goal of D is to accurately distinguish the real sample and produce samples; In other words, D aims to maximize $D(x)$ while minimize $D(G(z))$ in the condition of $D(x) \in [0,1]$ and $D(G(z)) \in [0, 1]$. Therefore, the objective function of D is:

$$\max_{D} V(D, G) = E_{x \sim p_{data}(x)}[\log D(x)] + E_{z \sim p_z(z)}[\log(1 - D(G(z)))] \tag{3}$$

Through adversarial learning, the generator and the discriminator are continuously optimized and improved in the competition, so the generative adversarial network has obvious advantages in a variety of generative models.

2.2 Research Status of Generative Adversarial Networks in Image-to-Image Translation

In recent years, with the deepening of related research, GAN has formed two main research directions: the stability research of GAN at the theoretical level and the application research of GAN in computer vision. Among all kinds of applications of GAN, the research on image generation is most extensive [6]. Image generation mainly includes image-to-image translation, fusion image generation, label-to-image mapping, and text-to-image conversion [7]. This research mainly involves the translation between the line drawing and the rendering image, which belongs to the research category of image-to-image translation. Therefore, We have conducted a related survey on the research status of generative adversarial networks in this subfield.

Image translation in order to convert an image from a source domain to a target domain, preserving the content information of the original image and assigning attribute information in the target domain to this inherent content [8]. Image-to-image translation aims to learn mappings between different image domains. Image-to-image translation can be divided into supervised learning and unsupervised learning according to whether the data is paired or not [9]. In order to solve the image translation task under different conditions, many variants of generative adversarial networks have been derived based on the original GAN.

Supervised image-to-image translation is commonly seen in dual-domain image translation, using aligned image pairs as source domains and target domains [10]. Isola et al. [11] improved the conditional generative adversarial networks and firstly applied it to the image-to-image translation task, and then proposed the image translation framework pix2pix. Pix2pix can achieve one-to-one mapping generation from source domain images to target domain images through supervised learning. To solve the problem of pix2pix in generating high-resolution images with realistic details, Wang et al. [12] proposed pix2pixHD, which can generate images with resolutions up to 2048×1024. For image translation tasks in specific fields, experts and scholars have proposed a targeted generative adversarial network framework. For the image to image translation problem of sketch to image, Chen et al. [13] proposed an end-to-end generative model Sketchy-GAN based on the expanded Sketchy dataset with the introduction of the masked residual unit to achieve unimodal generation of manual hand-drawn sketches to realistic images. The style2paints proposed by Zhang et al. [14] combines the residual U-net and AC-GAN to colorize the grayscale images of comic line drafts automatically. Supervised image-to-image translation improves the quality of image generation to a certain extent through strict constraints on pairwise data. However, the existing open source datasets can hardly meet the data requirements of supervised learning, and it is very hard to obtain large batches of paired data for a specified research direction, which requires a lot of time and research costs. Unsupervised image-to-image translation provides a new idea of training without the need of paired data, which has gained wide application and attention in recent years.

Unsupervised image-to-image translation can accurately find mapping relationships in the absence of paired data [8]. DualGAN proposed by Yi et al. [15] uses the loss form advocated by WGAN [16], which achieved translation between dual domains of unlabeled images. Zhu et al. [17] proposed CycleGAN to translate images from the source domain to the target domain by introducing adversarial loss and cyclic consistency loss without giving paired data. Huang et al. [4] encoded images into content codes and style codes, and combined the content codes in the shared space with the random style codes in the target domain. Based on that, an unsupervised multimodal image-to-image translation framework MUNIT was proposed, which realized the Diversified output of images.

2.3 The Application of Generative Adversarial Networks in Design Field

The generative adversarial network introduces the idea of adversarial learning, which can be continuously optimized and improved during the training process. Compared with other generative models, GAN has obvious advantages. It has triggered a wave of research on GAN-based design applications by researchers all around the world. In the field of clothing design, researchers from Sun Yat-sen University proposed a virtual clothing display method based on FashionGAN [18]. The virtual clothing image filled with fabric shapes and textures can be displayed by inputting clothing sketches and desired fabric images. In the field of traditional cultural design, based on the pix2pix model, a research team from Zhejiang University developed an interactive application interface that intelligently generates ancient glyph styles for personalized seal design [19]. Based on the deep learning model, Burnap et al. [20] of the University of Michigan realized the transformation of automobile modeling between different shapes, brands and angles in the estimated product form space, providing new inspiration for designers under subdivision conditions. The research team of Soochow University and the University of Hong Kong continued to optimize style2paintsV1. They proposed style2paintsV3 [21] based on a two-stage coloring model. Style2paintsV3 solved the problems such as blurring of watercolor, color distortion and dim texture in comic line rendering.

In summary, GAN is widely used in image-to-image translation tasks. In particular, unsupervised GAN avoids the problem of collecting a large amount of paired data and provides strong technical support for intelligent generative design. However, there is a lack of research on the generation of colour rendering for cars.

3   MUNIT Framework

MUNIT is a multimodal unsupervised image-to-image translation framework based on generative adversarial networks, which can map one input to multiple different outputs.

MUNIT assumed that image representations can be decomposed into domain-invariant content codes and style codes that characterize specific image domain attributes. The transformation of images from the source domain to the target domain is achieved by recombining content codes in the source domain with random codes sampled from the style space of the target domain. The overall objective function of MUNIT model includes adversarial loss, image reconstruction loss, style reconstruction loss and content reconstruction loss.

Adversarial loss aims to learn the data distribution in the target domain so that the generated image is infinitely close to the real image. The generation effect of the image is continuously optimized in the confrontation between the generator and the discriminator. Adversarial loss of G_2 and D_2 can be expressed as:

$$L_{GAN}^{x2} = \mathbb{E}_{c1 \sim p(c1), s2 \sim q(s2)}[\log(1 - D_2(G_2(c1, s2)))] + \mathbb{E}_{x2 \sim p(x2)}[\log D_2(x2)] \quad (4)$$

$x2$ represents a random image from the target domain. E represents the expected function. $c1$ and $s2$ represent its content code and style code respectively. G_2 aims to maximize $D_2(G_2(c1, s2))$, namely, minimize L_{GAN}^{x2}. D_2 aims to maximize $D_2(x2)$ and minimize $D_2(G_2(c1, s2))$, namely, maximize L_{GAN}^{x2}. Similarly, G_1 amis to minimize L_{GAN}^{x1} while D_1 aims to maximize L_{GAN}^{x1}.

Image reconstruction loss and latent reconstruction loss constitute bidirectional reconstruction loss, which aims to restrict the reverse relationship between encoder and decoder (generator). The style reconstruction loss in latent reconstruction loss provides the possibility for diversified output of images; The content reconstruction loss makes the translated image retain the content information of the original image. After the enconding by $E1$ and decoding by G_1, the image reconstruction loss of image $x1$ can be expressed as:

$$L_{recon}^{x1} = \mathbb{E}_{x1 \sim p(x1)}[||G_1(E_1^c(x1), E_1^s(x1)) - x1||1] \quad (5)$$

$x1$ represents a random image from the target domain. Image reconstruction loss allows the original image to be reconstructed after being processed by encoder and decoder. As a result, the reconstruction target of $x1$ is $G_1(E_1^c(x1), E_1^s(x1)) \approx x1$, namely, to minimize L_{recon}^{x1}. Similarly, the reconstruction target of $x2$ is to minimize L_{recon}^{x2}.

After the encoding process and decoding process, the content reconstruction loss and style reconstruction loss of can be expressed as follows respectively:

$$L_{recon}^{c1} = \mathbb{E}_{c1 \sim p(c1), s2 \sim q(s2)}[||E_2^c(G_2(c1, s2)) - c1||1] \quad (6)$$

$$L_{recon}^{s2} = \mathbb{E}_{c1 \sim p(c1), s2 \sim q(s2)}[||E_2^s(G_2(c1, s2)) - s2||1] \quad (7)$$

Whether the content code or the style code expects to be reconstructed furthest after encoding and decoding. In other words, $E_2^c(G_2(c1, s2)) \approx c1$ and $E_2^s(G_2(c1, s2)) \approx s2$ are expected. The total content reconstruction goal is to minimize L_{recon}^{c1} and L_{recon}^{c2}. While the total style reconstruction goal is to minimize L_{recon}^{s1} and L_{recon}^{s1}.

In conclusion, the total loss function is as follows:

$$\min_{E_1, E_2, G_1, G_2} \max_{D_1, D_2} L(E_1, E_2, G_1, G_2, D_1, D_2) = L_{GAN}^{x1} + L_{GAN}^{x2} + \lambda x(L_{recon}^{x1} + L_{recon}^{x2}) +$$

$$\lambda c(L_{recon}^{c1} + L_{recon}^{c2}) + \lambda s(L_{recon}^{s1} + L_{recon}^{s2})$$

$$(8)$$

4 Generative Design Method of Car Side Color Rendering Based on MUNIT

We proposed a generative method for car side colour rendering based on MUNIT. The method mainly includes five parts: the construction of car colour rendering inspiration dataset, the construction of car colour rendering object dataset, generation experiment based on MUNIT, generation evaluation and the prototype design. The flow chart is shown in Fig. 1.

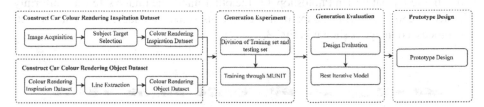

Fig. 1. Flow chart

4.1 Construction of Car Colour Rendering Inspiration Dataset

Image Acquisition. The images in car colour rendering inspiration dataset mainly consists of colored hand-drawn images of side view of the car. The initial images are mainly from various design portals such as carbodydesign, Puxiang Industrial Design Station, Huaban.com, Pinterest, and Behance. Hand-drawn images of the car were collected by the image acquisition program and the image acquisition tool Fatkun. The image acquisition program was run in the environment with python3.7. Based on this, 20,000+ initial images were collected as shown in Fig. 2.

Fig. 2. The collected pictures

On this basis, the duplicate file cleaning tool duplicatecleaner was used to screen and delete the duplicate images in collected images. Since that the quality of the images collected in batches is uneven, the unrelated images and the images with low definition were deleted. As a result, 562 images that met the collection requirements were obtained.

Subject Target Selection. The backgrounds of the collected hand-drawn images are complex and different. It's difficult to capture the shape information and the color rendering information. In order to remove the influence of the background of the image and ensure the effect of the subsequent generation experiments, the images were selected and extracted in batches in Photoshop. On the other hand, the image size was uniformly adjusted to 256×256 with 150dpi to ensure the consistency of images within the dataset. The processed image is shown in Fig. 3.

Fig. 3. The extracted car body image

4.2   Construction of Car Colour Rendering Object Dataset

The car color rendering object dataset is expected to be composed with clear ine drawings of the car side. Due to the limitation in quantity and quality of the available car side line drawings, we extracted the sketch line from the car colour rendering inspiration object dataset. In order to obtain high-quality line drawings, we have tried the following line drawing extraction methods, as shown in Fig. 4.

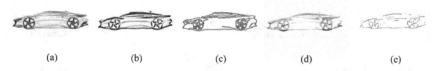

(a)   (b)   (c)   (d)   (e)

Fig. 4. Comparison of line drawing extraction methods

Stylizing the colored images to line drawings with Photoshop is one of the common processing methods. After the color adjusting procedure, the example image was processed with the minimum filter and photocopy filter respectively. The results are shown in Fig. 4 (a) and (b). Figure 4 (c) was generated by the edge detection algorithm Canny in OpenCV vision library. Anime2Sketch [22] provides a pre-trained model for extracting hand-drawn sketches from colored images, whose transformation was shown in Fig. 4(d). Figure 4(e) was generated through Sketch Simplification model proposed by Simo Serra et al. [23] Through comparison, it can be found that (a) clearly shows the characteristics of the line drawing; The light-dark relationship in (b) are excessively deepened and some of the details are missing; The contour with jagged lines in (c) has lost the sense of brush stroke. (d) shows the ability of reducing image noise and simplifying outlines effectively; The car shape has been changed in (e) with discontinuous lines. In summary, we use the following method to extract image line drafts: Firstly, process images in batches with the minium method in Photoshop. Then, for the images with much noise after batch processing, Anime2Sketch pre-trained model will be taken for simplified processing. Images in the car colour rendering object dataset are shown in Fig. 5.

Fig. 5. Images in car colour rendering object dataset

4.3   Generation Experiments

Training Config of Generation Experiments. In terms of data training environment configuration, the generation experiments in this research were performed with Pycharm IDE, using the programming language Python 3.7.11. In recent years, with the popularity of Pytorch, the percentage of top AI conference papers using Pytorch is increasing. Pytorch has gradually become one of the current mainstream deep learning frameworks. This research used the Pytorch 1.4.0 framework for generative adversarial training in anaconda environment based on the Nvidia GPU Drive Version and cuda version.

In terms of hardware configuration, the study was run on the laptop with GPU NVIDIA GeForce RTX 2060 with Max-Q Design and CPU AMD Ryzen 7 4800HS with Radeon Graphics.

Training Process of MUNIT Framework. Since the data samples involved in this study are few, car color rendering inspiration dataset and car color rendering object dataset were divided into training set and testing set according to the ratio of 7:3.

In the configuration file, modify the relevant parameters and file paths of the MUNIT. Create a new virtual environment named pytorch-MUNIT in anaconda environment and install the relevant python packages. According to the modified parameters, the MUNIT model will save four training effect images every 1000 iterations. The four images display the generated effect of source domain-target domain and target domain-source domain. Each image shows the transformed effect of 8 samples. The training interface is shown in Fig. 6.

Fig. 6. Training interface

Generation Results of MUNIT. This study uses the line drawing test.jpg as the test image. Pytorch models with 5000 iterations, 10000 iterations, 20000 iterations, 30000 iterations and 40000 iterations are selected to compare the generation effect. As a multimodal image translation framework, MUNIT will generate 10 new different colour rendering images of the car side after being input test.jpg. The generated representative images after different iterations are shown in Fig. 7.

input   sample translations

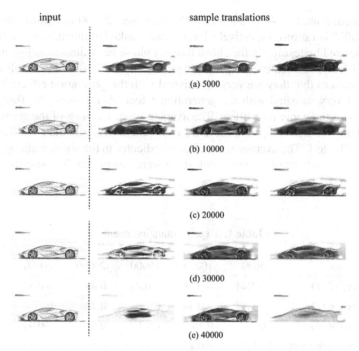

(a) 5000

(b) 10000

(c) 20000

(d) 30000

(e) 40000

Fig. 7. Generated representative images after different iterations

4.4 Generation Evaluation and Optimization

In this study, qualitative evaluation and quantitative evaluation are used to evaluate the generating effect of MUNIT framework. From the qualitative perspective, this study uses the qualitative observation method to evaluate the effect of image generation. From the quantitative perspective, this study adopts the expert evaluation method and FID index to evaluate the image generation results.

Qualitative Evaluation. The images generated at different training stages were observed and analyzed, as shown in Fig. 7. At the early stage of training, the rendering of the line drawings appeared to have blurred colors and lacked light-dark features. With the increasement of iterations, different structures of the side view of the car gradually differentiated into different rendering features. After 10,000–30,000 iterations, the generalization ability of model rendering has been significantly improved. The line drawings showed obvious brush touch and light-shadow changes. After that, the overall quality of the output images decreased as the number of training iterations increased. And some images showed overfitting features.

Quantitative Evaluation. Expert evaluation method and FID index were adopted to evaluate the image generation results.

Expert Evaluation Method. This study invited 15 graduate students majoring in industrial design and computer sciences as experts to rate images generated by the model

with 5000 iterations, 10000 iterations, 15000 iterations, 20000 iterations, 30000 iterations and 40000 iterations respectively. Experts were asked to rate the satisfaction of the
images generated by test.jpg in the above training phase according to follow indicators:
(1) clarity, (2) stylistic features, (3) diversity. The score is based on a five-level Likert
scale. - 2 indicates that they are very dissatisfied with the generation effect; 2 indicates
that they are very satisfied with the generation effect; And 0 indicates that they feel
generally about the generation effect. The average score for each of the above training
phases and the average composite score for each phase were calculated and the results
are shown in Table 1. The average score of each indicator in the above training stage and
the average comprehensive score of each stage were calculated. The results are shown
in Table 1.

Table 1. Expert evaluation result

Training Iteration	5000	10000	15000	20000	30000	40000
Average Score of (1)	−1.44	−0.78	−0.44	0.44	−0.22	−1.11
Average Score of (2)	−1.11	−0.33	0.11	0.78	0.22	−0.89
Average Score of (3)	0.44	0.78	0.67	0.56	−0.44	−1.22
Average Composite score	−0.7	−0.11	0.11	0.59	−0.15	−1.07

The results in Table 1. Shows that the images generated after 20,000 iterations
achieved the highest average overall score as well as the highest average score in terms
of sharpness and style features.

FID. FID is an index which measures the similarity between two groups of images. It
is measured by calculating the distance between the real sample feature vector and the
generated sample feature vector. The smaller the calculation result of the FID, the closer
the generated distribution and the real distribution are, that is, the higher the quality and
the better the diversity of the generated images. In the best case, the value of FID is 0.
The formula for calculating FID is shown below.

$$FID(x, g) = ||\mu x - \mu g||_2^2 + Tr(\Sigma x + \Sigma g - 2(\Sigma x \Sigma g)^{\frac{1}{2}}) \tag{9}$$

The FID value of the real and generated sample sets were calculated for each training
stage. The results are shown in Table 2.

According to the calculation results, the images generated by MUNIT model with
20000 iterations got the smallest FID value. Since the smaller the FID value, the closer
the style features of the generated samples are to the target domain image, and the quality
and diversity of the generated samples are also better. Therefore, according to FID, the
model with 20000 training iterations had the best generation result.

In summary, the Pytorch model with 20,000 iterations had the best generative effect
both in qualitative and quantitative perspectives.

Table 2. FID value in different training stages

Evaluation iteration	Training iteration					
	5000	10000	15000	20000	30000	40000
FID	263.73	231.95	212.15	167.11	206.10	216.67

4.5 Prototype Design

We integrated the generated experimental data to design the car color rendering generative design system Analogist based on the optimal iterative MUNIT model. The system interface of analogist is shown in Fig. 8.

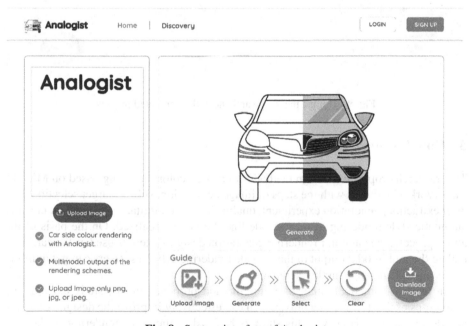

Fig. 8. System interface of Analogist

At the bottom of the system, the using process is explained in the way of graphic pointing. First, click the upload image button to upload the line drawing image of the car side. Next, click the generate button to generate 10 colored rendering schemes automatically based on the uploaded drawing. As shown in Fig. 9, users can check the generated image they want according to their preferences and click the download image button to download the images.

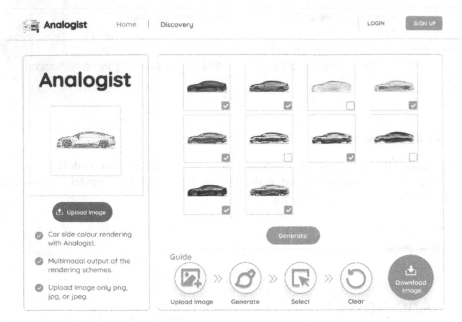

Fig. 9. Upload the image and check the generated images

5   Conclusions

This research proposed a design method for car side color rendering based on MUNIT framework. Combined with the steps of image acquisition, subject target selection, line draft extraction, generation experiment, qualitative and quantitative evaluation, etc., the automatic style rendering of the car side line drawing is realized. On the basis of the above process, the car color rendering generation design system is used as the carrier to realize the multimodal output of the car side rendering schemes. Users can get multiple rendering schemes by simple interactions.

In terms of practical application, the method proposed in this study expands the limitations of the designer's ability, which can effectively improve the design efficiency and design quality. However, this study only fixed in the color rendering of the side view of the car and failed to consider the rendering generation mechanism of other angles. In addition, the research only stayed at the 2D level, lacking the consideration for the rendering of 3D models. Therefore, future research will focus on the extension of rendering angles and rendering dimension.

Computer technology was used to empower design in this research. It realized the cross-integration of design and computer technology in the field of car rendering, which has certain guiding significance for the exploration of new research models of integration of science and art.

Acknowledgements. This study was partly supported by the National Natural Science Foundation of China (No. 51905175), the second Batch of 2020 MOE of PRC Industry-University Collaborative Education Program (Program No. 202101042012, Kingfar-CES "Human Factors and Ergonomics" Program), Shanghai Pujiang Talent Program (No. 2019PJC021), the Shanghai Soft Science Key Project (No. 21692196800) and the Smart Travel Art Design Innovation Laboratory (No. 20212679).

References

1. Winkenbach, G., Salesin, D.H.: Computer-generated pen-and-ink illustration. In: Proceedings of the 21st Annual Conference on Computer Graphics and Interactive Techniques, pp. 91–100 (1994)
2. Zhang, W.: Stylized Rendering Based On A Single Image. Doctor, Shanghai Jiao Tong University (2016)
3. Goodfellow, I., et al.: Generative adversarial nets. Adv. Neural Inf. Process. Syst. **27** (2014)
4. Huang, X., Liu, M.-Y., Belongie, S., Kautz, J.: Multimodal unsupervised image-to-image translation. In: Ferrari, V., Hebert, M., Sminchisescu, C., Weiss, Y. (eds.) ECCV 2018. LNCS, vol. 11207, pp. 179–196. Springer, Cham (2018). https://doi.org/10.1007/978-3-030-01219-9_11
5. Hong, Y., Hwang, U., Yoo, J., Yoon, S.: How generative adversarial networks and their variants work: an overview. Acm Comput. Surv. (csur) **52**(1), 1–43 (2019)
6. Chen, F., et al.: A survey about image generation with generative adversarial nets. Chin. J. Comput. **44**(02), 347–369 (2021)
7. Shamsolmoali, P., et al.: Image synthesis with adversarial networks: a comprehensive survey and case studies. Inf. Fus. **72**(1), 126–146 (2021)
8. Li, H.: Research and Application Implementation of Generative Adversarial Networks Based Image Translation. Doctor, Huazhong University of Science and Technology (2018)
9. Lin, Z., Yin, M., Yang, F., Zhong, C.: Survey of image translation based on conditional generative adversarial network. J. Chin. Comput. Syst. **41**(12), 2569–2581 (2020)
10. Pang, Y., Lin, J., Qin, T., Chen, Z.: Image-to-IMAGE translation: methods and applications. IEEE Trans. Multimedia **24**, 3859–3881 (2021)
11. Isola, P., Zhu, J., Zhou, T., Efros, A.A.: Image-to-Image translation with conditional adversarial networks. In: Proceedings of the IEEE Conference on Computer Vision and Pattern Recognition, pp. 1125–1134 (2017)
12. Wang, T.C., et al.: High-resolution image synthesis and semantic manipulation with conditional gans. In: Proceedings of the IEEE Conference on Computer Vision and Pattern Recognition, pp. 8798–8807 (2018)
13. Chen, W., Hays, J.: Sketchygan: towards diverse and realistic sketch to image synthesis. In: Proceedings of the IEEE Conference on Computer Vision and Pattern Recognition, pp. 9416–9425 (2018)
14. Zhang, L., Ji, Y., Lin, X., Liu, C.: Style transfer for anime sketches with enhanced residual u-net and auxiliary classifier gan. In: 2017 4th IAPR Asian conference on pattern recognition (ACPR), pp. 506–511. IEEE (2017)
15. Yi, Z., Zhang, H., Tan, P., Gong, M.: Dualgan: unsupervised dual learning for image-to-image translation. In: Proceedings of the IEEE International Conference on Computer Vision, pp. 2849–2857 (2017)
16. Arjovsky, M., Chintala, S., Bottou, L.: Wasserstein generative adversarial networks. In: International conference on machine learning, pp. 214–223. PMLR (2017)
17. Zhu, J.Y., Park, T., Isola, P., Efros, A.A.: Unpaired Image-to-Image translation using cycle-consistent adversarial networks. In: Proceedings of the IEEE International Conference on Computer Vision, pp. 2223–2232 (2017)

18. Cui, Y.R., Liu, Q., Gao, C.Y., Su, Z.: FashionGAN: display your fashion design using conditional generative adversarial nets. In: Computer Graphics Forum, pp. 109–119 (2018)
19. Yin, Y., Chen, Z., Zhao, Y., Li, J., Zhang, K.: Automated Chinese seal carving art creation with AI assistance. In: 2020 IEEE Conference on Multimedia Information Processing and Retrieval (MIPR), pp. 394–395. IEEE (2020)
20. Burnap, A., Liu, Y., Pan, Y., Lee, H., Papalambros, P.: Estimating and exploring the product form design space using deep generative models. In: International Design Engineering Technical Conferences and Computers and Information in Engineering Conference. American Society of Mechanical Engineers (2016)
21. Zhang, L., Li, C., Wong, T.T.: Two-stage sketch colorization. In: Association for Computing Machinery, pp. 1–14. Association for Computing Machinery (2018)
22. Xiang, X., et al.: Adversarial open domain adaptation for sketch-to-photo synthesis. In: Proceedings of the IEEE/CVF Winter Conference on Applications of Computer Vision, pp. 1434–1444 (2022)
23. Simo-Serra, E., Iizuka, S., Ishikawa, H.: Mastering sketching: adversarial augmentation for structured prediction. ACM Trans. Graph. (TOG) 37(1), 1–13 (2018)

Research on Training Model of Design Talents Based on Well-Being Cultural Industry

Xing Ji[1,2,3](✉), Jie Tang[1,2], and Jing Wang[1]

[1] Beijing Technology Institute, Zhuhai, Zhuhai City 519088, People's Republic of China
54619184@qq.com
[2] Studying School for Doctor's Degree, Bangkokthonburi University, Bangkok 10170, Thailand
[3] Institute of Innovation Design for Well-Being,
519088 Zhuhai City, People's Republic of China

Abstract. The development trend of the future design industry must be people-oriented, and the well-being of people's livelihood is the development direction of the future society. Based on the background of design education innovation, this paper puts forward suggestions and opinions on design professional theory and practical teaching, and organically combining colleges and society, strives to narrow the gap between college talent cultivation and social needs. It also analyzes and researches the current status of design education and the problems it faces, as well as the party and the state's policy on the welfare and cultural industry, to find out the development trend of design education in the future, which is also intended to cultivate applied innovative design talents for the industry and society to meet the needs of social development, promoting the healthy and sustainable development of art design majors in colleges and universities as much as possible, and meeting the requirements of current cultural and creative industries. This paper proposes the development direction of the people-oriented well-being design talent training model, analyzes its feasibility, and discusses the future innovation design education.

Keywords: Well-being cultural industry · Design talent · Training model · Design education

1 Background of University Design Education

1.1 Internationalization Background

Internationalization as a complex and dynamic process involves many factors such as economies, society, culture, science and nation. The impact of foreign culture and the development of post-modern culture make traditional culture gradually fade out of people's vision. Trendy art emerged in the 1960s and influenced Chinese college students at that time. They believe that everything is a work of art, art production does not need skills and techniques, and anyone can be an artist [4]. In this context, we fully understand and learn foreign art and culture. At the same time, we also need to fully explore local art design resources, so to form a development situation with Chinese regional cultural

© Springer Nature Switzerland AG 2022
V. G. Duffy and P.-L. P. Rau (Eds.): HCII 2022, LNCS 13522, pp. 435–444, 2022.
https://doi.org/10.1007/978-3-031-21704-3_29

characteristics. Similarly, design in the context of globalization is no longer a personal matter, but a must challenge facing the development trend of international trends.

In 2020, the United Nations put forward five challenges facing the world today at the 75th anniversary conference: first, geopolitical tension; second, the world does not trust each other; third, the climate crisis; fourth, the outbreak of the new crown virus; fifth, the dark side of the digital world. In December 2020, UNESCO held the first Future Literacy Summit, reminding people to face the challenges of human society, comprehensively reflect on the existing economic, social and health models, and provide solutions to overcome the current social situation by improving "future literacy" [1]. Higher education has entered a new era of quality improvement. Therefore China's higher education talent training model must undergo major changes, changing from a single to a more reasonable, complete variety and complete system. Many well-known design institutions and universities around the world are working hard in the face of ecological crisis, conflict relationship, human heart, technology, etc., and are actively transforming their research results into social transformation, so as to care for the world's human beings more widely.

1.2 Innovative Education is the Objective Demand of the Rapid Development of Creative Industry

Education has always been a key area of public concern. Now, in the context of innovation and the Internet, education in the future also presents a lot of innovative tendencies, which are often consistent with the innovative tendencies of future education. The development of creative industry and the demand for creative talents have created the reform direction of colleges: to run society-oriented college and to train applied talents. Design education should also timely respond, closely combine with the economic development of the region where the school is located, actively connect with relevant industries, start practical education reform, construct practical education system from the training objectives, education content, education mode and other aspects, train more applied creative design talents. Cultural creation industry is an emerging industry that is booming at present. It has strong development vitality and has brought huge social value and economic benefits. Cultural creation industry is a booming emerging industry, with strong development vigor, bringing huge social value and economic benefits. According to the growth path of talents, a precise education system with a combination of Chinese and Western education content is established, and an experiential education method is established based on the industry's demand for creativity. The requirements for talents are not only digital workers with excellent technology, but creative talents who are truly innovative and can adapt to changes in the industry. This also requires the establishment of an "experiential" education method for the future design education system. The inevitable requirements of the rapidly developing cultural creation industry for modern education include a precise education system, a combination of Chinese and Western education content, and an experiential education method. For China's education industry, it is an inevitable choice to devote itself to these three directions and carry out innovations in educational concepts, methods, channels and other aspects.

1.3 Demand for Innovative Design Talents for Industrial Upgrading

After the release of the "14th Five-Year Plan", the enterprise strategy has undergone great changes, with the trend of internationalization and digitization becoming increasingly obvious, the degree of design participation and demand rising significantly, and the shortage of design talents [7]. For example, in the well-being industry in recent years, the aging of the population is accelerating, and new cultural tourism projects such as cultural tourism, medical treatment and retirement towns are constantly emerging, which not only rapidly expand the demand for welfare talents, but also have high requirements for the comprehensive ability of welfare talents. At present, there are many design colleges in China, but they tend to cultivate traditional design talents in a single field. It is a solution of future design education to establish a new talent training system through the linkage of government, industry and colleges.

The first is to establish a close cooperative relationship between colleges and enterprises, establish a talent training base, and correctly meet the employment needs of students and enterprises [3]. The second is to establish an online training system, make full use of the Internet platform, mobilize high-quality education resources in various industries, and create an online education system to meet the theoretical and practical needs of professional knowledge. The third is to build an industry recognized talent evaluation system. Adopt certificates and training certificates to form practical certification standards for entry and promotion. Finally, the solution of providing talents continuously and stably is to provide talents for enterprises continuously and stably through proper docking and corresponding talent demand and professional training [2].

2 The Status Quo and Problems of Design Education Mode in Colleges

2.1 Bubble Development of Design Education

Manufacturing lies in creating, and its content lies in imitating design. China's rapid economic development has made us a world-class manufacturing power. After China becomes the world's factory, many things are made, such as appliances, furniture, clothes, toys. However, are there any outstanding home appliance designers, furniture designers, fashion designers, and toy designers? Most colleges now offer design majors. However, graduated students are more like the product of professional and employment-oriented vocational education. Design colleges in China have transformed into for-profit enterprises, which tend to be more technical than creative when recruiting students. Even after entering the school, problems will arise. For example, the expansion of university enrollment has made the growth of outstanding teachers slowly, resulting in the failure of teachers' teaching and students' learning to keep up with the development of the times, and there has been a bubble-like development of education.

2.2 Unreasonable Major and Course Setup

From the perspective of reality, there are two main reasons: one is from the early 1980s to the end of 1990s, the establishment of arts major can not ignore the influence of two great development opportunities. First, in the early 1980s, with the boom of reform and opening up, the art and design professional universities in art colleges, teacher training colleges and polytechnic universities developed rapidly, and the cultivation of art and design talents showed a trend of accelerating development. The other one was in 1999, with the comprehensive "enrollment expansion" of Chinese universities, the major of art and design increased sharply. The number of related majors not only increased 100 times than that of the early 1980s, but also expanded to include science colleges, agriculture and forestry colleges, economics colleges and comprehensive universities. However, in the two rapid development process, art and design major education coexists with the new and the old. Not only did many practical causes not be solved in time, but also overlapped with new problems and became very complicated. The reform of curriculum structure is imminent, and a series of educational countermeasures such as teaching plans are lacking. Therefore, the reform of curriculum structure of art design majors is still in a slump in the past eight years after the promulgation of "Catalogue of Undergraduate Majors of Ordinary Colleges and Universities" issued by the Ministry of Education [8].

From the perspective of system, the art design major formed under the planned economy system is a single counterpart curriculum structure, and the curriculum should be strictly implemented in accordance with the relevant plans formulated by the state. Therefore, a series of curriculum problems are unique to the planned economy system, that is, the single corresponding professional curriculum structure and fixed-line planning system are not conducive to the rapidly changing market demand of universities and the cultivation of diverse specifications and types of talents. Similarly, the initial establishment of the socialist market economic system is a major feature of the transformation of the university education system, but in this process, the unilateral pursuit of "market-oriented" economic interests leads to the emergence of the curriculum view of eager for quick success and instant benefits. The emergence of utilitarian educational goals quickly affected the whole educational field. However, there is no shortcut to educational reform and development. To achieve good educational results, we can not use the method of model project to pursue results, which directly affects the education quality of art design specialty in colleges and universities in China.

2.3   The Design Education System is Not Perfect and the Quality of Talents is Not High

Design is a highly comprehensive subject, which needs to be based on scientific theory and take science and technology as practice, and has high aesthetic value. This kind of design education is in a very awkward position for the two design colleges in China: art and science. The design process and method are completed under the guidance of rationality and with strict respect for the laws of nature and science. Art shows flexibility, creativity and full concern for humanity in dealing with problems [4]. However, in the current field of design, engineering and the training of technology are emphasized. No matter what kind of design it is, the knowledge structure of students will be single and incomplete.

If the design discipline does not pay attention to the curriculum construction and theoretical research of modern design theory and modern science and technology theory, it is difficult to make great progress and development. As early as the Barhouse School of

Design required the unification of art and technology. The United States, Britain and other countries attach importance to the combination of design education with economics, business and management, which aims to adjust the knowledge structure of students and improve their comprehensive quality.

2.4 Students' Practical Ability is Low

According to the response of design-related enterprises, newly graduated students cannot design and practice independently and can only be competent after two to three years of training [12]. In fact, design as a practical discipline, the accumulation of experience and precise thinking in social practice need to be constantly improved. These can also change the pure classroom learning into the combination of classroom learning and social learning to some extent.

Practical courses are an indispensable part of design education. Through the mutual combination of theoretical courses and practical courses, students not only become active and independent learners from passive learners, but also can make up for the deficiency of knowledge learned in college by checking what they have learned in practical work. However, from the actual situation, some colleges are laissez-faire to students' social practice courses and graduation projects, ignoring management. In addition, some internship companies in order to adapt to the needs of market operation, the content of internship, requirements and other aspects are often inconsistent with the educational content in college. This increases the distance between college and social production practice and creates an insurmountable gap. Students do not know the whole process of actual engineering at all, which requires students to go out into the society.

2.5 Unstable Faculty

With the rapid development of cultural and creative industry, the cultivation of design talents in universities is consistent with the needs of enterprises. Under the background of cultural and creative industry, the construction of college teachers is more urgent, and the demand of teachers for double-qualified quality is increasing. They need to have strict educational experience and scientific research ability, and rich practical ability and market operation ability. At present, from the teacher structure of high school design class, there are few such teachers. The reason why college teachers lack practical ability is that colleges put great pressure on teachers in education and scientific research, which is also one of the problems faced by the education team.

Art design majors in universities are the basic sources for cultural and creative industries to absorb innovative thinking talents. With the development of cultural and creative industry, in view of the needs of design-oriented talents and the situation of design majors themselves, strengthening the proportion of practical teaching in education can improve the innovative thinking ability of graduates, and it is also the inevitable direction to improve the dual-teacher ability of teachers. Through the fundamental reform of practical education, we can build a bridge between graduates and enterprises, reduce the gap between college talent training and enterprise demand, increase the connection between classroom teaching and market demand, art and technology, effectively improve the employment development potential of students, and provide sustainable development of innovative design talents for the cultural industry.

3 The Feasibility Analysis of the Training Mode of Well-Being Cultural Design Talents

3.1 The Status Quo of the Development of Well-Being Culture

Japan began the study of social well-being culture in the late 1980s. The Japanese Well-being Culture Society was founded in 1989, and the articles of association of relevant societies have been formulated [5]. It regularly carried out welfare cultural activities and academic exchanges, and made great achievements in academic and welfare design, which is of positive significance to the stability of society and the development of elderly products. In 1996, the Ministry of Health, Labor and Welfare of Japan set up a special policy research institution, "Japan National Institute of Social Security and Population Problems", which mainly conducts macro policy research on the increasing social burden caused by population aging and explores the direction of solving the problem, to meet the needs of the aging population [10].

South Korea has constantly opened the well-being cultural design major in universities such as Seoul Metropolitan University, Ewha Womans University and Soongsil University. More and more countries and design organizations are focusing on the perspective and focus of design on the well-being culture, taking more care of well-being of the people [5].

In the 1990s, China also carried out research on service design for the elderly, and successively set up service associations and societies for the elderly and the vulnerable groups. There is still a gap in the academic field of social well-being. In view of the current environment of aging society, we must propose solutions to the current aging problem, put forward constructive meanings to social welfare culture, welfare needs and people's happiness, and put forward counter-designs. Now, the college of Design of Statistical University has established the Service Design Research Institute to study the service design of the system, which greatly improve the system design of social service and demand service.

Currently, 39 percent of China's 85.02 million disabled people need to be equipped with rehabilitation AIDS, but the actual allocation rate is only 7.31 percent. In addition, according to the relevant data of China Working Commission on Aging, the current consumption demand of China's elderly service market is more than 3 trillion yuan, and the market demand will reach 5 trillion yuan in 2050. Where there is a demand, there is a market. A large-scale well-being industry is forming in China.

3.2 Future Development Trend of Welfare Cultural Industry

The 17th CPC Congress put forward the concept of "well-being", which reflects the party's political philosophy of caring about people's livelihood. There is a big difference between "well-being" and the "welfare" we use every day. "Welfare" is material assistance, which is provided to all kinds of vulnerable groups and is the product of the early stage of social and economic development. "Well-being" not only ensures material security for all people through state power and public power, but also, most importantly, spiritual security.

Xi said in his report to the 19th CPC National Congress, "We will actively respond to the aging of the population, build a policy system and social environment for the elderly, filial piety and respect for the elderly, promote the combination of medical care and elderly care, and accelerate the development of undertakings and industries for the elderly. On the basis of advancing development, we should address the problem of unbalanced development, improve the quality and effect of development, better meet the people's ever-growing economic, political, cultural, social and ecological needs, and promote all-round human development and social progress."

"Well-being" is for everyone in society, regardless of race, class, age or gender. By 2020, the number of people aged over 60 in China will have increased to about 255 million, and the number of people living alone or with empty nests will have reached 118 million, raising the dependency ratio to about 28%. The problem is that the effective supply of domestic pension service is insufficient, the quality and efficiency are not high, and the talent team is insufficient. The contradiction between supply and demand in the elderly goods market is prominent. It is of strategic significance to enhance the elder's sense of participation, gain and happiness and achieve the goal of well-off society in an all-round way.

3.3 Well-Being Designers Are the Future Needs of Well-Being Cultural Industry

Whether the elderly, the disabled and other vulnerable groups can be taken care of represents the level of social development and civilization. Both the old-age care industry and the rehabilitation assistive device industry started very slowly in China. In order to realize the healthy and rapid development of these vibrant "sunrise industries", we must focus on meeting the needs of the elderly and the disabled, so that they can live a comfortable and dignified life. These new industries are booming, contributing to the improvement of the quality of our economy.

The well-being industry is still a new industry in China and in its early stage of development, with late start, small scale, slow development, unreasonable industrial layout, single products and services, low technology and many other problems. The lag of talent training and the lack of well-being talents also affect the development of China's well-being industry. It is a comprehensive industry derived from other industries, providing products and services for special groups such as the elderly, the disabled, orphans and other general social mass groups such as women and children. Well-being products include not only traditional service products such as facilities for the elderly, children and the disabled, but also emerging service industries such as leisure, culture, entertainment, sports, tourism, information and psychological consultation; education industries such as education for the elderly, education for the disabled and re-employment education for the elderly; sales of special living AIDS, products for production and living, health care and rehabilitation for the elderly and the disabled; Residential space, public space and other renovation industries designed for the elderly and disabled.

China has entered a rapid aging society, the development of well-being industry for the elderly, training excellent well-being industry talents is an effective solution to the aging problem. The design major, with its unique artistic characteristics and social functions, has played a great role in promoting the healthy life and social development of the elderly under the premise of fully satisfying the use function of public space and personal aesthetic needs in an aging society [15]. With the overall development of the social economy and the improvement of democracy, the design needed by human beings overlaps with the clues needed by the country and society. In the field of design, design, emotional design, human design and other concepts have become hot words in the industry, reflecting the development of modern society in the process of paying more attention to human values and needs. The future is here. The design of the future is coming. At the arrival of new technology era, it is pointed out that humanistic care of design is the "constant" in future design education, and the "change" is the comprehensive penetration of technology. To "change" to promote "constant", follow the design of life logic.

3.4 Strategies for Universities to Cultivate Well-Being Design Talents

The cultural field of well-being covers life well-being, social well-being, needs well-being, spiritual well-being, service well-being, infant well-being, elderly well-being, disability well-being, social vulnerable groups well-being, etc. Ultimately, the well-being culture is based on people's needs and aims to improve the existing service experience, service innovation and service awareness to achieve greater social role of people.It encourages active participation in community and social activities; provides functional, practical products for vulnerable groups, and can live with dignity; improves the public environment and provides convenience for vulnerable groups; provides better health and social services; provides more opportunities to create value for society. The teaching of well-being culture design takes the well-being of the elderly as the starting point, and also includes the research category of children's well-being, the well-being of the disabled and the well-being of social vulnerable groups [13].

By understanding the demand level and characteristics of vulnerable groups for well-being culture, adjusting social forces at all levels in combination with service design concepts, building a well-being service innovation design system, timely integrating the needs of vulnerable groups for well-being culture, effectively planning research results in various fields, in-depth Life services, well-being product development and other aspects.It is so to meet the well-being needs of vulnerable groups, further demonstrate the characteristics of safety, interaction, flexibility and humanization of well-being design, and promote the development of social well-being in China through innovative research in the field of design [9]. We'll take the study of the elderly welfare as the breakthrough point, radiation to the social vulnerable groups (old, weak, sick, disabled, pregnant, etc.), take the Chinese excellent traditional culture as the center, to meet the basic needs of the vulnerable group, and supported by service design, with "well-being, research, collaborative and intelligent" design for breakthrough innovation main body of the barriers as the goal, build a bridge of cooperation between research fields and industrial practices, integrate the resource advantages of universities and enterprises, and fully release the vitality of their "talents, capital, information, technology" and other elements.

Education should be based on humanism, respecting for life and human dignity, equality of rights, social justice, cultural diversity, and international solidarity to create sustainable future design education [6]. The development and promotion of the well-being talent training model must firstly define the professional goals of the discipline, take serving the society as the direction, strengthen the international perspective to build a practical platform for college-enterprise cooperation, and apply the big design to the discipline construction, so that various disciplines are cross-integrated. At the same time, it also needs cooperation with each other to build an excellent teaching team in colleges and universities. During the process of expert training program formulation and course construction, it should take the project content and goals as important references, try to practice the yearning of cooperation between colleges and enterprises through multiple channels [14].

4 Conclusion

The focus of future design education is that the cultivation of talents is closely related to the society, and modern talents that are suitable for social development and urgent needs must be cultivated [11]. On the basis of industrial service, scientific research has made great progress along the track of national science and technology development. The curriculum settings and educational content are constantly updated with the development of science, which carries out the real sense of industry-university-research cooperation along with subject of specific project, responsibility of experts, professional docking, professional training, professional enterprises for the principle. It pays attention to the future society, assumes social responsibility, observes people's lifestyle and demand changes, finds out valuable design issues, so as to form innovative design scheme + student choice problem, from all aspects of life, whose expected results are related to the environment, products, and service process. In the era of global design, it means that the scope related to design is wider, and disciplines and personnel involved in design action are linked more closely and frequently across national boundaries. This raises a series of new problems for the reform of design education, but also creates a broad "soil".

References

1. The logical starting point of future education. Education. (47), 1 (2019)
2. Yonghua, J.: How to cultivate students' innovation ability in art design teaching in colleges and universities. New Course (II) (01), 119 (2016)
3. Lin, C., Zhang, H.: An analysis of art design Teaching reform in colleges and universities from the perspective of industry-education integration. J. China Multimedia Netw. Teach. (Top 10) (07), 211–213 (2021)
4. Li, Y.: Preliminary study on the reform path of design aesthetics in art design teaching in colleges and universities. J. High. Educ. (02), 139–141 (2020)
5. Sun, J.: Basic concept and purpose of Well-being and Well-being science. Health World (07), 49–51 (2020)
6. Tao, Y.: Research on CBE training mode of business welfare talents under the background of Aging in China. Mod. Educ. Sci. (2):129–134 (2017)
7. Tu, K.: A preliminary study on integrating the spirit of cultural creative industry into art design teaching. J. Jimei Univ. (Educ. Sci. Ed.) 19(01), 80–83 (2018)

8. Wang, Y.: Current situation of art design students' skills training and exploration of course teaching reform in colleges and universities. Chin. Writ. Artists (05), 153–154 (2021)

9. Xu, F.: Thoughts on the training of welfare talents. J. Northeast Normal Univ. (Phil. Social Sci. Ed.)(4), 179–182

10. Yi, Z.: Study on the design of community welfare facilities complex in Singapore and Japan from the perspective of "internal symbiosis". South China University of Technology (2020)

11. Zhang, X.: Education (18), 20–21 (2018)

12. Zhou, Z., Zhan, J., Yang, X.: Research on current Situation and Trend of Industry-education Integration in Design Education. Design **34**(19), 107–109 (2001)

13. Zong, M., Wang, Y., Li, C.: Design (11), 31–37 (2015)

14. Zong, M.M.: Development of well-being design education and cultural ecology -- facilitating the design momentum of guangdong-hong kong-macao greater bay area. Design (23), 70 (2018)

15. Zong, M.M.: Design 32(19), 72 (2019)

Use Persona and Semantic Differential Method to Assist Undergraduate Students Learning Product Design

Elena Carolina Li[✉]

Department of Visual Arts, University of Taipei, Taipei, Taiwan
elenali@utaipei.edu.tw

Abstract. Currently in design education in Taiwan, students may have the basic operational skills of design analysis, as well as good design practice capabilities, but lack the ability to apply design analysis and design practice together. This often makes design results unsuitable for user needs or consumer markets. To improve this problem, this study establishes a teaching mode that integrates design analysis into the design practice curriculum. This study mainly uses the Persona and Semantic Difference methods as the learning goal of design analysis, and we teach students how to use the two methods to produce a design that meets the user's needs. The research results show that integrating the Persona and Semantic Difference methods into the product design process can effectively help students get closer to the design goals, and help maintain students on their design paths. Moreover, students' self-evaluations have good learning effectiveness in the curriculums.

Keywords: Design education · Product design · Semantic Differential · Persona

1 Introduction

When college students are learning product design (particularly first-and second-year college students), they tend to start drawing up design proposals and developing sketch drawings during the third to fourth week after a design topic is announced in Taiwan. In order to lay a solid foundation for students' practical skills, teachers spend most of time focusing on practical skills training. Many students do not know that they can adopt systematic and objective design methods to identify user needs to complete their designs; as such, students may complete a beautiful prototype without meeting users' needs. As a teacher on the front line, I have tried to integrate relevant design methods into product design courses in the hope of connecting design analysis and design practice closely through appropriate course arrangement, thereby helping students adopt more objective and effective methods for design.

Before offering this practical course, I once offered another course with the SD method as the main tool, at which the author guided students to adopt the SD method to design product appearance, so that students could have an initial understanding that

© Springer Nature Switzerland AG 2022
V. G. Duffy and P.-L. P. Rau (Eds.): HCII 2022, LNCS 13522, pp. 445–460, 2022.
https://doi.org/10.1007/978-3-031-21704-3_30

the design method was effective in assisting with the product appearance design, including design analysis, design goal setting, design concept development, and prototyping. Afterwards, when conducting this research, the author included the concept of user-centered design in an advanced course, in an attempt to incorporate the Persona method, which could learn about user needs, and the SD method, which could assist with product appearance design. Then, the author explored whether the integrated application of the two methods could help students complete products that met their design goals (i.e. user needs).

Designers have been seeking key attractive points that can display product functions effectively or respond to users' recreational needs (Hassenzahl 2003). To identify these attractive points, designers may spend their energy on researching or planning the expected product impressions when designing products while other designers even apply their personal experiences to the design intuitively and focus too much product impressions rather than user impressions (Bloch 1995; Demir 2008; Hsiao and Chen 1997), making it impossible to design product functions or appearance in alignment with user needs. However, designers should try to reduce the difference between the two parties' perceptions of product semantics, to bridge the gap between users and designers (Khalaj and Pedgley 2019).

The above-mentioned issues are actually reflected in the current design education in Taiwan. In the process of designing products, students may have set their target users and conducted simple design analyses in the beginning; however, once they move onto the design practice stage, they ignore the importance of user preferences or needs due to excessive focus on the visual presentation of their products. Therefore, this research focuses on the analysis and practice of product design based on the concept of user-centered design (UCD). It is hoped that students will not only design the reasonable product appearance in the course, but their products must meet users' needs or expectations.

To objectively analyze target groups, one of the most commonly used methods is Persona. The author chose to adopt the Persona method to help students establish potential target users and establish the goals to be achieved through design. Next, the common method used in product appearance design to measure users' perception of appearance design is the SD method, which is an effective quantitative method (Osgood et al. 1957). Ahmed and Boelskifte (2006) adopted the SD method to point out the difference between the designer's original design intention and users' actual experience, and to define the semantic elements clearly or the goals of products that meet user needs first before the design stage. This research will also use the SD method to assess whether there is a gap between the students' design results and their design goals, and to understand the students' learning experience in a qualitative manner to inspect whether the integrated application of the Persona and the SD methods can help students achieve their expected design goals.

The purpose of this research is as follows: (1) To establish a teaching model for product design courses through the integration of the Persona and the SD methods. (2) To teach students to comprehensively apply the Persona and the SD methods to complete a product design. (3) To point out the gap between product design goals and design results through quantitative assessments, to examine the feasibility of the teaching model.

2 Literature Review

2.1 Persona

The designers design the product appearance in alignment with users' needs and ideas, and the appearance needs to be able to convey the desired image successfully (Chuang and Kao 1997). This is the reason this research chose the Persona method to analyze user needs first, and then adopted the SD Method as a tool for product appearance design.

Persona is not a real user, but a transformation and representation of a group of real users to help designers understand their target groups. Persona is also known as the user archetype, the user profile in the Persona method can also be used to represent users for product design (Sinha 2003). There are many advantages in the Persona method, such as role-playing, focusing on discussions on specific users, and identifying the priority needs of products to facilitate design decisions (Friess 2012).

Leifer et al. (2017) proposed 10 steps for the implementation of the Persona method: seek users, establish hypothetical users, confirm hypotheses, identify regular user patterns, profile users, define scenarios, test and verify, and disseminate knowledge, establish the scenarios, and continue to enhance the development. The main purpose of this research is to use the Persona method to help the students identify users' image and needs, and to invite the students to complete the first six steps in accordance with the design topic. Goltz (2014) proposed that the basic elements of a Persona should include at least name, demography, descriptive title, introduction, day-in-the-life narrative, and explicit or tacit end goals. To create a persona, interviews and observations are generally adopted to obtain the user's internal and external characteristics, goals, habits, and daily life problems or frustration (Nielsen 2012; Sinha 2003).

This research required the students not only to list a persona's basic internal and external characteristics, lifestyles, and habits but to list product issues and needs. The Persona method is highly flexible and can be combined with many design methods, such as brainstorming, scenario, design mapping, and mood boards, to facilitate design development (Adlin and Pruitt 2010). This research attempts to integrate the Persona and the SD methods in alignment with the objectives of the two courses on user-centeredness and product appearance.

2.2 Semantic Differential Method

Product appearance design is divided into the following two dimensions: (1) physical features, which refer to the features of product appearance, such as appearance, color, material, and other elements that can be analyzed and identified directly; (2) expressive features, which refer to the emotional features expressed by the appearance that are more difficult to be analyzed and identified directly (Chen 2000).

The SD method was developed by Charles E. Osgood in 1957. This method adopts adjectives that general users can understand to measure the semantic perception of stimuli quantitatively and presents abstract user experiences in a quantitative and visual manner (Hung and Nieh 2013). Participants need to evaluate the stimulus using pairs of bipolar adjectives with semantically opposite meanings to understand the attributes and the portion of the stimulus in each pair of bipolar adjectives, mostly measured on the Likert scale of 5, 7, or 9. It is generally suggested that at least three pairs of adjectives be provided to the participants to measure the semantics of a product (Khalaj and Pedgley 2019).

Adjectives that can be evaluated through visual perception are mainly selected for this practical course because vision is the major factor that affects the senses (Chang 2000). Khalaj and Pedgley (2019) mentioned that designers, in response to design practical needs, could establish pairs of bipolar adjectives in alignment with their product image goals, and design based on the pairs of bipolar adjectives as the design goals. After product design is completed, designers evaluate whether the product design has met their original image goals through the assistance of experienced experts. In this way, the SD method is not just used to analyze the product appearance, but it can also become the goal and basis of each design stage and help designers provide objective information to prove that their design is not based on personal intuition or is completed at will. The SD method has also been applied to product design analyses many times (Creusen and Schoormans 2005; Hassenzahl 2011).

The author asked students to play the role of "designers" in class to interview users based on a design issue (such as shoulder and neck massage tools for office workers) and to collect images related to the issue (such as images that include interviewees' daily necessities, lifestyle-related images, images of competitors' products, etc.). The students then identified their product image goals in alignment with target users' needs based on the images collected through Image Scale (such as an office massage tool that could help office workers relax with a decorative function), and then selected three pairs of bipolar adjectives as design principles and goals, such as "Decorative (1 points) - Functional (7 points)" and " Stressed (1 points) - Relaxed (7 points)". According to the image distribution in Image Scale, students decided to set "Decorative (2 points)" and "Relaxed (5.5 points)" as their design goals, and identified product features in alignment with the design goal before developing a design concept with reference to the image distribution of Image Scale.

After the design was completed, the author invited the students in this course, interviewees, and experts to conduct design evaluations to examine whether the design results were aligned with the design goals (Decorative [2 points]; Relaxed [5.5 points]). Through this model, students were guided to design products that met their target users' needs, and the design methods were applied throughout the stages of preliminary analysis, goal setting, design concept development, and design assessment.

2.3 Image Scale

Image map is often called Image Scale in the design field or the industry. Generally speaking, it is x- and y-axes with semantically opposite adjectives marked on them accordingly. It is mostly used in chromatics-related courses. After the "sample group (usually presented in the form of images)" is compared based on the semantic meanings of the pairs of adjectives and placed on the coordinates, the analyst can interpret and analyze the results of the sample group on the coordinates.

Image Scale is a commonly used analysis method in industrial design field. Designers focus on design issues in visual and systematic methods, or identify the design context and design opportunities through the image map (Chen 2003). Pan (2006) pointed out that the image map could be used in preliminary analysis and planning, prior to design concept development, and consensus building and management, such as comparison of advantages and disadvantages, design reference, internal consensus building, and external communication. Lin (2010) stated that the image map had the following functions: understanding and analyzing the product market, analyzing the future product trends, setting the product design direction, and examining whether the design results meet the expected goals.

In this research, only the x-axis was adopted for the image map to allow students to focus on a single pair of adjectives (see Fig. 1); the y-axis was not adopted because students who were new to product design would be distracted and confused due to the overlapping of semantic meanings due to the use of two pairs of adjectives to analyze the product appearance. After the students selected the pairs of adjectives to be analyzed based on their design goals, they placed the images collected from interviewees on the x-axis of the image map based on the meanings of the pairs of adjectives. After completing the placement of the images, they performed product image analyses, set design goals, and identified potential product features and elements.

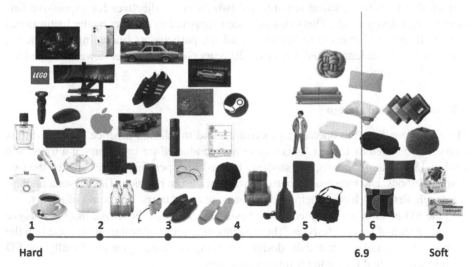

Fig. 1. Sample of Horizontal image map (Source: a student draws on coursework).

3 Research Method

The main teaching issues that this research aims to solve are that when students are learning product design, they often move onto the stage of sketching too quickly without a complete design analysis to identify user needs and clear design goals. In addition, the final grade of designing courses in the past was often decided through teachers' and experts' evaluations based on their subjective opinions, without an objective grading method. In the course offered by the author, the Persona and the SD methods were adopted as tools for design analysis, design goal setting, midterm/final design evaluations, and a set of teaching methods that allowed the two methods to be used throughout the design practice process was designed to assist students in developing design concepts by means of the two methods above, to help them obtain feedback from others for their design, and to enable them to understand the gap between their own design and expected design goals.

3.1 Research Scopes

The target students were the second-year students majoring in Visual Arts at the University of Taipei. The author taught the students to use the Persona method to design daily necessities and find user needs for one of their relatives or friends. Then, the SD method was adopted as a tool for appearance analysis. The author collected relevant studies (Bagus and Murata 2016; Chan 2013; Chen 1997; Lu and Chuang 2013; Guan and Lin 2002; Huang 2007; Lin 2014; Liu 2012; Syu 2014) and compiled a total of 97 pairs of adjectives. Chen (2000) divided the product appearance design into two categories: physical features and expressive features; each team in the course needed to choose one pair of adjectives for physical features and two pairs of adjectives for expressive features as their design goals. This study had been approved to conduct by the Institutional Review Board of University of Taipei and all the participants (including 18 students, parents of some students who did not over 20 years old, and 13 interviewees) signed the informed consents.

3.2 Instructional Design

The design method, the operating procedures, and the design practice process in this course are detailed in Table 1. This course was conducted for two hours at a time for a total of 18 weeks. In this course, students learned the operating procedures of the two design methods, and then moved onto the stage of design practice. The Persona method was taught first, which could help students analyze target users' needs and lifestyles, and then the SD method was adopted as the basis for the use of the image map to analyze the image map of users' lifestyles. The students then set their design goals based on the analysis results, and completed the design according to the design goals. Finally, the SD method was applied for midterm/final evaluations.

Each student/team of students needed to complete one piece of work, with one to two members per team. In the midterm evaluations, each team of students was required to draw an A3 color design drawing for the finalized design plan for experts, peers and their target users (interviewees) to evaluate. Product drawings from multiple angles needed to be provided in the design drawing to help evaluators understand the design proposal for midterm evaluations. The users were then asked to conduct a midterm evaluation (SD method) to understand their feelings and opinions about the design, and they could also provide their suggestions about the design plan.

At the end of the semester, each student/team needed to complete a prototype and an A2 poster. At this stage, the same experts, peers and interviewees in the midterm evaluations were invited to evaluate their final results. In the final evaluations (SD method), the prototype (optional) and the poster (with a 2D visual map of products) were adopted as

Table 1. Course practice process

Operation steps		Student's tasks
Design topic announcement		Choose a close relative/friend (user) and design a product for him/her
Persona method	What is Persona	Learn how to create a Persona once based on the slides and paper handouts
	Design scopes (Seek users)	Each student interviews a user to understand his/her needs and expectations
	Data collection (Create hypothetical users, confirm hypotheses)	Collect at least 50 images of the interviewee in daily life (including food, clothing, housing, transportation, entertainment, and branding) to get a preliminary understanding of the user's lifestyle and style preferences
	Persona settings (Find regular user patterns, describe users, define scenarios)	Divide students into teams according to the attributes of their interviewees. Each team can obtain at least three interviewees' interview results and images. Create a Persona based on the results and seek potential design opportunities
Persona and SD method combination	What is the SD method	Learn how to apply the SD method once based on the slides and paper handouts
	A library of pairs of adjectives provided	The teacher provides 97 pairs of adjectives (physical features and expressive features)
	Image analysis	Seek product image direction that meets the persona's preferences or needs based on the images of interviewees collected (at least 150 images in total from at least three images of interviewees for each team), and find pairs of adjectives with similar images from the library
	Decision of pairs of adjectives	Choose a pair of adjectives with physical features and two pairs with expressive features as the design goals

(*continued*)

Table 1. (*continued*)

Operation steps		Student's tasks
	Image map analysis	Sort the daily-life images of the interviewees collected into the image map (similar to Fig. 1) according to the meanings of the three pairs of adjectives, and complete three x-axis product image maps
	Decision of design target (Set image points)	Select the image categories that meet the design goals or the needs of the target group according to the three image maps, and set the design goals (image points), such as 2 points for decoration, 5.5 points for relaxed, and 4.5 points for elegance
Based on Persona and SD design targets (image points)	Form feature analysis	Analyze the visual features of the product for image points, including the form, structure, texture, color, pattern (motif and symbol), and size
	Concept development	Phase I: Five concept sketch drawings (divergence) Phase II: Three complete concept drawings (convergence)
	Design finalized	An A3 design drawing, which including appearance, operating process, use scenario, color, materials, etc
	Midterm evaluation (pretest)	An A3 complete design drawing, and fill out the SD method questionnaire by experts, peers, and interviewees
	Evaluation result announcement	Include two pieces of expert data, 18 pieces of peer data, and 13 pieces of interviewee data
	Modify	Adjust the designs based on the results of the questionnaire
	Mockup	Choose the appropriate material to make a 1:1 mockup
	Prototype	Choose appropriate materials to make a 1:1 prototype or make a complete product visual design drawing (adjusted the method due to the pandemic in 2021)

(*continued*)

Table 1. (*continued*)

Operation steps		Student's tasks
	Final evaluation (post-test)	An A2 poster, a prototype (optional), oral presentation, fill out the SD method questionnaire by experts, peers, and interviewees
Interview after the course		Interview with six students after this course, with the topic of weekly course progress and connotation, to understand the students' ideas about learning design methods

the stimulus for evaluation. When this course was conducted, the COVID-19 pandemic broke out in Taiwan, this course was switched online completely. As some students were unable to make prototypes due to limits of space, materials, and tools, they were not required to make prototypes.

The Likert 7-scale was adopted for both midterm and final evaluations. The examples of midterm/final evaluation questions are as in Table 2, including the evaluation items and three pairs of adjectives, without providing design goals (image points) set by each team of students. In the midterm evaluations, each evaluator measured the "A3 complete design drawing" based on their personal perception. The final evaluation method was the same as that of the midterm one, while the evaluation items were changed to a prototype and a poster. Participants in the evaluation were experts, peers in this course, and interviewees. Experts must have more than 10 years of experience in the field of product design.

Table 2. Sample of midterm/final evaluation items

When	Midterm			Final		
Evaluation items	A3 proposal image			A2 poster with prototyping (not be required)		
Scale	1 2 3 4 5 6 7			1 2 3 4 5 6 7		
Paired adjectives	Hard	☐☐☐☐☐ ☐☐	Soft	Hard	☐☐☐☐☐ ☐☐	Soft
	Functional	☐☐☐☐☐ ☐☐	Decorative	Functional	☐☐☐☐☐ ☐☐	Decorative
	Vulgar	☐☐☐☐☐ ☐☐	Elegant	Vulgar	☐☐☐☐☐ ☐☐	Elegant
Evaluators	2 experts, 18 peers, and 13 interviewees for each evaluation					

3.3 Data Analysis Method

The data collected in this course include (Table 3): The midterm data results, mainly descriptive statistics and design suggestions (in the form of texts), were provided to students to let them understand the gap between their own design goals and others' perception. In addition, because the total number of peers and interviewees exceeded 30, IBM SPSS 22.0 was used to conduct a single-sample T-test of the midterm and final data. There were three pairs of adjectives for each team's work, and the design goals set by the students themselves (image points) were the values tested so as to understand the rate of achieving their design goals. Furthermore, whether the final questionnaire data was better than the midterm results was examined through a dependent sample T-test, so as to infer whether the students would adjust their designs based on the experts', peers', and interviewees' evaluation results.

Table 3. Method of data analysis

Items	Method
Midterm/Final evaluation: experts, peers, and interviewees	Descriptive statistics
The gap between the design goal and the questionnaire data (Midterm and final)	Single sample T-test
Comparison of midterm and final design goal gaps	Dependent sample T-test
Analysis of Self-Evaluation Scale on Learning Effectiveness	Single sample T-test
Student interviews	Qualitative analysis

To understand how the students perceive their personal learning effectiveness, the students in this course were invited to fill out a self-evaluation scale for learning effectiveness at the end of the semester. With reference to Lin's (2019) learning effectiveness scale as a measurement tool, the questionnaire consisted of three dimensions measured with the Likert 7-scale: (1) cognitive with 5 items, one of item is "I understand the knowledge and skills taught by the teacher"; (2) affective with 5 items, one of item is "I can share the knowledge and skills taught by the teacher with others"; (3) psychomotor with 4 items, one of item is "I have learned different skills through the knowledge and skills taught by the teacher". The results of the questionnaire were analyzed by a single-sample T-test, and the results of the students' interviews after class were analyzed qualitatively. Six students from two teams that made progress, two that regressed, and two that remained flat in this course were selected for interviews.

4 Results and Discussion

There were 14 teams in this course, and the designed works included a hot compress tool, massage tool, flower pot, sleep aid product, wine packaging design, Hako toy, series of action figures, handbook, straw set, storage tool, a charm, etc. After the midterm assessment, there were two teams adjusting the set values of the image points based on feedback from the experts, peers, and interviewees.

Table 4 is a summary of the statistical analysis results of the course materials. First, both peers and interviewees were considered as target users, and the data of the two groups (N = 31) was combined; then, a single-sample T-test was conducted to calculate whether there was a significant difference between the questionnaire data and the set values of the image points of each team (p < .05). The statistical results showed that 21 pairs of adjectives in the entire class reached the design goals in the midterm evaluations; 22 pairs of adjectives of the total 42 pairs of adjectives reached the design goals in the final evaluations. Then, a dependent sample T-test was performed to compare whether the final results of each team of students were better than their midterm results. The results showed that two teams made significant progress, 10 remained flat, and the remaining two regressed. Of the teams that remained flat, two teams had two pairs of adjectives reaching the design goals, and seven teams had one pair of adjectives reaching the design goals. Of the 42 pairs of adjectives, the performance of six pairs of adjectives was improved, 20 remained flat, and six regressed. This showed that most of the students might strive to reach their design goals or to maintain a certain design direction through this course.

The experts evaluated the results and analyzed two pieces of data through descriptive statistics. Due to the small number of the experts (N = 2), when the difference between the experts' data and the students' set value of an image point was less than 0.5 points, it indicated that a design goal was achieved. The results showed that only eight pairs of adjectives reached the design goals in the midterm evaluations; nine pairs of adjectives reached the design goals at the final evaluations. Next, whether the final results of each team of students were better than their midterm performance for experts were compared, and the results showed that one team made progress, 11 remained flat, and two regressed. Of the 11 teams that remained flat, one team had two pairs of adjectives reaching the design goals, and three had one pair of adjectives reaching the design goals. There were 10 teams on which peers'/interviewees' evaluations and experts' evaluation reached a consensus. In this course, of the pairs of adjectives that reached the design goals, the number of pairs of adjectives with physical features and expressive features was close.

A single T-test was performed additionally to evaluate the students' self-evaluation of their learning effectiveness. The analysis results were as follows: cognitive (T = 10.24, $p = .000$; M = 6.21, Sd = 0.50), affective (T = 10.41, $p = .000$); M = 6.46, Sd = 0.59), and psychomotor (T = 11.53, $p = .000$; M = 6.47, Sd = 0.54). The three dimensions were all significant, and 18 students considered the learning effect of this course was positive in their self-evaluation. Based on teaching observations and interviews with six students, the author proposed the teaching reflections below:

- From the results of the interviews, the author discovered that the teams with improved performance or performance that remained flat had a better understanding and recognition of the operation of the design methods, and would continue to examine the gap between their design goals and the progress of their design during the design process. On the contrary, the teams with regressed performance had insufficient understanding and recognition of the design methods from the beginning of this course, or they were

Table 4. Summary of statistics analysis

No.	Paired adjectives	Peers and interviewees (N = 31)			Experts (N = 2)			
		Goal achievement items (Single sample T test)	Goal progress [P] or regression [R] (Paired samples T test)		Goal achievement items	Goal progress [P] or regression [R]		Total
			Single paired adjective	Total Midterm/Final	(Absolute value ≤ 0.5)	(Absolute value ≤ 0.5 = flat [F])		
1	Functional-Decorative	Final	P	P		-1.00	P	F
	Troublesome-Convenient		F			1.00	R	[One pair]
	Comfortable-Uncomfortable		F			0.00	F	
2	Functional-Decorative	Final	P	F [One pair]		0.00	F	F
	Original-High-tech	Midterm/Final	F			0.00	F	
	Troublesome-Convenient	Final	F			0.00	F	
3	Hard-Soft	Midterm/Final	F	F [Two pairs]		1.90	R	F
	Comfortable-Uncomfortable	Midterm/Final	F		Midterm/Final	0.00	F	[Two pairs]
	Relaxed-Stressed		F		Midterm/Final	0.00	F	
4	Functional-Decorative		R	F		1.10	R	P
	Nonmainstream-Mainstream	Midterm	F			-1.80	P	
	Relaxed-Stressed		F			-1.80	P	
5	Cold-Warm		P	P	Midterm	1.50	R	R
	Low-profile-High-profile	Midterm/Final	F			0.50	F	
	Childish-Mature		F			1.50	R	
6	Hard-Soft	Midterm	F	F [One pair]		0.00	F	F
	General-Personalized	Midterm/Final	F			0.00	F	
	Dark-Bright		F			-0.50	F	
7	Delicate-Rough	Midterm/Final	F	F [One pair]		-0.20	F	F
	Savage-Cute		F			1.50	R	[One pair]
	Close-Distant		F		Midterm/Final	0.00	F	
8	Round-Sharp	Midterm/Final	F	F [One pair]		0.00	F	F
	Savage-Cute		P			0.00	F	
	Lively-Dull		F		Final	-1.00	F	
9	Functional-Decorative	Midterm/Final	F	F [Two pairs]		-0.02	F	F
	Gentle-Strong		F			-0.50	F	
	Relaxed-Stressed	Midterm/Final	F			0.00	F	
10	Ugly-Beautiful	Midterm	F	F [One pair]		0.00	F	F
	Savage-Cute	Final	P			-0.10	F	
	Unsaturated-Saturated	Midterm/Final	F			1.00	R	

(continued)

less motivated to learn, so that they deviated from their design goals more and more in the process of developing their works.

Table 4. (*continued*)

No.	Paired adjectives	Peers and interviewees (N = 31)			Experts (N = 2)			Total
		Goal achievement items (Single sample T test)	Goal progress [P] or regression [R] (Paired samples T test)		Goal achievement items	Goal progress [P] or regression [R]		
			Single paired adjective	Total Midterm/Final	(Absolute value ≤ 0.5)	(Absolute value ≤ 0.5 = flat [F])		
11	Unpolished-Glossy	Final	F	F [One pair]		1.50	R	F [One pair]
	Unique-Ordinary	Final	F		Midterm/Final	0.00	F	
	Quality-Bad quality	Midterm/Final	F			0.50	F	
12	Mature-Unique	Midterm/Final	R	R [Two pair]	Final	−1.00	P	F
	Functional-Decorative	Midterm	F			0.00	F	
	Savage-Cute	Midterm/Final	R			0.00	F	
13	Functional-Decorative	Midterm	F	F [One pair]		−0.50	F	F
	Elegant-Vulgar	Midterm/Final	F			0.00	F	
	Unique-Ordinary	Midterm/Final	P		Final	−1.00	P	
14	Relaxed-Stressed		R	R	Midterm/Final	0.50	F	R [One pair]
	Unique-Ordinary		R		Midterm	1.50	R	
	Functional-Decorative	Midterm	R			1.00	R	

- The entire class reached nearly 50% of their design goals in the midterm evaluations (half of the pairs of adjectives reached the design goals), which indicated that most of the students identified their design direction quickly, probably due to their learning experiences in the last semester. This also showed the possibility of improvement in the design methods through multiple operations.
- Through the practice of this teaching model, some pairs of adjectives did achieve the expected design goals, but there were many factors influencing the design results. It is difficult to objectively infer whether the results were caused by the integrated application of the Persona and the SD methods. In addition, although more than half of the pairs of adjectives in the peers'/interviewees' evaluations reached the design goals, the data of the two experts were far from ideal. The factors that caused this gap need to be further studied.

5   Conclusion

Most students agreed that these two methods were significantly helpful to design practice. The Persona method could help students design according to the target groups set and user needs while the SD method could assist students in setting out the direction of product appearance; the combination of these two methods could help students integrate the two design directions of "user-centeredness" and "product appearance design" together. This teaching model can help students to get closer to the design goals.

Students agreed that the operation at each stage of this course was necessary. Each team of students also completed a design work under this teaching model. According to the students' feedback, the design topics of this course were moderately difficult and allowed them to leverage their design abilities. The 97 pairs of adjectives provided by the teacher were sufficient, and three pairs of adjectives set as the design goals were executable. In the process of design development and practice, the gap between the image points of the three pairs of adjectives and the design progress would be constantly reminded of throughout the process, which would help the students' designs to achieve their expected goals. The experts, peers, and interviewees helped point out design blind spots through the midterm evaluations, so the students had sufficient time to adjust their designs and to know users' insights again.

Due to the outbreak of the COVID-19 pandemic in Taiwan, the offline drawing review activity needed to be switched online. As a result, the evaluators could not feel or watch the physical works in person in the final. The student interviewees stated that their understanding and experience of other students' works online were less real and certain than in a physical display. In the future, we should think about how to improve the quality and the effect of the online drawing review process to be close to those in offline teaching.

Acknowledgements. This study was partially supported by the MOE Teaching Practice Research Program, Ministry of Education, Taiwan (PHA1090412), and thanks to Cheng, Yu-Ching for serving as a course teaching assistant. The author is grateful for this support.

References

Adlin, T., Pruitt, J.: The Essential Persona Lifecycle: Your Guide to Building and Using Personas: Your Guide to Building and Using Personas. Morgan Kaufmann, Burlington (2010)

Ahmed, S., Boelskifte, P.: Investigation of designers intentions and a users' perception of product character. In: Unnthorsson, R., Jonsson, M. (eds.) Proceedings of Nord Design Conference. University of Iceland, Reykjavik (2006)

Bagus, M.R.D., Murata, T.: Conjoint analysis of customers' preferences with kansei engineering system for product exterior design. In: Matsuo, T., Kanzaki, A., Komoda, N., Hiramatsu, A. (eds.) Proceedings of the 2016 5th IIAI International Congress on Advanced Applied Informatics, pp. 1026–1032. IEEE Computer Society, Kumamoto (2016)

Bloch, P.H.: Seeking the ideal form: product design and consumer response. J. Mark. **59**(3), 16–29 (1995). https://doi.org/10.2307/1252116

Chan, C.-Y.: A Study of Emotional Design Characteristics of Bentwood Chair (Unpublished master's thesis). Ling Tung University, Taichung City (2013)

Chang, C.-C.: Perceptual Factors Underlying Users' Image Perception toward Product Form (Doctor's thesis). National Chiao Tung University, Hsinchu City (2000)

Chen, C.-C.: The study on the application of style operation mode to product form design. Ind. Des. **28**(2), 111–115 (2000)

Chen, C.-K.: A Study on Design Methods Commonly Used in Industrial Design Industry of Taiwan (Unpublished master's thesis). National Taiwan University of Science and Technology, Taipei City (2003)

Chen, K.S.: Style recognition and description. J. Des. **2**(2), 123–143 (1997). https://doi.org/10.6381/JD.199712.0123

Chuang, M.-C., Kao, C.-H.: Exploring the image of products made in Taiwan. J. Des. **2**(2), 37–54 (1997). https://doi.org/10.6381/JD.199712.0037

Creusen, M.E.H., Schoormans, J.P.L.: The different roles of product appearance in consumer choice. J. Prod. Innov. Manag. **22**(1), 63–81 (2005). https://doi.org/10.1111/j.0737-6782.2005.00103.x

Demir, E.: The field of design and emotion: concepts, arguments, tools, and current issues. METU J. Fac. Archit. **25**(1), 135–152 (2008)

Friess, E.: Personas and decision making in the design process: an ethnographic case study. In: Proceedings of the SIGCHI Conference on Human Factors in Computing Systems (2012)

Goltz, S.: A closer look at personas: what they are and how they work (part 1). Smashing Magazine (2014)

Guan, S.-S., Lin, Y.-C.: A study of generating the web design system based on the Kansei Engineering process. J. Des. **7**(1), 59–74 (2002). https://doi.org/10.6381/JD.200206.0059

Hassenzahl, M.: User experience and experience design. In: Soegaard, M., Dam, R.F. (eds.) The Encyclopaedia of Human-computer Interaction. The interaction design foundation, Aarhus (2011)

Hassenzahl, M.: The thing and I: understanding the relationship between user and product. In: Blythe, M.A., Overbeeke, K., Monk, A.F., Wright, P.C. (eds.) Funology: From Usability to Enjoyment, pp. 31–42. Kluwer Academic Publishers, Dordrecht (2003)

Hsiao, S.W., Chen, C.H.: A semantic and shape grammar based approach for product design. Des. Stud. **18**(3), 275–296 (1997). https://doi.org/10.1016/S0142-694X(97)00037-9

Huang, T.-S.: The form element system design for portable multimedia digital products. J. Des. **12**(4), 59–77 (2007). https://doi.org/10.6381/JD.200712.0059

Hung, T.-F., Nieh, C.-K.: Semantic evaluation research on image of shop facade using SD-relationship between form features and kansei image. J. Arch. **84**, 55–75 (2013)

Khalaj, J., Pedgley, O.: A semantic discontinuity detection (SDD) method for comparing designers' product expressions with users' product impressions. Des. Stud. **62**, 36–67 (2019). https://doi.org/10.1016/j.destud.2019.02.002

Leifer, L., Lewrick, M., Link, P.: The Design Thinking Playbook. John Wiley & Sons, Hoboken (2017)

Lin, B.-R.: An Exploration of the Application of Image Map in Product Development (Unpublished master's thesis). Chaoyang University of Technology, Taichung City (2010)

Lin, C.-Y.: Relationships between Leisure Participations, Leisure Benefits and Learning Effectiveness of Students in a Private Junior High School in Pingtung (Unpublished master's thesis). Meiho University, Pingtung City (2019)

Lin, Y.-C.: The Study of Appearance and Functional Design of Garbage Can by Using Kansei Engineering (Unpublished master's thesis). National Kaohsiung University of Applied Sciences, Kaohsiung City (2014)

Liu, S.-H.: A Study of Product Image and Product Preference on Gender Product – a case of mobile phone (Unpublished master's thesis). National Taiwan University of Science and Technology, Taipei City (2012)

Lu, J.-C., Chuang, M.-T.: A study of using kansei engineering into the appearance design of the smartphone. J. Commer. Modern. **7**(2), 97–115 (2013). https://doi.org/10.6132/JCM.2013.7.2.05

Nielsen, L.: Personas-User Focused Design, vol. 15. Springer, Heidelberg (2012). https://doi.org/10.1007/978-1-4471-7427-1

Osgood, C.E., Suci, G.J., Tannenbaum, P.H.: The Measurement of Meaning. University of Illinois Press, Urbana (1957)

Pan, C.-Y.: A Study of the Process of Mature Period Product Differentiation-The Proposal of Multi-Image Features Deduction Method (Unpublished master's thesis). National Cheng Kung University, Tainan City (2006)

Sinha, R.: Persona development for information-rich domains. In: CHI 2003 Extended Abstracts on Human Factors in Computing Systems, pp. 830–831. ACM (2003)

Syu, S.-R.: The Objective Evaluation Method and Correlation Analysis of Product Images (Unpublished master's thesis). National Taipei University of Technology, Taipei City (2014)

The Packaging Design of Traditional Festival Products Based on Green Concept

Li Ouyang(✉), Nabin Chen, Xiansi Zeng, and Yonglin Zhu

Academy of Fine Arts Education, Guangzhou Academy of Fine Arts, Guangzhou 510261, China
228066765@qq.com

Abstract. Festival packaging has the characteristics of a short life cycle and fierce commercial competition. Nowadays, holiday gift packaging pursues luxurious and extravagant designs out of commercial interests. As a result, the sales of holiday products have caused an excessive economic burden to consumers and caused waste of social resources and environmental pollution. The concept of green design is gradually changing the packaging of festive products. The way to solve this problem is to reduce the energy consumption of product packaging, such as reducing the volume of packaging, rational selection of packaging materials and recyclability, and full use of intelligent technology. It is necessary to guide the contemporary festival product packaging with a new design concept and transition it from the luxury type to the ecological green environmental protection design concept.

Keywords: Holiday gifts · Product packaging · Green design

1 Introduction

There are thousands of ceremonies and customs in China, and the long-standing festival culture has profoundly affected people's daily life. With the development of the times, the changes in modern life and consumption concepts, and more importantly, the improvement of aesthetic taste, etiquette, and customs has also changed, and society has put forward higher requirements for holiday products. Today's holiday packaging is popular with luxury and the pursuit of taste, so excessive packaging of products causes unnecessary economic burdens to consumers, waste of resources, and environmental pollution to society. Due to the short life cycle characteristics and fierce commercial competition of festival packaging, new design concepts must guide the design and production of contemporary festival product packaging and lead the transition of festival product packaging from external waste to ecological green design concepts. This article will discuss solutions from three aspects: packaging volume, material, and structure, and explore the concept and direction of holiday product packaging design.

V. G. Duffy and P.-L. P. Rau (Eds.): HCII 2022, LNCS 13522, pp. 461–471, 2022.
https://doi.org/10.1007/978-3-031-21704-3_31

2   Traditional Culture and Gift Packaging

2.1   Ethics and Customs

"Book of Rites" and "Ritual Instruments" record: "Look at the utensils to know the skill of its work, and watch it to reveal the knowledge of its people. Therefore, it is said that the gentleman is careful about what he does with others." In the traditional Chinese etiquette culture, the gentleman and the value of the villain is valuable no matter how big or small. The number of gifts fully shows a person's character, cultivation, wisdom, and aesthetic taste, so people must be "prudent" and gradually evolve from "prudent" to "fine". Form a fresh, frugal, ingenious, and affectionate gift-giving style, expressing the sincere heart of "substituting things for love." In ancient China, people began to give gifts when they communicated and gave gifts to others. The relationship between relatives and friends is as important as choosing a gift, so the scale must be considered. This is a part of traditional cultural etiquette and the exchange of gifts between relatives and friends in the traditional festival period. After thousands of years of historical development, the traditional culture of etiquette and customs has been continuously completed and improved. Gifts are frugal but not lacking in impact. It is still the spirit advocated by people in today's society (Fig. 1).

Fig. 1. "New year's eve in the palace" Chinese new year gift box series. Source: https://www. sohu.com/a/506961000_120048229

2.2 Traditional Festival Culture

In Cross-Cultural Design: Communicating in the Global Marketplace (1994), Henry Steiner said: "Most people are unaware of their own culture.—as if they were una-ware of air, growth, and gravity. We live in culture that affects our thinking and behavior in a 'natural' way like water does to fish." Obviously, in order for designers to create "worldwide" packaging, they must first understand "their own culture" that they have never experienced. China's traditional festival culture has a long history, which can be fully utilized and carried forward through the design of festival products and can be used and promoted as traditional culture in people's daily lives. Facts have proved that the more folk and local design, the more global it is. Therefore, we need to deeply explore their cultural connotation of traditional festivals that traverses historical time and space, summarize and refine their cultural roots, and update and develop to adapt to contemporary cultural ecology and national cultural construction.

2.3 Holiday Gift Design

The festive packaging of the product presents the cultural character of the festival. The specific cultural connotation is one of the design's goals. The corresponding de-sign for the festival should not be simply imitating or cutting the surface elements of some designs but integrating the elements and cultural characteristics of the festival into the modern product packaging design. Therefore, product packaging design needs to have a traditional cultural spirit that resonates with the public. Only by deeply understanding the history of traditional festivals, the cultural connotation and appearance characteristics of festivals can the festival and etiquette culture be integrated into one, and the product packaging form with strong traditional cultural characteristics can be designed. In today's cultural context, contemporary designers have the responsibility and obligation to create festival packaging designs belonging to China through traditional cultural elements and lead new design trends and trends.

3 Changes in Festive Product Packaging

3.1 Diversification of Brands and Festival Products

Traditional mooncake brands usually come from hotels and restaurants, and most types of mooncakes are made from traditional ingredients in traditional flavors such as wu ren, lotus seed paste, and double yellow. In recent years, there have been many innova-tive concept cake shops, such as BreadTalk. The first concept mooncake product was launched, assembled into mini-shaped mooncakes. The brand has teamed up with hello kitty to launch a pouch kitty as a mooncake packaging with four mini bags inside. This mooncake stands out among many mooncake packaging brands, using its brand strategy to display and innovate its product concept effectively.

Another example is the famous ice cream brand "Haagen-Dazs," which launched ice cream mooncakes such as "Splendid Peony" and "Ruyi Mid-Autumn Festival," taking advantage of the unique advantages of its products to dominate the market. (See Fig. 2) During the Mid-Autumn Festival, not only bakeries and dim sum shops are innovating, but tea brands also want to take a share of this traditional festival and develop gift packaging with their characteristics: refreshments, moon cakes, tea combinations, product packaging from characters, colors and patterns are full of elements of the traditional Chinese Mid-Autumn Festival.

As a Mid-Autumn Festival product, in addition to traditional moon cakes, other products have gradually entered the festival market, which is a new business trend and direction. According to the survey, people are tired of moon cake products, it is no longer the only gift people yearn for, and it may even become a burden. Many merchants keenly seized this business opportunity and quietly entered this huge festival market competition using their brand advantages and characteristics. Godiva operates a series of Mid-Autumn chocolate packaging among the many Belgian chocolate brands during the Mid-Autumn Festival and has won a larger share of the Chinese market. The company uses the product advertising slogan "Cuihe invites the bright moon, the bright moon adds affection," integrates traditional Chinese culture, and combines different quantities and types of chocolate products through festive packaging design to form holiday gifts at different prices. Become a highlight of Mid-Autumn Festival gifts (Fig. 3).

Fig. 2. Haagen-Dazs mid-autumn mooncake packaging. Source: author's own photograph

Fig. 3. Godiva mid-autumn mooncake packaging. Source: author's own photograph

3.2 Multiple Functions of Holiday Product Packaging

Urban living requires dual or multiple functions, where land is expensive, and working principles are challenged by leisure and flexible hours. Now, Added value means extra functionality that makes the appliance feel like an improvement in saving time and money. Therefore, the functional requirements pursued by green design are to obtain maximum benefits with the least resources and to make the relationship between product packaging and products more diversified. There is also a functional connection between them. Figure 4 shows the gift packaging for red wine, assembled by disassembling the box. The first impression of the packaging is that it looks elegant and straightforward, with a particular class, which is a very decent holiday gift, but the biggest highlight is that the packaging can be reassembled into another product which is a wine rack for storing wine bottles. This product packaging design is multifunctional, allowing users to enjoy the conversion process of packaging functions. Gift wrapping has changed from an aesthetic and protective function to a display function. The original structure is modified to form new functions, the functions of the two products are completed, and the added value of the products is increased, which is easy to be loved by consumers. In addition to the modification function, there is also a combination function that is multiple gift packages can form a variety of combinations, and the collaborative design of a single package and multiple packages can be combined in various ways. This design method is diverse. First, the display effect is relatively affluent. Second, after receiving the gift, the recipient can make various combinations and place them in the family space.

Figure 5 The gift packaging for festivals in Guangdong, Hong Kong, and Macau draws inspiration from traditional festivals. It integrates the modern color elements of Guangdong, Hong Kong, and Macau to express the image of an international metropolis such as dynamic, charming, and fashionable capitals of the three places. The composite structure adopts a hexagonal shape, implying eternal life and infinity. The four-sided

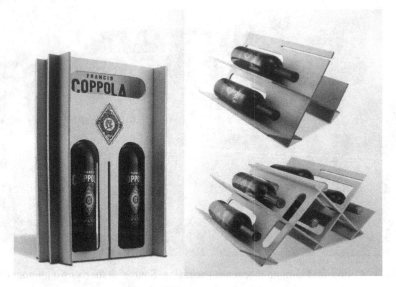

Fig. 4. Gift wrapping for wine

rhombus box and the combination of two rhombi can be combined to form a whole hexagon.

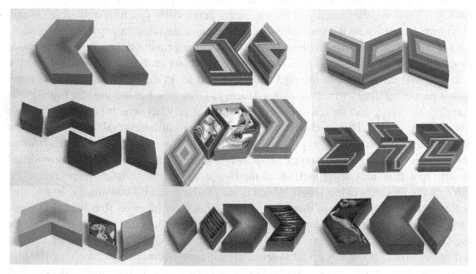

Fig. 5. Guangdong-Hong Kong-macao festival gift packaging. Author: Li Ouyang, Jie Ling

Gift packaging boxes are suitable for gift customization of silk scarves, ties, accessories, and other items, and both singleness and combination can be expanded. It is also especially suitable as a return gift during the Spring Festival. The packaging box of the series contains different gifts to give back to the gift-giving party, which is decent, generous, and fashionable.

3.3 Modernizing the Visual Expression of Festive Elements

Through visual information symbols, designers can transform the function, value, and meaning of information and invisible information such as human thinking and expressions into visible communication elements as words, colors, and graphics. On this basis, designers release information through the visual language formed by the organic combination of visual elements, and cultural information is transformed from one form to another. As far as the visual representation of festival elements is concerned, we first classify traditional cultural festival information and visual elements according to images such as words, animals, plants, objects, utensils, Etc., then extract and summarize texts and images and colors. The second is to transform the extracted information elements into visual expression and design and reproduce the visual form with contemporary aesthetics and market consumption tastes. In the process of information transformation, only by transforming these graphics into festive packaging graphics, transforming traditional cultural elements into visual elements in modern packaging design, and establishing an internal connection with the product can we correctly add value to the brand product.

Information graphics can be figurative or abstract. The novelty, folklore and modernization of the expression make the product establish the trend, fashion and modernity in the tradition while conveying the traditional festival culture. For example, brand colors must be obtained strictly, sticking to the same color. Designers must respect the brand's visual assets and create new design forms based on a pre-set color spectrum. The color design of the festival packaging and the original brand color body can handle the contradiction and unity of the product packaging design and the festival under the normal state. The color system of various traditional festivals is not particularly complicated; it is essential to find the most critical elements and the most representative colors (Fig. 6).

Fig. 6. Yamada Tu "Super Lucky Tiger" new year gift box packaging design. Source: https://mp. weixin.qq.com/s/sruVkPuDxAjQEt5JHEBJXQ

4   Green Design Principles for Festive Packaging

4.1   Reduced Design

One of the significant challenges of festive product packaging is to simplify packaging, reduce packaging aging materials, and achieve the best packaging results with the least amount of packaging materials while reducing the impact on the environment. For commercial benefit, merchants often design holiday packaging much larger than the product to make the gift more valuable. However, green design advocates reducing the space of the content packaging and improving the utilization of the inner space of the packaging - aging to reduce the volume of the packaging. The GODIVA brand has a relatively high utilization rate of packaging space. The packaging volume is determined by the content products' number, shape, and height, and there is almost no remaining space. Some gift packaging designs are large in size and empty inside to reflect the sense of the weight of the gift. This method is a design method that wastes resources. A large volume is no longer a trend that consumers like, because it increase the burden on the recipient and the environment. One of the principles of green design is the most convenient, least resource, and maximum packaging design for holiday gifts. Under this principle, there is a lot of design space to exert. Figure 7 shows the packaging of the New Year's chocolate gift box. The packaging is made of recycled paper and can be recycled. It can be folded into a rabbit according to the instructions on the back of the package, for it was the year of the rabbit. This chocolate gift packaging uses the least environmentally friendly materials, the least volume, directly wraps the chocolate products, and its functional design is completed on the back of the paper, which minimizes the gift packaging and maximizes the function.

Fig. 7. Godiva mid-autumn mooncake packaging. Source: author's own photograph

4.2 Material Utilization

Using recycled materials is far less damaging to the environment than new materials. There is much recyclable packaging after the holidays, but recycling holiday packaging is an issue right now. Because designers choose different packaging materials, matching recycling systems are minimal. A supermarket in Guangzhou once held an activity to recycle iron moon cake boxes. As a result, the campaign received a great response and was well received by the public. In this event, consumers lined up to work with the tin boxes of mooncakes left over from the past year at the event. It can be seen that the moon cake packaging box is very beautifully designed, but it is not conducive to recycling.

The use of materials considers the cost; designers should select and design materials according to the principles of easy recycling and degradation to save and utilize social resources. Different materials bring different emotions to the packaging, and new materials will also give the packaging a new look. Different packaging designs, changing from the material, can be one of the easy ways to achieve the effect. Distinguish another product packaging directly from the appearance and feeling of touch, and pull apart the difference between products. The eco-friendliness of the material is also a new difference in a festive packaging. Merchants treat the design of festive packaging and strengthen the high-quality materials and excessive packaging to enhance the commercial value of the packaging. With improved living standards, the aesthetics of people's cognition is also changing, and paper packaging is not necessarily cheaper than metal packaging. This cycle indeed reduces waste and pollution of resources and fully reuses resources.

Moreover, any design cannot increase the burden on society, nor can it create waste of resources and excessive packaging. As a part of society, contribute a little more to the energy and environment of society. Designing festive packaging not only does not increase the burden, but on the contrary, saves energy and designs festive packaging that is environmentally conscious (Fig. 8).

Fig. 8. Gift box wrapping paper folded rabbit

4.3　Multiple Structures

The green design uses the least resources and the minor force into the most significant effect. The structure is the most crucial element in packaging design and is closely related to materials. For a packaging design, the combination of multiple structures is equivalent to increasing the function and value of the packaging. The concept of green design is gradually guiding holiday product packaging to appear in front of people with an updated face.

4.4　Intelligent Technology

Innovative festive gift packaging brings new life and experience. The NFC radio frequency chip is implanted into the traditional gift packaging, and the gift packaging can be traced back to the source of the gift through the induction of the smartphone. It provides the recipient with new intelligent interaction and festival celebration scene, bringing the other party a new experience; Intelligent chips can analyze consumer behavior data, and feedback to designers and researchers on behavior data of consumer groups is also the basis for continued research and development.

The sensor chip received the gift package, and the mobile phone contacting the package can show the cordial blessing of the gift-giver, which can be video and voice, and even animation, VR, and other technologies.

The dynamic display of customs activities different festivals can be traced back to different festival information, traditional customs and festival cultural information appear, and gift packaging is no longer a product; it has become a medium and platform for communication between friends, conveying each other's thoughts. The development of technology will also bring breakthroughs to the design of holiday gifts. When technology becomes routine, and costs are controllable, gift packaging with an excellent experience will be the design trend.

5　Conclusion

The selection criteria of consumers' holiday gifts will guide the direction of the product design of merchants, and the careful planning of merchants will also guide consumers' choices and become a fashion. In the new era, the definition of traditional Chinese holiday gift customs and etiquette is gradually changing, and the design also faces the challenge of innovation. As a result, the green design concept will guide the transformation of holiday product packaging from extravagant waste to ecological green design and achieve the best experience of holiday product packaging design with the least resources through green design.

Acknowledgments. The author thanks the annual project library of Guangzhou Academy of Fine Arts for its financial support (No.: 20XSB07).

References

1. Wang, W.: History of Chinese Rites and Customs, 1st edn. China International Broadcasting Press, Beijing (2021)
2. Liu, X.: Chinese Festival Journal (Guangdong Volume), 1st edn. Guangming Daily Press, Beijing (2016)
3. Xiao, F.: Traditional Festivals and Intangible Cultural Heritage, 1st edn. Xueyuan Press, Beijing (2016)
4. Nachtwey, J., Mair, J.: Doing Ecological Design - New Green Brand Strategy. (Wang, H. Trans.). Tianjin University Press, Tianjin (2010)
5. Gordon, S.K.: Packaging Makeovers. (Hu, X., & Zhu, Q. Trans.). Shanghai People's Fine Arts Publishing House, Shanghai (2006). (Original work published 2005)
6. Barbero, S., Cozzo, B.: Ecodesign. Potsdam Ullmann (2009)
7. Design Center Stuttgart: Focus Green. Avedition, Ludwigsburg (2008)
8. Cheung, V., Viction, A.: Simply Packaging. Hong Kong Victionary (2008)
9. Scott, B.: Designing Sustainable Packaging.: Laurence King Publishing, cop, London (2009)
10. Campos, C.: Promotional Packaging and Design. Promopress, Spain (2010)

Morphological Design Method of Cave Karst Based on Biomorphic Algorithm - Digital Design of Guilin Cave

Qianhang Qin[1]([✉]), Wenda Tian[1]([✉]), Fei Yue[2], and Guan Lian[3]

[1] GXNU School of Design, Guangxi Normal University, Guilin 541000, China
tanqh17@tsinghua.org.cn, twd936474757@gmail.com
[2] Art and Design Academy, Tsinghua University, Beijing 100030, China
[3] School of Architecture and Transportation Engineering, Guilin University of Electronic Technology, Guilin 541000, China

Abstract. Karst is the general term for a series of underground or surface forms produced by the erosion of soluble rocks by water. Karst landforms are the masterpieces of nature, with high aesthetic, scientific and natural heritage values. Karst caves are landscapes composed of carbonate rocks dissolved and eroded by groundwater into cavities and secondary carbonate deposits, such as stalagmites, stalactites, stone pillars and stone mantles. The article takes Guilin, China, the most typical and universal representative place of karst evolution in the world as the research object, and proposes a new design method of karst cave geomorphology based on cave landscape characteristics and computerized morphogenetic algorithm with the help of interdisciplinary thinking and tools. Different landscape causes and characteristics of caves are analyzed and the elements of their morphogenetic design are summarized. The grasshopper platform combined with different algorithmic plug-ins to determine the morphology is introduced and the generation of shapes with cave landscape characteristics is realize. A real case is analyzed and its potential role in interactive design is discuss.

Keywords: Guilin cave · Digitalization · Algorithm design · Interactive design

1 Introduction

Karst landform is a unique geological landform, which is a general term for a series of subsurface or surface forms resulting from the erosion of soluble rocks by running water. Cave karst are cavities and secondary carbonate deposits made of carbonate rocks by dissolution and erosion of underground water, forming landscapes such as stalagmites, stalactites, stone pillars, stone mantles, etc. The caves of Guilin in the Karst World Natural Heritage Site of Southern China have extraordinary scientific, cultural, aesthetic and tourist values, such as examples of the main stages of the earth's evolutionary history. The karst region of Guilin, China, has developed a large number of large-scale cave systems and rich cave accumulations underground, and its karst features and geomorphological diversity are unique in the world. These treasures from nature show a thick image of the

© Springer Nature Switzerland AG 2022
V. G. Duffy and P.-L. P. Rau (Eds.): HCII 2022, LNCS 13522, pp. 472–483, 2022.
https://doi.org/10.1007/978-3-031-21704-3_32

world's historical civilization. Under the premise of protecting natural heritage, it is the rational use of natural heritage values that can bring scientific research results, aesthetic feelings and considerable economic feedback. As the world ushers in a comprehensive digital era, especially with the backlash of the new crown epidemic, it has become increasingly difficult for traditional, single form means of tourism to adapt to the new situation. Natural scenic spots urgently need to grasp the development opportunities of digital communication and vigorously promote the digital conservation, display and dissemination of natural heritage. Digital conservation, display and dissemination of natural heritage is not simply the application of digital technology, but through the organic integration of digital technology and natural heritage. The introduction of digital design and development thinking, to achieve the conservation, display and dissemination of natural heritage into a new era of digital.

The conservation and dissemination of natural world heritage is the source of strength for its sustainable development. In addition to ensuring the economic benefits of tourism development of heritage sites, Guilin karst landform caves should highlight the aesthetic value, cultural value and scientific value, comprehensively manifest the connotation of the world heritage brand as it should be, and establish the authentic brand image of the world heritage sites [1]. China is forming a corresponding conservation concept and development approach, but the traditional model is facing challenges in many aspects. Strengthening the digital presentation of natural heritage is of great significance to promote natural heritage conservation, natural heritage safety, natural heritage communication and natural heritage development. In this paper, a method is proposed to help the digital design of Guilin cave morphology through bionic algorithms. In this method, the karst features and topography of caves can be used as elements of the bionic algorithm. Different karst features will generate different paths, and then the designer can choose the next step to design a specific digitized morphology according to the paths. It increases the diversity of digital research, display and tourism of Guilin caves, and can better strengthen the link between natural heritage conservation and socio-economic development activities, and enhance World Heritage education and knowledge sharing. It is hoped that this approach can provide designers with different needs, different options and references.

2 Limitations of the Development of Guilin Cave Karst and Digital Future

2.1 Limitations of the Development of Guilin Cave Karst

At the 44th World Heritage General Assembly in 2021, the World Heritage Committee called in the Fuzhou Declaration for strengthening the links between heritage conservation and socio-economic development activities; enhancing the use of digital technologies; and strengthening World Heritage education and knowledge sharing for young people.

Natural heritage is the common wealth of human beings, in which mountains, water, forests, grass and air are closely related to human beings. Heritage conservation is to protect the common home of human beings. Natural cultural heritage is unique and non-renewable, and the rich variety of natural heritage specifically has a common cultural value. On the basis derives economic value, natural heritage tourism can bring huge social and economic benefits to the local community. The conservation and development of World Natural Heritage is now encountering new opportunities and challenges. Taking Guilin caves and rocks in the karst landscape of southern China as an example, there are many problems in its own development although it has rich cultural tourism resources.

The impact of the new crown epidemic, the lack of tourism communication and innovation, and weak cultural penetration. Located in the south of China, Guilin karst geomorphic caves are weakly connected between regions due to geographical restrictions, and the form of communication and educational materials is single and backward. Tourists and scientific staff from all over the country or even the world must experience and investigate in the field in order to more deeply perceive the value of cave caves and rocks in aesthetic and scientific aspects.

Guilin cave faces insufficient attractiveness and lack of core tourism competitiveness. Tourism products lack unique cultural value, do not highlight the advantages of Guilin lava cave world natural heritage, and lack of characteristic brand construction [2]. At present, Guilin caves karst are relatively weak in the sense of experience in publicity. The publicity should not be limited to a single media communication path, but should increase the design concept. The development and application of experience design and cultural and creative tourism product design enable people to have a richer sense of experience and reshape the connection between the participants of landscape activities and the overall landscape environment, which produces a continuous and long-lasting communication bridge [3].

2.2 Digital Future of Cave Solution Rock Development in Guilin

The rapid development of technology has brought the transmission mode into the digital era. The use of digital means of communication of the world's natural heritage culture is an inevitable choice. Digital natural heritage content has less depletion in the process of transmission. It can be effectively enhanced by perception of visualization and understandability in the presentation of the content [2].

Through digital interactive design technology, natural culture can be transformed into an entertaining and product-oriented cultural industry advantage. It can realize the transformation from natural cultural heritage to cultural and creative industry, provide in-depth user experience for the community. This can meet the public's cognitive demand for natural heritage, effectively disseminate and popularize related knowledge, bring brand effect and economic benefits, and at the same time achieve the purpose of protecting natural heritage. The museum in Kazan Kremlin, Russia, uses multimedia technology in the presentation of non-natural heritage items, which allowing visitors to access and download applications and displays related to non-natural heritage items via a wireless network environment. They can scan QR codes to access podcasts, images and texts related to the exhibition content. The use of new media has increased the number of young visitors to the museum. The number of online visitors accessed through the website platform is also increasing [4].

Digitalization has great advantages in realizing the dissemination of values and knowledge of natural heritage in fixed areas like Guilin caves karst by means of technology, which can get rid of the limitation of information access to people by space. Using the convenience and cross-domain nature of digital information technology can enhance the sense of participation, identification and access of people who are not located in the region in terms of scientific, cultural, aesthetic and tourism values of natural heritage while realizing a wide range of information coverage. It stimulates the curiosity and interactivity of the group and facilitates a better immersive experience of the cultural charm of cave karst [2].

2.3 Value Created by the Digitization of Guilin's Cave Karst

The fact that Guilin karst landform caves karst rocks can become a World Natural Heritage Site shows that its scientific significance and aesthetic value are outstanding and have a global status. At the technical level, Guilin caves karst rocks can achieve wider and deeper dissemination of cultural contents through digital media, thus creating a huge cultural data dividend, enhancing the global dissemination of its information and supplementing the cultural database of the World Natural Heritage.

The intervention of digital technology in the development of Guilin caves and karst has broken through the closed state of caves and rocks confined to geographical restrictions, providing more room for development for effective brand communication and economic revenue enhancement. Changing the single form of sightseeing tour mode, innovating Guilin landscape tourism concept, can innovate Guilin landscape aesthetics, develop new tourism products, expand tourism space, form new unconstrained tour modes and routes, and further enhanc the taste and image of Guilin international tourism city [5].

3   Analysis of Morphological Characteristics and Formation Principle of Guilin Caves

Cave karst are independent underground spaces with underground pipes of a certain size in diameter or with long continuous runoff space formed by the karst action of soluble rocks (some erosion may exist). These karstable rocks, under the action of dissolution and transport of groundwater, develop and form the most colorful cave resources in the world with rich dissolution and deposition forms in the cave. These karstable rocks mainly include stalagmites, stalactites, stone pillars, stone mantles, side stone dams, etc. [6].

Stalagmite, growing on the floor of the cave, is shaped like a bamboo shoot growing out of the ground. The stalagmite is formed by the infiltration of water from the limestone crevices into the cave, and during the infiltration process water reacts with carbon dioxide and limestone to form water droplets, which precipitate calcium carbonate crystals on the ground. Then, the stalagmite grows through continuous calcium carbonate deposition and accumulation.

Stalactites, stalactites and stalagmites grow in the opposite direction, hanging upside down from the top of the cave, shaped like milk, is a calcium carbonate-based sediment growing downward along the fissures and pores from the top of the cave. At the beginning, it appears as a gentle bump, then calcium carbonate water keeps adding, and the stalactite gradually increases and becomes longer.

Stone pillars, growing downward and stalagmites growing upward are joined together to form a stalagmite pillar. Because the deposition rate of stalagmites and stalactites is slow, the formation of stalagmite pillars takes a very long time.

Stone mantle, is formed by the thin layer of water full of calcium carbonate along the cave roof, cave wall fissures or level fissures in the outflow accumulation. It deposites out of the surface such as wave, skirt, multi-fold or stacked into a sedimentary form.

The side stone dam, in the process of downward flow of the water body with a certain slope, or cave drip water down the cave wall in the process of deposition of the formation of barrage, step-shaped calcium carbonate side stone.

Lotus, a calcium carbonate deposit formed by the synergistic deposition of dripping water, pond water and running water, is generally round or muddy in shape [7].

The formation environment of karst cave lava morphology is mainly dissolution under strong groundwater dynamics and chemical dissolution under weak groundwater dynamics [8]. According to the hydrodynamic genesis effects of different morphologies of cave lava, the analysis of the morphological characteristics and hydrodynamic genesis effects of cave lava was drawn (Fig. 1), which was used as a reference standard for the way of parametric realization of cave lava morphology in Guilin.

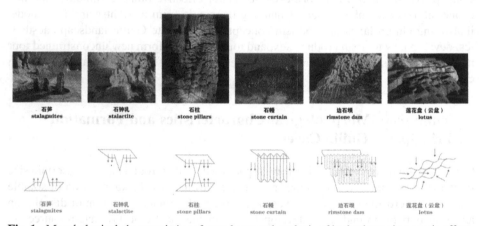

Fig. 1. Morphological characteristics of cave karst and analysis of hydrodynamic genesis effect.

4   Digital Realization of Karst Morphology in Guilin Caves

4.1   Criteria and Approach

Cave karst itself is a naturally occurring structure formed by the dissolution, deposition or scouring of thin layers saturated with calcium carbonate for a hundred or even a thousand years in the cave. It is one of the constituent elements of the karst landscape in southern China. The Grasshopper platform and its numerous algorithmic plug-ins have inspired the topic of cave lithology generation. Simply building a digital model of a cave is an extremely complex process, so we choose to complete the parametric model generation of cave morphology through the Grasshopper platform one by one. The ultimate goal is to obtain a 3D model that fits the cave lithology.

In this way, the Grasshopper platform is used to firstly generate contours with the characteristics of karst morphology by adjusting the parameters using the random point and contour tools, and then use the dendro plug-in to complete the materialization of the morphology so as to get the more desired structure as well as morphology. In the following calculations of karst morphology generation, four types of karst landscape generation methods, namely stalagmite and lotus, stalactite and Stone pillars, are selected to show, among which the generation methods of fitting stone mantle and side stone dam are still being explored.

4.2 Way of Stalagmites and Lotus Created

By analyzing the morphological characteristics of stalagmites, it can be found that the part of stalagmites near the cave wall can be summarized as a fusion of different circles (Fig. 2), and the stalagmites gradually become pointed from the bottom to the top during the growth process, with a larger ratio of height and bottom diameter. Since the location of stalagmite growth is also somewhat random due to the influence of space, material, humidity and other factors in the generation process, we locate the location center of stalagmites through the random point function in Grasshopper, and then arrange the circle with the random point as the center. Then transform these parameters into energy lines of different densities by MetaBall plug-in, endowed with vectors in the Z-axis direction. By adjusting the shape, height, number of layers, and the size of the top and bottom faces, the contour lines with stalagmite shape characteristics can be quickly obtained. This is an important advantage of the Grasshopper platform, which makes it easy and efficient to generate the stalagmite shapes we need (Fig. 3).

Fig. 2. Stalagmite morphology generated using random point and contour tools.

Unlike stalagmites, lotus is gradually widened during the formation process. The stalagmite disc has a wider chassis, and the ratio of its top to bottom area is closer, and the height is smaller than that of the stalagmite. Therefore, we can follow the same idea as the stalagmite to produce a variety of forms with lotus characteristics by adjusting the top area, height, and morphological parameters (Fig. 4).

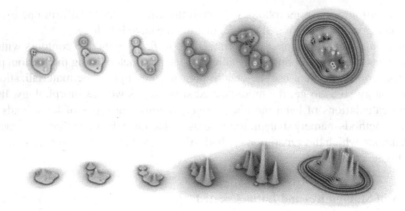

Fig. 3. Morphology of the generated stalagmite.

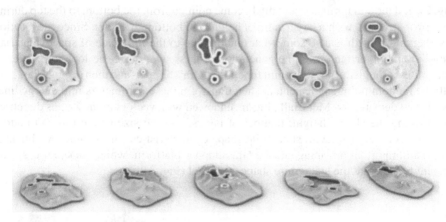

Fig. 4. Generated lotus form.

4.3 Way of Stalactites Created

In the exploration of generating stalactite morphology, the method of simulating electric fields is used to accomplish the generation of stalactite morphology. Firstly, to construct the electric field based on lines and points, we used the plug-in related to electric field and force in Grasshopper to construct a power plant with a plane as the reference plane. By adding interference lines, we can get the force relations of the points at different locations in the electric field (Fig. 5). Then the interference line as a curve is used to build the stalactite form. By observing the influence of the interference line on the points in the electric field, the force near the interference line changes the most, and we can get the points in space by giving these points a displacement in the negative direction of the Z-axis. By controlling the shape of the interference line and the electric field strength, the points distributed in space is got that can build the stalactite form. Finally, the points in space is used to build a Mesh grid to obtain a set of shapes with stalactite characteristics

(Fig. 6 and 7). Using this method, stalactite shapes are generated efficiently by adjusting a small number of parameters.

Fig. 5. Construction of electric field and interference lines.

Fig. 6. Stalactite morphology generation using electric field simulation plug-in and random point tool.

Fig. 7. Generated stalactite morphology.

4.4 Way of Stone Pillars Created

From the observation of the stone pillars morphology, it is found that the stone pillars morphology is supportive in the cave space, DESO algorithm is generated the initial stone pillars morphology by simulating the forces. Firstly, a basic force model in grasshopper is constructed, and Ameba plug-in is adopted to calculate the force and structure optimization of the model to obtain an initial model. Then symmetry and surface optimization on the initial model is performed. Finally, the model is imported into Zbrush for epidermal texture processing to obtain the final model of the stone pillars form (Fig. 8 and 9).

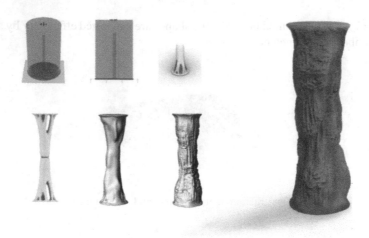

Fig. 8. The process of generating stone pillars and the morphology of the generated stone pillars.

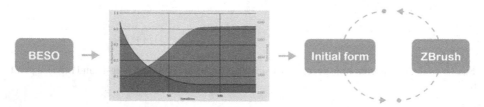

Fig. 9. Principle of generation of stone pillars form.

5 Application Scenarios and Interactions of Parametric Morphology of Guilin Cave Melting Rocks

5.1 Development of Tourism Products

The karst rock forms and landscapes with rich and diverse morphology are designed through parametric algorithm restoration with rich details. Tourists or other consumers can freely combine different forms and materials of karst landscapes to get personal customized cave replica tourism souvenir products (Fig. 10), which not only realize the economic value, but also complete the popularization and dissemination of scientific, cultural and aesthetic values of karst caves in Guilin, a world natural heritage.

5.2 Interactive Home Healing Products

According on the generated cave form, the product can be used to design a natural healing home product based on the profound audio-visual sensation that visitors experience in the cave. The lighting connected with the sensor can be placed in the bedroom or a specific place, and the user's touch and voice command can make the product change like the ambiguous light in the cave, while emitting the sound effects of dripping water and slow running water to assist the user to calm down and feel calm (Fig. 11).

Fig. 10. Cave-related tourism souvenir products.

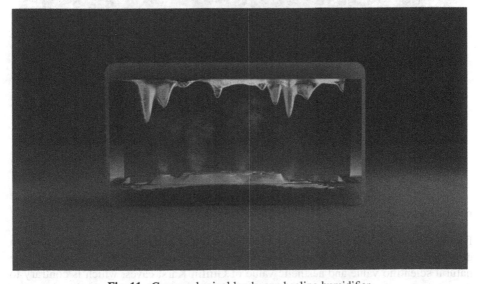

Fig. 11. Cave ecological landscape healing humidifier.

5.3 Immersive Scene Construction

The parameterized generation form we introduced is not only applicable to the design of material products, but also can be applied to the construction of virtual reality products and scenes to provide an immersive experience space. For example, online tours can be built as a new way for visitors to participate in the experience. Visitors can experience the mystery, beauty and charm of Guilin caves through mobile platforms and home video VR glasses, or mini-games can be designed based on algorithm-generated cave landscapes as experience scenes, and visitors can carry out collective "hide and seek" mini-games in scenes with complex terrain and strange shape of caves. In the end, the program generates a video of the process of the game for the visitors to remember (Fig. 12), so that the visitors get satisfaction and contribute to more social sharing and communication, and also provide a positive entrance to know the cave culture of Guilin karst landscape.

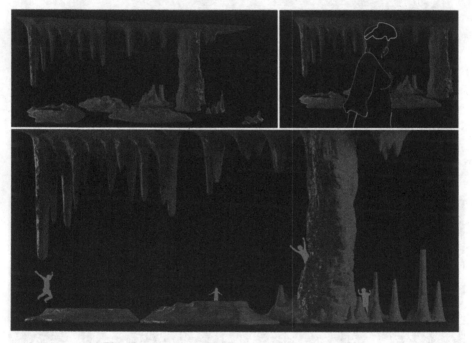

Fig. 12. Cave ecological landscape healing humidifier.

6   Conclusion

Due to the closed state of the geographical limitation of natural heritage, single tourism development activities and means of communication, the public lacks awareness of the natural scientific value and aesthetic value of Guilin Karst caves, which is contrary to the original purpose of protecting and recognizing the natural culture established by the World Heritage Site. We propose a new design method to restore the image of Guilin karst cave karst rocks through parametric design and combine digital technology with interactive design concept to productize the digital results, with the aim of being able to effectively enhance the value and dissemination of knowledge of Guilin karst cave, a World Natural Heritage site.

References

1. Xu, C., Huang, L.: Value structure of tourism image of karst natural heritage sites in southern China–a study based on reviews of tourism social networking sites. J. Nat. Sci. Hunan Norm. Univ. **43**(04), 26–34 (2020). [in Chinese]
2. Wang, W., Sun, Y., Yu, Q.: Research on the conservation and utilization of the world natural heritage in the perspective of the integration of cultural tourism in ssss–Jianglang Mountain in Quzhou City, Zhejiang Province as an example. Archit. Cult. **197**(08), 112–113 (2020). [in Chinese]
3. Liu, X., Li, X., He, R.: Digital inheritance and innovation of non-traditional culture based on interactive virtual reality technology perspective. Art Work (01), 93–98 (2022). [in Chinese]
4. Ma, X., Tu, L., Xu, Y.: The current situation of digital development of intangible cultural heritage. China Sci.: Inf. Sci. **49**(02), 121–142 (2019). [in Chinese]
5. Li, Z., Liang, F.: The necessity of expanding the science tour of Guilin Karst in the context of "world heritage". J. Guilin Norm. Univ. High. Educ. **30**(5), 4 (2016). [in Chinese]
6. Li, W., Wei, Y., Shi, W.: What makes Guilin's landscape unique. China Min. **30**(S1), 486–488 (2021). [in Chinese]
7. Li, W., Wei, Y., Shi, W.: Into the mysterious and beautiful cave. China Min. **30**(S2), 228–230 (2021). [in Chinese]
8. He, Y., Zou, C.: On the depth of karst cave development. China Karst (02), 72–80 (1997). [in Chinese]

Research on Cultural Tourism Product Design in Bay Area Based on Lingnan Traditional Culture

Bingxuan Shi[✉]

Beijing Institute of Technology, Zhuhai, No. 6, Jinfeng Road, Xiangzhou District, Zhuhai, Guangdong, People's Republic of China
13004935@qq.com

Abstract. The highly developed economic level of the Guangdong-Hong Kong-Macao Greater Bay Area has led the vigorous development of cultural tourism industry, and various cultural tourism products have also emerged. As a common cultural gene, Lingnan traditional culture plays an important role in the development of cultural tourism industry in Bay Area and is the engine of building "Humanistic Bay Area". In recent years, the cultural tourism product design industry in the Bay Area has made great progress, and the product types, product forms and industrial scale have been improved to a certain extent, but it is still in the preliminary stage. Many excellent traditional cultures have not been explored, and the needs of a new generation of young people have not been taken into account in product forms and product images. Teenagers are not only the main body to inherit and carry forward traditional culture, but also the key factor to build a "Humanistic Bay Area". Therefore, on the one hand, this paper deeply explores Lingnan traditional culture and explores the methods of its inheritance and development. On the other hand, it conducts extensive research among young groups to understand the needs of young groups, so as to provide some reasonable suggestions for the design research and design application of cultural tourism products in the Bay Area.

Keywords: Lingnan traditional culture · Product design · Needs of young people

1 Introduction

The Guangdong-Hong Kong-Macao Greater Bay Area, including Hong Kong Special Administrative Region, Macao Special Administrative Region, Guangzhou, Shenzhen, Zhuhai, Foshan, Huizhou, Dongguan, Zhongshan, Jiangmen and Zhaoqing (hereinafter referred to as the nine cities in the Pearl River Delta), is one of the regions with the highest degree of openness and the strongest economic vitality in China, and has an important strategic position in the overall situation of national development. The outline of the development plan of Guangdong Hong Kong Macao Great Bay Area proposes to "jointly build a cultural Bay Area", shape the humanistic spirit of the bay area, strengthen cultural self-confidence, jointly promote the inheritance and development of Chinese excellent traditional culture, give play to the advantages of close geographical proximity and cultural affinity between Guangdong, Hong Kong and Macao, support the promotion of Lingnan culture represented by Cantonese opera, Dragon Boat, Martial arts and Lion dance, and highlight its unique cultural charm. Enhance the cultural soft power of Bay Area, further improve the cultural literacy and social civilization of residents, and jointly shape and enrich the connotation of humanistic spirit of Bay Area [1].

With the high economic development of the bay area, the humanistic spirit construction of the Bay area should also develop simultaneously. As the common cultural gene of the Bay area, Lingnan traditional culture is an important link to connect the nine cities in the Bay area and enhance the cohesion of the Bay area. The inheritance and promotion of Lingnan traditional culture plays an important role in the development of cultural tourism design industry in the Bay area. It is an important means to highlight regional characteristics and create new value of cultural tourism industry. It is the core of the construction of humanistic Bay area and the engine of further economic development in the Bay area. To deeply explore more Lingnan traditional culture and apply it to the design of cultural and tourism products, carry forward excellent traditional culture and intangible cultural heritage, and enhance the cultural soft power of the Bay area is an important way to improve residents' cultural literacy and social civilization, and jointly shape and enrich the connotation of the humanistic spirit of the Bay area.

Individual Lingnan traditional culture is on the verge of disappearing. The reason is that the high development of modern commercial culture has had a great impact on traditional culture, greatly reducing the opportunities for young people to contact traditional culture and interrupting the inheritance of traditional culture. Therefore, the key to the inheritance and development of Lingnan traditional culture is to re explore more traditional culture and publicize and carry forward them through various means. On the other hand, applying traditional culture to cultural tourism products, combined with the development of cultural tourism industry, so that it can face more audiences, especially young audiences, which is an appropriate means for the inheritance and development of traditional culture. However, at present, the design of most cultural and tourism products still pays too much attention to the consumption scale and ignores the cultural connotation. The design of other cultural and tourism products only mechanically copy the traditional culture, resulting in its outdated form, which can not stimulate the consumption desire of contemporary young people, let alone promote young people's cognition and recognition of traditional culture, Thus, the purpose of inheriting Lingnan traditional culture cannot be achieved. Therefore, the design of these cultural tourism products must keep up with the trend of the times, meet the aesthetic and emotional needs of young people, and also consider the consumption ability of young people, so as to promote young people's understanding of traditional culture, inherit traditional culture, condense the cultural spirit core of the Bay Area and create the ultimate goal of the humanistic Bay area.

2 Literature Review

Nowadays, the term "Lingnan" is often used to talk about culture and economy, referring to Guangdong, Guangxi, Hainan, Hong Kong and Macao, that is, South China. The study of Lingnan traditional culture focuses on Guangdong. Lingnan traditional culture is mainly divided into three categories: Guangfu traditional culture, Chaoshan culture and Hakka culture. In order to integrate Lingnan traditional culture and cultural tourism products, we must extract rich Lingnan elements and integrate traditional culture into cultural and creative products. Cultural and creative products should not only seek sales, but also pay attention to its culture and establish brand characteristics [2].

Many researchers have made different attempts to apply Lingnan traditional culture to the design of cultural tourism products. Sheng Yuwen (2019), from Guangdong Construction Vocational and technical college, takes the ancient post road in southern Guangdong as the material for cultural and creative design. With the help of the way of "tourism + sports + cultural and creative + industry", she integrates the cultural, natural and other characteristic resources along the line, drives the development of rural tourism and economy, and achieves the fundamental purpose of studying the traditional culture of Lingnan and protecting the ancient post road in southern Guangdong [3]. Zhang Ying (2021), from Guangdong Baiyun University, integrated Lingnan Xingshi's cultural gene into product innovation design, improved users' use frequency and cultural transmission range, and realized better inheritance and protection of Xingshi culture. After studying Lingnan Xingshi culture through perceptual analysis and shape grammar, extract the genes in connotation, color and shape, copy and translate the extracted genes, and then implant cultural symbols into product design (see Fig. 1) [4].

Fig. 1. Tea set design of Lingnan Lion dance culture gene.

3 Methodology

There are two main research tasks in this paper. The first is to explore more Lingnan traditional culture; The second is the research on the design of cultural tourism products, which mainly refers to how to apply traditional culture to the design of cultural tourism products, so as to make it easier for young consumer groups to accept these cultural tourism products, so as to promote young people's cognition and recognition of traditional culture and inherit and develop traditional culture imperceptibly.

The research methods include field investigation, online questionnaire and online interview, and the research results are obtained through summary and analysis. The on-the-spot investigation is mainly to investigate the traditional culture and traditional handicrafts in the Pearl River Delta and Chaoshan areas of Guangdong, and interview the inheritors of intangible cultural heritage to understand the current situation and future trend of traditional culture and traditional handicrafts in Guangdong. Through the questionnaire star network platform, the online questionnaire survey investigated the young people's understanding of traditional culture and handicrafts and their needs for cultural tourism product design. A total of 63 valid questionnaires were collected. The survey content of online interview is roughly the same as that of the questionnaire. 20 young people from different regions of Guangdong were interviewed in writing or voice. The survey process shows that most young people still have a certain understanding of traditional culture, but the degree of understanding is not deep. The way of understanding is mainly oral or written records of their elders. However, those interviewees who have a better understanding of traditional culture also give many representative suggestions, which will have some enlightenment on the inheritance and development of traditional culture. In terms of the demand for cultural tourism product design, young people are very independent and put forward many specific requirements. These requirements have a good reference value for the future cultural tourism product design. At the same time, it also show that the means of inheriting and carrying forward traditional culture through cultural tourism products is highly feasible.

4   Results and Discussion

4.1   Current Situation of Lingnan Traditional Culture

Lingnan traditional culture is mainly divided into Guangfu culture, Chaoshan culture and Hakka culture.

Guangfu traditional culture: Guangfu area usually refers to the inhabited area of Han residents in Guangdong, mainly in Guangzhou, including the Pearl River Delta and some western and northern Guangdong. The traditional culture of Guangfu includes "Cantonese Opera", "Guangxiu", "Guangcai", "Guangdiao" and so on. In terms of architecture, the architectural technology in Guangfu area is influenced by the architectural style of Jiangnan area and Western culture, and there are garden buildings and blockhouses with unique Lingnan style. Among them, Duan inkstone in Zhaoqing, ivory carving in Guangzhou and ceramics in Foshan are the most characteristic of Guangfu [2]. According to the analysis results of field investigation, questionnaire and interview, in addition to the above representative traditional culture, Guangfu area also has lion dance, dragon dance, dragon boat racing, Xiguan copper public art, sandalwood fan, grey sculpture, mahogany palace lantern, Guangzhou flute, Guangzhou Opera costume, Guangzhou enamel, Guangzhou style furniture, etc. In the surrounding areas of Guangzhou, there are also Xingshi in Foshan, fish lanterns, Shiwan dolls, fragrant cloud gauze, paper cutting, boat porridge, etc.; Jiangmen Shenggong carp, Liang's wood carving, Xinhui sunflower art, Jade Flower Bonsai, Wing Chun boxing, etc.; Qianjiaodeng, guancao weaving and qiqiaogong cases in Dongguan; Tea fruit and puppet show in Zhongshan. According to the results of field investigation, some traditional cultures of Guangfu have been completely preserved, well inherited and recognized by many young people, such as lion dance, dragon dance, dragon boat racing, Shiwan doll, Wing Chun boxing, etc. There are lion dance clubs in many extracurricular activities in universities and middle schools, which has played a great role in the publicity and inheritance of lion dance culture. Dragon boat racing has also become a necessary program for the annual Dragon Boat Festival in many villages, attracting the participation of many young people. In Heshan City, Jiangmen District, the education department takes Wing Chun boxing as the recess exercise of primary schools in the city, and invites special Wing Chun coaches to teach Wing Chun boxing in primary schools. On the one hand, this measure can make primary school students strong and healthy. On the other hand, it is also the best way to inherit Wing Chun boxing.

Chaoshan traditional culture: there are famous Chaozhou Opera, English song and dance, Chaoshan puppet show, Chaozhou wood carving, art ceramics, etc. Chao embroidery is one of the four famous embroideries in China and an important part of Guangdong embroidery. Chaoshan has three architectural techniques: wood carving, stone carving and porcelain inlay, which makes the Chaoshan ancestral hall series buildings look very magnificent and magnificent [2]. Chaozhou Kung Fu tea is also a major feature. According to the field investigation results, in addition to the above traditional cultures, Chaoshan also has hand-held Vermilion clay pot, Dawu clay sculpture, Chaozhou lantern, Chenghai lantern riddle, centipede dance, bamboo weaving, etc. In addition, the unique sacrificial methods in Chaoshan area are also completely preserved, and many young people participate in the sacrificial activities, which is also a characteristic traditional culture of Chaoshan. During the on-the-spot investigation, I visited Mr. Xie Hua, the inheritor of intangible cultural heritage holding a Zhu clay pot, Mr. Lu Guangzheng, the inheritor of Chaozhou wood carving, and Mr. Wu Hongcheng, the inheritor of intangible cultural heritage of Dawu clay sculpture, to investigate the current situation and inheritance of these traditional handicrafts. They generally said that because these traditional cultures are purely hand-made and the process is cumbersome, they have very high requirements for technology. If an apprentice wants to skillfully make these handicrafts, he needs to study for at least 2–3 years. In the modern fast-paced economic and social environment, it is undoubtedly very difficult for young people to spend 2–3 years learning a skill and have no economic income before they learn it. Therefore, these factors will dissuade a large part of young people and make it difficult to inherit and carry forward these traditional cultures. They also said that because these traditional handicrafts are handmade and consume a lot of energy of craftsmen, the sales price is generally very high, which is not competitive compared with mass-produced cultural and tourism products. The vast majority of people who buy these handicrafts are elderly businessmen, usually for the purpose of collection. These phenomena will bring two bad effects. One is that many young people will no longer participate in the inheritance of these traditional cultures due to the long learning time and the lack of guarantee of income. The other is that due to the limited number of sales, these traditional cultures can not be well publicized and promoted. They will gradually fade out of the vision of the younger generation and may disappear slowly. In fact, their views also show a common dilemma of Lingnan traditional culture and traditional handicrafts, that is, they can not get good publicity opportunities, nor can they be recognized by young people, and they have lost their competitiveness in the face of mass production. Although many of them have become intangible cultural heritages at all levels, it is difficult to inherit these traditional cultures simply with the weak financial support of the government. Therefore, for these traditional cultures, adapting to the new social environment, seeking a new way out, cooperating with the government's policies and financial support, and making more measures are the right way for them to continue to inherit and carry forward.

4.2 Questionnaire Analysis Results

The analysis of the network questionnaire first studies the understanding of traditional culture and traditional handicrafts in different age groups (see Fig. 2). The results show that young people aged 18–25 have a relatively low understanding of traditional culture. Only 25% of the respondents know very much about traditional culture, more than half of the respondents only know generally, and nearly a quarter of the respondents don't know anything about traditional culture at all. In the group aged 26–35, the situation is even worse. Nearly half of the people do not understand traditional culture at all, and the other half only understand it in general. In the group over 35, the situation has changed. Nearly 60% of the people know traditional culture very well, and the other 40% also know it. There is only one survey sample under the age of 18, so it has no reference value. To sum up, the respondents aged 18–35 have a low understanding of traditional culture. More than a quarter of them do not know traditional culture at all, and more than half of them only know it in general. Therefore, it is very necessary to strengthen the publicity and promotion of traditional culture among young people and improve their cognition and recognition of traditional culture, which is the key to the inheritance and development of traditional culture.

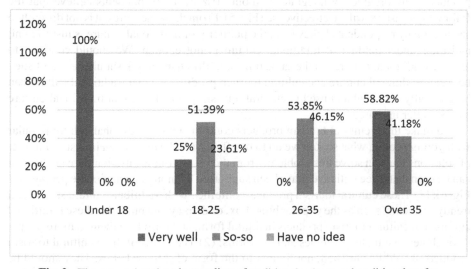

Fig. 2. The respondents' understanding of traditional culture and traditional crafts.

Then, the questionnaire understands the respondents' views on the market prospect of traditional handicrafts, and the results show that most people are not optimistic. Half of the people think the market prospect is general, and nearly 20% think the market prospect is bad (see Fig. 3).

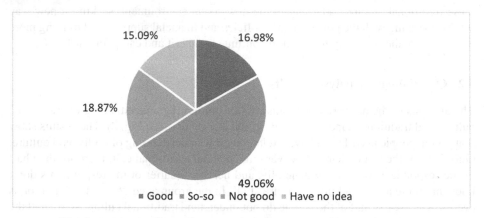

Fig. 3. Respondents' views on the sales prospect of traditional handicrafts.

So, what effective measures should be taken to promote traditional handicrafts into local cultural and tourism products? Through the questionnaire survey, the respondents agree with the following measures and believe that these measures are helpful to develop traditional handicrafts into local characteristic cultural and tourism products, and each measure is supported by more than 60% (see Fig. 4).

Next, the questionnaire continues to study how to apply traditional culture to cultural tourism products. What measures can make traditional culture and cultural tourism products truly organically integrated? About 70% of the respondents believe that the following measures will be effective (see Fig. 5). From these measures, it is not difficult to see that many respondents believe that the publicity of traditional culture is insufficient, and their understanding of traditional culture is not enough. We should continue to explore traditional culture. At the same time, a multi-channel link should be established between traditional culture and cultural tourism products, so that traditional culture can be gradually activated and used in cultural tourism products, so that traditional culture can be better inherited.

To make these cultural tourism products combined with traditional culture popular with young people, what should we do to be effective? The questionnaire lists a number of solutions that can solve this problem. From the results of the questionnaire analysis, it can be seen that three initiatives have been supported by more than half of the people (see Fig. 6): (1) These cultural tourism products combined with traditional culture should add trendy elements, such as the popular blind box, or display and publicize these traditional culture and cultural tourism products in digital form, and introduce them to more people through new media technologies and platforms; (2) The forms of these cultural tourism products should be enriched, not limited to the form of gifts or letters. They should be expanded to categories such as stationery, daily necessities, toys and so on, so that they

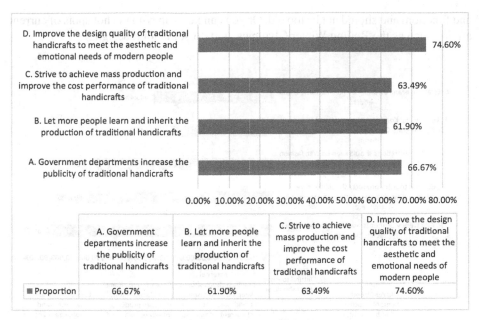

Fig. 4. Measures to make traditional handicrafts into cultural and tourism products.

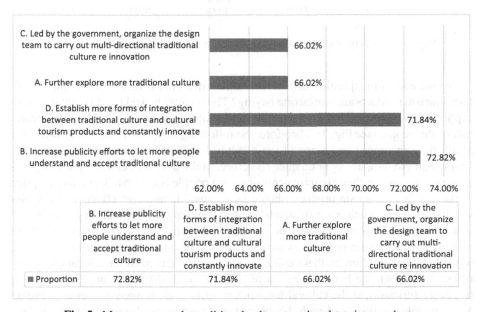

Fig. 5. Measures to apply traditional culture to cultural tourism products.

have certain practical value, not just ornamental; (3) These cultural and tourism products should also keep up with the fashion trend, keep pace with the times in terms of shape and function, and should not be too old. Or you can keep up with the hot spots of current affairs, such as the Beijing Winter Olympics, and do some joint design.

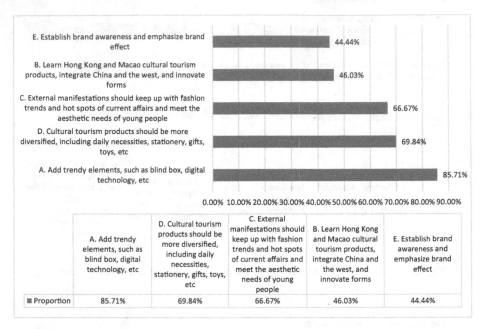

Fig. 6. Popularity of cultural tourism products combined with traditional culture.

At the end of the questionnaire, a more direct question is raised: what kind of cultural tourism products are most worth buying? The results showed that two options were supported by more than half of the people, and another option was supported by nearly half of the people (see Fig. 7). Therefore, the following conclusions can be drawn. First of all, the appearance and shape of these cultural tourism products must be pleasing, simple and modern, lovely or unique. Therefore, in the design of cultural tourism products, meeting the aesthetic requirements of young people is the first. Secondly, the price of these cultural tourism products should be reasonable and cost-effective. Generally speaking, young people have relatively limited spending power, and they may not be willing to spend too much money on cultural and tourism products. Therefore, don't design cultural tourism products as too expensive gifts. You can consider making some novel knickknack. Thirdly, these cultural tourism products must have local characteristics. At present, the homogenization of China's cultural tourism product market is relatively serious, and the cultural tourism products sold in many places are similar. Many people are disgusted with this phenomenon, so cultural tourism products must have local characteristics.

There is an interesting phenomenon in the conclusion of this topic. In the previous topic, the selection rate of option A (Add trend elements, such as blind box, digital technology, etc.) is 85.71%. However, the selection rate is only 17.46% when it reappears as option E in this topic. Therefore, I tried to make a cross analysis of these two topics,

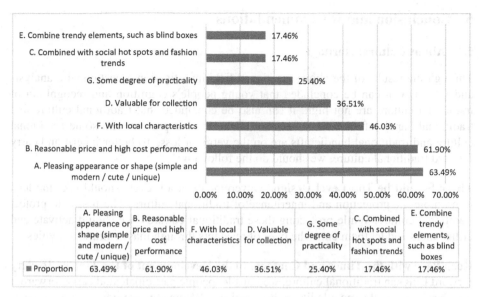

Fig. 7. Cultural tourism products worth buying.

and the results are as follows (Table 1). From the cross analysis results, it is not difficult to see that the correlation of the top three options of these two topics is still very high, indicating that the top three options of these two topics are still of great reference value in the design of cultural and tourism products.

Table 1. Cross analysis of the last two questions of the questionnaire.

X (Fig. 7)\Y (Fig. 6)	A	B	F	D	G	E	C	Subtotal
A	36 (66.67%)	34 (62.96%)	28 (51.85%)	19 (35.19%)	15 (27.78%)	9 (16.67%)	9 (16.67%)	54
D	29 (65.91%)	25 (56.82%)	21 (47.73%)	15 (34.09%)	12 (27.27%)	9 (20.45%)	10 (22.73%)	44
C	29 (69.05%)	27 (64.29%)	17 (40.48%)	15 (35.71%)	13 (30.95%)	6 (14.29%)	10 (23.81%)	42
B	16 (55.17%)	18 (62.07%)	15 (51.72%)	10 (34.48%)	10 (34.48%)	7 (24.14%)	5 (17.24%)	29
E	19 (67.86%)	16 (57.14%)	14 (50%)	12 (42.86%)	6 (21.43%)	4 (14.29%)	7 (25%)	28

5 Conclusion and Recommendations

5.1 About Cultural Heritage

Through the results of the above-mentioned field investigation, questionnaire analysis and interview, it can be concluded that young people's cognition and recognition of traditional culture are not high. It can also be concluded that traditional culture and traditional handicrafts have not been well developed at present, and some traditional culture and traditional handicrafts are on the verge of loss. To better inherit and carry forward traditional culture, we should do the following:

There Should be Top-Level Design. Governments at all levels should take the lead to promote the protection and inheritance of traditional culture. The first is to protect traditional culture. While protecting these traditional cultures, we should activate and utilize them and let them enter the lives of residents through mass cultural activities.

Keep Pace with the Times and Conform to the Development of the Times. To carry forward Lingnan traditional culture, we must let people participate and carry forward it together in a way that people like to hear and see. We must make good use of contemporary new media communication methods and the growing enthusiasm of good people to pursue spiritual satisfaction. The highly developed economy in Guangdong has not only laid a solid material foundation for cultural inheritance and dissemination, but also spawned a variety of new media technologies and new media platforms. Through these new media technologies and new media platforms, the public can better participate in traditional cultural activities, deepen their understanding of traditional culture and enhance their recognition of traditional culture through video teaching and offline interaction.

Teenagers are the Key to Inherit and Carry Forward Lingnan Traditional Culture. To build a "Humanistic Bay Area", it is necessary to establish a sense of identity among teenagers for the integration of Lingnan traditional culture. As the backbone of the future, the youth are the main body of the traditional culture. Only when they recognize and identify traditional culture can they carry forward the traditional culture, go out of Guangdong, and even go to the world, simultaneous interpreting the future development of the Bay area with cultural power. In order to improve teenagers' awareness of traditional culture, in addition to participating in social and cultural activities, school education is also essential. We should pay attention to the combination of local culture and school education, and pay attention to the inheritance of cultural genes among the young generation. Traditional cultural forms such as Cantonese Opera and folk minor can be integrated into the school music education system. Traditional handicrafts such as Guangdong embroidery, Canton carving, Shiwan doll and clay sculpture can be added to the manual class, and teaching contents such as dragon and lion dance and Wing Chun boxing can be introduced into the school physical education teaching. In university education, there are rich and colorful extracurricular community activities, which can integrate more Lingnan traditional culture into community activities under the organization and drive of the school.

5.2 About Cultural Tourism Product Design

In addition to the above three ways, the inheritance of traditional culture can also be carried out in a more intuitive and popular way, such as combining traditional culture with cultural tourism products, so that young people can accept the influence of traditional culture in the process of purchasing and contacting these cultural tourism products, and gradually form their recognition of the integration of traditional culture in Lingnan, Lay a solid foundation for building the "Humanistic Bay Area". In order for the younger generation to recognize these cultural tourism products and stimulate their purchase desire, the design of these cultural tourism products should meet the following requirements:

In Appearance or Modeling, We Must Meet the Aesthetic and Emotional Needs of Contemporary Young People. Some trendy elements, such as blind box, or digital media technologies, such as VR and AR, can be combined to make traditional culture and cultural tourism products keep up with the trend of the times and glow with new forms. These products can also keep up with the hot spots of current affairs, such as the Beijing Winter Olympic Games, and do some joint design. This way will make cultural and tourism products have a wider audience and higher popularity.

The Types of Cultural Tourism Products Should be Richer. These products can be more practical, such as some daily necessities, jewelry and stationery. On the one hand, these things are likable, on the other hand, the price is relatively cheap and will not be too high. The price comparison is in line with the consumption level of young people. Of course, while the price is cheap, we should also increase the cost performance and try to be good and cheap.

These Cultural Tourism Products Must Have Local Characteristics. At present, the homogenization of China's cultural tourism product market is relatively serious. On the one hand, it causes consumers' disgust and reduces their consumption desire. On the other hand, homogenization also makes traditional culture lose its space to play a role. Therefore, the design of cultural tourism products must have local characteristics and truly apply the local traditional culture to the product design.

References

1. State Council of China: Outline of development planning of the Guangdong-Hong Kong-Macao Greater Bay Area (2019)
2. Gao, P.: Research on the design of cultural and creative products based on Lingnan traditional culture. Tiangong (10), 80–81 (2021)
3. Sheng, Y.-W.: Research on cultural and creative design of ancient post road in southern Guangdong based on Lingnan traditional culture. Art Design (Theory) (9), 90–92 (2019)
4. Zhang, Y.: The integration of Lingnan lion culture gene and product design. Art Rev. (24), 84–85 (2021)

Research on Development Trend of Ceramic Product Design in Digital Media Era

Xiao Song[1,2](✉)

[1] Beijing Technology Institute, Zhuhai, People's Republic of China
842766039@qq.com
[2] Studying School for Doctor's Degree, Bangkok Thonburi University, Bangkok, Thailand

Abstract. Ceramic art is a kind of culture, is a both young and ancient art, ceramic product design is a branch of modern design, is a way to express and develop ceramic products according to people's needs. With the advent of the digital information age, computers have brought great changes to our lives. Information transmission is high-speed and convenient, and all kinds of information crisscross in all aspects of life. Among them, the technological products produced around the digital model have emerged constantly. In the field of modern ceramics industry industrial intelligent assembly line manufacturing, ceramic 3D printing molding technology to give priority to with the human cost of traditional ceramics such as manual manufacturing made a tremendous impact, in such a big trend how to through the change of design thinking, form conforms to the development of innovative and applied ceramic products is the focus of this paper wants to discuss.

The era of digital media is an era of science and technology and also an era that pays more attention to the development of "people". While the Internet economy and AI technology have changed people's way of life, they have also updated the requirements of the era for ceramic design. The research on ceramic design centered on the construction of ceramic technology as the leading and handicraft culture theme innovation is accompanied by technological leadership, urban cultural creativity and tourism industry is increasingly becoming an important part of China's national economy. The development of ceramics industry is faced with both challenges and opportunities, to reposition the development goal of ceramic design is the first way to explore the ceramic products in line with the future market demand, specific construction measures or to clarify the leading ideas of China's ceramic design development and the implementation of intelligent manufacturing technology. The digital media era has put forward higher standards for ceramic product designers, requiring them to keep pace with The Times and constantly improve their comprehensive ability through learning to meet the requirements of the era for designers.

Keywords: Digital media age · Ceramic product design · Ceramic cultural and creative products

1 Introduction

The design of the digital media era ceramic products mainly divided into two trends: a class on how to construct the ceramic technology of ceramic product design, is to

V. G. Duffy and P.-L. P. Rau (Eds.): HCII 2022, LNCS 13522, pp. 496–506, 2022.
https://doi.org/10.1007/978-3-031-21704-3_34

rely on modern ceramic mechanical equipment manufacture as well as the form of AI technology to design and develop ceramic product, main technology including intelligent production line of ceramic manufacturing as well as 3 d printing technology on the basis of design innovation; The other is the ceramic cultural creative product design centered on the construction of handicraft, which is based on the production method of handicraft and accompanied by the urban cultural creativity and tourism industry is increasingly becoming an important part of China's national economy (Fig. 1).

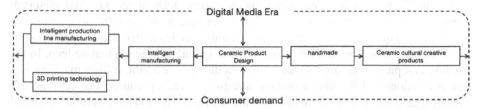

Fig. 1. Analysis of the future development trend of ceramic product design

2   Design of Intelligent Manufacturing Products in the Digital Era

The daily-use ceramics industry has manufacturing from the traditional to the modern manufacturing industry, the traditional ceramic production in molding and grouting process combined with the mode of production, grouting, grouting pressure, grouting process including artificial centrifugal grouting and ultrasonic methods, such as design methods are mainly hand-painted design drawing combined with years of production experience to master's, Technology also limited the innovation strength of ceramic products. Now some small batch ceramic factories in China still use these grouting methods, manual mold turning to complete. Modern Chinese ceramics manufacturing transition soon, daily-use ceramics industrial raw materials used in preparation of forming, sintering and other machinery and equipment have all realized the localization, can not only meet the demand of daily-use ceramics, and began to export to southeast Asia, central Asia, South America and other countries, realized the ceramic mechanical equipment across from import to export.

2.1   Ceramic Manufacturing Under Intelligent Production

Digital and intelligent mechanical production line has become the mainstream of the world ceramic industry research and development, a number of digital and intelligent mechanical equipment in the industry has been applied and promoted. With China's labor shortage and the increase of labor costs, the industry increased rolling, billet, glaze, the largest number of employment, bottle production etc.) of machinery and equipment research and development efforts, has developed a number of mechanization, automation, intelligent rolling production line, glazing equipment, fettling grouting machine, bottle machine, etc., to improve the production efficiency and product quality of ceramic products. With the development of intelligent manufacturing technology, the intelligent control of ceramic industrial production unit has not only contains only ceramic manufacturing system, including intelligent ceramic quality inspection system, intelligent process quality monitoring tracking system, intelligent central control system, intelligent warehouse system and so on have been vigorously promoted. Chinese enterprises are more and more aware that to solve the labor shortage and labor shortage and other practical problems, only by improving the intelligent degree of ceramic production line, can fundamentally improve the quality of products and brand competitiveness.

In modeling manufacturing, mold manufacturing technology was first changed, numerical control technology was applied in ceramic mold manufacturing, improve the processing quality and speed of ceramic mother mold, so that the ceramic production industry has been used for decades of mold manufacturing qualitative leap. In the molding equipment, the appearance of the digital daily ceramic rolling machine is a new, revolutionary daily ceramic rolling machine. China's production of ceramic roll forming machine can achieve molding technology has CAM, roll the head and the lateral movement and vertical movement and track of model have all adopt the digital control, in the process of forming with all parameters can be stored according to the different requirements of customers forming can be all kinds of specifications size of circular vessels, to satisfy the needs of individualized small batch customization (Fig. 2).

Fig. 2. Ceramic intelligent production line

In the aspect of decoration machinery, daily ceramic glaze process in the wall and floor tile automatic glaze equipment, developed a batch of ceramic spray glaze, dip glaze, glaze mechanical equipment, compared with the past more accurate, efficient. In the treatment of decorative patterns using ceramic inkjet printing technology principle, the promotion of spray glaze, spray dry powder technology inkjet printing technology, expanded the scope of application of ceramic inkjet printing. The introduction of this technology not only reduces the labor cost but also effectively protects the ecological environment. The firing effect is more natural and the decoration form is more abundant. The intelligent chain dryer is used in the drying process of ceramic products, which greatly improves the production efficiency and product quality. Science and technology is always the first productive force. In the intelligent digital era, the research and development of new technologies and materials has become the basis of design innovation, and also puts forward higher requirements for designers.

The appearance of ceramic sanitary ware intelligent manufacturing production line, "changed the most widely used gypsum mold micro-pressure grouting system in the industry, the adoption of mold car carrying system, relying on automatic operation of the crawling line system to achieve automatic circulation of gypsum mold; Special mold closing machine, mold opening machine, automatic billet out machine, to achieve automatic mold opening and closing, wet billet automatic billet out process; Tunnel mold drying room combined with kiln waste heat reuse technology, using hot air internal circulation system to achieve rapid drying of gypsum mold; Green solid storage drying storage system; The track type non-power transmission structure and the storage heat pump cycle technology of the kiln waste heat secondary conversion are adopted to realize the multi-quantity storage of green blanks, regionalize the temperature and humidity differential drying, and improve the drying spccd and pass rate of green blanks. Automatic manipulator glazing workstation, closed area for automatic glazing body, to ensure the stability of glaze quality, prevent pollution leakage. The research and development of a whole set of intelligent production lines strengthens the stability of product manufacturing and changes the current situation of high pollution and high labor cost manufacturing in the bathroom industry.

From the current development level of the world ceramic manufacturing industry, it is more and more urgent to study the whole line of intellectualization of ceramic machinery equipment in ceramic factories. It has become the core of China's ceramic machinery manufacturing industry to improve the intellectualization level of mechanical equipment and speed up the intellectualization research of sanitary ceramics and daily use ceramic machinery equipment. In China, computer-aided design began to rise from the 1990s. Western modern design concepts and methods are more widely cited with the improvement of China's modern ceramic manufacturing technology, and the progress of modeling and decoration technology expands the infinite possibilities of ceramic design. As a designer how to ceramic industry in the existing production experience, the level of machinery and equipment and intelligent manufacturing, on the basis of using big data platform and Internet to realize the data real-time digital collection demand for ceramic products, from the Angle of environment protection and used to the way people live, to explore the possibilities of the ceramic is the main tendency of the development of the production of ceramic design.

2.2 3D Ceramic Printing Technology

With the advent of the era of digital information, the computer bring great changes to our lives, the information transmission speed is convenient, and all kinds of information on all aspects of life, of which around digital model and technology products arises at the historic moment, in the field of modern ceramics industry in addition to the above mentioned intelligent assembly line manufacturing, Ceramic 3D printing molding technology is another pair of traditional ceramic manual manufacturing industry with labor cost has a great impact on the technology products in the digital era. Ceramic 3D printing molding technology can quickly prepare ceramic parts with complex shapes without molds. This technology has changed the process from the traditional hand-drawn drawings, mold making, mold turning, mold repairing, mold drying, grouting, firing and other design to production of ceramic design for a long time. Traditionally, a brand new ceramic product needs more than ten days or even a month to make, or even according to the actual situation while designing and making, resulting in a long development cycle of new products, high damage rate, human and material consumption, and unable to quickly achieve the development and quantitative production of new products. At present, the new product development mode of using 3D printing technology to manufacture mold type and remanufacture mold has become one of the mainstream technologies in the design and manufacture of China's ceramic products, especially daily-use ceramics and home furnishing ceramic products.

3D printers were invented in the 1980s and the first commercial 3D printers were developed in the United States. 3 d printing ceramic is the basic principle of "using the computer to carry on the model design, and then the model slicing software processing, become a kind of printer can identify the data, the import to the printer for printing technology, so that a series of processing will be the relationship between human and mud into the relationship between human and digital. At present, 3D printing technology that can be used for ceramic molding mainly includes liquid deposition ceramic 3D printing and ceramic powder printing. Indirect molding is the way to choose photosensitive resin 3D printing technology, hot melt plastic 3D printing technology, paper printing technology and other printing models after turning gypsum mold, the use of mold to assist the completion of ceramic modeling molding."[i] At present, the printing precision of 3D printer can reach 0.01mm, and the manufacturing structure is meticulous and the shape is clear (Fig. 3).

In the face of this technical field, 3D modeling is not only the core of 3D printing process but also the top priority in the design process. Therefore, designers' mastery of 3D modeling technology determines the technical requirements of ceramic design. Using computer software to generate product model has become the basic means of modern ceramic product modeling and functional design, the use of three-dimensional modeling software to design products, and then use the printer to make samples, for enterprises to carry out new product research and development, saving development costs and other aspects have benefited a lot. But at the same time, printing technology also puts forward higher requirements for design modeling. "3D printing has relatively strict requirements on models. Once the polygon surfaces of the data model overlap and penetrate during the design process, 3D printing will make errors in data analysis and the model cannot be printed smoothly. "[2] Currently, 3D digital modeling software commonly used in 3D printing technology includes 3DMAX, MAYA, Rhino, C4D, Inventor, Sketchup, Solid Works, and Zbrush for model carving and post-processing. Skilled mastery of modeling software has become a necessary tool for ceramic design.

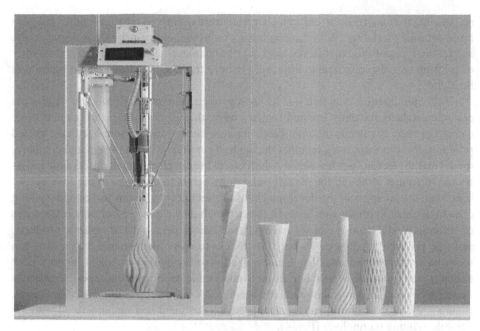

Fig. 3. 3D ceramic printing technology

In China's ceramic industry, 3D printing technologies mainly used for ceramic product design and production include 3D printing mold indirect ceramic molding and liquid deposition ceramic direct ceramic powder 3D printing technology. The 3D printing technology applied to model making is photocuring 3D printing and plastic hot melt deposition 3D printing. The printed model is used as mold type and then the artificial plaster mold is made. After the plaster mold is made, it can be grouting or printed, and then the ceramic mud can be repaired and glazed. Compared with the traditional hand-made mold turning mode, the 3D printing mold forming method reduces the error rate, saves the development cycle of new products, and also saves the amount of materials, which is conducive to the protection of resources and environment. At present, it has been widely used in the field of enterprise product development and ceramic product design teaching in colleges and universities.

"Liquid deposition ceramic printing technology is a relatively common 3D ceramic printing technology at present. The principle is to replace the raw material with thick mud material, and use the mud strip extrusion and similar to the way of mud strip plate building layer by layer to form three-dimensional modeling." [1] Similar to the traditional mud plate building manual molding. However, compared with the traditional printing method, the cost of consumables is relatively low, and the precision of mud plate construction is relatively high. The printed works have regular hierarchical texture and stable shape, and ceramic works of different colors can also be made according to the color of mud. The printing model can be directly glazed firing with a little drying treatment, shortening the ceramic process cycle and improving the rate of finished products. Liquid deposition 3D printing is a kind of 3D printing technology that is widely used in ceramic modeling at present. It can print not only small ceramic modeling, micro modeling, but also large ceramic modeling. With the continuous improvement of printing equipment, the increasing types of mud that can be used as printing materials, the precision and stability of printing will also continue to improve, I believe that the popularity of the future will be higher.

If the intelligent production line technology meets the needs of modern large-scale ceramic products for daily use and sanitary ware, the 3D ceramic printing technology can better meet the needs of small-batch ceramic design and personalized customized products. We can intuitively feel that the modern ceramic product design and computer model making technology has become the focus of the development of the ceramic industry in the future, although the overall technology needs to continue to improve but we have seen the prospect of the development of this technology. From foshan, guangdong chaozhou ceramic production areas of the city such as we can see not only mass, mass of ceramic products, also can see have differentiation, personalized ceramic products, and new product launch speed is very fast, thanks to more like ceramic 3 d printing can meet the demand of the small batch customization today market technical support. How to better make people and machine easier to communicate, how to make people easier to master technical products, has gradually become the main subject in front of designers. Figure 3 shows the cultural and creative products designed and manufactured with 3D ceramic printing technology (Fig. 4).

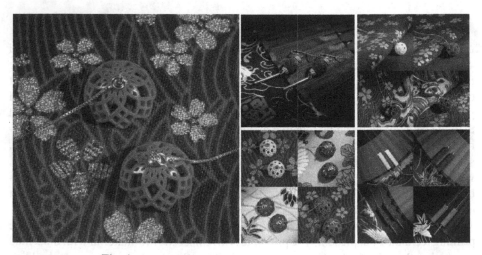

Fig. 4. 3D ceramic printing cultural and creative products

3 Handicraft Ceramic Cultural Creative Product Design

On the one hand, people are enjoying the convenience brought by high-tech electronic intelligent products in the information age. On the other hand, people are facing emotional and spiritual loss in the face of machinery. People increasingly hope that ordinary daily articles can also bring people more emotional and spiritual resonance. Functionalism of function first is no longer the only pursuit of contemporary people, the combination of humanized function and manual art, can cause emotional resonance with temperature products are more and more favored. As the Japanese ethnographer Munoyuki Naganagi said, "The difference in beauty between a machine-shaped object and a hand-made object is obvious. Mechanical molding is the completion of the established content, manual production is the activation of creative freedom. Compared with the infinite variety of the latter, the former is monotonous. No machine, however complex, can match the power of the human hand." [4] The household articles for use with the famous Italian brand alesi (Alessi), more than 90 years of development, design production of 3000 sets of household kitchen products, variety, style, style is various, but they always stick to, rooted in the product core concept is still a handicraft culture, emphasizes the pure art or craft limited edition model.

"After experiencing the baptism of industrial civilization, in today's information society, handicrafts with its mythic charm, for us to highlight the poetic life, for us to win back the perceptual experience. Handicraft, with its free play at the junction of art and technology, continues its tradition for thousands of years, declaring to us an indisputable fact that craftsmanship has always determined the value of products." [5] In the face of the coming digital media era, the warm and intelligent "manual" production has regained people's attention. Orderly, mechanized ceramic products began to be indifferent to people, handmade ceramics with extremely affinity materials and extremely handle temperature technology gradually return to people's life, we can see from the popularity of various cultural creation market people in leisure time eager to return to nature, return to the era of manual yearning.

"When the generality of the big industrial products for mechanical industry and the whole world the at the same time, the product features, various countries on each nationality in each region, handicraft art became the real national industry and national products to participate in the international cultural art exchange, as the representative of the national industry, culture and art in the whole human cultural exchanges play an important role in transmission structure". [6] World famous ceramic brand Wedgwood, Meissen mason, etc. are established in the industrial society period, until into the information age, now in some process of ceramic products remain on manual work, grasps the manual skills, these handcrafts passing on a technology that is full of originality, national history and cultural memory, It is also the continuation of cultural spirit and cultural emotion. The value created by manual creation is the dual wealth of material and spirit that naturally integrates function and emotion, practicality and aesthetics, art and culture, and we should cherish it. In this respect, the Chinese traditional craft thought has a deeper understanding, at the same time also has more can learn from the place.

Pioneer is a famous German economic history in the study of the creative economy and economic thinkers schumpeter put forward and was a great achievement, the creative economy has become the western cities such as London, Birmingham, Los Angeles,

USA motive force of the Renaissance, Asia, Singapore, Bangkok, Tokyo has gradually formed the cultural creative industry gathering place, attract tourists from all over the world to gravitate to. "The concept of cultural and creative industry is a cultural industry based on the copyright economy of the United States and the creative industry index of the United Kingdom. In terms of the definition of the concept, many countries have included traditional crafts into the category of cultural and creative industry."[7]"The promotion of cultural and creative industries has become the trend of economic development strategies of various countries. The traditional culture of each country has unique identification in its life style. In the global market competition, the design and application of cultural characteristics can enhance the uniqueness of products and increase consumption experience." [8].

In early 2011, our country is to promote cultural industry become a pillar industry of national economy in the national 12th five-year plan outline, many cities are developing creative industry development strategy, and put it as a future pillar industry to foster city, urban cultural creative industry is increasingly becoming an important part of China's national economy and the pillar of the tertiary industry. Ceramic cultural creative product design is a new ceramic product design concept formed with the cultural creative industry. "With the improvement of life demand levels, the consumer market has entered an era of emphasizing experience and aesthetic economy. The uniqueness of regional culture and the construction of creative knowledge have become the key to the development of ceramic products." [9].

"The development of projects themed with regional cultural construction has become the main construction content in the era of creative economy." [10] These cultural themes include regional intangible cultural heritage, local customs, museum culture, bookstore culture and urban and rural cultural tourism development projects, etc. The creative product development of these themed cultural projects is of great significance to the traditional ceramic art that emphasizes handwork, labor, technology, and time precipitation. It provides a broader space for design innovation while preserving traditional handicraft techniques. Therefore, the development of local cultural projects in each city provides a unique perspective for the development of China's urban cultural and creative industry with identification and market competitiveness, and also provides a source of innovative design for China's long-standing traditional ceramic technology. The proposal of cultural creative product design concept with handicraft as the core is helpful to balance the relationship between traditional craft and design. It constantly inspires designers to think about culture, creativity and technological innovation; It is of constructive significance to carry forward and inherit China's traditional culture and regional culture (Fig. 5).

Fig. 5. Ceramic cultural creative product design of Guangzhou Shawan Ancient Town.

4   Conclusion

The ceramic product design in digital media era is endowed with new requirements of The Times. The extensive application of AI intelligent manufacturing technology and 3D ceramic printing technology has subverted the traditional ceramic manufacturing model and put forward higher requirements for designers' design thinking and technical ability. On the other hand, with the promotion of the government and the development needs of urban tourism creative cultural industry, handicrafts return to the public's vision. Let designers come to realize that can compete with technology should be product to bring the warmth of modern craft and cultural influence, therefore in the field of digital media era ceramic product design presented on the basis of the modern science and technology of daily-use ceramics, ceramic sanitary ware products design and based on manual and product design trend of these two design. Today, the word "design" has multiple meanings, and the common point among them is "service". Therefore, the concept of ceramic art design is redefined under the trend of The Times: ceramic design is a service profession engaged in by designers. It is a creation process of function, shape and decoration by using ceramic materials in order to meet the needs of people's lifestyle and from the perspective of harmonious coexistence in nature.

References

1. Bo, Y.: Application of CERAMIC 3D Printing Technology in Ceramic Forming, Master thesis, School of Design, Jingdezhen Ceramic University, p. 9 (2019)

2. Qian, L.: Application of three-dimensional digital technology in ceramic product design. Design **11**(19), 45 (2015)
3. Liu, Z.: The Way of Craft. Guangxi University Press, p. 67 (2017). Translated by Xu, Y.
4. Hang, J.: The Idea of Handicraft. Shandong Pictorial Publishing House, p. 29 (2017)
5. Li, Y.: Introduction to arts and crafts, China Light Industry Press, 1 (1999)
6. Song, X.: Inspiration from the involvement of Japanese craft cultural and creative industry in urban tourism -- a case study of Zhuhai. Art Des. **11**(10), 64 (2019)
7. Xu, Q., Lin, R.: Design Program For Cultural Products. J. Des. **16**(4), 5 (2011)
8. Handa, R.: Against arbitrariness: architectural significance in the age of globalization. Des. Stud. **20**(4), 363–380 (1999)
9. Lin, R.T.: Transforming Taiwan aboriginal cultural features into modern product design: a case study of cross-cultural product design model. Int. J. Des. **1**(2), 45–53 (2007)

Research and Re Practice of Oyster Shell Architectural Culture

Jie Tang[1,2(✉)] and Xing Ji[1,2]

[1] Beijing Technology Institute, Zhuhai, 519088 Zhuhai, People's Republic of China
4448286@qq.com
[2] Bangkok Thonburi University, Bangkok 10170, Thailand

Abstract. As early as the northern and Southern Dynasties in China, it has been recorded that in villages near the seashore and rivers, oyster shells have high strength and hardness due to their unique structure, and have anti-theft, noise reduction and sound insulation effects. Therefore, they are often used in the wall construction of residence, also known as "oyster shell house". However, due to the development of materials and technology in the field of architecture, this local building material gradually disappears in the field of modern architecture. At the same time, with the coastal cities expanding a large number of marine aquaculture for economic development, oysters, known as "milk of the sea", have become the most important marine products in coastal cities. But as the main food material, oysters also make the waste of oyster shells become more and more serious. Facing the flooding of oyster shells, coastal cities spend a lot of human, material and financial resources every year to alleviate the environmental pollution caused by oyster shells. Therefore, how to deal with a large number of abandoned oyster shells has become a very serious problem in coastal cities. If oyster shell, a natural and renewable green material, can be widely used in product manufacturing as an industrial raw material, it will greatly alleviate the urban pollution caused by oyster shell.

Keywords: Oyster shell architectural culture · Destruction of sea area · Municipal pollution · Green materials

1 Introduction

China is a big country with a long history in the Marine product farming industry. Today, the total area of Marine product farming has exceeded one million hectares, accounting for 70% of the world's total production. In Marine product cultivation, shellfish cultivation accounts for 80% of Marine product cultivation due to its low input cost, high yield per unit area and large market demand [1]. As oysters are favored by consumers in shellfish, oyster cultivation accounts for the highest proportion in the shellfish cultivation industry. Oysters not only taste delicious, but also have rich nutritional value and fat smooth meat, which is called by many as the "milk of the sea. "Nowadays, oyster cultivation has not only become the main economic source of coastal fishers, but also made a great contribution to the economic development of coastal cities. However, the

V. G. Duffy and P.-L. P. Rau (Eds.): HCII 2022, LNCS 13522, pp. 507–515, 2022.
https://doi.org/10.1007/978-3-031-21704-3_35

expansion of oyster cultivation scale has also brought huge hidden dangers of urban pollution.

In this study, Zhuhai of Guangdong province as an example, from the study of the origin of oyster shells architectural culture, heritage and development, and analysis of the coastal city of disorderly aquaculture waters caused by hidden dangers and abandoned city pollution brought by the oyster shells, discusses how to reuse the oyster shell abandoned, develop and explore new materials and practical process and practice.

2   Literature Review

2.1   History of Oyster Shell Architecture Culture

Since the Song Dynasty in China, people in Shajing Town, Shenzhen, have been planting oysters with rods, making it the earliest area of artificial oyster cultivation in the world and known as the "hometown of oyster cultivation". At that time, oyster shells became the preferred construction material for coastal fishermen who could not afford to build tile-roofed houses with blue bricks, and they left a lot of oyster shells after eating them. They built 50-cm-high foundations out of stone to prevent flooding [2], and then they built oyster shells and mud on top of them, and eventually they became what we see today as oyster shell houses (see Fig. 1).

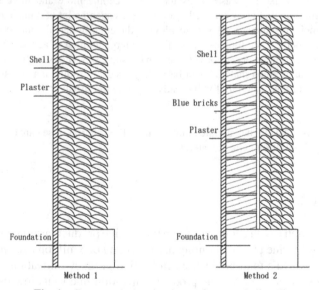

Fig. 1. Construction technology of oyster shell wall

In the Yuan Dynasty, oyster shells were found to have high strength and hardness, and oyster shell houses were resistant to moth, warm in winter and cool in summer. Oyster shell houses were not only strong but also did not collect rain, which was very suitable for the climate of Lingnan region. Therefore, oyster shells were gradually used as building materials. In the Ming and Qing dynasties, due to the improvement of architectural techniques and the growth of architectural experience, most southern Guangfu style mansions gradually used oyster shells for architectural collocation, and were favored by wealthy families. For example, compared with the oyster shell houses in Longan Village (see Fig. 2), Shunde District, Foshan city, the oyster shell walls of Bijiang Jinlou (see Fig. 3) are not only much more neatly arranged, but also much better in color. However, the oyster shell houses in Longan village are mostly because they are close to the seashore, so it is common to eat oysters and raise oysters. The local materials are convenient enough, so the arrangement of oyster shells is more random and random.

Fig. 2. Oyster shell house in Longan Village

Fig. 3. Oyster shell wall of Bijiang Jinlou

According to historical records, oyster shell powder particles as masonry adhesive can have a strong bonding force, often used for beating adobe, ramming earth to build walls or firing bricks and tiles, its function is relative to cement [3–6]. The wall of oyster shells consists of large pieces of oyster shells, which are then piled up layer by layer with yellow mud, brown sugar and steamed glutinous rice. Moreover, as the surface of oyster shell wall is sharp, it also has a certain anti-theft function. Moreover, due to the uneven shape of oyster shell itself, it can cause irregular reflection of sound waves, which makes oyster shell wall have excellent sound insulation effect. Oyster shell wall building is a living specimen of ecological technology applied by residents' regeneration in Lingnan coastal region. It is the folk wisdom selected through the evolution of time.

2.2 Artistic Value and Application of Oyster Shell

In the spirit of craftsmanship, oyster shell Windows have also become a representative of classical architecture. The ancients to choose large and flat light transmittance, high quality oyster shells, by cleaning and polishing, slicing, polishing process into a palm-sized white pervious to light glass, with a high quality bamboo piece shapes by pane fixed shape, with bolt finally fixed within the wooden window frame, adornment effect is strange (see Fig. 4), and can very good filter out the ultraviolet ray in sunshine, Moreover, when the sun shines on the window made of oyster shell, it can also present the grain like tree rings, which makes the whole window beautiful and elegant, and endows the building with extremely high decorative value [7–9].

Fig. 4. Oyster shell window

In modern times, the oyster shell has its own characteristics due to its shape. The simple and elegant nature of oyster, unique and refined, can be turned into practical articles or decorations with certain value after artificial treatment. Adding some attached decorative items on the surface of oyster shell can also make it more beautiful and noble, and the derived products are also unique, such as candlesticks and decorative paintings.

2.3 Damage of Disorderly Aquaculture Industry to Sea Area

As the shellfish farming industry has brought huge economic benefits to coastal cities, it is increasingly difficult to control disorderly and illegal oyster farming in coastal cities' sea areas. According to the investigation of aquaculture industry in Qiao Island, Zhuhai city, in the peripheral waters of Qiao Mangrove Provincial Nature Reserve, the floating row of oyster cultivation has densely surrounded mangroves, which not only seriously affected the navigation of ships in the sea, but also affected the scenery of the sea [10]. Located in Guandi Bay of Qiao Island, the Chinese White Dolphin National Nature Reserve also directly affects the positioning system of white dolphins because of the dense distribution of oyster piles underwater, because white dolphins use sonar backtracking positioning. Whether directly or indirectly, intensive oyster farming practices have an impact on the conservation of white dolphins.

2.4 Discarded Oyster Shells and Urban Pollution

In an adult oyster, the bulk of the weight is the shell. About one kilogram of flesh produces about 20 kg of shell. Therefore, the oysters consumed by consumers in the market every day will produce 20 times the quality of oyster shells. However, these discarded oyster shells have not been properly treated, and the untreated oyster shells are very difficult to decompose (see Fig. 5). Because even after many years, oyster shells remain the same, only becoming slightly brittle and fragile, but there is no fundamental solution.

Fig. 5. Oyster processing and breeding base

Zhuhai city in Guangdong Province is famous for Hengqin oysters, but the disposal of discarded oyster shells is the most prominent seafood product. In factories and breeding bases, a large number of oyster shells are accumulated after processing, and the relevant measures to deal with oyster shells are only to use the traditional method of centralized landfill when the number of oyster shells accumulates to a certain amount, but this can only solve the urgent problem, not a long-term solution. Because oyster shells have a huge impact on the land. There have been feed-mills in other cities that have bought fresh oyster shells for feed, but the economics have been so low that they have not done so again. Freshly discarded oyster shells, especially in the hot southern city of Zhuhai, can make the air smell very heavy and pungent, seriously affecting environmental health. For tourists who come to Zhuhai, it will greatly affect their interest and impression of Zhuhai.

Not only in Zhuhai city, but also in all the coastal cities that focus on oyster farming, these coastal cities need to spend a lot of manpower, material and financial resources to alleviate the environmental pollution caused by oyster shells every year [11–13].

3   Practice and Research

3.1   The Influence of New Materials on Design

With the continuous progress of world science and technology and design, the focus of design is no longer limited to modeling and function, more is to begin to process, materials, engineering and other directions of in-depth development. And the new environmental protection materials have also been paid attention to by the public, in the increasingly fierce industrial competition environment only to make enterprises and designers realize the importance of new environmental protection materials, in order to promote the enterprise to enhance the market competitiveness, in order to occupy the initiative in the development of the industry. At the same time, because design is the combination of science and technology and humanities and arts [14], realizing the function of products needs the support of science and technology, which also needs the innovation of materials to drive the development of design. Therefore, the study of discarded oyster shells as a new industrial raw material can make a large number of discarded oyster shells used from the perspective of environmental protection and recycling design.

3.2 Restudy on New Material of Oyster Shell

Oyster shells are composed of minerals, proteoglycans and other organic matters. Minerals are mainly calcium, which contains a large amount of $CaCO_3$, which can be used to prepare nitrogen fertilizer and improve acidic soil. In terms of structure, oyster shell is composed of three layers: cuticle layer, prism layer and pearl layer. SEM section scanning shows that oyster shell has a natural porous surface, loose texture, high strength and low thermal conductivity (see Fig. 6). The physical structure is relatively special, because of the interlacing and stacking of the leaf-like structure of the prismatic micropores, with strong adsorption and exchange catalytic characteristics, can be used as the adsorbent of some particles in the waste liquid, phosphorus removal, etc. [15–18].

Fig. 6. SEM section scanning of oyster

In the initial studies of oyster shell materials, oyster shells were ground into powder and then mixed with other adhesive materials to form. The successful exploration of oyster shell composition can account for 60% of the total content of new materials, which can preliminarily prove that a large number of discarded oyster shells can be reused as a kind of raw material (see Fig. 7). In addition, it is found that the external performance characteristics of the new material are very similar to those of the products made of clear water concrete. We can with the help of the basic research, and then through the design to solve part of the product on the market demand for new materials, at the same time the oyster shell new material widely used in the manufacturing process of production [19], not only enhance the value of the new material also helps to solve the problem

Fig. 7. Oyster shell powder and experiment

of environment pollution from oyster shells, etc., may even reach the integration of production resources, A new enterprise or industry that innovates the mode of production.

3.3 Re Practice of New Materials for Oyster Shell

As the new material in the process of research is more about how to use in the product, so in the process of practice, household products as the main direction of production. In the practice process that desk makes, spent a lot of time to try to search a few scale or law to the line layout of desktop, let reason and perceptual photograph union (see Fig. 8). This can also prove another design point of view, that is to use a certain proportion to deliberately constitute the plane, than the kind of messy plane more comfortable and balanced [20].

Fig. 8. Furniture making of new materials

In the production process of the desktop product series, considering that these products are closely related to the quality of people's life, so try to make the product model show a more delicate texture and surface effect (see Fig. 9). After several attempts, it was found that the texture effect on the surface of the product model would be coarser due to the large particles in the raw material of oyster shell. Meanwhile, the vacuum bubble extraction environment could not be achieved due to the relatively simple production conditions. The oyster shell powder was filtered through a thinner mesh filter and a chemical anti-bubble agent was added to create a smooth finish [21].

In the process of research, due to the limitations of various experimental conditions, the experimental results could not be further optimized, but we insist that oyster shell has more novel ideas and broader space in the extended use of materials.

Fig. 9. Production of household products with new materials

4   Conclusion

The flood of oyster shells has brought great impact on the ecological environment and people's life. It is the duty and responsibility of designers to explore a sustainable development path for the environment facing serious ecological crisis by studying discarded oyster shells as new raw materials for industrial products. Because design is to create a more reasonable and healthy lifestyle, design major should be a discipline leading social progress and people's healthy lifestyle [22]. Especially in the design education, we should train designers with social morality, overall outlook and sense of responsibility as the goal, which is also a long way for college teachers.

Under the guidance of global consumerism, most products in our daily life are just changed in appearance without much value improvement, which not only wastes a large amount of non-renewable resources on the earth but also damages the environment. Along with the social increasing energy consumption of non-renewable resources, environmental protection design concept has been all over the world advocate early, with the continuous improvement of the public on the quality of life and personal accomplishment, cognition of ascension, sacrifice the environment for economic development of the traditional development model is not sustainable, we should adhere to the resource conservation and environmental protection, adhere to the harmonious coexistence between man and nature.

References

1. Fisheries of ChinaReport: on the development of Oyster industry in China. **06**, 20–31 (2021)
2. Zhang, H., Li, L.: Study on materials of Quanzhou shell wall from the perspective of construction. Sino Foreign Architect. **09,** 76–78 (2016)
3. Zhang, W.S.: Research on the expression of Lingnan traditional materials in Contemporary Architecture. South China University of Technology (2015)
4. Zeng, L.J.: Ecological art of oyster shell. A traditional local architectural decoration material in Lingnan. Grand View Fine Arts **11**, 94–95 (2019)
5. Liang, J.J.: The use of oyster shells and the historical changes of oyster shell walls in Lingnan area. J. Huizhou Univ. **38**(05), 41–46 (2018)
6. Chen, J.Y., Wei, S.: On the preservation status and protection of oyster shell houses. Shanxi Architect. **39**(29), 3–5 (2013)
7. Wang, Z.Y.: On the architectural decoration art of ancient villages in Nanmen, Zhuhai. Beauty Times. **1**, 1 (2018)

8. Feng, Y.N.: Research on the decorative art of doors and windows of traditional buildings in Guangfu area. South China University of Technology (2020)
9. Huang, X.H.: Study on the color of windows in Lingnan landscape architecture. Res. Art Educ. **05**, 82–84 (2019)
10. Jia, X.P., Chen, T., Zhou, J.S., Guo, Z.: Preliminary investigation on Chinese white dolphins in the Pearl River Estuary. China Environ. Sci. **2000**(S1), 80–82 (2000)
11. Su, T., Wang, W.M., Zhang, L.Q., Su, Y.L.: Pollution problems and solutions of waste oyster shells. Environ. Protect. Circ. Econ. **37**(09), 20–22 (2017)
12. Zeng, Z.N., Ning, Y.: Current situation, problems and countermeasures of oyster breeding industry in Fujian. Marine Sci. **09**, 112–118 (2011)
13. Wei, Y., Yu, X.T.: Oyster shells are processed into feed to turn waste into treasure. Huizhou Daily, 27 November 2012
14. Niu, Y.Y.: Necessity of regeneration of traditional buildings. Design **29**(19), 53–54 (2016)
15. Liu, X.K., Zhang, L., Meng, Q.L., Li, C.S.: Field measurement of heat transfer coefficient of oyster shell wall. Build. Energy Conserv. **40**(12), 31–33 (2012)
16. Chen, W.T.: Study on composition characteristics and comprehensive utilization of Oyster shell. Fujian Agriculture and Forestry University (2013)
17. Lin, R.X.: Study on the preparation of water quality improver from oyster shell. Fujian agriculture and Forestry University (2013)
18. Huang, Y.: Development of phosphorus removal materials for oyster shell wastewater purification. Fuzhou University (2010)
19. Lu, F.: Research on oyster shell product design based on green design concept. Jingdezhen Ceramic University (2019)
20. Xia, B.: Harmonious formal beauty in design aesthetics. Xuelian **23**, 46 (2015)
21. Wang, B.X.: Study on aesthetic problems of waste renewable design. Design **29**(20), 112–113 (2016)
22. Liu, G.Z.: Thoughts on Chinese Industrial Design. Jiangsu Phoenix Art Press, Jiangsu Phoenix Art Publishing House, Jiangsu (2018)

A Form Design Method of Children's Slide Based on BESO Algorithm

Wenda Tian[1(✉)], Qianhang Qin[1(✉)], and Meilun Tan[2]

[1] Guangxi Normal University, Guilin 541000, China
twd936474757@gmail.com, tanqh17@tsinghua.org.cn
[2] Art and Design Academy, Tsinghua University, Beijing 100030, China

Abstract. The BESO algorithm is a bionic algorithm often used in the design of architectural structures. With the help of the BESO algorithm, designers can design structures for buildings, bridges, etc. that are reasonably stressed and consume less material, thus reducing material losses. The forms generated by this algorithm often have a unique aesthetic and bionic character, and from the perspective of an industrial designer, this unique aesthetic is applicable to a wider range of product form designs. Therefore, we propose a new design method for children's slide morphology by combining the BESO algorithm. First, we summarize the fallacies and causes of previous children's slide designs, and summarize the elements of an ideal children's slide form design. Secondly, we review the cases of application of BESO algorithm in building structure design, summarize the shape characteristics of its generated forms, and bring the algorithm into the process of generating the forms of various types of children's slides to obtain different children's slide forms. Third, we optimize the design of different slide shapes generated by the algorithm, and then obtain a series of children's slide shape design solutions with unique aesthetics. Finally, we bring these structures into the case study and discuss the impact brought by human-computer interaction in the design process.

Keywords: Children's slide · Bionic morphology design · Algorithm design · Interactive design

1 Introduction

The development of industrialization in recent years has boosted China's economy and accelerated the urbanization of Chinese society, but it has also revealed many social and educational activities problems. In China's development, educational resources for urban children are becoming more abundant and teachers are becoming more qualified while equipment is becoming more advanced. At the same time, A growing number of Chinese children are becoming distant from nature. More children have less access to learn nature during their education, even cannot recognize the common crops that are used as food in their daily lives. Therefore, the danger of being away from nature does not stop there.

In his book, Last Child in the Woods, Richard Louv describes the phenomenon of "nature deficit disorder," pointing out that prolonged absence from nature leads to a series

© Springer Nature Switzerland AG 2022
V. G. Duffy and P.-L. P. Rau (Eds.): HCII 2022, LNCS 13522, pp. 516–528, 2022.
https://doi.org/10.1007/978-3-031-21704-3_36

of problems such as distraction, reduced use of the senses, and increased incidence of emotional and physical illness. Many Western industrialized countries have responded to the problems of childhood "nature deficit disorder" by offering children's opportunity which learn and exposed to nature in a natural environment through the "forest school" approach to education. In fact, this approach has been effective, as Dabaja reveals in his review of the literature that forest schools allow children to better develop (1) social and cooperative skills; (2) physical fitness; (3) self-confidence and self-esteem; (4) academic performance and cognitive abilities; (5) emotional and mental health; (6) risk management skills; and (7) Environmental awareness and sense of belonging (citation needed) [1]. However, this format may be difficult to carry out in China due to population and land issues. Although China has a land area of 9.6 million square kilometers, it also has a population base of 1.4 billion and a large concentration of people in the central and eastern coastal cities of China, which makes it more difficult for children in cities to enjoy natural land space, and we can see that even kindergartens in developed areas of China are often in the midst of many tall buildings, and Chinese children face a serious problem of "nature deprivation".

Here, we propose the concept of "moving the forest into the school", and generate the design idea of children's slide form with the characteristics of natural form according to BESO algorithm. The children's slide design with the characteristic structure of trees can increase the natural elements in Chinese kindergartens. Interaction design related to the forest could draw the relationship between Chinese urban children and nature closely and alleviate the problem of the lack of nature in Chinese children's education.

2   A New Relationship Between Children and Nature

With the rise of cities and tall buildings made of steel and concrete blocking the connection between humans and nature, the educational meaning that can only be felt in nature is disappearing. The theory of "biophibia" suggests that humans have an innate instinct to be close to nature, and the instinct determines that children have a strong curiosity to acquire knowledge of natural cognition and to feel natural emotions with ecology form [2]. Outdoor playing is considered as an essential part of a "proper childhood" [3], but in modern society "idyllic childhoods" are becoming increasingly rare due to parental anxiety. As children become increasing dependent on their comfortable environment and less interested in nature, their physical and sensory minds are slowly deteriorating [4]. Some scholars have found that older people have better childhood experiences of nature than younger people, such as the memory and experience of flowering plants around the price.

Richard Love said, "For the new generation, nature is more abstract than reality. Nature is becoming something to be observed, consumed, worn, or even ignored" [5]. Children are alienated from nature, "imprisoned" indoors for long periods of time, and almost deprived of the freedom to be outdoors. There are complex socio-cultural changes behind the current alienation of children from nature: parental attitudes, guardianship and restrictions are among the main reasons, followed by safety issues, the spread of new technologies and screen media are also considered to be the main reasons for this phenomenon. In today's Chinese context, urban parents and grandparents tend to have mostly negative views on children's physical exposure to nature, believing that it is sufficient for children to be in nature but not in contact with it, and therefore children's activities in nature are mostly supervised. Children's nature experiences have changed from spontaneous play behaviors to organized and planned activity behaviors controlled by adults [3].

2.1 The Importance of Nature for Children

Children's experience of nature is an embodied process [3]. Children prefer to play freely in nature than participate in adult-organized activities because of the physical, emotional, and sensory aspects of nature [6]. Education in nature, the environment of nature can provide children with real feeling experiences, enrich children's emotional experiences and reduce physical health problems; through feeling nature to trigger children's curiosity about things and phenomena around them, enhance their courage to meet setbacks and difficulties, and at the same time stimulate interest in learning inside and outside the classroom; when children use all their senses to explore, question and discover nature, they have interaction with the surrounding environment, which is benefit to their logic, independent personality and creativity. The most important is cultivating children's concern for nature and their sense of responsibility.

Children's connection to nature can lead to healthy mental and physical growth, and the fun learning process can improve children's learning styles, efficiency and understanding, in addition to being more active in protecting the ecosystem after experiencing nature.

2.2 The Ideal Environment for Children's Nature Education in the City

In the context of such social research, a philosophy based on returning to nature and getting close to nature is being quietly integrated into the construction of children's nature education. However, how can children connect with nature in their daily lives in urban areas far away from woodlands and natural environments? This is where the "relationship between children, nature and the mediator" comes into play, as the mediator is an integral part of children's interaction with nature. This idea is based on Brad's new materialism [7, 8]. (Nonhuman) material objects can play a mediating role in children's interactive behaviors with nature, and technological devices can also be mediators in the interactions children use with nature.

Based on the research direction of "child-mediator-nature", we hope to generate a new design method to connect nature's intermediary-children's slide, providing children with the opportunity to get close to nature and forest education. We hope to generate a children's slide with the following characteristics: connected to the natural environment, that is, the structure and function of the children's slide need to be associated with the forest nature and other environments, which can motivate children to find more interactive ways to play and increase the fun under the premise of safety and security.

3 Simulation Generation of Children's Forest Education Environment

3.1 BESO Algorithm

The BESO algorithm is a topology optimization algorithm developed by Yimin Xie's team at RMIT. The original purpose of developing this algorithm is to reduce the cost of construction by minimizing the consumption of materials while ensuring the strength of the structure. During our research and application of the BESO algorithm, we found that the topologically optimized structure has an aesthetic shape similar to that of a tree, which is a very close to the natural shape of the structure. This discovery led us to introduce the BESO algorithm into some design activities related to children. Through a study of children's activity areas in China, we found that slides are the most common facilities in various children's playgrounds, and the relatively simple contour shape of slides is also suitable for structural morphology generation by BESO algorithm, and we expected to generate structural morphology related to the most basic elements of nature, such as forest trees, and started some experiments in this way.

3.2 Three Forms of Generative Tree Structural Morphology

By using the Chinese oracle bone characters "木 (wood)", "林 (woodland)" and "森 (forest)" as inspiration for our design (Fig. 1). In the oracle bone script, "Mu" means a tree, "Lin" looks like two trees from the character form, which also means a small forest, and "Sen" often represents a large forest with many tall and luxuriant trees. Through the form and meaning of the oracle bone pictograph "木 (wood)", "林 (woodland)" and "森 (forest)", we tried to create a shape that echoes these three ancient pictographs by designing different numbers of pivot points.

Fig. 1. "Wood", "Forest" and "Sen" in the oracle bone script.

In the specific morphological construction, A cube meshed the shape by Ameba is a prototype, setting the force planes with one, two, three support points and non-computed areas, then compared the final obtained morphology, discovering this morphogenetic method has operability (Fig. 2).

Generate a Pivot Point Tree Structure Form. In this section, using the tree structure morphology in the design of the slide, corresponding to the oracle word "木 (wood)". First, we summarize the basic form of a slide, determine the tree structure form using a

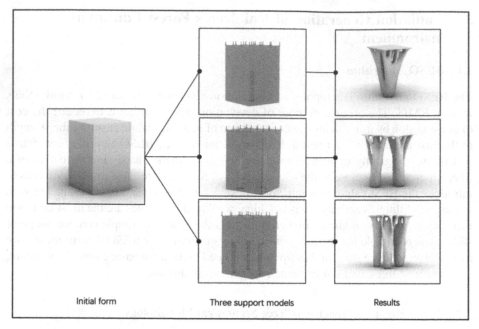

Fig. 2. Tree structure morphology generation method.

support point for a small slide, and apply the load to this form in Grasshopper through Ameba (Fig. 3).

Fig. 3. Morphological analysis of tree structure for one pivot point.

Through iterative calculations, obtained a slide structure shape supported by a large tree, after processed this shape, we obtain a small slide shape with natural features finally (Fig. 4).

Fig. 4. Calculation and generation process of tree structure morphology for one pivot point.

Secondly, by analyzing this slide structure with Ameba and found that it has good stability which can meet the needs of children playing (Fig. 5).

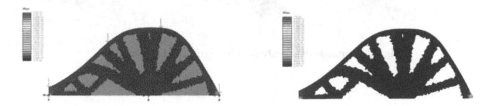

Fig. 5. Calculation and generation process of tree structure morphology for one pivot point.

By importing the shape into Zbrush to imitate the texture of the tree skin design, and rendered the effect in Keyshot software. Finally obtained a more realistic tree slide shape, the form and the meaning of the word "wood" to form a corresponding relationship (Fig. 6). It has the function of a slide and the structure of a tree, which is completely different from the previous children's slides.

Fig. 6. A pivot point tree structure children's slide.

Generate the Structural Form of the Tree with Two Pivot Points. In generating the tree structure slide form with two pivot points, we followed the idea of generating the first slide form. In the initial design process, the width and height of the basic form were increased so that the slide could accommodate two children sliding side-by-side, hoping that the final form would correspond to the meaning of the word "林 (woodland)" (Fig. 7, 8 and 9).

After processing and calculating the model, the shape of a children's slide supported by two tree structures were achieved, and the resulting result met our expectation (Fig. 10).

Generate the Structural Form of the Tree with Three Pivot Points. In generating the tree structure slide form with three pivot points, increased the width and height of the basic form further and echo the word "森 (forest)". Since the enlargement of the initial form size provided more space for designing support structures, we experimented with different structures by controlling the distance between the support structures (Fig. 11).

Fig. 7. Morphological analysis of tree structure for two pivots.

Fig. 8. Calculation and generation process of tree structure morphology for two pivot points.

Fig. 9. Tress analysis of slide structure with two pivot points.

Fig. 10. Two pivot points of the tree structure children's slide.

This approach was tried to give us two different tree structures, and found that the different structures provided more opportunities for children to play, therefore, both calculations are presented here (Fig. 12, 13 and 14).

Summary. By combining the BESO algorithm with the concepts of "木 (wood)", "林 (woodland)" and "森 (forest)" in Chinese oracle bone pictographs, generated four types of children's slides with the structure of trees (Fig. 15). They can meet the basic slide function and also have the structural shape of natural woodland features.

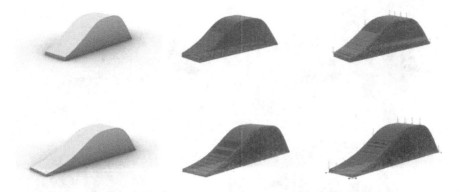

Fig. 11. Morphological analysis of tree structure with three pivot points.

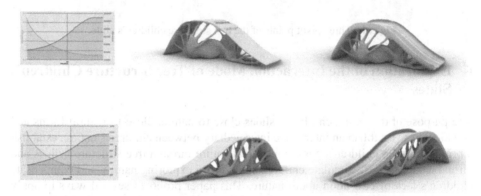

Fig. 12. Calculation and generation process of tree structure morphology for three pivot points.

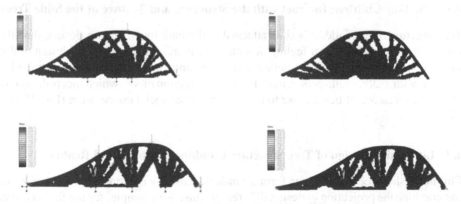

Fig. 13. Stress analysis of three pivot point slide structure.

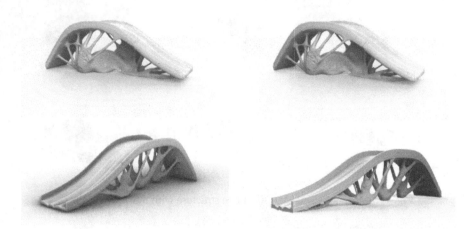

Fig. 14. Three pivot points of the tree structure children's slide.

4 Exploration of the Interaction Mode of Tree Structure Children's Slides

The purpose of designing children's slides close to nature, close to natural forms and situations is to establish an interactive intermediary between children - nature, establish a bridge between children's cognition of real nature through tree structured slides and virtual nature scenes, stimulate children's interest in exploring nature, and compensate children's lack of education about nature. This paper proposes several ways to apply interactive scenarios based on the generated tree structure children's slide facilities.

4.1 The Way Children Interact with the Structure and Texture of the Slide Trees

Tree structure of the children's slide attached to the bark touch texture design, directly for children to touch the real feeling of nature in the tree trunk bark. The design of the support structure with diverse structure, low height and even force distribution provides children with a safe, multi-person tree climbing interaction mode, which meets the needs of children's nature of being close to nature, active and social cooperation (Fig. 16 and 17).

4.2 Interaction Design of Tree Structure Combined with Virtual Reality

Children's slide tree structure can form the material basis for creating a natural forest, we can combine the projection to design different themes, for example, for the four seasons in the forest design "spring, summer, autumn and winter" theme of the situation (Fig. 18), the formation of immersive general virtual reality combined with the experience of space, to provide children with the most intuitive feeling of nature the four seasons change the feeling. Or, based on the structure of the slide, we can make a series of images of trees, forests, birds and insects to help children feel nature and understand nature knowledge

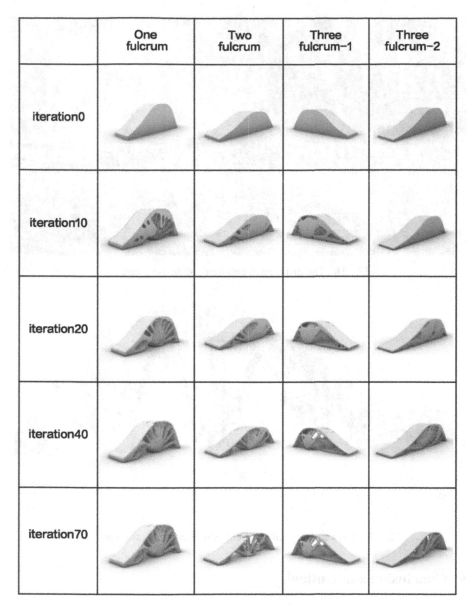

Fig. 15. Iterative process of tree structure with different support points.

(Fig. 19), replacing text, pictures and general video knowledge transfer with experiential interaction.

Fig. 16. The first type of children's slide use scenario.

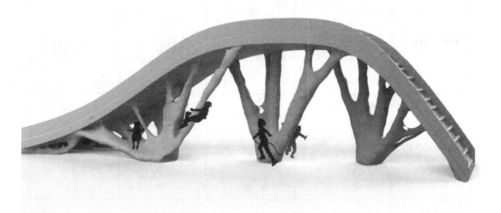

Fig. 17. The fourth type of children's slides and other use scenarios.

5   Conclusion and Outlook

This design practice is intended to provide a parametric design and interaction approach to nature education for urban children in China who lack access to woodland environments. We propose a bionic design method based on the BESO algorithm, which uses the bionic algorithm to generate four sets of three-dimensional children's slide designs based on the similarity between the structure of the Chinese character "木 (wood)", "林 (woodland)" and "森 (forest)". The design practice cases and methods still fall short in fully considering children's psychology and needs for playgrounds, but hopefully they can enrich and broaden the research content of children's nature education and fill the gaps between children and nature.

Fig. 18. Conceptual design of the "Spring, Summer, Autumn and Winter" themed virtual scene.

Fig. 19. Conceptual design of the "Forest-Animal" themed virtual scene.

References

1. Dabaja, Z.F.: The forest school impact on children: reviewing two decades of research. Education 3–13 (2021)
2. Xiang, H.: A study of children's human-earth relationship with nature: contact, cognition and emotion. Hum. Geogr. **35**(06), 9–17+75 (2020). (in Chinese)
3. Layard, R., Dunn, J.: A Good Childhood: Searching for Values in a Competitive Age: The Children's Society, p. 124. Penguin, London (2009)
4. Kaiyan, S.: Research on sensory education in forest schools. Sci. Educ. J. (Late) **21**, 50–51 (2018)

5. Louv, R.: Last Child in the Woods: Saving Our Children from Nature-Deficit Disorder. Algonquin Books, Chapel Hill (2005)
6. Skar, M., Gundersen, V., O'Brien, L.: How to engage children with nature: why not just let them play? Child. Geographies **14**(5), 527–540 (2016)
7. Barad, K.: Meeting the Universe Half Way: Quantum Physics and the Entanglement of Matter and Meaning, p. 28. Duke University Press, Durham (2007)
8. Anggard, E.: How matter comes to matter in children's nature play: posthumanist approaches and children's geographies. Child. Geographies **14**(1), 77–90 (2016)

An Investigation into the Weavability of Plants and Their Application in Fashion and Textile Design

JiChi Wu[1,2] and Ying Zhou[1]([envelope])

[1] Minzu University of China, Beijing 10081, China
553050756@qq.com
[2] Southwest Minzu University, Chengdu 610225, China

Abstract. In recent years, green and environment-friendly textile materials are more and more favored by the public. Making degradable textile materials from natural fibers is one of the means to reduce pollution and make rational use of resources. In this paper, plants such as fireweed, silvergrass and corn, which are easy to grow, have high yield, low raw material cost and broad market prospect, are selected as the research object. Through experiments on their cellulose content and spinnability technology, the influence of plant cellulose content on weavability is explored. It is expected that it can be better used in garment and textile design in the future.

Keywords: Wearable bio-textile · Sustainability · Plants · Weavability · Fashion design

1 Introduction

With the dwindling of resources, sustainable design[1] becomes increasingly important. Fashion and technology together often bring new materials and processing techniques

---

[1] Sustainable design is a design method which takes economy, environment, ethic and society into fully consideration. It aims to design products that satiate the current needs and guarantee the future development for the later generations. "In recent years, researchers and practitioners are devoted to environment sustainability in fashion and textile industry (Caniato et al., 2012)." Palomo-Lovinski and Hahn (2014) cited that "sustainable practices in clothing have not, thus far, created a significant impact and instead continue to be largely marginalized within the fashion industry." From this, we can conclude that the top priority should be about how to settle and improve these problems. Reiley and DeLong (2011) concluded that "sustainability in fashion is going to require transformative changes in the practices of all involved: designers, manufacturers, marketers, and consumers. But consumers especially need a vision for sustainable fashion practice." Under these conditions, it is difficult for companies to make changes in design methods, product qualities and materials. Thus, designers should take responsibility to seek other ways for change.

V. G. Duffy and P.-L. P. Rau (Eds.): HCII 2022, LNCS 13522, pp. 529–541, 2022.
https://doi.org/10.1007/978-3-031-21704-3_37

driving the industry towards a more sustainable future[2]. Many designers have conducted research within this field including Carmen Hijosa's Piñatex [1], Tanja Schenker's handbag brand 'Happy Genie' [2], Carole Collet's Biolace design of fruit, vegetable roots [3] and Dutch artist Diana Scherer's graminaceous root system [4]. The former two adopted methods to extract and remodel fibers to create leather-like textiles to find a new way to transform plant fiber into fabrics. However, their products were mostly accessories while only a few of them were utilized in clothing. Collet has spent years studying future bio-materials and Biolace to explore new types of plants (strawberry and tomato with potentially weavable roots). However, due to long growing period, these plants have low productivity and cannot meet the requirements. Regarding this, Scherer implemented mature root textile with short production period which could be utilized in fashion despite the lack of wearability and flexibility. However, harvesting roots may lead to excessive grass-loss causing environmental impact. Therefore, we put forward some suggestions on the weavability of plant fiber (Fig. 1), which is often used in textile engineering. Weavability here refers to the possibility of converting materials into fabrics. The ability to be woven is a practical engineering term. In weaving practice, it is very important to analyze the weavability of fabrics. Traditionally, with the help of compound technique, such as coating, spraying, binding or 3D printing, most materials could be weaved into fabrics.

Fig. 1. Interpretation of weavability

Weavability introduces the following questions: How to effectively obtain weavable fibers from plants? What are the main challenges in seeking new bio-textiles from

---

[2] "The increasing public awareness and sense of social responsibility related to environmental issues have led the textile industry to manufacture products with improved environmental profile (Chen and Burns, 2006)". This would require designers to develop new ideas to recycle products and use wasted materials for new designs. It could bring new ideas to products, save materials and also be economically beneficial. Such trends, together with a sustainable design concept, have gained popularity among the public. There is a consensual view that any new design should have minimal impact on the environment whilst achieving high standards.

plants and how can this be utilized in the fashion industry? How can we effectively transform economical bio-textiles into body-oriented, wearable products? This study mainly explores the weavability of several and environmental - friendly natural plants with low utilization, and the research plan is to deduce reversely from the physical and chemical properties (cellulose content/ fiber form) of ecological textiles to explore wearability. I will mainly focus on analyzing the prospect of bio-fabrics (weavable plants) in body-oriented fashion design and its contribution to sustainable fashion and textile design[3].

2   Literature Review

The development of bio-textiles has attracted the attention of a large number of scholars and designers, and a lot of research has been done in the early stage (Fig. 2). The natural fiber contains biodegradable yarn developed by biomaterials research company in New York with seaweed and kelp; The remaining materials are reused. There are fabrics made

Fig. 2. Research case tree. (2021)

---

[3] In this project, sustainable design refers to design that could make progress in nature, economy and science. It should also be beneficial to human environment and resources. The natural property of my design is to pursue an optimal combination of Eco-system and design concept. The key step is to discover in nature and recycle the waste by obtaining raw materials from wasted plants. Wastes could be design into products and its pollution could also be avoided. By recycling wastes could create maximum benefit, a risk-free return. Without putting any harm to natural resources, it maximally increases the products' economic benefits. For the technical part, with preference toward clean and effective technology, we aim to achieve real sustainable design by reducing the waste of energy and other natural resources in design process through establishing a craft and technical system which produces little waste and pollution.

by Dutch artists with the surplus materials of fruits and vegetables in the kitchen; Banana fiber made from the stem of banana tree can be used to make textiles of different weight and thickness. There is also organic leather made of mushrooms by German companies in the closed-loop design, which has been developed into a complete product line.

Foreign research institutions and scholars, such as: Ted-Ten (Tedresearch.net, 2017) [5], Nanollose Ltd (Nanollose.com, 2018) [6] and WRAP (Wrap.org.uk, 2017) [7] are some examples of cutting-edge research to find breakthroughs in the life-cycle of closed-loop products and innovative ways to recycle and upcycle. TED-TEN was jointly developed by several scholars and the textile environmental design research group of Chelsea School of art, London University of the arts. There are 10 topics (Fig. 3), each has identified important areas that need attention in the product life cycle, and proposed solutions to analyze and change strategies. When used together, these topics can be served as practical guidelines to examine, investigate and highlight sustainability issues and the role of designers in change and innovation. They are visual evidence of strategic thinking, as follows:

1. Design to minimize waste, which refers to the design to minimize the waste of production in the textile industry, whether before or after consumption;
2. Design for cyclability, which is also a recyclable design;
3. Design to reduce chemical impacts, this strategy is about the appropriate material selection and process of any product to minimize the impact on the environment;
4. Design to reduce energy and water use;
5. Design to explore clean and better technologies;
6. Design that take models for history and nature;
7. Design for ethical production;
8. Design to reduce the need to consume, this strategy is about making durable things, the things that you really want, since fashion is developing and changing rapidly. This strategy also involves exploring alternative forms of design and consumption, such as joint design and collaborative consumption;

1. DESIGN TO MINIMISE WASTE
2. DESIGN FOR CYCLABILITY
3. DESIGN TO REDUCE CHEMICAL IMPACTS
4. DESIGN TO REDUCE ENERGY AND WATER USE
5. DESIGN TO EXPLPRES CLEAN AND BETTER TECHNOLOGIES
6. DESIGN THAT TAKE MODELS FOR HISTORY AND NATURE
7. DESIGN FOR ETHICAL PRODUCTION
8. DESIGN TO REDUCE THE NEED TO CONSUME
9. DESIGN TO DEMATERIALISE AND DEVELOP SYSTEMS&SERVICES
10. DESIGN ACTIVISM

Textiles Environment Design 20

Fig. 3. Ten topics for textiles environment design by Ted-Ten

9. Design to dematerialise and develop system & services, this strategy introduces the concept of designing systems and services, rather than supporting products, such as leasing, sharing, maintenance, etc.;
10. Design activism, in this final strategy, we encourage designers to leave their products behind and work creatively with consumers and society.

Biological textiles' development has drawn numerous designers' attention like Carmen Hijosa, Tanja Schenker, Diana Scherer, etc. Domestic scholars such as LIU Lunlun mentioned that natural fiber comes from renewable resources and can be recycled. It is generally divided into two categories: one is to extract fiber from plants, and the other is to extract fiber from animals [8]. It can be seen that plant fiber is a very important part of natural environmental protection fabrics and has sustainable utilization value. For another example, ZHANG Yi and others pointed out that making degradable textile materials from natural fibers is one of the means to reduce pollution and make rational use of resources, especially using plants such as palm leaves, which are easy to grow, have high yield, low raw material cost and broad market prospects [9]. These provide a reference for our research. This study mainly tests the weavability of several natural plants with low utilization and environmental protection, such as silvergrass, corn and so on. CHEN Chen mentioned that clothing should not only have basic wearing performance, but also have the functions of environmental protection and health care [10]. Through the practice of utilizing natural plant fibers such as mint fiber, wormwood fiber and aloe fiber, he has successfully developed various functional fabrics. It can be seen that natural plant fiber as fabric raw material has great development potential in future design, which also brings new ideas to the closed-loop design of fashion products.

3 Main Concepts

Based on the above, we comb and think about this project as shown in Fig. 4. The core is wearable biological textiles. By studying the weavability of materials, the natural materials can be transformed into products that can be woven. Firstly, taking sustainability as the theoretical basis of research, sustainable design refers to the design that can make progress in nature, economy and science, which can be beneficial to the harmonious development of human environment and resource. Thus, conforms to the human and natural life community concept which President Xi put forward on World Leaders' Climate Summit (April 2021). Secondly, material research takes economy and environmental protection as the starting point, and pursues the best combination of an ecosystem and design concept. From the perspective of ecology, natural plants or surplus materials are selected as raw materials to explore the organic combination of ecological resources, art design and science and technology. Then, in the process of design and production, try to establish an effective process and technical system, which will hardly produce waste and pollution, so as to realize the real sustainable design. The end product in the project is a kind of clothing product that uses natural fiber, which can be regenerated and recycled without affecting the purity and performance. The design results are effectively transformed into products, which can be widely used in life and can bring social and economic benefits. Encourage and advocate designers to make full use of recyclable natural product material flow in source design and adopt flexible renewable closed-loop scheme. Thus, the raw materials are processed into finished products, applied to different fields, and then returned to the material itself, which is a series of flow charts for recycling and reuse.

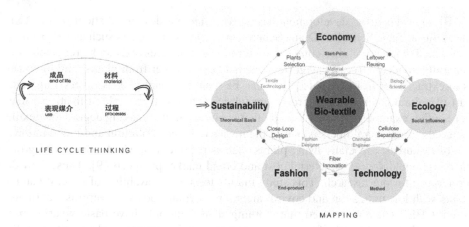

Fig. 4. Research keywords mapping. (2021)

Using our experience in clothing and sustainable textile design, we fully explore the characteristics of different plants and fibers, especially the species with low utilization rate that were neglected in the past. The results showed that the fiber content of stem and leaf was more considerable than that of plant root. The research combines interdisciplinary experimental methods to effectively test and analyze the properties of a variety of plant fibers, explore their wearability by inversely pushing the physical and chemical properties (cellulose content and fiber form) of biological textiles, deeply analyze the prospect of biological textiles (plant weavability) from a practical point of view, and explore their contribution to sustainable clothing and textile design.

The project will focus more on the body-oriented products and explore plants' unique features, especially low utilization plants and leftover fiber which could become biological textiles in fashion. Target plants include corn stigma/bran, silvergrass inflorescence and kudz vines (Fig. 5). These plants are high in yield and economical in cultivating, while their leftovers can be easily collected and reused as fiber sources. This process is much more sustainable in saving raw materials and reusing waste sources.

Fig. 5. Raw material selection. (2020)

Through the cooperation with the fruit and vegetable Laboratory of China Agricultural University and Jiangsu Jiaxin Testing Co., Ltd to research weavable plants[4], we succeeded in extracting cellulose from 10 different types of plants (Fig. 6 and 7). The analysis and comparison of the test results will contribute to narrow the selection range and pave the way for the further development of biological textiles.

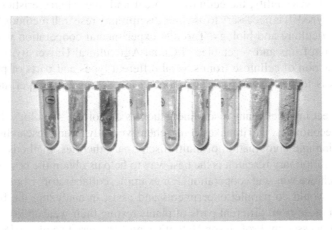

Fig. 6. Cellulose extraction experiment 1. (2021)

---

[4] By sifting raw material, extracting fiber, and further study in doctor's program, we intend to choose an appropriate method to mostly increase the weavability of plants, so raw materials could be more effectively changed into fabrics.

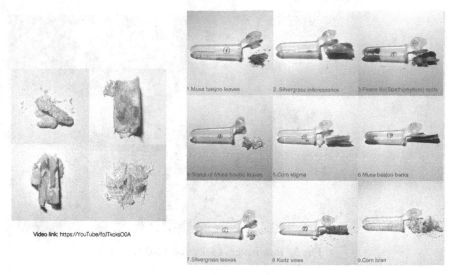

Video link: https://YouTube/foJTkoksO0A

Fig. 7. Cellulose extraction experiment 2. (2021)

4   Methodology

4.1   Interdisciplinary Research Method

Based on their weavability, the cellulose content and fiber characteristics of different plants are analyzed. It is necessary to use interdisciplinary research methods from botany, chemistry, agriculture and biology. Through experimental cooperation with the Ph.D. candidates from fruits and vegetables of China Agricultural University, we have realized the extraction of cellulose from several different types and parts of plants. Effective analysis is made by designing experiments and comparing experimental results [Appendix].

This subject involves many disciplines, such as ethnology, sociology, botany, ecology, design, economics, etc. it makes comprehensive analysis and research by means of the intersection and combination of multi-disciplinary theories, methods and achievements. Interdisciplinary research is the best way to help us obtain the best experimental results and achieve win-win cooperation. For example, collaborators from Imperial College London would do parallel experiments and assist in analyzing the best methods to extract cellulose from different parts of plants testing their weavability (Fig. 8, such as BioFlex processed by Prof. Jason Hallett's team) (Imperial.ac.uk, 2018) [11]. From this, experiment data will be collected, analyzed and interpreted into a description and visualization results. Their innovative bio flex process separates different natural chemical components in wood, namely lignin, cellulose and hemicellulose. Once separated separately, these components can be used in various applications, such as biochemistry, plastics or as new materials themselves. By analyzing cellulose content and fiber characters of different plants according to their weavability. Theoretical knowledge on botany, chemistry, agriculture and biology would be needed. A literature review and case study would be conducted throughout the project to supplement related interdisciplinary theories and the latest research. An exploratory case study (Yin, 2003) will be used to understand the existing practical bio-textile study. An evaluative case study (Yin, 2003) will be used to select the most feasible, effective and beneficial method [12].

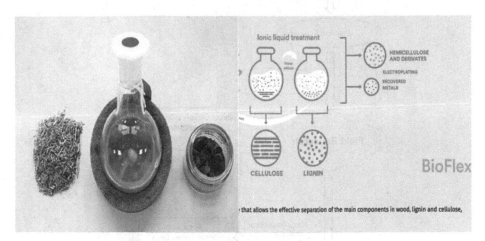

Fig. 8. Imperial College London website, BioFlex process. (2018)

4.2 Comparative Study Method

Based on the research results of the discipline, different investigation and practice results are combined with literature and theoretical data to conduct research and comparative analysis, so as to interpret the inevitability of the future existence of biological textile materials and textile technology and the sustainability of future development.

4.3 Case Study Method

Select relevant excellent cases at home and abroad for inquiry learning to find new innovation points. Among them, focus on the development context of typical and mature biological textile cases, conduct long-term and continuous investigation and attention, obtain the latest progress, and make records of the whole process.

4.4 Practical Research Method

Through experiments, narrow the scope of research and material selection, and pave the way for subsequent development. Practice is not only the best way and way to test the results, but also the most important link in the design discipline. It is a necessary skill for design practitioners and researchers. Therefore, it is very important and indispensable.

Meanwhile, fieldwork (Fig. 9), like trips to plantations and wilderness, would be conducted regularly.

Based on the results, we will start textile design from the weavability of materials (Fig. 10), trying to transform fiber into fabric for a mature and niche product attempting to design a fashionable and wearable collection of garments.

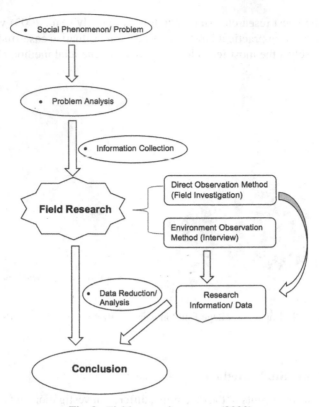

Fig. 9. Field research process. (2020)

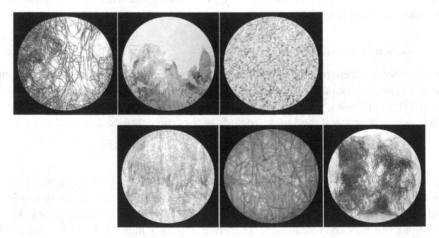

Fig. 10. Practical exploration of plant materials

5 Future Work

There is still a long way to go in the research on the weavability and sustainable utilization of materials. As a research hotspot, natural plant fiber has rich use value and sustainable utilization value. As the most potential biomass resource on the earth, natural plant fiber is rich in sources, cheap and easy to obtain, renewable and high strength. It also has excellent biocompatibility and full biodegradability which is often used as the matrix for the preparation of various materials. Among them, hemp fiber (HF), wood fiber (WF) and bamboo fiber (BF) have high mechanical properties and environmental friendliness [13]. If these materials are combined with bio-based materials (such as PLA, PCL, PA, etc.), the composite utilization is expected to improve some of the defects of bio-based synthetic fibers and expand their application scope. With the maturity of extraction technology of plant fiber extracts such as cellulose, hemicellulose and lignin, these extracts are being combined with polymers more and more widely and applied in more fields. By using the experience in clothing and sustainable textile design, we can fully explore the characteristics of different plants and fibers, practice in combination with interdisciplinary research methods and theoretical knowledge, transform biological materials into textile materials with weavability, and use non-woven technology to bring them into the garment and textile industry, so as to make green natural products and the concept of ecological environmental protection run through human life in the future.

Appendix

The Experiment of Cellulose
Location: China Agricultural University
Name: Jichi Wu

1. **Materials**
   Musa basjoo leaves, Silvergrass inflorescence, Peace lily(Spathiphyllum) roots, Stalks of Musa basjoo leaves, Corn stigma, Musa basjoo barks, Silvergrass leaves, Kudz vines, Corn bran
2. **Reagents**
   Sodium hydroxide solution (2%), Hydrogen peroxide solution (5%), Liquid nitrogen, Distilled water
3. **Devices**
   Mortar, Scissors, Precision balance (readability 0.0001 g), Centrifugal tube (50 ml), Centrifugal tube rack, Pipette, Beaker, Funnel, Filter paper, Titration flask, Centrifugal tube (2 ml), Water bath, Incubator
4. **Steps**
   Grinding: Scissor appropriate samples into mortar; add liquid nitrogen to freeze the samples and grind them into powder.
   Weighing: weigh 0.5–1.5 g of ground samples and put them into centrifugal tubes (50 ml).
   Heated bath: (1) add 10 ml of sodium hydroxide solution (2%) into centrifugal tubes mentioned above; shake the tubes well, put them into water bath(100 °C) for

90 min before taking them out; (2) add 10 ml of hydrogen peroxide solution (5%) into every tube; shake them well; let the tubes stand still at room temperature till large amount of colorless bubbles are produced; put the tubes into water bath (75 °C) for 30 min and take them out to cool to room temperature.

Filter: shake the samples well and slowly pour them into funnel to filter.

Drying: pack the filtered samples with filter paper and dry them in incubator (65 °C) for one night.

Weighing: weigh the dried samples and preserve them in centrifugal tubes (2 ml).

5. **Result:**

The experiment result is shown below:

Sample no	Name	Sample weight (g)	Final product weight (g)	Cellulose content (%)
1	Musa basjoo leaves	1.00	0.008	0.80
2	Silvergrass inflorescence	0.50	0.053	10.60
3	Peace lily (Spathiphyllum) roots	1.50	0.040	2.67
4	Stalks of Musa basjoo leaves	1.00	0.016	1.60
5	Fireweed	1.00	0.060	6.00
6	Corn stigma	0.50	0.087	17.40
7	Musa basjoo barks	1.00	0.180	18.00
8	Silvergrass leaves	1.00	0.005	0.50
9	Kudz vines	1.00	0.094	9.40
10	Corn bran	1.00	0.397	39.70

Video link: https://youtu.be/foJTkoksO0A.

References

1. Hijosa, C.A.A.: Piñatex, the design development of a new sustainable material. Ph.D. The Royal College of Art (2014)
2. Happy genie. Happy genie - luxury handbags made from apples (2018). https://happy-genie.com/. Accessed 13 Sept 2018
3. Designandlivingsystems.com. Biolace | Design & Living SystemsDesign & Living Systems (2018). http://www.designandlivingsystems.com/biolace/. Accessed 11 Apr 2018
4. Dianascherer.nl. Diana Scherer (2018). http://dianascherer.nl/. Accessed 05 June 2018
5. Tedresearch.net. The home of sustainable textile design research. Textiles Environment Design (2020). http://www.tedresearch.net/. Accessed 22 Dec 2020
6. Nanollose.com (2020). http://nanollose.com/. Accessed 30 Dec 2020

7. Wrap.org.uk. WRAP - Circular Economy & Resource Efficiency Experts (2020). http://www. wrap.org.uk/. Accessed 25 Dec 2020
8. Liu, L., Tang, Y., Bellavitis, A.D.-A., Shen, L.: Research on the development of sustainable fashion design. Wool Textile J. **47**(10) (2019)
9. Zhang, Y., Yang, B., Gao, J., Yu, C.: Production of needle punched nonwovens of palm leaf fiber and its properties. Shanghai Textile Sci. Technol. **49**(02) (2021)
10. Chen, C.: Production of mint fiber/flax/Tencel blended health care dyed shirt fabric. Shanghai Textile Sci. Technol. **49**(05) (2021)
11. Imperial.ac.uk. Separations | Faculty of Engineering | Imperial College London (2020). http:// www.imperial.ac.uk/chemical-engineering/research/researchthemes/separations/. Accessed 07 Oct 2020
12. Yin, R.: Case study Research. Sage Publications, Thousand Oaks (2003)
13. Yu, W., Jiao, Y., Zhou, Y., Lei, W.: Preparation and application status of plant fiber/PLA biomass composite. Plastics **49**(02), 90–94 (2020)

Smart-Color: Color-Interactive Device Design Based on Programmable Physical Color-Changing Materials and Motion Capture Technique

Chao Yuan[✉], Lyou Yeung, Xiao Zhang, and Song Qiu

Tsinghua University, Beijing, China
1037303749@qq.com

Abstract. Research background: Material Intelligence is a widely discussed topic in recent years. With the promotion of the manufacture, designers enable design patterns to create or change materials performance for their creative works. Material properties such as the color, texture and luster could show specific effects in different conditions. In the field, this paper focuses on the material color and human behaviors, and proposes a design method for creating a better interior environment.

Research question: Color is a significant part of our life. Many design cases use color widely to affect emotions to realize special functions. However, the dye is difficult to change in real-time, which unable to adapt to different emotion requires. Artificial lights are difficult to keep vivid in sunny conditions, and large-scale use of artificial light could also cause uncomfortable to people.

Approach: To implement the purpose in research, using laser films materials as the basic research object. Analyzing relationships between color produced through rotating films and the rotation angle, which transform programs to realize digital twin. Then, the overall equipment is fabricated by structural design and 3D printing technology, and the Arduino Open-source hardware control the device. Moreover, analyzing different postures of people by motion capture technique, realize positively change color by user-behavior.

Results: In this paper designing a color-interactive device to positively change color based on programmable physical color-changing materials and user-behavior analysis, which actively adapt human's behavior. And this creates a way for the interior environment of adaptive design.

Contributions: This research attempt to connect microstructures of materials and macro performance by programmable technology. From principles to design application, it is a practice of using design thinking to realize design innovation in longitudinal research. In this study, the color generated based on the principle of structure-color materials, compared with artificial light, this physical color-changing material has good display effect and real color in outdoor or strong light environment. And it can save energy of artificial light, which is also an exploration and experiment of sustainable intelligent design.

Keywords: Structural-color materials · Physical interaction design · Motion capture.

© Springer Nature Switzerland AG 2022
V. G. Duffy and P.-L. P. Rau (Eds.): HCII 2022, LNCS 13522, pp. 542–551, 2022.
https://doi.org/10.1007/978-3-031-21704-3_38

1 Introduction

Color is everywhere in human life, and different colors bring different feeling. In the perceptual understanding, people usually feel warm in a space with red or warm colors, and feel calm in the space with blue-green or cold colors. Color not only affect human sensation, but also affect working efficiency. In the studies of impacts of interior color on workers' mood and productivity (Nancy Kwallek 1988) [1] finding workers have more pressures in red environment, and maintain depression in blue environment. However, the research did not find obviously impacts of color on productivity. However, no significant effect was found in the one-hour typing survey (Rebecca A. Ainsworth 1993) [2]. But when the test time is increased, studies find that workers generate higher productivity in red environment than those in blue environment (Nancy Kwallek 1997) [3], which declare that different color in environment have different impacts on mood and productivity in long time work.

A large number of design practices contain the application of color, which can strengthen design goals or produce a specific function. For example, the influence of color on students' emotions is studied as the basis of color selection for campus buildings (Sevinc Kurt 2014) [4]. Designing color schemes for urban environment-architectural settings (Banu Manav 2017) [5]. And the survey on interior color and psychological functioning in a university residence hall (Marco Costa 2018) [6]. Above these color design cases based on user psychology, the final purpose is that determines and selects color used for design by many investigations and studies.

With the development of the electronic technology, color is widely applied to digital world, which use photoelectric technique and control means of digital RGB values. It is very convenient to change interior color by different light of color and to create different ambience. However, in the sunny outdoors, photoelectric color rendering is difficult to maintain vividness and brightness, and large-scale use of artificial light can also cause discomfort. Moreover, the building exterior wall and interior dec-oration are mostly the use of paint. The color will not to change in short time once it is determined, which is hard to meet peoples' different requirements.

This paper carried out research on these requirements, applicate the physical col-or-changing materials whose main principle is the structural color. Since reflection of light, the physical color-changing material shows better and the color is more real than artificial lights. So, using computer program to study programmable physical col-or changing materials is the focus of current research. The purpose is that designing a device to intelligently control color, then changing the color of the environment by cognition of human behaviors, which can better adapt to different requirements of people.

2 Method

2.1 Principles of the Structural Color

Color is a light wave essentially, and small domain in whole wavelength can be seen. The different wavelength of the visible light shows different color in human brains. The relationship of color and wavelength is shown below (Fig. 1): the shorter the wavelength is, the "colder" the color is, otherwise the "warmer" the color is. Generally, people can see the color whose wavelength between 360 nm and 760 nm. While the white light is a mixture of these colors. Therefore, it is the basic principle of all things in nature showing the color, that objects absorb some wavelengths when the sun shines on them, and remained wavelengths are reflected into eyes, which make people see the color of the object.

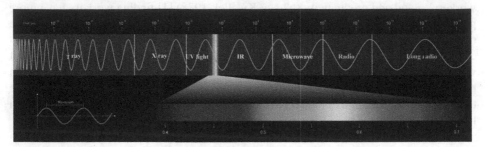

Fig. 1. The wavelength of the visible light

Based on the principle producing two mechanisms of showing color. One is the chemical color, such as the carrot, paint, etc. The other is the shown color presented by the microstructures of the materials, which called the structural color [7]. The basic principle is the interference effect that the light refracted and reflected repeatedly in the microstructure of the material surface when white lights shine on the object, and last reflected light waves superpose to form waves of greater or lower (greater waves are bright and lower waves are darker), then eyes capture waves of greater at a certain angle. The figure below represents the interference effect at the film of soap bubbles (Fig. 2). Color is influenced by the surface microstructure of materials, refractive index, light incidence Angle, viewing Angle and other factors, resulting in these materials are usually colored.

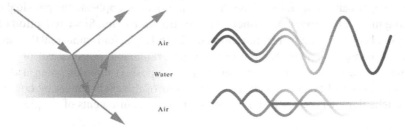

Fig. 2. The principle of the structural-color at films of soap bubbles.

These materials widely exist in nature, such as morpho butterfly scales [8] and peacock feathers [9]. The structural color can maintain the vivid color long time, and no oxidation to fade compared to the chemical color. These shown colors are bright outdoors due to the reflection of sunlight. And no uncomfortable feeling for eyes. These advantages are obvious when compared with artificial light.

2.2 Digital-Twin

With the development of the manufacturing process, laser films are widely applied to commercial design, art, and exhibition, which are produced according to the basic principle of structural color and holographic laser technology. In the research of ColorFolds (Jenny Sabin, 2016) [10], the film is applied to design as color-changing means, but the emphasis in the research is application to kirigami art (a type of origami means). The focus of this paper is to study and practice the characteristics of laser films.

Observing a laser film, there are many different colors since the angles of the viewing ray and normal of fragments of the film are different. Then testing a small square laser film (side length = 1mm), recording the rotation angle and color. The first test was recorded every 10° from 0° to 180°. The color of the film changes along with the angle of rotation, but the result is irregular since the angle too large result of the changing of color is not continuous. After repeated attempts, the color has a better gradient effect when recording per 2° in 40°. The colors are changed from red to purple, then the loop continues (Fig. 3).

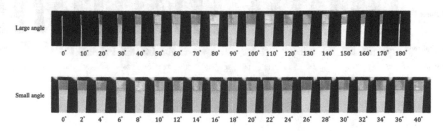

Fig. 3. The relationship between rotation angle and color

Therefore, Rhino and Grasshopper are used to design the computer program according to the law in the research. The basic process is that settings of viewports and recording the camera position, construction of a color-changing unit square (side length = 1) and recording the position and the normal, calculation of unit vector from the square position to camera position, calculation of angle values between square normal and unit vector. Calculation of color values by converting angle values, finally showing the color at the unit square. Then simulation of real color-changing effects by adjusting parameter. The whole process forms a digital-twin.

The core principle is calculation of viewing angle from the shader diffuse reflection algorithm [11], the expression is (1):

$$A = arcos\left(\frac{V - F}{|V - F|} \cdot N\right) \tag{1}$$

A is the value of the angle between the unit vector from the fragment position to the camera position and the fragment normal. V is the camera position. F is the position of the center of unit fragment. N is the fragment normal.

Calculation of every fragment color by angle values that are calculated by the dot product of two vectors, which can fit real color-changing effects of laser film. The color is composed of hue, purity, and lightness, and the range of these three parameters are from 0 to 1. The main computer program is shown in the figure below (Fig. 4), and it can be found that the calculated colors basically have good fitting effects (Fig. 5).

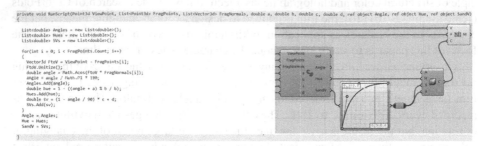

```
private void RunScript(Point3d ViewPoint, List<Point3d> FragPoints, List<Vector3d> FragNormals, double a, double b, double c, double d, ref object Angle, ref object Hue, ref object SandV)
{
    List<double> Angles = new List<double>();
    List<double> Hues = new List<double>();
    List<double> SVs = new List<double>();

    for(int i = 0; i < FragPoints.Count; i++)
    {
        Vector3d FtoV = ViewPoint - FragPoints[i];
        FtoV.Unitize();
        double angle = Math.Acos(FtoV * FragNormals[i]);
        angle = angle / Math.PI * 180;
        Angles.Add(angle);
        double hue = 1 - ((angle + a) % b / b);
        Hues.Add(hue);
        double sv = (1 - angle / 90) * c + d;
        SVs.Add(sv);
    }
    Angle = Angles;
    Hue = Hues;
    SandV = SVs;
}
```

Fig. 4. The C# script and the program of constructing color.

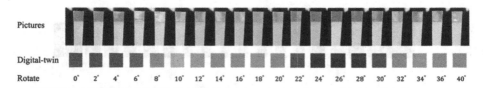

Pictures

Digital-twin

Rotate   0°   2°   4°   6°   8°   10° 12° 14° 16° 18° 20° 22° 24° 26° 28° 30° 32° 34° 36° 40°

Fig. 5. The fit between calculating color and the color of pictures.

2.3 Structural Design

As long as the rotation Angle of each unit is well controlled, color changes and uniform pattern generation can be achieved. Then, the hexagonal grid is used as the structure of the unit array since it is more denser compared to rectangle and triangle grid in the same space (Fig. 6), so the overall color is more integrated. As for the control of every unit, using the Arduino open-source hardware as control modules of the device, and controlling rotating angles by using servo. Therefore, the servo can be designed parameterized according to the real dimensions to generate the adapt assembly structure.

2.4 Fabrication and Test

Producing the designed parts through 3D printing technology (SLA) and assembly. Then, controlling the device by computer programs can change color and pattern generation (Fig. 7).

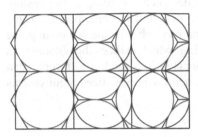
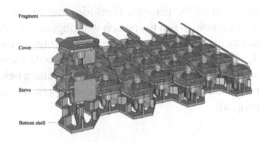

Fig. 6. The comparison of two structures that hexagonal grids and rectangular grids. Red circles represent spatial density of hexagonal grids, blue circles represent spatial density of rectangular grids. Hexagonal grids can contain more circles per unit area from the figure (Color figure online).

Fig. 7. 3D-print, fabrication and prototype test: the color is control by computer programs in real-time.

2.5 Behavior Recognition

It is a foundation of further research through the prototype test that change parameters in computer programs to change colors of the programmable device. Therefore, the data acquisition modules added can realize the function of the human-computer interaction by obtaining external data in real-time. In this paper, the Kinect motion capture device is used to capture the human postures in real-time, then the Grasshopper-based plug-in, firefly is used to obtain the Kinect data, and the data is converted into angle parameters through the program, which control the color of the programmable device. In this research, the human behavior is divided into two states, one is working state and the other is resting state. Then, summarizing the person's posture in these two states respectively. First, the human body is represented by some simple line segments. Then analyzing the corresponding actions of people in the two states. It can be found that people's postures are relatively consistent in the working state, while people have a variety of postures in the resting state (in this study the judgment is based on the relative distance between the head and the wrist of the person). Therefore, the program is designed according to the posture information. When the person working, the program will output the corresponding value to change to the color suitable for working, on the contrary, when the person resting, the device can be changed to the color suitable for resting, which realizes the autonomous adjustment to interior environment by human behavior (Fig. 8). In addition, the color can be customized according to the user's preferences to achieve personalized requirements (Fig. 9).

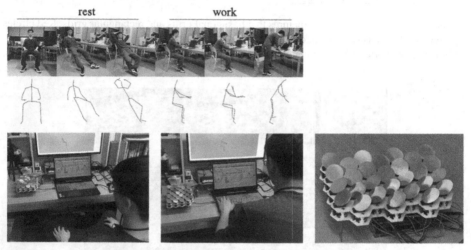

Fig. 8. Interaction of human with the Color-interactive device. Showing red when working, and showing blue when resting (Color figure online)

3   Expectation and Discussion

3.1   Application Prospect

Using this device by this principle, we can design building facades or big walls to inter-action with people. So, the new wall has the interactive function of showing the special color and pattern, which is a new interesting way of showing information distinguishing from digital electronic screen. it is suitable for use during the day or in strong light. And if each color-changing unit uses the self-adapt materials as control drive, such as accord-ing to temperature or humidity control the wall, this will become a good energy-saving design application. In addition, based on this research and prototyping, the device can be mass-produced and used for a variety of purposes, such as for interior spaces, art advertising board in public space and building facades, etc. Those can change the color according to different user behaviors. In general, it can serve specific needs by collecting specific data to realize the interaction between colors and people.

Fig. 9. Interactive device.

3.2 Future Research Directions

In nature world, the skin color of many organisms is the structural color. Scientists through these natural materials have developed many color-changing materials based on structural colors, and can change their colors by physical approaches such as the force, temperature, light, electronic and magnetic, etc. At present, these physical approaches are widely used in the field of smart wearables to realize the intelligence of wearable devices, such as (Irmandy Wicaksono, 2020) [12]. With the in-depth research on smart materials, color-changing materials based on the principle of structural colors can realize more convenient and accurate color control through these physical approaches and computer programs, which have the function by programs control to colors and patterns when applied to intelligent wearable devices. Therefore, the study and application of intelligent color-changing materials will be a direction with great development potential in field of the intelligent materials.

In the other hand, this research and design workflow is different from general design workflow that focus to the user research. The general design research indeed has more advantages to focus to good and suitable functions or goals for special users, but generally this belongs to a certain application research. However, the purpose of this article wants to discuss the design foundation problems and design potency through the whole product development process example. In this process, the research shows a new design mode from the principle to application by integration of cross-disciplines, which is a new cross-disciplinary way of integration of the principles research and design thinking. This process can bring about new experiences and provide a new possibility of interactive art and HCI [13]. So, the core points are below the follows:

A. The principles research to initial objects.
B. Discussing and predicting the design applications according to the principles.
C. Converting design goals to details of technology implementation.

The A process focus to finding inspiration from natural objects. This is the foundation of innovation and finding new experiences. The B process is the core importance to design, which is the process of divergent thinking, as a design thinking. The goal will have distinction according to different design requirements. The C process is the key point of realizing design goals by technique details. This process needs suitable connection of design goals and details of technology implementation. In conclusion, the research provides a new deeper collaborative way of design and technology, and the research mode belongs to the point-to-surface mode (Fig. 10).

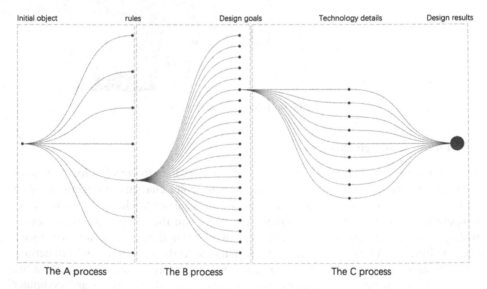

Fig. 10. The research mode.

4 Summary

This research attempt to connect microstructures of materials and macro performance by programmable technology. From principles to design application, it is a practice of using design thinking to realize design innovation in longitudinal research. Compared with artificial light, this physical color-changing material has good display effect and real color in outdoor or strong light environment. In conclusion, this research is about the application of design under the theory of the impact of color on human psychology. Combining intelligent data recognition and program control technologies, this research is also an exploration of adaptive and sustainable intelligent design.

References

1. Kwallek, N., Lewis, C.M., Robbins, A.S.: Effects of office interior color on workers' mood and productivity. Percept. Mot. Skills **66**(1), 123–128 (1988)
2. Ainsworth, R.A., Simpson, L., Cassell, D.: Effects of three colors in an office interior on mood and performance. Percept. Mot. Skills **76**(1), 235–241 (1993)
3. Kwallek, N., Woodson, H., Lewis, C.M., Sales, C.: Impact of three interior color schemes on worker mood and performance relative to individual environmental sensitivity. Color Res. Appl. **22**, 121–132 (1997)
4. Kurt, S., Osueke, K.K.: The Effects of Color on the Moods of College Students. SAGE Open (2014)
5. Manav, B.: Color-emotion associations, designing color schemes for urban environment-architectural settings. Color. Res. Appl. **42**(5), 631–640 (2017)
6. Costa, M., Frumento, S., Nese, M., Predieri, I.: Interior color and psychological functioning in a university residence hall. Front. Psychol. **9**, 1580 (2018)
7. Starkey, T., Vukusic, P.: Light manipulation principles in biological photonic systems. Nanophotonics. **2**(4), 289–307 (2013)
8. Kinoshita, S., Yoshioka, S., Kawagoe, K.: Mechanisms of structural colour in the Morpho butterfly: cooperation of regularity and irregularity in an iridescent scale. Proc. R. Soc. London. Ser. B. Biol. Sci. **269**(1499), 1417–1421 (2002)
9. Zi, J., et al.: Coloration strategies in peacock feathers. Proc. Natl. Acad. Sci. **100**(22), 12576–12578 (2003)
10. Sabin, J.E., Miller, M., Cellucci, D., Moorman, A.: ColorFolds: eSkin+ Kirigami-From Cell Contractility to Sensing Materials to Adaptive Foldable Architecture (2016)
11. Bishop, G., Weimer, D.M.: Fast phong shading. ACM SIGGRAPH Comput. Graph. **20**(4), 103–106 (1986)
12. Wicaksono, I., et al.: A tailored, electronic textile conformable suit for large-scale spatiotemporal physiological sensing in vivo. NPJ Flexib. Electron. **4**(1), 1–13 (2020)
13. Jeon, M., Fiebrink, R., Edmonds, E.A., Herath, D.: From rituals to magic: interactive art and HCI of the past, present, and future. Int. J. Hum Comput Stud. **131**, 108–119 (2019)

Research on Innovation and Development of Chinese Traditional Textile Technology Duntou Blue Based on Design

Jun Zhang[✉]

Beijing Technology Institute, Zhuhai, 519088 Zhuhai, China
81901765@qq.com

Abstract. Duntou Blue is produced in Heyuan, Guangdong Province, China. Hakka traditional hand weaving, dyeing and weaving techniques. It began in the mid-16th century and declined in the 1990s. Qualitative research methods such as field investigation, in-depth interview, questionnaire, case study and visual analysis were adopted. In-depth understanding of the Duntou Blue dyeing and weaving skills information. Starting from the historical development of Duntou Blue traditional handicraft, this paper combs the technological process and summarizes the technological characteristics. Visit the inheritor to learn about the current situation. Questionnaire method was used to obtain people's understanding and understanding of Duntou Blue, as well as reasonable development suggestions. The purpose is to study the economic value and cultural value of Duntou Blue. Explore the innovative design method of pier blue. This paper points out that design is an important means of cultural innovation and industrial development of Duntou Blue textile technology. Design innovative industrial chain strategy supported by consumption. Design Duntou Blue brand, make systematic formulation and layout of brand strategy, and promote the formation of the whole protection system. Design elements should be combined with the trend of The Times, in line with people's aesthetic. The design should not only respect the inherent law of Duntou Blue inheritance and development, but also be based on the reality of the development of Duntou Blue.

Keywords: Duntou Blue · Textile technology · Artistic characteristics · Innovation and development · Brand image design · Product design · Promotion design

1 Introduction

With the accelerated process of industry and urbanization. With the popularization of modern textile technology, traditional manual production has been abandoned. Young people are reluctant to engage in this traditional craft, which is on the verge of extinction. Research on Duntou Blue Hakka textile technology is very scarce in academic research and product market development. It is urgent to inherit and innovate Duntou Blue textile and dyeing technology. To this end, I will lead the student team to participate in the

© Springer Nature Switzerland AG 2022
V. G. Duffy and P.-L. P. Rau (Eds.): HCII 2022, LNCS 13522, pp. 552–563, 2022.
https://doi.org/10.1007/978-3-031-21704-3_39

"Innovation and Entrepreneurship Training Program for College Students" in 2020. The project aims at protecting and innovating the intangible cultural heritage of Duntou Blue. Duntou Blue is in urgent need of protection. The project investigated the status quo of Duntou Blue textile technology. Understand the technical characteristics and artistic characteristics of Duntou Blue textile technology. Study the economic value and cultural value behind Duntou Blue. Based on the practice of Duntou Blue brand visual image design, brand promotion and product development design are carried out. Expand product path, let Duntou Blue innovative products into life, extend the industrial chain of its products. Research product patterns that conform to the current aesthetic. In the Internet era, digital media technology is borrowed and diversified promotion methods are used to carry out online publicity. Information visualization design plays a role in the education and training of Duntou Blue skill inheritance. Deeply understand the cultural characteristics of Duntou Village in Heyuan and develop the regional culture of Duntou village. To protect intangible cultural heritage and promote rural development. Using design methods to complete the development of Duntou Blue traditional textile technology innovation strategy.

2   Status Quo of Duntou Blue Textile Technology

2.1   The History of Duntou Blue

Duntou Blue has a long history and has experienced more than 400 years of development. Combined with the local natural conditions, the formation of a unique textile and dyeing system. Duntou Blue is a kind of unique blue fabric produced by Hakka people by self-spinning, self-weaving, self-dyeing and self-spinning using cotton, linen and other raw materials cultivated at home. It is named Duntou Blue because of its origin. At one time, this textile technique was so popular that every family grew cotton textiles. Duntou Blue finished fabric has the advantages of strong and wear-resistant, crisp and smooth feel, simple and refreshing style, high color fastness, mostly plain color. It has a wide range of uses and is a must in Hakka's daily life, including: head cloth, Hakka embroidered hat, embroidered shoes, clothes, trousers, mosquito net, quilt, quilt cover, cloak, shoes, socks, suspenders, handkerchief, towel, tablecloth, tea bag, tofu bag, etc. [1]. Cloth art is also used in painting and calligraphy mounting, book binding. High quality products are exported to Guangzhou, Dongguan, Huizhou and other places in the Pearl River Delta. In Fujian, Jiangxi, Hunan and other provinces have sales. See Fig. 1.

Fig. 1. Duntou Blue traditional products.

2.2 Duntou Blue Status Quo

Today, the status quo of Duntou Blue traditional textile technology is not optimistic, and gradually withdraw from People's Daily life. By 2021, there are less than 10 craftsmen, most of whom are old. This makes the inheritance of this skill more serious, facing the embarrassing situation of no successor [2]. The fundamental reason for the decline of Duntou Blue from prosperity is: the production mode has changed. First of all, machines take the place of manual work, which increases productivity. However, Duntou Blue textile, which relies on pure manual work, has many processes, from planting cotton to weaving cloth, which consumes long time cycle, high cost, but low economic benefit. Second, modern chemical dyes, which are easy to color and fix, replace traditional vegetable dyes. Finally, more and more practitioners choose to abandon this traditional skill and find new ways to make a living. See Fig. 2.

Fig. 2. Duntou Blue textile site.

Of course, the change of people's aesthetic consciousness is also the reason for the decline of Duntou Blue. Duntou Blue takes blue as the basic tone, the fabric is simple, the pattern is rich and all has the good meaning, was once the industrious and simple Hakka people's favorite product. However, with the development of The Times, people have different pursuit of beauty. Duntou Blue can't provide colorful, ornate and unique clothing. Gradually lost consumer groups.

At present, in order to change this situation, innovation mode is also being explored, but the effect is not good. The main reasons are backward production technology, product development lag behind, single product type. The products are mainly made of soil woven fabric and tourist souvenirs produced in small batches. The designs and patterns are more traditional. Without brand support, cultural value and artistic value are out of touch with modern society. Secondly, the inheritance and protection of intangible cultural heritage lacks systematic management. In 2015, Duntou Blue textile technology was rated as intangible cultural heritage of Guangdong Province [3]. But only individual organizations are making efforts to protect Duntou Blue. Duntou Blue want more long-term development, but also need to establish a reasonable innovation mechanism.

3 Characteristics of Duntou Blue Textile Technology

Visit intangible cultural heritage inheritor Mr. Chunlei Zeng in Duntou Village. Based on the existing fabric remains and restored fabric. It is understood that the weaving technology of Duntou Blue is very complicated, and it is woven by crossing warp and weft. The textile process consists of five steps: spinning, tilling, weaving, dyeing and chuai (flattening) [4]. There are nearly thirty processes. In Duntou village, the master of this textile skill is mainly male, in the form of workshops. Because skills are taught only to men. Only local villagers are allowed to study.

3.1 Rigorous Process of Textile Technology

From a cotton thread woven into a piece of cloth, and then dyed into the Duntou Blue. To go through the first link - spinning. Refers to the process from growing cotton to spinning cotton yarn, making yarn and preliminary processing of textile materials. It involves the process of cooking pulp, sizing yarn, drying yarn and playing yarn tube. The second link - ploughing. It is the process of yarn finishing and yarn preparation before machine. It involves the process of tilling yarn, reeding, carding cloth, loading machine and wearing heald. The third link - weaving. It refers to the process of weaving the yarn through the heald, the machine, the cloth and the fabric. According to the different color of the fabric, weaving is done by dyeing before weaving or weaving before dyeing [5]. The fourth link - dye. It involves picking green leaves, soaking, natural fermentation, adding lime, condensation precipitation, blue and other processes to produce blue dye. The last link - flattening. It is the process of finishing the blue fabric later. It is mainly through the roller press to make the fabric smooth, while adjusting the skewed weft line. See Fig. 3.

Fig. 3. Rigorous process of textile technology

3.2 Textile Equipment

According to the large-scale weaving instruments preserved. It is found that each process is assisted by corresponding instruments. And form a complete weaving system. The weaving process has standardization requirements. In order to improve the weaving efficiency, the instrument design is ergonomic. For example, in the process of spinning, ergonomic warping frame, warp frame, bedroom spinning wheel is used [6]. At the same time, in order to avoid mistakes in the weaving process, it is necessary to concentrate on the operation of limbs and body.

3.3 Natural Weaving and Dyeing Raw Materials

Chinese folk cloth art mostly relies on local ecological environment and local materials. Adept at dyeing with vegetable and mineral dyes. Plant dyes are extracted from natural plants and have the characteristics of environmental protection and green. At the same time also has certain antibacterial, mildew effect. Heyuan area is rich in plant resources, which provides diversified dyeing materials for Duntou Blue [7]. Common dyes come from locally grown or wild plants such as blue, suzuki, and madder. Due to the diversity of materials, Duntou Blue has a distinctive blue and fabric look.

After soaking, natural fermentation, adding a certain proportion of lime, finally condensed into indigo. Soak the cotton cloth in indigo dye and place it under the sun. The indigo dye on the cotton cloth is fully oxidized in contact with the air, and the original green dye liquid on the cotton cloth is rapidly transformed into blue. It is dried to form an indigo-blue color that is not easy to fade. The cotton cloth color after dyeing is simple, quality of a material is soft, safe and durable, natural environmental protection.

3.4 Plant Color System

Duntou Blue although named blue, but the color of blue department, red department, brown department. It is Duntou Blue, Duntou Brown, Duntou Red as the main color of plant dyed fabrics collectively. The dyeing material used for blue fabric is horse blue. After soaking, fermenting and adding a certain proportion of lime, fresh marlin is condensed into indigo, and then the yarn or fabric is dyed. Different dyeing times have dark blue, blue, light blue. Red fabric is made of madder heated extract juice and dyed, with deep red, bright red, pink and other colors. The dyed material that brown fastens fabrics to use has yam, mineral and so on dye and become [8]. Duntou Blue fabric overall color is mainly blue, red, brown department auxiliary embellishment color. Presents the beauty of natural and fresh color, with the color system of local characteristics. See Fig. 4.

Fig. 4. Folium isatidis, Duntou Blue, Duntou Brown, Duntou Red.

3.5 The Geometry of the Pattern

Influenced by traditional Chinese culture, Hakka people pay much attention to the aesthetic effect of costume patterns. Current analysis of existing fabrics. The pattern is closely related to weaving and dyeing. Duntou Blue fabric pattern in addition to plain dyed fabrics. With the development of dyeing after weaving technology. A series of geometric patterns were created using blue, white and red yarn. The fabric presents a simple and harmonious artistic feature [9]. Composition is based on the combination of straight lines, rectangles and squares to form geometric patterns. Geometric fabric has long flowing water cloth, well orchid cloth, sesame cloth. See Fig. 5.

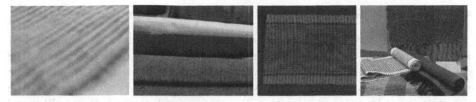

Fig. 5. Long flowing water cloth, well orchid cloth, sesame cloth.

The fabric of long flowing water cloth takes weft line as direction in the weaving process. The grain is like a stream, so it is named long flowing flowered cloth. The pattern is mainly fine stripe, the warp is white cotton thread or blue cotton thread, and the weft is distributed by 4 blue and 4 white intervals. The width of the finished product is about 52 cm. Well orchid fabric is thick and thin lines intersect to form a cross shape. Found from the existing pier head blue fabric, well orchid cloth is divided into coarse grid and fine grid two kinds. Using the method of dyeing after weaving, uniform texture. Chinese people like to use odd numbers as the ratio. The number of striped longitude and latitude lines is repeated in singular numbers. It has its own unique rhythm and rhythm, reflecting the artistic beauty after the pattern proportion and balance. Sesame cloth is blue warp, white weft, two color single yarn interwoven plain fabric. Each batch of yarn finish, thickness are subtle differences, fabric texture shows different natural texture, or fine, or coarse.

4 Design Duntou Blue Innovative Development Ideas

4.1 Research on Design Direction

In order to obtain the innovative design direction of Duntou Blue. In the early stage, literature and materials were collected and sorted out to deeply understand the history of Duntou Blue. At the same time, by the way of field investigation to understand the characteristics of textile technology, weaving tools. Visit the skill inheritor. Field investigation of textile technology development status, and the product derivatives have done detailed and careful analysis and research. In the later stage, questionnaires were issued on social platforms to collect people's understanding of Duntou Blue and suggestions for its future development [10]. The process is divided into three parts: part one, question setting and preparation. On the basis of determining the research theme, the relevant information of Duntou Blue culture was collected and analyzed in a large range. Several important keywords are analyzed and extracted: "awareness, Hakka, intangible cultural heritage culture, innovation and development". Set the question from these keywords. The second part, questionnaire delivery and collection. Fill in the questionnaire as Hakka and non-Hakka. Better understand how different people think about it. The third part analyzes the data. Analyze and review the collected 400 questionnaires, make statistics on data sources and answer division, conduct multi-dimensional analysis and discussion, and provide effective information for later program formulation.

4.2   Duntou Blue Textile Technology Innovation Design Direction

Through research, we can see a clear core context. How to save this intangible heritage? It's not simply copying; it's not simply developing lots of derivative designs. The economic value and cultural value of Duntou Blue should be studied [10]. Formulate systematic innovation strategies in line with market rules and product positioning. The use of design techniques and innovative ideas to do a combination of Duntou Blue and modern trends. Extract the cultural connotation and design elements in line with this era. Integrate tradition with the sense of The Times to create a chain of innovative industries supported by consumption.

4.3   Duntou Blue Brand Image Design

Market demand for brand building. Duntou Village has rich historical and cultural resources. The local villagers and the few artisans cherish and love this skill. I also hope that Duntou Blue can be passed on. At the same time, Duntou Blue inheritance and innovation. Promote the cultural development of Duntou Village through brand design. The innovation of Duntou Blue brand culture is centered on young literature and art, quiet and elegant, traceability and innovation, and protection of intangible cultural heritage. Brand building should be considered in all directions. We should combine the cultural background of Duntou Village in Heyuan. Drive the development of rural areas and form villages with cultural characteristics [11].

In the brand image design, the blue tone of Duntou Blue is adopted. In line with the spiritual needs of urban people homesickness. Meanwhile, regional cultural elements are extracted. Use design language for innovative design. Form a new aesthetic visual image in line with The Times. Based on the above factors, a brand image design named "Shike" was designed. Promote brand, enrich brand culture connotation. Expand market development value. (see Figs. 6 and 7).

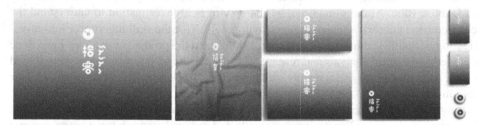

Fig. 6. Duntou Blue brand image design "Shike".

Fig. 7. Brand promotion application.

5 Industrial Design Development Paths

It is an important method to use design to intervene in cultural innovation and industrial development of Duntou Blue. Duntou Blue due to the green environmental protection, sustainable development and other characteristics back to the public vision. Based on the protection of intangible cultural heritage, restore Duntou Blue fabric technology [12]. After analyzing and summarizing the technological process and artistic performance characteristics. The design and development paths of Duntou Blue products are discussed from three aspects of technological innovation, product application and diversified promotion methods.

5.1 Innovation in Process Design

The core of Duntou Blue textile technology should be retained for its inheritance. The core technology of Duntou Blue is embodied in two aspects: improved weaving machine and set dyeing technology. From the perspective of technological innovation, the dyeing technology of Duntou Blue textile technology should be taken as the key development object. Because through special weaving and dyeing raw materials, the fabric dyed by plant color system has regional uniqueness. Developing cultural and creative product design based on dyeing is one of the ways to develop Duntou Blue product [13]. The weaving machine, influenced by modern machinery, has no advantage in the production process. See Fig. 8.

5.2 Cross - Boundary Design to Broaden the Scope of Product Application

Design and manufacture of derivative products to generate consumption chain. Combined with daily aesthetic and life consumption, attract people to consume, improve the influence and economic benefits of Duntou blue. In Duntou village to mobilize artisans engaged in this craft, attract more young people to learn this craft. Design intervention to broaden the scope of product application to solve the contradiction between Duntou Blue textile technology inheritance and economic development needs. In the design process to show the characteristics of the hand, the development of high-end hand series products. Combined with the characteristics of fabric art in home textiles, furniture soft decoration products, electronic products, tourism souvenirs and other fields, develop products [14]. Based on the market consumer groups, seeking more humanized design form, into modern life. See Fig. 9.

Fig. 8. Blue dye home textile design products by Yang Xiaoli, Gao Jie.

Fig. 9. Duntou Blue innovative product design by Du Wenfei.

For example, the use of Duntou Blue dyeing, combined with the local specialty plum tea, to develop cross-border packaging design. The design inspiration comes from the combination of plum garden tea culture and Duntou Blue culture. Consumers can not only touch the tea culture, but also feel Duntou Blue culture. Packaging design concept "green environmental protection as the premise, appearance combined with the regional characteristics of Duntou village." The structure of the package adopts the shaker box, and the architectural shape of the window is lined with dyed gradation [15]. The box body is mainly white, fresh and elegant. The inner box is mainly blue gradient, showing the dyeing and weaving process. Using dyeing changes as a starting point, blue is rooted in the product to form a unique color memory. In terms of design elements, the box extracts the typical buildings of Duntou village as the main graphics. Three pictures are combined to form a series of boxes for viewing. A blue gradient plum blossom pattern is enclosed in the inner box. On the top of the box, there is a famous quote about Duntou Blue. The number of products corresponds to the process of Duntou Blue dyeing and weaving technology. See Fig. 10.

Fig. 10. Duntou Blue crossover product design—Plum tea packaging design.

5.3 Design Diversity Promotion Methods

There are two ways to promote Duntou Blue textile technology: offline and online. Under the line of the Duntou Blue textile technology life. For the development of derivative products, we try our best to combine Duntou Blue with daily necessities, stationery, clothing, etc., to integrate into life and extend the industrial chain of its products. For example, the "Mini Version Duntou Blue Process Device" was developed to experience and promote textile skills. Let people understand the textile technology culture, enhance people's awareness of intangible cultural heritage protection. Combined with parent-child interactive education development of the "Chinese green leaves planting pot" toy [16]. Toys in the concept of advocating green natural pollution-free life. Inspire children's perception of vitality, exercise children's observation ability, hone their patience, and increase parent-child interaction between parents and children. Let more parents and children know Duntou Blue. Experience the time and patience aesthetics of Duntou Blue. To promote and develop the intangible heritage Duntou Blue culture.

Information visualization of Duntou Blue, combined with digital media, online propaganda, make the network become an important carrier of communication. Using information visualization design, the process of pier blue as the key diagram. Introduce the characteristics, inheritance, historical background, geographical location and representative buildings of Duntou Blue in turn. Let people further understand the Duntou Blue handicraft, rather than stay on the surface of the impression of blue dye [17]. See Fig. 11.

Holding "China · Duntou Blue Town Blue Festival" cultural display activities. Use cultural exhibitions to let people know about Duntou Village. Let Duntou Blue culture achieve sustainability. Let consumers feel the charm of Duntou blue culture, so that this handicraft more widely spread out. Thus, maintaining the spiritual memory and cultural heritage.

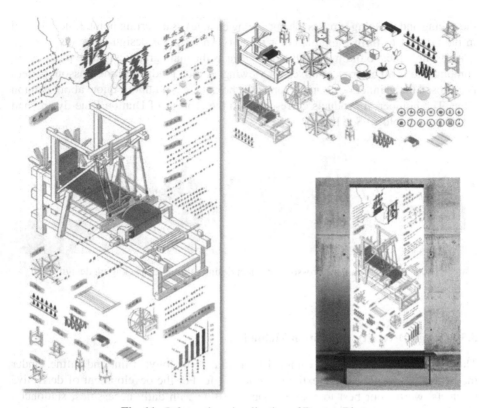

Fig. 11. Information visualization of Duntou Blue.

6   Conclusion

Duntou Blue textile technology has experienced more than 400 years of development, is the product of human civilization. Both practical and aesthetic. There is a textile system of excellence in craftsmanship. Local materials are used to form natural weaving and dyeing materials and unique plant color system. Aesthetically reflects the Chinese farming culture under the simple aesthetic thought, and human wisdom. At the same time, it is also an important product of local residents' economic development.

At present, people pursue the values of returning to the origin and craftsman spirit. Recognize the importance of protecting intangible cultural heritage. By analyzing and summarizing the technological process and artistic expression of textile technology. Study the economic value and cultural value of Duntou Blue. Design is involved in the cultural innovation and industrial development of Duntou Blue textile technology. From the process innovation, product application, brand image building, design diversity promotion. To develop a systematic innovation strategy in line with market rules. Using design techniques and innovative thinking, the traditional textile technology and the modern trend to do a combination. Extract the cultural connotation and design elements in line with this era. Integrate tradition with The Times to create a chain of innovative industries supported by consumption.

References

1. Guangdong Cultural Center. Skills-Duntou Blue textile skills. https://www.gdsqyg.com/agd fyzg/mingluinfo/mlproid=2018040410267538. Accessed 10 July 2020
2. Xiuli, H.: Structural characteristics and process analysis of Hakka "Duntou Blue" traditional clothing in Heyuan area. J. China. J. Fashion. **16**(4), 5 (2019)
3. Feng, Z.: "Duntou Blue" Hakka clothing cultural inheritance and innovation. J. Western Leather. **20**(4), 63–66 (2016)
4. Hai, H., Yang, H., Lan, C.: Investigation and practice of traditional crafts in cross-cultural context. J. Art Des. **57**(11), 137–139 (2015)
5. YanRen, S.: Annals of Heyuan County. Zhongzhou Ancient Books Publishing House, Zhongzhou (2017)
6. Zhigan, C.: Ntangible Cultural Heritage of Heyuan. China Literature and History Press, Beijing (2010)
7. Guiyuan, L.: On The Pattern Art of Lei Guiyuan. Shanghai Culture Press, Shanghai (2016)
8. Daoyi, Z.: On Auspicious Culture. Chongqing University Press, Chongqing (2011)
9. Yueqi, W.: Research on the design of Lingnan plant dyeing products. J. Pack. Eng. **37**(16), 39–43 (2016)
10. Wei, W.: Overview of the historical development of Chinese traditional dyeing of plants and trees. J. Sichuan Silk. **22**(3), 52–54 (2007)
11. Johnson, M.: Brand Design Book. Shanghai People's Fine Arts Publishing House, Shanghai (2020)
12. Bingnan, W.: Packaging Design. Cultural Development Publishing, Beijing (2016)
13. Xiaoqin, L., Liwen, W.: The inheritance dilemma of "Duntou Blue" in Heping county, Guangdong province. J. Jiamusi Voc. College. **27**(12), 49–50 (2017)
14. Sun, H.: Industry Interpretation of "Seeing People, Seeing Things, Seeing Life". Beijing China Textile Intangible Cultural Heritage Development Report, Beijing (2019)
15. Jinrong, X.: Innovative research of Duntou Blue in modern home design and soft decoration. J. Forest Prod. Ind. **57**(11), 60–64 (2020)
16. Yu, A.: Innovation, Integration and Practice of Cultural and Creative Industry. Beijing United Publishing Company, Beijing (2020)
17. Guanzhong, L.: The designer coordinator must take into account the interests of all parties. J. Des. **32**(2), 67–68 (2019)

How Can Design Help Improving Products During the Pandemic

Lu Zhang[3], Fei Yue[1,2(✉)], Qianhang Qin[3], and Yun Liang[3]

[1] School of Future Design, Beijing Normal University, Beijing 100091, China
fffei.yue@gmail.com
[2] Art and Design Academy, Tsinghua University, Beijing 100030, China
[3] GXNU School of Design, Guangxi Normal University, Guilin 541000, China

Abstract. The new crown pneumonia epidemic (COVID-19) has been a global pandemic for more than two years since the outbreak began in late 2019, with far-reaching effects on people's social lives as well as their mental health. At present, science and technology, bioengineering, materials and other disciplines have been integrated into protective materials, medical equipment and other items just needed for the epidemic from many aspects, but there are still not enough humane, direct technical interventions lack of human fit, not able to meet the user's sense of experience, etc., and design has the advantage of technical integration and system integration, which can assist in quickly and efficiently providing effective epidemic-related products, environments, and services solutions. This paper first analyzes and summarizes the transmission pathway and infection process of the new coronavirus, and divides the pre- and mid-epidemic period according to the data, and analyzes the design of protection and disinfection category in the pre-epidemic period, the design of treatment-related category in the mid-epidemic period, and the design of psychological healing category in the post-epidemic period. The purpose of this paper is to systematically review and analyze design research results related to the new crown epidemic at home and abroad, and then explore how design can better provide new solutions to the problems caused by the epidemic.

Keywords: Crown epidemic · Epidemic design · Intelligent technology · Humanization · Interdisciplinary

1 Overview of the Background of the New Crown Epidemic

Since the beginning of 2019, pneumonia caused by the new coronavirus (COVID-19) has been raging worldwide for more than two years, causing a cumulative total of more than 300 million infections and more than 5.5 million deaths worldwide [1]. This epidemic has severely disrupted social production and people's lives, resulting in serious threats to people's lives and safety. The global spread of the new crown epidemic has plunged countries around the world into a serious public health crisis, manifested by the unavailability of treatment technologies and drugs, the shortage of medical resources

© Springer Nature Switzerland AG 2022
V. G. Duffy and P.-L. P. Rau (Eds.): HCII 2022, LNCS 13522, pp. 564–584, 2022.
https://doi.org/10.1007/978-3-031-21704-3_40

and services, the failure of public health early warning systems, the delay in social isolation measures [2], and people's mental health problems, among others. The process
by which a new coronavirus invades the body and leads to new coronavirus pneumonia
is as follows: the virus first enters the cell and initiates a new coronavirus infection by
fusing with the associated cell membrane, (Fig. 1) which also leads to acute respiratory
distress syndrome due to increased inflammation during critical stages of disease progression in neo-coronavirus pneumonia. Initial infection of the upper respiratory cells
may be asymptomatic, but these patients can still transmit the virus. For those who
develop symptoms, up to 90% will develop pneumonia, which is caused by infection of
the lower respiratory cells [3]. More than two years into the epidemic, there is growing
evidence that New Crown is not just a respiratory disease, but affects multiple tissues
and organs in the body. For example, it causes loss of smell and taste, fatigue, cognitive
decline, and in some more severe cases, more serious symptoms such as stroke and
impaired consciousness, all of which are known as post-Neo-Con sequelae [4].

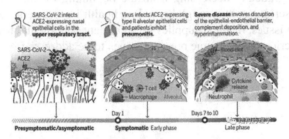

Fig. 1. SARS-CoV-2 invasion process in humans Image credits. (https://www.science.org/).

As a respiratory infection, the novel coronavirus is transmitted in three main ways:
droplet transmission, contact transmission, and aerosol transmission (Fig. 2). Droplet
transmission refers to infection caused by droplets produced by patients through sneez-
ing, coughing, talking and breathing, which are inhaled into the respiratory tract by
susceptible individuals or adhered to mucous membranes [5]. Contact transmission is
divided into direct contact transmission and indirect contact transmission. Direct contact refers to transmission caused by direct skin contact with the patient (e.g., shaking
hands); indirect contact transmission refers to transmission caused by a susceptible person through contact with environmental surfaces contaminated by the patient. Aerosol
transmission, also known as airborne transmission, is due to the fact that droplets with
SARS-Cov-2 exhaled by the patient have many small particle sizes, and when these
small particles evaporate if their radius is less than 5 μm, they can form tiny particles in
solid or liquid form and move with the airflow to long distances, thus causing aerosol
transmission [6].

For example, the global daily death toll of novel coronavirus 2020.1–2022.3 (Fig. 3)
indicates that the daily death toll stabilized at around 6000 from 2020.1–2020.10. While
the daily death toll peaked at 16900 (the highest) from 2020.11–2021.09, and the overall
daily death toll from 2020.10–2022.4 showed a decreasing trend. For example, the global
mortality rate and recovery rate of novel coronavirus from 2020.1–2022.3 (Fig. 4) shows

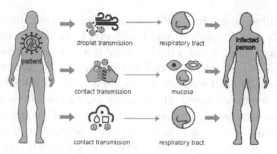

Fig. 2. Schematic diagram of SARS-CoV-2 transmission by droplet, contact and aerosol trans

that the mortality rate peaked at 42.27% in the initial period of 2020.1–2020.10, and then the mortality rate basically showed a decreasing trend to 1.41% until 2021.3. Based on the data in the above graphs, it can be concluded that the global daily death and mortality rates have been gradually decreasing from the beginning of 2020 to the present. In the face of this serious epidemic, global public health issues, personal protection and virus eradication issues, medical supplies for treatment, and mental health issues in the post-epidemic period have become pressing issues to be addressed.

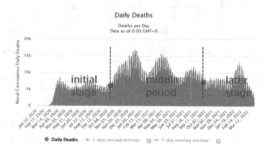

Fig. 3. Global daily death toll from new coronary pneumonia. (www.worldometers.info)

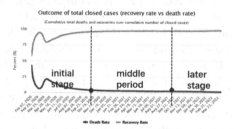

Fig. 4. Outcome of total closed cases (recovery rate vs death rate) (www.worldometers.info)

2   Citespace-Based Epidemic Design Study

2.1   Keyword Analysis Research Literature (Web of Science Database)

The high-frequency keywords for 2019–2022 are co-present (Fig. 5), where the larger keyword font represents the higher frequency of occurrence and the higher research heat. The most frequent keywords in the field of design related to the new crown epidemic are design, cellular cholesterol, molecular docking, and combinatorial effects. From this, we can see that design, biological science, medicine, big data, and applied statistics are all research hotspots among the epidemic, and the more keywords intersect on the graph, the more closely the keywords are connected, such as design and cellular cholesterol, molecular docking, and technical characteristics, etc. The overall picture shows multidisciplinary integration and becomes a cross-disciplinary research direction. Design, as a discipline characterized by technological integration and system integration, builds bridges to human fit on the basis of many scientific type disciplines.

Fig. 5. High-frequency keyword co-occurrence (web of science). (citespace)

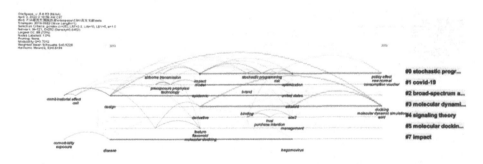

Fig. 6. Clustered words timeline (web of science). (citespace)

The analysis of clustered keywords as seen in Fig. 6, in which the keywords with high correlation are converged to form clustered words, and the larger the point on the chronological horizontal line, the higher the attention. It is divided into 8 groups of clustered words, and the new crown epidemic-related design appeared in 2019 until now, which has a smalltime span and presents a state of multidisciplinary cross-research integration during this period.

2.2   Keyword Analysis of Research Literature (CNKI Database)

The most frequently occurring keywords in the field of epidemic-related design were epidemic prevention and control, followed by level epidemic integration, healthy housing, design, ventilation systems, and retrofit design. This shows that during the New Crown epidemic, there are many connections between epidemic prevention and control and healthcare, architecture, services, and systems.

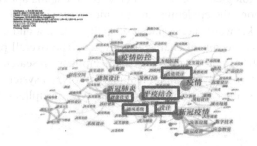

Fig. 7. High-frequency keyword co-occurrence (CNKI). (citespace)

The clustering keyword analysis is shown in Fig. 8, which is divided into seven groups of clustering words, namely, new crown epidemic, epidemic prevention and control, flat epidemic combination, new crown pneumonia, value, residential design, and healthy office building. In the early stage of the 2019 epidemic, "emergency supplies" and "epidemic prevention strategy" were the first hot spots, and in the middle and late stages, "artificial intelligence innovation design", "healthy housing" and "system design" are highly explored.

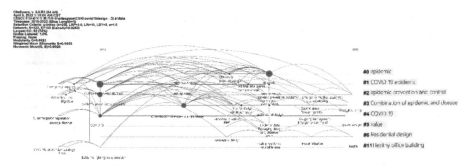

Fig. 8. Clustered word timeline (CNKI). (citespace)

The top 18 emergent keywords for 2019–2022 are shown in Fig. 9, from which the prominence of the keywords can be read, with higher prominence indicating greater influence of the keywords over time. 2019–2022 prominence of disaster waste, accounting queries, sewage treatment, new crown vaccine, air health, digital technology, green space effectiveness, intelligent transportation, HVAC, sensible engineering, and care management reached 1.06, these keywords are the series of problems generated by the epidemic and the solutions corresponding to them.

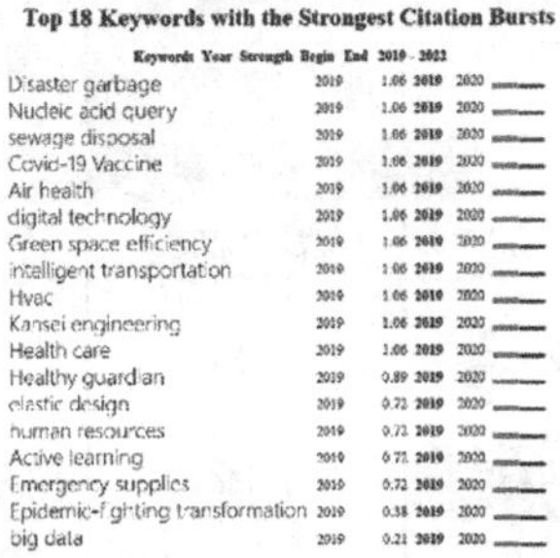

Fig. 9. Top 18 emergent keywords 2019–2022 (CNKI). (citespace)

April 2020 large-scale nucleic acid testing in China, the end of 2020, the world's first batch of new coronavirus vaccines developed by China approved for marketing, [7] March 2022 new coronavirus (2019-nCov) antigen detection kits released, [8] to meet people's self-testing needs, 2021 the emergence of healing landscape design and the combination of audio and warm stories and other forms of better healing of people's mental health.

Corresponding to this in the clustering words timeline (web of science and CNKI) (shown in Fig. 7/9) researchers in late 2019 early 2020, the research keywords made are around emergency supplies, epidemic prevention strategies. In 2020.10–2021.06, the research keywords made are modular square cabin, interior design ventilation system. In 2021.07–2022.4, the research keywords made are service design, emergency medical cloud monitoring, and system design.

From the above data analysis, we can conclude that the time period of pre-epidemic development is roughly 2020.1–2020.10, where people face unknown virus and can only strengthen information collection, sharing and prognosis, and at this stage people focus on protection and design mainly around sustainability and multifunctional design participation. In the middle of the epidemic development (outbreak period) time period roughly 2020.11–2021.09, the risk of accelerated spread of the epidemic to the whole country, people carry out strict prevention and control, with treatment and disinfection as the main focus, and design in this stage is mainly based on portability, modularity and simplicity. In the post-epidemic period, roughly 2021.10–2022.4, the epidemic situation tends to moderate, the public's mental health is not good, in this stage the design is mainly in the form of care and fun interactive forms of psychological healing for people (Fig. 10).

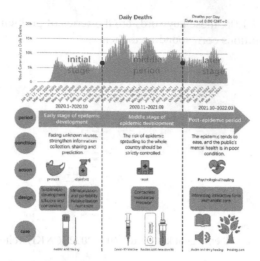

Fig. 10. Timeline image. (Self-drawn)

3   Pre-epidemic Development - Protection Class, Disinfection Class

On the basis of biological sciences and other disciplines providing technical services to solve the problems existing in epidemic prevention and control [9], design, as a non-technical means, supportively serves these technologies in a more humanized form for people and enhances the user's sense of friendly experience in using the products [10]. Whether we can carry out epidemic prevention design from a humanized perspective for epidemic prevention products and do a good job of humanized care for users will directly affect the epidemic prevention effect of epidemic prevention products and concern the efficiency of epidemic prevention war [11]. (Fig. 11) illustrates the relationship between human-machine-environment, where various problems arising from the epidemic affect people and lead to the demand for epidemic prevention products, and designers summarize the design direction and make design solutions that work for the epidemic environment. From [12], it is clear that design is a cyclical activity that begins with the generation of design concepts for people's behavioral needs, followed by design production and use, and then design iterations as people demand higher quality [13].

3.1   Type of Protection

The research and design of epidemic prevention and elimination products is a direct method and effective way to relieve public health stress, public environmental stress, and people's highly tense mental stress [14]. From a user-friendly perspective, design interventions as a non-medical tool better connect people and epidemic prevention products, and design provides diverse solutions from the human needs for epidemic prevention products [15]. For example, the general direction of protective masks is more comfortable, safer and more convenient [16]. The design needs to pay attention to the user's experience during the wearing process, which is the deeper demand of the people for the design at this stage of society, and the design of protective masks needs to analyze

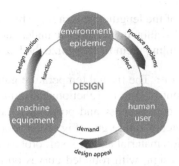

Fig. 11. Human-machine-environment relationship diagram (Self-drawn)

and study the users and the external objective environment, and even think about the social level in the production process of protective masks, and do its part in ecological environmental protection [17]. Next, we will analyze the design expressions of protective products from four aspects: user experience, technology application, application scenario, and design intervention.

Longevity Visualization Mask: AT the beginning of the epidemic, mask resources were extremely scarce and masks were often wasted. The "Lifetime Visualization Mask" (Fig. 13A) provides a solution to this problem by visualizing the lifespan of masks for the general public who often go out during the epidemic. The mask's breathing valve is equipped with a humidity paper that changes color to match the maximum humidity of the mask's meltblown fabric life, and changes from blue to pink when its life expectancy is reached. This design uses humidity sensitive color changing material in the mask to maximize the use of the mask and avoid wasting the mask or overusing it, thus saving the mask.

MH8 Disposable Thermometer: For people in quarantine, the MH8 thermometer with Bluetooth low-power technology (Fig. 13B) can monitor the user's body temperature for up to 14 days without interruption. The sensor can be fixed under the armpit with skin-friendly medical tape, and the data can be shared to a cloud server for data analysis through a gateway. LED lights indicate when the thermometer is on and when the battery is low, and the design is flat and soft to make it comfortable to wear.

Easy Pull Mask: The mask as a new medical mouth and eye integrated mask, (Fig. 13C) designed to focus on solving the problem of wearing cumbersome and protective loopholes of medical personnel. The mask is designed based on a new additive manufacturing idea without process restrictions, it can be formed in one piece, and the wearing process is simple and easy to use. At the same time, the future can be customized according to the facial characteristics of health care workers to do design, can greatly improve the mask on the face of the pressure.

Woobiplay Children's Masks: The mask (Fig. 13D) is made of translucent medical-grade silicone and can be reused for up to one month. The mask adopts a modular design with two large and small ports, respectively the outlet valve and intake valve, with a strap design for self-adjustment of the length, encouraging children and parents to assemble their own masks together, also allowing children to understand the structure and function of the product, and also enabling them to recognize the hazards of viral contamination.

Forehead Temperature Gun: The frontal temperature gun plays an important role in epidemic prevention and control with its functional advantages of non-contact infrared temperature measurement, compactness and portability, fast measurement speed and high accuracy. The frontal temperature gun (Fig. 13E) adopts medical grade mercury-free environmental protection material and new soft probe design. It adopts streamlined design style in modeling design, with rounded curves outlining the ergonomic form, simple human-machine operation interface, comfortable buttons, and easier and more comfortable one-handed operation, also with intelligent voice warning, which provides great convenience for temperature screening work.

From the above analysis, it is clear that among the protective products, mainly masks, masks, and measurement products, the design is mainly aimed at sustainability, efficiency and convenience, ease of use, and cognitive interest in such products, and assisted by the corresponding science and technology and biotechnology for design participation [18] (Fig. 12).

Product name	User Experience	technology application	Application scenario	Design intervention
Service life visualization mask	Visualize and save resources.	Concealment and display technology	public place	The respiratory valve and test paper are fixed at the proper position of the mask by structural design.
MH8 disposable thermometer	Skin sticking and intelligence	Bluetooth low power technology	Flexible scene	Make the shape flat and soft to make it comfortable to wear.
Easy pull mask	Convenience and safety	without	public place	With a new additive manufacturing idea, the design is not limited by the process and can be formed as a whole.
Woobi play Children's Mask	Cognition and interest	without	public place	Modular mask design needs hands-on assembly so that children can understand the structure and function.
Frontal warming gun	Fast and efficient	Infrared temperature measurement technology	Flexible scene	Streamline design is adopted to make the product conform to ergonomics.
Protection products				

The design is mainly aimed at sustainable development, high efficiency, convenience, ease of use and cognitive interest.

Fig. 12. Case study diagram of protection products. (Self-drawn).

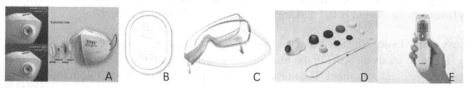

Fig. 13. Case of protection products. (A) Longevity visualization mask. (http://www.red-dot.cn/). (B) MH8 Disposable Thermometer. (http://www.red-dot.cn/). (C) Easy pull mask. (http://www.red-dot.cn/). (D) Woobiplay children's masks. (http://www.red-dot.cn/). (E) Forehead temperature gun. (BAIHU Industrial Design).

3.2 Type of Disinfection

Following the outbreak of a new coronavirus pneumonia outbreak in late 2019, the demand for disinfection products has increased dramatically [19]. With the diversified demand for disinfection forms, disinfection and purification and other epidemic prevention product designs continue to be updated and iterated, seeking to build a daily, accurate and humane way to prevent epidemics and maintain people's physical and mental health [20]. The next four aspects of disinfection product case design expressions will be analyzed in terms of user experience, technology application, application scenarios, and design interventions.

Disinfection Lamp: The disinfection lamp (Fig. 15 A) combines an ultraviolet light source with a tray for placing objects, and its specific use scenario is placed at the entrance of the user's home. Before the user enters the living room, he or she can subconsciously place cell phones, keys and other daily necessities in the tray, and press the cover to activate the ultraviolet light source. The hood will automatically pop open after 60 s of continuous disinfection. The design incorporates the user's subconscious habits into the disinfection process, making it more normalized and adding human-computer interaction to add interest.

Intelligent Disinfection and Cleaning Robot for Public Places: The cleaning and disinfection robot (Fig. 15B) disinfects surfaces of public transportation systems such as subways and buses, and guides passengers in and out of stations, avoiding the most crowded routes to prevent large gatherings of people. The smart disinfection robot is shaped with a modular design to optimize the layout of the multi-directional disinfection spray outlets, control interface, and walking wheels to meet the demand for a hygienic environment in public places.

Sterilization Stylus: The keepstick sterilization stylus (Fig. 15C) makes it easier for people to achieve sanitation and disinfection. It works like a stylus and enables users to perform daily activities without touching the surface of the object, such as pressing elevator buttons and using electronic touch screens. The built-in UVC light can sterilize contaminated surfaces and is also equipped with a plastic box into which users can place the small products to be sterilized. The styling of the sterilization stylus is designed with a simple pencil shape and cut-out details to give the user a comfortable grip and easy to carry on the go.

Intelligent Robot for Medical Waste Sterilization Treatment: At present, the garbage generated by treating new crown patients requires manual operation by staff, which poses a great threat to the life and health of staff. The medical waste disinfection treatment intelligent robot (Fig. 15 D) adopts unmanned transportation technology and systematically designs the robot workflow to realize medical waste collection-transportation-sealed disinfection-storage, avoiding direct contact with staff and protecting their personal safety. When the intelligent robot battery runs out, it automatically docks for wireless charging.

Big Eye Bubble Hand Washing Instrument: Children's groups lack awareness of hygiene and health, and washing hands adequately is a difficult task for children. The big eye bubble handwasher (Fig. 15E) is designed to solve the problem of children's inability to wash their hands properly, with the following highlights: timed handwashing, contact-free foam pickup, fun to use in multiple scenarios, and the ability to ensure that children wash their hands autonomously for 20 s before sterilization is achieved. The hand-washing instrument uses children's cognition and completion psychology to design the product, creating a broader imagination when children interact with the instrument.

From the above analysis, it can be seen that the design of disinfection products is primarily designed to engage with the specific disinfection methods in different scenarios[21], which can be broadly divided into public area disinfection products, home disinfection products, hand-held products on the go, and specific object disinfection products, with the design engaging in various scenarios from the perspective of small portability, integration into habits, humanization, fun, and systematization (Fig. 14).

Product name	User Experience	technology application	Application scenario	Design intervention
Disinfection lamp	Habit, interactive intelligence	Ultraviolet disinfection technology	Home use	The user's habits are skillfully designed to realize unconscious disinfection in the use process.
Intelligent disinfection and cleaning robot for public places	Peace of mind and intelligence	sensor technology	public place	Intelligent interactive interface design guides users to take the best route.
Sterilization stylus	Intelligent and convenient	Uvled technology	Flexible scene	Miniaturize the shape and facilitate carrying out.
Intelligent robot for medical waste disinfection and treatment	Automatic and systematic	Unmanned transportation technology	Medical environment	Systematically design the operation process to avoid contact with people.
Bubble hand washing instrument	Cognition and interest	auto-induction	Multi-scene	Combining interesting design with interaction to guide children to wash their hands healthily.

Disinfection products

The design is mainly aimed at small portability, habituation, humanization, interest and systematization.

Fig. 14. Case study diagram of disinfection products. (Self-drawn).

Fig. 15. Disinfection products case. (A) Disinfection lamp. (https://www.dezeen.com/). (B) Intelligent disinfection and cleaning robot for public places. (https://www.behance.net/). (C) Sterilization stylus. (https://www.behance.net/). (D) I Intelligent robot for medical waste sterilization treatment. (https://www.behance.net/). (E) Big Eye Bubble Hand Washing Instrument. (http://www.red-dot.cn/).

In the early stage of the epidemic, when the virus was raging, the supply of protective masks seriously exceeded the demand [22], and many "wild designs" (grapefruit peel with a string as a mask, mineral water bucket with the bottom removed as a mask, etc.) appeared to meet the most basic and urgent needs of people for epidemic prevention at that time. With the relative abundance of protective materials, people began to focus on a new problem: how to extend the life of masks? At this time, the innovation of design structure and materials solved such problems. At the same time, people began to focus on the tedious step of disinfection: how to make it less of a hassle? How to make disinfection a fun thing to do? At this time, the innovation of design for the use of the product form is to meet the needs of people at this time.

4 Mid-epidemic Development - Treatment Category

At the peak of the New Coronavirus epidemic, with the rapid increase in the number of confirmed and suspected cases, the increasing demand for medical products, wards, etc. was a major challenge for medical institutions at all levels [23]. At this stage in the field of medicine and biological sciences, the successful development of a vaccine for the neo-coronavirus has allowed people to take some initiative in the fight against the epidemic [24]. The advent of antigen detection technology has made the detection of neo-coronavirus faster and more efficient, allowing self-testing at home and easy operation [25]. Next, we will analyze the expression form of medical product case design from four aspects: user experience, technology application, application scenario, and design intervention.

MAC WARD Mobile Ward: The MAC WARD (Fig. 17A) allows a general ward to be transformed into a ward with isolation, negative pressure, and intensive care within 48 h depending on the use scenario. The modular design allows the ward to be resized and reshaped to fit different spaces and locations, and to revert to a general ward when the epidemic is over, without any waste of space or materials.

Six-Item Nucleic Acid Testing Product System: This system (Fig. 17B)requires only the collection of patient sputum pharyngeal swabs, sputum and other secretion samples, and it is the world's first system that can detect common respiratory viruses, including the 2019 novel coronavirus, in a single test within 1.5 h. In this system, the design team used a design solution of modular rapid assembly and high-throughput detection mode to give users a safer, smarter, and easier-to-use experience [26].

One-Shot CT Imaging Robot: Patients after diagnosis of new coronary pneumonia are required to undergo CT light film and other validity aspects of the examination. The OneShot CT imaging robot device innovatively introduces a dual robotic arm design (Fig. 17C). The robotic arm has multi-joint flexibility and precision, and the doctor does not need to contact the patient to avoid cross-contamination. The device can adopt elliptical or deformation track scanning according to the bed shape or patient's posture, truly realizing the bedside CT imaging mode of adapting the device to people. The design is ergonomically designed to shape the device to the most suitable position for patient shooting.

Patient Wearable Sensor Device: Wearable sensor devices (Fig. 17D) can contribute to this problem by using Bodynet technology with sensors made of transparent, stretchable, non-allergenic elastomers. It is designed to combine screen-printed metal-ink sensing electronics and flexible radio frequency identification (RFID) antennas with the elastomers, allowing them to track human health status and send data to a matching clothing RFID receiver on the garment.

EpiShuttle Isolation Device: The device (Fig. 17E), as a patient isolation and transport system, not only effectively protects patients from infection in the external environment, but also protects the environment from infection by patient viruses. It can provide maximum safety and comfort to patients. The modular design enables easy disassembly and handling, providing great convenience in the use of the device [27].

From the above analysis, it can be concluded that in therapeutic products, the design incorporates integrated design thinking based on various new technologies [28], allowing medical products to better serve the user community and provide more efficient solutions for the treatment of the new coronavirus. Design in therapeutic products is mainly involved in design from the perspectives of modularity, contactlessness, humanization, and precision to solve the problems of medical resource scarcity and cross-infection (Fig. 16).

Fig. 16. Case study diagram of Medical equipment. (Self-drawn).

Fig. 17. Medical equipment case. (A) MAC WARD mobile ward. (Fu Jen Catholic University Hospital). (B) Six-item nucleic acid testing product system. (Academy of Fine Arts, Tsing-hua University). (C) One-shot CT imaging robot. (Internet). (D) Patient wearable sensor device. (Internet). (E) EpiShuttle Isolation Device. (Internet)

The middle of the epidemic development is the period of large outbreak, which requires rapid response and fine management, and urgently needs to make scientific decisions with the help of analysis of data [29]. Designers no longer design based on active feedback from users, but by detecting the huge data stream formed by users' usage behavior. With the help of relevant technologies and models for statistical analysis, the potential value of data can be explored to guide product design [30], thus significantly improving the effectiveness of the entire product development cycle and upgrading the design iterations at the fastest speed to cope with complex epidemic forms. The new artificial intelligence technology is achieving "great harmony" through "great collection, great recognition, great calculation, great extraction, great construction, great prediction, and great strategy......" [31].

5   Post -Epidemic Period - Psychological Healing

The rapid form of the new pneumonia epidemic has caused serious harm to society as a whole, not only in economic terms, but also in terms of its great impact on people's physical and psychological health, and its impact is "long-term and far-reaching". The psychological health of the population and the pattern of changes throughout the epidemic, how to effectively intervene and protect them, and how to carry out psychological guidance in the late stage of the epidemic have become important factors in maintaining the psychological health of the population and ensuring social security and stability, and are also the focus of the current mental health work [33–36].

With the effective control of the epidemic, the form tends to ease and people's lives have basically returned to normal, but patients with palpitations, anxiety, insomnia, and depression due to the impact of the epidemic still continue to appear in hospitals, and some medical personnel involved in the treatment of the epidemic also have obvious emotional problems such as somatization, terror, and anxiety [37].

At this stage, the mental health problems of the population brought about by the new coronary pneumonia epidemic need urgent attention and diversion [38]. Mental health hotlines, fairy tale readings, lectures, and psychological counseling have been launched in various countries in the fields of psychology and psychiatry to address this issue [39], (Fig. 18) and many online virtual and figurative products for psychological healing have been created. For example, healing spaces are one of the virtual-reality healing modalities, and the term "healing space" was first introduced by Dr. Esther Sternberg in 2009 as a space that promotes stress reduction [40]. Studies have shown that under the guidance of the concept of healing space, the design optimization of color, space scale and other factors can meet the psychological needs of patients to a certain extent [41]. Next, we will analyze the design expression form of medical product cases from three aspects: user experience, application form, and design intervention.

Heal - Life - Source Healing Theme Park: IN the post-epidemic period, people are longing for natural space. The design of Heal-Bio-Source, a healing theme park in the "post-epidemic" era (Fig. 20A), has clear functional zoning and flexible road organization, with one above-ground entrance and two underground passages connecting the plots. The park is connected by an above-ground entrance and two underground passages. Visitors and residents can exercise, release their anxiety, blend in with nature, and find peace and belonging in the park. The design not only hopes that the green island in the city will heal the body and mind and lead a healthy life through the landscape, but also commemorates the epidemic through this healing park.

Game "Retrograde" "Pathogenic Battle: The game "Retrowalker" (Fig. 20B) is an interactive animation game based on the background of the period of the prevention and control of the new coronavirus. The main purpose is to show the difficulties of the front-line retrowalkers, and to popularize some tips on the prevention and control of the

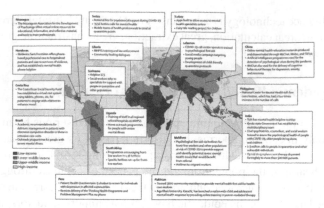

Fig. 18. Selected national responses to COVID-19 mental health measures. (https://www.scienc edirect.com/).

epidemic on the way to pass the interactive mini-game. Pathogens Battle" (Fig. 20C) is a "cut cut cut" game, in which the virus falling from the top is quickly removed by sliding the screen with the finger. The various psychological healing products presented through the design of fun interactions and humanistic interventions will have a positive effect on people with poor mental health in the post-epidemic period.

Metaphorical Audio Story: The series introduces four metaphorical stories: "A Beautiful Day", "The Fallen Tree", "I Love My White Shoes" and "The Nesting Swallow" (Fig. 20D), which combine audio and hand-drawn forms.

Life Education Picture Book: The illustrated book "The Cat Who Lived a Million Times" (Fig. 20E) tells users a story about exploring the meaning of life through illustration design. When anxiety arises from the epidemic, reading life-based educational picture books can have a healing effect. Through reading such picture books, users generate a rational perception of death, overcome their one-sided fear of death, and thus improve their understanding of the meaning of life.

Psychological Healing Mechanism of Sound Landscape: The radio broadcasts of the Square Cabin Hospital use sound as a medium to intervene in the psychological healing process of the audience. Using a cross-disciplinary approach to study the relationship between sound communication and the influence of audience trauma and brain neurocognition, a healing soundscape theoretical framework dominated by unique sound frequency, timbre, and content is proposed (Fig. 20F). The framework reveals that audiences gain psychological satisfaction after actively using radio sounds, which leads to subjective healing at the cognitive, psychological, and behavioral levels [42].

From the above analysis, it can be seen that psychological healing products can be mainly divided into audio, game, space, facility, and picture book categories, and the design is mainly designed to engage in humanistic and interesting interactive forms to help people get out of the anxiety state of the epidemic [43]. And the design can directly lead the healing of people's psychological trauma, combining psychology, spirituality, electronic computing software, etc. to present a variety of psychological healing methods (Fig. 19).

Name	User Experience	Application form	Design intervention
Yushengyuan Healing Theme Park	Relaxation and freedom	Realistic scene	Design thinking of integrating human, environment and cultural care
Interactive game	Decompression and cognition	Online virtual	Enhance the popularity of science while ensuring fun through game interaction.
Metaphorical audio story	Heal, inspire	Online audio	The combination of hand-painted design and audio makes people hope again.
Life education picture book	Education, understanding	Physical product	Psychotherapy for people in the form of illustration design
Sound psychological healing mechanism of landscape	Emotional memory	Online audio	The media constructs different images through emotional processing to effectively mobilize the audience's psychological activities.
Psychological healing products			
Design mainly takes part in design in the form of humanistic care and interesting interaction.			

Fig. 19. Case study diagram of Psychological healing products. (Self-drawn).

Fig. 20. Psychological healing products case. (A) Heal - Life - Source Healing Theme Park. (Wuhan University School of Urban Design). (B) "Retrograde". (Internet). (C) "Pathogenic Battle". (Internet). (D) Metaphorical audio story. (http://psy.ecnu.edu). (E) Life Education Picture Book. (Internet). (F) Psychological healing mechanism of sound landscape. (https://www.cnki. net/).

In the post-epidemic period, design research related to virus protection and treatment has been relatively well developed, and people are increasingly concerned about their physical and mental health, while design heals people's body and mind from various expressions such as architecture, landscape, home products, virtual products, art installations, etc. For these expressions, design uses healing design thinking to intervene directly, allowing users to fully release their own pressure and express emotions [44] (Fig. 21).

6   Conclusion and Outlook

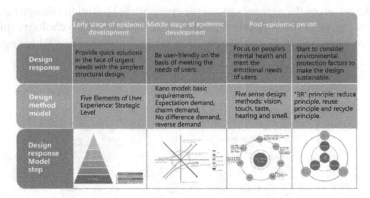

Fig. 21. Design method models corresponding to the three periods of the epidemic. (Self-draw).

Comprehensive analysis of the above research shows that the key to solving public health emergencies in the early stages of epidemic development is the rapid and sustainable supply of emergency medical supplies. The design is designed to provide rapid solutions to the emergency problems that arise during this period with the simplest structural design [45], with rapid testing and feedback iterations to reduce trial and error cycles and costs [46]. These designs can be applied to the strategic layer of the five elements of user experience, as mentioned in 3.1 of the paper, where the goal of the product is to solve the problem of cumbersome mask wearing and protective vulnerability of medical personnel, and the user needs to be able to use the protective mask and goggles in a quick and easy way.

In the middle of the epidemic development, the design pays more attention to the user's feeling of use and continuously optimizes and upgrades the user experience [47]. To achieving user-friendly and efficient on the basis of satisfying the user's needs, the Kano model can be applied, as mentioned in 4in the paper, the product system for nucleic acid detection of six respiratory diseases for neocrown pneumonia, analyzes the user's needs, and satisfies the sampling based on In addition, it is able to produce test results within 1.5 h to meet the expectation-based needs of users, and the modular and rapid assembly design substantially reduces the burden of nucleic acid testing staff.

In the post-epidemic period, the design mainly considers two aspects. One is people's psychological health to meetting the user's emotional needs. Another is the environmental protection factor, which is sustainable use of design and the design method model can be applied to the five senses design method and the "3R" principle. For example, in the 5 Healing - Life - Source theme park, the visual experience is presented in the form of a green island in the city. The auditory experience is reflected in the form of the whispering of wind and trees and the ecological water cycle. The olfactory experience is realized by aromatherapy, and the tactile experience is presented by people perceiving things in the park through their bodies. The 4MAC WARD movable wards in the text follow the principle of reduction: the use of in-situ material recycling and remanufacturing methods. The principle of reuse: the modular design can be adjusted in size and shape according to the space and can be restored to a normal ward after the epidemic is over. And the principle of recycling: the materials used are all recyclable and reused (Fig. 22).

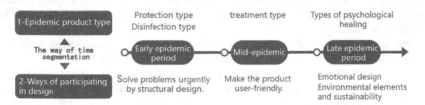

Fig. 22. Pre- and mid-epidemic segmentation approach. (Self-drawn).

As shown in the Fig. 39, this paper segments the pre- and mid-epidemic period by major product types and design engagement, respectively, while the approach used for segmenting the epidemic is not absolute and can even be staged in more different perspectives, such as the depth of design engagement and the combination of design and people's concerns.

Looking back at the relevant studies during the epidemic, the design studies related to the period of 2019–2022 epidemic occurrence are more abundant and the research dimensions are diversified. To better serve people to solve the problems in the epidemic, human-centered design and future ubiquitous technology should be supported to co-create healthy social systems and lifestyles [48]. Design is innovation and problem-solving oriented, as mentioned by the American scholar Jeremy Rifkin in his book The Third Industrial Revolution: In the era of the third industrial revolution, knowledge, data, and information become the most valuable resources [49]. In order to better serve "people", design needs to break away from the original professional or limited concept of design and enter a larger, holistic and systematic "design" based on a cross-fertilization approach of disciplines [50], in the epidemic. During the epidemic, design needs to uphold the principle of human-centeredness, considering the relationship between people, objects, and the environment [51], throughout the product life cycle chain.

References

1. Wang, P., Guo, C., Liu, J.: SARS-CoV-2 Variant of Concern: Omicron. SCIENCE. **74**(01), 26–31+4 (2022). (in Chinese)
2. Ming, Q., Zhen, W.: The triple dimension of science, industry and institutions in public health crises: a factual analysis based on the fight against new coronary pneumonia in the United States and the United Kingdom. Nankai J. (Philos. Soc. Sci. Edn.).**05**, 106–117 (2020). (in Chinese)
3. Matheson, N.J., Lehner, P.J.: How does SARS-CoV-2 cause COVID-19? Science. **369**(6503), 510–511 (2020)

4. Huang, L., et al.: Health outcomes in people 2 years after surviving hospitalisation with COVID-19: a longitudinal cohort study. Lancet Respir. Med. **10**, 863–876 (2022)
5. Chen, W., et al.: Short-range airborne route dominates exposure of respiratory infection during close contact. Build. Environ. **176**, 106359 (2020)
6. Lei, H., Zhang, N., Wei, J., Jin, T.: Major transmission routes of novel coronaviruses in the home environment. Sci. Technol. Rev. **39**(09), 78–86 (2021). (in Chinese)
7. Wei, S., Cai, S.: Exploring the advantages of the socialist system with Chinese characteristics–based on the practice of China's anti-epidemic struggle. Mod. Bus. Trade Ind. **43**(14), 118–120 (2022). (in Chinese)
8. Yong, L.: Heavy medical research and development of new crown antigen rapid test kit approved for marketing. Sci. Technol. Daily. 03-15(001) (2022). (in Chinese)
9. Wang, Q., Sun, H.: Study on the integration of the great anti-epidemic spirit into the cultivation of medical students' professionalism in the new era. Health Voc. Educ. **40**(08), 62–64 (2022). (in Chinese)
10. Zeng, J., Liu, C., Yang, Y., Cao, Q., Li, Q.: The new crown epidemic and the "economic singularity" of artificial intelligence - evidence based on big data on consumer behavior. Rev. Ind. Econ. **05**, 116–132 (2021). (in Chinese)
11. Li, Y., Liu, Y.: Humanized care in the design of epidemic prevention products. Design. **33**(06), 88–91 (2020). (in Chinese)
12. Gao, H., Pi, Y.: Research and practice on upgrading design of public epidemic prevention products based on folk wisdom. Design. **33**(06), 82–84 (2020). (in Chinese)
13. Jing, X.: Research on the Impact of Goal Progress Presentation and Internet Product Types on Users' Intention to Continue Using. Wuhan University (2021)
14. Yi, X.: Design of anti-epidemic and disinfection products based on 3R principles. Nanchang University (2021)
15. Product. Process. **02**, 47 (2022). (in Chinese)
16. Tian, J.: Face mask design and evolution of respiratory protection. Zhuang Shi. **02**, 30–37 (2020). (in Chinese)
17. Tang, X., Cong, W., Tao, X., Zhu, Y.: Research on the humanized design of protective masks based on user behavior observation. Design. **35**(05), 135–137 (2022). (in Chinese)
18. Guo, Y.: Application of science and technology to achieve product design innovation. Hangzhou Dianzi Univ. J. (Soc. Sci. Edn.) **13**(03), 53–57 (2017)
19. Lin, X., Cao, Y., Luo, W., Lin, Z., Zhang, Z., Wen, Y.: Study on the preparation and antibacterial properties of antibacterial hand sanitizers containing dodecyl dipropylene triamine. China Surfactant Detergent Cosm. **52**(04), 376–382 (2022). (in Chinese)
20. Pan, L., Yin, B.: Design: the endogenous power of cultural cohesion and national livelihood. China Lit. Art Critic. **2022**(02), 27–37 (2021)
21. Guo, Y., et al.: Air disinfection for SARS-CoV-2 and other pathogens: a review. J. Tsinghua Univ. (Sci. Technol.), **61**(12), 1438–1451 (2021). (in Chinese)
22. Zhou, J., Lang, N., Yuan, Y., Sun, C.: Respiratory protection and countermeasures of COVID-19 epidemic situation. Occup. Health Emerg. Rescue. **38**(02), 116119+182 (2020)
23. Li, Y., Chen, Z., Fei, R., Liao, W., Gong, Z.: Considerations and suggestions for medical social work intervention under the COVID-19. Chin. Med. Ethics (in Chinese) **34**(08), 959–965 (2021)
24. Jiang, P., Wang, T.: Immunogenicity of neocrown virus and progress of neocrown vaccine development. Chin. J. Pharm. (Web Version) **20**(01), 40–46 (2022)
25. Chen, C., Jinchao, H., Cao, S., Men, D.: The development of antigen testing for SARS-CoV-2. China Biotechnol. **41**(06), 119–128 (2021). (in Chinese)
26. Zhao, C.: Constant temperature amplification biochip detection system - six respiratory virus nucleic acid detection chip products. Des. Res. **10**(02), 2 (2020). (in Chinese)

27. Zhao, Y.: Industrial design assisting in epidemic prevention. Zhuang Shi. **2020**(02), 16–21 (2020). (in Chinese)
28. Qin, Y., Qin, J.: Artificial intelligence & innovation design for preventive treatment of disease leading to future great health. Design. **34**(10), 66–71 (2021). (in Chinese)
29. Viktor, M.: Big Date Era: Great Changes in Life Work and Thinking. Zhejiang People's Publishing House, Hangzhou (2013)
30. Xi, T., Zheng, X.: Iterative innovation design methods of internet products in the era of BigData. Pack. Eng. (in Chinese) **37**(08), 1–5 (2016)
31. Xu. K., Xu, K.: Designing enabling public health solutions. Design. **34**(08), 86–88 (2021). (in Chinese)
32. Xu, L., Lianrong, J.Y.: Research on archives service strategy in post-epidemic era. Lantai World. **2022**(05), 34–37 (2022)
33. Shi, K., et al.: The risk perceptions of SARS and SOCIO-psychological behaviors of urban people in China. Acta Psychol. Sin. **04**, 546–554 (2003). (in Chinese)
34. Liu, Z., Kankan, W., Wang, L.: Psychological and behavioral research after major disaster in China. Adv. Psychol. Sci. **19**(08), 1091–1098 (2011). (in Chinese)
35. Vardy, T., Atkinson, D.: Property damage and exposure to other people in distress differentially predict prosocial behavior after a natural disaster. Psych. Sci. **30**(4), 563–575 (2019)
36. Zhu, X., Jiang, L., Dong, C., Jin, W., Wang, Y.: Study on risk perception and early warning mechanism ofsevere disaster events such as typhoon etc. J. Catastrophol. **27**(02), 62–66 (2012). (in Chinese)
37. Wang, Q., et al.: Relationship between mental health, psychological resilience, and social support among medical staffs in the post·COVID·19 era in Wuhan [J/OL]. Med. J. Wuhan Univ. 1–5 (2022)
38. Chen, X., Xiaolan, F.: Urgently needed construction of public psychological service system in emergency management. Bull. Chin. Acad. Sci. **35**(03), 256–263 (2020). (in Chinese)
39. Kola, L., et al.: COVID-19 mental health impact and responses in low-income and middle-income countries: reimagining global mental health. The Lancet Psych. **8**(6), 535–550 (2021)
40. Geddes, L.: Review: healing spaces by Esther Sternberg. New Scientist. **202**(2707) (2009)
41. Xu, Y., Niu, Y., Qi, C.: Virtual reality: the future of healing space development. Archicreation. **2020**(04), 140–155. (in Chinese)
42. Lang, Y., Chen, K.: Ember in the dark: a study on the psychological healing mechanism of soundscape during the new crown epidemic - a statistical analysis and emotional examination based on the messages of the audience of Fang Pod Radio. In: 2021 Proceedings of the Annual Meeting of the Health Communication Committee of the Chinese Journalism History Society and the Fourth International Symposium on "Medicine, Humanities and Media: Health China and Health Communication Research, pp. 202–215 (2021). (in Chinese)
43. Xue, R.: Research on interaction design of art intervention mpsychotheraoy. North Central University (2021). (in Chinese)
44. Fang, Z.: The role of empathy in contemporary design perspective - taking Zhu Guangqian's aesthetic thought as a starting point. Beauty Times (above). **01**, 7–10 (2022). (in Chinese)
45. Jin, H., et al.: How China controls the Covid-19 epidemic through public health expenditure and policy? J Med Econ **25**(1), 437–449 (2022)
46. Miao, K.: Product design thinking and methods research in the internet & intelligent era. Pack. Eng. **38**(18), 166–170 (2017). (in Chinese)
47. Zhang, M.: Healthy China requires design upgrades. Design. **34**(10), 76–78 (2021). (in Chinese)
48. Zhao, C.: Health care design: the new paradigm of narrative-evidence based innovation. Zhuang Shi. **04**, 12–19 (2021). (in Chinese)
49. Jeremy, R.: Third Industrial Revolution. China Citic Press, Beijing (2012)

50. Yang, Y., Cheng, K., Yin, X.: Research on industrial design education reform based on design thinking. Ind. Des. **02**, 34–36 (2022). (in Chinese)
51. Wang, X., Wang, S.: The methods of product design based on the crossover design. Pack. Eng. **37**(04), 148–151 (2016). (in Chinese)

Author Index

Printed in the United States
by Baker & Taylor Publisher Services